DISCARDED
MILLSTEIN LIBRARY

THE FIRST FREEDOM

I have sworn upon the altar of God

eternal hostility

against every form of tyranny

over the mind of man.

THOMAS JEFFERSON

The first freedom

Liberty and justice in the world of books and reading

Edited by Robert B. Downs

American Library Association

323.445
D

Copyright © 1960 by the American Library Association

Manufactured in the United States of America

Library of Congress Catalog Card Number 59-13653

Fourth Printing, December 1969

CONTENTS

Introduction xi

Chapter I **We have been here before:
a historical retrospect**   1

     Leo M. Alpert   Naughty, Naughty!   4
     David Spitz   Milton's Testament   8
     Richard Hanser   Shakespeare, Sex . . . and Dr. Bowdler   15

Chapter II   **The issues at stake**   19

     Walter Gellhorn   Restraints on Book Reading   20
     William O. Douglas   Censorship and Prior Restraint   41
     Austin Harrison   Literature and the Policeman   46

Chapter III		**The courts look at books**	50
	Leo M. Alpert	Judicial Censorship of Obscene Literature	52
	Norman St. John-Stevas	Obscenity, Literature and the Law	67
	Augustus N. Hand	United States v. Dennett	76
	John M. Woolsey	United States v. "Married Love"	81
	John M. Woolsey and Augustus N. Hand	United States v. "Ulysses"	83
	William O. Douglas	Hannegan, Postmaster General, v. Esquire, Inc.	89
	Curtis Bok	Commonwealth v. Gordon et al.	93
	Jerome Frank	Roth v. Goldman	115
	Jerome Frank	United States v. Roth	119

Chapter IV		**Giving others the courage of our convictions: pressure groups**	133
	American Civil Liberties Union	Statement on Censorship Activity by Private Organizations and the National Organization for Decent Literature	134
	John Fischer	The Harm Good People Do	138
	Elmer Rice	New Fashions in Censorship	141
	John Lardner	Let 'em Eat Newspapers	146
	John Lardner	The Smut Detective	147
	John H. Griffin	Prude and the Lewd—Wherein the Bigger Peril?	148
	John Haynes Holmes	Sensitivity as Censor	152
	John Mason Brown	Wishful Banning	155

Chapter V		**Who or what is obscene?**	159
	Edward Weeks	Sex and Censorship	162
	Havelock Ellis	Obscenity and the Censor	168
	D. H. Lawrence	Pornography and Obscenity	171
	Paul Blanshard	Sex and Obscenity	181
	Eric Larrabee	The Cultural Context of Sex Censorship	193

Bernard De Voto	The Easy Chair	201
Bernard De Voto	The Case of the Censorious Congressmen	205
Max Lerner	On Lynching a Book	209
Aldous Huxley	Vulgarity in Literature	210
Ben Ray Redman	Is Censorship Possible?	213
John Courtney Murray	Literature and Censorship	215

Chapter VI Political subversion and censorship — 223

Julian P. Boyd	Subversive of What?	224
Henry Steele Commager	Free Enterprise in Ideas	230
Harold D. Lasswell	Politics and Subversion	235
Charles G. Bolte	Security through Book Burning	242
Emily Davie	"Profile" and the Congressional Censors	247

Chapter VII The writers fight back — 251

Authors League of America	Freedom To Write	252
George Bernard Shaw	The Rejected Statement	254
John Galsworthy	About Censorship	265
Osbert Sitwell	On the Burning of Books as Private Pastime and National Recreation	270
Aldous Huxley	Censorship	272
Heywood Broun	Censoring the Censor	273
H. L. Mencken	Comstockery	276
George Jean Nathan	On Censorship	278
George Jean Nathan	A Programme for Censorship	279
William Saroyan	A Cold Day	281
John Steinbeck	Some Random and Randy Thoughts on Books	284
A. B. Guthrie, Jr.	The Peter Rabbit Library?	285
James T. Farrell	The Author as Plaintiff: Testimony in a Censorship Case	286

Chapter VIII The librarians take a stand — 302

James Rorty	The Attack on Our Libraries	303
Robert B. Downs	The Book Burners Cannot Win	310
Leon Carnovsky	The Obligations and Responsibilities of the Librarian concerning Censorship	312
Margaret Culkin Banning	The Restricted Shelf: Censorship's Last Stand	320
Archibald MacLeish	A Tower Which Will Not Yield	323
John Anson Ford	We Will Gamble on the American	329
David H. Clift	Enduring Rights	331
American Library Association	Library Bill of Rights	336
American Library Association	Statement on Labeling	336
American Library Association and American Book Publishers Council	The Freedom To Read	337
American Library Association	Overseas Libraries Statement	339
Dwight Eisenhower	Letter on Intellectual Freedom	340
American Bar Association	Statement on the Freedom To Read	341

Chapter IX The schools under attack — 343

Harold Rugg	A Study in Censorship: Good Concepts and Bad Words	344
Benjamin Fine	The Truth about Schoolbook Censorship	349
The "New Yorker"	Comments on New York Textbook Censorship	352
Archibald W. Anderson	"The Nation" Case	353
Robert Shaplen	Scarsdale's Battle of the Books: How One Community Dealt with "Subversive Literature"	359
Mark Van Doren	If Anybody Wants To Know	370
Renwick C. Kennedy	Alabama Book-Toasters	375

Chapter X Censorship in Ireland — 378

Marion Witt	"Great Art Beaten Down": Yeats on Censorship	382
William Butler Yeats	The Irish Censorship	388
AE	The Censorship in Ireland	391
Francis Hackett	A Muzzle Made in Ireland	393

Margaret Barrington	The Censorship in Eire	398
Brian Inglis	Smuggled Culture	402
Heywood Broun	It Seems to Heywood Broun	404

Chapter XI Books under dictators red and black 407

G. E. R. Gedye	What a Book Famine Means	408
Carl Sandburg	Murderers of Books	410
George Orwell	The Prevention of Literature	411
Michel Gordey	What You Can Read in Russia	417
John MacCormac	Reading by Red Star Light	424

Chapter XII The broad view: past, present, future 429

Elmer Davis	Are We Worth Saving? And If So, Why?	430
Zechariah Chafee, Jr.	Why I Like America	437
Gerald W. Johnson	Freedom of Inquiry Is for Hopeful People	450
Curtis Bok	The Duty of Freedom	457

Index 461

INTRODUCTION

Why *The First Freedom?* There are notable historical precedents for the use of the phrase.

It is highly significant that when the Bill of Rights was added to the U.S. Constitution in December, 1791, after being ratified by the required three fourths of the states, the *First Amendment* specifically stated, in part, that "Congress shall make no law . . . abridging the freedom of speech or of the press."

One hundred and fifty years later, when America was on the verge of war with the Axis powers, Franklin D. Roosevelt addressed the U.S. Congress, enunciating the Four Freedoms: "In the future days, which we seek to make secure," he said, "we look forward to a world founded upon four essential human freedoms. The first is freedom of speech and expression everywhere in the world."

Reaffirmation from another distinguished source came on December 14, 1946, when the UN General Assembly resolved, "Freedom of information is a fundamental human right, and the touchstone of all the freedoms to which the United Nations is consecrated."

Few, if any, principles have inspired as eloquent statements of faith as the belief in free expression. The characteristic views of one of the greatest of American jurists, Justice Brandeis, in *Whitney* v. *California,* may be noted as an illustration:

"Those who won our independence believed that . . . the deliberative forces should prevail over the arbitrary. They valued liberty both as an end and as means . . . They believed that freedom to think as you will and to speak as you think are means indispensable to the discovery and spread of political truth; that without free speech and assembly discussion would be futile; that without them, discussion affords ordinarily adequate protection against the dissemination of noxious doctrine; that the greatest menace to freedom is an inert people; that public discussion is a political duty; and this should be a fundamental principle of the American government."

In an address before the Fund for the Republic, February 21, 1957, a leading American historian, Bruce Catton, restated this basic truth:

"The greatest of all American traditions is the simple tradition of freedom. From our earliest days as a people, this tradition has provided us with a faith to live by. It has shaped what Americans have done and what they have dreamed. If any one word tells what America really is, it is the one word—freedom . . . The secret of the American tradition is freedom—freedom unabridged and unadulterated, freedom that applies to everybody in the land at all times and places, freedom for those with whom we disagree as well as for those with whom we do agree."

An organization with a noteworthy record as champion of the freedom to read, freedom of inquiry, and related rights is the American Library Association. When the Fund for the Republic, in 1956, proposed the establishment of the American Library Association Liberty and Justice Book Awards, to draw especial attention to books that make distinguished contributions to the American tradition of liberty and justice, the Association unhesitatingly accepted sponsorship for a two-year program. The Awards were officially terminated in 1958. To serve as a permanent reminder of the nature and purpose of the series, however, it was agreed, with the approval of the Fund for the Republic, to assemble and publish an anthology of the most notable writings in the field of censorship and intellectual freedom over approximately the past half century. Hence, the present work.

The extent of publishing in the area selected is astonishing. It is a tribute to the publishers' recognition of the fundamental bearing of these themes on the great American heritage. Likewise, it is gratifying to find that so many first-rate writers are preoccupied with essential rights and freedoms, especially when such concepts are under attack and misunderstood. A quick survey of American and British writings since 1900 revealed over 1200 periodical articles and in excess of 100 books dealing directly with literary censorship. These figures exclude the large and important subject of freedom of the press—a specialized topic which, in itself, has inspired a massive literature.

Because of the mass of published materials available, certain limitations had to be placed on this compilation. The primary restriction is to censorship of the printed word, again excluding press freedom, thereby omitting the problems of censorship of motion pictures, of television, radio, and other mass media, except as they may impinge on the book. In addition to the date limits, the work is almost entirely confined to American and British authors.

More basic than any of the foregoing, perhaps, is the point of view or scope of the work. Admittedly it has a bias, reflecting the liberal view, as contrasted to the advocates of censorship. No attempt has been made to prepare a debater's manual, with the pros and cons nicely balanced. In any case, such a balance would be difficult to strike, for the weight of the evidence is on the other side. Strong statements expressing the sentiments of censorship proponents are not lacking, but, by and large, the writings of the leading American and British authors during the present century have reflected unyielding opposition to the idea and practice of censorship. With rare exceptions, the banners and burners of books have not been highly literate folk.

After the imposition of the limitations described, there remained a far larger body of pertinent and publishable literature than it has been practicable to include herein. In the final painful process of selection, an effort was made to eliminate the repetitious and to avoid the dull, the preachy, and the platitudinous. Even so, enough excellent material remained for another book of equal size.

The availability of reading materials to Americans and to the rest of the world is greater than ever before in history. In the United States alone, some 12,000 book titles in a total of three quarters of a billion copies are published annually. Three billion copies of magazines, exclusive of comic books, are issued each year, and about 55 million copies of newspapers appear every day. A preponderance of this vast quantity of printed matter is distributed without incident or interference. Most Americans believe that every adult should have freedom of choice to read whatever he wants to read whenever he wants to read it, except for treason, fraud, and pornography. Nevertheless, in recent years the American tradition of the freedom to read has been challenged by many groups and prominent individuals. Viewed objectively, we remain a free people in the field of reading, but as various contributors to this compilation constantly reiterate, it is a freedom that cannot be taken for granted, casually and indifferently. Instead, its protection requires "eternal vigilance."

No one of our freedoms is an island, standing separate and alone, but each is quite interdependent on others. As J. R. Wiggins, editor of the *Washington Post and Times Herald,* so aptly phrased it:

"A complex of many rights must co-exist unimpaired if the printed word is to be the effective agent of enlightenment. Men must have the right to discover the truth. They must have the right to print it without the prior restraint or precensorship of government. They must have access to printed materials. They must be able to print without fear of cruel or unusual punishment for publication alleged to be wrongful. They must have the right to put printed material into the hands of readers without obstruction by government, under cover of law, or obstruction by citizens acting in defiance of the law. Wherever these rights are threatened, the power of the printed word is incapable of performing its mission to mankind."

These are the great human rights which the present work is designed to support and to defend.

Chapter 1

We have been here before: a historical retrospect

As the French are fond of saying, *"Plus ça change, plus c'est la même chose,"* the more things change, the more they remain the same. Viewed in historical retrospect, censorship and all kinds of thought suppression are ancient phenomena, exhibiting the same characteristics in every era. One age may be predominantly concerned with religious heresy, another with political orthodoxy, and the next with obscenity and morality. Periods of rigorous, even ruthless repression have been followed by periods of freedom and liberality, after which the pendulum has again swung toward reaction and extreme conservatism. No longer is it customary to burn the victims at the stake, though under totalitarian regimes they may be imprisoned or exiled, and in democracies deprived of their livelihoods.

Most famous of all organized censorship efforts and in continuous operation over the longest period of time is the *Index Librorum Prohibitorum* of the Catholic Church. Writing nearly fifty years ago in the *English Review,* Sir Edmund Gosse, English poet and man of letters, examined the history and workings of this system:

"The idea of a censorship of books was a Papal invention, and has been carried out most firmly and consistently, not by any temporal authority, but by the Church of Rome. In the beginning of the fourth century, the Council of Carthage issued a decree forbidding Christians to circulate or to possess the writings of the authors of pagan antiquity. It would be difficult to exaggerate the loss which this act of fanaticism has entailed upon the modern world, and the spirit which inspired it is one which must always be regarded with suspicion. In times when books circulated only in manuscript, and within very limited areas, the actual destruction of a work of genius was not only possible, it was often easy. After the invention of printing, the work became more difficult, and was prosecuted with a fiercer zeal. The opening years of the sixteenth century are prominent in the annals of repression, but it took a different course. The Renaissance had done its work, and Roman prelates expended their enthusiasm and their money in the preservation of ancient literature, even though its tendency might be unfavourable to morals and religion. A new enemy was in the field, the reform inside the Church, and this was now pursued in all its literary emanations.

"The earliest list of censored books is said to be that drawn up under clerical advice, by Charles V. in Belgium in 1524. The theological faculty of the University of Louvain made itself dreaded throughout Europe by the fierce and reiterated attacks which it made on the freedom of the Press. In 1543 an elaborate list of prohibited books, now catalogued for the first time, was issued at Venice, and in the following year the faculty of theology in Paris produced a fuller Index, and contrived heavier penalties on the sale of improper works. Pope Paul IV. took advantage of the labours of the Inquisition in Venice, Milan, and Spain, to draw up the famous *Index Librorum Prohibitorum,* of which so much has since been vaguely heard. He delivered the list in 1559 to the Inquisition in Rome, and this most formidable engine of literary tyranny was circulated throughout the Catholic world. In this document there were three alphabetical sections; the first comprising a list of authors whose entire writings were prohibited; the second specified works by authors otherwise held innocuous; the third, anonymous writings. It is noticeable that an appendix contained almost all existing editions of the Holy Scriptures. This Index, after a delay during which the theological faculties in all parts of Europe were consulted, was at length published, in 1564, at the close of the Council of Trent.

"It would be tedious to continue the history of these Roman Indices, which those who are curious in the matter may follow in the learned compilations of such historians as Reusch and Mendham. A recent work by Hilgers (1904) may be indicated as a useful source of information. But it is interesting, in examining the early censorship of books, to notice that 'immorality,' except in a violent form, rarely attracted the censure of the inquisitors, which was directed mainly against theological and philosophical speculation. Heresy was the game which the censors went forth to hunt, and their principal prey were 'apostates, schismatics, and every species of sectary.' In 1586, the business was taken out of the hands of the Inquisition, and placed in those of the Index Congregation, a sort of committee whose duty was to keep the list of prohibited books up to date, and to grant learned and pious men special permission to read, for a holy purpose, this or that condemned work. This Congregation has never ceased its labours, and although the spread of liberal opinion has made its zeal more and more nugatory, and though that zeal has itself abated, yet its action remains of a kind which no citizen of a free community, unless biased by prejudice, can regard with satisfaction." [1]

Even more ancient than the censorious activities of the Catholic Church through its *Index* are several examples cited by George W. Lyon in his discussion of "Book Burners in History":

"Who could even attempt to estimate the loss to culture, literature, and civilization in the past caused by the world's book-burners? In some instances whole libraries containing the priceless wealth of accumulated knowledge gathered and preserved for centuries have been ordered burned.

"We might turn first to China, which very early in its history developed a high degree of culture. One of China's most famous monarchs was Tsin Chi Hwangti, who built the Great Wall of China (214 to 204 B.C.) which is said to be the one and only piece of man's engineering on the surface of our earth that could be seen through a telescope from the distance of the moon, no mean achievement as even Hitler or the Son of Heaven might admit. Great Builder as he was, Hwangti, by the same logic peculiar to all dictators, ancient or modern, conceived the notion that when men become too wise they become worthless.

"In keeping with this philosophy, Hwangti in

---

[1] Edmund Gosse, "The Censorship of Books," *English Review,* 4:621–23 (March, 1910).

the year 213 B.C. attempted the extinction of all literature, root and branch, with the exception of those books dealing specifically with medicine, agriculture, and science. Not only were the books burned, but five hundred of the *literati* who had offended him most were executed and thousands of others banished.

"But a better known example of book-burning, and indeed the classical one in all history, was the destruction of the great Alexandrian Library by the order of Omar in A.D. 642, when he was head of the Moslem religion. Omar exercised his sword arm through the ruthless and intrepid Amru, who in true Mahometan manner advanced on conquered nations with the Koran in one hand and the sword in the other.

"And almost four centuries before that, Aurelian visited destruction on the Bruchium quarter of the city. Later, 389 A.D., came the edict of Theodosius the Great for the destruction of the Serapeum. Theophilus, a fanatical Christian bishop, was his willing tool in this burning of pagan literature. It has always seemed a bit illogical to condemn a book as pagan literature just because it was written before the time of Christ, as obviously no other literature could have been written before the dawn of the Christian era.

". . . A long siege of seven months was required before Amru reduced the royal city of Alexandria. Here was the greatest library and museum of the then-known world. The books, or, more correctly, rolls of manuscripts, had been collected from every available source at great pain and expense. Omar did not burn the books in one great bonfire for spectacular effect, but, prompted by thrift, he used them as fuel to heat the luxurious baths for which the city was famous. The number of volumes has been given as 700,000, and we are told that this quantity was sufficient to heat the water for four thousand baths over a period of six months. One conservative scholar inclines to the belief that papyri and palm leaf manuscripts were very likely used for kindling the fires in these baths, and not as more substantial heat producing fuel, which seems quite probable. But in either case, kindling or fuel, the books were destroyed.

"If Omar could have had any slight compunction for so wanton a destruction of the world's most valuable library, he at least dismissed the whole matter with easy logic: 'The contents of these books are either in accordance with the teaching of the Koran or they are opposed to it. If in accord, then they are useless, since the Koran itself is sufficient, and if in opposition, they are pernicious and must be destroyed.' No dictator of our day could advance a neater bit of sophistry to justify an act of vandalism, unless it be Hitler's idea of extending 'protective custody' to Norway, Holland, Belgium, and the other conquered nations.

"Fortunately, a few books escaped the flames at Alexandria, just how we do not know; but it is safe to assume that there were book lovers of that day who did not relish the idea of giving valuable and beautifully handwritten and embellished manuscripts to the flames, decree or no decree. We know that a few books were salvaged, and among these were the 'Elements' of Euclid in thirteen books, the foundation of modern geometry, the 'Almagest' of Ptolemy, or more correctly, the *Syntaxis-megiste*. This was first translated by the Arabians about 800 A.D. at the direction of Calif Al Maimon, and then called 'Al-Maghesti,' i.e.: 'the megiste.' It is regarded as one of the world's rarest and most valuable volumes.

"Besides Ptolemy and Euclid many other great scholars advanced their theories and worked out their original ideas at Alexandria. Among these were Apollonius on the subject of conic sections, Archimedes, the great physicist, Eratosthenes, the scientific geographer, Hero and Philo in the field of dynamics, and Hipparchus in astronomy.

"Among other book-burners must be included the mighty Julius Caesar during the siege of Alexandria. The priceless collection suffered great loss at his hands in the so-called Alexandrine War (48 to 47 B.C.). If his 'Commentarii de Bello Gallico' were written at this time—as no doubt they were—many a schoolboy and schoolgirl has perhaps regretted that the 'Commentaries' were not tossed into the fire, but Caesar was not an author to burn his own writings, any more than Hitler would be likely to destroy 'Mein Kampf.' "[2]

In the selections which follow, Leo M. Alpert presents a general review of the history of book censorship, while David Spitz and Richard Hanser consider more specialized aspects.

---

[2] George W. Lyon, "Book Burners in History," *Saturday Review*, 25:12 (August 15, 1942).

⊂▷ Leo M. Alpert, a Miami attorney, examines in "Naughty, Naughty!" some historical phases of censorship over the past three hundred years, chiefly from the legal point of view and with particular reference to the courts' attitudes toward obscenity in Britain and America. A more detailed study of the "Judicial Censorship of Obscene Literature" by Mr. Alpert appears in a later chapter, "The Courts Look at Books."

Leo M. Alpert
NAUGHTY, NAUGHTY!

To go back of Judge Woolsey's now famous essay on the emetic rather than aphrodisiac qualities of Joyce's *Ulysses* means a brisk skip of almost three hundred years into the past—to the days of 1663 when the gay Sir Charles Sedley, "mannerly obscene" poet, was jailed, not for his literary exhibitions, but for his purely physical, accompanied by blasphemies and assaults "to the scandal of the Government." Whether this incident, bizarrely dubbed the first reported case on judicial censorship of obscene literature, benefitted or not the sale of Sedley's works (published, after his death in 1701, in six editions from 1702 to 1778) is shrouded in the mists of history. From the fact of six editions it would seem that Sedley's poetry caught on, regardless of what happened to him. But definitely Edmund Curll's tilts with the law, until in 1728 he was finally pilloried and promised to retire from "Publick Business," enhanced his piratical and flourishing trade in obscene literature. "Can Statutes keep the British Press in Awe, When that sells best that's most against the Law?" So also the prosecution of John Wilkes, just one hundred years after Sedley's disgraceful antics, for publishing the obscene poem, *Essay on Woman,* gave to that composition a still high notoriety.

It was not, however, until the second hundred years of the Three Hundred Years War against Obscene Literature that the skirmishes developed into broad battles affecting authors, publishers, and booksellers; and it is that phase of the War—the adventures of suppressed or sought-to-be-suppressed literature—which is the focus of this sortie.

Southey's *Wat Tyler* affords, perhaps, one of the most paradoxically amusing of the adventures. The drama—a rousing revolutionary piece—had been finished in 1794 and brought to London by one of Southey's friends who had placed it in the hands of Ridgeway and Symonds, publishers. They feared to print it, probably because of the High Treason trials in that year. For twenty-three years, *Wat Tyler* languished in manuscript. Then, with Southey no longer a comparatively obscure young man but poet laureate of England, the successors to Ridgeway and Symonds published the drama.

Southey was mortified and apprehensive. As poet laureate he bore the duty of swelling the traditions of a conservative England. The piece might destroy his official position. He brought suit to enjoin the publication. And the even more conservative Chancellor, Lord Eldon, who had been Attorney General in the High Treason trials, refused to grant an injunction against the piracy, declaring that the work was, in its very nature, calculated to do injury to the public. *Wat Tyler* therefore saw the light of day and enjoyed a popularity unalloyed by the author's reluctance to see it circulated or by the judicial decision that it was not fit for print. Though the avowed purpose of Lord Eldon was to keep the drama from publication, his decision, as every decision refusing the protection of the law of property to a pirated work because the writing is "obscene" or "indecent," resulted in many editions and wide distribution. Southey was forced to include the drama—with a preface apologizing for ever writing it—in his collected works which appeared in 1848. But he died before they appeared.

To cap the irony, Lord Eldon shortly afterward declined to prevent Byron's *Cain* from being pirated; and his vice, Sir John Leach, of whom it is said that litigants preferred the tardy justice of the chief, Lord Eldon, to the swift injustice of the Vice-Chancellor, similarly declined, on the ground of obscenity, to grant protection—copyright—to so much of Byron's *Don Juan* as had appeared by July, 1822, and was being hawked about by pirates. The court defeated itself, of course; a multitude of pirated editions swept the country, and Southey, who

---

Leo M. Alpert, "Naughty, Naughty!" *Colophon,* Ser. 3, v. 1, no. 3:47–54 (1939), copyright 1939 by Pynson Printers, Inc. Reprinted (without footnotes) by permission of the author and of Elmer Adler.

had attacked Byron and *Don Juan,* the one as founder of the "Satanic School" and the other as a "monstrous combination of horror and mockery, lewdness and impiety," found, to his chagrin, that he and Byron were regarded alike by the men of law.

Much the same happened to Shelley's *Queen Mab,* a tragic action in the War. Shelley started *Queen Mab* in 1812 and finished it in the spring of 1813. For one reason or another, however, mercurial Shelley decided he was too young to be a judge of religious controversies (he was twenty-one, though Mary Godwin believed him to have been but eighteen) and he therefore had 250 copies privately printed in the summer of 1813 for his own use.

It was one of those privately printed copies that Shelley's in-laws, the Westbrooks, used as evidence that the poet was not a fit father for his two children, Ianthe and Charles, born of his marriage with Harriet Westbrook. And it was from one of these copies that a pirated edition of *Queen Mab* was issued in 1821.

Shelley was furious. *Queen Mab* evoked the black memory of his unsuccessful contest in Chancery in 1817 for his children. *Queen Mab,* with its adolescent fervor of religion as the source of all evil, did not represent the more mature poet. Shelley wrote a letter to *The Examiner* to disavow participation in the appearance of the poem, and added: "I have directed my solicitor to apply to Chancery for an injunction to restrain the sale; but after the precedent of Mr. Southey's *Wat Tyler* (a poem written, I believe, at the same age, and with the same unreflecting enthusiasm), with little hope of success." Apparently further action against the piracy was not taken. Certainly no solicitor, aware of the view of *Queen Mab* taken four years before in the suit by Shelley to gain custody of his two children, would have advised resort to law; and so the poem, one of Shelley's earliest pieces of importance, despite its author, became one of his most popular.

The first authorized edition of *Queen Mab* did not appear until 1839, after Shelley's death, and then was considerably expurgated. Edward Moxon, a most reputable publisher, had not cared to have the entire poem printed and Mrs. Shelley had agreed. Before the end of the year, demand for a new edition was heard. Shelley's friends, Trelawney and Hogg, had raised a storm of protest over the emasculated edition and Mrs. Shelley now prevailed upon Moxon to print the entire poem in the second edition.

Also in the second edition, it is pertinent to note, *Swellfoot the Tyrant* made its first public appearance. Originally, it had been issued in 1820 and, as Mrs. Shelley wrote in her diary, been promptly "stifled at the very dawn of its existence by the Society for the Suppression of Vice."

To illustrate the malign and perverse turns of the Fates, hovering over all of the War like Greek gods, the fact that a Mr. Henry Hetherington had been convicted in April of 1840 for selling a libel on the Old Testament caused the prosecution of Moxon for the second edition of *Queen Mab* issued in 1841. Hetherington could see no consistency in his conviction for libelling the Old Testament and Moxon's freedom in publishing Shelley's attack on the Old Testament, the New Testament, God, priests, preachers, rabbis, and religion in general.

A mist envelops the precise outcome of the Moxon prosecution. Some writers say Moxon won the case; others that he lost it. What actually happened, to piece out dusty odds and ends, was that the Crown, seeing it might lose, professed itself as satisfied if Moxon were held liable for the court costs only. The jury, reassured that the judge would impose no fine, returned a formal verdict of guilty. Says an unofficial reporter of the case: "The pathetic and forcible arguments by which Serjeant Talfourd justified the intentions of Mr. Moxon would doubtless have succeeded in screening him from punishment, had not the prosecutor prudently chosen to abandon all further proceedings on payment of his costs. We may rejoice in the wise determination not to harass an unintentional offender, without impugning the propriety of the verdict." Withal, the costs incurred were enormous and repercussions were heard in 1866 when Swinburne involuntarily entered the lists.

Swinburne had placed the manuscript of his sensuous and magically moving *Poems and Ballads* in the hands of Edward Moxon and Company, at that time under the management of James Bertrand Payne. Payne, as Swinburne observed, "was terribly nervous in those days," a state not surprising in view of the heavy costs in the *Queen Mab* incident. Payne resolved upon a trial balloon in the shape of a limited edition of *Laus Veneris*. The edition passed unnoticed. The house of Moxon was reassured. "The full collection was printed by the beginning of June [1866], but the actual publication was delayed, owing to compositors' errors, till August."

On a memorable day in August, the *Saturday Review* carried a scathing criticism of the book. "And it was then that the thunder crashed upon the frightened head of Bertrand Payne. Fearing prosecution, which was already being mooted in some quarters, he withdrew the volume from circulation, thus breaking his contract. . . ." So Swinburne was forced into the hands of the Curll of the day, John Camden Hotten, who placed *Poems and Ballads* on the market in September while the attacks moved from criticism to viciousness.

To leave England now, though there have been many other engagements, and turn to the United States reveals similarly bitter battles. Why these fights have been almost exclusively confined to New York and Massachusetts and the Federal courts of those States is a sociological conundrum. Perhaps it is because New York has a Society for the Suppression of Vice and Massachusetts a New England Watch and Ward Society. This latter society began the Boston Book War of 1928–1930, and, in the melee, had suppressed Dreiser's *An American Tragedy*. Dreiser, however, had had tilts before.

In 1900 Dreiser submitted his first novel, *Sister Carrie,* to Doubleday. Frank Norris, the reader, enthusiastically pressed the book upon the publisher, who contracted to issue it and then decided the frank approach to sex would open him to a prosecution under the obscenity laws. Dreiser insisted on performance of the contract and Doubleday, after consultation with counsel, continued the publication of 1,008 copies, which, however, never saw the light of bookshops—the contract did not specifically call for sale, just for publication, suggested astute counsel—thus making Dreiser's first published novel a failure. For eleven years Dreiser was silent until *Jennie Gerhardt* came off the presses.

Then, in 1916, when Dreiser was getting on his feet, the New York Society for the Suppression of Vice warned the John Lane Company that *The Genius* was obscene and that action would be taken if the publishers would not agree to cease sale. The company decided to obey the extrajudicial ukase and Dreiser had no money to engage counsel for a persuasion opposite.

At this point a reputable New York law firm volunteered its services. After discussions, it was amicably agreed to bring a suit for damages against John Lane Company on an agreed statement of fact that, if the book be found obscene, the plaintiff, Theodore Dreiser, should not recover. In a riot of excitement the literary world and the Vice Society awaited the decision. For Dreiser had become the symbol of the revolt against Victorianism, and the conflict was the preliminary skirmish of the special Book War that came in the turbulent twenties.

The court, however, refused to decide the case—courts can always refuse to decide a controversy and frequently avail themselves of this out in a troublesome dispute—and Dreiser again became a victim of the War. In 1923, it should be added, *The Genius* was republished with the added sales blurb of the previous extrajudicial suppression. It sold. And in 1920 *Sister Carrie* was first published, in France, by Les Éditions des Sirènes.

Then came the prosecution in Massachusetts. *An American Tragedy* was judged, not in its entirety, but through passages and excerpts culled by the district attorney for the especial titillation of the jury.

Although statistics are not at hand it would seem an undeniable conclusion that the sale of Dreiser's books benefitted from the tilts.

The news of *Sister Carrie* was spread quickly and the whispers took voice, as they have always done. *The Genius* in its day aroused fever heat, and *An American Tragedy* was the rage for more than two years.

So, also, with D. H. Lawrence's *Lady Chatterley's Lover,* along with *An American Tragedy* officially banned in Boston in 1930. That book has since appeared in various editions of varying degrees of expurgation. But in 1929 it was banned by Customs; in 1930 it achieved nationwide prominence by the litigation in Massachusetts and by the Senatorial debate on the obscenity clause in the tariff bill in which Bronson Cutting infuriated Senator "Smoot from Ute" through innuendoes that *Lady Chatterley's Lover* was one of Smoot's private pleasures. In 1932 the book was suppressed in Ireland and Poland. In New York, nevertheless, neither *An American Tragedy* nor *Lady Chatterley's Lover* was touched by the censors.

From the mauve decade when Payne's edition of *The Arabian Nights,* Fielding's *Tom Jones, The Confessions of J. J. Rousseau, Tales from the Arabic, Aladdin, The Works of Rabelais, The Art of Love, The Decameron,* and *The Heptameron* were attacked but survived, many and strange books ran the gamut of the battle-line in New York, some to fall whilst others lived. Voltaire's *The Philosophical Dictionary* and *The Maid of Orleans, Madeleine,* the autobiography of a prostitute, *Memoirs of Mme. de Maupin,* Caldwell's *God's Little Acre,* Flaubert's *November* and Gide's *If It Die* survived. There fell Radclyffe Hall's *The Well of Loneliness,* Schnitzler's *Reigen* and *Casanova's Homecoming.*

To say flatly that these prosecutions benefitted sales seems a truism. To detail the statement would require arduous work, but some few observations can be made.

Despite the judicial damnation of *The Well of Loneliness* in 1929 the book has nevertheless since been republished and is freely on sale in New York with its appeal heightened by the dust-jacket blurb "Unexpurgated." It is said that the Court of Special Sessions in New York City later freed the tale, even though in England the Home Secretary declared the book obscene and ordered all copies destroyed. Likewise Schnitzler's *Reigen* was republished in a Modern Library edition, and Schnitzler's *Casanova's Homecoming* also appeared again.

Indeed, it is indicated, and truly by the record, that regardless of the activities of the censors no book of merit has ever been successfully suppressed.

"By 1930," say two interested writers speaking of the New York Society for the Suppression of Vice and its chief, Sumner, "he found himself in the embarrassing position of being forced to admit that during the decade he had not been able to suppress any book issued by a reputable publisher through the usual channels and considered by reputable critics to possess any literary merit."

But the difficulty of judging the actual result of attempted suppression is shown best in the instance of Erskine Caldwell's *God's Little Acre.* Shortly after the first edition of 2500 copies was published in February, 1933, the Vice Society moved in without first warning the publishers and obtained a warrant under the obscenity laws, summons being served. The pending litigation in this instance decreased sales because the publishers did not care to risk prejudicing their case by flaunting the fact that the book was under suspicion, and booksellers hesitated to sell for fear action might be taken against them.

When the decision gave the book a clean bill of health there was a substantial increase in sales, and it is probable that this increase was over what the book would have normally sold had there been no prosecution. The explanation of the use of the word "probable" lies, of course, in the continued run of Caldwell's *Tobacco Road* and the notoriety the play received on its road tour. The net result, however, must certainly be a longer life for *God's Little Acre* than the average novel.

On the other hand, the attempted suppression in 1936 of Gide's *If It Die* apparently had no effect on sales. An edition of 1600 copies was first published in October, 1935, and the records show that demand remained fairly steady throughout the years following. Though there was still some demand for the work after the limited edition was exhausted, no reprintings were made.

In the case of Joyce's *Ulysses* a boom market was produced by the attempt at suppression, but again a complicating factor entered in: the fact that *Ulysses,* in one form or another, had been circulating for some fifteen years before the actual decisive battle was fought. Early installments had appeared in this country in 1918 in *The Little Review* and copies had been burned by the Post Office Department. "Bobbed-haired Miss Beach" had her Shakespeare & Company bring out the first edition in Paris in 1922, and in that year copies were burned in Ireland and banned in Canada. In England, it is said, 499 copies were burned by the customs at Folkestone, and here five hundred copies were similarly treated by the ubiquitous postal authorities. Then, two years later, the manuscript was sold at auction for almost $2,000.

All this, coupled to the discussions by literary critics and allusions of book-reviewers running over such a long period as fifteen years, naturally made the *Ulysses* controversy a *cause célèbre* in literary history. A wide sale resulted.

The conclusions of this matter of attempted suppression are provocative. No book of merit

—however that word may be used—has ever been successfully suppressed. When public sale is halted by judicial decision, the climate of opinion, in its variable moods, sooner or later catches up with the book and the fiat is ignored. At that time the previous suppression is regularly employed as an additional sales argument. When an attacked piece survives the legal trauma, the battle has, of course, given to it notable publicity. In general as in particular, it may safely be said that the long-time effect of these battles is to ensure a wider distribution, knowledge and sale of the sought-to-be or actually-suppressed book. Literary history is proof sufficient. It might also be as safely hazarded, though this is a matter of speculation, that the short-time effect, looking to the country as a whole, is the same.

The practical fact (for hitherto it has been tacitly assumed that suppression means literal suppression) is that under our constitutional form of government—something probably not calculated by the omniscient Founding Fathers—judicial condemnation is not at all effective though the ink of the opinion still be wet.

True, the obscenity clause in the tariff law effectively bars foreign "obscene" imports. Nevertheless, the most used Federal statute prohibits only the use of the *mails* to obscene matter. When a Federal court declares that a book is "obscene, indecent, impure, disgusting, lewd and lascivious," the publisher still may circulate the work. Railway expresses, interstate motor trucks, are available and legal. It is then up to the State itself to act. So far, only the two States of New York and Massachusetts have done any real acting. And if the one holds a novel obscene, neither the other, nor any of the remaining forty-seven States, is bound to follow that decision. Indeed, even in the Federal courts one district is not bound by the decision of another, and one circuit—there are nine over the country—may, and often does, disregard the decision of another.

With this anarchy of "law" to the fore, is it not a reasonable supposition that the book-reading public of, say, Maryland may become enthralled over the prospect of reading a book "banned in Boston" and order quantities to the glee of the publisher and local booksellers? As a matter of living reality, everyone knows this occurs.

This business of suppression, usually only one forty-eighth effective at best, puts the judiciary and the vice societies on their sorry nags as a band of Don Quixotes tilting at windmills. The crusades may be fun for somebody but they are not particularly sensible.

⊂⊐ One of the most inspiring pleas for free thought ever penned was *Areopagitica: A Speech of Mr. John Milton for the Liberty of Unlicensed Printing to the Parliament of England* (1644). Milton was attacking, in this powerful pamphlet, the Order of Censorship imposed on printing by Parliament in 1643. His answer was modeled after the *Areopagiticus* of Isocrates (355 B.C.), in which the Greek philosopher-orator urged the restoration of the old freedom of the Areopagus, the place of public meeting and debate in Athens.

Milton's speech, full of memorable passages, is analyzed here by David Spitz, a member of the Ohio State University political science faculty and author of *Patterns of Anti-Democratic Thought* (New York: Macmillan, 1949).

David Spitz
MILTON'S TESTAMENT

Those who believe that the truth will make men free do not universally agree that men should be free to seek the truth. For the search for truth involves the discovery of error, and error when disclosed has sinful charms. Truth when known and enforced, on the other hand, ensures right conduct and precludes the possibility of evil deeds. Thus "true" freedom, in the minds of many men, implies not freedom of thought but freedom of *certain* thoughts. It is the freedom to entertain "right" ideas rather than the freedom to assert or to examine loathsome and erroneous ideas.

Freedom so conceived is the principle embraced by the dominant authoritarian movements of our time. Recently, and within the span of a single week, both the Roman Catholic Church and the Chinese branch of the Communist Party were revealed to have "curbed" once again the teaching or dissemination of "false" ideas. On May 25, 1952 it was reported

---

David Spitz, "Milton's Testament," *Antioch Review*, 13: 290–302 (Fall, 1953), copyright 1953 by the Antioch Review, Inc. Reprinted by permission of the author and of the publisher.

from Hong Kong that three prominent Chinese educators, each of whom had accepted and at an earlier stage had praised Mao Tse-tung's New Democracy, were now deemed ideologically incorrect and hence unfit to continue in their university positions. In accordance with Communist policy as previously enunciated and practiced in the Soviet Union and other countries, and in line with the proclaimed mission of Chinese teachers as defined by the Shanghai Ta Kung Pao on March 31 of the same year, which is to help youth "establish correct thought," the educators were purged.

On the basis of a like principle, the Sacred Congregation of the Holy Office, by a decree dated May 20 and published May 26, 1952, placed on the Catholic index of forbidden books all the works of Alberto Moravia, the Italian novelist. The Sacred Congregation deplored "the enormous damage that is done to souls both by the unbridled license to publish and divulge books, pamphlets and magazines that deliberately narrate, describe or teach lascivious or obscene things and by the wicked desire to read all this indiscriminately." They also considered it their duty to admonish:

All faithful that they should remember their very grave obligation to abstain completely from the reading and circulating of such books and periodicals.

All those who are engaged in the education of youth that, conscious of their very grave duty, they should keep young people entirely away from such writings as from a subtle poison.

Lastly, all civil authorities who are responsible for public morality, that they should not tolerate the printing and circulation of such books which subvert the very principles of natural honesty.

In this way, Catholics and Communists believe, men shall be stayed from error and directed to truth.

This principle is not, of course, the exclusive possession of the two groups mentioned above. It is common to all fanaticisms, to all orthodoxies. It is the basis of all varieties of fascist thought. It is the principle that underlies the current, if still largely informal, censorship of ideas that now threatens America—a censorship which certain individuals and groups, having themselves or through their ancestors found truth, now seek to have formally and permanently secured.

But apart from the difficulties of defining truth and compelling unbelievers to act in accordance with its precepts, there remains a contrary view of freedom. This is the principle that freedom can only be true to itself, not to a value outside of it. We can, under certain circumstances, force men to do good. We can even, perhaps, force them to do evil. But we cannot, without distorting the very meaning of our terms, force men to be free. On the contrary, by such efforts we restrain and coerce them in a cause other than freedom's own. For freedom strictly defined is still but the absence of chains. It is not the quality of being "true" or "false" but simply the quality of being free.

This truth was perceived and eloquently affirmed by the poet John Milton some three centuries ago. Faced in his day with a threat of conformity not unlike that which attends us today, he set forth in the *Areopagitica* a testament for intellectual freedom that is more than relevant to the problem of liberty in our own time. Normally, it is true, one does not look to a dour Puritan for a philosophy and defense of freedom; and Milton can be quoted in detail against anyone who seeks to make an exception in his case. He called, for example, for the suppression of "popery and open superstition" and "that also which is impious or evil absolutely, either against faith or manners." He argued that government does not exist to secure liberty but to assure "that good men enjoy the freedom which they merit, and the bad the curb which they need." He admitted, even in the *Areopagitica*, that a church or commonwealth ought "to have a vigilant eye how books demean themselves as well as men; and thereafter to confine, imprison, and do sharpest justice on them as malefactors." And he exempted "blasphemous and atheistical, or libellous" books from his plea for unrestrained freedom of publication.

Nevertheless, Milton's argument for the freedom of unlicensed printing—a freedom opposed by Communists, Catholics, and all who distrust man's capacity to be guided by his own reason—remains a noble and enduring statement of the free spirit. It assures him a permanent place in the history of liberal thought.

II

The occasion and purpose of the *Areopagitica* can be briefly stated. In 1643 Cromwell's Parliament renewed an old order forbidding unlicensed printing. This was not a period of religious toleration, and the fact that this order had originally been issued by royal decree and had been exercised through the odious Court of Star Chamber did not prevent its enactment. Milton's marital difficulties led him to publish, without license, several pamphlets on divorce. One of these was attacked before Parliament as "a wicked book," and Milton was named in another action as a violator of the licensing law. The *Areopagitica,* in the form of a speech to the Parliament of England, was his reply.

In it Milton was concerned to demonstrate four things. He sought, first, to prove that the Puritan attempt to control the publishing of books derived in its essentials from the Catholic Inquisition, with its resulting "catalogues and expurging indexes that rake through the entrails of many an old good author with a violation worse than any could be offered to his tomb" and that led in turn to the controls of the Imprimatur. He attempted, secondly, to demonstrate that while the reading of books is dangerous, the suppression or censorship of books is catastrophic, more devastating in a way than the taking of a human life. For he "who kills a man," wrote Milton, "kills a reasonable creature . . . ; but he who destroys a good book, kills reason itself, . . . slays an immortality rather than a life." He argued, thirdly, that an edict of censorship will not succeed in suppressing scandalous, seditious, and libellous thoughts. He concluded that the primary effect of such an order will be the discouragement of all learning, indeed the suppression of truth itself.

The argument is familiar but merits recapitulation: both to release it from Milton's stiff and involved style—though, as Macaulay said, there is "gorgeous embroidery" in it—and infrequent errors, and to commend it anew to a nation so overcome by hysteria that while it continues to praise Milton it ignores the meaning of his contribution.

III

Concerning the first of Milton's arguments, little need be said. The origin of a censorship or of any other policy has nothing to do with its validity. It may make for effective polemics, but it does not address itself directly to the merits of the case. Moreover, Milton's allegation that licensing will lead to the controls of the Imprimatur overlooks his own admission that books which ill demean themselves ought to be confined.

Now if books are to be imprisoned, there must be judges and acceptable grounds for imprisonment, in which case the principle of a free press is abandoned and the only meaningful questions concern the selection and control of the judges, and the determination of the rules according to which the judges shall be presumed to adjudicate. The mere threat of censure is no less an infringement of a free press than the act of censure itself. Men who know that failure to conform will result in punishment are unlikely to invite it. If they do, the suppression of their books removes what they have to say from the marketplace of ideas.

It is one thing to recognize that books are dangerous—that they have a life and activity of their own, that their potency might even be such as to drive men to arms. It is quite another to conclude from this that vigilance over them may require their banishment. Milton's references to, and defense of, "good books" at this stage of his argument is an evasion of the issue that yields a point to the case for censorship.

We arrive at the real meaning of his message, however, in his defense of freedom of publication. He is scornful of the argument that evil books will corrupt innocent minds, holding, with the Apostle, that "to the pure all things are pure." Knowledge, Milton asserts, whether of good or of evil, cannot defile, unless the will and conscience are already defiled. Among books, some are of good and some of evil substance; but the choice must remain a matter of individual discretion. For while "best books to a naughty mind are not unappliable to occasions of evil," bad books "to a discreet and judicious reader serve in many respects to discover, to confute, to forewarn, and to illustrate."

How, for that matter, asks Milton, are men to know good and truth and virtue unless they know also what is evil and false? Good and evil emerge and grow up together almost inseparably, as polar opposites. They are as twins cleaving together, the knowledge of one so involved and interwoven with the knowledge of the other as to make it an incessant labor to distinguish them. Without such labor, there is neither wisdom nor virtue in forbearing vice. "I cannot praise a fugitive and cloistered virtue," remarks Milton,

... that never sallies out and seeks her adversary, but slinks out of the race, where that immortal garland is to be run for, not without dust and heat.... That which purifies us is trial, and trial is by what is contrary. That virtue therefore which is but a youngling in the contemplation of evil, and knows not the utmost that vice promises to her followers, and rejects it, is but a blank virtue, not a pure; her whiteness is but an excremental whiteness.

Since, therefore, to know truth men must know error, and to be virtuous men must know vice, Milton concludes that of all ways to scout into the regions of sin and falsity the least dangerous is the reading of books and exposure to all manner of reason.

To the common objection that this course entails certain harm, notably the spread of infectious ideas, Milton replies that the alternative is to remove all human learning and controversy, even and particularly the Bible, which often relates carnal and blasphemous things. Moreover, it is not the book but the interpreter that corrupts; and

if it be true that a wise man like a good refiner can gather gold out of the drossiest volume, and that a fool will be a fool with the best book, yea, or without book, there is no reason that we should deprive a wise man of any advantage to his wisdom, while we seek to restrain from a fool that which being restrained will be no hindrance to his folly.

IV

Censorship, if effective, would thus destroy the virtue of reading even evil or dangerous books. But censorship, whether exercised through this or any other licensing order, cannot achieve the end for which the licensing order is framed. There are, Milton contends, two reasons for this. One is the difficulty of administering such laws fairly and intelligently; this Milton examines both as to complexity of detail and the quality of the licensers. The other, and more important, difficulty is that heresy is spread by other means.

Concerning the first of these factors, Milton is content to show that, if the licensing order is really to work, it must immediately catalogue and proscribe all scandalous and unlicensed books already published, and prohibit the importation of foreign books until they have been examined and approved. It must also expurgate those books which are partly useful and excellent, and partly pernicious. These arduous tasks require licensers of unusual quality—and many of them to boot.

But by the very nature of the task, Milton argues, licensers are likely to be "illiterate and illiberal individuals" who will refuse their sanction to any work which contains "views or sentiments" at all above the level of "the vulgar superstition." Men of worth would refuse such an assignment as tedious and unpleasant, and as an immense forfeiture of time and of their own studies. To assume that "ignorant, imperious, and ... basely pecuniary" licensers would be graced with infallibility and uncorruptibleness, is to close one's eyes to reality.

Even if these difficulties were overcome, the licensing order would still be fruitless. Condemned books always manage surreptitiously to reappear and to circulate, often to an audience enlarged and attracted by the very act of condemnation. Moreover, it is simply not true that the suppression of books ensures the suppression of heresy. The Christian faith began and flourished as a schismatic sect before any Gospel or Epistle was seen in writing. To close the gates against corruption requires that *all* the gates be closed.

No music must be heard, no song be set or sung, but what is grave and Doric. There must be licensing dancers, that no gesture, motion, or deportment be taught our youth, but what by their allowance shall be thought honest.... It will ask more than the work of twenty licensers to examine all the lutes, the violins, and the guitars in every house; they must not be suffered to prattle as they do, but must be licensed what they may say. And who shall silence all the airs and madrigals that whisper softness in chambers? The windows also, and the balconies, must be thought on; there are shrewd books, with dangerous frontispieces, set to sale: who shall prohibit them, shall twenty licensers? The villages also must have their visitors, to inquire what lectures the bagpipe and the rebec reads, even to the balladry and the gamut of every municipal fiddler....

Next, what more national corruption ... than household gluttony? Who shall be the rectors of our daily rioting? And what shall be done to inhibit the multitudes that frequent those houses where drunkenness is sold and harbored? Our garments also should be referred to the licensing of some more sober workmasters, to see them cut into a less-wanton garb. Who shall regulate all the mixed conversation of our youth, male and female together, as is the fashion of this country? Who shall still appoint what shall be discoursed, what presumed, and no further? Lastly, who shall forbid and separate all idle resort, all evil company? These things will be, and must be; but how they shall be least harmful, how least enticing, herein consists the grave and governing wisdom of a state.

Such wisdom, Milton is convinced, would eschew a mass of wearying and ridiculous licensing. It would acknowledge boldly that God, in giving men reason, gave him freedom to choose.

Wherefore did he create passions within us, pleasures round about us, but that these rightly tempered are the very ingredients of virtue? They are not skilful considerers of human things, who imagine to remove sin by removing the matter of sin. . . . Though ye take from a covetous man all his treasure, he has yet one jewel left: ye cannot bereave him of his covetousness. Banish all objects of lust, shut up all youth into the severest discipline that can be exercised in any hermitage, ye cannot make them chaste that came not thither so.

For goodness is personal and must be derived from right choices. To choose rightly, one must be free to choose—between good and evil, virtue and vice, truth and falsehood. To delegate such choice to others—whether state, church, or licensers—is to abandon goodness itself. It is to forsake individual reason and individual decision that alone constitute what we mean by man.

Goodness or morality, in fine, is not a matter to be legislated. Laws which eliminate or restrict freedom of choice prevent rather than promote virtue and thus defeat the very purpose they ostensibly seek to secure.

V

It is to the undesirability rather than the ineffectiveness of licensing that Milton addresses the bulk and core of his argument. He believes not only that licensing can do no good, but that it causes manifest harm. It is "the greatest discouragement and affront that can be offered to learning and to learned men." It hinders the discovery of new truth and makes existing truth heretical. It enslaves not only the citizens but the enslavers themselves. And in seeking political unity through uniformity rather than diversity of thought, it destroys the very hallmark of a free society.

Now it is understandable that a temperament as sensitive as Milton's should be shocked and humiliated by a law which stipulates, in effect, that "debtors and delinquents may walk abroad without a keeper, but unoffensive books must not stir forth without a visible jailer in their title." His excursus on this theme contains some of his most passionate and enduring prose . . . :

When a man writes to the world, he summons up all his reason and deliberation to assist him; he searches, meditates, is industrious, and likely consults and confers with his judicious friends; after all which done he takes himself to be informed in what he writes as well as any that writ before him; if in this, the most consummate act of his fidelity and ripeness, no years, no industry, no former proof of his abilities, can bring him to that state of maturity as not to be still mistrusted and suspected, unless he carry all his considerate diligence, all his midnight watchings, and expense of Palladian oil, to the hasty view of an unleisured licenser, perhaps much his younger, perhaps far his inferior in judgment, perhaps one who never knew the labor of book-writing; and if he be not repulsed, or slighted, must appear in print like a puny with his guardian, and his censor's hand on the back of his title to be his bail and surety that he is no idiot or seducer, it cannot be but a dishonor and derogation to the author, to the book, to the privilege and dignity of learning.

But men in power are generally prone to indulge their own sensibilities rather than the feelings of learned men. If Milton's defense of intellectual freedom is to persuade a Parliament, it must rest on other grounds.

These cannot be such trivia as the inconveniences and delays that are likely to attend an author anxious to correct and recorrect galley and page proofs before his manuscript is finally published, or the resort by timid and parochial ministers to stock or ready-made sermons with ideas that are unlikely to disturb the serenity of their parishioners' minds. Consequences such as these are not unique to lands where licensing orders prevail; nor are they vital to the argument.

In one other respect Milton renders his case vulnerable. His devotion to truth leads him to overestimate its powers. Thus he writes:

. . . though all the winds of doctrine were let loose to play upon the earth, so Truth be in the field, we do injuriously by licensing and prohibiting to misdoubt her strength. Let her and Falsehood grapple; who ever knew Truth put to the worse in a free and open encounter?

And again:

. . . who knows not that Truth is strong next to the Almighty? She needs no policies, nor stratagems, nor licensings to make her victorious; those are the shifts and the defences that error uses against her power: give her but room, and do not bind her when she sleeps.

It is to be noted that Milton does not say that truth will always prevail. He argues only that it will prevail if the encounter is "free and open," if truth is not bound. But even with this qualification, the doctrine is not altogether convincing.

In the first place, error or falsehood may rule

where men are in no mood to accept a truth that injures their interests or affronts their prejudices. Thus the technique of the big lie, the vile but highly developed art of character assassination, the disproportionate publicity given to sensational or scandalous falsehood as against the later and sobering truth, and the like—all these have in our own day made it very clear that truth seldom or only after an excessive delay catches up with falsehood. By that time a man's reputation may have been destroyed, a nation may have abandoned democracy for dictatorship, a judgment of men and events may have been formed that may never be completely erased. In the second place, not all men can recognize the truth when it is paraded before them. Whether for lack of knowledge or intelligence or ability in pleading, men on the side of truth do not always carry it to victory. Finally, a commitment to reason and the scientific method is a commitment to uncertainty; it compels us to view truth as a tentative rather than an absolute and final hypothesis. Truth is always subject to correction, and correction implies that the earlier truth was in error or was at best only a partial truth (and therefore perhaps a partial error). All that we have a right to say is that, under conditions of "free and open encounter," truth has its maximum if not its only chance to prevail.

These objections do not impair Milton's broader argument against censorship. In fact, they make his case all the more convincing; for if truth is not final, we must give range to the continuing search for real truth. Thus Milton's argument for freedom of the press remains eminently sound. It is difficult to see how learning can flourish in the absence of provocative ideas; and since licensers are likely to be men of no special merit or attainment, they will expunge such ideas from even the more famous books of deceased authors. New generations of students and writers, unacquainted with and unstimulated by those thoughts, can thus build not on the best of what has gone before but on that portion of past thinking which is staid, proper, and convenient to the minds of the licensers. Indeed, they will themselves restrict their own writings to things that flatter and do not rise above those narrow and traditional bounds, lest they sever the ever-present Damocletian sword. Out of such ignorance and fear will emerge nothing less than a new "tyranny over learning."

Truth, Milton believes, if it comes at all, comes from exercise, not from conformity to tradition. A man who believes only because he is told to believe and knows no other reason for doing so, is essentially "a heretic in the truth"; even "though his belief be true, yet the very truth he holds becomes his heresy." Consider, says Milton, the man who finds religion so great a burden of mysteries that, though he wants to be deemed religious, he refuses to tax his mind any further.

What does he therefore but resolves to give over toiling, and to find himself out some [agent], to whose care and credit he may commit the whole managing of his religious affairs, some divine of note and estimation that must be. To him he adheres, resigns the whole warehouse of his religion, with all the locks and keys, into his custody; and indeed makes the very person of that man his religion; esteems his associating with him a sufficient evidence and commendatory of his own piety. So that a man may say his religion is now no more within himself, but . . . goes and comes near him according as that good man frequents the house. He entertains him, gives him gifts, feasts him, lodges him; his religion comes home at night, prays, is liberally supped, and sumptuously laid to sleep; rises, is saluted, and after the malmsey, or some well-spiced brewage, . . . his religion walks abroad at eight and leaves his kind entertainer in the shop trading all day without his religion.

The licensing order, by delegating thought, establishes and dignifies this sort of nonsense; and by making truth heretical it renders the discovery of new truth difficult. For unless we assume that some men know the truth, and possess it whole—an impossible assumption for those who, like Milton, believe that perfect truth is known only to God—we must continue to seek it. But how are we to seek truth when the licensing order "enjoins us to know nothing but by statute"? What is generally forgotten, Milton adds, is "that if it comes to prohibiting, there is aught more likely to be prohibited than truth itself: whose first appearance to our eyes, bleared and dimmed with prejudice and custom, is more unsightly and unplausible than many errors."

As a result, liberty and the unity of the state are destroyed. It is not true, Milton argues, that uniformity binds and glorifies a state. On the contrary, licensers who prevent men from discovering and putting together fragments of the truth are themselves the destroyers of unity. They forget that perfection in a state, as in a building, consists in a symmetry of many varieties, that a rigid external formality is likely to produce a gross conforming stupidity, and that if all cannot—as all should not—think alike, it is more wholesome that they be tolerated than compelled to simulate conformity.

For if they are compelled, society suffers. Errors are made by even a good government, but if ideas are silenced magistrates are likely to be kept ignorant of proper remedies. Their continued misinformation, in fact, will commit them to continuing error. It is true, Milton admits, that wrong ideas might otherwise reach them, but in the absence of new and right doctrines they are already the victims of wrong ideas. The true answer to erroneous views is in any case "gentle meetings and gentle dismissions," in liberal and frequent debate. For if men want liberty, they must be prepared to live with the expression of grievances. Indeed, the very purpose of civil liberty is to assure that "complaints are freely heard, deeply considered, and speedily reformed." The suppression of complaints does not eliminate the grievances; but the enslavement of citizens enslaves the enslavers.

> Ye cannot make us now less capable, less knowing, less eagerly pursuing of the truth [Milton tells the Parliament], unless ye first make yourselves, that made us so, less the lovers, less the founders of our true liberty. We can grow ignorant again, brutish, formal, and slavish, as ye found us; but you then must first become that which ye cannot be, oppressive, arbitrary, and tyrannous, as they were from whom ye have freed us.

For these reasons and others, Milton demands above all other freedoms "the liberty to know, to utter, and to argue freely according to conscience."

VI

Milton as a spokesman for intellectual freedom is not, perhaps, to be praised too much. His tolerance was not always in evidence, and even in the *Areopagitica* it was essentially limited to those who were agreed on the fundamentals of the social order. He failed, as generations of his critics have never tired of pointing out, to distinguish the dangers of absolute or unbounded liberty and the dangers of circumscribing it. Moreover, while Milton was not himself prosecuted for publishing without license, and the licensing order became, in effect, a near-dead letter, his appeal of reason to authority did not produce an immediate and avowed reversal of policy. Indeed, more than half a century was to pass before licensing was to disappear from English legislation; while in other parts of the world, as in the totalitarian states of our own day, and in the authoritarian attitudes of certain religious and political orthodoxies, the principle of censorship has been retained, institutionalized, and even extended. Everywhere, of course, the censors, or those who seek to establish them, are "good" men—men who "know" what is right and who seek only to cleanse others of error and sin. But as is so often the case, he who applies the disinfectant may be himself possessed of the greater poison.

To avoid the evil that such "good" men do is, perhaps, an endeavor beyond human control. But to minimize that evil, to place obstacles in its desolating (and, because it plays God, desecrating) path, men can, at the very least, reaffirm their faith in reason and in the virtues of difference. For without reason and the freedom of choice that reason entails, the individual cannot hope to realize his stature as man. And without diversity—in thought, in manners, in human values—a society cannot be unified, free, or flourishing.

These considerations, so ably articulated in the *Areopagitica,* are today often obscured. We have few Miltons and many would-be or actual censors, and the voices of reason are small if not yet stilled. But those who are emancipated from the worship of authority and find no intolerable discomfort in uncertainty, will recognize in those small voices, as in Milton's *Areopagitica,* a wellspring of the liberal faith.

Thomas Bowdler, English editor, in 1818 published the *Family Shakespeare* in ten volumes, "omitting those words and expressions which cannot with propriety be read aloud in a family." To castigate the method, one of his detractors coined the term "bowdlerism," a synonym ever since for prudish and senseless expurgation. The last years of Bowdler's life were spent preparing an expurgated edition of Gibbon's *Decline and Fall of the Roman Empire*. His nephew, who published this work, maintained that his uncle had so purified Shakespeare and Gibbon that they could no longer "raise a blush on the cheek of modest innocence nor plant a pang in the heart of the devout Christian."

Richard Hanser was a psychological warfare

specialist in Europe during World War II, and later documentary film writer for RKO Pathe. He is now a free-lance writer who contributes frequently to the *Saturday Review* and other periodicals.

Richard Hanser
SHAKESPEARE, SEX . . .
AND DR. BOWDLER

A little group of Oxford scholars, moved by some obscure sense of literary piety, gathered in a Welsh graveyard not long ago to observe an anniversary which the rest of the world passed by with total unconcern. It was the 200th birthday of Dr. Thomas Bowdler, whose surgery on the works of Shakespeare won him the dubious immortality of having his name printed in lower case in all standard dictionaries and spoken with derision by succeeding generations.

The ceremonies at the Welsh grave may well have been disturbed by a muffled whirring underfoot, as of a body revolving rapidly. Not only has the lifework of the good doctor become a general joke but, to rub it in, contemporary scholarship has painstakingly searched out every naughty reference and obscene allusion in Shakespeare and called it to the attention of a public which might otherwise be unaware of it. Worse, it has been found that Bowdler was far too pure-minded, or ignorant, to accomplish the mission he set for himself. Many passages he left untouched and uncut teem with improprieties which would have made him squirm had he known they were there.

It was Bowdler's purpose to eliminate from Shakespeare "whatever is unfit to be read aloud by a gentleman in the company of ladies" and to suppress anything which could "raise a blush on the cheek of modest innocence." Accordingly he hacked and slashed and erased until, in 1818, he produced the ten-volume "Family Shakespeare" on which his peculiar celebrity rests and which remained a thumping best seller for years. For good measure, he then took up his scissors and had a go at Gibbon.

Thomas Bowdler was—by heredity, training, and inclination—the very prototype of the literary censor. He was a case history of the quivering moralist who is certain in his soul that others will be contaminated by what he himself reads with impunity, and is serenely sure that his mutilations and suppressions, far from being in any way blameworthy, deserve the praise and approbation of all right-thinking men.

Until the age of fifty-seven, when his great inspiration seized him, Thomas Bowdler led a rather footling and futile life, although he was doubtless under the impression that he was spending his time as a man of culture and refinement should. He studied medicine at Edinburgh and, after taking his degree, made the Grand Tour, from which he returned spouting praises to God for having made him an Englishman. He warned one and all of the pitfalls of France, where he sensed the "danger of contamination from the religious principles of the worthy part of the French people, and from the want of both religion and morality among the generality of them."

He tried practicing medicine for a while, but could hardly bear the sight of pain and blood. When a young friend whom he was treating died of a "putrid disease" Bowdler retired from his profession for good. His father having left him comfortably off, he was able to follow his own bent unhampered by the necessity of earning a living.

He moved in "the politest and most elegant" of London literary circles, became a member of the Royal Society and studied prison reform without doing anything much about it. He was keen on charitable works, joined committees "to improve the condition of the lower classes," and, as a hint of things to come, was especially active in the Society for the Suppression of Vice. With it all he seems to have been, unlike most moralists and do-gooders, a rather sweet and self-effacing character, and those who knew him personally spoke of him afterwards with affection.

It was at Rhydinngs, near Swansea, that he settled down to his major effort. As his introduction to the "Family Shakespeare" reveals, he did not unsheath his shears without a certain amount of diffidence. He felt the need to justify what he was doing. It would be presumptuous, he said, for anyone to tamper with the "Transfiguration" of Raphael or the Belvedere Apollo. If a painting or a sculpture were injured in the attempt to

---

Richard Hanser, "Shakespeare, Sex . . . and Dr. Bowdler," *Saturday Review*, 38:7–8+ (April 23, 1955), copyright 1955 by the Saturday Review Associates, Inc. Reprinted by permission of the author and of the publisher.

improve it, the damage done would be permanent and irreparable. Not so with the works of a poet, he argued, because the original will "continue unimpaired," whatever may be done to it. He was effusive in his admiration of Shakespeare as the greatest writer in the language, and generously attributed the Bard's many regrettable lapses into obscenity as concessions to "the bad taste of the age in which he lived." It was his wish, he explained, "to render the plays of Shakespeare unsullied by any scene, by any speech, or, if possible, by any word that can give pain to the most chaste, or offense to the most religious of readers." He found little to eliminate on the latter score, since Shakespeare generally spoke well of religion, but when it came to offending the chaste—well!

The difficulties were prodigious. As an example, he cited a speech of Iago's. "The word 'bolster' is as innocent a word as any in our language," Bowdler wrote, "but in 'Othello' it is so emphasized as to assume a meaning so grossly improper that no gentleman could venture to read it to a lady, or could think that the substitution of 'quilt' instead of it would be an injury to this matchless tragedy."

But the difficulty about the bolster was as nothing compared to the formidable problem posed by Falstaff. Even Bowdler, for all his smug self-certainty, was overawed by Falstaff and never quite knew what to do with him. Obviously, if Bowdler were to stick by his principles, so prodigious a scalawag as Falstaff would have to be annihilated, but Bowdler didn't dare. He contented himself with modifying the language somewhat and blotting out Doll Tearsheet entirely.

By the time Bowdler got around to rendering the Bard antiseptic, the plays had been pretty thoroughly knocked about by others for other reasons, and he used this circumstance to help justify his own depredations. Voltaire had expressed the opinion that Shakespeare was a "barbarous mountebank," conceding only that there were "a few pearls in Shakespeare's enormous dunghill." Nahum Tate had tacked a happy ending on "King Lear." Garrick had reduced "A Winter's Tale" to the length of an afterpiece and modernized "Hamlet," driving Gertrude mad with remorse and having Hamlet duel with the King.

But *The British Critic,* in April of 1822, lashed out at the growing practice of rejiggering Shakespeare according to the heart's desire of every theatrical tinker and literary meddler who came down the pike. "They have purged and castrated him, and tattooed and beplaistered him, and cauterized him and phlebotomized him with all the studied refinement that the utmost skill of critical barbarity could suggest," the magazine wrote. "Shakespeare is, of all poets, precisely that one of whom we can least afford to lose one iota . . ."

And it added:

> Here ran Johnson's dagger through;
> See what a rent envious Pope made,
> And here the well-beloved Bowdler stabbed.

Bowdler was hurt. He was, as always, genuinely baffled that anyone should fail to see what an admirable work he was doing in his literary laundry. "Am I to be classed with the assassins of Caesar," he cried in rebuttal, "for rendering these invaluable plays fit for the perusal of virtuous females?" As examples of what, in his opinion, had to go he cited among others the speeches of Hamlet to Ophelia in the Players Scene, the last line of Touchstone's verses to Rosalind in the forest, Celia's racy remark later in the same scene, and the porter in "Macbeth" whose "indecent description of the effects of drunkenness only serves to interrupt the most interesting part of the narration."

Here, perhaps, is the most objectional aspect of Bowdler's tampering the texts: his bland presumption in arrogating to himself not only moral judgment, but artistic also. He actually believed that he knew better than Shakespeare whether or not a scene, a line, a word belonged where Shakespeare put it. It never occurred to him that as a universal genius Shakespeare's scope was all-inclusive, embracing the whole man and the whole woman regardless of the "blush on the cheek of modest innocence"—a cheek which colors or fails to color in accordance with the changing mores of the passing day, while the truth of Shakespeare's characters remains steady and unchanging.

"Shakespeare is never filthy," says Eric Partridge, "he is broad, ribald, healthily coarse, unsqueamishly natural, and unaffectedly humorous. . . ." And: "Shakespeare never exclaims 'Oh, shocking!,' never sniggers: he fails—very naturally—to see that there is any occasion to be shocked: and to him the subject calls for a hearty laugh, not a prurient snigger."

Eric Partridge might be called the modern anti-Bowdler, the farthest extreme in the opposite direction in which Bowdler traveled. In "Shakespeare's Bawdy" (Dutton) he has made a careful and sober study of what he calls "a neglected, yet very important, aspect of Shakespeare's character and art"—sexuality and bawdiness in the plays and poems. Where Bowdler scoured Shakespeare word by word to cleanse him of every last smudge of impropriety, Partridge scrutinizes the plays with equal diligence for the diametrically opposed reason: to uncover and clarify every sexual reference, explain it, and illumine it in the context of the poet's work. It is Partridge's point that what Bowdler so laboriously abolished is a major element in Shakespeare's art, without which it is not only not improved, as Bowdler believed, but outrageously maimed. The eroticism is not something smeared on to truckle to the baser appetites of the audience, but a vitalizing and fermenting ingredient which contributes to making Shakespeare Shakespeare.

"In him, erotic wit often becomes so penetrating, so profound, so brilliant," Partridge writes, "that it would make us forget the eroticism, were it not that the eroticism itself is penetrating and profound; and certainly the degree of wit renders the eroticism aseptic and—except to prudes and prurients—innocuous."

Accordingly, Partridge, a University lecturer and former Fellow of Oxford, applies the same scholarly techniques that produced his "Usage and Abusage" and "The World of Words" to his exploration and analysis of the sex theme in Shakespeare. More than half of the book is devoted to a glossary clarifying the Bard's bawdy use of such seemingly innocent words as *traffic, treasury, trick, flower, flax, tumble, turrets, sunburnt, glib, glow,* and hundreds of others. He counts up the number of synonyms Shakespeare uses for the male sex organ (forty-five) and for the female (sixty-eight). He classifies the plays according to the varying degree of their erotic content: "Twelfth Night," "the cleanest comedy except 'A Midsummer Night's Dream' "; "Measure for Measure" and "Othello," "Shakespeare's sexually most bawdy plays"; "Pericles": (IV, ii) is perhaps the lowest scene in Shakespeare": "Macbeth," "the 'purest' of the tragedies," and so on.

Bowdler, for all his dogged insistence on suppression, was nowhere near the scholar that Partridge is in his work of illumination. When Shakespeare has the Nurse in Act II, Scene v, say to Juliet—

> . . . I must another way,
> To fetch a ladder, by which your love
> Must climb a bird's nest when it is dark:
> I am the drudge, and toil in your delight . . .

—Bowdler was sharp enough to catch the naughty allusion and bowdlerize the passage to read:

> . . . I must another way,
> I must go fetch a ladder for your love.
> I am the drudge, and toil in your delight.

But the following speech from "King Henry IV," Part I, and dozens like it, he unwittingly let stand—

> Come, come, you paraquito, answer me
> Directly unto this question that I ask:
> In faith, I'll break thy little finger, Harry,
> And if thou will not tell me all things true.

Bowdler was too innocent, or too dull-witted, to realize that Lady Percy is here using very unladylike language indeed; but Partridge knows, and he has no fear that his frank glossary note explaining the indelicate reference will seriously undermine the morality of his readers.

This attitude received sweeping confirmation one Sunday afternoon not many months ago when Orson Welles, as King Lear, bellowed—

> Let copulation thrive . . .

—and the rest of that bitter passage, unbowdlerized, into several million television homes without noticeably lowering the moral tone of the American public or corrupting any appreciable number of those virtuous females Bowdler was forever wringing his hands over. What Shakespeare judged could safely be absorbed by mixed company in sixteenth-century London can evidently be taken in stride by succeeding generations also, despite the prognosis of Dr. Bowdler.

"An examination of every passage of Shakespeare's sexual imagery," runs Eric Partridge's argument, "would show, once and for all, how picturesque and arresting were his imagination

18 *We have been here before*

and fancy; how concise and pregnant and vivid the manner in which he expressed those mental faculties; how apt the use of the sexual metaphor in any given context . . . how large and yet how exact his vocabulary; how rich his mind; his emotions how varied; how wide-scoped his esthetic purpose, expressing itself in purest poetry or the most pedestrian prose and ranging from ethereal delicacy to the most cynical and brutal coarseness, with subtlety and wit applied sometimes to the most unlikely subjects."

But when *The British Critic* insisted on having Shakespeare "placed before our eyes as he really was," Bowdler responded, in caps, with the eternal bleat of the censor:

IF ANY WORD OR EXPRESSION IS OF SUCH A NATURE THAT THE FIRST IMPRESSION IT EXCITES IS AN IMPRESSION OF OBSCENITY, THAT WORD OUGHT NOT TO BE SPOKEN NOR WRITTEN OR PRINTED; AND, IF PRINTED, IT OUGHT TO BE ERASED.

The climate of literature continually fluctuates between these extremes of Bowdler at one pole and Partridge at the other, from the "Family Shakespeare" to "Shakespeare's Bawdy" and all variations between. Bowdler, his successors, heirs, and assigns are always with us, bold when the atmosphere is right for their flourishing, running for cover when the wind blows the other way. The comfort is that Shakespeare, just as he is and without alteration, is certain to survive all weathers for all time.

Chapter II
The issues at stake

B   more specialized aspects of censor-
          ntellectual freedom are introduced,
          rs to the present chapter will offer a
          rview of the subject. These writers—
          llhorn, William O. Douglas, and Aus-
          on—all bring exceptional qualifica-
          e task of seeing the issues whole and
          ry one of wide experience and back-
          ey represent the law, political science,
          terature, the publishing world, and the
          al field.
          way or another, each of these three
          ls is vitally concerned with the freedom
          as indeed are all others whose writings

have been selected for this work. Unquestionably, here is the most basic issue of all. There may be onslaughts against the freedom to speak, the freedom to assemble, and against academic freedom, but when the right to read is taken away, the most fundamental freedom of all has been lost.

It is fitting, therefore, that Walter Gellhorn should analyze in full detail "Restraints on Book Reading"; Justice William O. Douglas examine efforts outside the law to place literature in a strait jacket; and an editor, Austin Harrison, comment on the dire effects of censorship on the serious writer and on national culture.

An outspoken and dedicated defender of civil rights and intellectual freedom, Walter Gellhorn with his active pen has been productive of several of the ablest statements of the liberal point of view on these subjects. "Restraints on Book Reading" is from his *Individual Freedom and Governmental Restraints,* one of a series of lectures at Louisiana State University, published in 1956. In addition, Gellhorn is author in whole or in part of *Security, Loyalty and Science* (1950), *Civil Liberties under Attack* (1951), *The States and Subversion* (1952), and *The Freedom To Read* (1957).

Gellhorn has a distinguished record of public service in various capacities with the federal government. Since 1933, he has been a member of the Columbia University faculty of law and, since 1937, also a member of the faculty of political science.

Walter Gellhorn
RESTRAINTS ON BOOK READING

Books are not big business in the United States. The gross annual receipts of all American publishers from the sales of all manner of books —including the *Bible, First-Grade Arithmetic, Aunt Emma's Cookbook,* and *How to Build Your Own Spaceship*—aggregated in 1955 only a bit more than half the net profits, after taxes, of the General Motors Corporation. If the term "bookstore" be given an extremely loose definition, there are perhaps 1,500 bookstores in the United States—as against 18,000 blacksmith shops. To be sure, there are other means of book distribution, including "book clubs" and public libraries. But Americans are not assiduous bookworms. Sweden, in relation to population, enjoys ten times as many public libraries as does the United States; Denmark has seven bookstores to our one; a recent series of interviews showed that while only one out of every five Americans shyly admitted that he was reading a book (or, at least, reading at a book) during the survey period, more than half the people questioned in Britain were so engaged at that time.

If quantitative measurements like these were to be given overriding significance, restraints on book reading might perhaps be unruffling. Books, however, have a special importance for the nation's health. Paradoxically, their significance derives in part from the economically "small time" character of the publishing business. The book trade is old-fashioned. It still resembles the nineteenth century more than it does the twentieth. Many small, personally operated firms compete actively with one another. Publishers of books unlike publishers of newspapers need not be press owners; so entry into business does not require a vast initial capital expenditure. The resulting entrepreneurial variety encourages the publication of books that might never appear if choice were entirely in the hands of a few industrial giants. Moreover, while best sellers are undoubtedly welcomed by even the most altruistic publisher, a small edition of a hard-cover book is economically feasible; an unsuccessful book is not a major catastrophe. In this respect book publishers are released from the pressure apparently felt by those who cater exclusively to a mass market that, they fear, might vanish if any part of it were antagonized or offended. Hence new ideas, which almost always antagonize or offend, are not so severely limited in books as elsewhere in our increasingly integrated society. And, apart from introducing ideas that may require extensive textual development, books remain the chief hope that diversity, and even elevation, of taste may survive the standardizing, leveling down influences of mass communications.

These considerations warrant particular attention to censorship of books, though all forms of censorship have certain common features and rest on similar hypotheses.

THE PHILOSOPHIC FOUNDATIONS OF CENSORSHIP

Censorship is a loosely used word. Strictly, it means prohibiting expression or communication. When legally enforcible, this connotes official action to prevent the writing or, if too late to prevent the writing, to prevent the publication or other circulation of what the censors deem objectionable. Today the term has been extended to wholly unofficial action as well. It embraces group activity aimed at eliminating

---

Walter Gellhorn, *Individual Freedom and Governmental Restraints* (Baton Rouge: Louisiana State University Press, 1956), pp. 49–104, copyright 1956 by Walter Gellhorn. Reprinted (without amplifying footnotes) by permission of the author and of the publisher.

particular works or kinds of works, or limiting their availability, after their publication. Official censorship, based on law or administrative regulation, usually observes the forms of legal procedures, though its permissible content has sometimes been defined so vaguely that the attendant procedures have given little real protection. Unofficial censorship derives its force not from legal mechanisms, but, at its best, from persuasion and, at its worst, from implacable economic or political pressure abetted by misuse of police authority.

Both kinds of censorship have long been applied to books. They generate problems that can be considered only in relation to the supposed needs that arouse demands for prohibitory controls and in the light of the dangers that the controls create.

Among the wise and good men of the world there have almost always been some who have felt that censorship advances rather than limits man's freedom. Plato, Augustine, and Spinoza among many others asserted that no man is free who acts erroneously because influenced by passion or mistaken ideas. When what is true and good is known, anything that would subvert it should be controlled—not to narrow man's freedom, but to save him from the unfreedom of immorality or harmful doctrine that might damage him or the community. In this view censorship rests in one or another degree upon the belief that those who are qualified to identify evil and mistake should be empowered to prevent their dissemination.

There is another appraisal, however, that leads to a different conclusion. Aristotle—and, in more recent times and in our own country, Dewey and Holmes among others—maintained that a man is free only so long as he may make his own choices. If choice is foreclosed by another's judgment about what is virtuous or wise, freedom is lost. More importantly, in this philosophic approach, the chances of discovering what really is virtuous or wise diminish when experimentalism and disagreement are impossible. Holmes' insistence that "the best test of truth is the power of the thought to get itself accepted in the competition of the market" is a reflection of Aristotle's democratic faith in the value of the individual's own search for virtue and his free action in association with others to secure the common good.

Censorship, in one view, aims at preserving freedom through reinforcing what its proponents regard as the true values and beliefs. Opposition to censorship, in the other view, does not derive from hostility to the virtues the procensors prize, but reflects, rather, a conviction that in the end the values of a free society will be attained through freedom rather than repression. The advocates of censorship, in other words, regard it as a means by which to prevent debasement of the individual virtues, the cultural standards, and the common security of democracy. Its opponents regard it, by contrast, as a danger to the freedom which fosters those virtues and standards, and without which democracy cannot survive. These two quite different conceptions must be kept in mind, because their adherents sometimes too readily believe that the other side is unconcerned with values or is uninterested in freedom. In fact, both seek the same general ends. The question remains whether censorship will advance or retard their attainment.

THE REVIVAL OF BOOK CENSORSHIP

The "omnicompetent and irrepressible" Lord Brougham strongly believed in popular education at sixpenny prices. In pursuit of that belief he organized a Society for the Diffusion of Useful Knowledge that brought forth works on, among other things, "Chemistry, Heat (with the theory of the thermometer and the steam engine), Hydraulics, Hydrostatics, Optics and Pneumatics and a Farmer's Series with something for every agricultural worker to read in the winter evenings." His enthusiasm was strong enough to carry across the Atlantic. In 1829 The Boston Society for the Diffusion of Knowledge began a low-priced venture similar to Brougham's, and two years later The American Library of Useful Knowledge began operations with the declared purpose of issuing "in a cheap form a series of works, partly original and partly selected, in all the most important branches of learning."

If the publishers of paperbound books had confined themselves to this laudable and unexciting purpose, their work would no doubt have passed unnoticed. In time, however, their operations became more ambitious. Approximately 1,500 out of a total of somewhat more than 4,500 titles published in this country in 1885 were paperbound. Many, perhaps most, of these were of foreign, and notably British, origin. Whether their charm lay in their intrinsic worth or in certain deficiencies in the copyright laws of that time is unclear. At any rate, the paperbound business did not survive strengthening of international copyright protection. Not until 1939 and the early 1940's did the paperbound books once more begin to make their presence sharply felt. During that period new high-speed printing and binding methods came to the fore, enabling the cheap production of soft-cover books at a time when the costs of hard-cover book production was markedly rising. By 1953 close to a thousand titles were being issued in paperbound editions annually, a tenth of all the titles published in America.

Mass production connotes mass distribution. In the case of the paperbound books this occurred through more than 100,000 outlets, where in most instances the books competed for sales with magazines whose flamboyant covers sought to catch customers' eyes. Soon the paperbound books were competing not only for customers but also for flamboyancy, both external and internal. In 1955 more than 200,000,000 copies were sold.

It would be manifestly unfair to the publishers of paperbound books to suggest that their products are typically unworthy. As a matter of fact, many (and their number is increasing) reflect the finest in western literary tradition. Even the "trash" is probably several cuts above the level of the pulp magazines, which have seemingly been deserted by millions of readers since the advent of cheap books. Much is said about the vulgarization of literary taste in modern times. But before becoming too despairing, let us recall that not long ago only one or two per cent of the population were among the elite who read any books at all. The ready availability of paperbound books has not debauched tastes that would otherwise have been refined by the steady reading of "good books." On the contrary, the paperbounds seem to have attracted many previous total abstainers who, having discovered that reading can be fun, may have gone ever upwards and onwards with the arts.

At any rate, whatever the merits of the matter, the appearance of paperbound volumes in the mass market drew the eyes of censors as well as customers. The zeal that had once fired the Watch and Ward Society, the Society for the Suppression of Vice, and other self-anointed guardians of the public soul had all but evaporated by 1940. A succession of judicial decisions had emancipated books from the rigorous test of obscenity laid down in 1868 by Lord Chief Justice Cockburn, who believed that words, phrases, or passages could be lifted out of context and then considered as abstractions to determine whether their tendency is to "deprave and corrupt those whose minds are open to such immoral influences"—a test, as one indignant litterateur exclaimed, that allows four letters to count for more than four hundred pages. The unwillingness of judges to condemn a literary work as a whole because some of its parts might offend the most sensitive reader was matched by an apparently mounting belief that anyone who could afford to spend money on books was probably past salvation, anyway. As a result, literary expression was increasingly free —and perhaps increasingly earthy.

Toleration reached the snapping point, however, when books fell within the reach of youthful and impecunious buyers. Then, in the words of Reverend James Pickett Wesberry, Chairman of the Georgia Literature Committee, "a few public-spirited citizens at last became alarmed" at the "display of salacious material freely accessible to the young and impressionable *at prices easily accommodated by young allowances,* and began to act." In this context, action meant censorial efforts.

THE IDENTIFICATION OF OBSCENITY

Those who urge increased repression of allegedly obscene books are of course convinced that "obscenity" can be identified. In reality, however, the word does not refer to a thing so much as to a mood. It is a variable. Its dimensions are fixed in part by the eye of the individual beholder and in part by a generalized opinion that shifts with time and place.

Partly, too, the concept of obscenity is itself a product of censorship and concealment. Our grandfathers, we moderns hear incredulously, strained hotly for a peek of a prettily turned ankle; their voyeurism was stimulated by clothing styles reflecting a moral conviction that the existence of female legs should be kept a secret. The Japanese, conditioned by their training to regard kissing as an entirely private exercise, are said to find American movies filled with obscenity because they unabashedly portray heterosexual osculation; and as a consequence films that do not bring a blush to the most demure Americans must be drastically edited before they are deemed appropriate for general exhibition in Japan. A hundred years ago Nathaniel Hawthorne's *Scarlet Letter* was thought unfit for modest maidens, a fact that probably led to its being read so eagerly and widely as to assure its becoming an American classic, now very grudgingly studied in high school courses from coast to coast. Nobody today cringes at mention of venereal disease, but not long ago it was one of the "dirty little secrets" that D. H. Lawrence insisted became dirty (and slyly cherished) only because of futile attempts to suppress mention of them—just as, in linguistics, words derive their deliciously vile connotations from restraints rather than from use. The late Harry Reichenbach, press agent extraordinary, put Lawrence's theory to practical commercial uses. He managed, by calling attention to a row of strategically placed asterisks, to persuade the Post Office Department to deny the mails to Elinor Glyn's *Three Weeks*. When the ban was lifted, as of course it eventually was, the demand for the shoddy novel moved it triumphantly to the best seller lists. According to one account, he made a "masterpiece" of an inferior painting called "September Morn," an innocuous representation of a nude woman standing up to her knees in sea water. Her arms were carefully intertwined to provide a reasonably chaste covering of her front, but only goose pimples covered her exposed flanks. Reichenbach bribed some boys to stand in front of a Brooklyn art dealer's window display, pointing and grimacing at this not very exciting spectacle. An anonymous telephone call brought the "vice crusader" Anthony Comstock storming to the scene, and, after him, the police. All this led to vast popularity for a picture that might otherwise have hung inconspicuously in the home of some Brooklyn burgher. Seven million copies were ultimately distributed, bringing the picture within the vision of almost every American male who patronized a barber shop; the original was sold for some $10,000.

But let us put aside for the moment the possibility that repression creates rather than stifles the evil of obscenity. The difficulty of definition remains. The Reverend Dr. James Wesberry says that "determining what is or is not obscene would not be difficult for me to do personally"—but he then quickly acknowledges with some puzzlement that what is obnoxious to him "would probably not get a guilty verdict in the courts." His perplexity is not unique. An international conference at Geneva on Suppression of the Circulation and Traffic in Obscene Publications accomplished much less than had been hoped, because the delegates could not agree upon what obscenity is. One prominent censor reportedly said a year or two ago: "I don't discriminate between nude women, whether or not they are art. It's all lustful to me." The remark shows, as Eric Larrabee has observed, that one man's sex may be another's psychoneurosis; it casts much more light on the censor than it does on obscenity.

It is easy to make fun of the untutored; but even the highly cultivated and literate person runs into real trouble when he seeks to define the undefinable. A very able and highly respected priest, for example, falls back upon "custom" and "common estimation" rather than upon precise definition to help in applying the principle that "if this object rouses to genital commotion, it is obscene"; but, recognizing that "it is not a matter of absolute certainty that this particular object will so arouse even the normal man," he urges acceptance of the idea that "even if it is not certain that such and such an object will arouse to sexual passion, nevertheless, if the probability swings in that direction, then the object is, for practical purposes, obscene." No doubt these words were not intended to be read literally, for a net cast so widely would bring in an unsuspected catch. Many persons profess, for example, to see a phallic symbol in the radiator ornamentation of motor cars; shall the ornamentation, which may thus arouse a "genital commotion" in one sensitive to symbols, be banned? In a carefully conducted survey 85 per cent of a group of boys between the ages of 12 and 16 (the tender years of adolescence about which censorial groups are particularly concerned) reported "genital commotions" resulting from such varied and seemingly non-erotic stimuli as carnival rides, playing a musical solo, fast car-driving, and seeing a column of marching soldiers. Perhaps we could tolerate doing away with such "obscenities"; but what would we do about the similarly "obscene" stimuli of taking school tests, receiving grade cards, and listening to the national anthem? Questioning of a large number of American college women disclosed that dancing, music, and, to some extent, reading had been among the sources of their sexual stimulation; but far and away the largest number very simply and directly stated that the chief stimulus was MAN—an obscene object susceptible of only a limited censorship. In truth, if the suggested test of obscenity were to be taken very seriously, it would lead to a fruitless effort to fetter life itself—and would certainly necessitate the censoring of brassiere advertisements, rock and roll music, and "sacrosanct institutions like the pin-up picture or the drive-in theater, which have done more to keep sex going in America than Steinbeck has." Unless the human race is to vanish entirely, we can scarcely afford to regard the arousing of normal sexual desires as a social danger to be curbed at all costs.

Federal Judge Ernest Tolin, faced with the perplexing question of what constitutes obscenity, decided to consult the settled authority of judicial utterances. His researches were more baffling than enlightening, for in 1954 he discovered fourteen different judicial definitions of the term. "No one seems to know what obscenity is. Many writers have discussed the obscene, but few can agree upon even its essential nature," complained Professors Lockhart and McClure after completing one of the most exhaustive studies yet made in this field.

Often coupled with obscenity as an object of censorial concern is the fictional portrayal of violence and "horror." These are somewhat more readily identified than obscenity, though, even as has been the case with obscenity, styles change from generation to generation. What was deemed outrageous yesterday may be taken for granted today. Thus, for example, an Illinois court only thirty years ago upheld a censorial refusal to permit the showing of "The Deadwood Coach," because "where gun-play, or the shooting of human beings . . . is for personal spite or revenge, and involves taking the law into one's own hands, and thus becomes a murder, the picture may be said to be immoral; it inculcates murder"—a belief that has seemingly had small effect on Hollywood producers or on movie-goers. The "czar" of the comic books industry now seeks to interdict "scenes of horror, excessive bloodshed, depravity, lust, sadism, or masochism," as well as scenes dealing with "'walking dead,' torture, vampires, ghouls and cannibalism." He has at least a fighting chance of identifying them, though what constitutes "*excessive* bloodshed" may be difficult to ascertain in a nation deeply addicted to detective stories, Western movies, highway fatalities, and the development of awesome devices for producing mass death.

In any event, the main theory of censorship in this respect is the same as in instances of alleged obscenity: suppression of the written word is necessary to forestall thoughts that the unsuppressed word might stimulate—and the theory back of this is that the stimulated thoughts are steps to socially undesirable actions.

THE IMPACT OF READING ON CONDUCT

The view that reading is readily translated into behavior is shared by many reputable persons. Mr. J. Edgar Hoover, as an example, has been quoted as contending that "the increase in the number of sex crimes is due precisely to sex literature madly presented in certain magazines. Filthy literature is the great moral wrecker. It is creating criminals faster than jails can be built." And Dr. Fredric Wertham, a psychiatrist of high standing, has waged a virtual crusade against comic books because his clinical observation has convinced him that the comics have sexually stimulated and emotionally brutalized many children.

With all respect to those who accept these assertions as self-evident truths, I doubt that the available evidence supports them. I think that they overstate the significance of words and pictures and understate the other elements of life that shape human behavior.

Admittedly, the premises underlying censorship have not as yet been fully tested by empirical research. Hence one cannot demonstrate unequivocally that books do not promote juvenile delinquency, sexual perversion, sadism, and the other evils the censors fear will flow from reading. Such objective evidence as does exist, does not sustain the fear.

We start with the proposition that an interest in pornography is seemingly not the molder of a man's personality but the reflection of it. Indeed, certain psychological experiments suggest that one who finds pornographic elements in allegedly obscene books is very likely to discover them also in apparently innocuous books, through a process of self-selection and emphasis that the reader himself brings to the words. This same process of self-selection—this tendency to read and see what accords with pre-existing interests—probably controls the effects of reading as well as the determination of what will be read. The fact that "sex maniacs" may read pornography does not mean that they became what they are because of their reading, but that their reading became what it is because of them. Their personality, according to modern scientific findings that confirm a proposition stated long ago by the Jesuit fathers, was probably basically formed before they ever learned to read.

So far as disclosed by the most exhaustive study of juvenile delinquency yet made in America, reading seems to be of small moment in shaping antisocial tendencies. Sheldon and Eleanor Glueck searchingly inquired into numerous cases to identify the influences that produced delinquency. Reading (if it was influential at all) was of such slight significance that it was altogether omitted from their statement of "factors with probable causal significance." Judge George W. Smyth, just retired after being for many years acclaimed as one of the nation's outstanding children's court judges, has described to the New York State Temporary Commission on Youth and Delinquency the causes that had seemingly contributed to delinquency in cases recently adjudged by him. Reading *difficulty* was mentioned as among the 878 causative factors that had had effect upon the troubled children before him; *reading,* no matter of what, found not a single place in his list.

Judge Smyth's observation is confirmed by other workers in the field of undesirable juvenile behavior. The Bureau of Mental Health Services of the Domestic Relations Court of New York has found a marked reading retardation among the children whose conduct has brought them before the court. Far from discovering that delinquency grew out of reading, the clinicians have discovered that among New Yorkers it is more likely to grow out of inability to read. This is no transitory condition, but, as a succession of studies has shown, has been true for decades. The importance of the "common sense" or "hunch" or "experience" that seeks to ascribe delinquent behavior to undesirable reading, should not be minimized. But heavily laying the finger of blame upon reading matter, even upon the despised comic books with all their crudities and offensiveness, is likely to divert attention from much more serious problems. Censorship is a nostrum rather than a remedy. Reliance on it will simply delay therapeutic and preventive steps that must be taken if youthful antisocial conduct is to be lessened.

Dr. Marie Jahoda and the staff of New York University's Research Center for Human Relations recently surveyed the available studies bearing on the impact of reading on human conduct, good and bad. Every indication points to a primary conclusion: "Direct experiences have a much greater directive power on human behavior than do vicarious experiences."

To say that one's personality is formed before he acquires reading habits is, of course, not the equivalent of saying that reading cannot conceivably affect behavior. Reading, like other environmental factors, may modify an individual's personality predispositions, though unlikely in itself to make a "bad" man out of a previously "good" one. The question remains, however, whether fiction will frequently provide what Dr. Wertham calls the "added impetus" to antisocial impulses, serving as a trigger mechanism to set off an explosion that otherwise might not have occurred.

Nobody is in a position, on the basis of what is now known about human beings, to deny this possibility. But there is at least one other possibility to be offset against it and, more importantly, a probability that diminishes its significance as an argument in support of censorship. The offsetting *possibility* derives from the Aristotelian concept of emotional catharsis, shared now by many psychiatrists who believe that aggressions and frustrations that might otherwise flare into overt conduct are not fanned to flame but, instead, are more often dissipated, or at least made temporarily quiescent, by reading. The *probability* is that fictional reading (even comic book reading) about sexual conduct or about violence and brutality has small behavioral consequence as compared with the more realistic impressions derived from reading newspapers—or even from seeing motion pictures or television that purport to mirror reality. Years ago, in commenting upon some of the classics that might be deemed obscene, Lord Macaulay said: "We find it difficult to believe that in a world so full of temptations as this, any gentleman whose life would have been virtuous if he had not read Aristophanes and Juvenal will be made vicious by reading them." Change Macaulay's illustrations and his point holds good today.

Unless all children are to be wrapped in cotton batting and utterly removed from the world, we cannot hope to immunize every one of them against contact with something that might conceivably energize his savage side. G. K. Chesterton once noted a complaint that a child had been induced to kill his father with a carving knife, through having seen a similar episode in a motion picture. "This may possibly have occurred," Chesterton conceded, "though if it did, anybody of common sense would prefer to have details about that particular child, rather than about that particular picture. But what is supposed to be the practical moral of it, in any case? It is that the young should never see a story with a knife in it? . . . It would be more practical that a child should never see a real carving-knife, and still more practical that he should never see a real father. . . . It is perfectly true that a child will have the horrors after seeing some particular detail. It is quite equally true that nobody can possibly predict what that particular detail will be . . . If the kinema exhibited nothing but views of country vicarages or vegetarian restaurants, the ugly fancy is as likely to be stimulated by these things as by anything else." Experts in abnormal psychology agree with Chesterton.

It is well, perhaps, to stress that in this branch of the discussion we are indeed talking about abnormal rather than normal psychology. Even if it be true that reading matter may activate the impulses of some twisted individual, can this possibility justify repressive policies that affect all alike? Should a nation's reading be tailored to fit the extremely uncertain contours of an hypothetical person with a supposedly lower threshold of resistance than is usual? A program of censorship aimed at that end must prove to be all but limitless. There is virtually no repression of expression that could not be justified as a necessary protection of isolated individuals with abnormal predispositions. Where the harmfulness of speech or writing is provable and certain, limitations in the form of penalties have always been upheld—as, for example, in the false labeling of foods, the uttering of defamations, and the inciting of riots. There is a world of difference, however, between speech (or writing) as a form of demonstrably dangerous action and, on the other hand, speech (or writing) that may conceivably though improbably have some unascertainable impact upon some unidentifiable and anomalous person. The stable and well adjusted members of the community must make many sacrifices because there are unstable and disturbed members as well. But freedom of communication and freedom to read ought not to be among the sacrifices when the gain is so dubious and the deprivation so plain.

Let this not be read as a plea for the preservation of "bad" books. It is a plea, rather, for the proposition that the accessibility of books should not be determined censorially but selectively; that the possibility of reader's choice should not be foreclosed, because the wisdom to make good choices may grow even out of bad choices; and that, above all, the public not be beguiled into hoping to curb delinquent behavior by curbing reading. Our better chance, so far as the problem of delinquency is concerned, is to discover how to persuade potential delinquents to commence reading good books, rather than to waste our energies in seeking to keep reading matter out of their hands.

THE SUPPRESSION OF BAD IDEAS

In another aspect of the matter, concern about obscenity merges into a more generalized concern about supposedly dangerous thinking. A Congressional committee, for example, has denounced a book that apparently made a serious argument in favor of polygamy, and entered another into its records because the "author is obviously trying to cash in on the Scottsboro pro-Negro agitation which was Communist-inspired." Elsewhere obscenity has been detected not so much in the wording as in the content of challenges to commonly accepted convictions about the desirability of chastity or monogamy. In such instances books are censorially threatened because they are the repositories of ideas deemed injurious to society, or, to put it in the more common speech of the day, because they are subversive. Opinions thought to be potentially subversive of governing authority and those thought to be subversive of the established social and moral order evoke an essentially similar reaction: They are too dangerous to be allowed to circulate! Thus the censorship of "obscenity" and the censorship of "sedition" or "propaganda" are seen to have a common core.

The Communist view, as expounded by Lenin, admits no argument about the desirability of suppressing unsettling thoughts. "Why should freedom of speech and freedom of the press be allowed?" Lenin asked. "Why should a government which is doing what it believes to be right allow itself to be criticized? It would not allow opposition by lethal weapons. Ideas are much more fatal things than guns. Why should any man be allowed to buy a printing press and disseminate pernicious opinions calculated to embarrass the government?"

I fear that there are non-Communist Americans who may share this particular bit of the hated ideology.

In my estimation the proscription of writings because of their feared effects on accepted beliefs is not only unconstitutional but, on the most pragmatic basis, unwise. Since 1791 the First Amendment has stood as a safeguard of the freedom of expression. The doctrine of political freedom it is intended to implement is not a bit of eighteenth-century muddleheadedness. It reflects, rather, the lesson learned from history that truth cannot be established by proclamation and that belief cannot be created by extirpating non-believers. It embodies the faith that whatever may be the short-run gains or losses along the way, in the end the national safety is endangered far less by political freedom than it is by political suppression.

Day-to-day decisions, however, are not shaped by constitutional absolutes. Nor do sons live always in the shadow of their fathers' faith. Excessive worry about disagreement, novelty, and heresy cannot be dispelled by the Spirit of 1776, but (if at all) by a cool appraisal of the contemporary scene.

What does that appraisal show? It shows, among other things, a perfectly amazing exaggeration of the extent to which dissent is abroad in the land. In the United States the main channels of communication are all but exclusively occupied by upholders of the established order. There are 1,860 daily newspapers—of which only one, with a circulation of 6,000, is Communist; *Life* magazine, which on the whole does not challenge the nation's fixed attitudes, sells more than 30,000,000 more copies than all the paperbound books put together and probably has an even larger influence than these numbers suggest upon the social attitudes of the day; *Time* magazine, which interlards the news with its own not very heretical views, has a circulation of 1,860,976 compared with the petty 33,006 of the *Nation* and the even paltrier 28,589 of the *New Republic,* two journals of critical though far from revolutionary opinion so unsettling to the good people of Bartlesville, Oklahoma, that they have discharged a public librarian after thirty years of service because she insisted the magazines had a legitimate place in the library.

Ah, yes, say some of our perturbed fellow citizens. That is all very well. But it fails to take into account the *propaganda*.

Differentiating propaganda from discussion or education is not simple. As David Riesman has noted, the distinction between the two may be as essentially subjective as the distinction between liberty and license; there is in general a tendency to regard as propaganda the dissemination of information or the statement of opinions we dislike. In any case, we Americans tend to overestimate the effectiveness of what we do identify as propaganda. A British professor teasingly explained to his own countrymen that "they [Americans] believe in machinery more passionately than we [British] do; and modern propaganda is a scientific machine; so it seems to them obvious that a mere reasoning man can't stand up to it. All this produces a curiously girlish attitude toward anyone who might be doing propaganda. 'Don't let that man come near me. Don't let him tempt me, because if he does I'm sure to fall.'"

Some of the observations made in earlier pages about the process of self-selection in reading matter has obvious pertinence here. Extensive researches have been made into the effectiveness of propaganda, political and other, disseminated by the mass media. Students of communication conclude that, as a rule, it is extremely difficult to impress a communication upon persons who do not already share the views it reflects. Republicans rarely listen to Democratic campaign speeches, and Democrats return the compliment; anti-Semites do not tune in on radio preachments about brotherly love; and Communist spokesmen do not attract large audiences of persons with emptily absorbent minds, ready to accept whatever they may hear. Propaganda seems to have its largest success as a reinforcer rather than as a disturber of existing convictions.

Moreover, a man's attitudes and courses of action are infinitely more significantly influenced by his face-to-face contacts than by what he reads or hears; this is the lesson consistently drawn from extensive analysis of voting behavior and racial prejudices. Ideas do not stick like burrs. Even when they are insistently pounded home by radio or television they still can be and, it seems, for the most part are "avoided by withdrawal, deflected by resistance and transformed by assimilation." The mass media have proved to be most effective when they operate in a situation of "psychological monopoly" (a situation in which books never find themselves); or when they seek to channel an already existent attitude (that is, for example, people who already brush their teeth might be persuaded to buy a particular toothpaste, but the idea of toothbrushing would not probably be adopted by those who had previously survived without it); or when they are conjoined with direct personal contacts. Surely there is even less reason to become exercised about the corrupting power of books, pallid things that are rarely taken up in the first place and that can always be put down and forgotten, than about the mass media.

In light of what we do know about these matters, suppressive efforts seem a misdirected expenditure of energy. I cannot understand, for example, why the Post Office Department is so vigilant to prevent Americans from receiving Russian publications to which, for one reason or another, they wish to refer. As former Ambassador George Kennan tartly remarked, there is probably "nothing sillier than the fear that American library users are going to be inclined toward communism by stumbling on communist publications in libraries. . . . I would know of no better cure for anyone who had illusions about communism or the Soviet Union than to be forced to read *Pravda* or *Izvestiya* over a certain length of time." Even if Communist writers were livelier and more persuasive than they have ever yet managed to be, enforced ignorance would not be the best way to offset their influence. The Advisory Committee on Prisoners of War, named by Secretary of Defense Charles E. Wilson on May 18, 1955, to analyze the problem of "brainwashing," concluded that the uninformed soldier, the man who had never had occasion or opportunity to know anything of communist conceptions and achievements, was the most likely prospect for enemy proselytizing. "The way to combat such a subject as Communism," the committee reported, "is not to hide it or hide from it. The way to combat it is to explode it. Americans have the means at hand—the Bill of Rights. Or call it Democracy or Republican Government, or the American Way. 'Armed with a knowledge of American principles—and a knowledge of the enemy's—the American fighting man possesses a sword and shield which cannot be wrested from him in combat or captivity.'"

That is a sound judgment. Nations do not lose their vitality because questions are asked, but because they remain unanswered. "I do not recollect that any civilization ever perished from an attack of doubt," commented José Ortega y Gasset. "Civilizations usually die through the ossification of their traditional faith, through an arteriosclerosis of their beliefs." Learned Hand reminds us that James Harvey Robinson, the American historian of ideas, advanced somewhat the same thought, but in the affirmative. Robinson used to say that we had risen from the ape because, like him, we had insisted on "monkeying around," always meddling with things as we found them. Judge Hand endorses the thesis, adding his own strong conviction that "any organization of society which depresses free and spontaneous meddling is on the decline, however showy its immediate spoils."

American democracy is not an inflexible thing of fixed components. It is, rather, a structure within which many persons of strongly opposed philosophies and aspirations can reach, for quite different reasons, commonly acceptable conclusions about the plans and actions required for organized living together. If ever the democratic system of the United States is overthrown, it will not be by words. It will be by acts of force and violence, made more forceful and more violent by the artificial stifling of the criticism, the controversy, and the compromise that invigorate our political institutions and make possible a peaceful coexistence of all the elements in our country. President Eisenhower well said in 1953: "As it is an ancient truth that freedom cannot be legislated into existence, so it is no less obvious that freedom cannot be censored into existence. And any who act as if freedom's defenses are to be found in suppression and suspicion and fear confess a doctrine that is alien to America."

THE MECHANICS OF RESTRAINT

Some years ago Boston theater owners risked revocation of their licenses if a majority of a board composed of the mayor, the police commissioner, and a member of the city art commission objected to a play on grounds of "public morality or decency." To avoid the economic gamble, the theater owners subjected themselves to the judgment of a censor appointed by the mayor. The system was efficient and simple. The only trouble with it, as it turned out, was that the officials who operated the system seemed to be altogether too simple. "I do not get the impression," Professor Chafee remarked mildly, "that the holder of this office [of censor] is usually a man of extensive literary training with an established reputation as a dramatic critic. Familiarity with the 'Oedipus Rex' of Sophocles or the 'Hippolytus' of Euripides might lessen his fears that a total collapse of family life will be caused by the presentation of incest on the stage in O'Neill's 'Desire Under the Elms.'" Nor were the mayor or the police commissioner or the art commissioner any better equipped. They were not chosen because they read widely and were accustomed to make literary evaluations. However admirable these officials might be in other respects and however honorably they might discharge their other duties, they remained (when it came to censoring plays) merely three untrained individuals in a position to transmute their tastes into edicts.

The Boston personnel problem is not unique in the annals of censorship. Probably very few official censors are warped and twisted beings of the Anthony Comstock type, neurotically preoccupied with the uncertain state of other people's morals. Still, all things considered, the post of censor is not likely to attract individuals of outstanding cultural attainments. The nature of their work, moreover, perforce bends their energies into finding what they are seeking.

Nor do matters improve when the work of identifying objectionable writings is passed into the hands of volunteer aides. No assurance can be given that the volunteers will be especially well equipped for their labors. In a Minnesota city where more than three hundred books were censored in a move quickly emulated in other communities, the "most responsible" person has been described by an admirer as "a white-haired grandmother, who manages a small grocery store. She looks on the task of censorship as a 'matter of salvation of souls.'" The National Organization for Decent Literature, which circulates lists compiled locally in some dioceses as well as a national list promulgated by the Archdiocese Council of Catholic Women of Chicago, depends upon volunteer readers to judge popular publications according to the organization's established criteria. The same is true of other citizens' groups that undertake to control the community's reading, usually with the help of local law enforcement officials who accept the unofficial lists as authoritative. In Detroit, where the Police Department's Censor Bureau seeks, as it says, to "skim off the filth" without reliance on volunteers, the police refer questionable items to the sole judgment of an assistant district attorney who determines whether they are "objectionable," only "partially objectionable," or fit for consumption. In Georgia a State Literature Commission whose original members were a Baptist clergyman and "two of the noblest and finest laymen God ever made" has been empowered to investigate "all sales of literature which they have reason to suspect is detrimental to the morals of the citizens of this State." The Commission is to hold hearings, to make findings, to "prohibit the distribution of any literature they find to be obscene," and to recommend prosecution if, notwithstanding their prohibitory order, sales continue. The members of the Commission need have no qualifications other than that they be Georgians "of the highest moral character." They must work rapidly, for they are limited to meeting for not more than thirty days in any one year; and they must be genuinely interested in their duties rather than in the rewards of office, for they receive a per diem fee of only ten dollars.

The essentially amateur status of the censors lends special significance to the practical observation that their judgments are rarely review-

Police Action and "Private" Censorship

Most state laws and municipal ordinances aimed at suppression of allegedly objectionable literature contemplate conventional criminal proceedings in which the issue of guilt or innocence may be tested. In point of fact, not very many prosecutions occur—partly, perhaps, because prosecutors fear that they may only succeed in advertising rather than suppressing the books they dislike.

In any event, convictions have become somewhat too difficult when guilt must be established through fair trials. The courts have evinced too liberal an insistence that a book be evaluated as a whole, instead of by examining isolated passages. Of course there are still occasional convictions of sellers of "under-the-counter pornography" and, even less frequently, of books with some pretensions to seriousness. But there is no present likelihood that scientific works on psychoanalysis or sexual behavior will provide the foundations of successful prosecutions, or that the books of modern writers like James T. Farrell, William Faulkner, and John O'Hara will be adjudged violative of the law.

Writings of these sorts, however, continue to be included among the books deemed objectionable by censorial elements who may not know much about art, but who know what they don't like.

This would be tolerable if the matter stopped there—if, that is, the objectors did no more than express their opinions concerning the merits of available reading matter. There is no reason why one must depend for advice upon the *Saturday Review of Literature* or the *New York Times Book Review* if, instead, one would prefer to receive his literary guidance from a religious source, from a circle of housewives, or from a veterans' organization.

Trouble arises only when the advisers insist that their advice be accepted. Precisely that trouble does arise today with considerable frequency, in the form of pressures upon distributors and sellers of books.

Application of pressure is especially easy in the case of paperbound books. In few cities are they distributed by more than two wholesalers, whose trucks also deliver magazines and comic books to news dealers and other retailers. The police need not attack upon a broad front, but can entirely control the situation by squeezing this narrow bottleneck. Truck operators are usually heavily dependent on police tolerance of brief violations of parking regulations, during unloading operations; wholesalers' warehouses are subject to being especially closely examined by building, fire, and health inspectors. Moreover, the retailers may be municipal licensees. Both wholesalers and retailers (who often combine ignorance of their rights with a disinclination to defend those of which they are aware) are therefore readily influenced by police "suggestions" that particular books be suppressed.

In mid-1955 the Detroit police department, upon request, was proudly distributing its list of banned books to at least a hundred other cities, where presumably the catalog of 275 "objectionable" and 60 "partially objectionable" paperbound titles is put to some sort of semi-official use. Similarly, private groups press vigorously for dealers' observance of their censorial judgments. Often this is done by awarding seals of approval to stores that remove listed publications from sale, the award to some shopowners being coupled with threatened or actual boycotting of others. Sometimes reliance is placed upon the police to "persuade" the recalcitrants. Mayors, police commissioners, and trade association executives have frequently called for "voluntary co-operation" with the "decent citizens of the community." This last phrase, being translated, means citizens who agitate for censorship. Those who do so are not always evenly motivated; they may include concerned parents, bigots of one brand or another, self-seeking officeholders who are looking for an "issue," and, often, newspapers that crusade against allegedly obscene books while simultaneously devoting their own columns to scandalism and crudities.

Even when formal legal processes have been prescribed as a prelude to repressive action, "voluntary co-operation" without the legal preliminaries may bulk larger in significance. Thus, for example, during the first year of its life the Georgia Literature Commission, presumably after complying with the statutory procedures, "suggested the withdrawal from sale of five pocket books, three so-called 'flapper' pamphlets and one picture pamphlet, and one art magazine"; but during the same period the distributors were led by "voluntary co-operation" to eliminate some thirty-odd additional publications. In Detroit, the police and the prosecutor read paperbound books that are voluntarily submitted for approval in advance of distribution—though one of the distributors "volunteered" only after the police notified retailers that they were handling books not yet cleared by the Censor Bureau, and might thus unwittingly expose themselves to the risk of prosecution under the obscenity laws. The result of all this co-operation is that Detroiters, young and old alike, are barred from obtaining cheap editions of many books of merit (as well as many whose authorship and titles cast doubt upon their value).

The test of what may be read in soft covers in Detroit is very simple. "If I feel that I wouldn't want my 13-year-old daughter reading it," the assistant prosecutor recently told a reporter, "I decide it's illegal." Then he added, "Mind you, I don't say that it is illegal in fact. I merely say that in my opinion it would be a violation of the law to distribute it. The distributors usually co-operate by withholding the book." Since the censorial rulings are not publicly announced, Detroiters do not, as it were, know what they are missing. The distributors seem content with a system that releases them from harassment by private censorial groups, and the retailers are little concerned since they are unaware of any loss. Interviews in Detroit lead one to conclude that dissatisfaction is largely confined to a few libertarian professors (who were especially aroused when students could not procure a paperbound edition of a book assigned for reading in an American literature course; the volume was readily available in hard covers at four dollars per copy) and, at the other extreme, a few clericals who think that religious pressures could, if given free reign, accomplish even more than the police.

But a warning lurks in the shadow of the Detroit experience. One publisher has already begun to submit book manuscripts to the Detroit Censor Bureau for approval before printing, in order to make such changes as may be required to assure distribution in that city. If the trend were to continue, the supposed needs of a thirteen-year-old girl in Detroit might determine the nation's book diet, for publishers are unlikely to prepare one edition for Detroit and another for the rest of the country.

The Government as Consumer and Distributor

To an extent only partially appreciated, the book trade is dependent for survival upon governmental purchases. Half of the hard-cover books sold in this country are either bought directly by federal, state, or municipal agencies or adopted pursuant to their instructions. Public library purchases account for a very large proportion of what the children and adults of America will voluntarily read, and textbook expenditures reflect what the children will have to read regardless of their wishes. The armed forces, through the post exchanges, control the accessibility of reading matter for purchase by nearly two million military personnel. School libraries, overseas information libraries, hospital libraries, and many other government programs involve official book buying.

Obviously, there must be selectivity in administering matters like these. Public agencies are under no duty to procure everything that is printed, or to underwrite the economic success of book publishers. Discretion must be granted broadly. Being broad, it is susceptible of misuse. The large choices necessarily involved in the selection process may be exercised censorially, sometimes without reference to the intrinsic merits of the books involved; and, when this does occur, the censorial judgment is essentially unreviewable.

Instances of debatable decisions abound. The Third Air Force, which controls the post exchanges for all American armed services in Britain, at one time forbade the sale in post exchanges of any books deemed objectionable by the Chicago Archdiocese Council of Catholic Women; and Dr. Kinsey's report on the alleged sexual behavior of human females was banned throughout the Army. The city manager of a large southwestern city recommended that the public library burn a large group of books (including an edition of *Moby Dick* that was suspect because it contained illustrations by the distinguished but "controversial" artist Rockwell Kent), after a "Minute Woman" had listed them as communist-connected. The Secretary of State of Illinois, responding to an indignant mother's protest that her teen-age daughter had been polluted by a book, directed a compilation of offensive volumes that should be removed from public libraries throughout the state; when the list had grown to 500 titles and had resulted in the disappearance of some six to eight thousand library volumes, suspicion arose that someone had been over-zealous or that there were imperfections in the litmus paper applied to books in Illinois, and in 1954 the volumes began to return to the shelves. In 1955 a general science textbook published by Houghton Mifflin was dropped from the public schools of Morehouse Parish, Louisiana, because it contained passages such as: "living things which belong to recognizable kinds, which are alike in most physical traits and which breed freely with each other, are said to belong to one species." This closely parallels the definition of "species" in Webster's Collegiate Dictionary; but it was objectionable in Morehouse Parish, according to the book's critics, because it insinuates that races "breed freely with each other" and is "a dangerous socialistic trend of thought to instill into the younger generation."

This episode illustrates in a small way one of the especially pressing problems in the publishing field. Much of the discussion in preceding pages has related to books that may be read or ignored, as each person may choose for himself. In that area, the words of the late Mr. Justice Jackson have especial pertinence: "It cannot be the duty, because it is not the right, of the State to protect the public against false doctrine. The very purpose of the First Amendment is to foreclose public authority from assuming a guardianship of the public mind through regulating the press, speech, and religion. In this field every person must be his own watchman for truth, because the forefathers did not trust any government to separate the true from the false for us." Textbooks, however, are in a special category. The reader has no choice about them. They are prescribed as the authoritative sources of schoolchildren's enlightenment. Somebody has to decide which book is the best one, all things considered, for compulsory study by a child who has neither the experience nor the resources to be "his own watchman for truth."

This fact justifies a most searching analysis and appraisal of textbook contents, to assure that the educational process will be effective. It also explains why textbook publishers—who, as one of their spokesmen likes to remark, do not thrive on controversy—often encounter irresistible pressures to produce books that no one will challenge. In every community there are articulate persons who oppose school teaching that causes children to question the attitudes they particularly cherish. Since these attitudes are not always uniform throughout the country, textbook editors and publishers are sometimes hard driven to anticipate each and every objection that might be voiced.

Foresight in this respect is highly necessary because an outcry raised against a book in one place induces wariness of it elsewhere. A publisher may therefore almost welcome the opportunity to submit to external editing. William E. Spaulding, former president of the American Textbook Publishers Institute, has addressed himself to the issue in blunt terms. "How many good books," he asks, "do school authorities refuse to consider for adoption just because those books have been subjected to attack? Many a superintendent of schools has quite naturally said to himself, if not to a bookman, 'I don't want a book that's been under fire. It may get me into trouble and I don't need to look for trouble these days.' He knows that attack and suspicion are enough and that no amount of vindication will positively ensure that the same book will not be attacked again. Thus, we seem to be moving closer and closer every day to a proscribing of textbooks on the basis of irresponsible and misguided criticism, to the defamation of textbook character merely by suspicion . . . As a result, teachers, authors, and publishers find themselves facing a mushroom growth of taboos. You can't say this or that any more, this or that author is out, avoid this topic, soft-pedal that, and so on."

Half of the 48 states have state-wide systems of textbook adoption, the others being "open territory." Even in those states that do require a centralized endorsement of texts, the trend is very strongly in the direction of compiling so-called multiple lists of three to five books in each subject, from which local school authorities are authorized to make their own selections. Only two states, Florida and North Carolina, adhere to the "basal book" plan, which involves prescribing a single text for state-wide use, thus entirely destroying the possibility of diversity and experimentation.

These legitimate mechanisms of book selection are readily convertible into illegitimate mechanisms of taboo-enforcement. The study of proposed texts is sometimes entrusted to professional advisers of highest standing or, at the least, to the teachers who must use the books. Often, however, the task is undertaken by persons of less apparent qualifications or by individuals who hold their posts for other than purely educational reasons. Much depends on the outcome of their work, for publishers aspire to universal adoption or at least to eligibility for it. This means, in essence, that they must observe everybody's taboo. If a book could not be adopted in, say, Texas or Indiana or California, there is strong likelihood that it would not be published at all. In a realistic sense, therefore, unprofessional judgments only loosely related to pedagogical needs may sometimes determine what may be available for teaching purposes in other states—and in private as well as in public schools.

No easy solution is at hand. The aims of textbook commissioners should not be to achieve a standardized innocuity, but, rather, to encourage variety as a means of developing fresh insights into educational materials. On the whole, diversity is more likely to result from pluralism than from centralism of authority to choose suitable school books. But when the topics taught in school strike close to the community's emotions and nerves, toleration does not come easily. At those times little patience may be shown toward books that raise questions the community regards as having already been answered.

Foreign Propaganda

The Foreign Agents Registration Act of 1938, as amended in 1942, requires "every person within the United States who is an agent of a foreign principal" to register with the Attorney General and to label as foreign propaganda any "communication or expression by any person which . . . influence[s] . . . any section of the public . . . with reference to the political or public . . . policies . . . of a foreign country or a foreign political party . . . [or the] foreign policies of the United States or promote[s] in the United States racial, religious, or social dissensions."

As the legislative background of the statute reveals, its purpose was to protect the American people against being tricked by persons in this country who, while pretending to be disinterested, were in fact employed by foreigners "to spread doctrines alien to our democratic form of government, or propaganda for the purpose of influencing American public opinion on a political question." Standing upon this narrow statutory base, and buttressed by an Opinion of the Attorney General in 1940 that certain Nazi materials were excludable from this country because of the interaction of the Foreign Agents Registration Act and the Espionage Act of 1917, the Customs Bureau of the Treasury and the Post Office Department have undertaken to withhold from American addressees large quantities of books and papers shipped or mailed from abroad. During one recent month 56,500 pieces of "foreign propaganda" are said to have been seized. In a single year 150,000 sacks of international mail are reported to have been specially processed through the Boston Post Office alone, and 800 different foreign publications are said to have been banned.

The mechanics of suppression are less complex than the questions they raise. As printed materials enter this country from abroad, they are initially examined by customs officers. If entry is otherwise than by the mails, the Customs Bureau itself exercises a final authority of decision, subject to an importer's petition for reconsideration. If entry is by mail, the printed matter is turned over to the Post Office Department, whose legal branch decides whether or not the items in question are "foreign propaganda." If so, the Department destroys the material or gives it to other government agencies. Neither the sender nor the addressee ordinarily receives any notice whatsoever. There appears to be an increasing rigidity in effectuating the present exclusionary policies.

The constitutional doubts created by this governmental action have been fully examined elsewhere. The wisdom of the action, apart from its debatable validity, warrants a few added words.

Administrative exclusion of printed matter from abroad is not necessary to protect Americans against being fooled about the origin of what they read. The foreignness of the sender is indicated at once by the geographical source of the material. As the *Harvard Law Review* puts it, "If the purpose of the Foreign Agents Registration Act is to alert recipients of political propaganda in the United States when the sender of it has foreign connections, that purpose would seem in no way circumvented by permitting the entry into this country of most, if not all, of the material currently excluded. Much of it states specifically the country of origin and the organization publishing it. In any case the very fact that it is sent from abroad presumably means that it bears a foreign postmark or shipping label. And when material is ordered or subscribed to, its recipient should be fully aware of its source."

The work of the customs and postal authorities, then, is not directed at assuring that the dispatcher of printed matter shall be suitably identified (which is the declared objective of the Foreign Agents Registration Act). It is directed, rather, against the printed matter itself, with the aim of insulating Americans against books and papers coming from other countries.

Why, one may ask, should any good American be concerned about the destruction of "foreign propaganda"? The answer, of course, is that the term has no fixed meaning, and may too readily be extended to almost anything of foreign origin. Little of the printed matter now being seized is propaganda that, in the interests of a foreign government, advocates the forcible overthrow of governmental authority in the United States. Much of it is descriptive, no doubt in overly sympathetic and artificially colored terms, of countries behind the Iron Curtain; some of it consists of the periodical publications that students and others read in order to remain in touch with overseas affairs; another portion consists of ideological writings (by no means exclusively communistic in character) that a customs officer thinks might raise unwelcome questions in the mind of a recipient; and some of it is objectionable for no apparent reason other than its having been printed abroad—no other explanation can readily be suggested for seizing issues of the London *Economist,* surely one of the most widely quoted and generally respected of all conservative publications.

As always happens, too, the original motivations of controls in this field are easily forgotten, and then the controls broaden far beyond their expected scope. In 1955, for example, the Post Office Department confiscated a thousand copies of a pamphlet printed abroad but written by the American pacifist A. J. Muste, head of the Fellowship of Reconciliation. Pacifism may be an unpopular and, in the eyes of some, even a dangerous philosophy, but it is not foreign propaganda. In 1954, to give another example, the Post Office Department ruled that an English book highly critical of the Roman Catholic Church was "foreign propaganda" and unmailable in this country because, presumably, it might "promote racial, religious, or social dissensions." The book may very possibly have deserved the oblivion to which the postal authorities sought to consign it. Its merits, however, ought to be judged by its readers rather than by officials who assume "a guardianship of the public mind." After protest had been made along this line, the Post Office Department rescinded its prohibitory action.

The Foreign Agents Registration Act never purported to interpose the government between the printed page and the reader. It undertook, merely, to assure that the reader should know the source of the printed page, so that its contents could be appraised in the light of that knowledge. The Supreme Court has more than once reminded us that the constitutional protection of free expression is intended to safeguard the opportunity to hear or read as well as the opportunity to speak or write. This opportunity vanishes when officials summarily determine the extent to which Americans may receive news and views from abroad.

Both the Post Office Department and the Customs Bureau, be it said to their credit, have begun to exercise a moderating discretion when satisfied that materials they regard as "foreign propaganda" are to be used for educational rather than propagandistic purposes. Columbia University, to state one example, had experienced great difficulty during a period of fifteen months beginning April, 1953, in securing delivery of books and other publications ordered from Russia, Hong Kong, and elsewhere. These were urgently needed by the University's Russian Institute and East Asian Institute, many of whose students were preparing for the diplomatic and military services. Finally, after strenuous efforts by university spokesmen, the governmental authorities were persuaded to deliver the impounded shipments of printed materials. Since July, 1954, the University's libraries have encountered little delay in obtaining publications, though individual instructors still occasionally fail to receive materials addressed to them.

The present Solicitor of the Post Office Department, who is responsible for this aspect of its activities, has been quoted as assuring that "no qualified recipients will be denied these publications. All they have to do is satisfy us that they have a legitimate reason for reading them" —though, as he comfortably adds, "We don't have much of a problem. Most Americans don't want the stuff." No doubt the Solicitor is entirely accurate in this appraisal of his fellow citizen's wishes. But individuals should be allowed to do their own discarding into wastebaskets. They should not be forced to declare in advance that they have "a legitimate reason" (or, indeed, any reason at all) for either reading or ignoring books, pamphlets, magazines, newspapers, or circulars. Whether a person reads or burns a publication is his business, not the government's.

Postal and Customs Administration

Neither the Post Office Department nor the Customs Bureau confines its administrative attention to foreign propaganda. Both of them possess broad additional powers with respect to books and writings deemed obscene or seditious. The Postmaster General may seek to eliminate objectionable matter from the mails; the Customs Bureau may seize attempted importations of offensive books.

These administrative powers lose their surface resemblance when their procedural aspects are considered.

Customs seizures are no longer, as once they were, the uncontrollable reflex actions of officials poorly trained as literary critics. For years the Customs Bureau had been accustomed to find intolerably obscene what others had for generations, or even centuries, regarded as important contributions to our cultural heritage— Ovid, Boccaccio, Rabelais, and Voltaire among others. Then, in 1930, upon the initiative of senators who thought the fun had gone far enough, the law was changed to provide that the importability of books should be made finally not by customs officers, but by courts.

The present procedure still involves an initial customs determination, of course. But if the Customs Bureau seizes an allegedly objectionable book, the seizure must be reported to the United States Attorney, who then begins a forfeiture proceeding in the local federal court. The importer of the book is suitably notified. A jury trial can be (but rarely has been) demanded by either the importer or the government. If the federal district judge determines that the book is "obscene" or otherwise prohibited by law, the seizure is upheld; otherwise, the book is released to the one who ordered it from abroad.

The 1930 statute encouraged a little freshet of litigation to test the validity of exclusionary rulings that had for long years been beyond challenge. Charming case titles began to appear in the law reports—*United States against Married Love,* for example—as publishers and importers hastened to ask the judges whether their books really were as bad as the customs officers had believed. The judges were unable to find the vices detected by the officials. In one ruling after another, culminating in the famous *Ulysses* case in which James Joyce was held to be an author rather than a pornographer, they upset the adverse determinations of the Customs Bureau.

Stung by criticism of the Bureau, the Treasury Department in 1934 began to improve its administrative vision. Now, as in the past, inspectors or other employees of subordinate rank examine imported books at ports of entry. If they are detained, the importer is notified of the detention. He may then, if he wishes, seek an overruling of the subordinate's decision by higher customs officers at the port. If he succeeds, the book enters and there is the end of the matter. If he fails, the question of admissibility must be referred to Washington. There it is considered by an exceptionally civilized censor, who, while he accords no formal hearings, is available for conference with the importer or others interested in the book. While the work at the ports seems to be carried on with much the same obtuseness that characterized the past (Kant's *Critique of Pure Reason* and a Spanish translation of the Bible have been among the casualties of recent years), the work in Washington has taken on a new dimension of sobriety.

Exclusionary rulings have not suddenly become rare. They are merely cautious. "Under-the-counter" writings, on the one hand, are identified and barred. Scientific and literary works, on the other, are identified and admitted. When the customs censor has doubt about the category in which a writing belongs, he consults the published authorities or seeks advice from acknowledged specialists in the relevant field.

Because the censorial judgment is now exercised with good sense and moderation, few adverse rulings are sought to be appealed. But if an exclusionary decision is not accepted, it is subject to a full re-examination in a federal court, where no weight will be accorded the prior administrative determination. The decision of the Customs Bureau to seize a book because of its character is analogous to a prosecutor's decision to press charges against a person suspected of crime; the trial takes place subsequently to find out whether the accusation is well founded.

The postal administration is strikingly different. The Post Office Department manages a gigantic enterprise, and on the whole does it well. The mail delivery business, monopolized by the government, is the "main artery through which the business, social, and personal affairs of the people are conducted"; and, naturally enough, the Department's energies are chiefly devoted to getting material into and through the artery, rather than keeping material out. As an exceedingly minor incident of the entire operation, however, the Department does have the responsibility and power to exclude matters that are objectionable either because of their physical properties (such as explosives or corrosives) or because of their ideological content (such as obscenity or seditious utterance). In theory, the postal authorities are not in the latter case engaged in censoring writings (which the First Amendment might be thought to forbid), but are merely deciding what sort of business the government will choose to transact.

This theory, it must be conceded, has some respectable underpinnings. In 1878 the Supreme Court upheld the power to exclude lottery circulars from the mails; this was thought not to be an abridgment of free speech because the use of the mails was a mere privilege, withdrawable when Congress willed. But the theory has been much weakened by critical analysis and by a succession of judicially expressed doubts. In 1878 the Supreme Court readily assumed that other suitable means of distribution were available to persons who were denied use of the mails. If this assumption was sound then, it is clearly not so now. All present signs point to a redirection of judicial analysis, with a probable conclusion that exclusion from the mails positively limits expression rather than merely withholds a privilege that may be granted or denied as whim may dictate.

As in other branches of this discussion, however, I wish to concentrate attention chiefly upon the merits of what is being done, rather than upon constitutional considerations. I turn therefore to the pertinent procedures, policies, and possible after-effects of postal censorship.

At the outset one must note the inaccessibility of information about the censorial practices of the Post Office Department. There are no published rules and regulations to suggest either the standards of judgment or the departmental procedures that will be followed in exclusionary cases. Even unofficial descriptions are infrequent and incomplete.

In fact, the postal censorship operates very informally. Any postal matter other than first-class mail is subject to inspection for "obscenity" by any person in the department, from rural-route carrier to clerk in the central station. Anything that is thought by anybody to be nonmailable because of its contents will be rejected or, if already in the mails, will be intercepted so as to forestall its delivery. If it is intercepted, the local postmaster sends it to Washington for review by the office of the department's Solicitor. There, it is again examined by members of the Solicitor's staff, with the ultimate decision (on behalf of the Postmaster General) in the hands of an Assistant Solicitor or the Solicitor. If this decision is adverse to the mailability of the intercepted matter, the person who sought to mail it is notified that he may within fifteen days seek to show cause why it should not be destroyed. This is the first regularized notice that anything is deemed amiss, though of course the addressor may have had less formal intimations that his mail has run into difficulties. No formal hearing is granted either before or after the solicitor has ruled on mailability.

Another departmental activity with censorial overtones is carried on rather more formally. Since 1950 the Post Office Department has had authority to refuse to make mail deliveries to a person who has been found to be using the mails to obtain payments for obscene matter. This is somewhat analogous to the Department's power to refuse its aid in effectuating a scheme adjudged to be fraudulent. In the latter case, the Department returns to the "suckers" the letters they have dispatched to the perpetrator of the fraud; in the former the Department issues an equivalent "stop order" against one who needs the mails in order to complete his sale of "any obscene, lewd, lascivious, indecent, filthy, or vile article, matter, thing, device or substance." In these cases, unlike exclusionary proceedings, the Department does accord the affected parties a fair hearing before branding their business as unlawful.

What sorts of judgments does the Post Office Department make under these broad powers, often so abruptly exercised? Is there in fact a general acceptance of its standards? One would like to report that all is for the best in this best of all possible worlds. Alas, satisfaction must be more restrained.

In 1909 an indignant editor denounced the prevailing social standards that, he said, had led cruelly to a young girl's death because she preferred to submit to an abortion rather than bear the stigma of mothering an illegitimate child. His indignation probably grew still stronger when he was convicted of having deposited an obscene writing in the mails. Few in the present Post Office Department would defend that distant prosecution commenced upon the complaint of some now forgotten predecessor. What will their successors say, however, about the judgments that are expressed today?—judgments that stigmatize Freud and Malinowski, Margaret Mead and Simone de Beauvoir, Alberto Moravia's *Woman of Rome* and Vivian Connell's *The Chinese Room* and James Jones' *From Here to Eternity?* What will they think of a determination that Aristophanes' *Lysistrata* should not be delivered to a dealer in rare editions because it "contains numerous passages which are plainly obscene, lewd and lascivious in character which are well calculated to deprave the morals of persons reading same and almost equally certain to arouse libidinous thoughts in the minds of the normal reader"?

The contrasts between the postal and customs administrations now become clear. First, the Customs Bureau avoids making as extreme decisions as those of the Post Office Department. Second, the decisions of the customs authorities are subject to an untrammeled re-examination by a judge and, if desired, by a jury. The decisions of the postal authorities, on the other hand, are not open to anyone's independent appraisals.

They are reviewed, if at all, in a proceeding to set aside the administrative determination; and in such a case, some courts believe as the United States Court of Appeals said only a few years ago, "judicial review channeled within the confines of a plea for an injunction should not be overextensive." If the sender of the allegedly obscene material were prosecuted for his offense, as the statute explicitly authorizes, then he would be entitled to a trial in which the community's notions of good sense might prevail over the administrative determination of objectionability. But so long as the Post Office Department proceeds only against the published matter rather than against its publisher or seller, the postal finding of obscenity may be virtually final.

When in reality there is so little opportunity for review, the importance of sound initial decisions is emphasized. In the Post Office Department a long-standing distrust of experts has prevented the sort of consultations that minimize the chance of mistakes in the administration of customs laws. Moreover, the Department has doggedly adhered to analytical methods long since in disfavor in almost all other American tribunals; for postal censors do not prove themselves capable of reading a whole work to determine its dominant purpose, but continue to be snagged by isolated words and phrases.

There is no good reason why the sort of judicial review provided in customs cases should not also obtain in postal proceedings involving the character of publications. Review of bad decisions will never take the place of good decisions in the first instance. But the possibility of review may stimulate heightened efforts to avoid arbitrariness in administration, and may thus render court proceedings unnecessary in fact. Extensive judicial re-examination of administrative factual determination is resisted in general on the ground that administrators acquire within the field of their specialization a competence that judges cannot claim. In the area of obscenity, however, this is not true. The administrators, to begin with, are not specialists. They are lawyers or party managers or, occasionally, old postal hands whose work has probably had nothing whatever to do with literature, history, psychology, and the other disciplines that may bear upon intelligent censorship. Nor does their main work after appointment provide them with pertinent experience or information. In this respect they differ from many other administrators who, though not especially trained at the outset of their careers, become educated through being immersed in their agency's practical affairs.

Moreover, the "fact" of obscenity is so illusory that bureaucratic methods are not peculiarly fitted to ascertain its existence. Especially when that "fact" may limit freedom of expression and may subject the press to a degree of governmental dictation, its existence should be verified by an independent examination.

Review in General

Preceding segments of this discussion have laid stress on the usual unavailability or inadequacy of procedures for testing censorial determinations. Still, a few cases do trickle into the zone of judicial cognizance. What happens to them when they do is not always reassuring.

Mention has already been made of the unduly narrow scope of review accorded to an adverse judgment of the postal authorities. Judges tend to sustain an exclusionary postal ruling so long as it lies within the outermost fringes of debatable soundness. If the administrative conclusion were the product of specialized insights denied the unspecialized judges, this deference would be not only courteous but functionally desirable. In the present context, however, no good reason appears for subordinating the judges' judgment —except that, in all likelihood, some judges prefer not to take upon themselves the responsibility for the dirty and unrewarding work of censorship. They know that if they rule against a writing, they will be accused of close kinship with Mrs. Grundy; while if they rule against censorship, Mrs. Grundy will take delight in denouncing them.

Appellate courts often exercise a similar self-restraint when called on to re-examine determinations of objectionability made by juries or by trial judges. If the finding below has a rational basis and does not obviously exhibit the application of legally impermissible tests, the reviewing judges are prone to wash their hands of the problem. Thus, for example, when a trial court in Massachusetts decided in 1944 that Lillian Smith's widely discussed and highly praised novel *Strange Fruit* was obscene, the Supreme Judicial Court declined to rely upon its own evaluation of the book, but sustained the adverse determination, remarking: "The test is not what we ourselves think of the book, but what in our best judgment a trier of the facts might think of it without going beyond the bounds of honesty and reason."

Professor Chafee has long espoused the view that a jury is the best tribunal, all things considered, for drawing a line between lawful and unlawful books. The subjective element inevitably remains uppermost in decisions about the permissibility of writings, whether determination be made by one man or twelve. If one man makes the decision alone, however, nothing forces him to dilute his personal prejudices or to achieve awareness that his value judgments may not be shared universally. When, on the other hand, twelve jurors grapple with the issue of objectionability, the very diversity of their backgrounds and tastes drives the jurors toward a cross-sectional and somewhat de-personalized opinion.

If this results in a judgment favorable to a book, an appellate court is warranted in relying upon the jurors' conclusion as dispositive of the question. Their verdict may be taken as a sampling, albeit a highly unscientific one, of community sentiment. Judges have no special competence that enables them to say that the community will be scarred by a book the jury has deemed harmless. Since the free flow of words is essential to the proper functioning of our governmental and intellectual institutions, restrictions upon that flow should be regarded as abnormalities requiring especially convincing justifications. Hence, given a determination by jury (or, for that matter, trial judge) in favor of freedom, an appellate court need not strain to find reasons for overturning the result.

It does not follow, however, that a higher court should accord the same measure of finality to a trial tribunal's adverse judgment, if review of it be sought.

In the ordinary run of things, litigated cases deal chiefly with past episodes. These must be re-created by testimony, often conflicting, which the initial trier of the facts is peculiarly well situated to appraise. The atmospherics of the trial, including the behavior of the witnesses, can be sensed by the jury or by the trial judge who sits without a jury; the appellate court, on the contrary, has before it nothing but cold typescript, entombing the echoes of spoken words. When, however, the issue to be tried is whether a book is obscene or otherwise unlawful, obviously the chief evidence is the book itself. This can be read and appraised by the judges of an appellate court, presumably with at least as much skill as was brought to the task in the inferior court.

There are two main reasons why appellate judges should exercise that skill, notwithstanding their accustomed reluctance to re-evaluate fact findings made in the lower court.

First, the consequences of an adverse judgment upon a book reach far beyond the immediate parties to the litigation. If a jury finds as a fact that the defendant's negligently operated automobile struck and injured the plaintiff, the verdict does of course have importance for the plaintiff and for the defendant (or his insurance company) in that particular case; but the verdict against the defendant has no impact on others. By contrast, a verdict against a bookseller for selling an allegedly obscene book may well determine the availability of that book throughout a community, or even throughout a whole state. Other booksellers may decline to assume the risk of continuing sales, even though the judgment in the case at bar does not affect them in any legal sense. Thus, the rights of innumerable book buyers and readers may be determined as a practical matter by what is done in a single case in which they have not participated and of whose very existence they are probably unaware. Recognizing this, reviewing courts should not hesitate to upset seemingly mistaken (even though debatably correct) decisions about the quality of books. Where communication between writers and readers is at stake, the state's most important judges must feel free to reappraise the need for restraints.

Second, in a field where strong feeling is regularly mistaken for knowledge, "findings of fact" may readily reflect predispositions rather than evidential analysis. Jurymen are not untouched by the passions of their time; and even judges may be intolerant of others' estimates of objectionability. Reviewing courts should not discharge their appellate functions as though wholly unaware of these realities.

A RETURN TO THE BEGINNINGS

The modern varieties of book censorship are not nearly so deeply rooted as most people suppose. Suppression in one guise or another is age-old. But the English obscenity law dates only from 1857, in the Victorian era, and the United States statutory framework began to be built only in 1873, when Congress was overcome by Anthony Comstock.

Before there were statutes in the Anglo-American system there was common sense—and common law. The heart of the common law approach, it seems to me, is this: No person should be deemed free to obtrude upon another an unwilling exposure to offensiveness—or, if you will, to obscenity.

The law of obscenity began, according to most legal scholars, with the case of young and bon vivant Sir Charles Sedley (or Sydlye, according to taste) in 1663. Sir Charles, still drunk after a spree of several days' duration, appeared nude on a balcony overlooking London's Covent Garden, from which vantage point he flung down upon a gaping crowd not only a torrent of profane and indelicate words, but also some bottles filled with what the judges described as an "offensive liquor." No matter what one may think of the later development of obscenity law, one can muster up no sympathy for young Sedley, who was duly found guilty of a criminal offense despite the absence of any statutory definition or direct judicial precedent.

The words Sedley used were probably not wholly unfamiliar to those who heard them. I doubt that they corrupted anyone's morals or coarsened any previously delicate taste. His offensiveness lay in his imposing his words upon auditors who, being about their lawful business in the neighborhood, had no choice but to listen. Few persons over the age of ten are likely to be baffled by four-letter words, but this does not mean that every foul-mouthed ruffian is at liberty to bellow them in the town square. The courts have long held, wholly independently of statutes, that utterances of obscene language in public places, near a dwelling, or in the presence of ladies could be punished. A decent regard for the sensibilities of others is all that makes communal life possible. Existence is difficult enough without the intrusions of wrongheaded nastiness upon a captive audience.

One may not with impunity dispatch letters to his political opponents, showering upon them words of a most distasteful character. One may not repeatedly telephone a respectable married woman, apparently a perfect stranger, and address to her a stream of "filthy, disgusting and indecent language" while persistently proposing acts of sexual intercourse and sodomy. Women may not parade unclothed on the highway—not, one might suggest, because doing so will destroy the moral fabric of society, but because, as Montaigne so strongly felt, nudity in humankind is too often aesthetically offensive: nakedness exposes the defects and imperfections that otherwise remain at least partly hidden, or remedied by the cantilever engineers who design underclothing. The poor wretches who suffer a compulsive need to expose their genitals in public are forbidden to yield to their compulsion—surely not because exposure will attract but because it will cause a revulsion of feeling.

These diverse cases have a single common element. In each, unwelcome conduct has been thrust by the defendant upon fellow-citizens who cannot escape it. Choice is gone. The community, or a part of it, is compelled to hear or see, without reference to its own standards of acceptability. This, in a true sense, is offensive. Many things not harmful in themselves and, indeed, entirely tolerable in some circumstances may be utterly shocking in other contexts. It may be only "social convention" that transforms the character of the thing in question. But convention is the rulebook by which the community plays the game, and the community is entitled to write the rules.

Not long ago the city of Pascagoula, Mississippi (population, 4,000) was outraged by a local humorist who adorned his ancient motor car with a prominently lettered sign: "All you ladies that smoke cigarettes throw your butts in here." The automobile, strategically parked in front of the local post office, drew the townspeople's eyes and, seemingly, stirred their indignation, for the owner was soon indicted for "showing and having in his possession an obscene writing." However deplorable may be the seeming mirthlessness of Pascagoula, is there not a good deal to be said for upholding local tastes in matters of this sort? A civilized being must refrain in public places from sexual or scatological behavior repugnant to the citizenry, just as he refrains in his neighbor's parlor.

Despite a strong personal preference for a society in which the idiosyncratic is accepted calmly, I think that courts should within rather generous limits sustain community attacks upon "public indecency." There is always, of course, a degree of danger that what purports to be the prevailing community sentiment may in fact itself be an idiosyncrasy—as seems to be the case when, as occasionally happens, some sex-mad constable charges that a pantalooned woman is indecently exposed. In the main, however, the community is entitled to demand external respect for its mores, allowing nonconformists the right to appeal for change in prevailing attitudes but not to flout them openly meanwhile.

Trouble arises when this permissible pressure for conformity spills over into censorship, where it has no justification at all. It is one thing to say that nobody should force upon everybody's unwilling eyes or ears a communication they deem outrageous. It is quite another to say that everybody must first approve the content of the communication before it may be transmitted to anybody who is willing to receive it. Books are voluntarily read. They are not obtruded upon the passer-by, regardless of his choice. To be let alone, as Justice Brandeis said, is the most precious of all human rights. In the one case it dictates that none should be compelled to read or listen to what he abhors. In the other it dictates that none should be precluded from writing or reading as his own rather than another's taste may determine.

PERSPECTIVE

Censorship is negative. It may conceivably prevent "bad" reading; but it never creates opportunities for "good" reading. Its proponents think it reduces the chances that individuals will develop antisocially; but it embodies no features that might actively enlarge their chances of developing healthily. A more positive program, though lacking the spectacular aspects of censorship, might take society farther toward the desired goals.

One's own interests are likely to determine what he reads, if anything. This man has a taste for biography, that one for adventure stories; this one for historical novels consisting mainly of bosoms, that one for Gide and Proust; that one for Spillane, this one for Saroyan. Self-selection largely controls not only the nature but the impact of reading matter. Anthony Comstock could boast of having spent forty busy years fishing for filthy literature in a sewer, without at the end being a jot or tittle worse than when he began. Why throw reformist energies into preventing the gratification of low tastes? Why not try instead to unravel the mystery of forming elevated tastes and interests, so that effective self-censorship may replace the clumsy external controls now attempted? Like any other freedom, the freedom to read can be used unwisely. But fear that freedom may be improvidently exercised does not justify its destruction. Foolish reading cannot be ended by force, but only by patient persuasion, by education rather than by edict.

A more pressing danger than bad reading is no reading at all. Many Americans, while able to read simple words and to write a decipherable signature, seem to be functionally illiterate. Another large part of the population is literarily starved. People cannot be compelled to discover the joy of books, even if, as is not the case, they should be forced. On the whole, however, little is done to entice them upon exploratory expeditions or, if the desire already exists, to gratify their wishes. Consider the plight of the public library as symptomatic of a broader problem. At a time when the cost of a "minimum" service was estimated to be $1.50 per capita, that of a "good" service was $2.25 per capita, and that of a "superior" service was $3.00 per capita, only seven states spent as much as $1.25 while twenty-nine spent less than $1.00 per capita; the average for the whole country was 96 cents. In 1950 less than half of the "professional jobs" in public libraries were filled by people trained for the tasks assigned them, because inadequate budgets made professionalism impossible in one community after another. One out of six counties in the United States has no public facilities whatsoever, and most of those that do exist have insufficient reading materials and inadequate personnel. "The American public library," asserted the New York State Library, "is facing a major crisis."

What we need in this country is not less reading, but more; not fewer poor books, but more good books; not repression, but liberation. After all, as President Whitney Griswold of Yale has well said, "Books won't stay banned. They won't burn. Ideas won't go to jail. In the long run of history, the censor and the inquisitor have always lost. The only sure weapon against bad ideas is better ideas."

One of the censor's most powerful weapons, if he is permitted to employ it, is prior restraint. If the police department in Boston or Detroit or a private organization, such as the NODL, can, by threats of arrest or boycott or other methods of intimidation, prevent the publication or distribution of a disputed book or magazine, the courts are bypassed. Over and over again, this kind of illegal or extralegal procedure has resulted in the suppression of publications without fair judicial process. Almost invariably, however, when the higher courts have had an opportunity to review any system of prior restraint, it has been ruled unconstitutional.

William O. Douglas, Associate Justice of the U.S. Supreme Court, has long been known as an individualist, unhesitatingly supporting unpopular causes if convinced of their merit. From the outset, he has been allied with the most liberal wing of the Supreme Court, a champion of labor rights; of full preservation of the rights of free speech, press, and assembly; and of a broad construction of civil rights.

"Censorship and Prior Restraint," from Justice Douglas' *The Right of the People,* was first presented as a lecture at Franklin and Marshall College in 1957.

William O. Douglas
CENSORSHIP AND PRIOR RESTRAINT

Censorship or prior restraint is anathema to the First Amendment, for it puts the hand of the censor in every editorial and in every news account. Once the censor enters the scene, he becomes by virtue of his power the dictator. One cannot engage in litigation over every editorial or news account as to which the author and the censor differ. The date of publication presses for release of news and editorials. The practical exigencies of a system of censorship mean that the author writes to the standards of the censor, who is beyond effective control. He writes to avoid the censor's prejudices and displeasure, if not to please him. The censor becomes the great leveler of thought. The censor sets a deadening

---

William O. Douglas, *The Right of the People* (New York: Doubleday & Co., 1958), pp. 66–78, copyright © 1958 by William O. Douglas. Reprinted by permission of the author and of the publisher.

pattern of conformity which one must meet or go out of business.

Moreover, jurisdiction feeds on itself and tends to expand. A censor's duty is to censor; and he is subject to the pressures of special groups demanding suppression. The tendency, I think, is for the censor to construe his powers liberally and freely and to expand his jurisdiction until he ends in stupid and silly rulings that often make his role a laughingstock. Milton in *Areopagitica* put his finger on this aspect of the problem when he wrote that there was no "more tedious and unpleasing journey-work" than a censor's job; that, therefore, we must expect the censor to be "either ignorant, imperious, and remiss, or basely pecuniary." He went on to say, "Truth and understanding are not such wares as to be monopolized and traded in by tickets and statutes, and standards." Yet through the ages conformity has been the great desire of every censor and his own jurisdiction an ever-broadening one.

Prior restraint, as contrasted to punishment for publication of illegal works, has other evils. Prosecution for what has been published requires much work and effort by the prosecutor. The censor need only use one stroke of the pen. A system of prior restraint makes it more likely that rulings adverse to freedom of expression will be made than does a system of subsequent punishment. Prior restraint gives the advantage to those who would suppress freedom of the press. Under a system of subsequent punishment, the advantage is with the author, editor, and publisher. A censor can always find what he's looking for, especially when he's looking for smut or earmarks of disloyalty.

Under a system of prior restraint the citizen loses many advantages he enjoys under a system of subsequent punishment. The system of prior restraint is an administrative one. Judicial review is narrow and limited and frequently impossible to obtain. Prior restraint tends to make the bureaucracy supreme. A system of subsequent punishment gives the citizen protection that prior restraint denies—the duty of the government to prove guilt beyond a reasonable doubt, a presumption of innocence, stricter rules of evidence, a challenge to the law on the grounds of vagueness, and a jury trial. These safeguards are not negligible. They are part of our hard-won rights against government that

over and again has proved to be obnoxiously officious.

Moreover, a judicial proceeding airs the merits as well as the demerits of a book. Censors do not like publicity. They prefer to work in secret, promulgating their decrees by easy strokes of the pen, and censoring work by work or *en masse* as the spirit moves.

These are some of the great vices of censorship and prior restraint that put them at war with the First Amendment.

The law involved in *Near* v. *Minnesota,* 283 U.S. 697, worked a prior restraint in a modern setting. The English-speaking world had had a special history of the prior restraint. Henry VIII put the entire press under a licensing system. Before one could publish he had to submit his intended work to the government for approval. This licensing system persisted in England until 1695. The Minnesota law, which came before the Court in 1931 in the *Near* case, carried the prior restraint one step further. A publisher who had a record of publishing "malicious, scandalous, and defamatory" material was put out of business completely. And scandalous and defamatory matter was defined as including charges against public officers of official dereliction, even though true. In a decision that is one of the great landmarks of freedom of the press, the Court held the Minnesota law unconstitutional as embodying "the essence of censorship." *Id.,* p. 713. Under the American system it would be unthinkable that a paper or magazine would first have to submit its pages to a censor before it could publish them. Yet if the government could close the paper or magazine down because of its tendency to publish stories that the government deemed dangerous or obnoxious, an indirect censorship would be attained, as Chief Justice Hughes said.

The power to stop the distribution of literature is as powerful a prior restraint as one imposed on the printing itself. Liberty of circulation is as much a part of freedom of the press as liberty of publication.

Historically, many literary purges have been conducted by tyrannical majorities. A religious group has often been strong enough to gain the support of judges in punishing the publication of books critical of the sect. Purity leagues have succeeded in banning such books as Theodore Dreiser's *An American Tragedy* and Edmund

Wilson's *Memoirs of Hecate County.* Federal officials, sitting astride the shipment of second-class mail, have sometimes been prone to act as censors. *Hannegan* v. *Esquire,* 327 U.S. 146. The Supreme Court in striking down the attempted censorship in the *Esquire* case said: "Under our system of government there is an accommodation for the widest varieties of tastes and ideas. What is good literature, what has educational value, what is refined public information, what is good art, varies with individuals as it does from one generation to another. There doubtless would be a contrariety of views concerning Cervantes' *Don Quixote,* Shakespeare's *Venus and Adonis,* or Zola's *Nana.* But a requirement that literature or art conform to some norm prescribed by an official smacks of an ideology foreign to our system." *Id.,* pp. 157–158.

In some States self-appointed groups either on their own or acting in concert with the police serve as unofficial censors in their effort to stop the distribution of literature deemed obnoxious. But since censorship is anathema to the First Amendment, the courts have been alert to enjoin those who threaten distributors with prosecution if they sell certain books, whether the censor be a self-appointed busybody or a police officer.

The dangers of censorship and prior restraint are the reasons why courts are wise in refusing to enjoin the publication of books or pamphlets that may, indeed, turn out to be defamatory and libelous. The point is illustrated by *Krebiozen Research Foundation* v. *Beacon Press,* 134 N.E. 2d 1, decided by the Supreme Judicial Court of Massachusetts. The book sought to be enjoined was said to contain wrongful and malicious statements about a drug which plaintiffs sold and whose commercial value would be impaired by the book. The court, following *Near* v. *Minnesota,* refused to enjoin the distribution. ". . . full information and free discussion are important in the search for wise decisions and best courses of action." *Id.,* p. 7. The court conceded that this attack on the drug, if false, might adversely affect its commercial value.

> But basing a rule on that possibility would end or at least effectively emasculate discussion in the very controversial fields where it is most important. And it is hard to believe that the publication of a critical book, even though it contains false statements and is of false tenor overall, will prevent the full testing of any substance which in fact shows to the profession any promise of curing or alleviating cancer. *Id.,* p. 7.

An injunction against publication of the book would bar the distribution of good and wholesome passages as well as the false portions, for the tail must go with the hide. If a judge could suppress all passages because he thought some were false, he would be a censor. That would be letting one man determine what should be read. Far better that the book be published and the plaintiff sue for libel and collect his damages than that a judge turn his talents to censorship. In so deciding, the Massachusetts court spoke in the great tradition of *Near* v. *Minnesota.*

The theatre and the movies differ from the press and the lecture platform only in form. The form, it is true, may make a vital difference in the impact of ideas conveyed. A play in cold print may be a lifeless thing. The human voice, gestures, facial expressions, body movements may bring it to life. A movie is more than the script. It is the harnessing of genius to awaken latent feelings, to challenge loyalties, to arouse prejudices, to instill courage or fear, and in a multitude of ways to arouse the emotions. A movie can carry an audience away more quickly than any orator. It has an impact in the raw that the other media usually lack.

These are the reasons usually advanced as grounds for censoring the theatre and particularly the movie. They are, I think, mistaken reasons. There is no room for censorship of any medium of expression in our society. Censorship is hostile to the First Amendment. That does not mean that the citizen can with impunity say what he likes, print what he likes, produce on the stage what he likes, draw or photograph what he likes for public showing. He is under restraints, as we have seen. But those restraints are carefully restricted and narrowly drawn to fit precise evils. They too operate as restraints in the manner in which all law tends to become a deterrent. But being narrowly drawn and being enforced by separate unrelated trials, they do not become a system whereby an individual, a board, or a committee subtly enforces its own moral, political, or literary code on the community. The Court has not gone so far as to strike down all censorship of the stage. It has been alert, however, to set aside orders of censors based on broad and inclusive powers.

Censorship assumes many forms. It has been a temptation for the Post Office to use the second-class mail privilege as an instrument to control the content of publications. This privilege is an extremely valuable one, being in substance a subsidy without which most magazines would be put out of business. Editors and publishers are extremely sensitive to the leverage that this privilege places in the hands of the Post Office. Unless restrained it could, indeed, become the power of life and death over a magazine. An Act of Congress states the conditions on which the privilege shall be granted: that the publication is "for the dissemination of information of a public character, or devoted to literature, the sciences, arts, or some special industry." The Post Office authorities ruled that this meant the magazine was "under a positive duty to contribute to the public good and the public welfare." *Hannegan* v. *Esquire,* 327 U.S. 146, 150. That ruling put the postal authorities in the seat of the censor, with the power of life or death over most magazines. The Court read the statute as granting no power of censorship. Whether a magazine meets the requirements of the statute is a decision that concerns primarily its format and whether its contents relate to "literature, the sciences, arts, or some special industry"—not "whether the contents meet some standard of the public good or welfare." *Id.,* p. 159.

Under other statutes the Post Office has undertaken vast powers of censorship. An Act of Congress, passed some eighty years ago when Grant was President, declares obscene publications "to be nonmailable matter and shall not be conveyed in the mails or delivered from any post office or by any letter carrier." It also makes the mailing of such literature a crime. A system of extensive surveillance grew up under that law. Literature was barred from the mails on the ground that it was obscene without any notice or hearing. It took *Walker* v. *Popenoe,* 149 F. 2d 511, to impose the duty to give notice and provide a hearing before barring the mails to a publication.

In 1950, Congress passed a new postal obscenity law which gave the Post Office power to return all mail, stamped "unlawful," sent to anyone who was mailing obscene literature and bar payment of any money order to such person. The power was construed by the Post Office to give it authority to stop indefinitely all mail addressed to a person whom the department found to be trafficking in obscene publications, whether or not the particular mail was offensive. A stop order of that breadth was held unlawful in *Summerfield* v. *Sunshine Book Co.,* 221 F. 2d 42. The court held that stop orders of the Post Office "must be confined to materials already published, and duly found unlawful." *Id.,* p. 47. Were that not true, a vast, pernicious system of censorship would be fastened on the citizen. He would in effect be driven out of the publishing business for perhaps a single transgression; his legitimate activities, as well as the unlawful ones, would be stifled.

Mr. Justice Holmes said in his dissent in *Milwaukee Publishing Co.* v. *Burleson,* 255 U.S. 407, 437, "The United States may give up the Post Office when it sees fit, but while it carries it on the use of the mails is almost as much a part of free speech as the right to use our tongues. . . ." That is why Mr. Justice Holmes and Mr. Justice Brandeis dissented in *Leach* v. *Carlile,* 258 U.S. 138, 140–141, from a decision which sustained a statute allowing the Post Office to cut off the delivery of mail to a person adjudged by the department to be engaged in fraudulent use of the mail in selling commodities. They dissented because the Post Office order was a prior restraint operating against the sender of literature or letters.

Their view did not prevail and a system of prior restraint operates in full force in the fraud field. It likewise operates in the field of obscenity. It was suggested by way of dictum in *Near* v. *Minnesota,* 283 U.S. 697, 716, that prior restraint was permissible when dealing with obscenity. That would seem to be untenable, since all forms of censorship are in conflict with our constitutional system, for the reasons I have given. Certainly a system of censorship operating through the Post Office is as obnoxious as any other type of prior restraint, for as Mr. Justice Holmes said, "the use of the mails is almost as much a part of free speech as the right to use our tongues."

Licensing, one of the most notorious types of censorship, has been quite consistently struck down by the Court when applied to the distribution of literature. An ordinance requiring permission from the city manager to distribute literature in the city was held invalid on its face in *Lovell* v. *Griffin,* 303 U.S. 444. "Legislation of the type of the ordinance in question would restore the system of license and censorship in its baldest form," said Chief Justice Hughes. *Id.,* p. 452. The *Lovell* case has been closely followed. Its holding is essential to a free society, for its repudiation would mean that some official could determine what ideas could and what ideas could not be carried to the homes of the citizens. Obviously a newspaper or magazine need not get a license from the local or national government in order to publish. The printing and publishing business is not dependent on any bureaucrat's discretion for its existence. That freedom extends to all branches of the press—to the pamphleteer and to the door-to-door solicitor as well as to the more conventional printer or publisher.

The Court in *Thomas* v. *Collins,* 323 U.S. 516, 540, went much further and held that mere registration as a condition for making a public speech was not consistent with the First Amendment. Mr. Justice Rutledge wrote, "The restraint is not small when it is considered what was restrained. The right is a national right federally guaranteed. . . . If the restraint were smaller than it is, it is from petty tyrannies that large ones take root and grow." *Id.,* p. 543.

So far as I know, the only system of licensing of the press which we have today in America is the Act of July 29, 1954, by which Congress requires communist printing presses to be registered.

We have, of course, a system of licensing for radio and television stations. But the problem there is quite different. The channels all lie in the public domain, the air space above the earth being under the exclusive control of Congress. The channels are restricted in number. It is necessary to regulate all if interference is to be kept at a minimum and service is to be efficient. What the government owns or controls in the airways it can regulate as it sees fit. The licensing of radio and television stations is therefore not inconsistent with the requirements of the First Amendment. Those stations could not, of course, be turned over to the licensees as their private mouthpieces. They are public channels burdened with the duty of carrying all sides of public issues to the people.

Certainly, the government as licensor cannot by its regulations allow stations to disseminate only one set of ideas. The audience is entitled to a diversity and balance of views in the fields of public controversy. Government, having the management of the airways of the nation, must within feasible limits allow equal access by all groups. Any other course would be as acute abridgment of freedom of expression as barring the mails to all political parties but one.

The principle that forbids the exaction of a license for exercising a constitutional right also forbids taxing the privilege. *Murdock* v. *Pennsylvania,* 319 U.S. 105. "The power to tax the exercise of a privilege is the power to control or suppress its enjoyment." *Id.,* p. 112. If the contrary were true, the constitutional right would turn on the ability to pay. But financial considerations have no relevancy to First Amendment rights.

Printers and publishers must pay all the taxes that other citizens pay. The modern newspaper, for example, is in business for profit. There is no reason, therefore, why it should not share with the community the burden of all taxes which others pay. When, however, the press is singled out for special taxation, other considerations apply. The power to tax is the power to destroy, especially when it is exercised with a discriminating eye. Huey Long in his quest for political power in Louisiana singled out the opposition press for discriminatory treatment. The Court struck it down in *Grosjean* v. *American Press Co.,* 297 U.S. 233, analogizing it to the ancient and despised "taxes on knowledge."

The liberal English point of view on censorship is presented in "Literature and the Policeman" by Austin Harrison (1873–1928), late editor of the *English Review.*

After five years as Berlin correspondent for Reuter's, Harrison acted as dramatic critic of the *Daily Mail* and subsequently became editor of the *Observer.* It was not until the founding of the *English Review* in 1910, however, that he discovered his true niche. Under his editorship the new journal flourished, attracting such contributors as John Masefield, H. G. Wells, Richard Middleton, Norman Douglas, D. H. Lawrence, and H. M. Tomlinson.

Harrison's philosophy is summed up in his declaration: "To strike at the creative section of the community to-day is national suicide. Our need is not of more politics, it is of more truth, more evocation, more spiritual guidance, and that only the artists can provide."

Austin Harrison
LITERATURE AND THE POLICEMAN

In literature every nation has its own policeman, and even the policeman has his "literature." We saw this aspect once more painfully emphasized at a recent trial where men of letters stepped into the box in defence of their art, impotent before the technicality of the law, which was out for blood. The case was a foreigner's book. Was it evil? Or, as the prosecuting counsel put it: "Do you regard such and such a passage as obscene or not?"

All things being relative in art, there was, of course, no answer. But in law things are not relative, and all lawyers are positive. As the Judge said, writers live in a world of their own; they are not moralists. And the Judge spoke truly in law though most untruly in fact. An artist is an explorer, a creator, he is not a juryman. He is, as artist, essentially the law-giver. But in the box he found himself confronted with the policeman's foot-rule, either or, yes or no, and the frown of the commercial librarian. His evidence was necessarily negative, and so the law ran its course, in the interests of society and of the *index expurgatorius*.

In a court of law morality cuts a comic figure, and evidence is reduced to an absurdity, because the fixed ideas of Puritanism still define our code and control our being. Puritanism has, or has had, such magnificent qualities; it does lead to such a pernicious and soulless hypocrisy. "Immoral," as George Moore has said, is a spring morning, far more so than any book. Immoral, one might imagine, was the electric theatre with its appeal to violence, crime, passion, and physical action. Immoral, surely, are the covers of the cheap magazines; immoral the realistic osculations on the stage, which in Paris would be deemed offensive. But Puritanism has a Nelsonic eye; its Copenhagen is print. Its pet abomination is the literary artist who dares to write truthfully about sex.

Austin Harrison, "Literature and the Policeman," *English Review*, 38:358–65 (March, 1924), copyright 1924 by English Review. Reprinted by permission of the publisher.

To quote George Moore again, that is, of course, why the novel in England is a stunted growth, and perhaps explains why to-day it is reputed to be dead. Sex is taboo. Such a taboo implies the elimination of the motive and promptings of life. Scott, Dickens, Thackeray, all wrote under the thumb of the policeman. In other words, there is no psychology. Only characterisation on a sexless canvas is permissible. Hence, perhaps, our humour—the escape. Hence, without a doubt, the poverty of our novels intellectually in comparison with the French and the Russians, which condition is shown even more conspicuously in our drama.

It is amusing to think that our first sex novel was *Jane Eyre,* the work of a clergyman's daughter, and that her quite melodramatic villain has been the prototype of Ethel Dell's gallery of sportsmen ever since. The book shook England at the time, and apparently frightened the men who, as if in despair, took to poetry. I suppose Byron was the first English psycho-analyst. Fortunately, for him, *Don Juan* rhymed. Puritans rather favour limericks. The fact saved him. Had *Don Juan* appeared in book-form it would no doubt have been suppressed—prose being far wickeder than verse; even as it was, the lord had to flee the country, like the saintly Shelley, who had offended the policeman of "divinity."

Even in Elizabethan times the policeman was apparently specific, and so Shakespearean women are Renaissance figures, types of types, taken obviously from reports of Italian women who figured prominently in the great masculine revival in Italy; thus Lady Macbeth, Juliet, Portia, and Cleopatra, whose famous cry, "O! happy horse," gives the imprint of them all in striking contradistinction to the Virgin Queen, last and the greatest of all women Renaissance figures. The study of Shakespeare seems to be curiously incomplete in this respect. How was it that Shakespeare missed (there is no other word) the character of his Queen, which must have been known to him, and must have excited widespread commentary? Why are his women dolls of the Italian Renaissance? How did he overlook the first new woman who remained unsung until Ibsen placed her in *A Doll's House?*

And so the history of English literature has been a long calvary. Byron, Shelley, Keats, were all three broken on the wheel of the index, since when the names of those who fell by the roadside have been many—far too many for the health and honour of a great race. One thinks of Vizetelly imprisoned for years for translating Zola. One recalls the sad failures of Middleton, of Davidson, of St. John Hankin, of Flecker, whose *Hassan* now delights a thoughtless mob, and of innumerable others. For the policeman acting upon the creative mind of man is not healthy. It antagonises. It leads to excesses. It makes rebels of such men. Hence, without a doubt, the reason of the sinister spectacle always with us of great literary artists who somehow appear to be at war with society and the State: who become, as it were, the Robin Hoods of English letters. This is a quite English peculiarity, and in nearly all cases the cause is sex, some book or statement which has placed the writer outside the pale of conventionality and driven him to rebellion and retaliation. There are many others. Indeed, at this moment some of our biggest living poets and writers are more or less under a social ban, live ostracised or outside the country, become, have become, or may become, pariahs and shipwrecks.

It is a curious paradox, for England is the home of individualism, and in no other country in the world has the individual, personally and creatively, played so noble a part. Our national spirit is freedom. Our national instinct is individualism—in commerce, in politics, in religion, in thought, and in action. Our national genius is man, not the State—man the explorer and founder of empires, man as poet, thinker, scholar, rhapsodist, weaver and practitioner of dreams, as sailor and soldier of fortune, as builder and architect of governance. We are the bankers of the world and the poets of the world, the conquerors and the dreamers of the world. Our whole gospel is sanction, our whole attitude is common-sense. Nothing is more galling to the English sense than authority based upon a truncheon. Everywhere the name of an Englishman is honoured for the law, which is his law, of liberty which has been his gift to civilisation, which may be said to be the fountain spring of all modern evolution. And yet at home the Puritan, with his policeman, acts like a blight upon the land, the kill-joy of art and its expression. And so to-day a ridiculous librarian is the policeman of English literature, and publishers quake before his opinion, and the commercialisation of books threatens to turn literature into the mere book-form of the Press. Can we wonder that so many of our great writers seem to "go wrong"? Artists are fighters. Blind acceptance is not their creed or mission. Driven down, they break out, only too frequently with unfortunate results. They become martyrs of a social hypocrisy. The net consequence of this Puritanism is to let in the tradesman who to-day controls. Books literally are at the mercy of the gentlemen who dispense them. A more inglorious position for the nation which has the grandest literature in the world it would be hard to conceive. The two favourite words in the trade to-day are "highbrow" and "best-seller," the former being suspect, the latter meaning business. One hears this sort of remark: "If So-and-So writes another sexy novel the librarians will boycott him; publishers have been warned"; or this: "Jackson, Tibbs and Co. have stopped ——'s novel, as he refuses to cut out the famous scene, etc." And so on. Mr. George Moore is reduced to publishing his works privately, yet I suppose it would be generally agreed that all the "naughty" (one must use the word) bits in all George Moore's books put together are not half so harmful, socially, morally and physically, as almost any film, or any newspaper pot-boiler, or any lurid melodrama in which the hero is a thief or confounded jackass. The objection will be raised: "Well, sex is not our genius," which no doubt is true. One effect of this attitude is the glorification of fairy stuff and grown-up boys' books, etc., the two great examples of which are *Robinson Crusoe* and *Peter Pan,* with Kipling running for third place. Our best fiction literature revolves around rainbow land, the alternative is action in which sex is eliminated. Our great writers are epicene. Bernard Shaw has managed to survive Socialism chiefly because he never offends Mrs. Grundy. He, Barrie, Arnold Bennett, Kipling, Chesterton, the late Mrs. Humphry Ward, are pre-eminently *couronnés* because of this one-sidedness. And the fact is all the more curious in a country where women first gained the vote in a fight which was admittedly a sex-liberating movement. Needless to say, it is the reason of our degenerate drama, which has become a business proposition.

A contributory cause is politics, we being the most politically-minded people in Europe, as opposed, say, to Tsarist Russia, where the taboo was specifically political. In a political country everything is free except art, and any form of politician is permissible; that is the Puritanical legacy. Morals do not apply to politics. A politician can cause incalculable harm with impunity, position, and a title; his one snag is sex, but, if he stumbles there, the axe falls relentlessly, as was the case with Parnell and Dilke. The starvation of our literature is unquestionably political in origin. Sex is the cardinal sin. The only fictional escape is humour or optimism—a book or play must end happily with a premium on the "ever after." As the commercial manager of a theatre will explain to the playwright whose play ends sorrowfully: "My dear sir, I'm not in this line for sentiment," and so the public thinks too —the most sentimental public in the world wants its books and plays to give them the feeling only too often absent in their real lives, and what the public wants is King. It wants the same old things, the same old superstitions, canons, climaxes and situations. It wants the policeman's idea of literature, and its purveyors see that it gets it.

But does the public always want the same thing? It is a very doubtful point. Our climate is partly responsible for our attitude towards letters, and for five months every year man thinks he needs a tonic after his day's work is done. The artist's retaliation is: "That's the stuff to give them," and if he puts it up in correct form it pays. But it also degrades. What has happened to Fleet Street is steadily taking place in letters. As the appeal widens and the market expands, the trade more and more acquires control. Newspapers have become a part of commerce. Already the novel threatens to follow suit. Even the most distinguished publishers will say warningly to a writer, "Rather highbrow, isn't it?" implying that it—the book—is rather over the heads of the mob which has become the criterion of merit, and out will come the passages that Alf and Susan are not expected to understand. Thus the process of levelling down proceeds. The prizes of successful fiction are to-day too big to refuse, and as, owing to prices, the public buys less and less, the libraries obtain more and more the control. They can, and do, set the standard. They are to letters what advertisers are to the Press. Their veto rules, and actually threatens to turn novelists into the jobbers of a trade.

People who complain about the effeminisation of Fleet Street and of the novel ought not to be surprised. The novel of action and of stock characterisation has almost reached the saturation point, and only variants of the old themes are possible. Hence the change in the form of the modern novel, which, if it is to survive as an art, will certainly have to become something more than a mere story of how a man and a woman came to marry. Mr. H. G. Wells has done yeoman service in this respect. The tendency to publish serious novels privately is on the increase, and we may even see an inner ring of writers who only sell to subscribers, as is done commonly in France.

But the question is wider than any art-form; it concerns living men, and here the need of reform is too obvious to insist upon. It is ludicrous that one cannot buy a book of George Moore, for instance. It is a national misfortune that so many great writers get pushed into the dock.

What can be done? We have no academy of letters, no forum. Nor do the universities, as in other countries, play any part as art and intellectual assizes, except, perhaps, in the sphere of political economy. It is characteristic of our insular politicism. At the same time, we might inaugurate a practical reform whereby literary offences should be tried either by a special jury of literary people or by a tribunal drawn from the universities and from public men convened solely for the purpose of dealing with art lapses, or even simply to decide whether such and such a case is to be submitted to the wooden absolutism of the law. Such a body would, at least, be intelligent and might be constructive. It would not decide upon a book merely from a few sentences strung together to look indictable; it would weigh the moral purpose of the writer; above all, the moral significance of the work as a whole. Librarians would gladly welcome any instance which relieved them of the necessity of taking a decision, and the policeman would not be sorry to see art left to artists. Writers could, of course, form such a body themselves, given authority. Anything, absolutely anything, would be preferable to the predicament in which authors now stand, liable at any moment to be condemned as felons for venturing to write a book containing some truth and wisdom about life and its meanings and manifestations. There must admittedly be a policeman or limit, yet when we look back and read the works of the literary martyrs—Ruskin was one—one feels inclined to laugh, so meek and mild do they appear in the orgy of our everyday life after a convulsion in which the highest duty of a hundred million men was to kill at any price. To stigmatise the artist, any artist, after such a blood-bath is only comic. It must be nationally and intellectually degrading.

It is really time we had a Ministry of the Fine Arts to straighten out this strange constriction of creative effort. Here one can rely on the women, whose cause, freedom of thought and expression, it is. Also it is the modern spirit. In a world unbound, such as exists to-day in Europe, we shall surely be left behind in the field of literature if the old Puritanical policeman is left to determine what may or may not be said in association with the necessarily timid because commercial tradesman, and those who advocate a Renaissance in England would do well to consider the causes which go to make any such movement possible. It was the artists who made the Italian Renaissance. It was the artists who made the great Elizabethan age. A country which neglects its artists and its art decays, as the poet says in *Hassan,* it loses its soul. To-day we need all the art impulse we can evoke, and perhaps only the artists, who are the true lawgivers, can give us the needful strength to win our way back and up in the difficult years before us.

To strike at the creative section of the community to-day is national suicide. Our need is not of more politics, it is of more truth, more evocation, more spiritual guidance, and that only the artists can provide. To fall back on the policeman to rid us of our turbulent priests of art is to indulge in cocaine. It is a new and great drama that we want, new thoughts, new tabernacles, new projections and horizons. The Old Bailey will only bring us more darkness, more politics, more herd commercialism, more stakes and martyrs. The evil of the policeman in art is the premium which his office puts upon bad art. As Sir Thomas Browne said: "Every man truly lives so long as he acts his nature, or some way makes good the faculties of himself." That is precisely what the writer cannot do, if he is to live. He has to be an entertainer, a jobber, or a compromiser, and the fact colours and permeates our whole life.

Because of this code, it is almost impossible to write truthfully about things in England, and this at a time when what we require, above all, are light and leading, truer explanations, surer diagnoses, finer appeals. Our political world sadly needs the indignant fire of the penman. As for the moral tone of the country, that surely will remain dumb and inarticulate under the pressure of materialism, until we get some spirituality and more inspiration. We shall not obtain those values through a dull trade outlook or futile political controversy. Vision is necessary. And that is the privilege which should be the business of the men who write.

Chapter III

The courts look at books

LEGAL literature relating to censorship of all varieties, but particularly the allegedly obscene, is prolific. For at least the past three centuries, according to Leo Alpert's historical résumé, English and American courts have been dealing with cases in this area, meanwhile groping for a consistent and workable definition of obscenity.

Modern Anglo-American law goes back almost exactly one hundred years to the statute of 20 and 21 Victoria, drafted and steered through the British Parliament in 1857 by Lord Chief Justice Campbell. Its author described the measure as "intended to apply exclusively to works written for the single purpose of corrupting the morals of youth, and of a nature calculated to shock the common feelings of decency in any well regulated mind."

About a decade after its enactment, the Campbell statute received a classic interpretation at the hands of Chief Justice Cockburn in the case of *Regina* v. *Hicklin* (1868). The case involved a pamphlet entitled *The Confessional Unmasked, Showing the Depravity of the Romish Priesthood; the Iniquity of the Confessional, and the Questions Put to Females in Confession,* an anti-Catholic publication being distributed by a member of a Protestant union. In connection with the case Justice Cockburn formulated his famous rule for judging obscenity: "I think the test of obscenity is this, whether the tendency of the matter charged as obscenity is to deprave and corrupt those whose minds are open to such immoral influences, and into whose hands a publication of this sort may fall."

As David Fellman recently pointed out in his "The Censorship of Books," "The objection to this test, of course, is that it fixes a standard for the community's reading matter geared to the feeblest mentality or most suggestible psyche in the community." Nevertheless, the Cockburn dictum has served as a guiding principle for a majority of English and American judges for the past ninety years.

The first serious challenge to Cockburn's doctrine came in 1933 in the celebrated *Ulysses* case, though strong doubts of the rule's validity had been stated twenty years earlier by Judge Learned Hand, in *United States* v. *Kennerley:* "I question," said Judge Hand, "whether in the end men will regard that as obscene which is honestly relevant to the adequate expression of innocent ideas, and whether they will not believe that truth and beauty are too precious to society at large to be mutilated in the interests of those most likely to pervert them to base uses."

In the case brought against James Joyce's *Ulysses,* in 1933, to prevent its importation into the United States, Judge John M. Woolsey decided that such a book "must be tested by the court's opinion as to its effect on a person with average sex instincts . . . who plays in this branch of legal inquiry, the same role of hypothetical reagent as does the 'reasonable man' in the law of torts . . . It is only with the normal person that the law is concerned."

The same point was driven home by Walter Gellhorn in his *Individual Freedom and Governmental Restraints:* "The stable and well adjusted members of the community must make many sacrifices because there are unstable and disturbed members as well. But freedom of communication and freedom to read ought not to be among the sacrifices when the gain is so dubious and the deprivation so plain."

The definitive word on the subject was expressed in 1957 by the U.S. Supreme Court decision in the case of *Butler* v. *Michigan.* As stated by Justice Felix Frankfurter, "The State [of Michigan] insists that, by thus quarantining the general reading public against books not too rugged for grown men and women in order to shield juvenile innocence, it is exercising its power to promote the general welfare. Surely this is to burn the house to roast the pig . . . The incidence of this enactment is to reduce the adult population of Michigan to reading only what is fit for children."

At almost precisely the same time as this American decision, a much publicized case involving a similar principle was being tried in England. There Sidney Kauffmann's *The Philanderer* was being prosecuted for obscenity. Justice Stable, in his charge to the jury, said:

"Remember the charge is a charge that the tendency of the book is to corrupt and deprave. The charge is not that the tendency of the book is either to shock or to disgust. That is not a criminal offense. Then you say: 'Well, corrupt or deprave whom?' and again the test: those whose minds are open to such immoral influences and into whose hands a publication of this sort may fall. What exactly does that mean? Are we to take our literary standards as being the level of something that is suitable for a fourteen-year-old school girl? Or do we go even further back than that, and are we to be reduced to the sort of books that one reads as a child in the nursery? The answer to that is: Of course not. A mass of literature, great literature, from many angles is wholly unsuitable for reading by adolescents, but that does not mean that the publisher is guilty of a criminal offence for making those works available to the general public."

On the basis of the two historic decisions in 1957 it is patent that enlightened judicial opinion in the Anglo-American world has moved far from the narrow Cockburn interpretation of obscenity. Further, as Judge Woolsey and others have stated, a book must be read in its entirety and the author's intentions recognized. This is the direct antithesis of Justice Cockburn's view that such factors as intent, and honest and laudable purposes, have no bearing on the question of obscenity.

Another landmark in the legal history of censorship dates from 1952 and concerns films rather than books. In the case of *Burstyn* v. *Wilson,* the U.S. Supreme Court for the first time extended to motion pictures the constitutional protections long since accorded printed media. In New York, under pressure from Catholic organizations, state authorities banned exhibition of an Italian film, *The Miracle,* which had previously been shown without clerical interference in Rome. New York's highest court had ruled in *The Miracle* case that "No religion . . . shall be treated with contempt, mockery, scorn and ridicule." This opinion was rejected by the Supreme Court on the ground that, as stated by Justice Clark, "In seeking to apply the broad and all-inclusive definition of 'sacrilegious' given by the New York courts, the censor is set adrift upon a boundless sea amid a myriad of conflicting currents of religious views, with no charts but those provided by the most vocal and powerful orthodoxies. New York cannot vest such unlimited restraining control over motion pictures in a censor."

In reversing the lower court, the Supreme Court decision concluded, "We hold only that under the First and Fourteenth Amendments a state may not ban a film on the basis of a censor's conclusion that it is sacrilegious." More broadly, it was the Court's opinion that, "It cannot be doubted that motion pictures are a significant medium for the communication of ideas. They may affect public attitudes and behavior in a variety of ways. The importance of motion pictures as an organ of public opinion is not lessened by the fact that they are designed to entertain as well as to inform." Obviously the Court's verdict in *The Miracle* and related cases sets some notable precedents, with clear implications for the censorship of books.

In the present chapter the legal aspects of censorship are reviewed from the American point of view by Leo M. Alpert and from the British by Norman St. John-Stevas. There follow detailed court reports on several American cases which have made legal history in this field during the past thirty years.

☞ Though written some twenty years ago, Leo Alpert's backward look at British and American censorship practices since the mid-seventeenth century remains the most adequate summary of legal developments. Mr. Alpert, a Miami lawyer, is represented elsewhere in the present compilation by a second piece, "Naughty, Naughty!" on the same topic, but in a lighter vein.

Leo M. Alpert
**JUDICIAL CENSORSHIP
OF OBSCENE LITERATURE**

History presents the facts of a Seven Years' War, a Thirty Years' War, and a Hundred Years' War, but the history of English literature would indicate the unparalleled extension of at least a Three Hundred Years' War—the war of words whose tented fields were the courts, whose hectic strategy revolved around the word "obscenity," whose weapons were legal strictures and classic retorts.

Legal pundits are agreed that the earliest reported case on obscenity is dated 1663 and is that of *The King v. Sir Charles Sedley*. Inebriated and nude, Sir Charles had exhibited himself on a London balcony overlooking Covent Garden and had hurled upon the populace bottles filled with an "offensive liquor," as judges later delicately indicated, the while he engaged in eloquent blasphemy. From this merry prank, perversely enough, was conceived our present obscenity law, with the sparkling figure of Sir Charles its innocent and unwitting progenitor.

Almost three hundred years later, in 1933, the legal forces of the United States had to confront *Ulysses,* an herculean novel by James Joyce. The decisions in this case, *United States v. One Book Called "Ulysses,"* held Joyce's book, although a strong draught for a sensitive person, not to have been written with pornographic intent and not to be obscene within the legal definition of the term. The book is an emetic perhaps, said District Judge Woolsey, but not an aphrodisiac; and thereby, with the assistance of the Second Circuit Court of Appeals which affirmed his opinion, he and they launched what may be interpreted as a new deal for literature.

What is the history of this Three Hundred Years' War? Concededly, it was Sedley who involuntarily opened offensives with his personal —not literary—behavior.

THE GENESIS OF THE LAW

Those gay days of wickedness and wit
When Villiers criticized what Dryden writ.
Fitzpatrick.

Among the roistering blades of Charles II's reign, none was more madly gay than young Sir Charles Sedley, Gentleman of Kent, intimate of the King, "as famous for his wit as he was notorious for the profligacy of his life." It took

---

Leo M. Alpert, "Judicial Censorship of Obscene Literature," 52 *Harvard Law Review* 40–76 (1938), copyright 1938 by the Harvard Law Review Association. Reprinted (without amplifying footnotes) by permission of the author and of the publisher.

the affair of the balcony, however, to fling Sedley squarely into the public eye and into the annals of English law. Accompanied by Charles Sackville, then Lord Buckhurst and later Earl of Dorset, Sedley and Sir Thomas Ogle engaged in a drinking spree at "The Cock," Oxford Kate's tavern in Bow Street by Covent Garden. Having achieved that degree of ecstatic inebriation which releases inhibitions, they mounted to the balcony of the tavern and, as Johnson dryly puts it, "exposed themselves to the populace in very indecent postures." Sedley was bolder. Naked as a jay, he harangued the hundreds of amazed men and women; captured their attention; preached a mountebank sermon; shouted, according to the ubiquitous Pepys, that he had for sale such a power as would cause all women to run after him; and culminated with rich profanities that "aroused publick indignation"—a general rage not dampened one whit by the bottles with which he gleefully showered the good folk.

Promptly a minor riot occurred. The doors and windows of Oxford Kate's tavern had hastily to be barricaded against the vicious onslaught of a populace turned mob. Balked of its prey, the mob drove stones at the performers until they fled from the balcony.

Legal reports of the incident supply passages both interesting and valuable. The first, titled *Le Roy v. Sr. Charles Sidley,* is in the motley legal language of the time. The second report of the case is in blunt, hearty English:

> He was fined 2000 mark, committed without bail for a week, and bound to his good behavior for a year, on his confession of information against him, for shewing himself naked in a balcony, and throwing down bottles (pist in) vi & armis among the people in Covent Garden, contra pacem and to the scandal of the Government.

Since Sir Charles reviled the law on at least three counts: he exhibited his person, he blasphemed, and he employed as missiles bottles containing a foul liquor, his scofflaw conduct is unquestioned. That the case, however, is accepted as the first milestone in the English common law of obscenity is sufficient illustration of the wisdom embodied in that Latin maxim often inscribed above library portals: *Prudentis est petere fontes.* A flimsier, more appallingly pointless foundation for the superstructure of law that was later erected could hardly have been deliberately laid.

For the existence of some of Sedley's obscene poems creates the diverting paradox that obscene literature made its appearance in the dockets as the consequence of the jailing of an obscene poet, not for obscene poetry, but for riotous personal behavior "contra pacem and to the scandal of the Government."

The "first" case, then, amounts to scarcely more than a creaking rumble of heavy artillery being shifted into position only to be found trained upon the wrong target. The first actual and incontrovertible case to establish obscenity in literature as a legal offense came almost half a century later, *The Queen v. Read.* Its printed report is meager:

> A crime that shakes religion, as profaness on the stage &c. is indictable; but writing an obscene book, as that intitled "Fifteen Plagues of a Maidenhead" is not indictable, but punishable only in the spiritual court.

This reference to the "spiritual court" lays bare the conflict of the time between the common-law courts and the ecclesiastical courts whose power was slowly waning. Astute counsel in the next obscenity case attempted to use *The Queen v. Read* to quash an indictment in the law court against Edmund Curll, bookseller, stationer, printer, pirate of literature, and specialist in the obscene. The case, *Dominus Rex v. Curl,* overruled *The Queen v. Read* by sustaining the indictment on the ground that religion was part of the common law; the offense was one against religion and was therefore to be tried in the common-law courts.

It may be summarized with safety that, up to this point, obscenity in literature had not been the concern of the courts; it is offenses against religion which have comprised the issues. This observation holds also in the case which closed the first hundred years of the Three Hundred Years' War Against Obscenity, *Rex v. Wilkes,* in which the manufactured bone of contention was a bawdy poem entitled "Essay on Woman."

"The Devil Wilkes," as George III labelled him, was thoroughly aroused over corruption of the Tory Government, and when Pitt and Temple, the most prominent Whigs of the time, asked Wilkes to unlimber his gall-tipped pen, he was but too eager to oblige. Upon Pitt's propulsion from office in 1762 by Lord Bute, Prime Minister, Wilkes inaugurated a bitter fight against the new government.

The publication of Wilkes' satirical introduction to the play, "The Fall of Mortimer," aroused the ire of George III not so much by the exposure of corruption in the government, or by the insinuation of the imbecility of the King, as by the oblique conveyance of a guilty relationship between his mother and the handsome Lord Bute.

England exploded. In Paris, Madame Pompadour inquired of Wilkes: "How far does the liberty of the press extend in England?" His answer was characteristic: "I do not know. I am trying to find out."

Lord Bute resigned. Wilkes, unappeased and relentlessly carried onward, forthwith suggested in his paper, the *North Briton,* that this move by Bute was one of convenience only, accomplished to facilitate his control of the government from behind the scenes. Thereupon Wilkes found himself arrested, jailed, and held for trial. He was then at the crest of his popularity: he was "the Liberty Boy." The reforms for which he then and later fought: the immunity from prosecution of political criticism; full publicity for legislative debates; the abolition of outlawry; the abolition of unreasonable searches and seizures; the right of a representative to both his opinions and his seat in Parliament if duly elected—his own particular combat with government officials—won "the Liberty Boy" huge personal acclaim in America as well as in England. As Professor Chafee notes: "One New England admirer had three sons, Wilkes, Pitt, and Liberty"; and one of the largest cities in Pennsylvania still bears his name.

The storms, the hue and cry and general furor drove the government into action. Desperately it attempted to bribe Wilkes into silence. That failed. It cast about for another method. Wilkes' "Essay on Woman" seemed made for the purpose; it furnished at once an instrument, a stratagem, and an excuse for hostilities in the guise of a crusade.

Doubtful of the adhesive qualities of such a charge as "seditious libel" as applied to the defamatory, highly unpleasant articles in the *North Briton,* the government gratefully accepted information from a dissolute clergyman relative to an obscene parody of Pope's "Essay on Man" written by Wilkes as an "Essay on Woman." It appeared that an ex-foreman in Wilkes' printing shop possessed a copy, the thirteenth and last to have been printed. In a short space this copy was purchased.

The immediate question is: Why was Wilkes writing obscene poetry? The answer exposes a part of Wilkes' private history fully as enthralling as his public activities. Early in life Wilkes had been initiated by a friend, Thomas Potter, into a strange society called the Medmenham Monks. The Monks—numbered twelve—devoted themselves zestfully to bacchanalia of supremely erotic frenzy in their architecturally significant house in the country. They pledged healths from a cup which discreet commentators described as "curiously shaped." The "Essay on Woman," written largely by Potter, it is said, with, however, Wilkes' hand palpably in it, seems to have been designed exclusively for the Monks, Wilkes having ordered the printing of but twelve copies. In secret, the ex-foreman ran off a thirteenth.

In secure possession of the thirteenth copy of the "Essay on Woman," Wilkes' foes planned a devastating campaign against him. Their guns were fully loaded and bristling ominously. It has been suggested that the case was "not merely worked up by bribery, but that an even more serious crime was committed"—apparently nothing less than forgery of certain sections of the "Essay" which were not sufficiently obscene.

Denunciations of Wilkes were simultaneously launched in the Houses of Commons and Lords. A resolution declaring that the "Essay" was "a most scandalous, obscene, and impious libel" came from Lords; in Commons, where Wilkes was sitting, he was so deliberately provoked by Sam Martin that only a duel could make honorable retort. The duel with his adversary, who had been indefatigably practicing with the pistol, drove a severely wounded Wilkes into retirement. Commons completed his defeat by expelling him from his seat, although he was both ill and absent.

Opposition to such a well-executed plan would ordinarily have been formidable enough for a healthy Wilkes; the ill Wilkes in Paris was easily vanquished. Lord Mansfield, a King's man, by the bye, who heard the case against Wilkes, was not impressed with the plea which admitted the printing of the "Essay" but denied its publication-circulation, and a judgment against the invalid was speedily followed by a warrant for his arrest.

The late Justice Holmes of the Supreme Court is reported to have said that a man may amuse himself in private as he desires. Publication, however, is an essential of obscenity. One may certainly print what one pleases, provided that it be not circulated. Wilkes' "Essay" was produced for private amusement. The decision, then, that encloses the Wilkes case in the annals of obscene literature is one radically unsound in law. The affair had been manufactured and was avowedly political (demonstrating also by what imperceptible degrees obscene grounds had shaded away from the previous religious ones) but, conceding *arguendo* the strongest position, that the case was not political but obscene, the Wilkes result still remains no precedent at all for later cases dealing with obscene literature; for, reasoning by these later cases, no offense had been committed by Wilkes since he had not circulated the "Essay."

In summary, then, the first hundred years which followed Sedley's cavortings on a Covent Garden balcony yielded scarcely anything conclusive as to literary obscenity. There is no definition of the term. There is no basis of identification. There is no unity in describing what is obscene literature, or in prosecuting it. There is little more than the ability to smell it. Throughout, the figures in the arena seem to have been doing little else than casual bloodletting; the few shots fired have been mostly blanks.

Hostilities had temporarily ceased, and the smoke of battle began to lift and drift off when, with something of a clatter, the general of staff arrived to direct the field work and to marshal his forces—The Lord High Chancellor, Lord Eldon.

THE GROWTH OF THE LAW

> I own, of our protestant laws I am jealous,
>   And long as God spares me, will always maintain,
> That *once* having taken men's rights or umbrellas,
>   We ne'er should consent to restore them again.
>
>   *Moore.*

Lord Eldon ranked infinitely higher than the typical Tory of his time; he was that perfect organism, the Tory of all time. Hazlitt has some now famous lines about the Lord High Chancellor:

There has been no stretch of power attempted in his time that he has not seconded: no existing abuse, so odious or so absurd, that he has not sanctioned it. . . . When the heavy artillery of interest, power, and prejudice is brought into the field, the paper pellets of the brain go for nothing: his labyrinth of nice, lady-like doubts explodes like a mine of gunpowder. The Chancellor may weigh and palter—the courtier is decided, the politician is firm, and rivetted to his place in the Cabinet! . . . In the whole of his public career, and with all the goodness of his disposition, he has not shown "so small a drop of pity as a wren's eye."

It was under the frowning brow of Lord Eldon that, in 1817, Southey, then Poet Laureate of England, pleaded that the publisher Sherwood be restrained from printing and selling Southey's stirring revolutionary drama, "Wat Tyler." The drama had been written in 1794 and brought to London by a friend of Southey's; there it had been placed in the hands of Ridgeway and Symonds, publishers, who had feared to print it, most probably because of the then recent trials for High Treason. "Wat Tyler" was, of course, a bold attack on sovereignty and power, asking —if not indeed threateningly demanding—a better lot for workers.

After a lapse of twenty-three years, Southey sued the successor to Ridgeway and Symonds' publishing house who had started to circulate the drama. Lord Eldon refused the relief prayed, declaring that Mr. Southey would first have to establish his right to the work by an action toward that end; in Lord Eldon's majestic opinion, this would fortunately be impossible of achievement since the drama was, in its very nature, calculated to do injury to the public.

To those unfamiliar with the circumstances of the case and the personalities involved, the decision appears most startling. In this regard *The Cambridge History of English Literature* says: "Southey failed in recourse to the law owing, perhaps, to one of the most extraordinary 'quillets' of a legal mind ever recorded." Those acquainted with Lord Eldon, however, find the decision easy to comprehend. The explanation for the decision is almost too human and warrants no comment: Lord Eldon had been Attorney-General in the High Treason trials of 1794.

The inevitable consequence of the decision was the publication of the drama—an end which both Southey and Lord Eldon were at least allied in wishing to prevent. But instead of Lord Eldon, the uncomfortable task of furnishing explanations fell to Southey; to him it proved doubly and painfully embarrassing since, as Poet Laureate, Southey bore the duty of maintaining and swelling the traditions of a conservative England.

Five years after he had so fulsomely distinguished himself in Southey's case, the noble Lord denied a prayer for relief against the piracy of Byron's poem, "Cain," because the work was a "profane libel"; and, as the opportunity to unbosom himself of literary criticism proved irresistible, the learned Judge proceeded to express his doubts also anent Milton's "Paradise Lost"; to him it appeared that the saving glory of those ponderous cadences was, "taking it altogether . . . that the object and effect was not to bring disrepute, but to promote the reverence of our religion."

"Cain," a powerful tragedy on man's doubts concerning his life and God's existence, and man's endeavors to lift himself to a higher plane of knowledge in this world, can hardly be described as obscene, lacking as it does all sexual connotations. It is blasphemous, possibly, in the sense that it attacks organized religion, pleading sympathy for one whom organized religion denounces. The leitmotif of this case, therefore, is still the religious.

The unfortunate Byron, so roughly handled by his peers, shook the dust of England from his heels forever when he started for the Continent and the later stirring episode in Greece which was to become the tale of his death. To his legal representatives, however, Byron had committed the task of enjoining the publisher, Dugdale, from pirating the Sixth, Seventh, and Eighth Cantos of "Don Juan," which had appeared in July of 1822.

The Vice-Chancellor of England, Sir John Leach, who in a previous unreported case had refused to protect "a foolish trifling song," since obliterated by history, now "exercising a kind of paternal censorship in copyright cases" declined, on the ground of its obscenity, to grant protection to the pirated work. Yet "Don Juan," while suggestive in sections, would scarcely be condemned today as obscene. Of the Sixth, Seventh, and Eighth Cantos—those which furnished the basis of the decision—the latter two, containing the siege and assault of Ishmail, are Byron's satire on warfare; it is the Sixth Canto which puts Don Juan, masquerading as a woman, into a harem for the night, but apparently nothing of great moment there transpires.

Ironical is the contrary effect achieved by these cases: when a court refuses to grant protection—copyright—to a literary product because it is immoral and likely to injure the public, the court at once defeats itself; for a multitude of pirated editions from mushroom publishers instantly swamp the country. Such was the actual experience of both "Wat Tyler" and "Don Juan."

That juries—the theoretical cross section of the population—were hardly more liberal than the judges is shown by *Moxon's Case,* dated 1841, in which the publication of Shelley's "Queen Mab" was found to be an indictable offense despite surrounding circumstances which, indubitably, would ordinarily have swayed a jury against conviction.

But that Lord Eldon's critiques and strictures did not represent the prevailing English attitude may be gleaned from Campbell's *Lives of the Lord Chancellors* in which he wrote:

. . . it must have been a strange occupation for a judge who for many years had meddled with nothing more imaginative than an Act of Parliament, to determine in what sense the speculations of Adam, Eve, Cain, and Lucifer are to be understood. . . .

This Campbell, an impoverished Scot who by dint of hard work rose to the woolsack himself, was a man of prolific if not of enduring literary ability and was, according to some commentators, "an arch enemy of censorship as it existed in its ordinary forms." If this be true, and with Campbell necessarily keenly perceptive of the universe lying beneath the judicial hat, it is surprising that he drafted and valiantly fought for the statute of 20 and 21 Victoria which, it has been stated, Lord Campbell intended as a protection for children against the abundant pornographic pamphlets, books, and picture postcards then, as now, in circulation. Under the date of 1858 Campbell writes in his diary that the success of his bill has been most brilliant: Holywell Street, which had long set law and decency at defiance, has capitulated after several assaults: "Half the shops are shut up, and the remainder deal in nothing but moral and religious books!" Even in Paris, jots Campbell in a wave of optimism, the influence of the bill has been felt, for the French police are purifying the *Palais Royal* and *Rue Vivienne.*

Queen v. Hicklin, in 1868, "interpreted"

Lord Campbell's Act. Henry Scott, member of a protestant union pledged, among other things, to defend England from Papish machinations, bought copies of the cumbersomely titled "The Confessional Unmasked, Showing the Depravity of the Romish Priesthood; the Iniquity of the Confessional, and the Questions put to Females in Confession," and sold them at cost. His barrister pleaded that the statute did not mean to cover the case of a book written honestly to reveal the evil suggestions and licentiousness prompted by a confessor's intimate questions, but the judges were not impressed; and, as the barrister's lucubrations apparently had not extended to the *Parliamentary Debates,* and with the judges apparently not caring to discuss the debates over the act, the cardinal question in statutory construction was not raised: precisely what evil was the statute designed to prevent or eradicate?

The case produced Lord Chief Justice Cockburn's test for obscenity: "whether the tendency of the matter charged as obscenity is to deprave and corrupt those whose minds are open to such immoral influences, and into whose hands a publication of this sort may fall." That the work may be written for an object both honest and laudable makes no difference, said the learned Lord; if a work is obscene, it is obscene—regardless of intent; and no one may break the law even to reach a worthy end.

And so the first two hundred years of the Three Hundred Years' War Against Obscenity came to a close. Again there was much manoeuvering as the accompaniment of several legal incidents, some ludicrous, some on occasion pathetic, culminating in the formulation of a "test" for obscenity. But, perhaps dogged by that same perverse turn with which the law on obscene literature seems historically to be afflicted, it is apparent that the "test" was evolved not from a case concerning a distinct and definite literary product, but from an attack upon the Catholic Church embodied in a book which was a blatant instrument of propaganda for a protestant society.

THE DEVELOPMENT OF THE LAW IN THE UNITED STATES

Thus "obscenity" is a function of many variables, and the verdict of the jury is not the conclusion of a syllogism of which they are to find only the minor premise, but really a small bit of legislation *ad hoc*. . . .
Judge Learned Hand.

I

For some untoward reason trenching upon the sociologist's domain, all the obscene literature cases come from two states, Massachusetts and New York, or arise in their Federal Courts.

In Massachusetts, home of Boston and the New England Watch and Ward Society, and hence father to the "Banned in Boston" dustjacket, literary casualties have been high and severe. The first conviction on record is dated 1821 for the sale of a book called *Memoirs of a Woman of Pleasure*. During the nineties, a "not reasonably specific" indictment for selling Boccaccio's *Decameron* was quashed on this technicality, the judge adding that since the book, well known to students of literature, had made its appearance long before the invention of printing, at a time when the illiteracy which prevailed would have given it a narrow circulation, it obviously had not been written to corrupt youth.

The Massachusetts judiciary, with this case, walked into the War from the opposite direction. Where the English test excluded the intent and called it irrelevant, the Massachusetts case searched the author for his intent and motive. The difference between the two approaches, or attitudes, is the—at least—verbal distinction between subjective and objective. The more liberal approach, however, can best be attributed to the leniency with which most courts have regarded publications heavy with the mosses of age.

The English test was at length duplicated and adopted in Massachusetts through the legal episode which resulted in the banning of Elinor Glyn's execrable novel, *Three Weeks*. Obscene, indecent, impure, and manifestly tending to corrupt the morals of youth were the sentiments of the judge as expressed in the so cherished, carefully comprehensive, legal jargon. The novel furnished a diverting incident to an English judge affected similarly but lightly, who refused to allow Elinor Glyn to recover against a film company which had produced a farcical picture based on the book, called, with characteristic English humor, *Pimple's Three Weeks (Without the Option)*. The gist of the Briton's sparkling opinion—he could not take the novel seriously despite all attempts—was simply that it was too trashy to be dignified by copyright. In gist, he described it as being a web of half-hysterical fancies such as are calculated to elicit sweet ejaculations and a shuddering ecstasy from parlormaids. "When it comes to immorality in books," said Theodore Dreiser, "the so-called 'best seller' type of fiction is vicious in the extreme...."

Yet the fourth, and most famous case in Massachusetts, decided in 1930, branded Dreiser's *An American Tragedy* as unfit for sale, to the accompaniment of the entire list of defamatory and harsh adjectives. The determination of the obscenity of this novel was effected by a court method unjust and unsatisfactory. Introduction of the complete book into evidence was denied, the only evidence permitted being chapters in which were located certain sections handpicked by the district attorney. The court's verbal justification for this procedure, which transformed the trial into a farce as gay as *Pimple's Three Weeks* (*Without the Option*), was, first, that the length of the book made a reading of it to the jury impossible (was the jury illiterate?); and, second, that a synopsis of the book would necessarily take color and emphasis from the mental predisposition of the abstractor.

Arthur Garfield Hays, in defending *An American Tragedy*, virtually used dynamite to explode the test for obscenity by pointing out that by it the most intelligent and cultured members of the community would be reduced to the same plane as their most mentally immature and lewd neighbors. No matter how high a man's head it would always be placed on the same level as another's feet. To this argument, the court, in the manner of those clothed in the purple, discreetly replied not.

However ill Dreiser might have felt in thus being rudely classed with Elinor Glyn, some consolation was surely his on finding D. H. Lawrence at his elbow.

Lady Chatterley's Lover, published in 1928 from the original unexpurgated English edition, was, at the request of an agent of the Watch and Ward Society, obtained and sold to him by a Cambridge bookseller. The bookseller was promptly indicted, tried and convicted, with his attorneys admitting on appeal that "by present standards" the novel was not fit for publication; and the court quickly held the book "obscene, indecent, and impure" and manifestly tending to corrupt the morals of youth. With the concession by the defense that the work was obscene, the case loses much of its value in the development of the law; but it is suggested that a cogent argument, probably useless in Massachusetts, might have been directed in favor of the book by explicating the theme of *Lady Chatterley's Lover* from a literary and social viewpoint.

In summary, the Massachusetts law on obscene literature is relatively simple, and, in its simplicity, harsh. The criminal statute, originally enacted in 1711, applying to any book "containing obscene, indecent, or impure language, or manifestly tending to corrupt the morals of youth" has been steadfastly construed as banning literary works, save possibly the older classics, containing a single passage or passages the tendency of which is to deprave and corrupt those whose minds are open to such immoral influences and into whose hands the publication might fall.

As a result of agitation in 1929 and 1930 an amendment to the statute was proposed by which the phrase "which considered as a whole is obscene" would be substituted for the existing words, "containing obscene language." The amendment was fought by the Watch and Ward Society and a compromise amendment, passed in 1930, with the words "which is obscene" is now the statutory law.

There have been no literature cases under the amended act; the present Massachusetts law is therefore a matter of conjecture, and it may be questioned whether the amendment will do more than cause the courts to write their opinions in a different style.

II

In New York not half so many pates have been cracked by the crusade. The courts have been "liberal"—a surprising tendency in a state the stamping ground of "Anthony Comstock, Roundsman of the Lord," founder, in 1873, of the New York Society for the Suppression of Vice, and destroyer of "something over fifty tons of vile books; 28,425 pounds of stereotype plates for printing such books; 3,984,063 obscene pictures; 16,900 negatives for printing such pictures."

Despite a brief in opposition filed in 1894 by this formidable slayer of dragons and knight valiant to virgins, Payne's edition of *The Arabian Nights,* Fielding's *Tom Jones, The Confessions of J. J. Rousseau, Tales from the Arabic, Aladdin, The Works of Rabelais,* Ovid's *Art of Love, The Decameron of Boccaccio,* and *The Heptameron of Queen Margaret of Navarre* were held salable and not obscene.

Although such a decision makes the man of letters laugh and play, it was not, in reality, especially astonishing, in view of certain factors which seem obvious to none but those of legal training: as has already been indicated, the courts measure "classics" with a yardstick which is not brought into use for contemporary creations; the editions in question here were choice—excellent examples of artistic bookbinding; the case was not an action by the state in the criminal courts, but arose on petition by trustees to dispose of the assets of Worthington Company.

An excellent illustration of the backhanded manner employed by the courts throughout the construction of the law of obscene literature is the next New York case, *St. Hubert Guild v. Quinn,* in which the obscenity issue was an obvious sham. The Guild, publishers of a forty-two volume set of Voltaire, was suing a purchaser for the contract price; the purchaser erected the defense that the contract was illegal because the books were immoral—and to support the point offered in evidence *The Philosophical Dictionary* and *The Maid of Orleans.* Of *The Philosophical Dictionary* an enlightened judge remarked:

> It is not only a reservoir of sarcasm and wit but it has exerted a profound influence in favor of a humane and rational administration of the law.

Of *The Maid of Orleans* the judge said:

> Offensive as some of the verses of this book undoubtedly are to the taste of our day, yet I do not think we can declare a contract for its sale illegal on this account.

Such liberality was finally capped with: "It is no part of the duty of the courts to exercise a censorship over literary productions."

This phenomenal generality must have caused Theodore Dreiser to wonder when he encountered the John Lane Company. About 1918, the John Lane Company, which had published Dreiser's *The Genius,* was warned by the Society for the Suppression of Vice that the book was obscene. The company decided to cease the sale of the novel. Dreiser promptly recalled the fate of his first book, *Sister Carrie,* which Doubleday, inspired by Frank Norris, had accepted and then feared to publish. Dreiser had insisted that the contract be carried out; Doubleday, after consultation with counsel, had continued the publication; some one thousand copies had been printed, but somehow never saw the light of day, thus making Dreiser's first published novel a failure. With this rankling in his heart, Dreiser was of course none too willing again to be hung up high and dry; but he lacked money. At this point a reputable New York law firm volunteered its services and it was amicably decided to bring suit against John Lane Company on an agreed statement of fact that, if the book be found obscene, the plaintiff, Theodore Dreiser, should not recover. H. L. Mencken, who had called the book "A Literary Behemoth," rallied to Dreiser's support and with great industry collected a list of *hommes de lettres* who declared they could see nothing obscene in the book. In a riot of excitement the literary world and the Vice Society awaited the decision.

But such commotion adversely affected the gazelles of jurisprudence, and it is an old adage that judges, like gazelles, never plunge into any situation they can avoid. The submitted question was refused adjudication. In the first place, said the court, the question of obscenity is one of fact, and questions of fact must be determined by a jury, not by the court. Further, since it is the jury which must decide, expert opinion—the opinion of men of letters, of literary critics, of distinguished people in the community—cannot be received. Third, the court would not give an advisory opinion. These legalisms, verbally neat though they may be, can be defined as little more than a makeweight.

To dismiss with but brief notice the case in 1920 which sustained a jury finding that *Madeleine,* the autobiography of a prostitute, issued by Harper & Brothers, was not obscene, presents, as the next development of the New York attitude, *Halsey v. New York Society for the Suppression of Vice.*

Here occurred one of those rare but delightful events known as the turning of the worm. John Sumner, the incumbent secretary of the Society, had Halsey arrested for selling a copy of Gautier's *Memoirs of Mademoiselle de Maupin*. Halsey was acquitted and promptly sued the Society for malicious prosecution—and recovered. The verdict was sustained by the Court of Appeals even though it was necessary to find that there had been no reasonable ground for the arrest.

Such an extreme holding was astounding; but more so was the extensive discussion of the literary merits of *Mlle. de Maupin* into which the court and dissent headlong plunged. Sainte-Beuve, Henry James, and George Saintsbury were among the critics quoted in the majority opinion; the dissent straightway cited in support of its view *The New International Encyclopaedia* and *The Encyclopaedia Britannica*. Although the court paid heed to the dangers of a censorship entrusted to men of one profession, of like education and similar surroundings, their Honors seemed not at all disinclined to engage in what Lord Eldon a century before had found to be a perilous pastime: literary criticism.

That vigorous sentence in the dissenting opinion, however, "Literary ability is no excuse for degeneracy," would seem to have been more impressive than the holding, for, in the next case, Judge Wagner, in sustaining a conviction for the possession of a copy of *Casanova's Homecoming,* emphatically wrote:

Charm of language, subtility of thought, faultless style, even distinction of authorship, may all have their lure for the literary critic, yet these qualities may all be present and the book be unfit for dissemination to the reading public.

One of the most thought-provoking opinions ever to emanate from any judge who met the problem of obscene literature came from City Magistrate Bushel in *People v. Friede,* where the bone of contention was Radclyffe Hall's *The Well of Loneliness,* a novel making an intense scrutiny of Lesbianism and presenting for sympathetic consideration the harrowing experiences of Lesbians derived from an hostile society. The conflict between restraint and liberty of literary expression was noticed; that the book had literary merit was admitted; but *The Well of Loneliness* was nevertheless adjudged obscene. The major ground of the decision was that although the book "pleads for tolerance . . . it does not argue for repression or moderation of insidious impulses." The argument was deftly turned by a quotation from Havelock Ellis, who had prefaced the novel with a laudatory comment, and who had written in his *Studies in the Psychology of Sex*: "We are bound to protect the helpless members of society against the invert." That duty, said Bushel, is imposed upon the courts; although the legislature of New York has not sought to set up a literary censorship, nor attempted to confine thought and discussion in a strait-jacket, it has endeavored to safeguard society.

The shift in emphasis observed in this case, from a forthright application of the English test for obscenity to a discussion of the duty imposed by the legislature upon the courts in those situations where a book may pervert society, had no effect on New York law; and in the next case, dated 1930, the philistines triumphed.

Arthur Schnitzler's *Reigen,* translated as *Hands Around,* privately printed for members of the Schnitzler Society, was the source of struggle. *Reigen* consisted of a series of ten dialogues: the first, between a prostitute and a soldier; the second, between the soldier and a parlormaid; the third, between the parlormaid and a young man; the fourth, between the young man and a young wife; the fifth, between the young wife and her husband; and so back to the prostitute. The court, thoroughly aroused by an indiscreet preface which held such phrases as "exquisite handling of the licentious" and "reflected the charms of a fastidious amatory technique," instantly applied the orthodox test.

The dissent, after having taken judicial notice of the fact that the book was universally accepted as being of definite literary merit, placed its disagreement solely on the ground that "it is no part of the duty of courts to exercise a censorship over literary productions." It might not be too amiss here to hazard the conjecture that the majority of the court exalted the preface beyond the book. At any rate, the decision was affirmed by the Court of Appeals: two judges dissented, and the literary Chief Judge Cardozo sided with the majority.

But the next following legal incident in New York gave Erskine Caldwell's *God's Little Acre* a clean bill of health on the strength of the sentiment entertained for the book by literary critics and persons prominent in the community. The result, however, had to be phrased in legal terminology and stated as if the purest of logic had impelled the decision. The court employed an artifice as old as man.

The false major premise of the decision was that courts have strictly limited the obscenity laws to pornography and have consistently declined to apply them to books of genuine literary merit. That the novel belonged in the category of merit was adduced from testimonials, solicited and unsolicited, signed by such men as Franklin P. Adams, William Soskin, Horace Gregory, Louis Kronenberger, and Gilbert Seldes; and was bolstered by numerous book reviews from the *New York Times* to the *San Francisco Chronicle.* When John Sumner, for the Vice Society, moved for the dismissal of such testimonials on the ground that obscenity must be judged by normal people and that these "literati" were "'abnormal people," the court, not a whit abashed, plucked forth more such evidence from the president of the Child Study Association of America, from a professor of English, from a clergyman, and from an executive and director of the Federation for the Support of Jewish Philanthropic Societies. Then, as if this were not sufficient to reduce the opposition to white heat, the court concluded: "To my way of thinking, *truth* should always be accepted as a justification for literature."

That the city magistrate in this case struck a spark going even beyond the Vice Society is exemplified in *People v. Berg,* a litigation involving so dirty a book that the court, which alleged it had read the work as a duty, refused to excite the curiosity of the prurient by naming it, and reaffirmed the doctrine of *Queen v. Hicklin* in every particular. The novel, "Female," was judged by the rigid test of Lord Chief Justice Cockburn with this amendation smacking of the Erskine Caldwell case:

In addition, it [the book] lacks literary merit. It teaches no lesson and points no moral. It describes no period of history and the people or characters of that time and their conduct and habits of life, such, for instance, as the "Elizabethan Age"; and no folklore or tales of primitive people living in isolated regions. *We cannot believe that the story is one even possibly true or representative of any individual or of any limited class.*

A slight digression at this point may be worthy and profitable. The orthodox test for obscenity had been formulated by the *Hicklin* case in 1868 as a consequence of an attack upon the Catholic Church by a book judged to be obscene. In 1907, the case of *People v. Eastman,* on all fours with the *Hicklin* case, reached an opposite conclusion. A "scurrilous and vile attack on a large and respected body of Christian clergymen"— the Catholic Church for its confessional—was held not to be obscene, although "improper, intemperate, unjustifiable and highly reprehensible." Judge O'Brien dissented strongly, averring that it seemed to him to be impossible to distinguish the *Hicklin* case from the one at bar. The logical implications of this situation are: either the *Hicklin* case with its test for obscenity is not followed in New York, or the test was a mere dictum not required by the decision. The first alternative is demonstrably false; the second cannot be seriously advanced. Peculiarly enough, however, none of the New York cases after 1907 has bothered about this curiously scrambled position occasioned by the application of a test for obscenity literally overruled at least *sub silentio.*

The two most recent cases in New York, in 1935 and 1936, respectively treated of Gustave Flaubert's *November* and André Gide's *If It Die.* Both books were held salable by city magistrates in opinions intriguing to the inquisitive legal theologian bent upon ascertaining whether the New York city magistrates follow their own law or that of the higher courts in their state.

City Magistrate Goldstein, in dismissing the complaint involving *November,* took the view of the Erskine Caldwell case that the obscenity statute was not intended to suppress bona fide literary effort but rather "dirt in the raw" and added that the test the book was required to meet was the "measure of public opinion in the city of New York in the year 1935," which the magistrate felt he must only observe and record, but not endeavor to regulate, else he would be another King Canute.

City Magistrate Perlman, in dismissing the complaint involving André Gide's *If It Die,* took a more legally consistent stand, noticing in his opinion both the statement of *St. Hubert Guild v. Quinn* that it was no part of the duty of courts to exercise a censorship over literary productions and the statement in *People v. Berg* that filth, however it may be bedizened, must remain plain filth in all ages. The result was this test:

Whether or not, recognizing the latitude afforded all works of literature and of art, and that tastes may differ, a reasonable, cautious and prudent man environed with the conditions of life as they exist today, and not in some past age, would be justified in believing that the book was obscene and lewd not in certain passages, but in its main purpose and construction and published for no useful purpose, but simply from a desire to cater to the lowest and most sensual part of human nature? In applying these tests, relevancy of the objectionable parts to the theme, the established reputation of the work in the estimation of approved critics, if the book is modern; and the verdict of the past, if it is ancient, are persuasive pieces of evidence.

In summary, while the New York courts have not by any means gone pagan, they have been far less severe than those of Massachusetts. As must already be patent, however, the New York law is a very welter of dissonances, although all the cases in New York save two (which were civil actions), have arisen under the present Section 1141 of the Penal Law (which has been in substantially the same form since 1884) prohibiting "any obscene, lewd, lascivious, filthy, indecent or disgusting book."

The "law" enunciated by the higher courts would seem in language to be the orthodox test for obscenity: whether the tendency of the matter charged is to deprave and corrupt those whose minds are open to such immoral influences and into whose hands the matter might fall. To this, however, are added four apparently subsidiary tests: whether the book lacks literary merit; whether it teaches a lesson or moral; whether it describes a period of history and the people and customs of that time; whether the story is true or representative of any individual or class. In making these tests, while the evidence of litterateurs will not be admissible as so-called expert opinion, the comment of critics will be heard in order to determine how the book affects different minds. Choice editions, falling within the category of classics, do not fall under the interdict of the law, nor do works offensive to taste but not libidinous.

In the application of these rules, the New York courts have been moderate; an attitude which demonstrates again that it is of prime importance in considering the law of obscene literature to establish the differential of what the courts have done, rather than said.

The magistrates in New York City, with a cheery waywardness, have created their own tests for obscenity in literature: the test of the duty to protect society from sexual perversions; of the duty not to restrain literary expression; the test of genuine literary worth; the test of "truth"; the test of the mere measure of public opinion; and the lengthy test (adopted in part from the *Ulysses* cases) of whether, affording latitude to literature, a reasonable man would believe the book to be obscene from its main purpose, in which case the established reputation of the work, the verdict of the past, and the relevancy of the obscene sections to the theme are all factors.

III

Until the *Ulysses* cases it might have been said, in respect of literature, that the federal courts were worthy aides and abettors of Comstockery. They exercise censorship through two media: regulation of importations under the tariff acts; and in criminal prosecutions under an act of 1873 declaring certain books, etc., nonmailable matter.

The Act of 1873 was the accomplishment of Anthony Comstock who, by virtue of an intensive campaign in which opponents were denounced as lechers and defilers of youth and American womanhood, succeeded in urging his bill through a busy Congress on the final day of its session. It was afterward signed by President Grant. Comstock then cleverly took a position with no salary as special agent of the Postoffice Department, and redoubled his spheres of influence with the effect already indicated.

The Act, as it stands today, deserves to be rendered *in extenso* since it excellently demonstrates the war cry of the Comstocks, "MORALS, Not Art or Literature," and illustrates also the myopia of the law which sees "obscene" literature as differing in no particular from illicit sexual intercourse, contraception, abortion, prostitution, and sheer unadulterated smut.

In addition to this sweeping statute which reads like a chunk of Rabelais, the orthodox test for obscenity as prescribed in *Queen v. Hicklin* was approved in the federal courts in 1879 by a case which held that *Cupid's Yokes, or the Binding Forces of Conjugal Life,* a book treating the sex side of marriage, was obscene.

Armed with this powerful weapon, the federal courts quickly struck down the first literary work which came before them by sustaining an indictment of the publishers of *Hagar Revelly,* a novel of manners centered on the life of a young woman in New York City compelled to earn her own living.

Judge Learned Hand overruled a demurrer to the indictment, but in a passage of comment singularly aware of social change, he took occasion to express his doubts regarding the obscenity law, declaring that the rule as laid down, however consonant with Mid-Victorian morals, did not seem to him to coincide with the understanding and morality of the time—prewar 1913. He continued frankly:

> I question whether in the end men will regard that as obscene which is honestly relevant to the adequate expression of innocent ideas, and whether they will not believe that truth and beauty are too precious to society at large to be mutilated in the interests of those most likely to pervert them to base uses.

Twenty years later came the *Ulysses* cases. James Joyce, in passionately seeking a new means of literary expression, had written "one of the strongest combinations of profanity, obscenity, and blasphemy ever published in English." Only Joyce had the "courage to lay back completely the epidermis of the soul and do it without a tremor or a hesitation" in describing with extraordinary fidelity some twenty hours in the life of an average man. Literary critics and reviewers of learning had already written long and profound expositions, drawing analogies between *Ulysses* and Homer's *Odyssey* on which it had been patterned. *Ulysses* was recognized in the world of modern literature, even by those who did not particularly care for it, as a powerful, stimulating literary work. Its legal entrance to the United States under the tariff laws, therefore, became a matter of intense concern. In what has been labeled an eloquent decision, District Judge Woolsey held that the huge novel was not obscene.

This holding was affirmed in an opinion, which, while not crystalline in its reflection of the court's position on the subject of obscene literature in general, is nevertheless outstanding as one of the best in the Three Hundred Years' War.

Two aspects of *Ulysses* were stressed by Circuit Judge Augustus N. Hand who spoke for the three judge court, Learned Hand concurring and Manton dissenting. First, he said, the erotic passages in the book were so submerged that the dominant effect produced on reading *Ulysses* was not one of lust. "In the end one feels, more than anything else, pity and sorrow for the confusion, misery, and degradation of humanity." Indeed, said the Judge, it may be questioned if the obscene parts in *Romeo and Juliet* were as necessary to the development of the play as those in the monologue of Mrs. Bloom are to the depiction of her tortured soul. Secondly, the depiction was "sincere, truthful, relevant to the subject, and executed with real art"; and even though Joyce dealt with things unattempted as yet—with things that very likely might better have remained unattempted, parenthetically commented Hand wryly—nevertheless the book as an experiment in a new art form should not be censored.

The Court took due cognizance of another censorship. It may be that *Ulysses* will not survive the test of time, Hand acknowledged, but that was not material.

> Art certainly cannot advance under compulsion to traditional forms, and nothing in such a field is more stifling to progress than limitation of the right to experiment with a new technique. The foolish judgments of Lord Eldon about one hundred years ago, proscribing the works of Byron and Southey, and the finding by the jury under a charge by Lord Denman that the publication of Shelley's "Queen Mab" was an indictable offense are a warning to all who have to determine the limits of the field within which authors may exercise themselves. We think that "Ulysses" is a book of originality and sincerity of treatment and that it has not the effect of promoting lust.

The precise significance of this decision as a precedent for later cases can best be unfolded by comparing a case which came some three years before, *United States v. Dennett,* and one which has followed the *Ulysses* opinion, *United States v. Levine.*

Mary Ware Dennett, when her two sons had reached the respective ages of eleven and fourteen, wrote for them a small pamphlet, "Sex Side of Life." Later she published it for the benefit of other parents and institutions faced with the necessity of educating young people. As a result she was indicted for sending the pamphlet through the mails and subsequently convicted by a jury which had been charged with the *Queen v. Hicklin* test for obscenity. The Second Circuit Court, speaking through Augustus Hand, J., reversed the conviction in holding that, as a matter of law, the pamphlet was not obscene. Lord Cockburn's test for obscenity, however, was not referred to more than indirectly; the opinion going off on the tangent that Comstock's Act was "never thought to bar from the mails everything which *might* stimulate sex impulses . . . it must not be assumed to have been designed to interfere with serious instruction regarding sex matters unless the terms in which the information is conveyed are clearly indecent." In saying that no case had been made for submission to the jury the court concluded: ". . . we hold that an accurate exposition of the relevant facts of the sex side of life in decent language and in manifestly serious and disinterested spirit cannot ordinarily be regarded as obscene."

Similarly, in the *Ulysses* case, the test for obscenity as enunciated by Lord Cockburn was not dealt with squarely; much the same talk of "sincerity" and "has not the effect of promoting lust" formed the cutting edge of the decision. Both the *Dennett* case and the *Ulysses* cases indicated, however, that the orthodox test was being circumscribed.

In *United States v. Levine,* Learned Hand, J., in speaking for the court, came out bluntly to say that *Regina v. Hicklin* had been overruled. One Levine had been indicted for posting circulars advertising obscene books. *Black Lust* was the only one of the books falling within the category of literature. The trial judge had charged the jury that Comstock's Act was directed against stimulating the sensuality of the usual, average mind, and also that the statute was designed to protect the young and immature, the ignorant and those who are sensually inclined, and that if the book contained a single passage such as would excite lustful desires in those into whose hands the book might fall, the statute was applicable.

On the defendant's appeal from a conviction, the court conceded *Black Lust* to be of considerable merit, but patently erotic in describing the adventures of an English girl captured by Dervishes at Khartoum and immured in a harem until her death at the Battle of Omdurman. And the court continued to say that the charge of the trial judge, *i.e.,* the charge of *Regina v. Hicklin,* was incorrect and had been overruled by the *Dennett* and *Ulysses* cases.

The gloss therefore put on the *Ulysses* case is that it has overruled the once orthodox test for obscenity; that a questioned book must be taken as a whole; if old, its accepted place in the arts must be regarded; if new, the opinions of competent critics; what counts is its effect, not upon any particular class, but upon all whom it is likely to reach. "The standard must be the likelihood that the work will so much arouse the salacity of the reader to whom it is sent as to outweigh any literary, scientific or other merits it may have in that reader's hands; of this, the jury is the arbiter."

For all the liberality of this, the last shot so far fired in the War Against Obscenity, the conflict cannot be supposed to have thus ended. True that the ancient and jejune "test" has been discarded, that an inclination toward the opinion of litterateurs has been manifested, that, after much travail, a sort of social balance of convenience test has been stated. The law, in its ponderous generalities, still remains as a weapon of censorship with the only safeguard the mercy of a judge. It is therefore not only apposite but necessary to consider the problem of censorship, as it now stands, from a broader base.

A CRITIQUE

"Give your evidence," said the King; "and don't be nervous, or I'll have you executed on the spot."
Alice in Wonderland.

From any point of view, the salient factor is that there are no rules of law on obscene literature, despite the professed preoccupation of this study with literature only; there are rules only on obscenity.

The first shell, therefore, to be discharged in the robed ranks of the legal divines contains the gunpowder of their own failing to consider literature as *sui generis,* of its own kind. They have failed to consider the nature and function of literature; they have sought to compress literature into one of the pre-established categories of the law. Using the mails to propose an adulterous liaison is no different in legal principle from using the mails to ship an obscene novel. The rule applying to the advertisements of prostitutes in a newspaper is identical with the rule applying to a translation of Schnitzler's *Reigen.* An endeavor to portray faithfully the lives of the degenerate Georgia "crackers" is governed by the rule forbidding the exposure of "one's private parts in public." The literary stream of consciousness receives the same legal contemplation as exhibitionistic sex orgies.

Such purblind lack of discrimination cannot be condoned by the cases, many of them cases in liberal jurisdictions, which pragmatically reach sound conclusions. The compressive force exerted on literature is created by a mere application of the obscenity laws irrespective of the result. This attempt to straitjacket literature into a legal category cannot be laid at the door of an inelastic juridical method alone; the fault is inherent in any system of literary review by a body equipped to adjudicate disputes of a different character.

Not only is the general law of obscenity absurd as applied to literature, and not only is the task of judging literature beyond the average judge's capacity and ability, but as a matter of physical organization courts are not able to do justice to literature, in the main, even had they such capacity and ability. Thus, the Massachusetts debacle at once comes to mind: *An American Tragedy,* because it was too long to be read to the jury, was judged not in its entirety but through passages culled by the district attorney for the especial delectation of the jury.

Yet all great literature contains the elements we call obscene. Certain portions of the Bible have been termed "obscene." When a lady objected to the presence of "improper" words in Samuel Johnson's dictionary, he is reported to have said: "Madam, you must have been looking for them."

One is driven, as a consequence, to a consideration of the feasibility of a literary board of review or administrative body comprising reputable men of letters. An obstacle which instantly erects itself may be that raised by Horace B. Liveright: ". . . it is obvious that no man or woman of fine intelligence will act in any way as a censor of the arts. . . ."

The argument is not inconsiderable, but one of even greater proportions is furnished by the disagreements characteristic of critics themselves. Literary critics and authors battle fiercely in internecine warfare while the public reads and is amused. Which of the critics will be chosen for the board? Which school of criticism? It was Swinburne, whose "Poems and Ballads" shocked England and was so viciously and successfully attacked by John Morley, while admired by Lytton and not offensive at all to the moralist critic, John Ruskin; it was Swinburne who was shocked by Shakespeare's "Venus and Adonis" and "had a good word to say for Bowdler . . . declaring that this editor made it possible for imaginative children to read Shakespeare." And what of Byron, Byron so harshly attacked in his time, called a fiend "laughing with detestable glee over the whole of the better and worse elements of which human life is composed." Keats, thought almost universally to be free of the slightest sexual taint, is said by one writer to be actually more voluptuous than Byron because Keats, with a middle-class upbringing, was possessed of a greater delicacy of touch in dealing with sex.

Conceding, *arguendo,* that a literary board of review or an administrative body of the best men of letters of the day could be created, reputable and able as the board might be, it would still not be infallible. And worse, would there not be the risk that a work which breaks with past literary traditions might be censored by them—yet hailed by posterity if posterity were to see it? Would not a powerful attempt to blast away the prevailing technics, styles, moods, language, and attitude be met with prompt suppression? Literary history would seem to afford proof sufficient.

Since neither the court nor the critic can properly and with justice censor literature, the question that remains is whether literature should be left uncensored. Unless a case can be made for an affirmative answer to the question, the better of the two evils—judge or literary board—would have to be considered. It is suggested that the case for removal of censorship of literature is far more cogent than the arguments for prohibition.

It is of prime importance, first, to detect a piece of bad reasoning which has clouded the issue. When one in vindictive mood tears a bit of paper to shreds, the shreds do not thereby become "vindictive" shreds of paper; the actor in the transaction was vindictive. Similarly many bits of paper bound together in the form of a book cannot be made vindictive, or pleasant, moral, or immoral, by the acts of persons who have read the book. Once it is perceived that people are moral or immoral—not books—the real issue comes to light, the real issue being the effect of a book upon that sum total of peculiarities known as the human being. It is amazing to realize that regarding this actual connection very little is known—hardly that there is or is not such a connection. Yet it is this untested, preconceived, perhaps groundless theory of a cause and effect which forms the basis for the censorship statutes and the myriads of essays by judges.

Over ten years ago the Bureau of Social Hygiene of New York City sent questionnaires to ten thousand college and normal school women graduates. Twelve hundred answers were received; and of those seventy-two persons who replied that the source of their sex information came from books, mentioning specific volumes, not one specified a "dirty" book as the source. Instead, the books listed were: the Bible, the Dictionary, the Encyclopaedia, novels from Dickens to Henry James, Shakespeare, circulars for venereal diseases, medical books, and Motley's *Rise of the Dutch Republic*. In answer to the question of what things were most stimulating sexually, of the 409 replies, 9 said "Music," 18 said "Pictures," 29 said "Dancing," 40 said "Drama," 95 said "Books," and 218 noted very simply "Man."

The American Youth Commission's study of the conditions and attitudes of young people in Maryland between the ages of sixteen and twenty-four, which has recently come off the press under the title *Youth Tell Their Story,* is even more enlightening. For this study Maryland was deliberately picked as a "typical" state, and, according to the Commission, the 13,528 young people personally interviewed in Maryland can speak for the two hundred and fifty thousand young people in Maryland and the twenty millions in the United States.

The chief source of sex "education" for the youth of all ages and all religious groups was found to be the youth's contemporaries. . . . Sixty-six per cent of the boys and forty per cent of the girls reported that what they knew about sex was more or less limited to what their friends of their own age had told them.

After "contemporaries" and the youth's home, the source that is next in importance is the school, from which about 8 per cent of the young people reported they had received most of their sex information. A few, about 4 per cent, reported they owed most to books, while less than 1 per cent asserted that they had acquired most of their information from movies. Exactly the same proportion specified the church as the chief source of their sex information.

These statistical results are not offered as conclusive; but that they do more than cast doubt upon the assertion that "immoral" books corrupt and deprave must be admitted. These statistical results placed in the scale against the weight of the dogma upon which the law is founded lift the counterpan high.

Add this: that "evil manners" are as easily acquired without books as with books; that crowded slums, machine labor, barren lives, starved emotions, and unreasoning minds are far more dangerous to morals than any so-called obscene literature. True, this attack is tangential, but a social problem is here involved, and the weight of this approach should be felt. The counterpan is lifted a trifle higher.

Add again the curious dissociative process within our national mentality which permits half-nude women and bathing beauties to bedeck advertisements; and which permits burlesques, leg shows, and frankly erotic motion pictures. Add all those things like newspapers with their deluge of sensational scandal which demonstrate symptoms a psychiatrist would quickly group as a sex neurosis or psychosis in an individual but which, because of their national extent, are not treated or considered.

Finally add to the weight in the scale opposing censorship the nature and function of literature. Literature is a social function, and its values, first and last, social values. Indeed, Gertrude Buck ingeniously makes the hit that a book is "the writer's action transforming itself into the reader's reaction at the point of print"; that "literature in this sense is no finished material object—a pill to be swallowed by the reader, or a sugar-plum to be eaten by him. Rather is it a great continuous activity, which goes on through and by the reader, his participation constituting its final stage, as organically related to it as the writer's function itself."

Now ultimate ends and ultimate values are beyond man's perspective. "Human experience," as Underhill Moore beautifully wrote in another, but not unrelated, connection, "discloses no ultimates. Events are related to events so that each is at once an end and a means. Ultimates are phantoms drifting upon the stream of day dreams."

Literature, therefore, should not be asked to embody the values of the time. Literature should disseminate ideas, not moralities. If the author's ideas jar the prevailing mores, it is not the ideas which must be suppressed: both can exist coetaneously, and both must so exist if society is not to stagnate, decay, and die. Moralities change; ideas develop; and the change in morals springs from the development of ideas. In this sense, to limn with a broad brush, poets *are* the unacknowledged legislators of the world.

To say that a substantial amount of the normal person's time is occupied with sex is neither to admit a brooding over original sin nor to bellow with Freudian fury about man and woman. It is the statement of an actuality. If, therefore, literature is to be "pudibund," to be closely restrained in the enunciation of sex ideas, one of the social functions of literature will be vitiated to society's loss.

CONCLUSION

The case for freedom, it is suggested, at least balances the dogma of the present law. The suggestion for a literary board of review has been seen to be quite as dangerous and lacking in justice as present judicial censorship, if, indeed, not more so. Personal predilections founded upon individual experience may, in this equipoise, vie for censorship or outright freedom. On the one hand, therefore, the proposal for a legal system which would exclude any attempt to censor literature, or perhaps even pornography, would appeal to many; while, on the other hand, the puritan neurosis is still prevalent.

This conflict of interests wherein judges are forced to seek passable compromises might well be ended by the decision, supported by this study, that there is no evidence establishing the need for censorship; that, on the whole, the evidence points the other way. Strongly rooted feelings, however, lying deep within the present social organization, cannot be so swept away. The judicial judgments within the field of censorship, judgments more irrational and more isolated from the realities of living than in most other fields of law are open demonstrations of this deeply rooted, ofttimes inarticulate, emotion on obscene literature.

It is therefore sensible, and practical, insofar as such a result may be achieved in the present climate of opinion, to ask only that the approach to the problem be confined within the borders of the nature and function of literature with due regard to the pertinent psychological and sociological aspects of the effect of literature. Such an approach would likely result in freedom banishing the censor, if not now, then in a more perfect or less neurotic world; but, more material at this time, would create a new, lifelike law on obscene literature in step with the march of events in an ever-changing world.

Norman St. John-Stevas, English barrister and lecturer, and author of an excellent book in this field, *Obscenity and the Law* (1956), here points up the inconsistencies, conflicting interpretations, and other difficulties confronting the British courts in the application of existing laws governing obscenity. Legal practice and precedents, still under the dead hand of Chief Justice Cockburn, can be freed, Mr. St. John-Stevas emphasizes, only by a thoroughgoing revision of the present statutes.

Norman St. John-Stevas
OBSCENITY, LITERATURE AND THE LAW

The law governing obscene publications in England has recently been subjected to severe criticism owing to the prosecutions launched against a number of reputable authors and publishers for "publishing obscene libels." This wave of prosecutions has now subsided, but the law has remained unchanged and there is nothing to prevent the recurrence of another series of indictments. It is still, therefore, of some value to examine the provisions of the existing law and the principles on which it is based.

Some maintain that there should be no law for the suppression of obscenity, because far from being an evil, it is a necessity in modern conventional society. Havelock Ellis held this view, arguing that the conditions of contemporary society require relief from oppressive conventions just as the conditions of childhood create the need for fairy stories. Obscene books, therefore, are not aphrodisiac, but act as safety valves protecting society from crime and outrage. A more convincing argument is that obscenity forms a necessary and valuable part of human life. The sexual appetite must be satisfied and find expression both in art and in life.

Half the great poems, pictures, music, stories of the whole world [wrote D. H. Lawrence] are great by virtue of the beauty of their sex appeal. Titian or Renoir,

---

Norman St. John-Stevas, "Obscenity, Literature and the Law," *Dublin Review* 230, no. 471:41–56 (Summer, 1956), copyright 1956 by the Dublin Review. Reprinted by permission of the author and of the publisher.

68 *The courts look at books*

the *Song of Solomon* or *Jane Eyre*, Mozart or Annie Laurie, the loveliness is all interwoven with sex appeal, sex stimulus, call it what you will. Even Michael Angelo, who rather hated sex, can't help filling the Cornucopia with phallic acorns. Sex is a very powerful, beneficial and necessary stimulus in human life, and we are all grateful when we feel its warm, natural flow through us like a form of sunshine.

Thus to outlaw obscenity is to falsify life, to separate the sexual appetite from everyday living and ultimately to degrade it. Lawrence spent the greater part of his life struggling against this attitude and its consequences, and was branded as an obscene writer, whereas his attitude to sex was essentially an integrated and ultimately a moral one. He was attacking the whole industrial and urban society of modern England which alone makes possible the separation of life and sex, converting life's greatest mystery into "a dirty little secret."

Obscenity raises the whole problem of censorship and freedom of discussion in contemporary society. The one point on which those involved in the obscenity debate are agreed is that a censorship of books before publication is undesirable. "The liberty of the press," wrote Blackstone, "is indeed essential to the nature of a free state: but this consists in laying no previous restraints upon publications and not in freedom for criminal matter when published."

The experience of the Irish Censorship Board confirms the opinion of those who are opposed to a previous censorship. Up to the present time over four thousand books and nearly four hundred periodicals have been banned. In the list of banned books, titles like *Hot Dames on Cold Slabs* and *Gun Moll for Hire* are found side by side with Proust's *Remembrance of Things Past* and André Gide's *If It Die.* Four winners of the Nobel Prize for Literature, and nearly every Irish writer of distinction, including St. John Gogarty, Liam O'Flaherty, Kate O'Brien and Sean O'Faolain appear in the list. Irishmen may not read Charles Morgan's *The Fountain,* Somerset Maugham's *The Painted Veil,* Aldous Huxley's *Point Counter Point,* or George Orwell's *1984.* Until released by the Appeal Board, Graham Greene's novels *The Heart of the Matter* and *The End of the Affair* were also forbidden to Irish readers. The British Government's *Report of the Royal Commission on Population (1949)* was placed on the list because it advocated birth control, and the same fate overtook Halliday Sutherland's *Laws of Life,* despite the fact that it carried the imprint of the Censor of the Archdiocese of Westminster. Senator Kingsmill Moore was fully justified when he described the Board's list as "Everyman's guide to the modern classics," during a Senate Debate of 1945, adding that the Board had "affronted the general opinion of decent and responsible men: the effect of it has been to impose the view of five persons as a kind of fetter upon the intellect and information of the nation." Undoubtedly, the Board has succeeded in keeping out of Ireland a great mass of pornography of a filthy and corrupting kind, but this has only been achieved at the price of depriving Irish readers of many of the best works of contemporary literature.

Censorship is rejected in England on grounds of principle, and the wisdom of this principle is confirmed by contrary practice elsewhere. Whatever may be the theoretical arguments in favour of censorship—and Plato has shown that they can be weighty—the practical advantages that follow from a wide freedom of publication are far greater than those benefits which might be gained by a system of censorship. Freedom of discussion is perhaps the basic doctrine of the liberal society, and springs not from any cynical contempt for truth, but from the conviction that no one man or body possesses truth in its entirety. To attain to truth the human mind must be free: free to speculate, to express, to make mistakes and to try again. Further, the liberal ethic presupposes an adult society with a certain minimum of education and the ability if left to itself to choose the right thing freely. Such freedom has, however, always been limited, although the limits have varied from decade to decade. Orators speak of the difference between "liberty" and "licence," but how does one distinguish? No logical point exists at which liberty can be distinguished from licence, just as there is no numerical point at which the number of constraints imposed by the State changes a free into a slave society. The liberal doctrine is one of the "minimum" State in which constraints are kept to the minimum necessary for good government and not imposed for their own sake. Thus a man may publish what he pleases subject to the constraints of the law of civil and criminal libel. He must not defame, he must not blaspheme, he must not be seditious and he must not be obscene, but within these limits he is free to publish what he pleases. Blasphemous and seditious libel are now dead letters, and the worst features of the libel law have been modified by the Defamation Act of 1952. Today obscene libel is the only effective legal limitation on freedom of discussion, although there are obviously many non-legal limitations from prevailing standards of taste to the existence of monopoly institutions such as the B.B.C.

Underlying the dispute about obscenity is a real clash of social interests. Authors have a right to communicate their thought and work freely. They must feel free if they are to give of their best, and they cannot feel this if they are in continual fear of prosecution.

> The police magistrate's opinion is so incalculable [wrote Virginia Woolf], he lets pass so much that seems noxious and pounces upon so much that seems innocent—that even the writer whose record is hitherto unblemished is uncertain what may or may not be judged obscene and hesitates in fear and suspicion. What he is about to write may seem to him perfectly innocent—it may be essential to his book; yet he has to ask himself what will the police magistrate say: and not only what will the police magistrate say, but what will the printer say and what will the publisher say? For both printer and publisher will be trying uneasily and anxiously to anticipate the verdict of the police magistrate and will naturally bring pressure to bear upon the writer to put them beyond the reach of the law. He will be asked to weaken, to soften, to omit. Such hesitation and suspense are fatal to freedom of mind and freedom of mind is essential to good literature.

Recent events have proved Virginia Woolf to be right. After the 1954 prosecutions printers all over the country employed extra readers to hunt through manuscripts, especially novels, and to mark passages which some old lady or police magistrate might consider obscene. Until such passages had been deleted they refused to print the books. One of America's most distinguished contemporary novelists was unable to find an English printer for her book—widely praised on its publication in the United States—because it contained certain passages which, taken out of their context, might fall within the present legal definition of obscenity. Another American novel has been abandoned by a well-known publisher because of the impossibility of obtaining a printer. In its American edition this novel of 450,000 words ran to over 900 closely packed octavo pages, and its price in the English market would have been not less than thirty-five shillings. The publisher's readers were convinced that the book showed great talent and had no doubt of its moral purpose since it criticized severely the life which it depicted. Nevertheless because for 2 per cent of its total length the book described sexual incidents in coarse language no printer could be found. The result of the police prosecutions has thus been to establish an unofficial censorship which is continuing.

Freedom to discuss every sphere of life is especially important today, since literature, and in particular the novel, is closely concerned with psychological problems and the realistic portrayal of sex. It can hardly be suggested that the Victorian solution of omitting sex from literature or confining the representation to those of an impeccably regular kind, which a reverend mother could contemplate with equanimity, should be re-adopted today. Such an attitude would maim contemporary literature by artificially restricting its range and shutting off from its vision what François Mauriac has called "that place of desolation, the human heart." Not all authors, of course, find conventions cramping. Dickens was happy to accept those of his own time, and a skilful writer like Thackeray was able to exploit them. It is true also, as C. S. Lewis has written, that to banish prudery from literature is to "remove one area of vivid sensibility" and "to expunge a human feeling." The obscenity problem is, however, not a curse for these writers but for those such as Lawrence who are not following but leading their readers in directions to which they have not grown accustomed. For such writers literary reticence and obscenity laws can be destructive.

If authors have a special position in society they also have duties, since they are not writing in a vacuum but writing to be read. Literature may or may not have a social purpose, but it certainly has social implications and writers cannot be totally emancipated from the customs of the community in which they live. If a great literature cannot be created without freedom, neither can it be sustained without a sense of responsibility on the authors' part. The greater the power and the less the external restraint, the more urgent the need of interior sanctions voluntarily imposed. Ultimately, the working of a free society is dependent on this intangible, a sense of self-discipline, the only alternative to which is regimentation. A free and, therefore, a great literature has grown up in England because of the high sense of responsibility felt by authors for their work. Freedom and responsibility go together, one extending the other, so that freedom is possible only in a confident and mature society. It is no accident that the three great English contributions to civilization have been law, literature and parliamentary government, all dependent upon self-restraint and an unwritten law of liberty.

Those authors who pretend that there is no problem, and that the whole obscenity question has been created by a group of unenlightened Grundys and Comstocks only bring discredit on their own cause. Nor is the inevitable carefully selected quotation from Milton—out of its historical and literary context—of any practical utility in the social conditions of the present time.

> The whole problem of propaganda [said Sir Ifor Evans at the P.E.N. Congress of 1944], the dissemination of opinion, the distribution of printed matter, has changed entirely since Milton's day. Milton's conception of the circulation of ideas was that which might have prevailed in Greece—a small audience all of whom are capable of forming their own judgements, with discussion to correct false emphasis. He has in mind the formulation of an adequate judgement by the Socratic method. Even the England of his own day did not fit into that picture altogether, and the world of our day does not fit into it at all. One man or group of men can by subtle psychological methods, and by use of the newspaper and radio, effect a secret tyranny over the minds of millions.

To use the language of Milton to defend the immunity of commercial interests whose only object is to make money by the sale of degrading pornography is only to mislead.

On the other hand those who pose the question as a clash between a group of irresponsible intellectuals, leaders of a minority literary coterie, striving to impose their extravagances on the virtuous and sober-living majority, are equally wide of the mark. Authors certainly have an interest in a free literature, but it is one shared by the rest of society. Consciously or unconsciously a nation's literature mirrors its life and values, being at once the repository of its culture and the guarantee of its continuance. If authors have an interest in writing freely, the public in general has an equal interest in being able to choose what to read. Society, however, also has an interest in preventing the exploitation of literature by those who wish to make money through the stimulation of the baser appetites and passions. Racketeers are especially tempted today by the emergence in every modern state of a new public who can read, but who are only semi-literate. On the whole, perverts excepted, educated people do not read pornography, since their taste for reading is fully formed, and they find it dull and uninteresting, but the barely literate masses have had no such opportunity and here the purveyors of filthy sub-literature find a profitable market.

Presumably it is this consideration which determines the policy of prosecuting only those books which are sold at popular prices. Publishers certainly act on the presumption that a high-priced book will not be prosecuted, and sometimes produce editions of the same book, one bowdlerized at a low price, and the other unexpurgated at a high one. Thus *The Mint,* by T. E. Lawrence, recently published, came out in two editions: the "popular" edition at seventeen shillings and sixpence "from which certain Anglo-Saxon words have been omitted," and a full edition at three pounds thirteen shillings and sixpence, which included the offending words. The latter edition was heavily oversubscribed. Some see in this practice a certain class discrimination, distinguishing an *élite* who can be trusted from the majority who cannot. It would be absurd, however, to suggest that the rich are either incorruptible or even beyond further corruption, and the Director of Public Prosecutions is probably actuated by the belief that the social gain in suppressing a high-priced book with a limited circulation is not worth the trouble of launching a prosecution. When this practice is extended to deprive the general public of literary works it is indefensible, but the protection of the mass of the people from the corrupting effects of pornography is not so much class prejudice as a realistic recognition that the present educational level leaves them open to victimization.

It has been assumed that pornography does have a corrupting effect on its readers, but this assumption must be further examined. Such an assertion rests not on scientific evidence but on what is called "common sense." A further assumption is made that even if there are legitimate doubts about the effect of reading upon adults there can be no doubt that reading does have a positive effect on youth and especially children.

Undoubtedly, the general moral standards and social customs prevailing in a community are frequently formed or changed by the influence of books. "I am convinced," wrote Bernard Shaw in his preface to *Mrs. Warren's Profession,* "that fine art is the subtlest, the most seductive, the most effective instrument of moral propaganda in the world, excepting only the example of personal conduct." In our own time we have the example of André Gide, whose books changed the outlook of a generation. The law, however, cannot be invoked to protect prevailing moral standards, first because this assumes a finality which such standards do not always possess, since much of what passes for morality is merely convention, and secondly because in a country such as England there is no common agreement on ultimate moral attitudes. A book advocating divorce will appear "obscene" or "corrupting" to one group, while another will regard it as an argument for a necessary freedom. Similar considerations apply to books about subjects such as birth-control or homosexuality on which there is no agreed opinion. Unless there is universal agreement on any subject, such as, for example, compulsory education, the liberal state cannot impose coercive sanctions. The situation is different in a state such as Southern Ireland, where there is an almost universal agreement on certain moral principles, and which enables a censorship to be imposed which would be intolerable in England.

Even where there is general agreement on a moral issue the dangers of using the law as a means of moral enforcement are very great. The concepts of law and morality become confused and morality is thought to draw its validity from legal sanctions. Furthermore the attempt to enforce morals by law frequently leads to greater evils than those the law seeks to prevent. On this point the words of Pius XII in his "Discourse to the National Convention of Italian Catholic Jurists" in 1953 are of interest:

> It is plainly true that error and sin abound in the world today. God reprobates them but He allows them to exist. Wherefore the statement that religious and moral errors must always be impeded, when it is possible, because toleration of them is in itself immoral, is not valid absolutely and unconditionally. Moreover, God has not given even to human authority such an absolute and universal command in matters of faith and morality. . . . The duty of repressing moral and religious error cannot, therefore, be an ultimate norm of action. It must be subordinate to higher and more general guiding principles, which in some circumstances allow, and even perhaps seem to indicate as the better policy, toleration of error in order to promote a greater good.

The greater good—in this case the freedom of literature—makes it necessary to tolerate some obscenity, just as the greater good of the freedom of the Press makes it necessary to tolerate worthless and even harmful papers.

The justification for the laws against pornographic books is the belief that such books have a directly undesirable effect on sexual behaviour. Unhappily, there is little scientific evidence to support this view, since very little research has been carried out on the causal relation between reading and behaviour. Social sciences can never hope to be as exact as the natural sciences since their study is man not matter, and with regard to sexual behaviour man is subject to so many differing stimuli that it is difficult to isolate one and to gauge its effect. Furthermore, it is at least as probable that it is sexual desire, especially if frustrated, that creates the taste for pornography and not pornography which stimulates sexual desire.

One of the very few investigations into this field was carried out by Dr. Kinsey, and he gives the result of his researches in the second of his two reports (*Sexual Behaviour in the Human Female*). He concludes that for the pre-adolescent and the late teenager erotic literature is not an important factor in arousing sexual desire. The age group most likely to be aroused by vicarious experience is that of the adult male. Women are less likely to be aroused by erotic literature than men. He further stressed that sex information comes as much from experience and word of mouth as from reading matter. Unfortunately he grouped together information from the verbal and printed word, and it is not possible to establish from his tables the proportion between these two sources of information. However, in 1938, the New York City Bureau of Social Hygiene carried out some researches, and showed that books play a very small part in the dissemination of sex information among women. One thousand two hundred women out of 10,000 college and school graduates were questioned about the sources of their sex knowledge. Of the 1200 only 72 mentioned books and none of these were of the pornographic type—one was

Motley's *Rise of the Dutch Republic*. Asked what they found most sexually stimulating, 95 of the 409 who replied answered "Books"; 208 said "Men"!

Behaviour is a function of both personality and environment, the dominant influence being personality. However, as the Jesuits have long known and modern psychologists stress, the personality is formed at a very early age, normally before the reading habit is formed. Environment, of course, influences behaviour, but direct experiences have a much greater influence on human behaviour than vicarious experiences through books. Once again there is no direct evidence in point, but the research into drug addiction and voting which has been carried out in the United States shows that reading matter and even mass mediums of communication have much less influence on attitudes than is generally supposed. Mass communications confirm and reinforce existing attitudes, but they rarely cause a fundamental change of outlook.

Youth and children are probably more open to influence because their attitudes have not yet been fully formed, and they have little residue of past experience on which to draw. There is no evidence that the reading of horror comics, for instance, leads directly to the committing of delinquent acts, but they may well have the more general effect of deadening a child's sensitivity and accustoming him to accept brutality and violence as a normal part of human conduct. In 1946, George Orwell noted the change which had come about in boys' papers after the war, and pointed out that bully worship and the cult of violence entered into the comics in a way they never did in the old *Gem* and *Magnet* and even the *Hotspur* and the *Wizard*. Dr. Wertham, in his book, *Seduction of the Innocent,* stressed the brutalizing effect that horror comics have on children, and supported this view by experiments carried out by himself and other psychologists.

> The most subtle and pervading effect of crime comics on children [wrote Dr. Wertham], can be summarized in a single phrase: moral disarmament. To put it more concretely it consists chiefly in a blunting of the finer feelings of conscience, of mercy and sympathy for other people's sufferings and of a respect for women as women and not merely as sex objects to be bandied around, or as luxury prizes to be fought over. Crime comics are such highly-flavoured fare that they affect children's taste for the finer influences of education, for art, for literature, and for the decent and constructive relationships between human beings and especially between the sexes.

He refuted the argument that such reading provides a necessary "catharsis" for children's emotions because emotion is stimulated without being given any adequate outlet. The child identifies itself with the characters in the comic and is left with only a limited scope for release in actions. These actions, he wrote, can only be "masturbatory or delinquent."

His argument that the reading of horror comics leads to juvenile delinquency is less convincing. He gives numerous examples of juvenile delinquents who had many comic books in their possession, but so have many children who never commit a delinquent act. The argument is the old one of "post hoc propter hoc" and is open to the same objections. Sheldon and Eleanor Glueck in their study, *Unravelling Juvenile Delinquency,* gave little prominence to reading among the ninety factors they listed as causes of juvenile delinquency. They showed, in fact, that delinquent children read much less than the law-abiding.

Horror comics have now been banned in England and in many Commonwealth and European countries. Such a step can be justified as a precautionary measure, if only to protect abnormal children, since there is no literary or social interest in the horror comic to be weighed against its possible harmful effect. Further, children are clearly in need of protection, whereas adults can be expected to choose for themselves. The irony of the horror comic situation is that they are read—at any rate in the United States—as much by adults as by children. Forty-one per cent of male adults and twenty-eight per cent of females in the United States read horror comics regularly.

The causal relation between reading and behaviour is so uncertain, the number of sexual stimuli so diverse, and the subjective factors are so numerous, that the law in the sphere of obscenity should proceed with caution. One point seems evident, that literary standards should not be regulated by law. Literature is creative, imaginative and aesthetic, with no extrinsic purpose, its one criterion being fidelity to its own nature. It is the study of the universal, but in the light of the individual and the particular, an expression of man's creative faculty, intent on beauty not on utility. Law is not creative but regulative, seeking not a special ideal harmony but a generalized justice and the application of universally valid principles. Thus it is impossible to attempt to confine literature within the Procrustean bed of the law.

On the other hand the law is rightly used to suppress the social evil of pornography and to punish those who seek to benefit by its distribution. The point has been clearly put by Virginia Woolf:

> There can be no doubt that books fall in respect of indecency into two classes. There are books written, published and sold with the object of causing pleasure or corruption by means of their indecency. There is no difficulty in finding where they are to be bought nor in buying them when found. There are others whose indecency is not the object of the book but incidental to some other purpose—scientific, social, aesthetic, on the writer's part. The police magistrate's power should be definitely limited to the suppression of books which are sold as pornography to people who seek out and enjoy pornography. The others should be left alone. Any man or woman of average intelligence and culture knows the difference between the two kinds of book and has no difficulty in distinguishing one from the other.

George Moore made the same distinction in *Avowals*. He denied that pornography and literature overlap.

> On the contrary the frontiers are extremely well defined, so much so, that even if all literature was searched through and through it would be difficult to find a book that a man of letters could not instantly place in one category or the other. The reason is that real literature is concerned with description of life and thoughts about life rather than with acts. The very opposite is true in the case of pornographic books.

George Moore and Virginia Woolf rather over-simplify the problem, but they do suggest a rational principle on which the law should be based. The Herbert Committee of 1955 took this principle as the basis of their deliberations and came to the conclusion that since the existing law was far from achieving its implementation in practice, the law should be reformed. Under the present law there are two distinct means of proceeding against obscene publications. At common law it is an offence to publish an obscene libel, and for this offence any author, publisher, printer, or distributor, may be prosecuted and sent to prison for an unspecified period of time. The test of obscenity was laid down in 1868 by Chief Justice Cockburn in Hicklin's case. "The test of obscenity is this, whether the tendency of the matter charged as obscenity is to deprave and corrupt those whose minds are open to such immoral influences, and into whose hands a publication of this sort may fall." The meaning of this formula is by no means clear, although it has always been followed by the courts. One point seems established that the courts will consider not the "intention" of the publisher but the "tendency" of the matter published to "corrupt and deprave." What do these last words mean? Clearly a book which shocks or disgusts by the offensiveness of its language does not come within the scope of the test. "Deprave" and "corrupt" are both strong words, and cannot be equated in meaning with writing that is merely offensive or shocking. The words can have any or all of three meanings. First, they can mean that the tendency of the book is to arouse impure thoughts in the mind of the reader or viewer. Secondly, they can mean that such a person would be encouraged to commit impure actions. Thirdly, they can mean that the reading of the book or looking at the picture would endanger the prevailing standards of public morals. The courts have used the words in all three senses.

A further question which must be answered is to whom the words "corrupt" and "deprave" apply? The answer may be normal adults, abnormal adults, normal children, or abnormal children. The English law has always stressed the importance of protecting the young. Thus the old form of indictment invariably contained an averment about the "morals of youth," and in the Hicklin case Chief Justice Cockburn specifically mentioned the need to protect youth. Such a consideration seems to have been uppermost in the minds of most judges and counsel who have taken part in obscenity trials, but in the *Philanderer* case Mr. Justice Stable rejected the youth criterion. "A mass of literature," he said, "great literature, from many angles is wholly unsuitable for reading by adolescents, but that does not mean that the publisher is guilty of a criminal offence for making those works available to the general public."

The Herbert Committee drafted a Bill which abolishes the old common law offence of obscene libel and this Bill was given a unanimous first reading by the House of Commons in March 1955, although it has not yet obtained a second reading. In place of the misdemeanour the Bill substitutes a new offence of "distributing, circulating, selling, or offering for sale any obscene matter." No person can be convicted of this offence unless it is affirmatively proved that he did so with an intent to corrupt, or was "reckless" as to the matter having this effect. "Reckless" is here used in the legal sense, meaning foresight of consequences, although there is no desire that the consequences shall take place. The prosecution must prove that the accused person actually foresaw the consequences of his action, not merely that he ought to have done so. In framing this provision the Committee had in mind the fundamental maxim of the criminal law: *actus non facit reum nisi mens sit rea*—the intent and the act must both concur to constitute the crime. They also considered that "intention" was the only effective way of distinguishing pornography from serious works with an incidental obscene content.

A second major reform proposed by the Bill is a new test of obscenity. No attempt is made to define the exact meaning of the word, but the jury must consider certain factors in deciding whether or not a book is obscene. Strictly interpreted the Hicklin case means that a book can be held obscene if it contains only one obscene passage. This interpretation was decisively rejected by the American judge, Judge Hand, when he lifted the ban on *Ulysses* in 1934:

> We believe that the proper test of whether a given book is obscene is its dominant effect. In applying this test, relevancy of the objectionable parts to the theme, the established reputation of the work in the estimation of approved critics, if the book is modern, and the verdict of the past, if it is ancient, are persuasive pieces of evidence; for works of art are not likely to sustain a high position with no better warrant for their existence than their obscene content.

In each of the recent prosecutions the jury was requested to read the whole book, and the Bill puts the matter beyond all doubt by requiring the jury to consider the "general character and dominant effect" of the publication concerned.

Juries must also take into consideration the "literary or artistic merit" of the work and its "medical, legal, political, religious or scientific character." The Committee's view that such matters are relevant is supported by the authority of Mr. Justice Stephen. In his *Digest of the Criminal Law* he wrote:

> A person is justified in exhibiting disgusting objects or publishing obscene books, papers, writings, prints, pictures, drawings or other representations, if their exhibition or publication is for the public good, as being necessary or advantageous to religion or morality, to the administration of justice, the pursuit of science, literature or art or other objects of general interest: but the justification ceases if the publication is made in such a manner, to such an extent or under such circumstances as to exceed what the public good requires in regard to the particular matter published.

This point was judicially approved by the Recorder of London in the De Montalk case (1932) and is incorporated in the New Zealand legislation covering obscene publications which came into force in 1954.

To assist the jury in assessing a book's literary or artistic merit, the Bill makes expert evidence on these matters admissible. At present "experts" are admitted to give evidence of scientific or medical value, but evidence of literary merit has always been excluded. Mr. Desmond Mac-Carthy was prevented from testifying in the *Well of Loneliness* case, and a similar exclusion operated in both the *Philanderer* and the *Image and the Search* cases. In the Federal courts of the United States, however, such evidence is freely admitted. The Committee felt that the distinction between scientific and literary evidence was both arbitrary and illogical and it is abolished by the Bill.

Juries must also consider the class of persons to whom the book was sold or distributed and any evidence of its in fact having had a corrupting effect. "Tendency to corrupt," the old Hicklin test, is thus abolished. Finally the meaning of the word "obscene" is extended to cover matter "which whether or not related to any sexual context, unduly exploits horror, cruelty or violence, whether pictorially or otherwise." This clause has been criticized, but the Committee felt it could not ignore a problem which has caused such widespread anxiety, and which in the "horror comic" constitutes a new form of pornography.

Apart from the common law offence of obscene libel there are also statutory powers for destroying obscene books under Lord Campbell's Act of 1857. This Act created no new punishable offence and no penalties are laid down save the destruction of the obscene matter. Under the Act any person can lay an information on oath before a stipendiary magistrate or any two justices, that he believes that obscene matter is being kept in premises within the jurisdiction for the purpose of sale or distribution, and that an actual sale has occurred. The magistrates, if they are satisfied that "publication of the matter would amount to a misdemeanour proper to be prosecuted as such," may issue a warrant giving authority for the premises to be entered by a police officer and the obscene matter to be seized. The magistrates, when the seized articles have been brought before them, must issue a summons calling upon the occupier to appear within seven days to show cause why the matter seized should not be destroyed. They may order matter so seized to be destroyed immediately after the expiration of the seven days allowed for appeal.

When Lord Campbell introduced this Act into the House of Lords in 1857 anxiety was expressed lest the Act should be used to attack literary works. He emphatically denied that this was his intention: "The measure is intended to apply exclusively to works written for the single purpose of corrupting the morals of youth and of a nature calculated to shock the common feelings of decency in a well regulated mind." Lord Lyndhurst's comment in view of the subsequent use made of the Act to suppress novels such as D. H. Lawrence's *The Rainbow* and Radclyffe Hall's *Well of Loneliness* was prescient: "Why, it is not what the Chief Justice means, but what is the construction of an Act of Parliament." The Bill re-enacts the main provisions of Lord Campbell's Act. Two reasons lay behind the Committee's decision to retain these powers. First they felt that the police needed such a weapon to check pornography, and secondly, they thought it undesirable to leave the police no alternative but to proceed with a criminal prosecution in every case. The Act is, however, amended in important respects. A duty is placed upon the prosecution to indicate why they consider any publication obscene, and the magistrate must make his finding of obscenity in court. Procedure under these sections is speeded up, and the injustice whereby a book can be condemned as obscene without author or publisher being able to speak in its defence is ended. In all proceedings under the Bill authors, publishers, and printers are given the right to give and call evidence. In *The Well of Loneliness* case Miss Radclyffe Hall was prevented from giving evidence about her book, and on protesting was threatened by the magistrate with ejection. The provisions of the 1857 Act are extended to cover seizure by the Customs Authorities, who must obtain a destruction order from a magistrate or return the seized publications "forthwith."

Uniformity in administering the law is ensured by making all proceedings subject to the consent of the Attorney-General. At the present time the police are bound to consult the Director of Public Prosecutions before they bring criminal proceedings, but they are not obliged to listen to his advice. Furthermore there is no obligation even to consult him when the 1857 Act procedure is used. Private persons are free to bring prosecutions and in the past this power has been abused. In the Bradlaugh case of 1877, when Charles Bradlaugh and Annie Besant were prosecuted for publishing a manual on birth-control, Chief Justice Cockburn pointed out the danger of leaving this power in the hands of the public. On one point, he said, they were all agreed: "A more ill advised and injudicious prosecution was never instituted." The Bill ensures that such abuses shall not occur in the future. A further change in the law is the fixing of maximum penalties for all offences under the Bill.

The Bill gives legal effect to the Committee's view that the essential requirement is to distinguish pornography from serious works that may by contemporary standards be considered shocking or obscene. Pornography should be suppressed by the law, but literature is best regulated by prevailing standards of taste. These standards are constantly changing and the law only brings itself into disrepute by attempting to enforce them by means of legal sanctions. At different times Mrs. Gaskell, Charlotte Brontë, George Eliot, Thomas Hardy, George Moore and James Joyce, amongst novelists, and poets such as Byron, Shelley, Swinburne and even Tennyson, have been denounced by contemporaries as obscene, an accusation which later generations have failed to sustain. The Victorians, although foolish in many ways in their attitude to sex in literature, were wiser than ourselves, for, with the single exception of Zola, prosecutions were never instituted to suppress books of literary merit. Lord Campbell was emphatic during the debate on his Act in the House of Lords that such books should remain free of the law. By this Bill the Committee hope to restore the law to its traditional position and at the same time to bring it into accord with the changed conditions and needs of modern times.

The Age of Enlightenment in the judicial treatment of censorship of obscenity in the United States may be said to have begun in 1930 with the case of *United States* v. *Dennett*. The opinion was written by Judge Augustus N. Hand.

Mary Ware Dennett had been convicted in the U.S. District Court for the Eastern District of New York on a charge that she had circulated a pamphlet, entitled *The Sex Side of Life: An Explanation for Young People*, written originally for her own children. The essay was later published in the *Medical Review of Reviews* and proved so popular that distribution in pamphlet form to meet the public demand was decided upon. Use of the mails for this purpose resulted in Mrs. Dennett's arrest and trial.

Mrs. Dennett's appeal of her conviction to the U.S. Circuit Court of Appeals was heard by Judges Hand, Swan, and Chase. Judge Hand pointed out, in the unanimous decision of the three judges, that the motive of the defendant in mailing the pamphlet was immaterial and that the only thing to be determined was whether the pamphlet was obscene and had a tendency to corrupt the morals of those whose minds are open to such suggestions. "We hold," stated Judge Hand, "that an accurate exposition of the relevant facts of the sex side of life in decent language and in manifestly serious and disinterested spirit cannot ordinarily be regarded as obscene . . . The direct aim and the net result [of the Dennett pamphlet] is to promote understanding and self-control." The judgment of the lower court was therefore reversed.

Augustus N. Hand
UNITED STATES v. DENNETT

Appeal from the District Court of the United States for the Eastern District of New York.

Mary W. Dennett was convicted of mailing obscene matter in contravention of section 211 of the United States Criminal Code (18 USCA § 334), and she appeals.

Reversed.

The statute under which the defendant was

Augustus N. Hand, "United States v. Dennett," 39 *Federal Reporter*, 2d Series, 565–69, copyright 1930 by West Publishing Co. Reprinted by permission of the publisher.

convicted reads as follows: "Every obscene, lewd, or lascivious, and every filthy book, pamphlet, picture, paper, letter, writing, print, or other publication of an indecent character, and every article or thing designed, adapted, or intended for preventing conception or producing abortion, or for any indecent or immoral use; . . . is hereby declared to be nonmailable matter and shall not be conveyed in the mails or delivered from any post office or by any letter carrier. Whoever shall knowingly deposit, or cause to be deposited, for mailing or delivery, anything declared by this section to be nonmailable, or shall knowingly take, or cause the same to be taken, from the mails for the purpose of circulating or disposing thereof, or of aiding in the circulation or disposition thereof, shall be fined not more than $5,000, or imprisoned not more than five years, or both."

The defendant is the mother of two boys. When they had reached the respective ages of eleven and fourteen, she concluded that she ought to teach them about the sex side of life. After examining about sixty publications on the subject and forming the opinion that they were inadequate and unsatisfactory, she wrote the pamphlet entitled "Sex Side of Life," for the mailing of which she was afterwards indicted.

The defendant allowed some of her friends, both parents and young people, to read the manuscript which she had written for her own children, and it finally came to the notice of the owner of the Medical Review of Reviews, who asked if he might read it and afterwards published it. About a year afterwards she published the article herself at twenty-five cents a copy when sold singly, and at lower prices when ordered in quantities. Twenty-five thousand of the pamphlets seem to have been distributed in this way.

At the trial, the defendant sought to prove the cost of publication in order to show that there could have been no motive of gain on her part. She also offered to prove that she had received orders from the Union Theological Seminary, Young Men's Christian Association, the Young Women's Christian Association, the Public Health Departments of the various states and from no less than four hundred welfare and religious organizations, as well as from clergymen, college professors, and doctors, and that the pamphlet was in use in the public schools at

Bronxville, N. Y. The foregoing offers were rejected on the ground that the defendant's motive in distributing the pamphlet was irrelevant, and that the only issues were whether she caused the pamphlet to be mailed and whether it was obscene.

The pamphlet begins with a so-called "Introduction for Elders" which sets forth the general views of the writer and is as follows:

"In reading several dozen books on sex matters for the young with a view to selecting the best for my own children, I found none that I was willing to put into their hands, without first guarding them against what I considered very misleading and harmful impressions, which they would otherwise be sure to acquire in reading them. That is the excuse for this article.

"It is far more specific than most sex information written for young people. I believe we owe it to children to be specific if we talk about the subject at all."

"From a careful observation of youthful curiosity and a very vivid recollection of my own childhood, I have tried to explain frankly the points about which there is the greatest inquiry. These points are not frankly or clearly explained in most sex literature. They are avoided, partly from embarrassment, but more, apparently, because those who have undertaken to instruct the children are not really clear in their own minds as to the proper status of the sex relation.

"I found that from the physiological point of view, the question was handled with limitations and reservations. From the point of natural science it was often handled with sentimentality, the child being led from a semi-esthetic study of the reproduction of flowers and animals to the acceptance of a similar idea for human beings. From the moral point of view it was handled least satisfactorily of all, the child being given a jumble of conflicting ideas, with no means of correlating them—fear of venereal disease, one's duty to suppress 'animal passion,' the sacredness of marriage, and so forth. And from the emotional point of view, the subject was not handled at all.

"This one omission seems to me to be the key to the whole situation, and it is the basis of the radical departure I have made from the precedents in most sex literature for children.

"Concerning all four points of view just mentioned, there are certain departures from the traditional method that have seemed to me worth making.

"On the physiological side I have given, as far as possible, the proper terminology for the sex organs and functions. Children have had to read the expurgated literature which has been specially prepared for them in poetic or colloquial terms, and then are needlessly mystified when they hear things called by their real names.

"On the side of natural science, I have emphasized our unlikeness to the plants and animals rather than our likeness, for while the points we have in common with the lower orders make an interesting section in our general education, it is knowing about the vital points in which we differ that helps us to solve the sexual problems of maturity; and the child needs that knowledge precisely as he needs knowledge of everything which will fortify him for wise decisions when he is grown.

"On the moral side, I have tried to avoid confusion and dogmatism in the following ways: by eliminating fear of venereal disease as an appeal for strictly limited sex relations, stating candidly that venereal disease is becoming curable; by barring out all mention of 'brute' or 'animal' passion, terms frequently used in pleas for chastity and self control, as such talk is an aspersion on the brute and has done children much harm in giving them the impression that there is an essential baseness in the sex relation; by inviting the inference that marriage is 'sacred' by virtue of its being a reflection of human ideality rather than because it is a legalized institution.

"Unquestionably the stress which most writers have laid upon the beauty of nature's plans for perpetuating the plant and animal species, and the effort to have the child carry over into human life some sense of that beauty has come from a most commendable instinct to protect the child from the natural shock of the revelation of so much that is unesthetic and revolting in human sex life. The nearness of the sex organs to the excretory organs, the pain and messiness of child birth are elements which certainly need some compensating antidote to prevent their making too disagreeable and disproportionate an impress on the child's mind.

"The results are doubtless good as far as they go, but they do not go nearly far enough. What else is there to call upon to help out? Why, the one thing which has been persistently neglected by practically all the sex writers,—the emotional side of sex experience. Parents and teachers have been afraid of it and distrustful of it. In not a single one of all the books for young people that I have thus far read has there been the frank unashamed declaration that the climax of sex emotion is an unsurpassed joy, something which rightly belongs to every normal human being, a joy to be proudly and serenely experienced. Instead there has been all too evident an inference that sex emotion is a thing to be ashamed of, that yielding to it is indulgence which must be curbed as much as possible, that all thought and understanding of it must be rigorously postponed, at any rate till after marriage.

"We give to young folks, in their general education, as much as they can grasp of science and ethics and art, and yet in their sex education, which rightly has to do with all of these, we have said, 'Give them only the bare physiological facts, lest they be prematurely stimulated.' Others of us, realizing that the bare physiological facts are shocking to many a sensitive child, and must somehow be softened with something pleasant, have said, 'Give them the facts, yes, but see to it that they are so related to the wonders of evolution and the beauties of the natural world that the shock is minimized.' But none of us has yet dared to say, 'Yes, give them the facts, give them the nature study, too, but also give them some conception of sex life as a vivifying joy, as a vital art, as a thing to be studied and developed with reverence for its big meaning, with understanding of its far-reaching reactions, psychologically and spiritually, with temperant restraint, good taste and the highest idealism.' We have contented ourselves by assuming that marriage makes sex relations respectable. We have not yet said that it is only beautiful sex relations that can make marriage lovely.

"Young people are just as capable of being guided and inspired in their thought about sex emotion as in their taste and ideals in literature and ethics, and just as they imperatively need to have their general taste and ideals cultivated as a preparation for mature life, so do they need to have some understanding of the marvelous place which sex emotion has in life.

"Only such an understanding can be counted on to give them the self control that is born of knowledge, not fear, the reverence that will prevent premature or trivial connections, the good taste and finesse that will make their sex life when they reach maturity a vitalizing success."

After the foregoing introduction comes the part devoted to sex instruction entitled, "An Explanation for Young People." It proceeds to explain sex life in detail both physiologically and emotionally. It describes the sex organs and their operation and the way children are begotten and born. It negatives the idea that the sex impulse is in itself a base passion, and treats it as normal and its satisfaction as a great and justifiable joy when accompanied by love between two human beings. It warns against perversion, venereal disease, and prostitution, and argues for continence and healthy mindedness and against promiscuous sex relations.

The pamphlet in discussing the emotional side of the human sex relation, says:

"It means that a man and a woman feel that they *belong* to each other in a way that they belong to no one else; it makes them wonderfully happy to be together; they find they want to live together, work together, play together, and to have children together, that is, to marry each other; and their dream is to be happy together all their lives. . . . The idea of sex relations between people who do not love each other, who do not feel any sense of belonging to each other, will always be revolting to highly developed sensitive people.

"People's lives grow finer and their characters better, if they have sex relations only with those they love. And those who make the wretched mistake of yielding to the sex impulse alone when there is no love to go with it, usually live to despise themselves for their weakness and their bad taste. They are always ashamed of doing it, and they try to keep it secret from their families and those they respect. You can be sure that whatever people are ashamed to do is something that can never bring them real happiness. It is true that one's sex relations are the most personal and private matters in the world, and they belong just to us and to no one else, but while we may be shy and reserved about them, *we are not ashamed*.

"When two people really love each other, they don't care who knows it. They are proud of their happiness. But no man is ever proud of his connection with a prostitute and no prostitute is ever proud of her business.

"Sex relations belong to love, and love is never

a *business*. Love is the nicest thing in the world, but it can't be bought. And the sex side of it is the biggest and most important side of it, so it is the one side of us that we must be absolutely sure to keep in good order and perfect health, if we are going to be happy ourselves or make any one else happy."

The government proved that the pamphlet was mailed to Mrs. C. A. Miles, Grottoes, Va.

Upon the foregoing record, of which we have given a summary, the trial judge charged the jury that the motive of the defendant in mailing the pamphlet was immaterial, that it was for them to determine whether it was obscene, lewd, or lascivious within the meaning of the statute, and that the test was "whether its language has a tendency to deprave and corrupt the morals of those whose minds are open to such things and into whose hands it may fall; arousing and implanting in such minds lewd and obscene thought or desires."

The court also charged that, "even if the matter sought to be shown in the pamphlet complained of were true, that fact would be immaterial, if the statements of such facts were calculated to deprave the morals of the readers by inciting sexual desires and libidinous thoughts."

The jury returned a verdict of guilty upon which the defendant was sentenced to pay a fine of $300, and from the judgment of conviction she has taken this appeal.

Greenbaum, Wolff & Ernst, of New York City (Morris L. Ernst, Newman Levy, and Alexander Lindey, all of New York City, of counsel), for appellant.

Howard W. Ameli, U. S. Atty., of Brooklyn, N. Y. (Herbert H. Kellogg, James E. Wilkinson, and Emanuel Bublick, Asst. U. S. Attys., all of Brooklyn, N. Y., of counsel), for the United States.

Before SWAN, AUGUSTUS N. HAND, and CHASE, Circuit Judges.

AUGUSTUS N. HAND, Circuit Judge (after stating the facts as above).

[1, 2] It is doubtless true that the personal motive of the defendant in distributing her pamphlet could have no bearing on the question whether she violated the law. Her own belief that a really obscene pamphlet would pay the price for its obscenity by means of intrinsic merits would leave her as much as ever under the ban of the statute. Regina v. Hicklin, L. R. 3 Q. B. 360; United States v. Bennett, Fed. Case No. 14,571; Rosen v. United States, 161 U. S. at page 41, 16 S. Ct. 434, 480, 40 L. Ed. 606.

[3] It was perhaps proper to exclude the evidence offered by the defendant as to the persons to whom the pamphlet was sold, for the reason that such evidence, if relevant at all, was part of the government's proof. In other words, a publication might be distributed among doctors or nurses or adults in cases where the distribution among small children could not be justified. The fact that the latter might obtain it accidently or surreptitiously, as they might see some medical books which would not be desirable for them to read, would hardly be sufficient to bar a publication otherwise proper. Here the pamphlet appears to have been mailed to a married woman. The tract may fairly be said to be calculated to aid parents in the instruction of their children in sex matters. As the record stands, it is a reasonable inference that the pamphlet was to be given to children at the discretion of adults and to be distributed through agencies that had the real welfare of the adolescent in view. There is no reason to suppose that it was to be broadcast among children who would have no capacity to understand its general significance. Even the court in Regina v. Hicklin, L. R. 3 Q. B. at p. 367, which laid down a more strict rule than the New York Court of Appeals was inclined to adopt in People v. Eastman, 188 N. Y. 478, 81 N. E. 459, 11 Ann. Cas. 302, said that "the circumstances of the publication" may determine whether the statute has been violated.

[4] But the important consideration in this case is not the correctness of the rulings of the trial judge as to the admissibility of evidence, but the meaning and scope of those words of the statute which prohibit the mailing of an *"obscene, lewd or lascivious . . . pamphlet."* It was for the trial court to determine whether the pamphlet could reasonably be thought to be of such a character before submitting any question of the violation of the statute to the jury. Knowles v. United States (C. C. A.) 170 F. 409; Magon v. United States (C. C. A.) 248 F. 201. And the test most frequently laid down seems to have been whether it would tend to deprave the morals of those into whose hands the publication might fall by suggesting lewd thoughts and exciting sensual desires. Dunlop v. United States,

165 U. S. at page 501, 17 S. Ct. 375, 41 L. Ed. 799; Rosen v. United States, 161 U. S. 29, 16 S. Ct. 434, 480, 40 L. Ed. 606.

It may be assumed that any article dealing with the sex side of life and explaining the functions of the sex organs is capable in some circumstances of arousing lust. The sex impulses are present in every one, and without doubt cause much of the weal and woe of human kind. But it can hardly be said that, because of the risk of arousing sex impulses, there should be no instruction of the young in sex matters, and that the risk of imparting instruction outweighs the disadvantages of leaving them to grope about in mystery and morbid curiosity and of requiring them to secure such information, as they may be able to obtain, from ill-informed and often foul-minded companions, rather than from intelligent and high-minded sources. It may be argued that suggestion plays a large part in such matters, and that on the whole the less sex questions are dwelt upon the better. But it by no means follows that such a desideratum is attained by leaving adolescents in a state of inevitable curiosity, satisfied only by the casual gossip of ignorant playmates.

The old theory that information about sex matters should be left to chance has greatly changed, and, while there is still a difference of opinion as to just the kind of instruction which ought to be given, it is commonly thought in these days that much was lacking in the old mystery and reticence. This is evident from the current literature on the subject, particularly such pamphlets as "Sex Education," issued by the Treasury Department United States Public Health Service in 1927.

[5, 6] The statute we have to construe was never thought to bar from the mails everything which *might* stimulate sex impulses. If so, much chaste poetry and fiction, as well as many useful medical works would be under the ban. Like everything else, this law must be construed reasonably with a view to the general objects aimed at. While there can be no doubt about its constitutionality, it must not be assumed to have been designed to interfere with serious instruction regarding sex matters unless the terms in which the information is conveyed are clearly indecent.

We have been referred to no decision where a truthful exposition of the sex side of life, evidently calculated for instruction and for the explanation of relevant facts, has been held to be obscene. In Dysart v. United States, 272 U. S. 655, 47 S. Ct. 234, 71 L. Ed. 461, it was decided that the advertisement of a lying-in retreat to enable unmarried women to conceal their missteps, even though written in a coarse and vulgar style, did not fall within prohibition of the statute, and was not "obscene" within the meaning of the law.

[7] The defendant's discussion of the phenomena of sex is written with sincerity of feeling and with an idealization of the marriage relation and sex emotions. We think it tends to rationalize and dignify such emotions rather than to arouse lust. While it may be thought by some that portions of the tract go into unnecessary details that would better have been omitted, it may be fairly answered that the curiosity of many adolescents would not be satisfied without full explanation, and that no more than that is really given. It also may reasonably be thought that accurate information, rather than mystery and curiosity, is better in the long run and is less likely to occasion lascivious thoughts than ignorance and anxiety. Perhaps instruction other than that which the defendant suggests would be better. That is a matter as to which there is bound to be a wide difference of opinion, but, irrespective of this, we hold that an accurate exposition of the relevant facts of the sex side of life in decent language and in manifestly serious and disinterested spirit cannot ordinarily be regarded as obscene. Any incidental tendency to arouse sex impulses which such a pamphlet may perhaps have, is apart from and subordinate to its main effect. The tendency can only exist in so far as it is inherent in any sex instruction, and it would seem to be outweighed by the elimination of ignorance, curiosity, and morbid fear. The direct aim and the net result is to promote understanding and self-control.

No case was made for submission to the jury, and the judgment must therefore be reversed.

⊂ℬ Foreshadowing his famous decision in the *Ulysses* case about three years later was Judge John M. Woolsey's ruling on the importation of Dr. Marie C. Stopes's book entitled *Married Love*. This was the first major case arising from federal censorship of books under the Smoot-Hawley Tariff Act of 1930. The Stopes book, which had sold 800,000 copies abroad prior to the trial, was being imported by G. P. Putnam's Sons for publication purposes. Actually the copy on trial was an expurgated one, all birth-control information having been eliminated before shipment from England.

It is of interest to note that, in dismissing the libel, Judge Woolsey cites the Dennett case as a precedent, commenting, "The present book may fairly be said to do for adults what Mrs. Dennett's book does for adolescents."

John M. Woolsey
**UNITED STATES
v. "MARRIED LOVE"**

I dismiss the libel in this case.

[1] I. The first point with which I shall deal is as to the contention that the section of the Tariff Act under which this libel was brought, title 19, U. S. C., § 1305 (19 USCA § 1305), is unconstitutional as impinging on the right of the freedom of the press. I think there is nothing in this contention. The section does not involve the suppression of a book before it is published, but the exclusion of an already published book which is sought to be brought into the United States.

After a book is published, its lot in the world is like that of anything else. It must conform to the law and, if it does not, must be subject to the penalties involved in its failure to do so. Laws which are thus disciplinary of publications, whether involving exclusion from the mails or from this country, do not interfere with freedom of the press.

[2] II. Passing to the second point, I think that the matter here involved is res adjudicata by reason of the decision hereinafter mentioned.

This is a proceeding in rem against a book entitled "Married Love," written by Dr. Marie C. Stopes and sent from England by the London branch of G. P. Putnam's Sons to their New York office.

The libel was filed under the provisions of title 19, U. S. C., § 1305 (19 USCA § 1305),

---

John M. Woolsey, "United States v. 'Married Love,'" 48 *Federal Reporter*, 2d Series, 822–24, copyright 1931 by West Publishing Co. Reprinted (without footnotes) by permission of the publisher.

which provides, so far as is here relevant, as follows:

"§ 1305. *Immoral Articles—Importation Prohibited.* (a) *Prohibition of importation.* All persons are prohibited from importing into the United States from any foreign country . . . any obscene book, pamphlet, paper, writing, advertisement, circular, print, pictures, drawing, or other representation, figure, or image on or of paper or other material, or any cast, instrument, or other article which is obscene or immoral, or any drug or medicine or any article whatever for the prevention of conception or for causing unlawful abortion. . . . No such articles, whether imported separately or contained in packages with other goods entitled to entry, shall be admitted to entry; and all such articles . . . shall be subject to seizure and forfeiture as hereinafter provided: . . . *Provided further,* that the Secretary of the Treasury may, in his discretion, admit the so-called classics or books of recognized and established literary or scientific merit, but may, in his discretion, admit such classics or books only when imported for noncommercial purposes."

Then it goes on:

"Upon the appearance of any such book or matter at any customs office, the same shall be seized and held by the collector to await the judgment of the district court as hereinafter provided. . . . Upon the seizure of such book or matter the collector shall transmit information thereof to the district attorney of the district in which is situated the office at which such seizure has taken place, who shall institute proceedings in the district court for the forfeiture, confiscation, and destruction of the book or matter seized. Upon the adjudication that such book or matter thus seized is of the character the entry of which is by this section prohibited, it shall be ordered destroyed and shall be destroyed. Upon adjudication that such book or matter thus seized is not of the character the entry of which is by this section prohibited, it shall not be excluded from entry under the provisions of this section.

"In any such proceeding any party in interest may upon demand have the facts at issue determined by a jury and any party may have an appeal or the right of review as in the case of ordinary actions or suits."

The book before me now has had stricken

from it all matters dealing with contraceptive instruction and, hence, does not come now within the prohibition of the statute against imports for such purposes, even if a book dealing with such matters falls within the provisions of this section—which I think it probably does not—and the case falls to be dealt with entirely on the question of whether the book is obscene or immoral.

Another copy of this same book, without the excision of the passages dealing with contraceptive matters, was before Judge Kirkpatrick, United States District Judge for the Eastern District of Pennsylvania, on a forfeiture libel under the Tariff Act of 1922, and he ruled that the book was not obscene or immoral, and directed a verdict for the claimant.

Although the government took an exception to this ruling at the time of the trial, it did not mature this exception by an appeal, and the case therefore stands as a final decision of a coordinate court in a proceeding in rem involving the same book that we have here. The answer in this case is amended and pleads res adjudicata on the ground of the proceedings had before Judge Kirkpatrick which involved exactly the same question as that now before me.

The only difference between the Philadelphia case and this case is that another copy of the same book has been here seized and libeled.

[3] I think that the proper view of the meaning of the word "book" in title 19, U. S. C., § 1305 (19 USCA § 1305), is not merely a few sheets of paper bound together in cloth or otherwise, but that a book means an assembly or concourse of ideas expressed in words, the subject-matter which is embodied in the book, which is sought to be excluded, and not merely the physical object called a book which can be held in one's hands.

Assuming it is proper so to view the meaning of the word "book" in the statute under consideration, Judge Kirkpatrick's decision at Philadelphia in a proceeding in rem against this book is a bar to another similar proceeding such as this in this district.

I hold that Judge Kirkpatrick's decision established the book "Married Love" as having an admissible status at any point around the customs' barriers of the United States. In this connection, see Gelston v. Hoyt, 3 Wheat. 246, 312 to page 316, 4 L. Ed. 381; Waples on Proceedings in Rem, §§ 87, 110, 111, 112, and cases therein cited.

It is perfectly obvious, I think, that, if a vessel had been libeled on a certain count for forfeiture at Philadelphia, and there acquitted of liability to forfeiture, on her coming around to New York she could not properly be libeled again on the same count. That is the real situation in the present case. Cf. United States v. 2180 Cases of Champagne, 9 F.(2d) 710, 712, 713 (C. C. A. 2).

[4, 5] III. However, in case the Circuit Court of Appeals, to which I presume this case will eventually be taken, should disagree with my construction of the word "book," and should consider that it was a copy of the book that was subject to exclusion, and not merely the book regarded as an embodiment of ideas, or should disagree with my application of the admiralty law to a situation of this kind, I will now deal with the case on the merits.

In Murray's Oxford English Dictionary the word "obscene" is defined as follows:

"Obscene—1. Offensive to the senses, or to taste or refinement; disgusting, repulsive, filthy, foul, abominable, loathsome. Now somewhat arch.

"2. Offensive to modesty or decency; expressing or suggesting unchaste or lustful ideas; impure, indecent, lewd."

In the same Dictionary the word "immoral" is defined as follows:

"Immoral—The opposite of moral; not moral.

"1. Not consistent with, or not conforming to, moral law or requirement; opposed to or violating morality; morally evil or impure; unprincipled, vicious, dissolute. (Of persons, things, actions, etc.)

"2. Not having a moral nature or character; non-moral."

The book "Married Love" does not, in my opinion, fall within these definitions of the words "obscene" or "immoral" in any respect.

Dr. Stopes treats quite as decently and with as much restraint of the sex relations as did Mrs. Mary Ware Dennett in "The Sex Side of Life, An Explanation for Young People," which was held not to be obscene by the Circuit Court of Appeals for this circuit in United States v. Dennett, 39 F.(2d) 564.

The present book may fairly be said to do for

adults what Mrs. Dennett's book does for adolescents.

The Dennett Case, as I read it, teaches that this court must determine, as a matter of law in the first instance, whether the book alleged to be obscene falls in any sense within the definition of that word. If it does, liability to forfeiture becomes a question for the jury under proper instructions. If it does not, the question is one entirely for the court.

"Married Love" is a considered attempt to explain to married people how their mutual sex life may be made happier.

To one who had read Havelock Ellis, as I have, the subject-matter of Dr. Stope's book is not wholly new, but it emphasizes the woman's side of sex questions. It makes also some apparently justified criticisms of the inopportune exercise by the man in the marriage relation of what are often referred to as his conjugal or marital rights, and it pleads with seriousness, and not without some eloquence, for a better understanding by husbands of the physical and emotional side of the sex life of their wives.

I do not find anything exceptionable anywhere in the book, and I cannot imagine a normal mind to which this book would seem to be obscene or immoral within the proper definition of these words or whose sex impulses would be stirred by reading it.

Whether or not the book is scientific in some of its theses is unimportant. It is informative and instructive, and I think that any married folk who read it cannot fail to be benefited by its counsels of perfection and its frank discussion of the frequent difficulties which necessarily arise in the more intimate aspects of married life, for as Professor William G. Sumner used aptly to say in his lectures on the Science of Society at Yale, marriage, in its essence, is a status of antagonistic co-operation.

In such a status, necessarily, centripetal and centrifugal forces are continuously at work, and the measure of its success obviously depends on the extent to which the centripetal forces are predominant.

The book before me here has as its whole thesis the strengthening of the centripetal forces in marriage, and instead of being inhospitably received, it should, I think, be welcomed within our borders.

As in the *Married Love* case, the issue of customs control was involved in *United States v. One Book Called "Ulysses."* Judge John M. Woolsey was again the key figure.

Censorship by customs officials had long been a sore point with its opponents. Such classics as Rousseau's *Confessions,* Casanova's *Memoirs,* the *Golden Ass* of Apuleius, Rabelais, Boccaccio's *Decameron, The Arabian Nights,* Voltaire's *Candide,* and numerous more modern books had been stopped at the border and denied entry into the United States. Confiscation and destruction had usually been the fate of books thus banned. The Smoot-Hawley Tariff bill, enacted by Congress in 1930, gave some relief from arbitrary customs rulings by authorizing the Secretary of the Treasury to admit classics and books of recognized scientific or literary merit when imported for noncommercial purposes. Further protection was provided by a requirement that the customs collector was to notify the federal district attorney when a book was seized, and action would then begin for forfeiture of the book. A jury trial could be demanded by any interested party.

This was the prevailing legal situation when customs officials prevented entry of James Joyce's *Ulysses* into the United States, on the basis of obscenity. Judge Woolsey, presiding in the Federal District Court, ruled that the book was not obscene within the meaning of the governing federal statute. His highly literate and civilized decision was taken to the U.S. Circuit Court of Appeals, resulting in another outstanding opinion from the pen of Judge Augustus N. Hand, affirming the lower court's decree. These two decisions, combined, went far to emancipate books from customs censorship.

*John M. Woolsey
and Augustus N. Hand*
**UNITED STATES
v. "ULYSSES"**

JOHN M. WOOLSEY, District Judge.

The motion for a decree dismissing the libel herein is granted, and, consequently, of course,

---

John M. Woolsey and Augustus N. Hand, "United States v. 'Ulysses,' " 5 *Federal Supplement* 182–85, copyright 1933 by West Publishing Co., and 72 *Federal Reporter,* 2d Series, 706–9, copyright 1934 by West Publishing Co. Reprinted by permission of the publisher.

84 *The courts look at books*

the government's motion for a decree of forfeiture and destruction is denied.

Accordingly a decree dismissing the libel without costs may be entered herein.

I. The practice followed in this case is in accordance with the suggestion made by me in the case of United States v. One Book, Entitled "Contraception" (D. C.) 51 F.(2d) 525, and is as follows:

After issue was joined by the filing of the claimant's answer to the libel for forfeiture against "Ulysses," a stipulation was made between the United States Attorney's office and the attorneys for the claimant providing:

1. That the book "Ulysses" should be deemed to have been annexed to and to have become part of the libel just as if it had been incorporated in its entirety therein.

2. That the parties waived their right to a trial by jury.

3. That each party agreed to move for decree in its favor.

4. That on such cross-motions the court might decide all the questions of law and fact involved and render a general finding thereon.

5. That on the decision of such motions the decree of the court might be entered as if it were a decree after trial.

It seems to me that a procedure of this kind is highly appropriate in libels such as this for the confiscation of books. It is an especially advantageous procedure in the instant case because, on account of the length of "Ulysses" and the difficulty of reading it, a jury trial would have been an extremely unsatisfactory, if not an almost impossible method of dealing with it.

II. I have read "Ulysses" once in its entirety and I have read those passages of which the government particularly complains several times. In fact, for many weeks, my spare time has been devoted to the consideration of the decision which my duty would require me to make in this matter.

"Ulysses" is not an easy book to read or to understand. But there has been much written about it, and in order properly to approach the consideration of it it is advisable to read a number of other books which have now become its satellites. The study of "Ulysses" is, therefore, a heavy task.

[1] III. The reputation of "Ulysses" in the literary world, however, warranted my taking such time as was necessary to enable me to satisfy myself as to the intent with which the book was written, for, of course, in any case where a book is claimed to be obscene it must first be determined, whether the intent with which it was written was what is called, according to the usual phrase, pornographic, that is, written for the purpose of exploiting obscenity.

If the conclusion is that the book is pornographic, that is the end of the inquiry and forfeiture must follow.

But in "Ulysses," in spite of its unusual frankness, I do not detect anywhere the leer of the sensualist. I hold, therefore, that it is not pornographic.

IV. In writing "Ulysses," Joyce sought to make a serious experiment in a new, if not wholly novel, literary genre. He takes persons of the lower middle class living in Dublin in 1904 and seeks, not only to describe what they did on a certain day early in June of that year as they went about the city bent on their usual occupations, but also to tell what many of them thought about the while.

Joyce has attempted—it seems to me, with astonishing success—to show how the screen of consciousness with its ever-shifting kaleidoscopic impressions carries, as it were on a plastic palimpsest, not only what is in the focus of each man's observation of the actual things about him, but also in a penumbral zone residua of past impressions, some recent and some drawn up by association from the domain of the subconscious. He shows how each of these impressions affects the life and behavior of the character which he is describing.

What he seeks to get is not unlike the result of a double or, if that is possible, a multiple exposure on a cinema film, which would give a clear foreground with a background visible but somewhat blurred and out of focus in varying degrees.

To convey by words an effect which obviously lends itself more appropriately to a graphic technique, accounts, it seems to me, for much of the obscurity which meets a reader of "Ulysses." And it also explains another aspect of the book, which I have further to consider, namely, Joyce's sincerity and his honest effort to show exactly how the minds of his characters operate.

If Joyce did not attempt to be honest in developing the technique which he has adopted in

"Ulysses," the result would be psychologically misleading and thus unfaithful to his chosen technique. Such an attitude would be artistically inexcusable.

It is because Joyce has been loyal to his technique and has not funked its necessary implications, but has honestly attempted to tell fully what his characters think about, that he has been the subject of so many attacks and that his purpose has been so often misunderstood and misrepresented. For his attempt sincerely and honestly to realize his objective has required him incidentally to use certain words which are generally considered dirty words and has led at times to what many think is a too poignant preoccupation with sex in the thoughts of his characters.

The words which are criticized as dirty are old Saxon words known to almost all men and, I venture, to many women, and are such words as would be naturally and habitually used, I believe, by the types of folk whose life, physical and mental, Joyce is seeking to describe. In respect of the recurrent emergence of the theme of sex in the minds of his characters, it must always be remembered that his locale was Celtic and his season spring.

Whether or not one enjoys such a technique as Joyce uses is a matter of taste on which disagreement or argument is futile, but to subject that technique to the standards of some other technique seems to me to be little short of absurd.

Accordingly, I hold that "Ulysses" is a sincere and honest book, and I think that the criticisms of it are entirely disposed of by its rationale.

V. Furthermore, "Ulysses" is an amazing tour de force when one considers the success which has been in the main achieved with such a difficult objective as Joyce set for himself. As I have stated, "Ulysses" is not an easy book to read. It is brilliant and dull, intelligible and obscure, by turns. In many places it seems to me to be disgusting, but although it contains, as I have mentioned above, many words usually considered dirty, I have not found anything that I consider to be dirt for dirt's sake. Each word of the book contributes like a bit of mosaic to the detail of the picture which Joyce is seeking to construct for his readers.

If one does not wish to associate with such folk as Joyce describes, that is one's own choice. In order to avoid indirect contact with them one may not wish to read "Ulysses"; that is quite understandable. But when such a great artist in words, as Joyce undoubtedly is, seeks to draw a true picture of the lower middle class in a European city, ought it to be impossible for the American public legally to see that picture?

To answer this question it is not sufficient merely to find, as I have found above, that Joyce did not write "Ulysses" with what is commonly called pornographic intent, I must endeavor to apply a more objective standard to his book in order to determine its effect in the result, irrespective of the intent with which it was written.

VI. The statute under which the libel is filed only denounces, in so far as we are here concerned, the importation into the United States from any foreign country of "any obscene book." Section 305 of the Tariff Act of 1930, title 19 United States Code, § 1305 (19 USCA § 1305). It does not marshal against books the spectrum of condemnatory adjectives found, commonly, in laws dealing with matters of this kind. I am, therefore, only required to determine whether "Ulysses" is obscene within the legal definition of that word.

[2] The meaning of the word "obscene" as legally defined by the courts is: Tending to stir the sex impulses or to lead to sexually impure and lustful thoughts. . . .

[3] Whether a particular book would tend to excite such impulses and thoughts must be tested by the court's opinion as to its effect on a person with average sex instincts—what the French would call *l'homme moyen sensuel*—who plays, in this branch of legal inquiry, the same role of hypothetical reagent as does the "reasonable man" in the law of torts and "the man learned in the art" on questions of invention in patent law.

The risk involved in the use of such a reagent arises from the inherent tendency of the trier of facts, however fair he may intend to be, to make his reagent too much subservient to his own idiosyncrasies. Here, I have attempted to avoid this, if possible, and to make my reagent herein more objective than he might otherwise be, by adopting the following course:

After I had made my decision in regard to the aspect of "Ulysses," now under consideration, I checked my impressions with two friends of mine who in my opinion answered to the above-stated requirement for my reagent.

These literary assessors—as I might properly

describe them—were called on separately, and neither knew that I was consulting the other. They are men whose opinion on literature and on life I value most highly. They had both read "Ulysses," and, of course, were wholly unconnected with this cause.

Without letting either of my assessors know what my decision was, I gave to each of them the legal definition of obscene and asked each whether in his opinion "Ulysses" was obscene within that definition.

I was interested to find that they both agreed with my opinion: That reading "Ulysses" in its entirety, as a book must be read on such a test as this, did not tend to excite sexual impulses or lustful thoughts, but that its net effect on them was only that of a somewhat tragic and very powerful commentary on the inner lives of men and women.

[4] It is only with the normal person that the law is concerned. Such a test as I have described, therefore, is the only proper test of obscenity in the case of a book like "Ulysses" which is a sincere and serious attempt to devise a new literary method for the observation and description of mankind.

I am quite aware that owing to some of its scenes "Ulysses" is a rather strong draught to ask some sensitive, though normal, persons to take. But my considered opinion, after long reflection, is that, whilst in many places the effect of "Ulysses" on the reader undoubtedly is somewhat emetic, nowhere does it tend to be an aphrodisiac.

"Ulysses" may, therefore, be admitted into the United States.

AUGUSTUS N. HAND, Circuit Judge.

This appeal raises sharply the question of the proper interpretation of section 305 (a) of the Tariff Act of 1930 (19 USCA § 1305 (a)). That section provides that "all persons are prohibited from importing into the United States from any foreign country . . . any obscene book, pamphlet, paper, writing, advertisement, circular, print, picture, drawing, or other representation, figure, or image on or of paper or other material, . . ." and directs that, upon the appearance of any such book or matter at any customs office, the collector shall seize it and inform the district attorney, who shall institute proceedings for forfeiture. In accordance with the statute, the collector seized "Ulysses," a book written by James Joyce, and the United States filed a libel for forfeiture. The claimant, Random House, Inc., the publisher of the American edition, intervened in the cause and filed its answer denying that the book was obscene and was subject to confiscation and praying that it be admitted into the United States. The case came on for trial before Woolsey, J., who found that the book, taken as a whole, "did not tend to excite sexual impulses or lustful thoughts, but that its net effect . . . was only that of a somewhat tragic and very powerful commentary on the inner lives of men and women." He accordingly granted a decree adjudging that the book was "not of the character the entry of which is prohibited under the provision of section 305 of the Tariff Act of 1930 . . . and . . . dismissing the libel," from which this appeal has been taken.

James Joyce, the author of "Ulysses," may be regarded as a pioneer among those writers who have adopted the "stream of consciousness" method of presenting fiction, which has attracted considerable attention in academic and literary circles. In this field "Ulysses" is rated as a book of considerable power by persons whose opinions are entitled to weight. Indeed it has become a sort of contemporary classic, dealing with a new subject-matter. It attempts to depict the thoughts and lay bare the souls of a number of people, some of them intellectuals and some social outcasts and nothing more, with a literalism that leaves nothing unsaid. Certain of its passages are of beauty and undoubted distinction, while others are of a vulgarity that is extreme and the book as a whole has a realism characterisitc of the present age. It is supposed to portray the thoughts of the principal characters during a period of about eighteen hours.

We may discount the laudation of "Ulysses" by some of its admirers and reject the view that it will permanently stand among the great works of literature, but it is fair to say that it is a sincere portrayal with skillful artistry of the "streams of consciousness" of its characters. Though the depiction happily is not of the "stream of consciousness" of all men and perhaps of only those of a morbid type, it seems to be sincere, truthful, relevant to the subject, and executed with real art. Joyce, in the words of "Paradise Lost," has dealt with "things unattempted yet in prose or rime"—with things that very likely might better have remained "unattempted"—but his book shows originality and is a work of symmetry and excellent craftsmanship of a sort. The question before us is whether such a book of artistic merit and scientific insight should be regarded as "obscene" within section 305 (a) of the Tariff Act.

That numerous long passages in "Ulysses" contain matter that is obscene under any fair definition of the word cannot be gainsaid; yet they are relevant to the purpose of depicting the thoughts of the characters and are introduced to give meaning to the whole, rather than to promote lust or portray filth for its own sake. The net effect even of portions most open to attack, such as the closing monologue of the wife of Leopold Bloom, is pitiful and tragic, rather than lustful. The book depicts the souls of men and women that are by turns bewildered and keenly apprehensive, sordid and aspiring, ugly and beautiful, hateful and loving. In the end one feels, more than anything else, pity and sorrow for the confusion, misery, and degradation of humanity. Page after page of the book is, or seems to be, incomprehensible. But many passages show the trained hand of an artist, who can at one moment adapt to perfection the style of an ancient chronicler, and at another become a veritable personification of Thomas Carlyle. In numerous places there are found originality, beauty, and distinction. The book as a whole is not pornographic, and, while in not a few spots it is coarse, blasphemous, and obscene, it does not, in our opinion, tend to promote lust. The erotic passages are submerged in the book as a whole and have little resultant effect. If these are to make the book subject to confiscation, by the same test "Venus and Adonis," "Hamlet," "Romeo and Juliet," and the story told in the Eighth Book of the Odyssey by the bard Demodocus of how Ares and Aphrodite were entrapped in a net spread by the outraged Hephaestus amid the laughter of the immortal gods, as well as many other classics, would have to be suppressed. Indeed, it may be questioned whether the obscene passages in "Romeo and Juliet" were as necessary to the development of the play as those in the monologue of Mrs. Bloom are to the depiction of the latter's tortured soul.

It is unnecessary to add illustrations to show that, in the administration of statutes aimed at the suppression of immoral books, standard works of literature have not been barred merely because they contained *some* obscene passages, and that confiscation for such a reason would destroy much that is precious in order to benefit a few.

[1-4] It is settled, at least so far as this court is concerned, that works of physiology, medicine, science, and sex instruction are not within the statute, though to some extent and among some persons they may tend to promote lustful thoughts. United States v. Dennett, 39 F.(2d) 564, 76 A. L. R. 1092. We think the same immunity should apply to literature as to science, where the presentation, when viewed objectively, is sincere, and the erotic matter is not introduced to promote lust and does not furnish the dominant note of the publication. The question in each case is whether a publication taken as a whole has a libidinous effect. The book before us has such portentous length, is written with such evident truthfulness in its depiction of certain types of humanity, and is so little erotic in its result, that it does not fall within the forbidden class.

In Halsey v. New York Society for Suppression of Vice, 234 N. Y. 1, 136 N. E. 219, 220, the New York Court of Appeals dealt with "Mademoiselle de Maupin," by Theophile Gautier, for the sale of which the plaintiff had been prosecuted under a New York statute forbidding the sale of obscene books, upon the complaint of the defendant. After acquittal, the plaintiff sued for malicious prosecution, and a jury rendered a verdict in his favor. The Court of Appeals refused to disturb the judgment because the book had become a recognized French classic and its merits on the whole outweighed its objectionable qualities, though, as Judge Andrews said, it contained many paragraphs which, "taken by themselves," were "undoubtedly vulgar and indecent." In referring to the obscene passages, he remarked that: "No work may be judged from a selection of such paragraphs alone. Printed by themselves they might, as a matter of law, come within the prohibition of the statute. So might a similar selection from Aristophanes or Chaucer or Boccaccio, or even from the Bible. The book, however, must be considered broadly, as a whole." We think Judge Andrews was clearly right, and that the effect of the book as a whole is the test.

In the New York Supreme Court, Judge Morgan J. O'Brien declined to prohibit a receiver from selling "Arabian Nights," Rabelais, Ovid's "Art of Love," the "Decameron" of Boccaccio, the "Heptameron" of Queen Margaret of Navarre, or the "Confessions" of Rousseau. He remarked that a rule which would exclude them would bar "a very large proportion of the works of fiction of the most famous writers of the English language." In re Worthington Co. (Sup.) 30 N. Y. S. 361, 362, 24 L. R. A. 110. The main difference between many standard works and "Ulysses" is its far more abundant use of coarse and colloquial words and presentation of dirty scenes, rather than in any excess of prurient suggestion. We do not think that "Ulysses," taken as a whole, tends to promote lust, and its criticized passages do this no more than scores of standard books that are constantly bought and sold. Indeed a book of physiology in the hands of adolescents may be more objectionable on this ground than almost anything else.

But it is argued that United States v. Bennett, Fed. Cas. No. 14,571, stands in the way of what has been said, and it certainly does. There a court, consisting of Blatchford, C. J., and Benedict and Choate, D.JJ., held that the offending paragraphs in a book could be taken from their context and the book judged by them alone, and that the test of obscenity was whether the tendency of these passages in themselves was "to deprave the minds of those open to such influences and into whose hands a publication of this character might come." The opinion was founded upon a dictum of Cockburn, C. J., in Regina v. Hicklin, L. R. 3 Q. B. 360, where half of a book written to attack alleged practices of the confession was obscene and contained, as Mellor, J., said, "a great deal . . . which there cannot be any necessity for in any legitimate argument on the confessional. . . ." It is said that in Rosen v. United States, 161 U. S. 29, 16 S. Ct. 434, 480, 40 L. Ed. 606, the Supreme Court cited and sanctioned Regina v. Hicklin, and United States v. Bennett. The subject-matter of Rosen v. United States was, however, a pictorial representation of "females, in different attitudes of indecency." The figures were partially covered "with lamp black, that could be easily erased with a piece of bread." Page 31 of 161 U. S., 16 S. Ct. 434. The pictures were evidently obscene, and plainly came within the statute prohibiting their transportation. The citation of Regina v. Hicklin and United States v. Bennett, was a support of a ruling that allegations in the indictment as to an obscene publication need only be made with sufficient particularity to inform the accused of the nature of the charge against him. No approval of other features of the two decisions was expressed, nor were such features referred to. Dunlop v. United States, 165 U. S. 486, 489, 17 S. Ct. 375, 41 L. Ed. 799, also seems to be relied on by the government, but the publication there was admittedly obscene and the decision in no way sanctioned the rulings in United States v. Bennett which we first mentioned. The rigorous doctrines laid down in that case are inconsistent with our own decision in United States v. Dennett (C. C. A.) 39 F.(2d) 564, 76 A. L. R. 1092, as well as with Konda v. United States (C. C. A.) 166 F. 91, 92, 22 L. R. A. (N. S.) 304; Clark v. United States (C. C. A.) 211 F. 916, 922; Halsey v. N. Y. Society for Suppression of Vice, 234 N. Y. 1, 4, 136 N. E. 219; and St. Hubert Guild v. Quinn, 64 Misc. 336, 339, 118 N. Y. S. 582, and, in our opinion, do not represent the law. They would exclude much of the great works of literature and involve an impracticability that cannot be imputed to Congress and would in the case of many books containing obscene passages inevitably require the court that uttered them to restrict their applicability.

[5] It is true that the motive of an author to promote good morals is not the test of whether a book is obscene, and it may also be true that the applicability of the statute does not depend on the persons to whom a publication is likely to be distributed. The importation of obscene books is prohibited generally, and no provision is made permitting such importation because of the character of those to whom they are sold. While any construction of the statute that will fit all cases is difficult, we believe that the proper test of whether a given book is obscene is its dominant effect. In applying this test, relevancy of the objectionable parts to the theme, the established reputation of the work in the estimation of approved critics, if the book is modern, and the verdict of the past, if it is ancient, are persuasive pieces of evidence; for works of art are not likely to sustain a high position with no better warrant for their existence than their obscene content.

It may be that "Ulysses" will not last as a substantial contribution to literature, and it is certainly easy to believe that, in spite of the opinion of Joyce's laudators, the immortals will still reign, but the same thing may be said of current works of art and music and of many other serious efforts of the mind. Art certainly cannot advance under compulsion to traditional forms, and nothing in such a field is more stifling to progress than limitation of the right to experiment with a new technique. The foolish judgments of Lord Eldon about one hundred years ago, proscribing the works of Byron and Southey, and the finding by the jury under a charge by Lord Denman that the publication of Shelley's "Queen Mab" was an indictable offense are a warning to all who have to determine the limits of the field within which authors may exercise themselves. We think that "Ulysses" is a book of originality and sincerity of treatment and that it has not the effect of promoting lust. Accordingly it does not fall within the statute, even though it justly may offend many.

Decree affirmed.

In 1943 Postmaster General Frank C. Walker summoned *Esquire* magazine to show cause why its second-class mailing privileges should not be revoked on the ground that it contained allegedly obscene matter. Later the government added the charge that the magazine was not entitled to second-class mail rates because it did not contain "information of a public character or devoted to literature, the sciences, arts or some special industry," as required by law. Accordingly, the Postmaster General revoked *Esquire's* mailing privileges as of February 28, 1944.

Long litigation followed. The Postmaster General's ruling was upheld in the U.S. District Court for the District of Columbia, reversed by Justice Thurman Arnold in the U.S. Circuit Court of Appeals, and finally reached the U.S. Supreme Court.

On February 4, 1946, in a unanimous decision, the Supreme Court ruled that the Postmaster General had no right to bar *Esquire* from the mails, regardless of its value or lack of value to the public. In the opinion read by Justice William O. Douglas, the Court declared, "Congress has left the Postmaster General with no power to prescribe standards for the literature or the art which a mailable periodical disseminates." The Court added, "A requirement that literature or art conform to some norm prescribed by an official smacks of an ideology foreign to our system." Further, "To withdraw the second-class rate from this publication today because its contents seemed to one official not good for the public would sanction withdrawal of the second-class rate tomorrow from another periodical whose social or economic views seemed harmful to another official."

Thus was another attempt at censorship through post-office control turned back at the highest judicial level.

William O. Douglas
HANNEGAN, POSTMASTER GENERAL, v. ESQUIRE, INC.

Congress has made obscene material nonmailable (35 Stat. 1129, 18 U. S. C. § 334), and has applied criminal sanctions for the enforcement of that policy. It has divided mailable matter into four classes, periodical publications constituting the second-class . . . And it has specified four conditions upon which a publication shall be admitted to the second-class . . . The Fourth condition, which is the only one relevant here, provides:

> Except as otherwise provided by law, the conditions upon which a publication shall be admitted to the second class are as follows . . . Fourth. It must be originated and published for the dissemination of information of a public character, or devoted to literature, the sciences, arts, or some special industry, and having a legitimate list of subscribers. Nothing herein contained shall be so construed as to admit to the second-class rate regular publications designed primarily for advertising purposes, or for free circulation, or for circulation at nominal rates.

Respondent is the publisher of Esquire Magazine, a monthly periodical which was granted a second-class permit in 1933. In 1943, pursuant to . . . 39 U. S. C. § 232, a citation was issued to respondent by the then Postmaster General (for whom the present Postmaster General has now been substituted as petitioner) to show cause why that permit should not be suspended or revoked. A hearing was held before a board designated by the then Postmaster General. The

---
William O. Douglas, "Hannegan, Postmaster General, v. Esquire, Inc.," 327 U.S. 146-60. Reprinted without amplifying footnotes.

board recommended that the permit not be revoked. Petitioner's predecessor took a different view. He did not find that Esquire Magazine contained obscene material and therefore was nonmailable. He revoked its second-class permit because he found that it did not comply with the Fourth condition. The gist of his holding is contained in the following excerpt from his opinion:

> The plain language of this statute does not assume that a publication must in fact be "obscene" within the intendment of the postal obscenity statutes before it can be found not to be "originated and published for the dissemination of information of a public character, or devoted to literature, the sciences, arts, or some special industry."
>
> Writings and pictures may be indecent, vulgar, and risque and still not be obscene in a technical sense. Such writings and pictures may be in that obscure and treacherous borderland zone where the average person hesitates to find them technically obscene, but still may see ample proof that they are morally improper and not for the public welfare and the public good. When such writings or pictures occur in isolated instances their dangerous tendencies and malignant qualities may be considered of lesser importance.
>
> When, however, they become a dominant and systematic feature they most certainly cannot be said to be for the public good, and a publication which uses them in that manner is not making the "special contribution to the public welfare" which Congress intended by the Fourth condition.
>
> A publication to enjoy these unique mail privileges and special preferences is bound to do more than refrain from disseminating material which is obscene or bordering on the obscene. It is under a positive duty to contribute to the public good and the public welfare.

Respondent thereupon sued in the District Court for the District of Columbia to enjoin the revocation order. The parties stipulated at a pre-trial conference that the suit would not be defended on the ground that Esquire Magazine was obscene or was for any other reason nonmailable. The district court denied the injunction and dismissed the complaint. 55 F. Supp. 1015. The court of appeals reversed. 151 F. 2d 49. The case is here on a petition for a writ of certiorari which we granted because of the importance of the problem in the administration of the postal laws.

The issues of Esquire Magazine under attack are those for January to November, inclusive, of 1943. The material complained of embraces in bulk only a small percentage of those issues. Regular features of the magazine (called "The Magazine for Men") include articles on topics of current interest, short stories, sports articles or stories, short articles by men prominent in various fields of activities, articles about men prominent in the news, a book review department headed by the late William Lyon Phelps, a theatrical department headed by George Jean Nathan, a department on the lively arts by Gilbert Seldes, a department devoted to men's clothing, and pictorial features, including war action paintings, color photographs of dogs and water colors or etchings of game birds and reproductions of famous paintings, prints and drawings. There was very little in these features which was challenged. But petitioner's predecessor found that the objectionable items, though a small percentage of the total bulk, were regular recurrent features which gave the magazine its dominant tone or characteristic. These include jokes, cartoons, pictures, articles, and poems. They were said to reflect the smoking-room type of humor, featuring, in the main, sex. Some witnesses found the challenged items highly objectionable, calling them salacious and indecent. Others thought they were only racy and risque. Some condemned them as being merely in poor taste. Other witnesses could find no objection to them.

An examination of the items makes plain, we think, that the controversy is not whether the magazine publishes "information of a public character" or is devoted to "literature" or to the "arts." It is whether the contents are "good" or "bad." To uphold the order of revocation would, therefore, grant the Postmaster General a power of censorship. Such a power is so abhorrent to our traditions that a purpose to grant it should not be easily inferred.

The second-class privilege is a form of subsidy. From the beginning Congress has allowed special rates to certain classes of publications. The Act of February 20, 1792, 1 Stat. 232, 238, granted newspapers a more favorable rate. These were extended to magazines and pamphlets by the Act of May 8, 1794, 1 Stat. 354, 362. Prior to the Classification Act of 1879, periodicals were put into the second-class, which by the Act of March 3, 1863, 12 Stat. 701, 705, included "all mailable matter exclusively in print, and regularly issued at stated periods, without addition by writing, mark, or sign." That Act plainly adopted a strictly objective test and left no discretion to the postal authorities to withhold the second-class privilege from a mailable newspaper or periodical because it failed to meet some standard of worth or value or propriety. There is nothing in the language or history of the Classification Act of 1879 which suggests that Congress in that law made any basic change in its treatment of second-class mail, let alone such an abrupt and radical change as would be entailed by the inauguration of even a limited form of censorship.

The postal laws make a clear-cut division between mailable and nonmailable material. The four classes of mailable matter are generally described by objective standards which refer in part to their contents, but not to the quality of their contents. The more particular descriptions of the first, third, and fourth classes follow the same pattern, as do the first three conditions specified for second-class matter. If, therefore, the Fourth condition is read in the context of the postal laws of which it is an integral part, it, too, must be taken to supply standards which relate to the format of the publication and to the nature of its contents, but not to their quality, worth, or value. In that view, "literature" or the "arts" mean no more than productions which convey ideas by words, pictures, or drawings.

If the Fourth condition is read in that way, it is plain that Congress made no radical or basic change in the type of regulation which it adopted for second-class mail in 1879. The inauguration of even a limited type of censorship would have been such a startling change as to have left some traces in the legislative history. But we find none. Congressman Money, a member of the Postal Committee who defended the bill on the floor of the House, stated that it was "nothing but a simplification of the postal code. There are no new powers granted to the Department by this bill, none whatever." 8 Cong. Rec. 2134. The bill contained registration provisions which were opposed on the ground that they might be the inception of a censorship of the press. *Id.*, p. 2137. These were deleted. *Id.*, pp. 2137, 2138. It is difficult to imagine that the Congress, having deleted them for fear of censorship, gave the Postmaster General by the Fourth condition discretion to deny periodicals the second-class rate, if in his view they did not contribute to the public good. Congressman Money indeed referred to "the daily newspapers, with their load of gossip and scandal and every-day topics that are floating through the press" as being entitled without question to the second-class privilege. *Id.*, p. 2135. To the charge that the bill imposed a censorship, he pointed out that it only withheld the privileged rate from publications "made up simply of advertising concerns not intended for public education"; and added:

> We know the reason for which papers are allowed to go at a low rate of postage, amounting almost to the franking privilege, is because they are the most efficient educators of our people. It is because they go into general circulation and are intended for the dissemination of useful knowledge such as will promote the prosperity and the best interests of the people all over the country. Then all this vast mass of matter is excluded from that low rate of postage. I say, instead of being a censorship upon the press, it is for the protection of the legitimate journals of the country. *Id.*, p. 2135.

The policy of Congress has been clear. It has been to encourage the distribution of periodicals which disseminated "information of a public character" or which were devoted to "literature, the sciences, arts, or some special industry," because it was thought that those publications as a class contributed to the public good. The standards prescribed in the Fourth condition have been criticized, but not on the ground that they provide for censorship. As stated by the Postal Commission of 1911, H. Doc. 559, 62d Cong., 2d Sess., p. 142:

> The original object in placing on second-class matter a rate far below that on any other class of mail was to encourage the dissemination of news and of current literature of educational value. This object has been only in part attained. The low rate has helped to stimulate an enormous mass of periodicals, many of which are of little utility for the cause of popular education. Others are of excellent quality, but the experience of the post office has shown the impossibility of making a satisfactory test based upon literary or educational values. To attempt to do so would be to set up a censorship of the press. Of necessity the words of the statute —"devoted to literature, the sciences, arts, or some special industry"—must have a broad interpretation.

We may assume that Congress has a broad power of classification and need not open second-class mail to publications of all types. The categories of publications entitled to that classification have indeed varied through the years. And the Court held in *Ex parte Jackson*, 96 U. S. 727, that Congress could constitutionally make it a crime to send fraudulent or obscene material through the mails. But grave constitutional questions are immediately raised once it is said that the use of the mails is a privilege which may be extended or withheld on any grounds whatsoever. See the dissents of Mr. Justice Brandeis and Mr. Justice Holmes in *Milwaukee Publishing Co.* v. *Burleson,* 255 U. S. 407, 421–423, 430–432, 437–438. Under that view the second-class rate could be granted on condition that certain economic or political ideas not be disseminated. The provisions of the Fourth condition would have to be far more explicit for us to assume that Congress made such a radical departure from our traditions and undertook to clothe the Postmaster General with the power to supervise the tastes of the reading public of the country.

It is plain, as we have said, that the favorable second-class rates were granted periodicals meeting the requirements of the Fourth condition, so that the public good might be served through a dissemination of the class of periodicals described. But that is a far cry from assuming that Congress had any idea that each applicant for the second-class rate must convince the Postmaster General that his publication positively contributes to the public good or public welfare. Under our system of government there is an accommodation for the widest varieties of tastes and ideas. What is good literature, what has educational value, what is refined public information, what is good art, varies with individuals as it does from one generation to another. There doubtless would be a contrariety of views concerning Cervantes' "Don Quixote," Shakespeare's "Venus and Adonis," or Zola's "Nana." But a requirement that literature or art conform to some norm prescribed by an official smacks of an ideology foreign to our system. The basic values implicit in the requirements of the Fourth condition can be served only by uncensored distribution of literature. From the multitude of competing offerings the public will pick and choose. What seems to one to be trash may have for others fleeting or even enduring values. But to withdraw the second-class rate from this publication today because its contents seemed to one official not good for the public would sanction withdrawal of the second-class rate tomorrow from another periodical whose social or economic views seemed harmful to another official. The validity of the obscenity laws is recognition that the mails may not be used to satisfy all tastes, no matter how perverted. But Congress has left the Postmaster General with no power to prescribe standards for the literature or the art which a mailable periodical disseminates.

This is not to say that there is nothing left to the Postmaster General under the Fourth condition. It is his duty to "execute all laws relative to the Postal Service." Rev. Stat. § 396, 5 U. S. C. § 369. For example, questions will arise as they did in *Houghton* v. *Payne,* 194 U. S. 88; *Bates & Guild Co.* v. *Payne,* 194 U. S. 106, and *Smith* v. *Hitchcock,* 226 U. S. 53, whether the publication which seeks the favorable second-class rate is a periodical as defined in the Fourth condition or a book or other type of publication. And it may appear that the information contained in a periodical may not be of a "public character." But the power to determine whether a periodical (which is mailable) contains information of a public character, literature or art does not include the further power to determine whether the contents meet some standard of the public good or welfare.

Affirmed.

Mr. Justice Frankfurter, concurring.

The case lies within very narrow confines. The publication under scrutiny is a periodical. It is therefore entitled to the special rates accorded by Congress provided it is published "for the dissemination of information of a public character, or devoted to literature, the sciences, arts . . ." If it be devoted to "literature" it becomes unnecessary to consider how small an infusion of "information of a public character" entitles a periodical to the second-class mail rates when the bulk of its contents would not otherwise satisfy the Congressional conditions.

Congress has neither defined its conception of "literature" nor has it authorized the Postmaster General to do so. But it has placed a limitation upon what is to be deemed "literature" for a privilege which the Court rightly calls a form of subsidy. Matters that are declared nonmailable (Criminal Code § 211; 35 Stat. 1129, 36 Stat. 1339; 18 U. S. C. § 334) are of course not "literature" within the scope of the second-class privilege. But the Postmaster General does not contend that the periodical with which we are concerned was nonmailable. He merely contends that it was not devoted to the kind of "literature" or "art" which may claim the subsidy of second-class matter. But since Congress has seen fit to allow "literature" conveyed by periodicals to have the second-class privilege without making any allowable classification of "literature," except only that nonmailable matter as defined by § 211 of the Criminal Code is excluded, the area of "literature, the sciences, arts" includes all composition of words, pictorial representation, or notations that are intelligible to any portion of the population, no matter whether their appeal is extensive or esoteric. Since the Postmaster General disavows the nonmailability of the issues of the periodical he had before him and since Congress did not qualify "literature, the sciences, arts" by any standards of taste or edification or public elevation, the Postmaster General exceeded his powers in denying this periodical a second-class permit.

It seems to me important strictly to confine discussion in this case because its radiations touch, on the one hand, the very basis of a free society, that of the right of expression beyond the conventions of the day, and, on the other hand, the freedom of society from constitutional compulsion to subsidize enterprise, whether in the world of matter or of mind. While one may entirely agree with Mr. Justice Holmes, in *Leach v. Carlile,* 258 U. S. 138, 140, as to the extent to which the First Amendment forbids control of the post so far as sealed letters are concerned, one confronts an entirely different set of questions in considering the basis on which the Government may grant or withhold subsidies through low postal rates, and huge subsidies, if one is to judge by the glimpse afforded by the present case. It will be time enough to consider such questions when the Court cannot escape decision upon them.

☞ Ranking in importance with Judge Woolsey's *Ulysses* opinion, and perhaps equally influential, was the decision delivered by Judge Curtis Bok of the Court of Quarter Sessions in Philadelphia in the *Commonwealth* v. *Gordon* case.

The Bok opinion, dated March 18, 1949, ably summarizes the conflict of authorities in the interpretation and application of obscenity laws. Since the early days of Anthony Comstock in the 1870's, authors, publishers, and booksellers have been harassed by a maze of state criminal statutes and local ordinances relating to allegedly obscene publications. Enforcement of the laws has ordinarily been placed in the hands of local police officials with little understanding of and no special training for the assignment.

It was in such a situation that Judge Bok's notable opinion was delivered. Five booksellers had been indicted by the Commonwealth of Pennsylvania for selling certain specific titles of books charged with obscenity. The indictments grew out of police raids a year earlier against some fifty Philadelphia newsstands and bookstores, from which more than two thousand books had been seized.

The Bok decision was subsequently affirmed by the Pennsylvania Superior and Supreme courts, though the latter court did not approve the "clear and present danger" test proposed by Judge Bok.

Curtis Bok
COMMONWEALTH v. GORDON ET AL.

The evidence consists of nine books and an oral stipulation at bar that defendants are booksellers and that they possessed the books with the intent to sell them on the dates and at the times and places set forth in the indictments. This constituted in full the Commonwealth's evidence, to which defendants have demurred.

I have read the books with thoughtful care and find that they are not obscene, as alleged. The demurrers are therefore sustained.

THE STATUTE

The indictments are drawn under section 524 of The Penal Code of June 24, 1939, . . . which reads as follows:

"Whoever sells, lends, distributes, exhibits, gives away, or shows or offers to sell, lend, distribute, exhibit, or give away or show, or has in his possession with intent to sell, lend, distribute or give away or to show, or knowingly advertises in any manner, any obscene, lewd, lascivious, filthy, indecent or disgusting book, magazine, pamphlet, newspaper, storypaper, paper, writing, drawing, photograph, figure or image, or any written or printed matter of an indecent character, or any article or instrument of indecent or immoral use or purporting to be for in-

---

Curtis Bok, "Commonwealth v. Gordon et al.," 66 *Pennsylvania District and County Reports* 101–56, copyright 1949 by the Legal Intelligencer. Reprinted by permission of the publisher.

decent or immoral use or purpose, or whoever designs, copies, draws, photographs, prints, utters, publishes, or in any manner manufactures or prepares any such book, picture, drawing, magazine, pamphlet, newspaper, storypaper, paper, writing, figure, image, matter, article or thing, or whoever writes, prints, publishes or utters, or causes to be printed, published or uttered, any advertisement or notice of any kind giving information, directly or indirectly, stating or purporting to do so, where, how, of whom, or by what means any, or what purports to be, any obscene, lewd, lascivious, filthy, disgusting or indecent book, picture, writing, paper, figure, image, matter, article or thing named in this section can be purchased, obtained or had, or whoever prints, utters, publishes, sells, lends, gives away, or shows, or has in his possession with intent to sell, lend, give away, or show, or otherwise offers for sale, loan or gift, or distribution, any pamphlet, magazine, newspaper or other printed paper devoted to the publication and principally made up of criminal news, police reports or accounts of criminal deeds, or pictures of stories of deeds of bloodshed, lust or crime, or whoever hires, employs, uses or permits any minor or child to do or assist in doing any act or thing mentioned in this section, is guilty of a misdemeanor, and upon conviction, shall be sentenced to imprisonment not exceeding one (1) year, or to pay a fine not exceeding five hundred dollars ($500), or both."

The particular and only charge in the indictments is that defendants possessed some or all of the books with the intent to sell them. . . .

It should be noted at once that the wording of section 524 requires consideration of the indicted material as a whole; it does not proscribe articles or publications that merely contain obscene matter. This is now true in all jurisdictions that have dealt with the subject. . . .

. . . In Commonwealth v. New, 142 Pa. Superior Ct. 358 (1940), the court said:

"We have no fault to find with the statement that in determining whether a work is obscene, it must be construed as a whole and that *regard shall be had for its place in the arts.*" (Italics supplied.)

RÉSUMÉ OF THE OPINION

Section 524, for all its verbiage, is very bare. The full weight of the legislative prohibition dangles from the word "obscene" and its synonyms. Nowhere are these words defined; nowhere is the danger to be expected of them stated; nowhere is a standard of judgment set forth. I assume that "obscenity" is expected to have a familiar and inherent meaning, both as to what it is and as to what it does.

It is my purpose to show that it has no such inherent meaning; that different meanings given to it at different times are not constant, either historically or legally; and that it is not constitutionally indictable unless it takes the form of sexual impurity, i. e., "dirt for dirt's sake" and can be traced to actual criminal behavior, either actual or demonstrably imminent.

RÉSUMÉ OF THE BOOKS

1, 2 and 3. The Studs Lonigan trilogy ("Young Lonigan," "The Young Manhood of Studs Lonigan," "Judgment Day"), by James T. Farrell; Vanguard Press, 1932–1935.

This is the story of the moral and physical disintegration of a young man living in Chicago between the years 1916 and 1932. Nothing that he attempted ever quite came off, and his failures became more and more incisive. He left school to hang around the streets with others of his kind; he was too young to enlist for war service; he loved Lucy since they were in school together, but avoided her for four years and finally alienated her by making drunken advances to her; he worked for his father as a painter, but, on a casual tip, invested his savings in a dubious stock, which failed; he fell halfheartedly in love with Catherine, and they were engaged to be married, but she became pregnant by him before the ceremony; looking for a job on a stormy day a few weeks before the wedding, he caught cold and died of pneumonia and a weakened heart.

The background of the semi-slum district in which Lonigan was born and lived was the outward counterpart of his own nature, and both together were too much for such decency of soul as he had. His drift downhill was relentless and inevitable. On the theory that no literature is vital that cannot be vulgarized, this trilogy may rank as an epic, for our criminal courts and prisons and many of our streets are peopled by Studs Lonigans. The characters in these books act and speak the kind of life that bred them, and Mr. Farrell has brought to the surface the ground swell of thought and inclination that move more people than, if they were honest, would admit to them.

It is not a pleasant story, nor are the characters gentle and refined. There is rape and dissipation and lust in these books, expressed in matching language, but they do not strike me as being out of proportion. The books as a whole create a sustained arc of a man's life and era, and the obvious effort of the author is to be faithful to the scene he depicts.

No one would want to be Studs Lonigan.

4. "A World I Never Made," by James T. Farrell; Vanguard Press, New York, 1936.

This book could well be the beginning of another series, for it takes a minor character from the Lonigan books, Danny O'Neill, and shows him as a child. The milieu is the same—Chicago in 1911—but there is a discernible effort to show Danny's struggle uphill against the same factors that pushed Lonigan down.

This is the one book of the nine that does not end tragically; it merely stops in midstream, but the people who surround Danny do and say the same things that appear in the Lonigan series. Unlike the latter, this book is plastered with the short Saxon words of common vulgarity; they are consistent with the characters who use them and with the quality of the lives and actions that are the subject of the author's scrutiny.

I am not of a mind, nor do I have the authority, to require an author to write about one kind of people and not about another, nor do I object to his effort to paint a complete picture of those whom he has chosen. Certainly I will not say that it is not a good thing to look deeply into life and people, regardless of the shadows that are to be found there.

5. "Sanctuary," by William Faulkner; Random House, 1931.

This is a powerful and dreadful story about a gay but virginal girl of 17 who accidentally falls into the hands of a sadistic man called Popeye, who is sexually impotent. He kills a half-witted boy who is informally guarding the girl, and ravishes her with a corncob. He then keeps her imprisoned in a house of prostitution and takes pleasure in watching her have intercourse with a man whom he kills when she tries to escape with him. Terrified of Popeye, she testifies that another man committed the murder, and is taken from court by her father, who has finally been able to locate her. Popeye is later apprehended on another charge of murder and is convicted.

There are no vulgar Saxon words in the book, but the situations are stark and unrelieved. It makes one shudder to think of what can happen by misadventure.

6. "Wild Palms," by William Faulkner; Random House, 1939.

This book concerns a wife who left her husband and children to seek integrity of experience, in terms of vitality, with her lover; "hunger is in the heart," she says, when the next meal seems uncertain, "not in the stomach." They wander about the country together, living as they must or as they wish, and she finally becomes pregnant. Her lover, a former doctor, attempts to abort her but mishandles it and she dies. He pleads guilty and is sentenced to 50 years in prison. He refuses a gift of cyanide from the woman's husband, saying: "Between grief and nothing I will take grief."

The redeeming feature of this tale is that an acid loneliness comes through, the awful loneliness that pervades lost people, even in company. No one could envy these two miserable creatures.

7. "God's Little Acre," by Erskine Caldwell; Random House, 1933.

An able companion to the same author's "Tobacco Road," it is the story of a poor and illiterate farmer's family in Georgia. The central figure is the father, who for 15 years has dug holes in his farm in search of gold. God's Little Acre is a part of the farm which he mentally moves about in order to keep it from getting in the way of his search for treasure; his idea is to give all that comes from it to the church, but he never works it. His daughters and sons and their wives get variously tangled up in sexual affairs which are taken as being in the nature of things. One brother kills another over his wife. The final and despairing cry of the father, who has always tried to keep peace, is, "Blood on my land!"

It is a frank and turbulent story, but it is an obvious effort to be faithful to the locality and its people.

8. "End As a Man," by Calder Willingham; Vanguard Press, 1947.

Life in a southern military academy. A drinking party and crooked poker game finally result in the expulsion of several cadets, including the wily and unmoral ringleader. The retired general in charge of the academy is the stereotype of military martinet, whose conception of the narrow and rigid discipline necessary to produce "a man" is set in bold relief against the energy of growing boys. The result is a fair picture of the frustration inherent in an overdose of discipline and in the license and disobedience that is largely engendered by it.

No one would care to send his son to such an institution.

This is perhaps the foulest book of the lot, so far as language is concerned, but it is the language of vulgarity and not of erotic allurement.

9. "Never Love a Stranger," by Harold Robbins; Knopf, 1948.

The story of a boy brought up in an orphanage who finds that he has an uncle and is Jewish. After losing touch with his uncle he has various experiences and is finally down and out because he can find no work. He then becomes head of New York City's gambling racket, which he ultimately leaves in order to marry a childhood friend. She dies in childbirth and he is killed in the war; his friends take over the child, who will presumably have a better chance in life than he had.

It is a swift story that covers a great deal of ground, its point being to portray a hard and lonely man who could not fully trust or give himself to anyone. Its last and least convincing part is also the least open to attack for obscenity; the rest, particularly the section dealing with New York City during the depression of the early 1930's, is very moving, not because there are sexual incidents but because the lines of the story are deep and authentic.

GENERAL COMMENT

Three of these books have already been judicially cleared in New York City.

"A World I Never Made" was before Magistrate Curran in 1937, under the caption of Bamberger v. The Vanguard Press, Inc., docket no. 329. The opinion was impromptu and is in the perceptive magistrate's best style.

"God's Little Acre" was the subject of People v. Viking Press, Inc., 147 N. Y. Misc. 813 (1933). In the course of his opinion Magistrate Greenspan said:

"The Courts have strictly limited the applicability of the statute to works of pornography and they have consistently declined to apply it to books of genuine literary value. If the statute were construed more broadly than in the manner just indicated, its effect would be to prevent altogether the realistic portrayal in literature of a large and important field of life. . . . The Court may not require the author to put refined language into the mouths of primitive people." (Italics supplied.)

Magistrate Strong held "End As a Man" not obscene in People v. Vanguard Press, 192 N. Y. Misc. 127 (1947), and observed:

"The speech of the characters must be considered in relation to its setting and the theme of the story. It seems clear that use of foul language will not of itself bring a novel or play within the condemnation of the statute."

After clearance by the magistrates, these books could have been brought before the grand jury, but no such indictments were attempted.

As I have indicated above, all but one of these books are profoundly tragic, and that one has its normal quota of frustration and despair. No one could envy or wish to emulate the characters that move so desolately through these pages. Far from inciting to lewd or lecherous desires, which are sensorially pleasurable, these books leave one either with a sense of horror or of pity for the degradation of mankind. The effect upon the normal reader, "l'homme moyen sensuel" (there is no such deft precision in English), would be anything but what the vice hunters fear it might be. We are so fearful for other people's morals; they so seldom have the courage of our own convictions.

It will be asked whether one would care to have one's young daughter read these books. I suppose that by the time she is old enough to wish to read them she will have learned the biologic facts of life and the words that go with them. There is something seriously wrong at home if those facts have not been met and faced and sorted by then; it is not children so much as parents that should receive our concern about this. I should prefer that my own three daughters meet the facts of life and the literature of the world in my library than behind a neighbor's barn, for I can face the adversary there directly. If the young ladies are appalled by what they read, they can close the book at the bottom of page one; if they read further, they will learn what is in the world and in its people, and no parents who have been discerning with their children need fear the outcome. Nor can they hold it back, for life is a series of little battles and minor issues, and the burden of choice is on us all, every day, young and old. Our daughters must live in the world and decide what sort of women they are to be, and we should be willing to prefer their deliberate and informed choice of decency rather than an innocence that continues to spring from ignorance. If that choice be made in the open sunlight, it is more apt than when made in shadow to fall on the side of honorable behavior.

The lesson to be learned from such books as these is not so facile as that the wages of sin is death, or, in Hollywood's more modern version, that the penalty of sinning is suffering. That is not enough to save a book from proper censorship. The tragedy of these books is not in death but in the texture of the slope that leads to death —in the inner suffering that comes at times from crimes against oneself as much as from crimes against society. That has been the green pastures of storytellers ever since the Greek dramatists, especially when the pressures on a character are not, as they are not always, of his own making or within his control. Sin is too apt a word to take in the full reach of circumstance, and I venture to say that in human experience suffering does not automatically follow sinning. Our laws have a good deal to do with that guarded notion. It is necessary to know what our laws are up to, and it is my conviction that, outside the police power, the laws of Anglo-Saxon countries are made less as absolute mandates than as clinical experiments. Democratic nations prefer checks and balances to absolute authority, and it is worthy of notice that the jury system exists only in those countries where the law is not considered to have been drawn, as Cicero put it, from the forehead of the gods, but rather from the will of the people, who wish to keep an eye on it. The eighteenth amendment to the Constitution is a case in point.

Such sumptuary laws, and some economic ones, differ from obscenity statutes only in the degree of danger to society inherent in the appetite in question. The need for decency is as old as the appetites, but it is not expressed in uniform law or custom. The ancient Hebrews had a rigid moral code which, for example, excluded bastards from the congregation up to the tenth generation, for the combined reasons of preserving their ancient tradition of tribe and family and of increasing the number of effective warriors. The Greeks, more cosmopolitan in a country whose sterile soil could not support many people comfortably, approved pederasty and a restricted form of concubinage in order to keep the population down. Standards of sexual behavior, as well as of the need to censor it, have shifted from age to age, from country to country, and from economy to economy. The State of New Mexico has no obscenity statute. South Carolina has no divorce law.

Censorship, which is the policeman of decency, whether religious, patriotic, or moral, has had distinct fashions, depending on which great questions were agitating society at the time. During the Middle Ages, when the church was supreme, the focus of suppression was upon heresy and blasphemy. When the State became uppermost, the focus of suppression was upon treason and sedition. The advent of technology made Queen Victoria realize, perhaps subconsciously, that loose morals would threaten the peace of mind necessary to the development of invention and big business; the focus moved to sexual morality. We are now emerging into an era of social ideology and psychology, and the focus is turning to these. The right to speak out and to act freely is always at a minimum in the area of the fighting faiths.

The censorship of books did not become a broad public issue until after the invention of printing in the fifteenth century. The earliest real example of it was the first Index Librorum Prohibitorum of the Catholic Church in 1559, and the church was broadly tolerant of sexual impurity in the books that it considered; its main object was the suppression of heresy. I think it is a fair general statement that from ancient times until the Comstockian laws of 1873 the only form of written obscenity that was censored was "dirt for dirt's sake."

I do not regard the above as apart from the decisional purpose of this case. The words of the statute—"obscene, lewd, lascivious, filthy, indecent, or disgusting"—restrict rather than broaden the meaning of a highly penal statute. The effect of this plethora of epithets is to merge them into one prevailing meaning—that of sexual impurity alone, and this has been universally held . . .

In Swearingen v. United States, 161 U. S. 446 (1896), a case involving the mailing of obscene matter, the court said:

"The offence aimed at, in that portion of the statute we are now considering, was the use of the mails to circulate or deliver matter to corrupt the morals of the people. The words 'obscene,' 'lewd' and 'lascivious,' as used in the statute, signify that form of immorality which has relation to sexual impurity, and have the same meaning as is given them at common law in prosecutions for obscene libel. As the statute is highly penal, it should not be held to embrace language unless it is fairly within its letter and spirit."

This view has been adopted in Pennsylvania, for the court said in Commonwealth v. New . . . :

"The test for obscenity most frequently laid down seems to be whether the writing would tend to deprave the morals of those into whose hands the publication might fall by suggesting lewd thoughts and exciting sensual desires."

The statute is therefore directed only at sexual impurity and not at blasphemy or coarse and vulgar behavior of any other kind. The word in common use for the purpose of such a statute is "obscenity." The great point of this case is to find out what that word means.

Nowhere in the statute is there a definition of it or a formula given for determining when it exists. Its derivation, *ob* and *scena,* suggests that anything done offstage, furtively, or lefthandedly, is obscene. The act does not penalize anyone who seeks to change the prevailing moral or sexual code, nor does it state that the writing must be such as to corrupt the morals of the public or of youth; it merely proscribes books that *are* obscene and leaves it to the authorities to decide whether or not they are. This cannot be done without regard to the nature and history of obscenity. It is unlike the fundamental laws of property, of crimes like murder, rape, and theft, or even of negligence, whose meaning has remained relatively constant. That of obscenity has frequently changed, almost from decade to decade within the past century; "Ulysses" was condemned by the State courts in New York just 10 years before it was cleared by Judge Woolsey in the District Court for the Southern District of New York. I must determine what this elusive word means now.

Something might be said at the outset about the familiar four-letter words that are so often associated with sexual impurity. These are, almost without exception, of honest Anglo-Saxon ancestry, and were not invented for purely scatological effect. The one, for example, that is used to denote the sexual act is an old agricultural word meaning "to plant," and was at one time a wholly respectable member of the English vocabulary. The distinction between a word of decent etymological history and one of smut alone is important; it shows that fashions in language change as expectably as do the concepts of what language connotes. It is the old business of semantics again, the difference between word and concept.

But there is another distinction. The decisions that I shall cite have sliced off vulgarity from obscenity. This has had the effect of making a clear division between the words of the bathroom and those of the bedroom: the former can no longer be regarded as obscene, since they have no erotic allurement, and the latter may be so regarded, depending on the circumstances of their use. This reduces the number of potentially offensive words sharply.

With such changes as these, the question is whether the legal mace should fall upon words or upon concepts—language or ideas.

Obscenity is not like sedition, blasphemy, or open lewdness, against which there are also criminal statutes. These offenses not only have acquired precise meaning but are defined specifically in the act. Sedition (Act of June 24, 1939, P. L. 872, section 207, 18 PS § 4207), which includes writing and publication, is carefully defined in eight subheadings. Blasphemy (same act, section 523, 18 PS § 4523) is stated as speaking "loosely and profanely of Almighty God, Christ Jesus, the Holy Spirit, or the Scriptures of Truth." Open lewdness (same act, section 519, 18 PS § 4519) is "any notorious act of public indecency, tending to debauch the morals or manners of the people." Other crimes, involving restriction on free speech and having their scope or purpose set forth with particularity in The Penal Code, include blackmail (section 801), libel (section 412), anonymous communications (section 414), false letters of recommendation (section 856), false advertising (section 857), advertising without publisher's consent (section 858), and fortune telling (section 870).

No such definition of standard or legislative intention occurs in section 524, and I am convinced that without a declaration of the legislature's intention as to what obscenity means or of what the lawmakers sought to prevent, there is no constant or reliable indication of it to be found in human experience.

The argument is often made that anyone can tell by instinct what is obscene and what is not, even if it is hard to put the difference into words. The same might be said of sedition, blasphemy, and open lewdness, but the legislature was careful to specify. With regard to obscenity, however, the argument does not hold water. When he was an editor, Walter Hines Page deleted the word "chaste" because it was suggestive, and the play "Sappho" was banned in New York City because a man carried the leading lady up a flight of stairs. A librarian once charged Mark Twain's "Tom Sawyer" and "Huckleberry Finn" with corrupting the morals of children. In 1907 Richard Strauss's "Salome" was banned in Boston. Charlotte Brontë's "Jane Eyre," when first published, was called "too immoral to be ranked as decent literature." Hawthorne's "Scarlet Letter" was referred to as "a brokerage of lust." George Eliot's "Adam Bede" was called "the vile outpourings of a lewd woman's mind." Others to suffer similarly were Elizabeth Barrett Browning's "Aurora Leigh," Hardy's "Tess" and "Jude," Du Maurier's "Trilby," and Shaw's "Mrs. Warren's Profession." Walt Whitman lost his job in the United States Department of the Interior because of "Leaves of Grass."

It is presumed that Mr. Page and the others who attacked this imposing array of classics could tell by instinct what was decent and what was not. The idea that instinct can be resorted to as a process of moral stare decisis reduces to absurdity.

It is a far cry from the examples just cited to what society accepts as innocuous now. The stage, literature, painting, sculpture, photography, fashions of dress, and even the still pudibund screen tolerate things that would have made Anthony Comstock turn blue. In its issue of April 11, 1938, Life magazine ran a series of factual and dignified pictures called "The Birth of a Baby." It was attacked in the courts but was exonerated. Dr. Kinsey's report on the sexual behavior of men is now current. Truth and error, as Milton urged in his "Areopagitica," are being allowed to grapple, and we are the better for it.

In addition to the books whose banning is the subject of cases cited later in this opinion, I suggest a short list of modern books that have not been banned, so far as I can find out. All of these books contain sexual material, and all of them can be found in the Boston Public Library. I defy anyone to provide a rational basis for the distinction between these two sets of books. My list includes: Fannie Hurst's "Back Street"; Arthur Koestler's "Arrival and Departure"; Erich Maria Remarque's "All Quiet on the Western Front" and "Arch of Triumph"; Eugene O'Neill's "Anna Christie" and "Hairy Ape"; John Dos Passos's "U. S. A."; Ernest Hemingway's "For Whom the Bell Tolls"; Somerset Maugham's "Of Human Bondage"; Charles Morgan's "The Fountain" and "The Voyage"; Richard Wright's "Black Boy."

It is no answer to say that if my point about the books just listed be sound, then by analogy the law against murder is useless because all murderers are not caught. The inherent evil of murder is apparent, but by what apparent, inherent standard of evil is obscenity to be judged, from book to book? It is my purpose to provide such a standard, but it will reduce to a minimum the operation of any norm of indefinite interpretation.

Before leaving this point, research discloses a curious but complete confusion between the post office and the customs over what constitutes obscenity. No unanimity of opinion unites these two governmental services in a common standard. Books have cleared the port only to find the mails closed to them: others, printed here, have circulated freely while foreign copies were stopped at the ports. One would expect greater uniformity than this if obscenity could be unmistakably detected.

There is a bale of literature on obscenity and the history of censorship, i.e., suppression of the right of free expression. It is best represented by two books by Morris L. Ernst, Esq., entitled "To The Pure" (Viking Press, 1929) and "The Censor Marches On" (Doubleday, Doran & Co., 1940), with William Seagle and Alexander Lindey, respectively, collaborating. In addition to the brilliant and scholarly text, there is a large bibliography and appendices. These two books should be required reading, of at least equal importance with legal authority, in deciding a censorship case.

An interesting volume on literary censorship is "Banned Books," by Anne Lyon Haight (R. R. Bowker Co., New York, 1935), which lists the principal suppression of books, for various reasons, at various times and in various places, from Caligula's attempt to suppress "The Odyssey" in A.D. 35 to the lifting of the ban on "Ulysses" in 1934.

The legal authorities on obscenity may be found well collected in 76 A. L. R. 1099, and 81 A. L. R. 801.

It is my conclusion that the books before me are obvious efforts to show life as it is. I cannot be convinced that the deep drives and appetites of life are very much different from what they have always been, or that censorship has ever had any effect on them, except as the law's police power to preserve the peace in censorship. I believe that the consensus of preference today is for disclosure and not stealth, for frankness and not hypocrisy, and for public and not secret distribution. That in itself is a moral code.

It is my opinion that frank disclosure cannot legally be censored, even as an exercise of the police power, unless it is sexually impure and pornographic, as I shall define those words. They furnish the only possible test for obscenity and its effect.

These books are not, in my view, sexually impure and pornographic.

THE PENNSYLVANIA CASES

I venture a long and detailed opinion because this is the first case in Pennsylvania that deals with current literature in book form. Our authorities on the censoring of obscenity are so few that they can all be referred to.

The earliest case is that of Commonwealth v. Sharpless, 2 S. & R. 91 (1815), in which defendant was convicted of exhibiting an indecent picture. The case has importance because of the holding by Tilghman, C. J., that since there was no act of assembly on the matter, the case had to be decided on common-law principles, which he found covered such an indictment. The chief justice did not doubt that the publication of an indecent book was also indictable at common law, and cited the English case of Rex v. Curl, 2 Str. 788, 93 E. R. 849 (1727).

The Sharpless case can be taken as authority that obscenity was a common-law offense in England at the time of the American Revolution and hence became part of the common law of Pennsylvania. The status of the common law on many points often depends on the date to which one opens the books, and it should be observed that obscenity was not a part of English common law until Rex v. Curl, supra: in Regina v. Read, Fortescue, 98, 92 E. R. 777 (1707), only 20 years earlier, the lords wished that there were a law to punish the publication of "The Fifteen Plagues of a Maidenhead," but decided that they couldn't make one—it was a matter for the ecclesiastical courts.

In Rex v. Wilkes, 4 Burr. 2527, 98 E. R. 327 (1770), defendant was indicted and convicted of printing an obscene libel entitled "An Essay on Women." Jurisdiction was assumed, for there was no discussion of it nor was any objection made to the indictment: the reported proceedings have to do with procedural matters and with the propriety of a sentence of outlawry for a misdemeanor.

It is on these two cases—Rex v. Curl and Rex v. Wilkes—and on Blackstone that indictable obscenity as a part of the English common law depends.

Blackstone, who began his Vinerian lectures on October 25, 1758, after labors "of so many years" in collecting his material, says, in Book IV of the Commentaries, pp. 150 and 151, that libels in their largest and most extensive sense signify any writings, pictures, or the like, of an immoral or illegal tendency, and are punishable in the interest of the preservation of peace and good order. It is interesting to note that he goes on at once to make the point that freedom of the press is not involved, since the right exists to publish anything, but only the abuse of it, established by trial after publication, is punishable.

While Blackstone had only Rex v. Curl (1727) to support him as authority, he is regarded as authority himself, and it must therefore be held that obscene publication was indictable at common law.

It is important to observe that there are few, if any, obscene book cases in the English reports between the time of Rex v. Curl, in 1727, and Regina v. Hicklin, in 1868; that in Pennsylvania no act was passed against obscenity until 1860, and that no case involving an obscene book appeared until Commonwealth v. Landis, infra, in

1870. Commonwealth v. Sharpless, in 1815, mentioned books by dictum only.

This removes from the doctrine of indictable obscenity much of the veneration that is usually given to common-law doctrines because of their hoary age. The plain fact is that the period of the Renaissance, in both countries, was a lusty one, and that concern over sexual purity did not begin to arise until Victorianism really took hold in the middle 1850's. One need only recall that the father of the post office, Benjamin Franklin, wrote and presumably mailed his "Letter of Advice to Young Men on the Proper Choosing of a Mistress"; that Thomas Jefferson worried about the students at his new University of Virginia having a respectable brothel; that Alexander Hamilton's adultery while holding public office created no great scandal, or that the morals of Southern chivalry provided us with mulattoes until the abolition of slavery at least made the matter one of free choice on both sides.

The formulation of the common-law proscription of obscene publication did not, therefore, amount to very much. It is a good example of a social restriction that became law and was allowed to slumber until a change of social consciousness should animate it. It is the prevailing social consciousness that matters quite as much as the law. Between 1870 and 1930 the obscenity law was on the social anvil: since then society has found other irons in the fire and has lost its interest in what Shaw has called Comstockery.

The next Pennsylvania case was Commonwealth v. Landis, 8 Phila. 453 (1870), in which defendant was convicted of selling a book called "Secrets of Generation." This case is interesting because it holds that it was for the jury to say whether the book was obscene, and that "that which offends modesty, and is indecent and lewd, and tends to the creation of lascivious desires, is obscene." Not only is this the first book case in the State, but it is the first example of showing the effort by both legislature and courts to define the libidinous synonyms in terms of each other: obscenity is filthiness, filthiness is indecency, indecency is lewdness, lewdness is lasciviousness, and lasciviousness is obscenity. The opinion also states "that to justify a publication of the character of this book they [the jury] must be satisfied that the publication was made for a legitimate and useful purpose, and that it was not made from any motive of mere gain or with a corrupt desire to debauch society." It ends with a warning that a book, obscene in itself, might be used either for a proper purpose, such as medical instruction, or for an improper one, such as general publication, and that in the latter case the utterer would have to answer.

In Commonwealth v. Havens, 6 Pa. C. C. 545 (1889), the constitutionality of the Act of May 6, 1887, was upheld, on the one ground advanced, that its title was broad enough. The case involved "The National Police Gazette" and "The Illustrated Police News." A conviction resulted. The court restricted the evidence to the specific advertisements complained of and refused to allow testimony as to what their real purpose was. Their inherent indecency was the only issue. The test of obscenity finally approved by the opinion was: "Would the articles or the pictures here . . . suggest impure and libidinous thoughts in the young and inexperienced?"

In re Arentsen, 26 W. N. C. 359 (1890), dealt with Count Leo Tolstoy's "Kreutzer Sonata." This case also holds that selling an obscene book was a common-law offense, and Judge Thayer cited Regina v. Hicklin, L. R. 3 Q. B. 360 (1868), of which more hereafter. Defendant was acquitted because the book was found to condemn marriage, not in favor of free love but of complete celibacy.

In Commonwealth v. Dowling, 14 Pa. C. C. 607 (1894), defendant was convicted of selling immoral newspapers to minors. The case is of little interest, except for the affirmance of one of defendant's points for charge: "The law does not undertake to punish bad English, vulgarity, or bad taste, and no matter how objectionable the jury may consider the papers referred to on those grounds, they have no right to convict on account of them."

In Commonwealth v. Magid & Dickstein, 91 Pa. Superior Ct. 513 (1927), the subject matter was indecent pictures. The court stated that the purpose of the Acts of 1887 and 1897 was "to shield minors and young children from obscene and indecent books and pictures."

In Commonwealth v. Kutler, 93 Pa. Superior Ct. 119 (1928), and Commonwealth v. Kufel, 142 Pa. Superior Ct. 273 (1940), the only question was whether defendants were the ones who sold certain pamphlets, the obscene character of which was conceded.

In Commonwealth v. New, supra (142 Pa.

Superior Ct. 358 (1940)), the matter involved was certain pictures in a magazine called "Tipster." The test of obscenity adopted by the court shows a virtual abandonment of the harsh rule of Regina v. Hicklin, infra, and is stated thus: "Whether the writing would tend to deprave the morals of those into whose hands the publication might fall by suggesting lewd thoughts and exciting sensual desires." The purpose of the act is again stated to be the prevention of "appealing to those of depraved tastes or to the curiosity of adolescents."

In Commonwealth v. Mercur, 90 Pitts. L. J. 318 (1942), the court applied the "as a whole" rule of Commonwealth v. New, supra, and held that certain pictures appearing in a book of instruction for photographers called "U. S. Camera 1942," did not render the volume obscene.

This exhausts the Pennsylvania cases.

It is therefore clear that section 524 of our act has not yet been applied to serious current literature. There has not been the opportunity to form a modern test for obscenity in Pennsylvania as there has been in the lower Federal courts, and in the highest appellate courts of New York and Massachusetts.

Despite the scarcity of literary obscenity cases in this State, the trend has been away from and beyond the English common law. The range in growth of doctrine is from the dictum in the Sharpless case, that the common-law rule of obscene libel would apply to a book, to the opinion in the New case, that a book must be considered as a whole and regard be given to its place in the arts. The English appellate courts have not gone so far, as will be seen.

The first articulate test appears in the leading English case of Regina v. Hicklin, L. R. 3 Q. B. 360 (1868), and the American jurisdictions have had to face it before they could disregard it and forge the modern rule. In Pennsylvania, the rule for which it has become famous was cited with approval in Commonwealth v. Havens, supra (6 Pa. C. C. 545 (1889)), and again in In re Arentsen, supra (26 W. N. C. 359 (1890)), but the modern American rule has not yet been squarely adopted here.

THE ENGLISH CASES

Regina v. Hicklin is an example of judge-made law quite at variance with the parliamentary intent behind the act on which it was based. Lord Campbell's act provided for search and seizure warrants that would enable the police to take and destroy obscene publications. The report of the debates in Hansard shows the lords' difficulties in deciding what an obscene publication might be. Lord Campbell, who was lord chief justice at the time, explained that the act was to apply exclusively to works written for the purpose of corrupting the morals of youth and of a nature calculated to shock the common feelings of decency in any well regulated mind. He was ready to make whatever was then indictable a test of obscenity in his new act. He made it clear that any work that even pretended to be literature or art, classic or modern, had little to fear.

All of this was nullified by Lord Chief Justice Cockburn in the Hicklin case, where the subject matter was a pamphlet entitled "The Confessional Unmasked," and containing a diatribe against the Catholic Church; its purpose was to show the depravity of the priesthood and the character of the questions put to women in the confessional. This is the now famous rule of the case:

"I think the test of obscenity is this, whether the tendency of the matter charged as obscenity is to deprave and corrupt those whose minds are open to such immoral influences, and into whose hands a publication of this sort may fall."

Strictly applied, this rule renders any book unsafe, since a moron could pervert to some sexual fantasy to which his mind is open the listings in a seed catalogue. Not even the Bible would be exempt; Annie Besant once compiled a list of 150 passages in Scripture that might fairly be considered obscene—it is enough to cite the story of Lot and his daughters, Genesis 19, 30–38. Portions of Shakespeare would also be offensive, and of Chaucer, to say nothing of Aristophanes, Juvenal, Ovid, Swift, Defoe, Fielding, Smollett, Rousseau, Maupassant, Voltaire, Balzac, Baudelaire, Rabelais, Swinburne, Shelley, Byron, Boccaccio, Marguerite de Navarre, Hardy, Shaw, Whitman, and a host more.

As will be seen later, the classics—whatever that may mean precisely—are considered exempt from censorship, but many of them are hounded in England, despite Lord Campbell's assurances, as a result of the rule of the Hicklin case.

The next English case—passing Regina v.

Read, Rex v. Curl, and Rex v. Wilkes, which have been examined above—was Steele v. Brannan, L. R. 7 C. P. 261 (1872), which involved the report of the trial of one George Mackey for selling a pamphlet called "The Confessional Unmasked." The report set forth the pamphlet in full, and the court held not only the publication was not privileged as a report of legal proceedings but that it was obscene, despite its purpose to expose what the author considered dangerous religious practices. The court followed Regina v. Hicklin, without quoting the rule, and placed its point of emphasis upon the effect of the pamphlet "on the young and inexperienced."

The next case was Bradlaugh v. Regina, L. R. 3 Q. B. 607 (1878), in which a conviction for publishing a book called "Fruits of Philosophy" was reversed. The point was whether the allegedly obscene matter should be included in the indictment instead of being referred to by name only. The Court of Error held that it should be, and expressly avoided passing upon the character of the book.

The lower court case of Regina v. Thomson, 64 J. P. 456 (1900), in which the jury found defendant not guilty in an issue of whether or not the "Heptameron," by Queen Margaret of Navarre, was obscene, is interesting because of the charge of Bosanquet, C. S. It is the first mention that I have found in the English reports of the idea that fashions in obscenity change. After mentioning that in the Middle Ages things were discussed which would not be tolerated now, if given general publicity, Sergeant Bosanquet left it to the jury to say "whether the book is a fit book to put into people's hands in these days at the end of the nineteenth century." The jury felt that it was.

Sergeant Bosanquet was referred to with respect in Rex v. Barraclough, L. R. 1 K. B. 201 (1906), but the opinions, while mentioning Regina v. Hicklin indirectly, decided a point under a new act of Parliament as to what the indictment should contain. A conviction for publishing an obscene typewritten document that libeled one Edith Woodhead was upheld.

In Rex v. Montalk, 23 Cr. App. Rep. 182 (1932), a conviction for publishing a typewritten libel was sustained, the lord chief justice citing Regina v. Hicklin in a very brief opinion. In the court below, the recorder charged the jury that if it was of the opinion "that this can be for the public good as an advancement of literature, in my opinion that would be a defense." The libel was not a book but a series of verses on half a dozen sheets of paper.

This exhausts the reported English cases that are in point. They show continued adherence to the Hicklin rule, but the paucity of authority is noteworthy. It is as if the English public does not want to risk the severity of the common law, and it is clear proof to me of the clinical nature of the laws that are made to cover social situations. While the higher English courts were kept relatively idle on the question, private censorship in England has been very active; the most effective censor of the Victorian era was Mudie's circulating library. It was the time of the three-decker novel—ponderous, dull, and pure as the driven snow. When Mudie's power was finally broken, smaller circulating libraries continued to wield the same sort of influence and to reflect the general desire of the public for no disturbing material of an emotional nature. England was the pioneer in the advance of the Industrial Age, and the nation of shopkeepers was unwilling to be diverted from making money by sidetrips into erotica; what individuals did in the dark was their affair, but bad morals could not profitably become a matter of public concern.

The rule of Regina v. Hicklin suited the English, and presumably still does—not as a satisfying standard but as an effective policeman to take over and tone down the situation when the social experiment threatens to get out of hand.

Censorship should be the proper activity of the community rather than of the law, and the community has never been lazy upholding what it believes to be inherently decent at the moment. With a legal policeman handy, the market place is the best crucible in which to distil an instinctive morality. We have the evidence of Milton that there is no authoritative example of the suppression of a book in ancient times solely because of obscenity, but this does not mean that private criticism was not alert. Plato thought that Homer should be expurgated before Greek children should be allowed to read him. In Plutarch's opinion the comedies of Aristophanes were coarse and vulgar.

This is healthy, for it is the struggle of free opinion: it is not suppression by law. In the English community the people argue and Hicklin stands guard in case of trouble. The Ameri-

104 *The courts look at books*

can method is different: the rule has been modernized.

THE AMERICAN CASES

1. *The Federal Courts*. There are two important opinions involving James Joyce's "Ulysses." Judge Woolsey's, in the district court, is reported as United States v. One Book Entitled "Ulysses," 5 F. Supp. 182 (S. D. N. Y., 1933), and Judge Hand's, affirming Judge Woolsey, is reported in 72 F.(2d) 705 (C. C. A. 2d, 1934).

Judge Woolsey's decision may well be considered the keystone of the modern American rule, as it brings out clearly that indictable obscenity must be "dirt for dirt's sake." He said:

"It is because Joyce has been loyal to his technique and has not funked its necessary implications, but has honestly attempted to tell fully what his characters think about, that he has been the subject of so many attacks and that his purpose has been so often misunderstood and misrepresented. For his attempt sincerely and honestly to realize his objective has required him incidentally to use certain words which are generally considered dirty words and has led at times to what many think is a too poignant pre-occupation with sex in the thoughts of his characters.

"The words which are criticized as dirty are old, Saxon words known to almost all men and, I venture, to many women, and are such words as would be naturally and habitually used, I believe, by the types of folk whose life, physical and mental, Joyce is seeking to describe.... As I have stated, 'Ulysses' is not an easy book to read. It is brilliant and dull, intelligible and obscure, by turns. In many places it seems to me to be disgusting, but although it contains, as I have mentioned above, many words usually considered dirty, I have not found anything that I consider to be dirt for dirt's sake. Each word of the book contributes like a bit of mosaic to the detail of the picture which Joyce is seeking to construct for his readers.

"If one does not wish to associate with such folk as Joyce describes, that is one's own choice. In order to avoid indirect contact with them one may not wish to read 'Ulysses'; that is quite understandable. But when such a great artist in words, as Joyce undoubtedly is, seeks to draw a true picture of the lower middle class in a European city, ought it to be impossible for the American public legally to see that picture?"

In affirming Judge Woolsey, Judge Hand said, in the circuit court of appeals:

"That numerous long passages in 'Ulysses' contain matter that is obscene under any fair definition of the word cannot be gainsaid; yet they are relevant to the purpose of depicting the thoughts of the characters and are introduced to give meaning to the whole, rather than to promote lust or portray filth for its own sake. The net effect even of portions most open to attack, such as the closing monologue of the wife of Leopold Bloom, is pitiful and tragic, rather than lustful. The book depicts the souls of men and women that are by turns bewildered and keenly apprehensive, sordid and aspiring, ugly and beautiful, hateful and loving. In the end one feels, more than anything else, pity and sorrow for the confusion, misery, and degradation of humanity.... The book as a whole is not pornographic, and, while in not a few spots it is coarse, blasphemous, and obscene, it does not, in our opinion, tend to promote lust. The erotic passages are submerged in the book as a whole and have little resultant effect."

In the circuit court Judge Manton dissented, and his opinion reviews the earlier Federal cases which he asserts approve the rule of Regina v. Hicklin . . .

These cases were individually and carefully distinguished by Judge Hand in the majority opinion, who held them not to represent the law:

"But it is argued that United States v. Bennett, Fed. Cas. No. 14,571, stands in the way of what has been said, and it certainly does. There a court, consisting of Blatchford, C.J., and Benedict and Choate, D.JJ., held that the offending paragraphs in a book could be taken from their context and the book judged by them alone, and that the test of obscenity was whether the tendency of these passages in themselves was 'to deprave the minds of those open to such influences and into whose hands a publication of this character might come.' The opinion was founded upon a dictum of Cockburn, C.J., in Regina v. Hicklin, L. R. 3 Q. B. 360, where half of a book written to attack the alleged practices of the confession was obscene and contained, as Mellor, J., said 'a great deal . . . which there cannot be any necessity for in any legitimate argument on the confessional. . . .' It is said that in Rosen v. United States, 161 U. S. 29, 16 S.

Ct. 434, 480, 40 L. Ed. 606, the Supreme Court cited and sanctioned Regina v. Hicklin, and United States v. Bennett. The subject matter of Rosen v. United States was, however, a pictorial representation of 'females, in different attitudes of indecency.' The figures were partially covered 'with lamp black that could be easily erased with a piece of bread.' P. 31 of 161 U. S., 16 S. Ct. 434. The pictures were evidently obscene, and plainly came within the statute prohibiting their transportation. The citation of Regina v. Hicklin and United States v. Bennett, was in support of a ruling that allegations in the indictment as to an obscene publication need only be made with sufficient particularity to inform the accused of the nature of the charge against him. No approval of other features of the two decisions was expressed, nor were such features referred to. Dunlop v. United States, 165 U. S. 486, 489, 17 S. Ct. 375, 41 L. Ed. 799, also seems to be relied on by the government, but the publication there was admittedly obscene and the decision in no way sanctioned the rulings in United States v. Bennett, which we first mentioned. The rigorous doctrines laid down in that case are inconsistent with our own decision in United States v. Dennett, (C. C. A.) 39 F.(2d) 564, 76 A. L. R. 1092, as well as with Konda v. United States, (C. C. A.) 166 F. 91, 92, 22 L. R. A. (N. S.) 304; Clark v. United States, (C. C. A.) 211 F. 916, 922; Halsey v. New York Society for the Suppression of Vice, 234 N. Y. 1, 4, 136 N. E. 219; and St. Hubert Guild v. Quinn, 64 Misc. 336, 339, 118 N. Y. S. 582, and, in our opinion, do not represent the law. They would exclude much of the great works of literature and involve an impracticability that cannot be imputed to Congress and would in the case of many books containing obscene passages inevitably require the court that uttered them to restrict their applicability."

It is quite clear that the harsh rule of Regina v. Hicklin has been supplanted by the modern test of obscenity, namely, whether the matter in question has a substantial tendency to deprave or corrupt by inciting lascivious thoughts or arousing lustful desire in the ordinary reader. This has been stated in various ways.

It has been said that the matter charged, to be obscene, must "suggest impure or libidinous thoughts," must "invite to lewd and lascivious practices and conduct," must "be offensive to chastity," must "incite dissolute acts," must "create a desire for gratification of animal passions," must "encourage unlawful indulgences of lust," must "attempt to satisfy the morbid appetite of the salacious," must "pander to the prurient taste." . . .

In Walker v. Popenoe, 149 F.(2d) 511 (1945), it was held:

"The effect of a publication on the ordinary reader is what counts. The Statute does not intend that we shall 'reduce our treatment of sex to the standard of a child's library in the supposed interest of a salacious few.'"

This test, however, should not be left to stand alone, for there is another element of equal importance—the tenor of the times and the change in social acceptance of what is inherently decent. This element is clearly set forth in United States v. Kennerley, 209 Fed. 119 (D. C., N. Y., 1913), where Judge Hand said:

"If there be no abstract definition, such as I have suggested, should not the word 'obscene' be allowed to indicate the present critical point in the compromise between candor and shame at which the community may have arrived here and now? . . . Nor is it an objection, I think, that such an interpretation gives to the words of the statute a varying meaning from time to time. Such words as these do not embalm the precise morals of an age or place; while they presuppose that some things will always be shocking to the public taste, the vague subject matter is left to the gradual development of general notions about what is decent."

In his The Paradoxes of Legal Science, Mr. Justice Cardozo said: "Law accepts as the pattern of its justice the morality of the community whose conduct it assumes to regulate" (p. 37). In Towne v. Eisner, 245 U. S., 418, 425, 62 L. Ed. 372, 376 (1918) Mr. Justice Holmes said: "A word is not a crystal, transparent and unchanged, it is the skin of a living thought and may vary greatly in color and content according to the circumstances and the time in which it is used." And in the same vein, Professor Wormser wrote in The Development of the Law, 23 Columbia Law Review, 701, 702 (1923): "Increasingly—ever increasingly—the community is beginning to require of the law that it justify its own administration of its resources before the bar of public opinion. And in order to justify itself before this critical bar, the law must be brought to evidence the mores of the times, to which it must conform, or it will fail to fulfill its function as the judicial expression of the community passion for justice and right dealing."

2. *The New York Courts.* The modern test was applied in People v. Wendling, 258 N. Y. 451 (1932), which involved the dramatization of the song "Frankie and Johnnie." In holding that the courts are not censors of morals and manners, Judge Pound said:

"The language of the play is coarse, vulgar and profane; the plot cheap and tawdry. As a dramatic composition it serves to degrade the stage where vice is thought by some to lose 'half its evil by losing all its grossness.' 'That it is "indecent" from every consideration of propriety is entirely clear' (People v. Eastman, 188 N. Y. 478, 480), but the court is not a censor of plays and does not attempt to regulate manners. One may call a spade a spade without offending decency, although modesty may be shocked thereby. (People v. Muller, 96 N. Y. 408, 411). The question is not whether the scene is laid in a low dive where refined people are not found or whether the language is that of the bar room rather than the parlor. The question is whether the tendency of the play is to excite lustful and lecherous desire. (People v. Eastman, supra; People v. Muller, supra)."

Since the New York cases are generally in line with the modern Federal rule above stated, it is necessary only to cite the principal ones: Halsey v. N. Y. Society for the Suppression of Vice, 234 N. Y. 1 (1922), which involved Theophile Gautier's "Mademoiselle de Maupin"; People v. Brainard, 192 App. Div. (N. Y.) 816 (1920), where the subject was "Madeleine," the anonymous autobiography of a prostitute.

3. *The Massachusetts Courts.* Boston has long been the center of book suppression in this country. Before 1930 the Massachusetts obscenity statute forbade the sale of any book "*containing obscene, indecent language.*" The Supreme Court upheld convictions for the sale of Dreiser's "An American Tragedy" and D. H. Lawrence's "Lady Chatterley's Lover." After a general wave of censorship that swept over Boston in 1929 and resulted in the suppression of 68 books, the law was changed to proscribe the sale of "a book which *is* obscene, indecent," etc.

The result was the modern rule, but the Massachusetts courts were still severe with individual books. Commonwealth v. Isenstadt, 318 Mass. 543 (1945), upheld a conviction for the sale of "Strange Fruit," and while it announced the modern rule to great extent, it refused to sanction the idea that sincerity of purpose and artistic merit would necessarily dispel obscenity. But it clearly held that the time and custom of the community are important elements. . . . :

"Since effect is the test, it follows that a book is to be judged in the light of the customs and habits of thought of the time and place of the alleged offense. Although the fundamentals of human nature change but slowly, if indeed they change at all, customs and habits of thought do vary with time and place. That which may give rise to impure thought and action in a highly conventional society may pass almost unnoticed in a society habituated to greater freedom."

In the very recent case of Attorney General v. Book Named "Forever Amber," decided October 11, 1948, and reported in 81 N. E. (2d) 663, the court repeated the stand it took in Commonwealth v. Isenstadt, supra, but it goes further on the question of sincerity and artistic purpose when the court said:

"It (the book) undoubtedly has historical purpose, and in this is adequately accurate in achievement. . . . The paramount impression is of an unfortunate country and its people as yet unfreed of the grasp of the Stuarts. . . . As to the individual characters, the reader is left with an estimate of an unattractive, hedonistic group, whose course of conduct is abhorrent and whose mode of living can be neither emulated nor envied."

THE MODERN TEST OF OBSCENITY

From all of these cases the modern rule is that obscenity is measured by the erotic allurement upon the average modern reader; that the erotic allurement of a book is measured by whether it is sexually impure—i.e., pornographic, "dirt for dirt's sake," a calculated incitement to sexual desire—or whether it reveals an effort to reflect life, including its dirt, with reasonable accuracy and balance; and that mere coarseness or vulgarity is not obscenity.

Forging such a rule from the precedents does not fully reach the heart of the matter, for I am sure that the books before me could be declared obscene or not obscene under either the Hicklin or the modern rule. Current standards create both the book and the judgment of it.

The evil of an indefinite statute like our section 524, however, is that it is also too loose. Current standards of what is obscene can swing to extremes if the entire question is left open, and even in the domestic laboratories of the States such freedom cannot safely be allowed. It is no longer possible that free speech be guaranteed Federally and denied locally; under modern methods of instantaneous communication such a discrepancy makes no sense. If speech is to be free anywhere, it must be free everywhere, and a law that can be used as a spigot that allows speech to flow freely or to be checked altogether is a general threat to free opinion and enlightened solution. What is said in Pennsylvania may clarify an issue in California, and what is suppressed in California may leave us the worse in Pennsylvania. Unless a restriction on free speech be of National validity, it can no longer have any local validity whatever. Some danger to us all must appear before any of us can be muzzled.

In the field of written obscenity this principle has met oblique acceptance with regard to what is called "the classics," which are now exempt from legal censorship. Just how old a work must be before it can enjoy this immunity is uncertain, but what we know as classics are the books by remarkable people that have withstood the test of time and are accepted as having lasting value; they have become historical samples, which itself is important. This importance could not be as great if the screening process were not free.

Current literature, good, bad, or indifferent, goes into the hopper without any background for judgment; it is in the idiom of the moment and is keyed to the tempo of modern life. I do not believe that such considerations should result in removing any of the output from the hopper before the process of screening can begin. What is pure dirt to some may be another's sincere effort to make clear a point, and there is not much difference, from the historical angle, between censoring books before publication and suppressing them afterwards, before there has been a reasonable chance to judge them. Blackstone's neat distinction may satisfy an exact legal mind, but it has no meaning for history. The unworthy books will die soon enough, but the great work of genius has a hard enough time to make its way even in the free market of thought. James Joyce, whose work is difficult to understand, even after years of study, has evolved a new form of communication, by his method of using words, that will some day be a shorthand for complexity. The public was deprived for years of this work of genius because someone found objectionable passages in it.

I can find no universally valid restriction on free expression to be drawn from the behavior of "l'homme moyen sensuel," who is the average modern reader. It is impossible to say just what his reactions to a book actually are. Moyen means, generally, average, and average means a median between extremes. If he reads an obscene book when his sensuality is low, he will yawn over it or find that its suggestibility leads him off on quite different paths. If he reads the Mechanics' Lien Act while his sensuality is high, things will stand between him and the page that have no business there. How can anyone say that he will infallibly be affected one way or another by one book or another? When, where, how, and why are questions that cannot be answered clearly in this field. The professional answer that is suggested is the one general compromise—that the appetite of sex is old, universal, and unpredictable, and that the best we can do to keep it within reasonable bounds is to be our brother's keeper and censor, because we never know when his sensuality may be high. This does not satisfy me, for in a field where even reasonable precision is utterly impossible, I trust people more than I do the law. Had legal censorship been as constant throughout the centuries as the law of murder, rape, theft, and negligence, a case for the compromise could be made out; as it is, legal censorship is not old, it is not popular, and it has failed to strengthen the private censor in each individual that has kept the race as decent as it has been for several thousand years. I regard legal censorship as an experiment of more than dubious value.

I am well aware that the law is not ready to discard censorship altogether. The English keep their policeman handy, just in case, and the modern rule is a more efficient policeman. Its scope, however, must be defined with regard to the universal right of free speech, as limited only by some universally valid restriction required by a clear and present danger. For this we must consider the Constitution and the cases lately decided under it.

CONSTITUTIONAL QUESTIONS

The fourteenth amendment to the Federal Constitution prohibits any State from encroaching upon freedom of speech and freedom of the press to the same extent that the first amendment prevents the Federal Congress from doing so . . .

The principle of a free press covers distribution as well as publication . . .

These guarantees occupy a preferred position under our law to such an extent that the courts, when considering whether legislation infringes upon them, neutralize the presumption usually indulged in favor of constitutionality . . .

And article 1, sec. 7 of the Pennsylvania Constitution states that:

"The free communication of thoughts and opinions is one of the invaluable rights of man, and every citizen may freely speak, write and print on any subject, being responsible for the abuse of that liberty."

When the first amendment came before the Supreme Court for interpretation in Reynolds v. United States, 98 U. S. 145 (1878), the court declared that government had no authority whatsoever in the field of thought or opinion: only in the area of conduct or action could it step in. Chief Justice Waite said: (p. 164)

"Congress was deprived of all legislative power over mere opinion, but was left free to reach actions which were in violation of social duties or subversive of good order."

Quoting from Jefferson's bill for establishing religious freedom, the Chief Justice stated:

" 'That to suffer the Civil magistrate to intrude his powers into the field of opinion, and to restrain the profession or propagation of principles on supposition of their *ill tendency,* is a dangerous fallacy which at once destroys all religious liberty . . . it is time enough for the rightful purposes of civil government for its officers to interfere *when principles break out into overt acts against peace and good order.' In these two sentences is found the true distinction between what properly belongs to the church and what to the State.*" (Italics supplied.)

The now familiar "clear and present danger" rule, first stated by Mr. Justice Holmes in Schenck v. United States, 249 U. S. 47 (1918), represents a compromise between the ideas of Jefferson and those of the judges, who had in the meantime departed from the forthright views of the great statesman. Under that rule the publisher of a writing may be punished if the publication in question creates a clear and present danger that there will result from it some substantive evil which the legislature has a right to proscribe and punish.

The famous illustration in the Schenck case was:

"The most stringent protection of free speech would not protect a man in falsely shouting fire in a theater and causing a panic. It does not even protect a man from an injunction against uttering words that may have all the effect of force."

Mr. Justice Brandeis added, in Whitney v. California, 274 U. S. 357 (1927), the idea that free speech may not be curbed where the community has the chance to answer back. He said:

"Those who won our independence by revolution were not cowards. They did not fear political change. They did not exalt order at the cost of liberty. To courageous, self-reliant men, with confidence in the power of free and fearless reasoning applied through the processes of popular government, *no danger flowing from speech can be deemed clear and present, unless the incidence of the evil apprehended is so imminent that it may befall before there is opportunity for full discussion.* If there be time to expose through discussion the falsehood and fallacies, to avert the evil by the processes of education, *the remedy to be applied is more speech, not enforced silence. Only an emergency can justify repression.* Such must be the rule if authority is to be reconciled with freedom. Such, in my opinion, is the command of the Constitution. It is therefore always open to Americans to challenge a law abridging free speech and assembly by showing that there was no emergency justifying it. (Italics supplied.)

"Moreover, even imminent danger cannot justify resort to prohibition of these functions essential to effective democracy, unless the evil apprehended is relatively serious. Prohibition of free speech and assembly is a measure so stringent that it would be inappropriate as the means for averting a relatively trivial harm to society. A police measure may be unconstitutional merely because the remedy, although effective as means of protection, is unduly harsh or oppressive. Thus, a State might, in the exercise of its police power, make any trespass upon the land of another a crime, regardless of the results or of the intent or purpose of the trespasser. It might, also, punish an attempt, a conspiracy, or an incitement to commit the trespass. But it is hardly conceivable that this Court would hold constitutional a statute which punished as a felony the mere voluntary assembly with a society formed to teach that pedestrians had the moral right to cross unenclosed, unposted, waste lands and to advocate their doing so, even if there was imminent danger that advocacy would lead to a trespass. The fact that speech is likely to result in some violence or in destruction of property is not enough to justify its suppression. There must be the probability of serious injury to the State. Among free men, the deterrents ordinarily to be applied to prevent crime are education and punishment for violations of the law, not abridgment of the rights of free speech and assembly."

It is true that subsequent to the decision of the court in the Schenck case, Justices Holmes and Brandeis fought what for a time appeared to be a losing battle. To them the "clear and present danger" rule was a rule of the criminal law, and they applied it only to prohibit speech which incited to punishable conduct. See the dissenting opinion in Gitlow v. New York, 268 U. S. 652 (1925), where they say:

"If the publication of this document had been laid as *an attempt* to induce an uprising against government at once and not at some indefinite time in the future it would have presented a different question. The object would have been one with which the law might deal, subject to the doubt whether there was any danger that the publication could produce any result, or in other words, whether it was not futile and too remote from possible consequences. *But the indictment alleges the publication and nothing more.*" (Italics supplied.)

The history of the Supreme Court, since its decision in Gitlow v. New York, has been marked by gradual progress along the path staked out by Justices Holmes and Brandeis, culminating finally in the complete acceptance of their views. . . .

As was said in Martin v. Struthers, 319 U. S. 141 (1943):

"The right of freedom of speech and press has broad scope. The authors of the First Amendment knew that novel and unconventional ideas might disturb the complacent, but they chose to encourage a freedom which they believed essential if vigorous enlightenment was ever to triumph over slothful ignorance. This freedom embraces the right to distribute literature, Lovell v. Griffin (citation), and necessarily protects the right to receive it."

There are other milestones in the judicial re-establishment of freedom of speech and freedom of the press. We cite the language of the Supreme Court in some of those cases:

In Herndon v. Lowry, 301 U. S. 242 (1937), the court said:

"The power of a state to abridge freedom of speech and of assembly is the exception rather than the rule and the penalizing even of utterances of a defined character must find its justification in a reasonable apprehension of danger to organized government. The judgment of the legislature is not unfettered."

In DeJonge v. Oregon, 299 U. S. 353 (1937), the court said:

"These rights may be abused by using speech or press or assembly *in order to incite to violence and crime*. The people through their legislatures may protect themselves against that abuse. But the legislative intervention can find constitutional justification only by dealing with the abuse. The rights themselves must not be curtailed." (Italics supplied.)

In Thornhill v. Alabama, 310 U. S. 88 (1940), the court said:

"Every expression of opinion on matters that are important has the potentiality of inducing action in the interests of one rather than another group in society. But the group in power at any moment may not impose penal sanctions on peaceful and truthful discussion of matters of public interest merely on a showing that others may thereby be persuaded to take action inconsistent with its interests. Abridgement of the liberty of such discussion can be justified only where the clear danger of substantive evils arises *under circumstances affording no opportunity to test the merits of ideas by competition for acceptance in the market of public opinion.*" (Italics supplied.)

The nature of the evil which the legislature has the power to guard against by enacting an obscenity statute is not clearly defined. As Jefferson saw it, the legislature was restricted to punishing criminal acts and not publications. To Holmes and Brandeis the bookseller could be punished if his relation to the criminal act was such that he could be said to have incited it. In neither view could the bookseller be punished if his books merely "tended" to result in illegal acts and much less if his books "tended" to lower the moral standards of the community. A much closer relationship was required. The legislature may validly prevent criminal acts and legislate to protect the moral standards of the community. But the threat must in either case be more than a mere tendency. The older cases which upheld obscenity statutes on the "tendency" theory would appear to be invalid in the light of the more recent expressions of the Supreme Court.

Thus the opinion of the Supreme Court in Bridges v. California, 314 U. S. 252 (1941) says: (p. 273)

"In accordance with what we have said on the 'clear and present danger' cases, neither 'inherent tendency' nor 'reasonable tendency' is enough to justify a restriction of free expression."

In Pennekamp v. Florida, 328 U. S. 331 (1946), a case in which the resulting evil was said to be that of improperly influencing the administration of justice, the Supreme Court said, in discussing the Bridges case:

"In the Bridges Case the clear and present danger rule was applied to the stated issue of whether the expressions there under consideration prevented 'fair judicial trials free from coercion or intimidation.' Page 259. There was, of course, no question as to the power to punish for disturbances and disorder in the courtroom. Page 266. The danger to be guarded against is the 'substantive evil' sought to be prevented. Pages 261, 262, 263. In the Bridges Case that 'substantive evil' was primarily the 'disorderly and unfair administration of justice.' Pages 270, 271, 278."

In addition to being substantive, the evil which the legislature seeks to control must be substantial: Bridges v. California, supra. The evil consequence must be serious and the imminence high; the proof must be clear, that is to say, "a solidity of evidence should be required": Pennekamp v. Florida, supra. Or, as was said in a contempt of court case (Craig v. Harney, 331 U. S. 367 (1947)):

"The fires which it kindles must constitute an imminent, not merely a likely, threat to the administration of Justice. The danger must not be remote or even probable; *it must immediately imperil.*" (Italics supplied.)

These principles have not been applied specifically to an obscenity statute by any recent opinion of the United States Supreme Court, but as Mr. Justice Rutledge said orally when the "Hecate County" case, Doubleday & Co., Inc. v. People of New York, 93 L. Ed. 37 (an obscenity case), was recently argued before the court:

"Before we get to the question of clear and present danger, we've got to have something which the State can forbid as dangerous. We are talking in a vacuum until we can establish that there is some occasion for the exercise of the State's power."

"Yes, you must first ascertain the substantive evil at which the statute is aimed, and then determine whether the publication of this book constitutes a clear and present danger."

"It is up to the State to demonstrate that there was a danger, and until they demonstrate that, plus the clarity and imminence of the danger, the constitutional prohibition would seem to apply." (Italics supplied.) (Quoted in 17 U. S. Law Week (Supreme Court Sections 3118).)

This appears to me much closer to a correct solution of obscenity cases than several general dicta by the Supreme Court to the effect that obscenity is indictable just because it is obscenity. For example, in Near v. Minnesota, 283 U. S. 697 (1931), Chief Justice Hughes remarked: "On similar grounds, the primary requirements of decency may be enforced against obscene publications."

It seems impossible, in view of the late decisions under the first amendment, that the word "obscene" can any longer stand alone, lighted up only by a vague and mystic sense of impurity, unless it is interpreted by other solid factors such as clear and present danger, pornography, and divorcement from mere coarseness of vulgarity.

In Chaplinsky v. New Hampshire, 315 U. S. 568 (1942), however, Mr. Justice Murphy said this: (p. 571)

"There are certain well-defined and narrowly limited classes of speech, the prevention and punishment of which have never been thought to raise any constitutional problem. These include the lewd and obscene, the profane, the libellous, and the insulting or 'fighting' words—those which by their very utterance inflict injury or tend to incite an immediate breach of the peace."

It is not clear to me, nor, I venture to assert, would it be to the Supreme Court, if faced directly by an appropriate case of literary obscenity, what words inflict injury by their very utterance or how such injury is inflicted. As for the notion of an obscene book tending to incite to an immediate breach of the peace, the proper point of emphasis is the breach of the peace. That is different from saying that obscenity automatically tends to a breach of the peace, for the idea is unreal.

The latest dictum on this subject is in Kovacs v. Cooper, decided on January 31, 1949, and reported in 17 U. S. Law Week 4163, where Mr. Justice Reed said:

"But in the *Winters* case (Winters v. New York, 333 U. S. 507 (1948)) we pointed out that prosecutions might be brought under statutes punishing the distribution of 'obscene, lewd, lascivious, filthy, indecent and disgusting' magazines. P. 511. We said, p. 518:

"'The impossibility of defining the precise line between permissible uncertainty in statutes caused by describing crimes by words well understood through long use in the criminal law—obscene, lewd, lascivious, filthy, indecent or disgusting—and the unconstitutional vagueness that leaves a person uncertain as to the kind of prohibited conduct—massing stories to incite crime—has resulted in three arguments of this case in this Court.'"

The difficulty here is that insofar as they apply to literature, obscenity and its imposing string of synonyms do *not* have a fixed meaning through long use in the criminal law—or to put it the other way, that they have a very narrow and restricted meaning quite at variance with the assumption that obscenity debauches public morals by a mysterious and self-executing process that can be feared but not proved.

Certainly the books before me do not command, or urge, or incite, or even encourage persons to commit sexual misconduct of a nature that the legislature has the right to prevent or punish. Nor are they an imminent threat to the morality of the community as a whole. The conduct described in them is at most offensive. It does not incite to unlawfulness of any kind. These facts are important in view of the following language of Justice Rutledge, speaking for Justices Murphy, Douglas and himself (the other members of the court did not reach the question) in Musser v. Utah, 333 U. S. 95 (1948):

"The Utah statute was construed to proscribe any agreement to advocate the practice of polygamy. Thus the line was drawn between discussion and advocacy.

"The Constitution requires that the statute be limited more narrowly. *At the very least the line must be drawn between advocacy and incitement, and even the state's* power to punish incitement may vary with the nature of the speech, whether persuasive or coercive, the nature of the wrong induced, whether violent or merely offensive to the mores, and the degree of probability that the substantive evil actually will result." (Italics supplied.)

Freedom of expression is the touchiest and most important right we have; it is asserted frequently and vigorously, for the democratic process rests fundamentally on the need of people to argue, exhort, and clarify. Thomas v. Collins, supra (323 U. S. 516) speaks of ". . . the preferred place given in our scheme to the great, the indispensable democratic freedoms secured by the First Amendment," and went on to say, at page 530:

"For these reasons any attempt to restrict those liberties must be justified by clear public interest, threatened not doubtfully or remotely, but by clear and present danger. The rational connection between the remedy provided and the evil to be curbed, which in other contexts might support legislation against attack on due process grounds, will not suffice. These rights rest on firmer foundation. Accordingly, whatever occasion would restrain orderly discussion and persuasion, at appropriate time and place, *must have clear support in public danger, actual or impending.* Only the gravest abuses, endangering paramount interest, give occasion for permissible limitation." (Italics supplied.) . . .

Mr. Justice Frankfurter sounds the warning that the phrase "preferred position" should not be allowed to become a rigid formula, lest another one grow beside it—that any legislative restriction on free speech be considered "presumptively invalid." The warning is well taken, for there are too many kinds of restriction as well as vehicles of free speech to warrant such rigidity. The Kovacs and Sara cases involve loud speakers and sound trucks, which are perilously close to nuisances and even to threats to public health.

112 The courts look at books

There are many instances where the police power may be used, at the expense of free expression, where the threat to order or health is directly and imminently demonstrable. The point is to see and understand the danger, and to keep particular cases within or without the justifiable area of the police power.

Short of books that are sexually impure and pornographic, I can see no rational legal catalyst that can detect or define a clear and present danger inherent in a writing or that can demonstrate what result ensues from reading it. All that is relied upon in a prosecution, is an indefinable fear for other people's moral standards—a fear that I regard as a democratic anomaly.

Finally, the Supreme Court, in Winters v. New York, supra (333 U. S. 507), held subdivision 2 of section 1141 of New York's Penal Law unconstitutional because it was vague and allowed punishment of matters within the protection of free speech. The court said:

"The appellant contends that the subsection violates the right of free speech and press because it is vague and indefinite. *It is settled that a statute so vague and indefinite, in form and as interpreted, as to permit within the scope of its language the punishment of incidents fairly within the protection of the guarantee of free speech is void, on its face, as contrary to the Fourteenth Amendment.* Stromberg v. California, 283 US 359, 369; Herndon v. Lowry, 301 US 242, 258. A failure of a statute limiting freedom of expression to give fair notice of what acts will be punished and such a statute's inclusion of prohibitions against expressions, protected by the principles of the First Amendment, violates an accused's rights under procedural due process and freedom of speech or press." (Italics supplied.)

I am clear that the books before me are within the protection of the first and fourteenth amendments of the Federal Constitution, and of article 1, sec. 7 of the Pennsylvania Constitution. They bear obvious internal evidence of an effort to portray certain segments of American life, including parts that more refined people than the characters may deplore, but which we know exist. The vulgarity and obscenity in them are inherent in the characters themselves and are obviously not set forth as erotic allurement or as an excuse for selling the volumes. Nor can it be said that they have the effect of inciting to lewdness, or of inciting to any sexual crime, or that they are sexually impure and pornographic, i. e., "dirt for dirt's sake."

DEFINITION OF OBSCENITY AS SEXUAL IMPURITY

Sexual impurity in literature (pornography, as some of the cases call it) I define as any writing whose dominant purpose and effect is erotic allurement—that is to say, a calculated and effective incitement to sexual desire. It is the effect that counts, more than the purpose, and no indictment can stand unless it can be shown. This definition is in accord with the cases that have restricted the meaning of obscenity and its synonyms to that of sexual impurity, and with those cases that have made erotic allurement the test of its effect.

This excludes from pornography medical or educational writings, whether in technical or layman's language, and whether used only in schools or generally distributed, whose dominant purpose and effect is exegetical and instructional rather than enticing. It leaves room for interpretation of individual books, for as long as censorship is considered necessary, it is as impossible as it is inadvisable to find a self-executing formula.

Sex education has been before the courts in many cases. In United States v. "Married Love," 48 F. (2d) 821 (1931), Judge Woolsey said:

"It makes also some apparently justified criticisms of the inopportune exercise by the man in the marriage relation of what are often referred to as his conjugal or marital rights, and it pleads with seriousness, and not without some eloquence, for a better understanding by husbands of the physical and emotional side of the sex life of their wives. I do not find anything exceptionable anywhere in the book, and I cannot imagine a normal mind to which this book would seem to be obscene or immoral within the proper definition of these words, or whose sex impulses would be stirred by reading it."

Judge Woolsey held similarly in United States v. "Contraception," 51 F. (2d) 525 (1931). Both of the above books were by Dr. Marie C. Stopes.

The case of United States v. Dennett, 39 F. (2d) 564 (C. C. A. 2d, 1930), involved a pamphlet written by a woman for the education of her children. Sections of it appear in the reporter's summary of the case, and show that it gave full and frank information, together with the view that the sexual impulse is not a base passion but is a great joy when accompanied by love between two human beings. In reversing a conviction, Judge Hand said:

"It also may reasonably be thought that accurate information, rather than mystery and curiosity, is better in the long run and is less likely to occasion lascivious thoughts than ignorance and anxiety. Perhaps instruction other than that which the defendant suggests would be better. That is a matter as to which there is bound to be a wide difference of opinion, but, irrespective of this, we hold that an accurate exposition of the relevant facts of the sex side of life in decent language and in manifestly serious and disinterested spirit cannot ordinarily be regarded as obscene. Any incidental tendency to arouse sex impulses which such a pamphlet may perhaps have, is apart from and subordinate to its main effect. The tendency can only exist in so far as it is inherent in any sex instruction, and it would seem to be outweighed by the elimination of ignorance, curiosity, and morbid fear. The direct aim and the net result is to promote understanding and self-control."

The definition of sexual impurity given above brings literary obscenity into workable analogy with sedition, blasphemy, open lewdness, and the other examples set forth earlier, as those terms are used in our Penal Code, except for one remaining point. Sedition, blasphemy, and open lewdness, by definition, carry their own threat of danger to the public peace. The deep and peculiar nature of religious faith is such that people are entitled to protection against those who call their gods in vain; religion has too recently and for too long been one of the greatest of the fighting faiths to assume that disorder will not follow from public irreverence. He who is publicly lewd is in himself an open and immediate invitation to morally criminal behavior. The pressing danger inherent in sedition speaks for itself.

A book, however sexually impure and pornographic, is in a different case. It cannot be a present danger unless its reader closes it, lays it aside, and transmutes its erotic allurement into overt action. That such action must inevitably follow as a direct consequence of reading the book does not bear analysis, nor is it borne out by general human experience; too much can intervene and too many diversions take place. It must be constantly borne in mind that section 524 does not include the element of debauching public morals or of seeking to alter the prevailing moral code. It only proscribes what *is* obscene, and that term is meaningless unless activated by precise dangers within legal limits. Since section 524 provides no standard, the danger and the limits must be found elsewhere, and the only clear and discernible ones are those having to do with the police power and the preservation of the peace.

THE CLEAR AND PRESENT DANGER

I have pointed out above that any test of the effect of obscenity is bound to be elusive. Section 524 is therefore vague, indefinite, and unconstitutional unless some exact definition can be found for the "clear and present danger" to be prevented that will satisfy the constitutional protection of free speech. There are various types of cases in which definition is clear because the need is clear. The police power operates in pure food cases because people can sicken and die from eating bad food; in traffic cases because people can be injured or killed unless there is regulation; in weights and measures cases because of the ease with which the consumer can be cheated, and in conventional crimes because of the threat to persons and property. The list could be extended.

Mr. Justice Holmes's example in Schenck v. United States is no test for the case before me; the public does not read a book and simultaneously rush by the hundreds into the streets to engage in orgiastic riots. Mr. Justice Brandeis's discussion in Whitney v. California is a better yardstick, for in the field of the printed word the community has full opportunity to answer back. How can it be said that there is a "clear and present danger"—granted that anyone can say what it is—when there is both time and means for ample discussion?

These words of Jefferson should not be forgotten:

"I deplore . . . the putrid state into which our newspapers have passed, and the malignity, the vulgarity, and the mendacious spirit of those who write them. . . . These ordures are rapidly depraving the public taste.

"It is, however, an evil for which there is no remedy: our liberty depends on the freedom of

114 *The courts look at books*

the press, and that cannot be limited without being lost."

Who can define the clear and present danger to the community that arises from reading a book? If we say it is that the reader is young and inexperienced and incapable of resisting the sexual temptations that the book may present to him, we put the entire reading public at the mercy of the adolescent mind and of those adolescents who do not have the expected advantages of home influence, school training, or religious teaching. Nor can we say into how many such hands the book may come. Adults, or even a gifted minor, may be capable of challenging the book in public and thus of forwarding the education and enlightenment of us all by free discussion and correction. If the argument be applied to the general public, the situation becomes absurd, for then no publication is safe. How is it possible to say that reading a certain book is bound to make people behave in a way that is socially undesirable? And beyond a reasonable doubt, since we are dealing with a penal statute?

We might remember the words of Macaulay: "We find it difficult to believe that in a world so full of temptations as this, any gentleman, whose life would have been virtuous if he had not read Aristophanes and Juvenal, will be made vicious by reading them."

Substitute the names of the books before me for "Aristophanes and Juvenal," and the analogy is exact.

The only clear and present danger to be prevented by section 524 that will satisfy both the Constitution and the current customs of our era is the commission or the imminence of the commission of criminal behavior resulting from the reading of a book. Publication alone can have no such automatic effect.

THE RULE OF DECISION

Thus limited, the constitutional operation of section 524 of our act rests on narrow ground.

The modern test of obscenity, as I have stated it above (page 106), furnishes a means of determining whether a book, taken as a whole, is sexually impure, as I have defined that term (page 112, ante).

I hold that section 524 may not constitutionally be applied to any writing unless it is sexually impure and pornographic. It may then be applied, as an exercise of the police power, only where there is a reasonable and demonstrable cause to believe that a crime or misdemeanor has been committed or is about to be committed as the perceptible result of the publication and distribution of the writing in question: the opinion of anyone that a tendency thereto exists or that such a result is self-evident is insufficient and irrelevant. The causal connection between the book and the criminal behavior must appear beyond a reasonable doubt. The criminal law is not, in my opinion, "the custos morum of the King's subjects," as Regina v. Hicklin states: it is only the custodian of the peace and good order that free men and women need for the shaping of their common destiny.

There is no such proof in the instant case.

For that reason, and also because of the character of the books themselves, I hold that the books before me are not sexually impure and pornographic, and are therefore not obscene, lewd, lascivious, filthy, indecent, or disgusting. The sustaining of the demurrers follows.

The same defendant and the same judge figured in two different censorship cases of unusual interest. The cases are noteworthy for the opinions produced by Judge Jerome Frank, rather than because of the fairly ordinary and routine issues involved.

The defendant, Samuel Roth, doing business in New York City, has had, according to the *Publishers' Weekly*, "a long career of publishing and mail-order selling materials skirting and, at times, crossing the borderline of the questionable." During his 1956 trial the prosecution contended that Roth had "been in this business almost 40 years and is one of the biggest dealers in obscenity in the nation," adding that he had distributed "more than 10,000,000 obscene circulars through the mails in the past 25 years." Roth's record revealed a number of federal and state convictions for trafficking in obscene literature.

In 1949, the Postmaster General excluded from the mails as "obscene, lewd, or lascivious" a small book, *Waggish Tales from the Czechs*, being distributed by Roth. Ostensibly these were stories "brought down from another era and clime," but according to the Postmaster General's charge they were "in fact American-made or shared smoking room jests and stories, obscene by any refined standards." When the U.S. District Court for the Southern District of New York held against Roth, he carried this case to the U.S. Court of Appeals, where it was heard before Circuit Judges Augustus N. Hand and Jerome Frank. The lower court's judgment was affirmed, but Judge Frank used the occasion to express certain views which he was forming on the subject of censorship and obscenity.

About seven years later, Judge Frank heard another Roth appeal—on this occasion from a conviction for mailing books, periodicals, and photographs alleged to be "obscene, lewd, lascivious, filthy and of an indecent character." Again the Court of Appeals sustained the District Court's verdict, with Judge Frank concurring. In the intervening years, however, Frank had apparently thought deeply about what he described as "a purely punitive obscenity statute." His views, he conceded, had been strongly influenced by Judge Curtis Bok, for Bok's "brilliant opinion, which states arguments that (so far as I know) have never been answered, nudged me into the skeptical views contained in this opinion and the Appendix." In the Appendix to the decision, to which Judge Frank referred, he explored in detail the difficulties in framing obscenity laws within the constitutional commitments to free speech.

Jerome Frank
ROTH
v. GOLDMAN

This is the first case in which I have sat where the validity of an administrative order suppressing a book allegedly obscene has been contested. Because of my judicial inexperience in this field, I yield in this case to the more experienced judgment of my colleagues. But I do so with much puzzlement, and with the hope that the Supreme Court will review our decision, thus dissipating the fogs which surround this subject. For, as I shall try to show, those fogs are indeed thick, and I find no clear light penetrating them either in my colleagues' opinion in this suit or elsewhere.

My private tastes are such that I think the American people will suffer no great loss if deprived of the opportunity to read "Waggish Tales from the Czechs." But far more is here involved than this particular book: Our decision will become a precedent—in a circuit which includes America's great publishing center—affecting the exercise of the right of free press guaranteed by the First Amendment. Our decision may put in peril other writings, of a higher order of excellence, which any man who happens at the moment to be Postmaster General happens to find offensive.

For my colleagues allow small room for court review, saying that the determination of obscenity "is committed in the first instance to an administrative office; and, under normal rules, therefore, judicial review channeled within the confines of a plea for an injunction should not be overextensive." That ruling vests immense administrative censorship authority in one fallible man, makes him an almost despotic arbiter of literary products. If one day he bans a mediocre book, another day he may do the same to a work of genius. Originality is not so common that we should lightly contemplate its potential stifling. And censorship does more than to keep finished books from being sold: it keeps many from ever being written. Tolstoy and other Russians of the Czarist era have told how fear of the censor impeded their creative writing. An American author's imagination may be severely cramped if he must write with one eye on the Postmaster General; authors must cope with publishers who, uncertain about that official's judgment, may refuse to accept the manuscripts of contemporary or future Shelleys or Whitmans.

Such a condition is compatible with the ideologies of Hitlers, Czars and Commissars. It does not accord with democratic ideals which repudiate thought-control. "Freedom of thought," it has been wisely said, ". . . is worthless unless it goes with freedom of expression. Thought is impossible without expression; thought is expression; an unexpressed thought, like an unlaid egg, comes to nothing. Given this freedom, then, other freedoms follow." The "right of expression beyond the conventions of the day," wrote Mr. Justice Frankfurter three years ago, is "the very basis of a free society." It would seem desirable that, in this industrial age, when economic pursuits will, perforce, become increasingly regulated by government, the realm of art should remain free, unregimented, the domain of unrestricted competition, free enterprise, and un-

---

Jerome Frank, "Roth v. Goldman," 172 *Federal Reporter*, 2d Series, 790–98, copyright 1949 by West Publishing Co. Reprinted (without amplifying footnotes) by permission of the publisher.

hampered individual initiative at its maximum. De gustibus non disputandum represents a cherished democratic maxim. Governmental control of the individual's taste may insidiously expand into menacing widespread anti-democratic practices. "Man," warned Goethe, "is easily accustomed to slavery and learns quickly to be obedient when his freedom is taken from him."

In that vein, President Franklin Roosevelt said: "The arts cannot thrive except where men are free to be themselves and to be in charge of the discipline of their own energies and ardors. The conditions for democracy and for art are one and the same. What we call liberty in politics results in freedom in the arts. . . . American artists . . . have no compulsion to be limited in method or manner of expression." Disturbed by the way my colleagues' ruling runs counter to that ideal, I think it not inappropriate to ask some questions.

1

In the light of the First Amendment, it is not, I think, frivolous to ask a question about the constitutional power of Congress to authorize an official to bar from the mails, and probably thus largely to suppress, any book or writing he finds obscene. For Mr. Justice Holmes, dissenting, with Mr. Justice Brandeis' concurrence, in Leach v. Carlile, 258 U.S. 138, 140, 141, 42 S.Ct. 227, 229, 66 L.Ed. 511, asserted the unconstitutionality of one of the very suppression statutes before us in this case, for the reason that the First Amendment was "intended to prevent restraints" except those needed "for the safety of the nation." Mr. Justice Frankfurter, concurring in Hannegan v. Esquire, Inc., 327 U.S. 146, 160, 66 S.Ct. 456, 90 L.Ed. 586, cited with approval the dissent in Leach v. Carlile. The majority of the Court in the Esquire case, speaking through Mr. Justice Douglas, remarked, 327 U.S. 156, 66 S.Ct. 461, that "grave constitutional questions are immediately raised once it is said that the use of the mails is a privilege which may be extended or withheld on any grounds whatsoever." It is germane here that several times the Supreme Court has with seeming approval referred to the distinction first proposed by Mr. Justice Stone in United States v. Carolene Products Co., 304 U.S. 144, 152 note, 58 S.Ct. 778, 783, 82 L.Ed. 1234: "There may be a narrower scope for operation of the presumption of constitutionality when legislation appears on its face to be within a specific prohibition of the Constitution, such as those of the first ten Amendments. . . ." Some there are who doubt the wisdom of that distinction; but members of an inferior court, like ours, may not judicially act on such doubts. Mr. Justice Frankfurter, concurring in the recent Kovacs case, objected to what he described as the oversimplified and dogmatic formulation of the distinction; yet he said that, since "without freedom of expression, thought becomes checked and atrophied," he would adhere to the views of Mr. Justice Holmes who "was far more ready to find legislative invasion [of the Constitution] where free inquiry was involved than in the debatable area of economics."

If we were dealing here with that part of the statute providing not for administrative suppression of an obscene book but for criminal punishment of one who had already published it, the question might be different (although in a case a few weeks ago, four Supreme Court Justices, out of the eight who participated, may perhaps have held even such punitive legislation, enacted by a State, violative of the constitutional right of free press and free speech).

The "safety of the Nation" exception would today, I think, be given a broader interpretation than Holmes'. It would, for example, include readily demonstrable social mischiefs such as commercial fraud and the like. It would doubtless justify suppression of a book if there were a "clear and present danger" that its words would bring about grave "substantive evils" adversely affecting the public interest. In terms of that exception, it may be urged that the reading of obscene books demonstrably entails such socially dangerous effects on normal persons as to empower Congress, notwithstanding the First Amendment, to direct suppression of those writings.

I think that no sane man thinks socially dangerous the arousing of normal sexual desires. Consequently, if reading obscene books has merely that consequence, Congress, it would seem, can constitutionally no more suppress such books than it can prevent the mailing of many other objects, such as perfumes, for example, which notoriously produce that result. But the constitutional power to suppress obscene publications might well exist if there were ample reason to believe that reading them conduces to socially harmful sexual conduct on the part of normal human beings. However, convincing proof of that fact has never been assembled. It may be exceedingly difficult to obtain. Perhaps in order to be trustworthy, such proof ought to be at least as extensive and intensive as the Kinsey Report. Macaulay, replying to demands for suppression of obscene books, said: "We find it difficult to believe that in a world so full of temptations as this, any gentleman, whose life would have been virtuous if he had not read Aristophanes and Juvenal, will be made vicious by reading them." Substitute "Waggish Tales from the Czechs" for "Aristophanes and Juvenal," and those remarks become relevant here.

Psychological studies in the last few decades suggest that all kinds of stimuli—for instance, the odor of lilacs or old leather, the sight of an umbrella or a candle, or the touch of a piece of silk or cheese-cloth—may be provocative of irregular sexual behavior in apparently normal men,—for all we know, far more provocative than the reading of obscene books. Perhaps further research will disclose that, for most men, such reading diverts from, rather than stimulates to, anti-social conduct (which, I take it, is what is meant by expressions, used in the cases, such as "sexual impurity," "corrupt and debauch the minds and morals").

Some dictionary definitions of "obscene"— as "disgusting," "loathesome," "repulsive"— may suggest that there is serious social danger, constitutionally justifying suppression, in the shock of obscene writings to normal susceptibilities. But there are indications that Thomas Jefferson and James Madison, no mean authorities when it comes to interpreting the First Amendment, recognized no such limitations on the free-press right.

It is not altogether impossible, then, that the Supreme Court, following the lead of Mr. Justice Holmes and Mr. Justice Brandeis, will strike down this suppression statute. But I do not venture so to prophesy.

2

If, however, it be true that "grave constitutional questions are immediately raised" by a statute authorizing an official to suppress books, one would suppose that such a statute, verging as it does on unconstitutionality, should at least contain unusual safeguards against arbitrary official incursions on the rights guaranteed by the First Amendment, and should be strictly interpreted so as to preclude doubts about its validity. To avoid unconstitutionality it might seem that the statute should provide some fairly precise standard to guide the officials' action, a standard far more precise than is necessary in those statutes, providing for administrative action, which do not come close to the very edge of constitutional power. If anyone regards as precise the standard in the obscenity statute, he cannot have read the pertinent cases. For see: At one time, the courts held that the existence of obscenity turned on the subjective intention of the author, regardless of the book's probable effect on readers. This test has now been abandoned; now the courts consider solely the author's "objective" intention, which equates with the book's effect on others. In other words, an author does not violate an obscenity statute if he writes and publishes a dainty ditty which he alone, of all men, believes obscene; his private, unsuccessfully communicated, thought and purposes are not a wrong. Also, at one time, a writing was held obscene if it would probably have a socially undesirable effect on the abnormal; but now the test has shifted and become that of the way the words will probably affect normal persons. A standard so difficult for our ablest judges to interpret is hardly precise. Nor are there any Supreme Court decisions which clarify it.

3

Let us assume, however, that we have a standard sufficiently precise to render the statute constitutional if it be interpreted to mean that a book is obscene which will probably have socially undesirable effects on normal readers. Even so, it is arguable that with a statute which, at best, skirts unconstitutionality, the finding of fact that such will be the probable results must be supported by evidence of an unusually clear and convincing kind—in other words, it is arguable that the evidence ought to be of a far stronger character than is required as the basis of ordinary administrative action. But, in the case at bar, the sole evidence to support the finding consists of the book itself.

However, although the Supreme Court has never passed on this question, the lower courts have held that direct proof of such harmful effects is not necessary. Perhaps because the primitive state of our psychological knowledge makes convincing proof of any such effects almost unobtainable, the lower courts have, instead, taken the current mores, "the social sense of what is right," the "average conscience of the time," i.e., what at the time is the attitude of the community in general. Maybe, then, the Postmaster General's finding will suffice, if based upon a not irrational determination of the contemporary public attitude towards books like this. But here he made no express finding about that attitude.

We thus do not know how he arrived at his conclusion as to obscenity. To sustain his order, we must, at a minimum, read into the record an implied administrative determination that the book is at odds with the "average conscience of the time." He has not told us how he ascertained that average conscience. In effect, we are asked to infer that he invoked something like judicial notice. That, however, can mean no more than a guess as to public opinion. And the recent Presidential election teaches that such a guess, even when assisted by so-called public-opinion polls, may go badly astray.

Because the state of our knowledge of psychology and the inadequacy of our procedures for determining public opinion make this question less susceptible of expert, objective, and explainable administrative determination than most questions passed on by administrative bodies, and noting again how closely this suppression statute approaches unconstitutionality, I would think that a reviewing court should scrutinize with more than ordinary care such an administrative determination with respect to public opinion. Engaged in such scrutiny, the judges must fall back on their own judicial notice, must by that means decide whether the official's guess is rational enough to be supportable. But where will the judges gather the facts to inform their judicial notice? Those whose views most judges know best are other lawyers. It would seem not improper to take judicial notice that tales such as those the Postmaster General here found obscene are freely told at many gatherings of prominent lawyers in meetings of Bar Associations or of alumni of our leading law schools. I doubt whether we ought arrogantly, undemocratically, to conclude that lawyers are a race apart, or an intellectual elite (like Plato's totalitarian "guardians" or "guards") with a "sense of what is right" for themselves, which has no relation to what is right for the vast multitude of other Americans, whom (à la Plato) they may look upon as children.

The truth of the matter is that we do not know, with anything that approximates reliability, the "average" American public opinion on the subject of obscenity. Perhaps we never will have such knowledge. For many years we have heard talk of "social science," and some may believe that from that source we may obtain the needed enlightenment. But, if "science" connotes a fairly high degree of accuracy, most studies of society, although by no means useless for all purposes, are further away from the "scientific" than were alchemy or astrology. Maybe some day we will attain scientific data about community opinion. One wonders whether free speech and free press may validly be suppressed when their suppression turns on the dubious data now available.

4

I can think of no better way, in the present state of our ignorance, to decide the rationality of the finding that this book is obscene than to compare it with other books now accessible to all American readers. On that basis, I have considerable difficulty in believing the Postmaster General's finding correct. For anyone can obtain for the asking, from almost any public library, a copy of Balzac's "Droll Stories," translated into English. That easy accessibility of that book might well serve as a persuasive indicator of current public judgments about the type of acceptable—i.e., not obscene—writing. Within the past few days, I have re-read "Droll Stories." For the life of me, I cannot see, nor understand how anyone else could see, anything in that book less obscene than in "Waggish Tales" which the Postmaster General has suppressed.

This court, per Judge A. N. Hand, has held that the passages alleged to be obscene in Joyce's "Ulysses" played a subordinate role. The same cannot possibly be said of "Droll Stories," which one deceased conservative critic described as "tales in which the lusts of the flesh are unleashed, satisfied and left to run riot amid a bacchanalia of flushed Priapi." Were that critic the Postmaster General, and were he to set up his own opinion of obscenity in disregard of the most readily available manifestations of American attitudes (i.e., public-library usages), he would suppress the Balzac book.

It will not do to differentiate "Waggish Tales" on the ground that "Droll Stories" is a "classic" which comported with the mores prevailing at the time and place of its publication. Balzac's own comments on this work show his awareness that it would, as it did, offend many of his contemporaries, such as George Sand who called it indecent. More important, where we seek to discover the attitude prevailing in this country today, the question is not what those living in Balzac's day thought of that book but how the "average" American now regards it. Wherefore (perhaps because I am without experience or am overly obtuse), I do not understand just how the "average conscience of the time" test of obscenity can be reconciled with the notion that a "classic"—defined as a work which has an "accepted place in the arts"—is not obscene, no matter what its contents and regardless of whether it is in tune with that current "average conscience."

Nor will it do to say that "Droll Stories" possesses unusual artistry which I chance to think "Waggish Tales" lacks. For this argument cuts just the other way: If a book is dominantly obscene, the greater the art, the greater the harmful impact on its "average" reader. If superior artistry—or what my colleagues call "literary distinction"—were to confer immunity from official control, then someone would have to determine which books have that quality. The Postmaster General's function would then be that of literary critic, with the reviewing judges as super-critics. Jurisprudence would merge with aesthetics. Authors and publishers would consult the legal digests for legal-artistic precedents. We might some day have a Legal Restatement of the Canons of Literary Taste. I cannot believe Congress had anything so grotesque in mind.

In sum, as "Droll Stories" appears obviously acceptable to the American public, and by that test is not obscene, no more, one would incline to think, is "Waggish Tales."

5

I agree that the fraud orders concerning the circulars which advertise Self Defense For Women and Bumarap must stand, for the evidence—the circulars themselves—support the findings on which those orders are based. But, as they rest on the ground that a person commits a fraud who advertises a book as if its dominant theme resembled that of "Waggish Tales" when in fact it does not, these orders tend to show that a considerable number of the reading public, and especially those who would buy and would probably read "Waggish Tales," want books like it. If so, then these orders strongly indicate that that book is not out of line with our present mores, and thus those orders may well be inconsistent with the finding that "Waggish Tales" is obscene.

I repeat, however, that, since, as a novice, I am unwilling in this case to oppose my views to those of my more experienced colleagues, I concur in their decision, but with bewilderment.

Jerome Frank
UNITED STATES v. ROTH

In a concurring opinion in Roth v. Goldman, 2 Cir., 1948, 172 F.2d 788, 790, I voiced puzzlement about the constitutionality of administrative prior restraint of obscene books. I then had little doubt about the validity of a purely punitive obscenity statute. But the next year, in Commonwealth v. Gordon, 1949, 66 Pa. Dist. & Co. R. 101, Judge Curtis Bok, one of America's most reflective judges, directly attacked the validity of any such punitive legislation. His brilliant opinion, which states arguments that (so far as I know) have never been answered, nudged me into the skeptical views contained in this opinion and the Appendix.

APPENDIX

As a judge of an inferior court, I am constrained by opinions of the Supreme Court concerning the obscenity statute to hold that legislation valid. Since, however, I think (as indicated in the foregoing) that none of those opinions has carefully canvassed the problem in the light of the Supreme Court's interpretation of the First Amendment, especially as expressed by the Court in recent years, I deem it not improper to

---

Jerome Frank, "United States v. Roth," 237 *Federal Reporter*, 2d Series, 805-27, copyright 1956 by West Publishing Co. Reprinted (without amplifying footnotes) by permission of the publisher.

120 The courts look at books

set forth, in the following, factors which I think deserve consideration in passing on the constitutionality of that statute.

1.

Benjamin Franklin, in 1776 unanimously designated Postmaster General by the First Continental Congress, is appropriately known as the "father of the Post Office." Among his published writings are two—*Letter of Advice to Young Men on the Proper Choosing of a Mistress* and *The Speech of Polly Baker*—which a jury could reasonably find "obscene," according to the judge's instructions in the case at bar. On that basis, if tomorrow a man were to send those works of Franklin through the mails, he would be subject to prosecution and (if the jury found him guilty) to punishment under the federal obscenity statute.

That fact would surely have astonished Jefferson, who extolled Franklin as an American genius, called him "venerable and beloved" of his countrymen, and wrote approvingly of Franklin's *Polly Baker*. No less would it have astonished Madison, also an admirer of Franklin (whom he described as a man whose "genius" was "an ornament of human nature") and himself given to telling "Rabelaisian anecdotes." Nor was the taste of these men unique in the American Colonies: "Many a library of a colonial planter in Virginia or a colonial intellectual in New England boasted copies of Tom Jones, Tristram Shandy, Ovid's Art of Love, and Rabelais. . . ."

As, with Jefferson's encouragement, Madison, in the first session of Congress, introduced what became the First Amendment, it seems doubtful that the constitutional guaranty of free speech and free press could have been intended to allow Congress validity to enact the "obscenity" Act. That doubt receives reinforcement from the following:

In 1799, eight years after the adoption of the First Amendment, Madison, in an Address to the General Assembly of Virginia, said that the "truth of opinion" ought not to be subject to "imprisonment, to be inflicted by those of a different opinion"; he there also asserted that it would subvert the First Amendment to make a "distinction between the freedom and the licentiousness of the press." Previously, in 1792, he wrote that "a man has property in his opinions and free communication of them," and that a government which "violates the property which individuals have in their opinion . . . is not a pattern for the United States." Jefferson's proposed Constitution for Virginia (1776), provided: "Printing presses shall be free, except so far as by commission of private injury cause may be given of private action." In his Second Inaugural Address (1805), he said: "No inference is here intended that the laws provided by the State against false and defamatory publications should not be enforced . . . The press, confined to truth, needs no other restraint . . . ; and no other definite line can be drawn between the inestimable liberty of the press and demoralizing licentiousness. If there still be improprieties which this rule would not restrain, its supplement must be sought in the censorship of public opinion."

The broad phrase in the First Amendment, prohibiting legislation abridging "freedom of speech, or of the press," includes the right to speak and write freely for the public concerning any subject. As the Amendment specifically refers to "the free exercise [of religion]" and to the right "of the people . . . to assemble" and to "petition the Government for a redress of grievances," it specifically includes the right freely to speak to and write for the public concerning government and religion; but it does not limit this right to those topics. Accordingly, the views of Jefferson and Madison about the freedom to speak and write concerning religion are relevant to a consideration of the constitutional freedom in respect of all other subjects. Consider, then, what those men said about freedom of religious discussion: Madison, in 1799, denouncing the distinction "between the freedom and the licentiousness of the press" said, "By its help, the judge as to what is licentious may escape through any constitutional restriction," and added, "Under it, Congress might denominate a religion to be heretical and licentious, and proceed to its suppression . . . Remember . . . that it is to the press mankind are indebted for having dispelled the clouds which long encompassed religion . . ." Jefferson, in 1798, quoting the First Amendment, said it guarded "in the same sentence, and under the same words, the freedom of religion, of speech, and of the press; insomuch, that whatever violates either, throws down the sanctuary which covers the others." In 1814, he wrote in a letter, "I am really mortified to be told that in the United States of America, a fact like this (the sale of a book) can become a subject of inquiry, and of criminal inquiry too, as an offense against religion; that (such) a question can be carried before the civil magistrate. Is this then our freedom of religion? And are we to have a censor whose imprimatur shall say what books may be sold and what we may buy? . . . Whose foot is to be the measure to which ours are all to be cut or stretched?"

Those utterances high-light this fact: Freedom to speak publicly and to publish has, as its inevitable and important correlative, the private rights to hear, to read, and to think and to feel about what one hears and reads. The First Amendment protects those private rights of hearers and readers.

We should not forget that, prompted by Jefferson, Madison (who at one time had doubted the wisdom of a Bill of Rights) when he urged in Congress the enactment of what became the first ten Amendments, declared, "If they are incorporated into the Constitution, independent tribunals of justice will consider themselves in a peculiar manner the guardian of those rights; they will be an impenetrable barrier against every assumption of power in the Legislative or Executive; they will be naturally led to resist every encroachment upon rights expressly stipulated for in the Constitution by the declaration of rights." In short, the Bill of Rights, including the First Amendment, was not designed merely as a set of admonitions to the legislature and the executive; its provisions were to be enforced by the courts.

Judicial enforcement necessarily entails judicial interpretation. The question therefore arises whether the courts, in enforcing the First Amendment, should interpret it in accord with the views prevalent among those who sponsored and adopted it or in accord with subsequently developed views which would sanction legislation more restrictive of free speech and free press.

So the following becomes pertinent: Some of those who in the 20th Century endorse legislation suppressing "obscene" literature have an attitude towards freedom of expression which does not match that of the framers of the First Amendment (adopted at the end of the 18th Century) but does stem from an attitude, towards writings dealing with sex, which arose decades later, in the mid-19th Century, and is therefore labelled—doubtless too sweepingly—"Victorian." It was a dogma of "Victorian morality" that sexual misbehavior would be encouraged if one were to "acknowledge its existence or at any rate to present it vividly enough to form a life-like image of it in the reader's mind"; this morality rested on a "faith that you could best conquer evil by shutting your eyes to its existence," and on a kind of word magic. The demands at that time for "decency" in published words did not comport with the actual sexual conduct of many of those who made those demands: "The Victorians, as a general rule, managed to conceal the 'coarser' side of their lives so thoroughly under a mask of respectability that we often fail to realize how 'coarse' it really was . . . Could we have recourse to the vast unwritten literature of bawdry, we should be able to form a more veracious notion of life as it (then) really was." The respectables of those days often, "with unblushing license," held "high revels" in "night houses." Thanks to them, Mrs. Warren's profession flourished, but it was considered sinful to talk about it in books. Such a prudish and purely verbal moral code, at odds (more or less hypocritically) with the actual conduct of its adherents was (as we have seen) not the moral code of those who framed the First Amendment. One would suppose, then, that the courts should interpret and enforce that Amendment according to the views of those framers, not according to the later "Victorian" code.

The "founding fathers" did not accept the common law concerning freedom of expression

It has been argued that the federal obscenity statute is valid because obscenity was a common law crime at the time of the adoption of the First Amendment. Quite aside from the fact that, previous to the Amendment, there had been scant recognition of this crime, the short answer seems to be that the framers of the Amendment knowingly and deliberately intended to depart from the English common law as to freedom of speech and freedom of the press. . . .

Of course, the legislature has wide power to protect what it considers public morals. But the First Amendment severely circumscribes that power (and all other legislative powers) in the area of speech and free press.

Subsequent punishment as, practically, prior restraint

For a long time, much was made of the distinction between a statute calling for "prior restraint" and one providing subsequent criminal punishment; the former alone, it was once said, raised any question of constitutionality *vis-à-vis* the First Amendment. Although it may still be true that more is required to justify legislation providing "preventive" than "punitive" censorship, this distinction has been substantially eroded. . . .

The statute, as judicially interpreted, authorizes punishment for inducing mere thoughts, and feelings, or desires

For a time, American courts adopted the test of obscenity contrived in 1868 by Cockburn, L.J., in Queen v. Hicklin, L.R. 3 Q.B. 360: "I think the test of obscenity is this, whether the tendency of the matter charged as obscenity is to deprave and corrupt those whose minds are open to such immoral influences, and into whose hands a publication of this sort might fall." He added that the book there in question "would suggest . . . thoughts of a most impure and libidinous character."

The test in most federal courts has changed: They do not now speak of the thoughts of "those whose minds are open to . . . immoral influences" but, instead, of the thoughts of average adult normal men and women, determining what these thoughts are, not by proof at the trial, but by the standard of "the average conscience of the time," the current "social sense of what is right." . . . Yet the courts still define obscenity in terms of the assumed average normal adult reader's sexual thoughts or desires or impulses, without reference to any relation between those "subjective" reactions and his subsequent conduct. The judicial opinions use such key phrases as this: "suggesting lewd thoughts and exciting sensual desires," "arouse the salacity of the reader," " 'allowing or implanting . . . obscene, lewd, or lascivious thoughts or desires,' " "arouse sexual desires." The judge's charge in the instant case reads accordingly: "It must tend to stir sexual impulses and lead to sexually impure thoughts." Thus the statute, as the courts construe it, appears to provide criminal punishment for inducing no more than thoughts, feelings, desires.

No adequate knowledge is available concerning the effects on the conduct of normal adults of reading or seeing the "obscene"

Suppose we assume, *arguendo,* that sexual thoughts or feelings, stirred by the "obscene," probably will often issue into overt conduct. Still it does not at all follow that that conduct will be anti-social. For no sane person can believe it socially harmful if sexual desires lead to normal, and not anti-social, sexual behavior since, without such behavior, the human race would soon disappear.

Doubtless, Congress could validly provide punishment for mailing any publications if there were some moderately substantial reliable data showing that reading or seeing those publications probably conduces to seriously harmful sexual conduct on the part of normal adult human beings. But we have no such data.

Suppose it argued that whatever excites sexual longings might *possibly* produce sexual misconduct. That cannot suffice: Notoriously, perfumes sometimes act as aphrodisiacs, yet no one will suggest that therefore Congress may constitutionally legislate punishment for mailing perfumes. It may be that among the stimuli to irregular sexual conduct, by normal men and women, may be almost anything—the odor of carnations or cheese, the sight of a cane or a candle or a shoe, the touch of silk or a gunnysack. For all anyone now knows, stimuli of that sort may be far more provocative of such misconduct than reading obscene books or seeing obscene pictures. Said John Milton, "Evil manners are as perfectly learnt, without books, a thousand other ways that cannot be stopped."

Effect of "obscenity" on adult conduct

To date there exist, I think, no thorough-going studies by competent persons which justify the conclusion that normal adults' reading or seeing of the "obscene" probably induces anti-social conduct. Such competent studies as have been made do conclude that so complex and numerous are the causes of sexual vice that it is impossible to assert with any assurance that "obscenity" represents a ponderable causal factor in sexually deviant adult behavior. "Although the whole subject of obscenity censorship hinges upon the unproved assumption that 'obscene' literature is a significant factor in causing sexual deviation from the community standard, no report can be found of a single effort at genuine research to test this assumption by singling out as a factor for study the effect of sex literature upon sexual behavior." What little competent research has been done, points definitely in a direction precisely opposite to that assumption.

Alpert reports that, when, in the 1920's, 409 women college graduates were asked to state in writing what things stimulated them sexually, they answered thus: 218 said "Man"; 95 said books; 40 said drama; 29 said dancing; 18 said pictures; 9 said music. Of those who replied "that the source of their sex information came from books, not one specified a 'dirty' book as the source. Instead, the books listed were: The Bible, the dictionary, the encyclopedia, novels from Dickens to Henry James, circulars about venereal diseases, medical books, and Motley's 'Rise of the Dutch Republic.'" Macaulay, replying to advocates of the suppression of obscene books, said: "We find it difficult to believe that in a world so full of temptations as this, any gentleman, whose life would have been virtuous if he had not read Aristophanes and Juvenal, will be made vicious by reading them." Echoing Macaulay, "Jimmy" Walker remarked that he had never heard of a woman seduced by a book. New Mexico has never had an obscenity statute; there is no evidence that, in that state, sexual misconduct is proportionately greater than elsewhere.

Effect on conduct of young people

Most federal courts (as above noted) now hold that the test of obscenity is the effect on the "mind" of the average normal adult, that effect being determined by the "average conscience of the time," the current "sense of what is right"; and that the statute does not intend "to reduce our treatment of sex to the standard of a child's library in the supposed interest of a salacious few"; United States v. Kennerley, D.C., 209 F. 120, 121.

However, there is much pressure for legislation, designed to prevent juvenile delinquency, which will single out children, i.e., will prohibit the sale to young persons of "obscenity" or other designated matter. That problem does not present itself here, since the federal statute is not thus limited. The trial judge in his charge in the instant case told the jury that the "test" under that statute is not the effect of the mailed matter on "those comprising a particular segment of the community," the "young" or "the immature"; and see United States v. Levine, 2 Cir., 83 F.2d 156, 157.

Therefore a discussion of such a children's protective statute is irrelevant here. But, since Judge Clark does discuss the alleged linkage of obscenity to juvenile delinquency, and since it may perhaps be thought that it has some bearing on the question of the effect of obscenity on adult conduct, I too shall discuss it.

The following is a recent summary of studies of that subject: "(1) Scientific studies of juvenile delinquency demonstrate that those who get into trouble, and are the greatest concern of the advocates of censorship, are far less inclined to read than those who do not become delinquent. The delinquents are generally the adventurous type, who have little use for reading and other nonactive entertainment. Thus, even assuming that reading sometimes has an adverse effect upon moral behavior, the effect is not likely to be substantial, for those who are susceptible seldom read. (2) Sheldon and Eleanor Glueck, who are among the country's leading authorities on the treatment and causes of juvenile delinquency, have recently published the results of a ten-year study of its causes. They exhaustively studied approximately 90 factors and influences that might lead to or explain juvenile delinquency; but the Gluecks gave no consideration to the type of reading material, if any were read by the delinquents. This is, of course, consistent with their finding that delinquents read very little. When those who know so much about the problem of delinquency among youth—the very group about whom the advocates of censorship are most concerned—conclude that what delinquents read has so little effect upon their conduct that it is not worth investigating in an exhaustive study of causes, there is good reason for serious doubts concerning the basic hypothesis on which obscenity censorship is dependent. (3) The many other influences in society that stimulate sexual desire are so much more frequent in their influence and so much more potent in their effect that the influence of reading is likely, at most, to be relatively insignificant in the composite of forces that lead an individual into conduct deviating from the community sex standards. . . . And the studies demonstrating that sex knowledge seldom results from reading indicates the relative unimportance of literature in sexual thoughts and behavior as compared with other factors in society."

Judge Clark, however, speaks of "the strongly held views of those with competence in the premises as to the very direct connection" of obscenity "with the development of juvenile delinquency." He cites and quotes from a recent opinion of the New York Court of Appeals and an article by Judge Vanderbilt, which in turn, cite the writings of persons thus described by Judge Clark as "those with competence in the premises." One of the cited writings is a report, by Dr. Jahoda and associates, entitled The Impact of Literature: A Psychological Discussion of Some Assumptions in the Censorship Debate (1954). I have read this report (which is a careful survey of all available studies and psychological theories). I think it expresses an attitude quite contrary to that indicated by Judge Clark. In order to avoid any possible bias in my interpretation of that report, I thought it well to ask Dr. Jahoda to write her own summary of it, which, with her permission, I shall quote. (In doing so, I am following the example of Mr. Justice Jackson who, in Federal Trade Commission v. Ruberoid Co., 343 U.S. 470, 485, 72 S.Ct. 800, 809, 96 L.Ed. 1081, acknowledged that he relied on "an unpublished treatise," i.e., one not available to the parties. If that practice is proper, I think it similarly proper to quote an author's unpublished interpretation of a published treatise.) Dr. Jahoda's summary reads as follows:

"Persons who argue for increased censorship of printed matter often operate on the assumption that reading about sexual matters or about violence and brutality leads to anti-social actions, particularly to juvenile delinquency. An examination of the pertinent psychological literature has led to the following conclusions:

"1. There exists no research evidence either to prove or to disprove this assumption definitively.

"2. In the absence of scientific proof two lines of psychological approach to the examination of the assumption are possible: (a) a review of what is known on the causes of juvenile delinquency; and (b) review of what is known about the effect of literature on the mind of the reader.

"3. In the vast research literature on the causes of juvenile delinquency there is no evidence to justify the assumption that reading about sexual matters or about violence leads to delinquent acts. Experts on juvenile delinquency agree that it has no single cause. Most of them regard early childhood events, which precede the reading age, as a necessary condition for later delinquency. At a later age, the nature of personal relations is assumed to have much greater power in determining a delinquent career than the vicarious experiences provided by reading matter. Juvenile delinquents as a group read less, and less easily, than non-delinquents. Individual instances are reported in which so-called 'good' books allegedly influenced a delinquent in the manner in which 'bad' books are assumed to influence him.

"Where childhood experiences and subsequent events have combined to make delinquency psychologically likely, reading could have one of two effects: it could serve a trigger function releasing the criminal act or it could provide for a substitute outlet of aggression in fantasy, dispensing with the need for criminal action. There is no empirical evidence in either direction.

"4. With regard to the impact of literature on the mind of the reader, it must be pointed out that there is a vast overlap in content between all media of mass communication. The daily press, television, radio, movies, books and comics all present their share of so-called 'bad' material, some with great realism as reports of actual events, some in clearly fictionalized form. It is virtually impossible to isolate the impact of one of these media on a population exposed to all of them. Some evidence suggests that the particular communications which arrest the attention of an individual are in good part a matter of choice. As a rule, people do not expose themselves to everything that is offered, but only to what agrees with their inclinations.

"Children, who have often not yet crystallized their preferences and have more unspecific curiosity than many adults, are therefore perhaps more open to accidental influences from literature. This may present a danger to youngsters who are insecure or maladjusted who find in reading (of 'bad' books as well as of 'good' books) an escape from reality which they do not dare face. Needs which are not met in the real world are gratified in a fantasy world. It is likely, though not fully demonstrated, that excessive reading of comic books will intensify in children those qualities which drove them to the comic book world to begin with: an inability to face the world, apathy, a belief that the individual is hopelessly impotent and driven by uncontrollable forces and, hence, an acceptance of violence and brutality in the real world.

"It should be noted that insofar as causal sequence is implied, insecurity and maladjustment in a child must precede this exposure to the written word in order to lead to these potential effects. Unfortunately, perhaps, the reading of Shakespeare's tragedies or of Andersen's and Grimm's fairy tales might do much the same."

Most of the current discussion of the relation between children's reading and juvenile delinquency has to do with so-called "comic books" which center on violence (sometimes coupled with sex) rather than mere obscenity. Judge Vanderbilt, in an article from which Judge Clark quotes, cites Feder, Comic Book Regulation (University of California, Bureau of Public Administration, 1955 Legislative Problems No. 2). Feder writes: "It has never been determined definitely whether or not comics portraying violence, crime and horror are a cause of juvenile delinquency."

Judge Vanderbilt, in the article from which Judge Clark quotes, also cites Wertham, "Seduction of the Innocent" (1954). Dr. Wertham is the foremost proponent of the view that "comic books" do contribute to juvenile delinquency. The Jahoda Report takes issue with Dr. Wertham, who relies much on a variety of the *post-hoc-ergo-propter-hoc* variety of argument, i.e., youths who had read "comic books" became delinquents. The argument, at best, proves too much: Dr. Wertham points to the millions of young readers of such books; but only a fraction of these readers become delinquents. Many of the latter also chew gum, drink coca-cola, and wear soft-soled shoes. Moreover, Dr. Wertham specifically says (p. 298) that he is little concerned with allegedly obscene publications designed for reading by adults, and (pp. 303, 316, 348) that the legislation which he advocates would do no more than forbid the sale or display of "comic books" to minors. As previously noted, the federal obscenity statute is not so restricted.

Maybe some day we will have enough reliable data to show that obscene books and pictures do tend to influence children's sexual conduct adversely. Then a federal statute could be enacted which would avoid constitutional defects by authorizing punishment for using the mails or interstate shipments in the sale of such books and pictures to children.

It is, however, not at all clear that children would be ignorant, in any considerable measure, of obscenity, if no obscene publications ever came into their hands. Youngsters get a vast deal of education in sexual smut from companions of their own age. A verbatim report of conversations among young teen-age boys (from average respectable homes) will disclose their amazing proficiency in obscene language, learned from other boys. Replying to the argument of the need for censorship to protect the young Milton said: "Who shall regulate all the . . . conversation of our youth . . . appoint what shall be discussed . . . ?" Most judges who reject that view are long past their youth and have probably forgotten the conversational ways of that period of life: "I remember when I was a little boy," said Mr. Dooley, "but I don't remember how I was a little boy."

The obscenity statute and the reputable press

Let it be assumed, for the sake of the argument, that contemplation of published matter dealing with sex has a significant impact on children's conduct. On that assumption, we cannot overlook the fact that our most reputable newspapers and periodicals carry advertisements and photographs displaying women in what decidedly are sexually alluring postures, and at times emphasizing the importance of "sex appeal." That women are there shown scantily clad, increases "the mystery and allure of the bodies that are hidden," writes an eminent psychiatrist. "A leg covered by a silk stocking is much more attractive than a naked one; a bosom pushed into shape by a brassiere is more alluring than the pendant realities." Either, then, the statute must be sternly applied to prevent the mailing of many reputable newspapers and periodicals containing such ads and photographs, or else we must acknowledge that they have created a cultural atmosphere for children in which, at a maximum, only the most trifling additional effect can be imputed to children's perusal of the kind of matter mailed by the defendant.

The obscenity statute and the newspapers

Because of the contrary views of many competent persons, one may well be sceptical about Dr. Wertham's thesis. However, let us see what, logically, his crusade would do to the daily press: After referring repeatedly to the descriptions, in "comic books" and other "mass media," of violence combined with sadistic sexual behavior, descriptions which he says contribute to juvenile delinquency, he writes, "Juvenile delinquency reflects the social values current in a society. Both adults and children absorb these social values in their daily lives, . . . and also in *all the communications through the mass media* . . . Juvenile delinquency holds up a mirror to society . . . It is self-understood that such a pattern in a mass medium does not come from nothing . . . Comic books are not the disease, they are only a symptom . . . The same social forces that made comic books make other social evils, and the same social forces that keep comic crime books keep the other social evils the way they are." (Emphasis added.)

Now the daily newspapers, especially those with immense circulations, constitute an important part of the "mass media"; and each copy of a newspaper sells for much less than a "comic book." Virtually all the sorts of descriptions, of sex mingled with violence, which Dr. Wertham finds in the "comic books," can be found, often accompanied by gruesome photographs, in those daily journals. Even a newspaper which is considered unusually respectable, published prominently on its first page, on August 26, 1956, a true story of a "badly decomposed body" of a 24 year old woman school teacher, found in a clump of trees. The story reported that police had quoted a 29 year old salesman as saying that "he drove to the area" with the school teacher, that "the two had relations on the ground, and later got into an argument," after which he "struck her three times on the back of the head with a rock, and, leaving her there, drove away." Although today no one can so prove, one may suspect that such stories of sex and violence in the daily press have more impact on young readers than do those in the "comic books," since the daily press reports reality while the "comic books" largely confine themselves to avowed fiction or fantasy. Yet Dr. Wertham, and most others who propose legislation to curb the sale of "comic books" to children, propose that it should not extend to newspapers. Why not?

The question is relevant in reference to the application of the obscenity statute: Are our prosecutors ready to prosecute reputable newspaper publishers under that Act? I think not. I do not at all urge such prosecutions. I do suggest that the validity of that statute has not been vigorously challenged because it has not been applied to important persons like those publishers but, instead, has been enforced principally against relatively inconspicuous men like the defendant here.

Da capo: Available data seem wholly insufficient to show that the obscenity statutes come within any exception to the First Amendment

I repeat that, because that statute is not restricted to obscene publications mailed for sale to minors, its validity should be tested in terms of the evil effects of adult reading of obscenity on adult conduct. With the present lack of evidence that publications probably have such effects, how can the government discharge its burden of demonstrating sufficiently that the statute is within the narrow exceptions to the scope of the First Amendment? One would think that the mere possibility of a causal relation to misconduct ought surely not be enough.

Even if Congress had made an express legislative finding of the probable evil influence, on adult conduct, of adult reading or seeing obscene publications, the courts would not be bound by that finding, if it were not justified in fact. See, e.g., Chastleton Corp. v. Sinclair, . . . where the Court (per Holmes, J.) said of a statute (declaring the existence of an emergency) that "a Court is not at liberty to shut its eyes to an obvious mistake, when the validity of the law depends upon the truth of what is declared." And the Court there and elsewhere has held that the judiciary may use judicial notice in ascertaining the truth of such a legislative declaration.

If the obscenity statute is valid, why may

Congress not validly provide punishment for mailing books which will provoke thoughts it considers undesirable about religion or politics?

If the statute is valid, then, considering the foregoing, it would seem that its validity must rest on this ground: Congress, by statute, may constitutionally provide punishment for the mailing of books evoking mere thoughts or feelings about sex, if Congress considers them socially dangerous, even in the absence of any satisfactory evidence that those thoughts or feelings will tend to bring about socially harmful deeds. If that be correct, it is hard to understand why, similarly, Congress may not constitutionally provide punishment for such distribution of books evoking mere thoughts or feelings, about religion or politics, which Congress considers socially dangerous, even in the absence of any satisfactory evidence that those thoughts or feelings will tend to bring about socially dangerous deeds.

2. The Judicial exception of the "classics"

As I have said, I have no doubt the jury could reasonably find, beyond a reasonable doubt, that many of the publications mailed by defendant were obscene within the current judicial definition of the term as explained by the trial judge in his charge to the jury. But so, too, are a multitude of recognized works of art found in public libraries. Compare, for instance, the books which are exhibits in this case with Montaigne's "Essay on Some Lines of Virgil" or with Chaucer. Or consider the many nude pictures which the defendant transmitted through the mails, and then turn to the reproductions in the articles on painting and sculpture in the Encyclopedia Britannica (14th edition): Some of the latter are no less "obscene" than those which led to the defendant's conviction. Yet these Encyclopedia volumes are readily accessible to everyone, young or old, and, without let or hindrance, are frequently mailed to all parts of the country. Catalogues, of famous art museums, almost equally accessible and also often mailed, contain reproductions of paintings and sculpture, by great masters no less "obscene."

To the argument that such books (and such reproductions of famous paintings and works of sculpture) fall within the statutory ban, the courts have answered that they are "classics,"—books of "literary distinction" or works which have "an accepted place in the arts," including, so this court has held, Ovid's "Art of Love" and Boccaccio's "Decameron." There is a "curious dilemma" involved in this answer that the statute condemns "only books which are dull and without merit," that in no event will the statute be applied to the "classics," i.e., books "of literary distinction." The courts have not explained how they escape that dilemma, but instead seem to have gone to sleep (although rather uncomfortably) on its horns.

This dilemma would seem to show up the basic constitutional flaw in the statute: No one can reconcile the currently accepted test of obscenity with the immunity of such "classics" as e.g., Aristophanes' "Lysistratra," Chaucer's "Canterbury Tales," Rabelais' "Gargantua" and "Pantagruel," Shakespeare's "Venus and Adonis," Fielding's "Tom Jones," or Balzac's "Droll Stories." For such "obscene" writings, just because of their greater artistry and charm, will presumably have far greater influence on readers than dull inartistic writings.

It will not do to differentiate a "classic," published in the past, on the ground that it comported with the average moral attitudes at the time and place of its original publication. Often this was not true. It was not true, for instance, of Balzac's "Droll Stories," a "classic" now freely circulated by many public libraries, and which therefore must have been transported by mail (or in interstate commerce). More to the point, if the issue is whether a book meets the American common conscience of the present time, the question is how "average" Americans now regard the book, not how it was regarded when first published, here or abroad. Why should the age of an "obscene" book be relevant? After how many years—25 or 50 or 100—does such a writing qualify as a "classic"?

The truth is that the courts have excepted the "classics" from the federal obscenity statute, since otherwise most Americans would be deprived of access to many masterpieces of literature and the pictorial arts, and a statute yielding such deprivation would not only be laughably absurd but would squarely oppose the intention of the cultivated men who framed and adopted the First Amendment.

This exception—nowhere to be found in the

statute—is a judge-made device invented to avoid that absurdity. The fact that the judges have felt the necessity of seeking that avoidance, serves to suggest forcibly that the statute, in its attempt to control what our citizens may read and see, violates the First Amendment. For no one can rationally justify the judge-made exception. The contention would scarcely pass as rational that the "classics" will be read or seen solely by an intellectual or artistic elite; for, even ignoring the snobbish, undemocratic, nature of this contention, there is no evidence that that elite has a moral fortitude (an immunity from moral corruption) superior to that of the "masses." And if the exception, to make it rational, were taken as meaning that a contemporary book is exempt if it equates in "literary distinction" with the "classics," the result would be amazing: Judges would have to serve as literary critics; jurisprudence would merge with aesthetics; authors and publishers would consult the legal digests for legal-artistic precedents; we would some day have a Legal Restatement of the Canons of Literary Taste.

The exception of the "classics" is therefore irrational. Consequently, it would seem that we should interpret the statute rationally—i.e., without that exception. If, however, the exception, as an exception, is irrational, then it would appear that, to render the statute valid, the standard applied to the "classics" should be applied to all books and pictures. The result would be that, in order to be constitutional, the statute must be wholly inefficacious.

3. How censorship under the statute actually operates:
(a) Prosecutors, as censors, actually exercise prior restraint.

Fear of punishment serves as a powerful restraint on publication, and fear of punishment often means, practically, fear of prosecution. For most men dread indictment and prosecution; the publicity alone terrifies, and to defend a criminal action is expensive. If the definition of obscenity had a limited and fairly well known scope, that fear might deter restricted sorts of publications only. But on account of the extremely vague judicial definition of the obscene, a person threatened with prosecution if he mails (or otherwise sends in interstate commerce) almost any book which deals in an unconventional, unorthodox, manner with sex, may well apprehend that, should the threat be carried out, he will be punished. As a result, each prosecutor becomes a literary censor (i.e., dictator) with immense unbridled power, a virtually uncontrolled discretion. A statute would be invalid which gave the Postmaster General the power, without reference to any standard, to close the mails to any publication he happened to dislike. Yet, a federal prosecutor, under the federal obscenity statute, approximates that position: Within wide limits, he can (on the advice of the Postmaster General or on no one's advice) exercise such a censorship by threat, without a trial, without any judicial supervision, capriciously and arbitrarily. Having no special qualifications for that task, nevertheless, he can, in large measure, determine at his will what those within his district may not read on sexual subjects. In that way, the statute brings about an actual prior restraint of free speech and free press which strikingly flouts the First Amendment.

(b) Judges as censors.

When a prosecution is instituted and a trial begins, much censorship power passes to the trial judge: If he sits without a jury, he must decide whether a book is obscene. If the trial is by jury, then, if he thinks the book plainly not obscene, he directs a verdict for the accused or, after a verdict of guilt, enters a judgment of acquittal. How does the judge determine whether a book is obscene? Not by way of evidence introduced at the trial, but by way of some sort of judicial notice. Whence come the judicial notice data to inform him?

Those whose views most judges know best are other lawyers. Judges can and should take judicial notice that, at many gatherings of lawyers at Bar Associations or of alumni of our leading law schools, tales are told fully as "obscene" as many of those distributed by men, like defendant, convicted for violation of the obscenity statute. Should not judges then set aside such convictions? If they do not, are they not somewhat arrogantly concluding that lawyers are an exempt elite, unharmed by what will harm the multitude of other Americans? If lawyers are not such an elite then, since, in spite of the "obscene" tales lawyers frequently tell one another, data are lacking that lawyers as a group become singularly addicted to depraved sexual conduct, should not judges conclude that "obscenity" does not importantly contribute to such misconduct, and that therefore the statute is unconstitutional?

(c) Jurors as censors.

If in a jury case, the trial judge does not direct a verdict or enter a judgment of acquittal, the jury exercises the censorship power. Courts have said that a jury has a peculiar aptitude as a censor of obscenity, since, representing a cross-section of the community, it knows peculiarly well the "common conscience" of the time. Yet no statistician would conceivably accept the views of a jury—twelve persons chosen at random—as a fair sample of community attitudes on such a subject as obscenity. A particular jury may voice the "moral sentiments" of a generation ago, not of the present time.

Each jury verdict in an obscenity case has been sagely called "really a small bit of legislation ad hoc." So each jury constitutes a tiny autonomous legislature. Any one such tiny legislature, as experience teaches, may well differ from any other, in thus legislating as to obscenity. And, one may ask, was it the purpose of the First Amendment, to authorize hundreds of divers jury-legislatures, with discrepant beliefs, to decide whether or not to enact hundreds of divers statutes interfering with freedom of expression? (I shall note, infra, the vast difference between the applications by juries of the "reasonable man" standard and the "obscenity" standard.)

4. The dangerously infectious nature of governmental censorship of books

Governmental control of ideas or personal preferences is alien to a democracy. And the yearning to use governmental censorship of any kind is infectious. It may spread insidiously. Commencing with suppression of books as obscene, it is not unlikely to develop into official lust for the power of thought-control in the areas of religion, politics, and elsewhere. Milton observed that "licensing of books . . . necessarily pulls along with it so many other kinds of licensing." J. S. Mill noted that the "bounds of what may be called moral police" may easily extend "until it encroaches on the most unquestionably legitimate liberty of the individual." We should beware of a recrudescence of the un-democratic doctrine uttered in the 17th century by Berkeley, Governor of Virginia: "Thank God there are no free schools or preaching, for learning has brought disobedience into the world, and printing has divulged them. God keep us from both."

The people as self-guardians: censorship by public opinion, not by government

Plato, who detested democracy, proposed to banish all poets; and his rulers were to serve as "guardians" of the people, telling lies for the people's good, vigorously suppressing writings these guardians thought dangerous. Governmental guardianship is repugnant to the basic tenet of our democracy: According to our ideals, our adult citizens are self-guardians, to act as their own fathers, and thus become self-dependent. When our governmental officials act towards our citizens on the thesis that "Papa knows best what's good for you," they enervate the spirit of the citizens: To treat grown men like infants is to make them infantile, dependent, immature.

So have sagacious men often insisted. Milton, in his Areopagitica, denounced such paternalism: "We censure them for a giddy, vicious and unguided people, in such sick and weak (a) state of faith and discretion as to be able to take down nothing but through the pipe of a licensor." "We both consider the people as our children," wrote Jefferson to Dupont de Nemours, "but you love them as infants whom you are afraid to trust without nurses, and I as adults whom I freely leave to self-government." Tocqueville sagely remarked: "No form or combination of social policy has yet been devised to make an energetic people of a community of pusillanimous and enfeebled citizens." "Man," warned Goethe, "is easily accustomed to slavery and learns quickly to be obedient when his freedom is taken from him." Said Carl Becker, "Self-government, and the spirit of freedom that sustains it, can be maintained only if the people have sufficient intelligence and honesty to maintain them with a minimum of legal compulsion. This heavy responsibility is the price of freedom." The "great art," according to Milton, "lies to discern in what the law is to bid restraint and punishment, and in what things persuasion only is to work." So we come back, once more, to Jefferson's advice: The only completely democratic way to control publications which arouse mere thoughts or feelings is through non-governmental censorship by public opinion.

5. The seeming paradox of the First Amendment

Here we encounter an apparent paradox: The First Amendment, judicially enforced, curbs public opinion when translated into a statute which restricts freedom of expression (except that which will probably induce undesirable conduct). The paradox is unreal: *The Amendment ensures that public opinion—the "common conscience of the time"—shall not commit suicide through legislation which chokes off today the free expression of minority views which may become the majority public opinion of tomorrow.*

Private persons or groups may validly try to influence public opinion

The First Amendment obviously has nothing to do with the way persons or groups, not a part of government, influence public opinion as to what constitutes "decency" or "obscenity." The Catholic Church, for example, has a constitutional right to persuade or instruct its adherents not to read designated books or kinds of books.

6. The fine arts are within the First Amendment's protection

"The framers of the First Amendment," writes Chafee, "must have had literature and art in mind, because our first national statement on the subject of 'freedom of the press,' the 1774 address of the Continental Congress to the inhabitants of Quebec, declared, 'The importance of this (freedom of the press) consists, beside the advancement of truth, science, morality and *arts* in general, in its diffusion of liberal sentiments on the administration of government.'" 165 years later, President Franklin Roosevelt said, "The arts cannot thrive except where men are free to be themselves and to be in charge of the discipline of their own energies and ardors. The conditions for democracy and for art are one and the same. What we call liberty in politics results in freedom of the arts." The converse is also true.

In our industrial era when, perforce, economic pursuits must be, increasingly, governmentally regulated, it is especially important that the realm of art—the non-economic realm—should remain free, unregimented, the domain of free enterprise, of unhampered competition at its maximum. An individual's taste is his own, private, concern. *De gustibus non disputandum* represents a valued democratic maxim.

Milton wrote: "For though a licenser should happen to be judicious more than the ordinary, yet his very office . . . enjoins him to let pass nothing but what is vulgarly received already." He asked, "What a fine conformity would it starch us all into? . . . We may fall . . . into a gross conformity stupidly . . ." In 1859, J. S. Mill, in his essay on Liberty, maintained that conformity in taste is not a virtue but a vice. "The danger," he wrote, "is not the excess but the deficiency of personal impulses and preferences. By dint of not following their own nature (men) have no nature to follow . . . Individual spontaneity is entitled to free exercise . . . That so few men dare to be eccentric marks the chief danger of the time." Pressed by the demand for conformity, a people degenerate into "the deep slumber of a decided opinion," yield a "dull and torpid consent" to the accustomed. "Mental despotism" ensues. For "whatever crushes individuality is despotism by whatever name it be called . . . It is not by wearing down into uniformity all that is individual in themselves, but by cultivating it, and calling it forth, within the limits imposed by the rights and interests of others, that human beings become a noble and beautiful object of contemplation; and as the works partake the character of those who do them, by the same process human life also becomes rich, diversified, and animating . . . In proportion to the development of his individuality, each person becomes more valuable to himself, and is therefore capable of being more valuable to others. There is a greater fullness of life about his own existence, and when there is more life in the units there is more in the mass which is composed of them."

To vest a few fallible men—prosecutors, judges, jurors—with vast powers of literary or artistic censorship, to convert them into what J. S. Mill called a "moral police," is to make them despotic arbiters of literary products. If one day they ban mediocre books as obscene, another day they may do likewise to a work of genius. Originality, not too plentiful, should be cherished, not stifled. An author's imagination may be cramped if he must write with one eye on prosecutors or juries; authors must cope with publishers who, fearful about the judgments of governmental censors, may refuse to accept the manuscripts of contemporary Shelleys or Mark Twains or Whitmans.

Some few men stubbornly fight for the right to write or publish or distribute books which the great majority at the time consider loathsome. If we jail those few, the community may appear to have suffered nothing. The appearance is deceptive. For the conviction and punishment of these few will terrify writers who are more sensitive, less eager for a fight. What, as a result, they do not write might have been major literary contributions. "Suppression," Spinoza said, "is paring down the state till it is too small to harbor men of talent."

> 7. The motive or intention of the author, publisher or distributor cannot be the test

Some courts once held that the motive or intention of the author, painter, publisher or distributor constituted the test of obscenity. That test, the courts have abandoned: That a man who mails a book or picture believes it entirely "pure" is no defense if the court finds it obscene. United States v. One Book Entitled "Ulysses," 2 Cir., 72 F.2d 705, 708. Nor, conversely, will he be criminally liable for mailing a "pure" publication—Stevenson's "Child's Garden of Verses" or a simple photograph of the Washington Monument—he mistakenly believes obscene. Most courts now look to the "objective" intention, which can only mean the effect on those who read the book or see the picture; the motive of the mailer is irrelevant because it cannot affect that effect.

> 8. Judge Bok's decision as to the causal relation to anti-social conduct

In Commonwealth v. Gordon, 1949, 66 Pa. Dist. & Co.R. 101, Judge Bok said: "A book, however sexually impure and pornographic . . . cannot be a present danger unless its reader closes it, lays it aside, and transmutes its erotic allurement into overt action. That such action must inevitably follow as a direct consequence of reading the book does not bear analysis, nor is it borne out by general human experience; too much can intervene and too many diversions take place . . . The only clear and present danger . . . that will satisfy . . . the Constitution . . . is the commission or the imminence of the commission of criminal behavior resulting from the reading of a book. Publication alone can have no such automatic effect." The constitutional operation of "the statute," Judge Bok continued, thus "rests on narrow ground . . . I hold that (the statute) may constitutionally be applied . . . only where there is a reasonable and demonstrable cause to believe that a crime or misdemeanor has been committed or is about to be committed as the perceptible result of the publication and distribution of the writing in question: the opinion of anyone that a tendency thereto exists or that such a result is self-evident is insufficient and irrelevant. The causal connection between the book and the criminal behavior must appear beyond a reasonable doubt."

I confess that I incline to agree with Judge Bok's opinion. But I think it should be modified in a few respects: (a) Because of the Supreme Court's opinion in the Dennis case, 1951, 341 U.S. 494, 71 S.Ct. 857, 95 L.Ed. 1137, decided since Judge Bok wrote, I would stress the element of probability in speaking of a "clear danger." (b) I think the danger need not be that of probably inducing behavior which has already been made criminal at common law or by statute, but rather of probably inducing any seriously anti-social conduct (i.e., conduct which, by statute, could validly be made a state or federal crime). (c) I think that the causal relation need not be between such anti-social conduct and a particular book involved in the case on trial, but rather between such conduct and a book of the kind or type involved in the case.

> 9. The void-for-vagueness argument

There is another reason for doubting the constitutionality of the obscenity statute. The exquisite vagueness of the word "obscenity" is apparent from the way the judicial definition of that word has kept shifting: Once (as we saw) the courts held a work obscene if it would probably stimulate improper thoughts or desires in abnormal persons; now most courts consider only the assumed impact on the thoughts or desires of the adult "normal" or average human being. A standard so difficult for our ablest judges to interpret is hardly one which has a "well-settled" meaning, a meaning sufficient adequately to advise a man whether he is or is not committing a crime if he mails a book or picture....

If we accept as correct the generally current judicial standard of obscenity—the "average conscience of the time"—that standard still remains markedly uncertain as a guide to judges or jurors—and therefore to a citizen who contemplates mailing a book or picture. To be sure, we trust juries to use their common sense in applying the "reasonable man" standard in prosecutions for criminal negligence (or the like); a man has to take his chances on a jury verdict in such a case, with no certainty that a jury will not convict him although another jury may acquit another man on the same evidence. But that standard has nothing remotely resembling the looseness of the "obscenity" standard.

There is a stronger argument against the analogy of the "reasonable man" test: Even if the obscenity standard would have sufficient definiteness were freedom of expression not involved, it would seem far too vague to justify as a basis for an exception to the First Amendment....

In United States v. Rebhuhn, 2 Cir., 109 F.2d 512, 514, the court tersely rejected the contention that the obscenity statute is too vague, citing and relying on Rosen v. United States, 161 U.S. 29, 16 S.Ct. 434, 480, 40 L.Ed. 606. However the Rosen case did not deal with that subject but merely with the sufficiency of the wording of an indictment under that statute.

Chapter IV

Giving others the courage of our convictions: pressure groups

THE "do-gooders," a term satirically coined several years ago by the *Chicago Tribune* for another purpose, aptly describes the ubiquitous organizations, invariably representing minority interests, whose main aim in life is to force their views on the majority. Through skillful use of pressure and influence, they have been directly responsible in recent years for some of the most obnoxious activity in the censorship field. Presuming to speak for millions, they have persuaded congressional committees, state legislatures, local police departments, and other official agencies to enact unconstitutional laws, to adopt extralegal measures for the suppression of disapproved literature, and to besmirch the names of reputable authors and publishers. In so doing, they have been intent on depriving the majority of certain basic rights that are guaranteed by law.

As a well-known educator, Willard E. Goslin, so eloquently pointed out:

"No particular special interest group makes up the people. The people are not the Chamber of Commerce, or the labor unions, or the league for constitutional governments, or the Methodists, or the Parent Teacher Association, or the Catholics, or the Liberty Belles, or the American Legion, or the Protestants, or the Sons of the Golden West, or the Jews, or the American Association of University Women, or the Presbyterians, or the Rotarians, or the farmers, or the college graduates, or the whites, or the Republicans, or the poor, or the Negroes, or the teachers, or the bankers, or the Democrats, or the commentators, or any other segmented or spe-

134 *Giving others the courage of our convictions*

cial interest group in America. The people, as we use the term, are that broad base of citizens representative of the diversity and strength of this nation." [1]

Two organizations long leaders in the field of censorship—the New England Watch and Ward Society and the New York Society for the Suppression of Vice—have in late years been quiescent. These stormy petrels of the past have been largely replaced by such groups as the National Organization for Decent Literature, under Catholic sponsorship; the American Legion and other veterans' organizations; branches of the National Association for the Advancement of Colored People; certain Jewish organizations; and local police officers following what John Lardner facetiously describes as the "Detroit Line." Highly laudable efforts, in the eyes of these groups, to limit adult reading to books suitable for children, to bar the writings of "subversive" authors, or to eliminate all works containing derogatory references to minority races have occasionally been hampered by courts of law and by counterpressures from, for example, the American Library Association, the American Book Publishers Council, and the American Civil Liberties Union. Undeterred, they push onward along what they conceive to be the path of righteousness, determined to give other people the courage of their own convictions.

An indefatigable watchdog over the constitutional rights of the American people—of all classes, rich or poor, without regard to race, creed, or color—the American Civil Liberties Union has gained wide respect among conservatives and liberals alike. While defending and supporting the freedom of any individual or group to express disapproval of a book, a play, or a motion picture, the ACLU stands in unyielding opposition to efforts by such individuals or groups to force others to conform to their views. This statement of the Union's attitude toward censorship activity by private organizations was issued in 1957 and signed by a distinguished list of over 150 authors, playwrights, composers, critics, editors, and publishers who were in agreement with the principles set forth therein.

American Civil Liberties Union
STATEMENT
ON CENSORSHIP ACTIVITY
BY PRIVATE ORGANIZATIONS
AND THE NATIONAL
ORGANIZATION FOR
DECENT LITERATURE

Throughout the United States, private organizations concerned with the morality of literature are increasingly going beyond their legitimate function of offering to their members, and calling to public attention, opinion or instruction about books, and are in effect imposing censorship upon the general public. And since any kind of censorship infringes the principle of that constitutionally guaranteed freedom of the press which protects the free exchange of ideas in our country, it is imperative that the American people be warned of the danger in which their freedom stands. In discussing this kind of censorship, we make a clear distinction between the right of all organizations to express their opinion, which we defend, and acting in such a manner as to deny those who do not agree with their opinion an opportunity to read the literature themselves.

BACKGROUND OF THE PROBLEM

1. *The constitutional guarantee.* The First and Fourteenth Amendments to the United States Constitution, and the constitutions of the several states, prohibit governmental abridgment of freedom of the press. If one may read, one must be able to buy; if one may buy, others must be able to print and sell.

2. *Legal basis for limiting freedom of the press.* If curbs are to be placed on freedom of the press, and these curbs must be based on a clear and present danger of a substantive evil from the publication, they can be imposed only by our courts, through full legal process. And the courts, not private literature-reviewing organizations, are the proper tribunals for determining the existence of such danger.

---

[1] Willard E. Goslin, "The People and Their Schools," *Forces Affecting American Education.* 1953 Yearbook. (Washington, D.C.: Association for Supervision and Curriculum Development, NEA, 1953), pp. 143–44.

Reprinted (without amplifying footnotes) by permission of the American Civil Liberties Union.

3. *Existing pressures for further limitation of freedom of the press.* It is an historical fact that the travail and tension of our time has adversely affected our society and raised particular problems of juvenile delinquency. We share with other Americans deep concern about this problem, which has been a problem in other ages as well, but we do not believe that it is desirable to try to cure the evil by unwise or unlawful abridgment of our civil liberties.

4. *The form now assumed by further, improper limitation of freedom of the press.* First, some state legislatures, after vigorous demands by religious and other private organizations, have passed laws so sweeping as to permit censorship of any publication which administrators of the law may disapprove of. Rhode Island and New York now prohibit the display, sale or circulation to any person under 18 of any book dealing with "illicit sex or sexual immorality." This ban could affect the *Odyssey,* half of Shakespeare, the *Divine Comedy;* the *Scarlet Letter* and parts of the Bible; Henry James' *The Turn of the Screw* was cited by the Rhode Island commission as an example of a book thought harmful to minors. In South Carolina, the legislature passed a resolution directing the removal from public libraries of "books that are inimical to the traditions of South Carolina."

Second, less formal governmental censorship is illustrated by the fact that the Detroit Police Department has made such representations to the only two wholesalers of paperbound books and magazines in Detroit that they have agreed not to offer any magazine or paperbound book for sale in that city until it has been submitted to the police and cleared by them or in doubtful cases by the prosecuting attorney. The list of books disapproved by the prosecuting attorney for that jurisdiction has been frequently sent to the police in other cities and used as a quasi-official "banned" list. This situation displays the particularly abhorrent practice of pre-publication censorship, because, although the books have been printed, publication is not completed if there is a barrier to distribution.

Such formal and informal censorship actions by official authority violates the First Amendment. In nearly every instance where it has been possible to test the constitutional issue in a court, censorship has been defeated.

Third, a number of private groups, particularly church-related organizations have prepared blacklists, threatened and imposed general boycotts, and awarded unofficial certificates of compliance. The most active of these groups is the National Organization for Decent Literature, a group within the Roman Catholic Church established in 1938 by the Catholic bishops of the United States. In 1955, the bishops set up a National Office for Decent Literature in Chicago, in order to coordinate the work nationally. There are other religious organizations, as well as racial, labor, parent-teachers and women's groups, who also engage in censorship activity, but our attention in this statement is focused on the NODL because of the prominence it has achieved and the great influence it has wielded in removing books from circulation.

THE NATIONAL ORGANIZATION
FOR DECENT LITERATURE

The NODL is a nationwide organization whose membership is largely made up of Roman Catholic laymen; it has active units in several towns and cities. The national and local membership receives guidance from officers and priests of the Roman Catholic church. The purpose of the NODL, as enunciated by the Bishops' Episcopal Committee, was "to organize and set in motion the moral forces of the entire country . . . against the lascivious type of literature which threatens moral, social, and national life"; it has emphasized its efforts to protect youth. The NODL Code, in addition to the negative pledge of removal of "objectionable" literature, also contains the positive pledge to "encourage publishing and distribution of good literature" and "to promote plans to develop worthwhile reading habits during the formative years." To evaluate the literature of our day in terms of its suitability for youth, the NODL, at last report, uses a reading committee of mothers of the Roman Catholic faith in the Chicago area. The NODL's focus has been on magazines, comic books, and paperbound books. It should be noted that the founders of the NODL sought from the beginning to enroll non-Catholics in their efforts. The NODL, says the Bishops' Committee, "appealed to all moral forces to combat the plague of indecent literature. The NODL office was, and is, merely a service organization to coordinate activities and supply information to all interested groups regardless of race, color or creed." The NODL's instruction manual, while listing procedures for individual committees to conduct Parish Decency Crusades, invites the cooperation of non-Catholic groups in the organization of local Decent Literature Committees to carry on the NODL work; such cooperation has not thus far been widespread.

It should be emphasized beyond the possibility of misunderstanding that the ACLU does not presume to object to the NODL's advising communicants of the Roman Catholic Church about any publication. Nor does the Union see any element of censorship in the NODL's informing the general public of its opinion that certain writings are immoral. Such criticism is a right of private freedom, and must immediately be protected when threatened.

From many towns and cities, come reports of extended NODL action which constitutes nothing less than censorship of what the American people as such may read. For example:

1. Roman Catholic parish groups, armed with the NODL list, call upon booksellers (bookstores, drug stores, tobacconists, etc.) and ask that the condemned titles not be offered for sale.
2. The NODL group informs a non-complying bookseller that they will refuse to buy any goods from him, in flagrant contradiction of its own assertion that its list is "merely an expression of a publication's non-conformity with the NODL Code, and that the list is not being used for purposes of boycott or coercion."
3. Newsdealers, druggists, and others who agree in advance not to sell anything to which the NODL objects are given monthly certificates of compliance.
4. Lists of complying, and often of non-complying, dealers are widely publicized, and parishioners are strongly urged to confine their purchases of all commodities to complying dealers. Check-ups are suggested at fortnightly intervals, i.e., a private morals-police force is encouraged to come into being.
5. In many cases police, prosecuting attorneys, and military commanders on Army posts have issued instructions or orders that no books or magazines on the NODL list shall be sold within their jurisdiction, thus putting the authority of the state in the service of a private sectarian group. However, in a recent newspaper article, the Very Reverend Monsignor Thomas J. Fitzgerald, who directs the NODL work, stated, "We request government officials not to use the list. . . . It is up to the courts to decide if a book is obscene."

If these were the acts of government officials, they would at once be challenged in court. That they are the acts of a non-official group makes them more difficult to attack, but they are nonetheless seriously violative of the principle of freedom.

A fundamental objection to these extended activities of the NODL is that the judgment of a particular group is being imposed upon the freedom of choice of the whole community. The novel which may be thought by a committee of Catholic mothers to be unsuitable for a Roman Catholic adolescent is thus made unavailable to the non-Catholic. It is plainly necessary to challenge the NODL as keeper, by self-election, of the conscience of the whole country.

THE NODL BOOK LIST

The argument against censorship applies to all lawfully published books, but it is important to note that many of the authors and titles on the NODL list are considered among the most distinguished in literature. (See the appendix to this statement.)

Books by recipients of the Nobel Prize, the Pulitzer Prize, and the National Book Award have been made markedly less available to the reading public by the censorship of a private and anonymous jury acting under its own standards of morality and taste. And these are books which have been the object of responsible literary criticism and studied in hundreds of literature courses throughout the country.

The ACLU is gratified to record that Roman Catholic opinion is by no means unanimous in support of the activities of the NODL. Father John Courtney Murray, S.J., in recent public statements admirably setting the tone for national discussion of the problem, observes that: ". . . in a pluralist society no minority group has the right to impose its own religious or moral views on other groups, through the methods of force, coercion or violence." (The ACLU emphasizes that this prescription applies as well to majority groups.) Father Murray adds: "Society has an interest in the artist's freedom of expression which is not necessarily shared by the family. If adult standards of literature would be dangerous for children, a child's standard of literature is rather appalling to an adult." He questions, as we do, the use to which the NODL list is put, particularly by public authorities and local zealots who substitute "coercion for cooperation."

The American Civil Liberties Union, which has prepared this statement and solicited signatures in support, is opposed to censorship, official or private, by police authority or by the NODL or any other group. It is our conviction that the people of this country should enjoy to the fullest extent the freedom embodied in the principle of the First Amendment. Specifically, the Union intends to expose in every way it can

---

APPENDIX: NODL BANNED BOOKS

A partial list prepared by the American Book Publishers Council of authors whose works have been or are included on the list of magazines and paperbound books listed as "objectionable" by the National Organization for Decent Literature since 1952.

Nelson Algren
　The Man with the Golden Arm
Louis Auchincloss
　A Law for the Lion
Vicki Baum
　Grand Hotel
Paul Hyde Bonner
　Hotel Talleyrand
Paul Bowles
　The Sheltering Sky
John Horne Burns
　A Cry of Children
James M. Cain
　The Butterfly; Serenade
Erskine Caldwell
　God's Little Acre; Tobacco Road; A House in the Uplands; Tragic Ground; Trouble in July
Joyce Cary
　Herself Surprised
John Dos Passos
　1919; 42nd Parallel
James T. Farrell
　Father and Son; My Days of Anger; A World I Never Made
William Faulkner
　Sanctuary; Soldiers' Pay
Radclyffe Hall
　The Well of Loneliness

Thomas Heggen
　Mister Roberts
Ernest Hemingway
　To Have and Have Not
Aldous Huxley
　Antic Hay
Christopher Isherwood
　The World in the Evening
James Jones
　From Here to Eternity
Arthur Koestler
　The Age of Longing
D. H. Lawrence
　The First Lady Chatterley; Women in Love
Norman Mailer
　Barbary Shore
F. Van Wyck Mason
　Three Harbours
John Masters
　Bhowani Junction; Nightrunners of Bengal
Alberto Moravia
　The Time of Indifference
John O'Hara
　Butterfield 8; The Farmer's Hotel; A Rage to Live
Will Oursler
　N.Y., N.Y.

Ann Petry
　The Narrows
Harold Robbins
　Never Love a Stranger; A Stone for Danny Fisher
J. D. Salinger
　The Catcher in the Rye
Budd Schulberg
　What Makes Sammy Run?
Margery Sharp
　The Stone of Chastity
Irwin Shaw
　The Young Lions
William Styron
　Lie Down in Darkness
Leon Uris
　Battle Cry
Gore Vidal
　The City and the Pillar
Nathanael West
　The Day of the Locust
Kathleen Winsor
　Forever Amber
Ira Wolfert
　Act of Love
Richard Wright
　Native Son
Frank Yerby
　Pride's Castle
Emile Zola
　Nana

NODL LIST AUTHORS WHO ARE LITERARY PRIZE WINNERS

Nelson Algren
　National Book Award, 1950
William Faulkner
　1949 Nobel Prize; National Book Award, 1951 and 1955; O. Henry Short Story Award, 1949; Limited Editions Club (Silver Jubilee Medal), 1954; Joines Award, Award for Merit for the Novel, 1954; 1955 Pulitzer Prize
Ernest Hemingway
　Pulitzer Prize, 1953; Nobel Prize, 1954
James Jones
　National Book Award, 1952
John O'Hara
　National Book Award, 1956
Leon Uris
　California Award (Silver Medal, unclassified), 1955

the use of lists of books as tools of general boycott, and to intervene on behalf of writers, publishers, vendors and purchasers who have the will to explore legal avenues for the maintenance of their freedom. We reiterate, meanwhile, that we will at all times defend the right of such an organization as the NODL to express its views.

This statement is signed by the officers of the American Civil Liberties Union who thereby indicate the intention of the Union to thwart censorship. Other persons who will not necessarily take part in the action of the ACLU have appended their signatures, because of their concern with the freedom of the press and literature and their general agreement with the principles herein set forth.

Another broadside aimed mainly at the National Organization for Decent Literature was fired by John Fischer, editor of *Harper's Magazine*. His scathing analysis of the sometimes disastrous consequences of good intentions brought enthusiastic applause from numerous readers—and the expected screams of protest from friends and supporters of the NODL.

John Fischer
THE HARM GOOD PEOPLE DO

A little band of Catholics is now conducting a shocking attack on the rights of their fellow citizens. They are engaged in an un-American activity which is as flagrant as anything the Communist party ever attempted—and which is, in fact, very similar to Communist tactics. They are harming their country, their Church, and the cause of freedom.

Their campaign is particularly dangerous because few people realize what they are up to. It can hurt you—indeed, it already has—without your knowing it. It is spreading rapidly but quietly; and so far no effective steps have been taken to halt it.

Even the members of this organization probably do not recognize the damage they are doing. They are well-meaning people, acting from deeply moral impulses. They are trying, in a misguided way, to cope with a real national problem, and presumably they think of themselves as patriots and servants of the Lord. Perhaps a majority of Americans, of all faiths, would sympathize with their motives—though not with their methods.

They do not, of course, speak for all Catholics. On the contrary, they are defying the warnings of some of their Church's most respected teachers and theologians. The Catholic Church as a whole certainly cannot be blamed for their actions, any more than it could be held responsible a generation ago for the political operations of Father Coughlin.

This group calls itself the National Organization for Decent Literature. Its headquarters are in Chicago; its director is the Very Reverend Monsignor Thomas Fitzgerald. Its main purpose is to make it impossible for anybody to buy books and other publications which it does not like. Among them are the works of some of the most distinguished authors now alive—for example, winners of the Nobel Prize, the Pulitzer Prize, and the National Book Award.

Its chief method is to put pressure on news dealers, drug stores, and booksellers, to force them to remove from their stocks every item on the NODL blacklist. Included on this list are reprint editions of books by Ernest Hemingway, William Faulkner, John Dos Passos, George Orwell, John O'Hara, Paul Hyde Bonner, Emile Zola, Arthur Koestler, and Joyce Cary. In some places—notably Detroit, Peoria, and the suburbs of Boston—the organization has enlisted the local police to threaten booksellers who are slow to "co-operate."

This campaign of intimidation has no legal basis. The books so listed have not been banned from the mails, and in the overwhelming majority of cases no legal charges have ever been brought against them. Indeed, it seems that the National Organization for Decent Literature deliberately prefers to ignore the established legal channels for proceedings against books which it thinks improper. Its chosen weapons are boycott and literary lynching.

For example, early last year committees of laymen from Catholic churches in the four northern counties of New Jersey—Union, Hudson, Essex, and Bergen—began to call on local

---

John Fischer, "The Harm Good People Do," *Harper's Magazine*, 213:15–20 (October, 1956), copyright 1956 by Harper & Bros. Reprinted by permission of the author.

merchants. These teams were armed with the NODL lists. They offered "certificates," to be renewed each month, to those storekeepers who would agree to remove from sale all of the listed publications. To enforce their demands, they warned the merchants that their parishioners would be advised to patronize only those stores displaying a certificate.

Contact, a bulletin published by the Sacred Heart Parish Societies of Orange, New Jersey, listed fourteen merchants in its March 1955 issue. "The following stores," it said, "have agreed to co-operate with the Parish Decency Committee in not displaying or selling literature disapproved by the National Organization for Decent Literature. . . . Please patronize these stores only. They may be identified by the certificate which is for one month only."

Similar tactics have been followed in scores of other communities. Even in Nevada—a state not noted for Puritanical temper—the Council of Catholic Men has asked booksellers to purge from their shelves a list of books which included such widely read novels as *Mister Roberts* and *From Here to Eternity.* When an Associated Press reporter pointed out that millions of people already were familiar with these works, in print and on film, the state chairman of the campaign, Paul Laxalt of Carson City, replied:

"We've got to stand by the list. If we make one exception the list would be chopped up."

Such tactics are highly effective. Most news dealers, druggists, and similar merchants carry paper-bound books only as a minor side line. Moreover, they receive from the wholesalers more books than they have space for; if they remove one title from their racks, there are plenty of others to take its place. They don't want trouble. It is never good business to argue with a customer—so most of them readily comply with this form of private censorship. After all, their other customers, who might want to read a book by Faulkner or Hemingway or Zola, will never know that it has been suppressed, and when they don't find it on the shelves they probably will buy something else.

For these reasons it was possible for the Archdiocesan Council of Catholic Men in St. Louis to report recently that it had "obtained the consent of about one-third of the store owners approached in a campaign to ask merchants to submit to voluntary screening. . . ."

Something—but not much—can be said in defense of the National Organization for Decent Literature and its local campaigners. A good many tawdry and disreputable magazines, paper-bound reprints, and comic books have been offered for sale on a lot of newsstands. A few publishers unquestionably have tried to base their sales appeal on sex and violence; the pictures and text on the covers of their publications often hint that the contents are far more salacious than they are in fact. (Such misrepresentation, however, is less common now than it was a few years ago, and both the contents and the covers of most pocket-size books seem to be growing less lurid.)

It can be argued, too, that law enforcement agencies in some cities have not been vigorous in enforcing the statutes against obscene publications. Finally, the "decent literature" campaigners apparently feel that their main mission is to protect young people, whose judgment is unformed and who might be attracted to sleazy reading matter by a provocative newsstand display; they seem to take far less interest in the hard-bound editions of the same books available in libraries or regular book stores. The Detroit NODL, for example, states that its list is "not intended as a restrictive list for adults"—though it does not explain how adults could purchase the books if merchants have been persuaded not to stock them.

But the motives of these zealous people are not the issue. The real issue is whether any private group—however well-meaning—has a right to dictate what other people may read.

Clearly any church, or any sub-group within a church, has a right to advise its own members about their reading matter.

Clearly, too, anybody has a right to try to *persuade* other people to read or to refrain from reading anything he sees fit.

The National Organization for Decent Literature, however, goes much further. Its campaign is not aimed at Catholics alone, and it is not attempting to *persuade* readers to follow its views. It is *compelling* readers, of all faiths, to bow to its dislikes, by denying them a free choice in what they buy.

(No doubt unconsciously, the Catholic War Veterans, Our Lady of Sorrows Post No. 1046, underlined the similarity between these tactics and those of the Communists. In a February 25,

1956, mailing to book dealers in Hartford, Connecticut, it enclosed the NODL list of "objectionable" publications—and it quoted the Chinese Communists who have been conducting a campaign of their own against "objectionable" literature: "'These books and pictures seriously harm those workers who by constantly looking at them can easily become degenerate in their thinking,' cautions the *Peking Worker's Daily* as quoted by *Newsweek* magazine, January 23, 1956. We have to hand it to the Communists . . . who have launched a nationwide campaign against pornographic trash. . . . Should not this example provoke a similar literary clean-up in our land where the morality of our actions is gauged by service to God and not to an atheistic state?")

This principle is of course unacceptable to Catholics—as it is to all Americans—if they take the trouble to think about it for a moment. How would Catholics react if, say, a group of Jewish laymen were to threaten merchants with boycott unless they banned from their shops all publications which referred to the divinity of Christ? Some religious denominations believe that gambling is immoral; most Catholics do not, and many of their parishes raise considerable sums by means of bingo games and raffles. What if some Protestant sect were to try to clean out of the stores all publications which spoke tolerantly of gambling, and to boycott every merchant who bought a raffle ticket?

The principle at stake was set forth with admirable clarity by Father John Courtney Murray, S.J., professor of moral theology at Woodstock College, Maryland, in a recent address on "Literature and Censorship." He listed four rules, which ought to command the enthusiastic support of all Americans regardless of religious belief:

1 "Each minority group has the right to censor for its own members, if it so chooses, the contents of the various media of communication, and to protect them, by means of its own choosing, from materials considered harmful according to its standards." (He also pointed out that in the United States "all religious groups . . . are minority groups.")

2 "No minority group has the right to demand that government should impose a general censorship" on material "judged to be harmful according to the special standards held within one group."

3 "Any minority group has the right to work toward the elevation of standards of public morality . . . through the use of the methods of persuasion and pacific argument."

4 "No minority group has the right to impose its own religious or moral views on other groups, through the use of methods of force, coercion, or violence."

And Father Murray went on to warn that methods of coercion are especially imprudent for Catholic associations.

"The chief danger," he said, "is lest the Church itself be identified in the public mind as a power-association. The identification is injurious; it turns into hatred of the faith. And it has the disastrous effect of obscuring from the public view the true visage of the Church as God's kingdom of truth and freedom, justice and love."

He quoted from Jacques Leclercq "of the Catholic University of Louvain, who is no slight authority" the dictum that "no government has ever succeeded in finding a balanced policy of combating unhealthy sexual propaganda without injuring legitimate freedom or provoking other equally grave or worse disorders."

Finally, Father Murray emphasized that "censorship in the civil order must be a judicial process," carried out under the statutes and according to the due processes of law.

The conclusions which flow from Father Murray's teachings seem plain enough:

1. *For the National Organization for Decent Literature*. It should stop immediately its campaign of threats, blacklisting, and boycott. It should then pursue its aims by the legitimate methods of persuasion, propaganda, and action through the courts. Most states have adequate laws against the publication and sale of indecent literature. In cases where the law seems inadequate, the legislature can be persuaded to amend it, by the normal means of lobbying and petition. In cases where the law is not enforced, public officials should certainly be reminded of their duty—and opposed at the polls, in the democratic way, if they fall down on their jobs.

Above all, the NODL ought to consider the possibility of guiding young readers by positive rather than negative techniques. Youngsters are not likely to read trash whenever they have good books readily available. If they are brought up in homes where good literature is a constant part of their environment—where parents read to them from infancy, and encourage them to build up their own libraries—then there is scant chance that they will be attracted by comics or two-bit horrors.

What has the NODL done to urge parents to give their children such basic moral training? Has it done all it can to foster topnotch libraries—public, school, church, and family? In how many communities has it sponsored campaigns to stimulate good reading?

2. *For news dealers, booksellers, and other merchants.* They should muster the courage to defy any group of private citizens which tries to impose its own brand of censorship on the publications they offer for sale. And, with equal courage, they should set their own house in order; they should refuse to sell any publication which—in their own untrammeled judgment—falls below their own standards as responsible business men.

3. *For the patriotic citizen.* He should protest against the lynching of books just as vigorously as against the lynching of people. He should go out of his way to support the merchants who resist such coercion. He should point out to the members of the National Organization for Decent Literature (and to any other self-appointed censors in his community) the immeasurable damage they are doing to the American way of life, to the very foundations of democratic government.

For the gravest harm done here is not to the Catholic Church—though as Father Murray noted, that is dangerous enough—or to the individual who is denied the right to choose his own books. The great peril is to the fabric of orderly government. It is always injured when any group takes the law into its own hands. And whenever such a band of vigilantes succeeds in imposing its will by force, some other—and perhaps more sinister—group is encouraged to try the same thing.

Dean Joseph O'Meara of the Notre Dame Law School recently put it like this:

"Unfortunately many sincere people do not comprehend the genius of our democracy . . . such people would deny free speech to those with whom they are in fundamental disagreement. . . . They would establish a party line in America—*their* party line, of course. This is an alien concept, a totalitarian concept; it is not consonant with the American tradition; it is antidemocratic; it is, in short, subversive and it should be recognized for what it is."

Still another eminent Catholic—Senator John F. Kennedy of Massachusetts—summed up the case in even more prophetic terms.

"The lock on the door of the legislature, the parliament, or the assembly hall," he said, "by order of the King, the Commissar, or the Führer—has historically been followed or preceded by a lock on the door of the printer's, the publisher's, or the bookseller's."

⊂**≣** A veteran of many campaigns in the eternal war against the censors is the Pulitzer Prize-winning playwright, Elmer Rice. As a speaker, writer, and participant in the affairs of the American Civil Liberties Union, he has always been outspoken against attempts to restrict literary freedom. In "New Fashions in Censorship," he reviews the activities of some of the special-interest pressure groups, letting the chips fall where they may.

Elmer Rice
NEW FASHIONS IN CENSORSHIP

Censorship in the United States used to consist mainly of governmental action such as customs seizure of imported publications; denial or revocation of mailing privileges by the Post Office; raids on bookshops; arrests of actors and producers. The motivation was almost invariably an allegation of obscenity—a term virtually impossible of definition.

With the growth of the motion picture industry, censorship boards were established in many states, and municipal authorities were vested with censorial powers or arbitrarily assumed them.

Since censorship was official, it was out in the open and easily recognizable. Since it violated the free speech and free press guarantees of the Constitution, it was relatively easy to attack on

---

Elmer Rice, "New Fashions in Censorship," *Survey*, 88:112–15 (March, 1952), copyright 1952 by the Survey Associates, Inc. Reprinted by permission of the author.

legal grounds. Since it dealt mainly with so-called "indecency," it was often possible to show that public standards of propriety were less rigid than those of the censors.

The obsolescence of Victorian conceptions of morality, and the persistent efforts of the American Civil Liberties Union and other organizations, resulted in court decisions that sharply curtailed the unconstitutional exercise of power by state legislatures and administrative officials. Book publishers fought and won many important cases; and actors, dramatists, and theatrical producers contested the improper use of the licensing power and defeated periodic attempts to set up a censorship.

In the motion picture field, however, state censorship boards (with vested interests of political patronage), continue to flourish, and numerous local censors exercise arbitrary control over the exhibition of motion pictures. Proponents of civil liberties contend that the operation of these agencies violates the Bill of Rights.

Forty years ago, the Supreme Court of the United States ruled that motion pictures were merely a form of entertainment, and were not protected by the First Amendment. But in view of the present-day importance of the motion picture, it seems unlikely that the Court now would take this view. In fact, in a recent decision, Justice William O. Douglas intimated that, given the opportunity, the Court would modify its position. Such an opportunity may be found when the pending case of "The Miracle" (to which I shall refer later), comes before the Court. Should the Court hold the First Amendment applicable to motion pictures, the state boards would have to go out of business, and local censors would be in a highly vulnerable position.

This might indicate that progress is being made and that bit by bit restraints upon freedom of expression are being loosened. And, in a sense, it is encouraging to find that, at a time when so many people are alarmed by the encroachments of bureaucracy, official interference with freedom of expression actually is abating.

Unfortunately, with the decline of official censorship, there has grown up a great, complex structure of what may be called unofficial censorship. This works deviously and far more effectively, than the easily assailable acts of public officials.

The reason books and plays remain relatively free from censorship, is that publishing and play-producing are small, individualistic enterprises, serving a limited market. They are still in the handicraft stage of industrial development, in which craftsmanship and personal idiosyncrasy are more important than standardization and merchandising.

The other channels of public communication —the press, the national circulation magazines, motion pictures, radio, and television—largely have been taken over by big business. These industries (for that is what they are) depend, like automobiles and canned goods, upon quantity output, assembly-line production, and mass distribution. The craftsman and the creator are still there; the industries could not function without them. There are many brilliant journalists, and magazine, scenario, and radio writers, but few of them now function as free and independent creators. They are employes, and as such they must write what they are bidden to write, or—and it amounts to the same thing—what conforms to their employer's prejudices or to his conception of what is good business.

Of course, a theatrical manager does not produce a play he does not like; nor does a publisher bring out a book that offends him. But in these fields there is still great diversity, and a good book, no matter how unorthodox, seldom goes unpublished, nor a good play unproduced. On the other hand, the more the mass communications industries expand, the more their control tends to become concentrated in fewer and fewer hands.

First, take the press. The forthright and often wrongheaded editor, who used to use his paper as a sounding-board for his own opinions, has almost ceased to exist. As the population grows, the number of newspapers declines and the independent newspaper tends to disappear entirely. The big syndicates—Hearst, Scripps-Howard, McCormick-Patterson, Gannett—are in full command. They are run impersonally from headquarters, with one eye fixed on circulation and the other on advertising linage. Even the small town newspaper has almost completely lost its identity. Its meager general news is fed to it by the wire services. Except for a few local items, all the rest is boiler-plate stuff—tear out the local page, and you will have a hard time discovering whether you are in Florida, Ohio, or Oregon.

Technically, of course, this is not censorship. The Constitution is not violated, no law is broken (unless possibly the anti-trust law). Theoretically, anybody can start a newspaper, and say anything he pleases. But unless he is a multimillionaire, the individual who tries it will end up in the lunatic asylum, or on the relief rolls.

In the periodical field, the situation is much the same. To pay their way, most magazines depend upon advertising. To get advertising, they must have circulation. To get circulation, they must appeal to the largest possible number of potential readers. That is to say, they must not only cater to the tastes (actual or hypothetical) of millions, but they must avoid anything that might conceivably run counter to the beliefs, prejudices, or superstitions of any considerable segment of the population, or of any well organized minority.

The production of motion pictures is dominated almost entirely by seven or eight large companies, which not only own the mechanical facilities, but control, directly or indirectly, the essential outlets: the 15,000 motion picture theaters of the country. Since the same considerations of mass appeal govern as in the newspaper and magazine fields (except that here the audience is measured not by millions but by tens of millions) it is not surprising that the product is conventional, standardized, and on a low level of intelligence and perception. Besides being restricted by official censorship agencies, the motion picture industry operates under a "code" which is a fantastic hodge-podge of taboos and prohibitions.

There is so much creative talent in Hollywood, that, in spite of all restraining influences, a vital, original, or unorthodox motion picture manages, now and then, to get produced. Barring these few honorable exceptions, it is apparent that the Hollywood product consists almost entirely of routine stuff manufactured in accordance with preconceived formulas, and designed for mass consumption. Since the motion picture audience consists largely of adolescents (perhaps because of the failure of the industry to provide fare for adults), the false values and standardized ideas which are disseminated play an important, and often harmful, part in shaping the minds and feelings of the immature. Equally harmful is the false impression of American life created by our films in other countries, millions of whose people have no other source of information about us. Any traveler can testify to the grotesque misconceptions held by those abroad who have been fed on a diet of American films.

With respect to radio, and its gargantuan baby brother, television, the situation, though apparently somewhat different, is essentially the same. Physical control of the outlets is concentrated in the hands of a few nationwide networks. Scattered independent stations, most of them in large metropolitan areas, manage to maintain a hand-to-mouth existence, but their influence is largely local and their programing restricted by lack of capital. Furthermore, the total number of stations is restricted by the limitation of wavelengths and channels.

Paradoxically, however, it is this very limitation that is largely responsible for such freedom as exists on the air. Since the number of applicants for station licenses exceeds the available wave-lengths, the Federal Communications Commission is empowered to allocate wavelengths on the basis of public service rendered by the applicant. Hence, the station licenses must allot a certain percentage of air time to programs of public interest and must restrict somewhat the excesses of the advertisers.

Because of this licensing system, there is a certain amount of freedom of discussion on the air; and also some cultural window-dressing—particularly at hours which are not desirable to advertisers. In the relatively noncontroversial field of music, there is considerable diversity. News coverage, on the whole, is good, as long as the news program is unsponsored. But when there is commercial sponsorship, the reporter is faced only too often with the alternatives of conforming to the opinions of the advertiser or seeking other employment.

To sum up the radio and television situation: it is the advertiser who pays the piper and hence calls the tune. In this field, creativeness, self-expression, and freedom of communication are mere incidentals to the selling of merchandise. The persons and material employed by the advertiser are used only for the purpose of subjecting the viewer or listener to an appeal to hurry to the corner drugstore. The value and importance of what is communicated by the participants in the program are judged in terms of effectiveness in increasing the advertiser's sales. Hence, the opportunity to be seen or heard on the air is mainly determined by the advertiser's judgment of what is or is not good business.

This brief survey brings us to a consideration of the new techniques of propaganda which result in the establishment of an elusive, but highly effective form of censorship. These techniques have been developed by the organization of individuals with common interests, into what are called pressure groups. They may be political, economic, professional, religious, racial, national or whatever. They consist of individuals, comprising a minority of the population, banded together for the purpose of asserting or defending some particular interest of their own.

There can be no doubt that these groups play a useful part in the life of the community. In our heterogeneous society, the rights of minorities are often ignored or brutally overridden. It is necessary for minorities to organize in order to better their condition and to redress the social and economic injustices to which they often are subjected. Every believer in democracy and in human welfare must applaud and support the efforts of Roman Catholics, Jews, Negroes, veterans, the foreign-born, wage earners, and of many other groups to win equality before the law, freedom from discrimination, and a fair share of the good things of our society.

But no group, no matter what its grievances or its objectives, should insist upon the protection of its own rights and interests at the expense of the rights and interests of the majority of the community. Every individual, in so far as his particular interests are concerned, is both a member of a minority group, *vis-à-vis* the majority; and a member of the majority, *vis-à-vis* any particular special interest group. As a responsible citizen, he therefore has an obligation not only to respect the rights of all minorities, but also to recognize that in a democracy, no minority can press its claims to the point of violating the rights of the majority.

Unfortunately, minority groups, in an excess of zeal, have become more and more insistent that anything which runs counter to their beliefs or which might conceivably reflect unfavorably upon their members, shall be denied a public hearing. They have learned only too well the efficacy of pressure upon the pocketbook nerve and by direct or implied threats of boycott and other forms of economic reprisal only too often have succeeded in getting the profit-minded controllers of the channels of communication to yield to demands for suppression. (It has become a grim joke among writers, for example, that, to play safe, you have to make your villain a native-born, white Protestant.)

A few instances, picked almost at random, will show how this censorship by pressure groups works. One of the most important, at the moment, is the banning of the motion picture, "The Miracle." This foreign film, which received awards in Europe and was acclaimed by the press and public here (after having been licensed by the New York State Censorship Board) was banned by court action, instituted by the Roman Catholic hierarchy, upon the ground of sacrilege, after the failure of an attempt by the New York City Commissioner of Licenses to use his power without legal justification.

In spite of the fact that the picture was highly recommended by Protestant clergymen and by well-known Roman Catholic laymen, the suppression of the picture was upheld by a majority of the Court of Appeals, which denied the applicability of the free speech guarantee of the Bill of Rights, upon the basis of the forty-year old decision of the Supreme Court of the United States, previously referred to. The "Miracle" case is now before the Supreme Court and its determination may have very important effects upon the future of free speech in this country. According to *The New York Times,* the Court is expected to hear the arguments in early April and to hand down its decision before its summer recess in June.

The Roman Catholic Church, perhaps because of its numerical strength and efficient organization, is one of the most influential pressure groups. The Church succeeded in banning *The Nation* from the New York City public schools because that magazine carried articles criticizing the activities of the Church in such fields as education, public health, and municipal government. In Philadelphia, a Roman Catholic priest prevented the exhibition of a motion picture by threatening that his parishioners would boycott not only that particular picture, but any picture exhibited by the offending theater. In Providence, Rhode Island, the Chief of Police forbade the reissue of a twenty-year old picture (which he admitted he had not seen) on the ground that no picture objectionable to the Catholic Legion of Decency could be shown in the city.

Other groups are equally culpable. For two years, Jewish organizations prevented the exhibition of the film version of "Oliver Twist," a faithful transcription of the Dickens classic, which had been shown successfully in England and Canada. (None of the objectors had seen the film, but based their protest upon its denunciation by a newspaper columnist, who afterwards wrote me that he felt he had made a serious mistake in demanding the suppression of the film.) Margaret Webster had to withdraw "The Merchant of Venice" from her projected Shakespearean repertory, when several large universities threatened to cancel their bookings if she included it. At a forum on civil liberties at which I presided, a representative of a Jewish organization advocated that any book which depicted a Jew in an unfavorable light should be excluded from school curricula and public libraries.

Branches of the National Association for the Advancement of Colored People (a splendid organization) have attempted to prevent the exhibition of "The Birth of a Nation," and to suppress touring companies of "Uncle Tom's Cabin"; and the organization itself has used threats of economic boycott in an attempt to force the television programs of "Beulah," and "Amos 'n Andy" off the air. During a recent revival on Broadway of "The Green Pastures," a play of outstanding excellence, a Negro bishop preached a sermon in which he demanded the banning of the play upon the ground that it brought discredit to the Negro race.

Veterans' organizations have been conspicuously successful in attempts to suppress everything and everybody with political opinions that run counter to their dogmas. In Oklahoma, the American Legion forced a librarian out of her job solely because she subscribed to *The Nation*. In Illinois, the Legion tried to prevent performances of "The Death of a Salesman" upon the ground that its author was listed in *Red Channels*. The play went on, but most of the would-be patrons were frightened away.

Due in large part to the activities of small units of the American Legion, scores of well known actors and writers are unable to find employment in radio, television, or motion pictures.

The organized alumni of a large eastern college prevented the exhibition of a film in which undergraduates of the college were unflatteringly portrayed. Organized social agencies served notice on Hollywood that in the screen version of a successful play, an unsympathetic character must not be identified as a social worker—and Hollywood obeyed.

Public utilities interests see to it that favorable reference to public ownership does not creep into textbooks.

Business and veterans' organizations are successfully agitating for a weeding out of school books that contain "subversive" ideas.

Left-wing groups tried to prevent the release of a film unfavorable to the Soviet Union.

Under pressure from Christian Scientists, the New York State Board of Regents this academic year ordered that questions dealing with the germ theory of disease be omitted from biology examination papers.

Each of these groups, of course, offers plausible reasons for its actions, and undoubtedly each has the right to agitate for its particular interests. But to anyone who views the whole picture objectively, it must be apparent that the total effect of all these pressures, impinging upon the relatively few focal areas of control, is to restrict freedom of expression in the mass media of communication and to reduce all expression to an innocuous, sterile, deadly uniformity, characteristic of totalitarianism rather than of democracy.

Without free speech, democracy cannot continue to exist; and free speech means the unlimited and unimpeded right to say anything. It does not matter whether what is said is Right or Left, right or wrong. What is important is the unrestricted ventilation of ideas, opinions, dogmas, prejudices. It is from the clash and competition of these multiple expressions that we learn, develop, and progress. Eventually, we must hope, the truth will prevail. There is no other hope for humanity.

To assure the realization of this ideal of free speech, two conditions are necessary. The first is diversity of outlet; the second, non-interference by influential minorities. It is easy enough to state these conditions; their establishment is not so easy.

There can be diversity of outlet only if there is diversity of ownership and control. The development of industrial organization is in the direction of more, rather than less, centralization of power. Legal remedies against monopoly are not very effective. Anti-trust laws are easily evaded, and most business men are inclined to put business considerations first. Since writers tend more and more to become employes, rather than independent creators, necessarily they must conform more and more to the rules laid down by their employers. It is utopian to hope that there will arise a group of leading executives in the communications industries who will put devotion to free speech above everything else.

It remains then for the militant minority groups to modify their demands and to change their tactics. Even from a purely selfish point of view, that would be advisable. For the rights of any minority are conditioned by the rights of all. To demand restrictions upon another's right to expression is to invite restrictions of one's own. He who comes into equity must come with clean hands; and he who demands the freedom of the market place for himself must not attempt to deny it to others.

Looking at the problem in terms of the general good, it must be obvious to any clear-thinking person that censorship springs from fear. And those who have not learned by now that fear is our worst enemy had better learn it before it is too late.

Ring Lardner's extraordinary talent for exposing the cheap, the shoddy, and the meretricious has been inherited by his son John. A regular contributor to *Newsweek,* John Lardner aimed his sharpest barbs for two consecutive issues at the city (Detroit) which has lately taken over Boston's old title of "Censorship Capital of America," and, in particular, at Inspector Herbert W. Case of the Detroit Police License and Censor Bureau, who directed the censorship program.

John Lardner
LET 'EM EAT NEWSPAPERS

When a horse-player wants to know what is what, he consults the selections, the "line," of an expert handicapper. When a police chief or city censor wants to know what books to ban, he sends for the "Detroit Line"—which is the obscenity list compiled and rechecked from month to month by Inspector Herbert W. Case of the Detroit police license and censor bureau, who is the country's foremost handicapper of dirty literature, such as Farrell, Hemingway, Simenon, and Hans Christian Andersen.

Case, the Detroit handicapper, has been in the smut-detection game for nearly twenty years. He began following and clocking "sexed-up" books —a censors' trade expression—in 1937, when he was a patrolman, or buck censor. He worked his way up through the ranks, as a sergeant censor and a lieutenant censor, till he became an inspector, and the editor in chief of the red-hot, nationally respected Detroit Line on books.

The Detroit Line came into being in 1951, which was a key year in the history of book-banning. Up to then, Inspector Case had to "wait books out"—that is, he had to wait till "Strange Fruit," or "To Have and Have Not," went on sale, before he could ban it. In 1951, he got the idea of censoring books at the source, by telling the distributors what not to distribute.

"Voluntary censorship is the ideal method of suppression," the inspector said one day a couple of years ago, while talking shop.

Today, his policy is to "skim off the filth, so to speak, at the top." Once the distributors get the Line, the stores don't get the books. In size, the Line runs to about 150 "banned" books, and 200 "objectionable" books—the "objectionable" books, as handicapped by Case, being books that are not legally banned, but why try to sell them? As a result of the growing popularity of the Line with wholesalers, all of whom are fans and readers of Case, there are regularly more than 300 books which Detroiters not only never have seen, but never have heard of, since the censorship list is censored, or, anyway, unannounced.

Twelve cops, or assistant clockers, work night and day reading books for the Detroit Line. In an average year, they put in 750 hours of overtime, at the risk of corrupting their own minds to save the public's. When the filth has been skimmed off, as the inspector puts it, it is sent

---

John Lardner, "Let 'em Eat Newspapers," *Newsweek,* 45:92 (March 14, 1955), copyright 1955 by Weekly Publications, Inc. Reprinted by permission of the publisher.

over in sanitary containers to the prosecutor's office, for a legal ruling. In a sense, the prosecutor is the unsung hero of the Case censorship operation, because he never gets to read anything in business hours but pure, distilled pornography. Not a nickel's worth of context. Just dirt, or what the clockers think is dirt.

A feature of the Case handicapping service is that it censors nothing but paperback books. The buyer of hardback, $3.95 books is free to ruin his morals on his own time. Critics of the Detroit Line have called this rule undemocratic —the rich can have books, the poor can't. In short, let 'em eat newspapers.

But Inspector Case does not think of buyers of paperback books as "poor"; he thinks of them as "the adolescent, the weak, and susceptible." In other words, the whole concept of low-cost literature, of bringing reading to the masses, is unsound. The inspector spotted it back in 1950. He looked at the "sexed-up" covers on the paperbacks. Then he looked inside, and saw that the books were sexed-up, too. The inspector has pretty well reached the conclusion of the Gathings Committee, in Congress, in 1952, that the whole low-cost book dodge is rotten; that "pocket-size books, which originally started out as cheap reprints of standard works, have largely degenerated into media for the dissemination of artful appeals to sensuality, immorality, filth, perversion, and degeneracy."

As noted above, the Detroit Line is now standard for local book-banners around the country. Censors in some 70 or 80 towns are said to have subscribed to the Line, which Case sends to fellow salacity-sleuths on request. The beauty of the service is that it stimulates new ideas. How else would the womanhood of San Antonio, Texas, have thought of banning Chaucer, and "Moby Dick"?

John Lardner
THE SMUT DETECTIVE

Inspector Herbert W. Case, of the Detroit police license and censor bureau, the country's leading handicapper of literature, or smut sleuth, has often said that he will be glad to send his Detroit Line (of pocket-size books to be banned) to any town where the local censor asks for it.

He and his team of twelve censors think of themselves as "big brothers," the inspector said one time, to smaller communities who don't have the time and money to find out for themselves that Andersen's fairy tales are obscene. Or that Havelock Ellis is a dirty writer. Case's clockers are willing to shoulder the load of the work, if they have to—even when it means reading pornographers like Dos Passos and Hemingway so late into the night that these honest cops see verbs before their eyes as they stagger to bed.

"Inspector," a congressman asked Case a couple of years ago, "your men do not resent having to go through the stuff?"

The inspector replied that they were all dead game.

"We are in the middle of the stream, and swimming," he said, "and we want to keep on for a while."

But that doesn't mean that they like it. The question that burns in Case's mind, he has said, is, why do the publishers force the trouble and expense of saving the country on him? In other words, why do they go on publishing books?

It is not as though the license and censor bureau—Case's handicapping service—had nothing else to do. In the year 1951 alone, the bureau inspected 241 juke boxes, cleaned up 69 burlesque scripts, and passed out seven warning tickets to saloons for improper lighting. This was in addition to 721 man-hours of "home reading" of filthy-minded novelists, and the banning of 39 books.

It was in 1951 that Case began "skimming off the filth, so to speak, at the top"; that is, keeping books off the stands to begin with, instead of letting them go on sale and knocking them down one by one. Between that time and the beginning of this year, 265 different books have been banned in Detroit. That does not include several hundred titles on the "objectionable," or I-wouldn't-sell-this-if-I-was-you, list. It's not illegal to display the books on the second list. It's just that no dealer in Detroit ever has.

Books banned by the Detroit Line—and recommended for banning to out-of-town censors who play the Line—include Ellis's "Psychology of Sex," Dos Passos's "1919," Salinger's "The

---

John Lardner, "The Smut Detective," *Newsweek,* 45:95 (March 21, 1955), copyright 1955 by Weekly Publications, Inc. Reprinted by permission of the publisher.

Catcher in the Rye," Hemingway's "Across the River and Into the Trees," O'Hara's "The Farmer's Hotel," Willingham's "End as a Man," Andersen's "Fairy Tales," Norman Mailer's "Barbary Shore," Russell Thacher's "The Captain," Lillian Smith's "Strange Fruit," Jones's "From Here to Eternity," Uris's "Battle Cry," and Farrell's "A World I Never Made"—all in the pocket size designed to be read by the evil-minded nonrich.

The thought of Case's cops turning tiny page after tiny page in search of four-letter words, when they might be out fingerprinting stripteasers, is saddening—as Case says, "I think it definitely is the publisher's responsibility" to delouse literature in advance.

But there is relief, and a better day, in sight. Already, Case says, at least one paperback publisher has begun to play ball with society by sending his manuscripts to Case's copy desk for editing before publication. This does not mean, as yet, less work for the cops. They still have to read, in order to advise the publisher what to do. The chances are, however, that under their firm but kindly discipline, the publisher—and other publishers, as they, too, begin to avail themselves of Case's literary tips—will cut down their output considerably, and eventually cure themselves of publishing altogether. Like smoking or drinking, it's just a habit.

A Congressional investigator once asked Case if a publisher, having put out a special, clean Detroit edition of the book, could afford to print up the original, dirty version for other towns? Or would the Detroit model be national?

MR. CASE: It probably would.

He said a mouthful.

☞ Another broadside at the "Detroit Line" and various private organizations engaged in book censorship is John H. Griffin's "Prude and the Lewd." Mr. Griffin is a blinded war veteran and a Catholic. The paperback edition of his *The Devil Rides Outside* has been confiscated by police in Detroit and elsewhere. As John Fischer so cogently expressed the matter earlier, Mr. Griffin maintains that good intentions are not sufficient to balance the evil done by sectarian and other groups operating as censors.

John H. Griffin
PRUDE AND
THE LEWD—
WHEREIN THE
BIGGER PERIL?

Obscene, lewd, lascivious, filthy, indecent, and disgusting—these are the six adjectives connected with censorship. No two persons agree on their precise definition, as Ernst and Seagle point out in their book "To the Pure." The League of Nations was unable to arrive at a legal definition of obscenity, the most frequently used adjective of all.

In the new wave of censorship that is sweeping all English-speaking countries, we are seeing familiar patterns repeated. Beginning with the laudable purpose of suppressing pornography, censorship historically ends up by engulfing more and more works of legitimate value and by spreading beyond the realm of creative literature to technical and philosophical works as well.

In this process, since no one has ever defined obscenity in a satisfactory manner, the general test is based on Chief Justice Cockburn's ruling in the case of *Regina v. Hicklin* in 1868:

> The test for obscenity is this: whether the tendency of the matter charged as obscenity is to deprave and corrupt those whose minds are open to such immoral influences, and into whose hands a publication of this sort may fall.

This sounds reasonable enough, but it only takes a moment's study to see that it actually means nothing insofar as legal precision is concerned, since it is predicated upon unascertainable, indefinite standards. For who can say whether the tendency of such and such a work is to deprave and corrupt one person, not another? And how does one determine who exactly are those "whose minds are open to such immoral influences"? And, of course, who is to know "into whose hands a publication of this sort may fall"?

This evaluation is supported by the decision of Judge Curtis Bok in *Commonwealth v. Gordon,* Philadelphia, 1949:

John H. Griffin, "Prude and the Lewd—Wherein the Bigger Peril?" *Nation,* 181:382–84 (November 5, 1955), copyright 1955 by the Nation Associates, Inc. Reprinted by permission of the publisher.

Strictly applied, this [Cockburn's] rule renders any book unsafe, since a moron could pervert to some sexual fantasy to which his mind is open the listings of a seed catalogue. Not even the Bible would be exempt.... Who can define the clear and present danger to the community that arises from reading a book? If we say that it is that the reader is young and inexperienced and incapable of resisting the sexual temptations that the book may present to him, we put the entire reading public at the mercy of the adolescent mind and of those adolescents who do not have the expected advantages of home influence, school training, or religious teaching. If the argument be applied to the general public, the situation becomes absurd, for then no publication is safe.

The Cockburn test is still used as the basis for censorship legislation and for the judging of a work as obscene. A number of states have statutes which define as obscene "any publication *containing* obscene, immoral, lewd, or lascivious material tending to incite *minors* to violent or depraved or immoral acts, manifestly tending to the corruption of the morals of youth" (Emphasis added).

This again sounds admirable, except that under this ruling virtually every major author, including Nobel and Pulitzer prize-winners, has been banned from public sale as obscene. It is even more faulty than the original Cockburn statement and appears to be a clear violation of the rights guaranteed under the First and Fourteenth Amendments to the Constitution of the United States in that it: (1) prohibits the distribution of any book to any member of the public because of the hypothetical effect the book might tend to have merely on minors; (2) permits books to be banned merely on the basis of *containing* questionable passages; (3) offers no express definition of what constitutes obscenity, and therefore many passages of legitimate realistic description can be proscribed merely on the basis of differing tastes.

Few people realize the far-reaching aspects of the statement: "... any publication containing obscene, immoral, lewd, or lascivious material." Art, in order to have any influence on man's understanding, must exist whole. Unless a work be considered as an entity, there is obviously no way of judging its validity. Isolated words and phrases torn out of context from the Bible, for example, sound exactly like those same words and phrases lifted from some pornographic book, and on the basis of merely *containing* such words and phrases the one is as subject to banning as the other. This is essentially what happens. So-called objectionable words and phrases are copied out of context, a list of them is handed to the censor, and he is obliged to decide the obscenity of the work on the basis of whether or not a fourteen-year-old child should be allowed books *containing* such words and phrases. The answer is as obvious as the process is puerile. It is like taking a photograph of the navel of Michelangelo's David and asking someone unfamiliar with the entire figure if he would like to have his fourteen-year-old daughter see a statue containing such realistic details.

In his testimony before the Gathings committee, Inspector Herbert Case, in charge of the Detroit police department's censor bureau, stated: "We in our municipality feel that the law and the statutes and everything are intended to protect the adolescent, the weak, and susceptible." This, again, is admirable, but it becomes vicious when the adult public is denied the right to any book on the basis of its possible harm to the "adolescent, the weak, and susceptible," and in passing it might be added that the Detroit blacklist reads like a Who's Who of our most respected novelists. Yet you can still walk into hotels and drugstores and buy the same old "Violent Honeymoon" and "Midnight Passion" trash because publishers have simply deleted the objectionable words and phrases. Actions such as Detroit's succeed effectively in banning everything except the innocuous and the mediocre.

Judge Learned Hand in *United States v. Kennerley* observed that this type of obscenity test would "reduce our treatment of sex to the standard of a child's library in the supposed interest of a salacious few" and "forbid all which might corrupt the most corruptible." Accordingly, authors of the caliber of Faulkner, Hemingway, Mauriac, Huxley, Greene, Dos Passos, Zola, and even Boccaccio, plus many others, are being branded as pornographers and their works dismissed as "obscene."

Although, as we shall see, all censorship can be lumped together, since all of it commits the same errors and is based on the same fallacy of juvenile behavior, it is necessary to point out that there are three general types of censorship currently practiced in the English-speaking world.

First, there is the police censor who derives

his authority to ban books from such statutes as the one I have discussed. An assigned policeman goes through new books, or reprints of old ones, and rejects from public sale those which he thinks might conceivably harm the young, the weak, and susceptible. He is often "aided" in making up his blacklist by lists furnished him by religious and sectarian organizations. Then there is the censorship board, such as that in effect in Georgia, where a three-man group of private citizens does the filth-hunting. And finally there is the so-called hidden censorship, consisting of religious and civic groups, leagues for and against this and that, which use a technique of pressures on bookshop owners in somewhat this manner: A representative of the group visits the local bookstores, presents them with lists of works which the group finds objectionable, promises them a plaque of cooperation if the blacklisted books are removed from sale, and indicates that lists of cooperating and non-cooperating stores will be published. Thus, through furnishing lists to tired police censors and to bookstores, these groups apply very effective censorship, replacing the "due processes of law" by extra-legal pressures to attain their ends. This practice is followed by many religious organizations of laymen, such as, for example, the National Organization for Decent Literature.

No one would deny the right of any sectarian group to discourage its members from reading books which are offensive to it, but such a prerogative becomes vicious when it is used to deprive others, who are not members of that particular group, from access to work to which they have a perfect right, according to the legal standards of the United States. Speaking of this, Victor Weybright, in his testimony before the Gathings committee, said:

> The fact that these groups act from the best of motives does not alter the fact that their attempt to pose such extra-legal standards is a clear infringement of the right of the reading public to select for itself what it will read. When the action of local or sectarian groups takes the form of pressure applied to distributors and dealers, whether or not with the assistance of local law-enforcement agencies, it becomes a secondary boycott which may be actionable as an illegal restraint of trade.

Censorship, by depriving the community of the right of access to serious works because it cannot distinguish pornography from realism, thereby commits mankind to a cultural and ethical hara-kiri. The list of abuses is far too long to be presented here, but it must be apparent that wherever these censorship drives have started they have invariably spread to works that could not conceivably be considered obscene. In one English community recently, "The Decameron" was banned along with trash such as "Foolish Virgin Says No." In another English community, a novel highly respected in America and Europe was banned because, according to the censor, "there is an insidious, sneaking Roman Catholic propaganda in it which I detest." The censor added that he would keep it "even from septuagenarians," which somewhat removes us from the criterion, false though it may be, of "the young, the weak, and susceptible."

The difference between pornography and the legitimate and necessary treatment of evil in literature is one which appears to escape these censoring agents. Every great artist, whether he is conscious of it or not, in some way illuminates the mystery of evil. But the pornographer wallows in evil, illuminating nothing. Unable to distinguish art from pornography, the average censoring body simply denies that the distinction exists. Reverend Dr. James Wesberry, chairman of Georgia's three-man censorship board, has said: "I don't discriminate between nude women, whether or not they are art. It's all lustful to me."

There is, then, particularly among the clergy and religious groups of all sorts, a growing clamor based on good intentions and a total disrespect for accepted artistic standards, which denounces anything not totally innocuous as "contemporary" or "new," with the implication that it depraves our children—or they presume it does, for it is odd that none of these youths has ever been presented in evidence as having been corrupted by banned works of literary stature. No, what is "new," of course, is the idea that we can no longer exercise parental control over our children. We do not ban essentially adult products in the pharmaceutical lines, we do not ban alcohol and cigarettes on the basis of our not desiring our fourteen-year-olds to use them. It is therefore intriguing that in what concerns literature and art, parental control mysteriously vanishes and we must deprive everyone of these works, which range from the Latin classics through Shakespeare and Shaw and the real contemporaries, some of which are admittedly adult fare, sometimes even the fare of scholars, theologians, and scientists—as the recently banned "Phallic Worship," a noted work in its field—on the formula of their possible harm to our children.

And what about this juvenile corruption of which we hear so much? Where does the problem really lie? It lies squarely in the home, the school, and the church. By the time the corruptible youth reaches an age to understand what he is reading and to be sensitive enough to it to be corrupted, his background training and moral development will have already been fairly well established; and if this has been properly done, art, no matter how realistic, will serve for him the same function it has for all men in the past: the dissemination of truth and the creation of perspective and compassion. Blaming truthful art for juvenile corruption is like blaming one's mother for original sin—the harm will have been done before either enters the picture. Does not this banning, making literature the scapegoat, indicate only one thing: defeat within the home? Another very new thing, of course, is that you build resistance to temptation by hiding it under a barrel. The legitimacy of these new ideas is richly indicated by the juvenile crime rates, which are high in banning countries and low in those where great art, and frank art, is a part of daily life under the guidance and control of parents. This is indisputable. Too many bishops and saints were reared on works now subject to banning. Cardinal Newman said:

> We cannot have a sinless literature about sinful men, and nothing is barred per se.

Huntington Cairns, one of the most astute critics of censorship in this country, observes:

> In general such men [police censors] have had little or no contact with science and art, have had no knowledge of the liberty of expression tacitly granted to men of letters since the beginnings of English literature, and have been, from the point of view of expert opinion, altogether incompetent to handle the subject.

How much less qualified as experts are those chosen at random from church and community groups on the basis of some fervor to "clean things up." This cleaning is producing an error of national proportions of which the average layman is more or less unaware.

Leon Bloy ascribes the error to two causes: ". . . the astounding unintelligence of modern Christians and their deep aversion to the beautiful." More detailed causes might be these:

That a problem of the most profound significance is attacked in its most superficial aspects;

That the censors appear innocent of any awareness of the supreme importance of art in the maintenance of a culture, particularly when that art offends some cherished prejudice, and are therefore willing and glad to sacrifice highly regarded works "to the good cause."

It has always been so, and there is little hope that the cycle will not again complete itself without going to an extreme that will make the demands for freedom of press and pen the subject of bitterly fought battles; for the public is always late in realizing that between the two evils, the prude does it ultimately greater harm than the lewd person. The prude and the bigot are what they are precisely because they lack qualities of prudence and understanding. Moral virtue, behind which they hide, is impossible without these intellectual virtues of prudence and understanding which direct man to the *proper means* of achieving his goals. Power, then, in the hands of people who are currently embracing censorship with neither prudence nor understanding, must inevitably result in abuse. Seemingly admirable motives obscure the true damage caused by such people until it reaches commanding dimensions —dimensions which it is now reaching in our English-speaking countries.

To the author, viewing this situation, it is indeed a source of some confusion that tempts him to throw up his hands and say: "What's the use? What's the use when such innocents are waiting to pounce on the lowest elements within a work without viewing those elements in the light of their function or treatment?" Pascal long ago described this tendency:

> No, no, if they are great it is because their heads are higher—a thing which we cannot see if we look only at their feet which are on the same ground as ours.

But to some, this situation in itself is a challenge, a challenge to discover how in this most advanced of all technological ages, when the degree of literacy is higher than ever before, how in this enlightened age a whole mass of people can have reached such a pitch of fervor over such a patently self-destructive ideal. Here, for the author who would illuminate the mystery of evil, is an evil of magnitude.

152 Giving others the courage of our convictions

The attitudes of American minority groups toward censorship are analyzed in these two articles by John Haynes Holmes and John Mason Brown. The Jews and the Negroes, in particular, perhaps because they themselves have so often been victims of misrepresentation, defamation, and oppression, have been abnormally sensitive to any literary works which appeared to malign them.

John Haynes Holmes, for over forty years pastor of the Community Church in New York, has seen long service as an officer of the American Civil Liberties Union and the National Association for the Advancement of Colored People. He was awarded the Gottheil medal in 1933 for his services to the Jewish people.

John Mason Brown is widely known as a dramatic critic, prolific author of works relating to the theater, and popular lecturer.

John Haynes Holmes
SENSITIVITY AS CENSOR

A serious situation is arising in the field of civil liberties, through the current attempt of well-organized pressure groups to suppress the presentation of material in theatres, movies, and radio which seems to be offensive to their feelings or dangerous to their interests. Something like an informal and yet drastic censorship is now appearing, and is already assuming power to dictate what shall, and shall not, be made available to the general public.

The case of Shakespeare's "The Merchant of Venice" is much to the point. Some years ago Jewish individuals and groups began to object to the presentation of this great play upon the stage, or even to the study of its pages by boys and girls in high school or college. The reason for this action is, of course, Shylock, a Jew, not a very pleasant Jew, in fact a villain, rather a magnificent villain. To exhibit this character, it is argued, is to defame the Jews. It tends to persuade people that all Jews are Shylocks. But does it? Are people generally so stupid as to transform a single personality into a general type? If so, then Italians must object, in sheer self-defense, to Iago in "Othello," and Englishmen to Falstaff in "Henry IV." If bad characters are not to be depicted as belonging to any especial race, religion, or nationality, then how can evil ever be presented in its eternal fight against good? Are we to return to the old morality plays, wherein characters are not persons at all, but abstract qualities, clothed upon for the moment in unidentifiable flesh?

What was begun so successfully with "The Merchant of Venice" has now been continued with Dickens's "Oliver Twist." An English version of this famous story has been made into a movie, after the pattern of "Great Expectations," and now has been refused entrance into this country because of the protests of Jews, including the American Board of Rabbis and various other powerful organizations. The trouble in this instance, of course, is Fagin, unmistakably a Jew, and an ugly Jew at that. But if all Jews are going to rise up against Dickens's novel because of Fagin, why should not all Englishmen rise up against the book because of Bill Sikes? Of these two villains, Bill is by all odds the more terrible. But I have yet to hear of anybody objecting to the work on this account.

The latest victim, a kind of *reductio ad absurdum,* is Scott's "Ivanhoe," a mammoth movie production now in preparation. Rumors come from Hollywood that already Jewish opposition is threatening this film. Objection must center about Isaac of York and his daughter Rebecca, but it seems incredible that this can be true. For Isaac, as I remember him, is a heroic character who suffers horribly at the hands of Anglo-Saxon persecution. As for Rebecca, she is the real heroine of the story, and it is a rare reader who is not sorry that at the end she does not marry Ivanhoe. One has only to think of Rebecca's hymn, the greatest of all Jewish hymns, to know that there is not a trace of offense in this book.

But the Jews are not the only people who are mistakenly sensitive. Some time ago, for example, Negroes in certain sections of the country undertook to suppress a musical version of the classic play "Uncle Tom's Cabin." Their contention was that the old sentimentalized plantation Negro was a slander on the race. As the Negro had been emancipated from slavery, so he had a right to be emancipated as well from the tradition of surrender and shame attaching to

---

John Haynes Holmes, "Sensitivity as Censor," *Saturday Review*, 32:9–10+ (February 26, 1949), copyright 1949 by the Saturday Review Associates, Inc. Reprinted by permission of the author and of the publisher.

this institution. To be sure, Uncle Tom had remarkable qualities—patience, forbearance, long-suffering, kindness, forgiveness. But these are all negative or passive virtues. The Negro today, we are reminded, has dignity and courage, and the elements of free manhood, and is so to be represented. Which means that from the literary and dramatic point of view, the suppression of "Uncle Tom's Cabin" may be all to the good! But there remains nonetheless the question of liberty in a democracy, which is not to be lightly cast aside.

"Uncle Tom" was matched more recently by the case of Walt Disney's "Uncle Remus," which, for much the same reason, was condemned by many Negroes. Their opposition must have contributed heavily to the failure of this picture. But the supreme example in this field is "The Birth of a Nation." Here is a screen play which must stand technically memorable in the history of the movie. Its appearance marked the opening of a new era on the screen. But the material of the picture is vicious. It undoubtedly was a contributing factor in the revival of the Ku-Klux Klan. What more natural than the fact that our colored friends have for years sought to suppress this picture wherever it has appeared? Its revival is now practically impossible. This is understandable enough, but what about the principle of freedom? Are we going to consent to the suppression of art at the hands of private or group interest?

Other instances of what may not inaccurately be called unofficial censorship, suppression by terrorization, are easily available. A recent one is the exclusion of the weekly magazine *The Nation* from the public schools of New York City, at the instance of the Roman Catholic Church, which has long been busy in this unhappy business. The organization of the Legion of Decency, so-called, and its quiet but nonetheless effective work behind the scenes in Hollywood, is a conspicuous, and today perhaps the most impressive, illustration of what I mean by unofficial group censorship. The ban of the League upon moving pictures is of enormous effect, and may well ruin the small local theatre by the interdiction laid upon the Catholic flock which may constitute a major part of its clientele. But ordinarily it has not been necessary to impose this ban. The mere presence of the League, like a secret police lurking in the background, prevents production at the source, and an unwelcome picture is stopped before it is begun.

What these minority groups desire, in such cases as I have cited, is not unworthy and is wholly natural. By banishing all unfavorable presentation of their part in our common world, they strive to escape the prejudice and persecution, the mean misunderstandings and horrid hates, which are all too often made their tragic lot.

What these minority groups are afraid of, in such cases as I have cited, is prejudice and persecution which they should not in decency be asked to endure. Returning to the opposition of Jewish people to "The Merchant of Venice," on grounds that it is defamatory and anti-Semitic, I am inclined to believe they are unduly sensitive. I heard the other day that my grandson was reading "The Merchant of Venice" at school. I took pains to question him closely, and found a vast enthusiasm for the play and no feeling at all against Jews. As for the stage, I saw Henry Irving, years ago, play the greatest of Shylocks. His interpretation of the character was along heroic and tragic lines. I recall how outraged I was by the elopement of Jessica, daughter of Shylock, and by her stealing of her father's jewels, which were all wrapped up with his touching love for Leah, his deceased wife. In the trial scene my pity was all for the Jew, in the hands of his persecutors, on whom was played so dirty a legal trick. I was profoundly moved by the famous "hath not a Jew eyes" speech, and still recall and record it as the noblest statement in our literature of the Jew's case. Irving, as well as other actors of our time, while hiding nothing of Shylock's rancor, explained it sympathetically, and thus saved the drama from anti-Semitism.

The same is true of Charles Dickens when he wrote "Oliver Twist," and placed a Jew, Fagin, at the heart of the story. Is this a case of anti-Semitism? If so, then we must believe that all Jews are saints, and that no evil must ever be ascribed to any one of them. Other men, of other race or religion, may commit crimes, but not members of the house of Israel. These latter are outside the pale of frail and faulty human nature, and thus never guilty of debasing qualities of character. The logic here, in other words, is that the Jew shall have literary immunity from the sins that do so easily beset the rest of the human family. Dickens was a good hater. He ripped the hide off his own countrymen, and left some supreme villains—Bill Sikes, Uriah Heep, Mr. Pecksniff, Steerforth, Quip—wrapped up in the integuments of English flesh. What Dickens did to America and Americans is still something fearful to think of, but he still lives in the admiration and grace of us all. We bear no grudge against him. We would certainly resent and oppose in this country any attempt to suppress "Martin Chuzzlewit" or "American Notes." These books may be unfair—I think they are! But they are the works of a novelist who is immortal and a part of a literature which is precious.

As for Walter Scott and his great heart, I have only to quote one passage from "Ivanhoe," which we are told the Jews don't like. On page 74 of my edition of this book, Scott writes of the Jews that:

except perhaps the flying fish, there was no race existing on the earth, in the air, or the waters, who were the object of such an unintermitting, general, and relentless persecution as the Jews of this period. Upon the slightest and most unreasonable pretenses, as well as upon accusations the most absurd and groundless, their persons and property were exposed to every turn of popular fury; for Normans, Saxons, Dane, and Briton, however adverse these races were to each other, contended which should look with greatest detestation upon a people whom it was accounted a point of religion to hate, to revile, to despise, to plunder, and to persecute. The kings of the Norman Race, and the independent nobles who followed their example in all acts of tyranny, maintained against this devoted people a persecution of a more regular, calculated, and self-interested kind.

No anti-Semitism or other wickedness appears in these masterpieces of fictional or dramatic art. In the case of Negroes and Catholics, as little as of Jews, great writers are not concerned, in any spirit of evil delight or intent, with prejudice against their fellow-beings. They treat these groups, in other words, just as they treat the rest of the human race—as complexes of flesh and spirit, to be presented without apology or reproach. They present their works as transcripts of life, in which evil contends with good for the conquest of man's heart.

Any serious production of genius, which penetrates deep into the soul, and studies sympathetically the incidence of vice and virtue in the vast range of human experience, is certain sooner or later to hit and hurt somebody. And, in the natural course of events, this impact of interpretation and criticism will fall now and then upon more or less helpless minority groups, who, goaded to desperation, will feverishly demand protection. If granted out of respect or pity, and some form of official or unofficial censorship established, then the flood of tyranny is loose. Suppression never intended or imagined in the beginning becomes in the end inevitable. An endless chain of dictatorship is suddenly unwound, and entwines in its fetters all the operations of the human mind. Thus, if we ban from this country the "Oliver Twist" film, out of deference to Jews who don't like Fagin, then we lay the foundation for banning from the public schools *The Nation* magazine out of deference to Catholics who don't like certain articles by Paul Blanshard. If we shut a lecturer off the air because he is an atheist and thus distasteful to Christians, then we prepare the way for silencing Unitarians because they are distasteful to Fundamentalists. A law enacted some years ago in New Jersey against the Nazi Bundists of that time caught for its first victims the innocent Jehovah's Witnesses.

Thus does suppression spread, like a disease. Smaller and smaller becomes the area in which the mind can operate. Man's noblest gift, the creative imagination, finds itself confined at last as in a prison cell, for there is now nothing for the novelist and dramatist to write about but robots, or such fantastic specimens of life as Gulliver encountered in his travels. "The proper study of mankind is man," wrote Alexander Pope, and succeeding generations of students and writers have said Amen. But this study cannot be carried on with any success, or indeed at all, if branch after branch of the human family is to be lopped off from consideration. And never, under any circumstances, if it is agreed that no weak or wicked character is ever to be identifiable as belonging to any particular class or clan of humans! Right at that point would freedom end, and man's higher life be left to atrophy and decay.

For all this, in the last analysis, is only the old familiar question of liberty. Shall a man be free to speak and publish his ideas, however disagreeable or even dangerous they may appear to be? Shall other men be free to hear these ideas, in their own inquiry after truth, or perhaps in curious interest in the fallacies and fantasies of the human mind? Or shall we turn to the iron hand of censorship, and dictate what men shall or shall not think and speak? To the true libertarian, who trusts in the essential integrity of human nature and the well-tried processes of democracy, the challenge is easy. He will not resort to censorship under any circumstances. He knows too well that censorship means:

First, the assumption of infallible personal judgment—the amazing ability to know what is false for oneself is false for everybody. Where such ability comes from, and how it is guaranteed—this is never told.

Second, the imposition of this personal judgment upon the entire community by group pressure, by duly enacted law, or, in the last analysis, by force and violence. By what right such suppression is exercised, is not stated.

Third, the arrogance of a minority in using its power to control and even persecute the majority. It is apparently not remembered that the majority, exactly like a minority, has rights which are entitled to recognition and respect.

Such is the character of censorship, which makes its use indefensible under any conditions, by reason of any provocation, in a free society.

But does this mean that men are to do nothing when they are viciously misrepresented or cruelly attacked? Are they to stand helpless against slander, false witness, and all untruth? The Jews, for example—are they to endure, as they endured the fires of the Inquisition, the danger and damage of a Shylock on the stage, and a Fagin on the printed page? Is a wicked picture, like "The Birth of a Nation," to be left to run its course, and the Negroes of the country seek no defense or redress? And are Catholics, because they are so accustomed to abuse, to enjoy no protection from what they regard as wanton attack upon the sanctities of their faith and works in the New York *Nation?* Does freedom, in other words, mean the exposure of the weak to the strong, and the license of error to wreak its utmost havoc without interference?

Such assertion, or suggestion, is natural, but quite absurd. Not in a free society are any to be left defenseless against enemies or traducers. Instead of outlawing serious literary and dramatic works in which offensive or careless material appears, let the sensitively maimed rise up and protest. In a country such as ours, the very atmosphere is hospitable to truth. Platform, pulpit, and printing press are everywhere available to reach and educate the public mind. Picket lines may be formed, and public meetings held, to challenge and correct error. Nothing is more unfair than to asssume that all the varied instrumentalities of freedom in a democracy are at the disposal only of the misguided and misinformed, even the wicked. As a matter of fact, every means for the expression of free opinion is as available for good as for evil uses. It is only when such means are fanatically denied us, that we need be afraid. Truth, and the liberty to speak it, is our whole case. And how events, when trusted, prove it! Thus, "The Birth of a Nation" may not inaccurately be described as a turning point in the history of the Negro in America, for with this picture and the reaction against it began the sudden emergence of Negro artistry in music, literature, and the drama. Shylock has helped more Jews than he ever hurt, since Shakespeare, with his inimitable genius of humanity, presented in this character not only the avaricious money-lender, but a psychological and spiritual martyr who bore on his person all the scars inflicted upon his suffering tribe. It is all a matter of confronting error with truth. So long as men are free thus to bear witness against defamation, they need not be afraid. John Milton said it all:

> Truth is strong next to the Almighty. . . . She needs no policies, no stratagems to make her victorious. These are the shifts and the defenses that error uses against her power. . . .
>
> So Truth be in the field, we do injuriously, by suppressing and prohibiting, to misdoubt her strength. Let Truth and Falsehood grapple. Whoever knew Truth put to the worse in a free and open encounter!

John Mason Brown
WISHFUL BANNING

Mr. Churchill's is the right approach. Explaining in "Their Finest Hour" why epidemics did not sweep London when millions were crowded in air-raid shelters, he says, "Man is a gregarious animal, and apparently the mischievous mi-

---

John Mason Brown, "Wishful Banning," *Saturday Review,* 32:24–26 (March 12, 1949), copyright 1949 by the Saturday Review Associates, Inc. Reprinted by permission of the author and of the publisher.

crobes he exhales fight and neutralize each other. They go out and devour each other, and Man walks off unharmed." Then Mr. Churchill adds, "If this is not scientifically correct, it ought to be."

There are so many things that ought to be, even if they are not. The microbes which assail men's minds are as mischievous as those which attack their bodies. One wishes that they, too, would fight and neutralize each other, allowing Man to walk off unharmed. Unquestionably they should, but they do not, as is proved by the epidemic of odd and sorry suppressions which has swept the world with increasing fury since V-J Day and the coming of the "cold war" or, more accurately, the hot peace.

Freedom was a big and beckoning word in wartime. There were even the Four Freedoms, the first of which was dedicated to "freedom of speech and expression—everywhere in the world." The fourth—who can have forgotten it?—promised freedom from fear. The source of fear it suggested did not go far enough. It was limited to aggressive warfare. It failed to include those other fears which can destroy freedom of speech. I mean those fears to which minorities and special groups appear to be heir; those fears born of insecurity, false pride, hypersensitivity, or a strange, self-deluding surrender to the notion that safety and esteem can be guaranteed by the placing of a ban or the action of a censor.

Take the now notorious case of "Oliver Twist." This British film has provoked rioting among displaced Polish Jews in Berlin. Protests against it have been lodged by Jews in Vienna and other Old World cities. So far its public release is not planned in the United States. Indeed it has been prohibited in New York due to the action taken by the New York Board of Rabbis under the leadership of Rabbi Theodore N. Lewis, who admits he has not seen the film.

Why this rioting, these protests, and this suppression? Of course because of Fagin; because some Jews there and here have objected to the alleged indignity done their people by showing on the screen a Jew who is such a deep-dyed villain. Their fear is that Fagin will arouse anti-Semitism; that movie audiences will forget Fagin is a caricature of an individual and be persuaded that all Jews are Fagins. Precious few of the millions still free to read Dickens's novel have, I will wager, succumbed to such an error. Yet this is the point of view as stated by Rabbi Lewis. The Rabbi, incidentally, is as adamant on the subject of "The Merchant of Venice" as he is on "Oliver Twist." He is determined to have it kept off the stage and banned from schoolrooms for the same reasons—because in his eyes Shylock and Fagin are equally insulting, unbearable, and dangerous as characterizations of Jews.

I know this is the Rabbi's attitude because I heard him state it when, some two months back, he appeared on ABC's television program "Critic-at-Large" with Morris Ernst, Louis Kronenberger, and myself. In combating the Rabbi's stand, the three of us found ourselves as one. All of us abhorred the idea of such censorship. All of us felt that it was contrary to the American tradition. All of us insisted that the film was entitled to be shown before being condemned and that, if it proved offensive, the case could and should be carried to the courts. All of us expressed our conviction that the Rabbi, with the best of good intentions, was doing his people greater harm than good. All of us believed that more anti-Semitism would result from such a banning by a minority pressure group than would ever be created by Fagin.

Mr. Ernst was the only one of us who had seen the film, a fact which did not subtract from his right to an opinion. Instead of being offended by "Oliver Twist," he had found it commendable as a transference of a classic to the screen. Mr. Kronenberger's judgment was that literature could not get along without its villains, and that a villain role in "Oliver Twist" on or off the screen just happened to be Fagin's, precisely as it was Bill Sikes's or the Artful Dodger's.

When I asked the Rabbi if, on the basis of his logic, the Danes would not be justified in picketing "Hamlet," since it shows that a Danish prince can be indecisive, Mr. Kronenberger pointed out that the Danes had an even more valid reason for suppressing the play—*i.e.,* it specifically states that there is something rotten in the state of Denmark.

The Jews who have protested against "Oliver Twist" and sought to have it, "The Merchant of Venice," and now it seems "Ivanhoe," banned are not the only persons who have reached for censorship as a weapon with which to combat the horrors of racial or religious discrimination. Some Negro groups appear to be equally touchy, just as humorless, no less given to trying to change what is past, or pretending that classics, written long ago and still available, can be unwritten and erased from man's minds by the edict of a censor.

There was, for example, the case of "Uncle Tom's Cabin"—of all things. Three years ago in Bridgeport a new musical version of it was temporarily banned because of the protests sent in by CIO Negro groups, the Bridgeport Pastors' Association, and the Communist Party. Their incredible objection was that "Uncle Tom's Cabin" "refreshed memories that tend to portray only the weaknesses of a racial minority," and held up to ridicule "peoples who in the early days of our country were unfortunately subjected to exposures that today would be considered atrocious." In other words, the desire of these protesting Negroes was to forget, and have others forget, that their people had even been slaves.

What they forgot, however, was that it was the slave owner, not the slave, who came out badly in Mrs. Stowe's pages. They also seemed willing to overlook entirely how much "Uncle Tom's Cabin" had done for their people. Yes, and to deny the encouragement it offers today by making clear how far both the whites and the Negroes in this country have advanced since the novel first needed to be written. Booker T. Washington did not attempt to dodge history when he wrote his autobiography. He called his volume "Up from Slavery." The significant word in his title is not the "Slavery." It is the "Up."

There are, too, some well-meaning Negroes, working for that true realization of democracy which should be every American's preoccupation, who object even to "The Green Pastures," I am told, because they find its naïveté offensive and because the young people in Mr. Deshee's Sunday School class have not a sufficiently enlightened conception of the Bible. There are other Negroes, just as well-meaning and just as falsely sensitive, whose hope is said to be to have "Little Black Sambo" suppressed. Their reason, I gather, is that Little Black Sambo, so endearing as a figure of all childhood, has a rather wholesale appetite for pancakes and is afraid of tigers!

The pressures of Catholic groups are no less evident. The suppression of *The Nation* in the public schools of New York City, because it ran a series of articles critical of the Catholic Church, is a case in point. So, of course, are the operations of the Legion of Decency in the realm of filmdom. The Legion does not have to ban to make itself felt. Fear of its disapproval exerts a constant influence upon motion-picture producers. Perhaps it was dread of this disapproval which resulted in the unfrocking of Cardinal Richelieu in the latest filming of "The Three Musketeers." In the picture the Cardinal, a gifted and not unworldly cleric, though allowed to be as worldly as Dumas and history demand, is denied his robes, apparently in order to give no offense. Such pressures from other religious groups are, no doubt, continuous even if they are not so well organized.

In Chicago recently Jean-Paul Sartre's "The Respectful Prostitute" was banned. A police captain in charge of the Crime Prevention Bureau reported to his superior that the play was likely to provoke interracial troubles. This, in spite of the fact that it had run in New York for many months without having done so. One explanation which I read, and certainly an odd one, was that Sartre's script was "unfair to the Negro." Perhaps the final word about "The Respectful Prostitute" in Chicago came from Mayor Martin Kennelly. His enlightened statement was, "The title alone would ban it."

As further proof of the growing tendency to believe that abuses can be corrected by running away from the facts, let me cite two other examples. The first of these is the campaign which, out of the highest of motives, Walter Winchell conducted some time back against any comedians who dared to tell stories in dialect. As if all of us did not speak with dialects; as if dialects were not part of the truth as well as the vigor of our speech! It is not the dialect—Jewish, Yankee, Southern, Western, Italian, Irish, or Scotch—which is offensive. It is the story told, the uses to which the dialect can be put.

For my second illustration I must come a little nearer home. In fact, to the *SRL* itself and an editor's note which appeared on the letters page on January 15. A well-intentioned reader from Charleston, S. C., had written in to ask when the magazine was going to stop "Jim Crowing" Negro writers. "If you always say a book is by a Negro, etc., you should, to be consistent, say another is by a white, etc.," wrote this correspondent. This was followed by one of those thunderous generalities, seemingly so fine in their liberalism, which unfortunately are apt to be as fuzzy-minded as they are untrue. "Only where literature has no race or religion will it be completely free."

Although I cannot speak for anyone else, I know I was saddened and distressed to read the editor's answer. It said, "After having applauded various publishers for omitting racial identification in their promotion of Negro authors, we are ashamed of ourselves. It won't happen again." Rot!

Certainly I would agree that nothing is gained and only harm done by insisting upon cataloguing a writer as a Negro, if his book has nothing to do with the problems which he himself has faced as a Negro. But I do not see how anyone could make an intelligent or just approach to such volumes, say, as Richard Wright's "Black Boy," Walter White's "A Man Called White," William Gardner Smith's "The Last of the Conquerors," or Ann Petry's "The Street," without mentioning the fact that the Americans who wrote these books are Negroes. The whole point of their writing and the reason for their having been written as they are is that they reflect the handicaps and humiliations to which Americans who are Negroes are heir. The source of their authority is that their authors are what they are.

As I see it, any citizen of the United States is an American. It is as simple as that. Yet it is absurd to pretend that all Americans, just because they live here, are sprung from the same race, are of the same color and the same religion, have the same accents, enjoy identical opportunities, are equally endowed, and have been exposed to the same agonies or privileges. These differences are facts. To ignore them is to surrender to the silliest and most self-deluding form of ostrichism.

We get nowhere by banning books just because they contain characters which do not flatter us. We get nowhere by pretending that there are not heroes and villains of all creeds and colors. We get nowhere by allowing any minorities to enjoy what John Haynes Holmes has admirably described in these pages as a "literary immunity from the sins that beset the rest of the human family." Our one hope is to face the facts.

Nowadays we appear to be misled by the best of good intentions. To conquer the horrors of intolerance and racial or religious discrimination, we seem more and more inclined to turn to the book-burning tactics of our enemy in the last war or to the gross suppressions of our opponent in the present peace. Neither literature nor freedom gains anything by such means. "Ye shall know the truth, and the truth shall make you free." Apparently there are those today who would reverse this, and have it read: avoid the truth and such avoidance shall make you free.

Chapter v

Who or what is obscene?

Differences of opinion as to what is and what is not obscene are as diverse among laymen as in the legal fraternity. The question was posed in amusing fashion by Marghanita Laski in a tongue-in-cheek letter to the *New Statesman*. Mrs. Laski, niece of Harold Laski, mother of two children, novelist and critic, wrote:

"I find myself stupidly confused over this question of obscene literature, and write in the hope that some of your correspondents may be able to clear my mind. What particularly puzzles me is the meaning of corruption. I read that five million copies of a particularly corrupting series have been sold. Now with the very modest estimate of two readers per book, this means that one-fifth of the population is already corrupt, and the need for a definition becomes urgent.

"Many references have been made to the possibility of *young* people being corrupted by obscene books, but no corrupted young person has ever been offered in evidence. If corruption means becoming interested in sex, then one must admit that this often happens as a result of reading, but most usually at a very early age and from books like fairy-tales and the *Encyclopædia Britannica*. And is being interested in sex the same thing as being corrupt?

"It can't mean, can it, that people have been persuaded by reading certain books to become homosexuals? For one thing, I doubt that a fifth of the population is homosexual, and for another, no one, in the recent spate of articles on the subject, has suggested that reading obscene books is a cause. The same goes for cosh-boys since these, according to the press, are either illiterate or read only comics. It could be, of course, that reading obscene books leads to Unspeakable Sexual Practices, but as these, in addition to being unspeakable, are necessarily committed in privacy, I don't see how the courts can tell. Maybe these books lead people to adultery, but a far more usual cause, I think, is attractive members of the opposite sex (of course, these could be banned). I *have* wondered whether what these books do is to teach people how to copulate, but since so many marriages fail because people *don't* know how to, and the birth-rate is causing anxiety, one can't feel such knowledge can be called corrupting or even anti-social. Or is it just that these books make people *want* to copulate, like war and music and the time of year? But if that were so, we'd surely start by banning war.

"I suppose evidence could be heard on all these points, and I do wonder that it isn't. Or couldn't some research be done to find out whether there is a positive correlation between, say, adultery and reading books recently banned? I have read obscene books myself, and it may be that I am corrupt, but I am a wife and mother, and have appeared on television." [1]

A flood of British court cases over obscenity in books during the year 1954 led to a joint letter of protest, addressed to the London *Times,* from seven of the nation's leading authors, including Somerset Maugham, Bertrand Russell, and J. B. Priestley. "It would be disastrous to English literature," they declared, "if authors had to write under the shadow of the Old Bailey if they failed to produce works suitable for teenagers." Perhaps more effective than this impressive array of signers was what *Time* described as a "burst of verse" from the pen of Sir Alan Herbert, M.P. To a lawyer who asked a jury: "Would you give this book to your daughter of 25?" Sir Alan replied:

"She's not an infant or an elf:
I let her choose her books herself.
But, since you ask me, I should not
Give her a racehorse, or a yacht,
A billiard-table, or a course
Of easy lectures on divorce.

Though none of these should I describe
As dangers to the British tribe.
Nor should I draw my child's attention
To certain bits I will not mention
In Holy Writ, in Shakespeare's plays,
And other works of olden days.
I should not give her Law Reports
(O dear, the things they say in courts!),
And I should give her, even less,
Some portions of the Sunday Press,
Some papers you might well condemn—
Though no one's prosecuting them.
'The law's a hass'—that's nothing new:
But let me keep my faith in you." [2]

English writers are not alone in seeing the humorous side of censorship. The following brief essay by E. B. White, "Censorship," from his delightful *The Second Tree from the Corner,* more tellingly exposes, in a few words, the ridiculous aspects of censorship than could be accomplished by a heavy treatise on the subject. In his usual gently ironical vein, Mr. White commented:

"We are delighted with the recent censorship ruling in the matter of motion-picture harems. Some scenes in a Paramount picture now in production are set in a harem, and after careful deliberation the censors have decided to allow this type of polyform allure *provided* the boudoir does not contain the sultan. The girls can mill about among the pillows, back and side having gone bare, but no male eye must gaze upon them —save, of course, yours, lucky reader. This harem-but-no-sultan decision belongs in the truly great body of opinion interpreting the American moral law. It takes its place alongside the celebrated 1939 ruling on the exposure of female breasts in the Flushing World of Tomorrow, which provided that one breast could be presented publicly but not two, and thereby satisfied the two seemingly irreconcilable groups: the art-lovers, who demanded breasts but were willing to admit that if you'd seen one you'd seen them both, and the decency clique, who held out for concealment but were agreed that the fact of concealing one breast established the essential reticence of the owner and thereby covered the whole situation, or chest. That subtle and far-reaching ruling carried the Fair, as we know,

---

[1] Marghanita Laski, in the *New Statesman,* 47: 634 (May 15, 1954).

[2] Alan Herbert, "No, Sir," in the London *Sunday Graphic,* 1954.

safely through two difficult seasons, and we imagine that the aseptic harem will do as much for Hollywood." [3]

Both the law and the laity, it would appear, find the chief justification for censorship in the protection of children and young people. When all other arguments favorable to censorship are demolished, its proponents fall back on this as the last line of defense. Is any reconciliation possible between the point of view, on the one hand, that anything capable of contaminating or corrupting our youth must be repressed, and, on the other, that adult reading should not be restricted to reading only what is fit for children? In a recent editorial by Walter Goodman, entitled "How To Deal with Obscene Books," *Redbook* magazine suggested a possible solution:

"An article in this issue of REDBOOK dramatizes the confusion that can result in a community from the discovery that children are reading pornographic material. Naturally, we all wish to safeguard our children from such unhealthy influences. But this normal wish may tempt some parents to resort to measures that are in conflict with our cherished freedom of the press. It is important, REDBOOK believes, that Americans become aware that there are proper and improper ways of dealing with obscene publications.

"In recent decisions, the Supreme Court has upheld Federal and state laws outlawing the sale and distribution of pornographic material. These decisions place heavy responsibility on local officials to exercise discrimination and common sense in enforcing such laws. For better or worse, the responsibility is theirs.

"Of particular danger to our freedom of the press today are private organizations whose representatives have set themselves up in some areas to act as judge, jury and police force over their communities' reading matter. Some of these groups have undertaken not only to pass publicly on the morality of literature—a quite legitimate role—but also to put pressure on booksellers not to distribute the works which they have labeled 'objectionable.' In some instances, they have threatened to boycott dealers who refused to abide by their judgment.

"This type of extralegal pressure has been scored many times by persons concerned with our civil liberties. As a prominent theologian, Father John Courtney Murray, S.J., has stated, '. . . in a pluralist society no minority group has the right to impose its own religious or moral views on other groups, through the methods of force, coercion or violence.'

"Some of the most respected names in world literature have had their books blacklisted by self-appointed censors. Among the authors whose works have been included on the 'objectionable' list of the National Organization for Decent Literature—the most active of the unofficial groups engaged in such activity—have been the following: Nobel Prize winners William Faulkner and Ernest Hemingway; outstanding American novelists such as James T. Farrell and John Dos Passos; distinguished European writers like Emile Zola, Aldous Huxley, D. H. Lawrence and Arthur Koestler, and such popular authors as James Jones, Norman Mailer, John O'Hara, J. D. Salinger, Budd Schulberg and Irwin Shaw.

"Of course, parents have a responsibility for watching over what their children read. But they have other responsibilities as well.

"As citizens in a democracy, they are obligated to protect the expression of ideas that are contrary to their personal views. And if they wish to continue to enjoy the works of free artists, they must help safeguard the freedom of those artists to have their books published and sold.

"Certainly, some books are printed simply to capitalize on the appeal of pornography. State officials are now equipped to deal with such books. But many works which may not be suitable for minors can be extremely rewarding for adult minds. An alert parent will find sensible means of keeping his children from reading books for which they are not yet ready—without resorting to bans and boycotts." [4]

The chief legal issues in the treatment of allegedly obscene publications were dealt with in a preceding chapter, The Courts Look at Books. The views of authors, editors, and a well-known churchman are among those represented in the following selections. Aside from the general public and the book trade, these individuals are typical of the interests most directly concerned with censorship and the free flow of information.

---

[3] E. B. White, *The Second Tree from the Corner* (New York: Harper & Bros., 1954), pp. 112–13.

[4] Walter Goodman, "How To Deal with Obscene Books," editorial, *Redbook*, November, 1957.

▣ For some thirty-five years Edward Weeks has served as editor or associate editor of the *Atlantic Monthly*. Under his able direction, the *Atlantic* has maintained its influential position and high prestige in the literary world. Mr. Weeks's "Sex and Censorship" first appeared in his *This Trade of Writing* in 1935. He emphasizes therein changing styles in writing which make the literary mores of one generation passé in the next. The law eventually recognizes the new order of things, though frequently some years after the fact. Mr. Weeks endorses wholeheartedly the test for obscenity applied by Judge Woolsey in the *Ulysses* case, i.e., intrinsic and extrinsic features, community acceptance, the book to be judged as a whole, and its purpose determined.

Edward Weeks
SEX AND CENSORSHIP

If literary prizes are the most available form of patronage,—the pot of gold at the rainbow's end,—then censorship is the shadow, the sudden thunderstorm which may descend upon the author without warning and with ruination to his hopes. Censors, and those who invoke the power of censorship, are touchy folk of rigid mentality whose wrath may be roused by a variety of provocations. They have forgotten—if indeed they ever knew—that standards of morality are not of cast iron. They have shut their eyes to the fact that things deemed indecent in one generation may be approved as decent in another. "The law," said Judge Cardozo, "will not hold the crowd to the morality of saints and seers. It will follow, or strive to follow, the principle and practice of the men and women of the community whom the social mind would rank as intelligent and virtuous." But the dictator or the reformer thinks that he alone is the right-minded member of his community.

In our time censorship is easily provoked: it may be leveled at a writer thought to be outspoken against the existing political machine, as is the case in Russia, Germany, and Italy to-day.

France and Switzerland now shelter those brilliant German exiles, Remarque, Neumann, Zweig, and Feuchtwanger, whose books were proscribed by Hitler. And the Soviet Government on coming into power condemned Russian classics—Dostoievsky, Tolstoy, and others—which in turn but a few decades earlier had been suppressed by the Tsarist Government for being too revolutionary. Censorship may be clamped upon such a book as *Greek Memories* by Compton Mackenzie, which was held to violate the Espionage Act in England. Censorship is sometimes called forth by representatives of the Roman Catholic Church who see, in novels or plays, material too subversive or too profane for the good of their communities. I believe that the banning in Boston of two plays, *Strange Interlude* by Eugene O'Neill, and *Within the Gates* by Sean O'Casey, both proceeded from this origin. A Penal Code may prohibit the sending or even the possession of literature dealing with contraception: such with minor reservations is the law now in effect in many of the United States—a law so contrary to public opinion that it is openly winked at. Finally, censorship may be enforced not because the printed matter is profane or unorthodox, but simply because it touches upon sex with a candor that shocks the reader. America is still free from the compulsion of either Communism or Fascism; the threat of espionage concerns us very little, and the ignorance of birth control is being steadily combated by common sense. Hence it is to the latter phase of censorship, the delineation and the policing of sex in fiction, that I shall devote the major part of my argument.

There is ample evidence to show that the presence of sex in literature troubled our grandparents quite as much if not more than it does us to-day. The grilled bookcases with lock and key (so often seen in old rectories) certainly suggest that there were a good many books which—though read by the elders—were kept out of reach of the younger generation. I have heard my mother describe how she read Hardy's novels by candlelight, the book being kept under the mattress by day for fear of parental discovery.

Of course Thomas Hardy was not the only novelist *défendu*. Ladies first. Shortly after its publication *Jane Eyre* by Charlotte Brontë "was pronounced too immoral to be ranked as decent

---

Edward Weeks, *This Trade of Writing* (Boston: Little, Brown, 1935), pp. 126–47, copyright 1935 by Edward Weeks, Jr. Reprinted (without footnotes) by permission of the author and of the publisher.

literature"; George Eliot's *Adam Bede* was condemned as "the vile outpouring of a lewd woman's mind"; and Elizabeth Barrett Browning's *Aurora Leigh* was happily said to be the "hysterical indecencies of an erotic mind." Du Maurier's *Trilby* was attacked as obscene. *Leaves of Grass* by Walt Whitman is said to have cost him his position in the Interior Department. *Ann Veronica* by H. G. Wells, *Jennie Gerhardt* by Theodore Dreiser, Hamlin Garland's *Rose of Dutcher's Coolly, Jurgen* by James Branch Cabell, were all, when the dew was fresh on them, considered "bad books," too bad for many a respectable household. I have myself heard a parent argue that *All Quiet on the Western Front* was not a fit book for a boy in his teens.

If it would serve any purpose I could easily double this list of shortsighted and prudish judgments. But such evidence should be enough to prove, first, that the nineteenth-century readers followed a fashion in fiction—as in speech and dress—which has by now been almost wholly discarded. They made as much of a fetish of reticence and propriety as we make of plain speaking. Any fashion dies when it is overdone. Such evidence also shows that readers in protesting against surface unconventionality often lost sight of the literary values within, values which established some of the condemned books as "classics" twenty years later.

Novelists as a class are more advanced in their thinking, more liberal in their tendencies, than the people who read them. This has always been so. At times it causes trouble. Fifty years ago novelists had arrived at a policy acceptable to their readers for treating those scenes which, being true to life, should be within the legitimate domain of the novel. In general I should say that they adhered to the "closed-door policy." When the lovers in a Victorian novel reached a point where temptation could no longer be resisted, they retired to a tower, to a deserted barn, to a clandestine bedroom, closed the door—and there the chapter ended. This formality you will see observed again and again in Hardy. The closed-door policy left the reader in the rather uncomfortable position of a gossip. He had been led to believe that something illicit had taken place. Should he think the best or the worst? And when a few chapters later it appeared that the young lady was in distress, the reader took the cue and proceeded to picture the sordid details for himself. For in Victorian fiction the wages of sin were inevitably a baby.

But in the early years of the twentieth century novelists began to shift to the "open-door policy." Young writers no longer felt themselves bound to respect the reticence maintained by their elders. They felt it perfectly legitimate to introduce into their stories—as novelists have done since the days of *Pamela*—passages which would show the passions unleashed and which, incidentally, would convey a certain erotic stimulus to the reader. This change was in progress by 1910: the war with its aftermath of realism hastened the transition. Freud and the new psychologists sped it still further. As the door opened the descriptions of sex in fiction have become more and more explicit. This has, not unnaturally, shocked readers of a generation used to reticence, and these citizens from time to time have raised their voices in protest against certain books.

But I would suggest that the open-door policy has also left our novelists in a state of confusion. We have had the blunt honesty of Theodore Dreiser, the faintly murky suggestiveness of Michael Arlen, the impassioned rationalism of D. H. Lawrence, and then in *Ulysses* James Joyce carried the conscious delineation of sex to what might be regarded as its ultimate conclusion. The door was pushed open to the full extent of its hinges. But the still younger novelists, the novelists emerging to-day—what shall they do? Is there any standard recognition of what is acceptable in the treatment of sex to-day? I don't think so. Accordingly a writer making a name for himself must decide either to describe his erotic scenes in terms that have been made conventional and perhaps a little stale by use, or else, like William Faulkner, to seek for the expression of still newer sensations. If he chooses the latter course his episodes may seem to many of us no better than aberrations, so extravagant in their detail as to be ludicrous rather than passionate. Thus a rift occurs between the reader who tends to be conventional and the writer who goes to extremes. And when the ultra-conservative reads the book of the ultra-extremist a demand for censorship is apt to arise.

II

Time was when the phrase "Banned in Boston" was actually used to advertise a list of books in more enlightened parts of our country. Between 1928 and 1930 sixty-eight books were suppressed in Boston. Of this number only two —*An American Tragedy,* by Theodore Dreiser, and *Oil!* by Upton Sinclair—were brought to trial and defended by their publishers. The other sixty-six were thought to be subject to the then existing Massachusetts statute, and so, according to the strict letter of the law, they may have been. Complaints, however, were lodged against them only in Suffolk County (which contains the city of Boston), where, in most cases, the volumes were promptly withdrawn from sale. Since officials throughout the other districts of the Commonwealth did not feel called on to take any parallel action, we had the anomalous situation of books being banned in Boston yet being sold openly in Cambridge, only three miles away.

For three years I served on citizens' committees which endeavored to reform the Massachusetts laws "relating to obscene literature." The fight was a bitter one, involving hard-shell puritans and liberals, the Watch and Ward Society, and certain religious bodies, and terminating of course in our hearing before the Legislature. Eventually we were successful in altering the law, and in the process I came to have a close view of the actual practice of censorship. Here is the machinery of enforcement.

The Law

First, of course, the law. As a matter of fact there are three sets of laws. One of them originates in the Tariff Act, is enforced by the Federal Customs Bureau, and governs the literature imported into this country. A second set of laws empowers the Federal Post Office to exclude matter from the mails. Thus, Mr. Farley may if he so chooses prove to be a good deal of an obstruction to the proponents of birth control. Remember that in the fall of 1928 the officials of the United States Customs Bureau and the postal authorities held a conference, as a result of which 739 books were blacklisted from importation into this country. Of these books, 379 were written in the Spanish language, 231 were in French, 5 were in Italian, 10 were in German, and the remaining 114 were in English. The choice was somewhat eccentric. *Mademoiselle de Maupin,* by Gautier, was allowed by the censors to enter the country in its original print and in English translation, but in Spanish it was forbidden. Pietro Aretino, the sixteenth-century Italian, was admitted when he spoke his original tongue or was translated into English, but in Spanish he was forbidden. On the other hand, *The Arabian Nights* in its literal English translations by Payne and Burton is perfectly passable, but when it has been translated into French by Mardrus it is a book no American citizen can touch. Finally, such books as the novels of Balzac, the *Confessions* of Rousseau, and the works of Voltaire and Rabelais were declared ineligible to enter the country under this provision in the Tariff Act.

Two episodes add their humor to the situation. In February 1929, thirteen copies of Voltaire's *Candide* destined for use in a Harvard classroom were confiscated by a customs official on their entry into Boston. A protest was entered and the decision referred back, presumably, to a higher expert in Washington. But it was not till August that the books were released. The classroom, of course, by that time was empty. In April 1929, a copy of Rabelais being imported by the book collector A. Edward Newton of Philadelphia was confiscated by a New York customs inspector "acting under Section 305-A of the Tariff Act." In his letter of protest to the Customs Mr. Newton wrote in part as follows:—

> The action of your representative is positively glorious! Rabelais is one of the world's classics; it is no more obscene than are Shakespeare and the English Bible. In order that you may not be the laughing-stock of the world, I beg that the volume be sent to me immediately; but for no other reason, for one can secure a copy at any well-ordered bookshop or library in the United States.
>
> I am not a youth seeking to gloat, surreptitiously, over a smutty book, but a student of mature years, the possessor of an important library, and the author of *The Amenities of Book-Collecting, A Magnificent Farce, Doctor Johnson* (a play), *The Greatest Book in the World* (a study of the Bible), *This Book-Collecting Game.* Moreover, I have a copy of the first edition of Rabelais, which is worth several thousand dollars.
>
> If you keep or destroy my Rabelais, it will be in my power to make you and your department ridiculous the world over. This would afford me much greater pleasure than the possession of the book.

It was such absurdities as these, practised alike by the designated censors of the Customs Bureau and the Post Office, that led the late Senator Bronson Cutting of New Mexico to propose a liberalizing amendment to a section of the Tariff Act of 1930.

The third set of laws are those designed, with slight variations, to control the circulation of obscene literature within the forty-eight states. Broadly speaking, the phrasing of all "censorship" statutes follows one of two models. The fairer version declares in so many words

that all persons are prohibited from importing, printing, publishing, distributing or selling any obscene book, pamphlet, paper, writing, advertisement, circular, etc., etc., etc.

The more severe variant—it should be obsolete in any self-respecting community—declares

that all persons are prohibited from importing, printing, publishing, distributing or selling any book, pamphlet, paper, writing, advertisement, circular *containing obscene, indecent or impure language* manifestly tending to corrupt the morals of youth.

Obviously, were the "containing" clause strictly applied, the Bible, the plays of Shakespeare, and all of the great novels could be suppressed; for, since a book to be suppressed need only contain "obscene language,"—that is to say, an "obscene or indecent" reference, paragraph, or page,—and since, to paraphrase English and American judicial opinions, that is obscene which tends to create obscene thoughts in the minds of those who are susceptible, it takes very little arguing to show that most contemporary novels, many contemporary biographies, and most of our great classics, when found in the hands of a moron, could be banned on the strength—or weakness—of a single isolated passage.

In 1895 one John B. Wise of Clay Center, Kansas, was convicted of sending obscene matter through the U. S. mails. The matter consisted of quotations from the Bible.

The Censors

Some are appointed officials—officers of the Customs Bureau, the Post Office; some are elected: I mean district attorneys before whom complaints are registered in the various states.

Some are members of benevolent societies: Anthony Comstock, and his successor, John S. Sumner, of the New York Society for the Suppression of Vice, and their counterparts in the Watch and Ward Society of Boston and the Western Society for the Suppression of Vice.

Some are genuinely outraged citizens.

A few are contentious, small-minded busybodies.

The Operation

That you may see censorship at its worst let me give you a hypothetical illustration of what might happen in a district governed by the stricter of the two statutes.

Discovering in the hands of my little daughter a copy of Fielding's *Tom Jones,* I am made curious to see what it is that is amusing her. I read a few pages and am properly shocked. Reaching for my hat, I march indignantly down to the bookseller who sold my child this trash and figuratively throw the book in his face. The bookseller defends himself by saying that he did not publish the book and has not read it. That does not give me the satisfaction I want, so I seek a policeman. With my pencil I mark the outrageous passages and ask him to read them. He is as shocked as I am and says he will take the matter up with his chief. He takes the book with him to headquarters and I go home to cool off.

Now the superintendent of police or the district attorney—should my marked copy of *Tom Jones* be relayed to him—has it in his power, if he believes the book is actionable, to descend without warning on my bookseller and arrest him for selling a book "containing obscene, indecent or impure language." The victim will be brought to trial and compelled to defend the book under the terms of the statute. The jury, almost certainly, will be picked from those who have never read *Tom Jones*. But the lawyer for the defense may not read the whole book to them or defend the whole book before them. His defense must be centred on those passages which I complained of and those alone. Such was the procedure in the Massachusetts trials of *Oil!* by Upton Sinclair, and Dreiser's *American Tragedy*. Both books were examined and finally condemned on the strength—or again the weakness —of certain isolated passages.

My sympathies go to the bookseller. In the last twenty years there have been perhaps a dozen court cases, and in many instances the verdict has gone against the bookseller. Yet he does not publish the books, and in buying, often from dummy copies, the five or six thousand new titles that are shown to him by salesmen each year it must be apparent that he can have at the outset, and often for a long time thereafter, only the vaguest notion of the contents of the books on his counters. Realizing that benevolent "vice societies" will be on the lookout for what they consider obnoxious books, he anticipates their complaints by asking them to notify him in advance of their taking any action. Upon their notification he is left with the choice of withdrawing the suspected book from circulation or running the risk of arrest and trial. He is human if he does the former and a martyr if he does not—and martyrs are rare in any community. Yet the former action on his part helps to establish the societies as the unofficial censors of any state.

I do not wish to give the opinion that vice societies are the only crusaders involved. In Massachusetts they were responsible for eleven suppressions in the two black years. The complaints which withdrew the other fifty-seven books from circulation were made by zealots, the police, and, in one case, the librarian of the Athenæum. Under the absurdly strict terms of the then existing law only one publisher felt justified in exposing his book and himself to a test case. A book could not be defended as a whole, and the fine and punishment—for this is a criminal law and gives one a criminal record—were hardly such as one would wish to incur even as a martyr. That is the reason why books like *The World of William Clissold,* by H. G. Wells, *Dark Laughter,* by Sherwood Anderson, *Elmer Gantry,* by Sinclair Lewis, *As It Was,* by H. T., *The Sun Also Rises,* by Ernest Hemingway, and *The Wayward Man,* by St. John Ervine,—to mention a few,—were suppressed in the city of Boston, and, if authorities wished, could have been suppressed anywhere within the Commonwealth, without trial. The only result of such absurdity was to set people to reading in search of a licentiousness that did not exist.

In England and in the United States our book censorship laws have been derived from statutes originally framed as a protection against deliberate pornography. Of course no one wants to see slimy pamphlets sold in school districts by representatives of pirate publishers: such men should be hounded and prosecuted to the full extent of the law. But unfortunately the laws were extended by misguided zealots until they were applied against books innocent as well as guilty, classics as well as the *Memoirs of Fanny Hill.* Erratic judgments are as much to be expected in bureaucratic censorship as under the crusading fervor of benevolent vice societies.

I believe that there must be a legal control of books. I believe that the law courts are a logical place for their examination and that our judges, if not our juries, are qualified to decide upon the question of whether or not they are obscene. But I believe very earnestly that the law should be so worded *as to take the whole book into account.* Such a law is enforced in New York; such a reform was urgently needed in Massachusetts. I must say I take some personal satisfaction in the campaign that ended in the law's revision.

When the statute is so worded as to allow the consideration of the whole book rather than the consideration of isolated passages, publishers will feel justified in defending, as they do in New York, books which have been the subject of complaint. If the complaint is borne out by the decision of the jury and judge, the publisher may be considered to have received fair warning against such continued practice, and if the book is given a clean bill of health no more will be thought about it.

III

If my words have not been in vain it should by now be clear that, as Morris Ernst says, "the test of obscenity is a living standard." The simplest of comparisons demonstrate that we live in a world of change: compare the bathing suit of 1900 with the bathing suit of to-day; compare the tennis shorts the women wear at Forest Hills with the tennis longs they wore a generation ago at Longwood. Clothes have given us the freedom of movement we desired without corrupting our physical standards: is it not logical to assume that the freedom of thought in modern literature has been attained without coarsening or corrupting the mind? It is told that Walter Hines Page once refused to print a book because it contained the suggestive word "chaste." Page was moved by the same impulse which prompted George H. Doran to remove some of the excess profanity in *Three Soldiers* by John Dos Passos—an impulse which in all likelihood gives concern to the editors of Ernest Hemingway's and William Faulkner's manuscripts to-day. From 1910 to 1935, in the intervening quarter of a century, there has been a shift from prudery to plain speaking, a shift so decided that one must distinguish very thoughtfully between that which is healthy and that which may be contaminating. This fluctuation was well expressed by Judge Learned Hand when in *U. S.* v. *Kennerley,* 209 Fed. 119, he remarked:—

> If there be no abstract definition, such as I have suggested, should not the word "obscene" be allowed to indicate the *present critical point* in the compromise between candor and shame at which the community may have arrived *here and now?*

So before you allow yourself to condemn a book ask yourself first whether the volume might conceivably be classified as literature or whether it belongs in the class of contemporary sensations. Ask yourself whether—despite your dislike of it—you can conscientiously believe that the book might contaminate not the moron but the average healthy mind in your neighborhood. Above all, ask yourself whether conceivably you may have misconstrued what the author has said. Remember that sage piece of advice handed down by a fastidious English novelist. "It is desirable," said E. M. Forster, "that people should not be corrupted, but there is no reason why they should not be shocked."

No test has meant more to literature than the trial and vindication of James Joyce's *Ulysses* which, in 1933, took place before Judge John M. Woolsey in the United States District Court of New York. Here was a book which has exerted a more widespread influence on contemporary literature than that of any other living author. It has been well said that "there is not a single modern psychological novel worthy of mention which does not bear some trace of the Joycean method." The book took seven years to write, it was a long book—as long as seven ordinary novels—and unlike any that had preceded it. Despite its colossal length the story recounts but a single day in the life of Leopold Bloom,—who is Ulysses,—an advertising solicitor of Dublin. The style has been tagged as "stream-of-consciousness"; its involution and its symbolic association with Homer's *Odyssey* make the reading of Joyce's work too complex for the consumer of easy fiction. In his admirable decision, which has now been reprinted in the Random House edition of *Ulysses,* Judge Woolsey made this defense of Mr. Joyce's style:—

> It is because Joyce has been loyal to his technique and has not funked its necessary implications, but has honestly attempted to tell fully what his characters think about, that he has been the subject of so many attacks and that his purpose has been so often misunderstood and misrepresented. For his attempt sincerely and honestly to realize his objective has required him incidentally to use certain words which are generally considered dirty words and has led at times to what many think is a too poignant preoccupation with sex in the thoughts of his characters.
>
> The words which are criticized as dirty are old Saxon words known to almost all men and, I venture, to many women, and are such words as would be naturally and habitually used, I believe, by the types of folk whose life, physical and mental, Joyce is seeking to describe. In respect of the recurrent emergence of the theme of sex in the minds of his characters, it must always be remembered that his locale was Celtic and his season Spring.
>
> Whether or not one enjoys such a technique as Joyce uses is a matter of taste on which disagreement or argument is futile, but to subject that technique to the standards of some other technique seems to me to be little short of absurd.
>
> Accordingly, I hold that *Ulysses* is a sincere and honest book and I think that the criticisms of it are entirely disposed of by its rationale.

The Judge's argument deserves to be read in its entirety. But for those who must take short cuts, be it said that the court found (1) that the intrinsic features of *Ulysses* by James Joyce, as well as certain extrinsic facts, negative any charge of obscenity; (2) that *Ulysses* has been generally accepted by the community; (3) that *Ulysses* when judged as a whole and its purpose determined must be cleared.

I should like to believe this test has created a precedent which will stand for a long time to come.

In reviewing Morris Ernst and William Seagle's *To the Pure,* Havelock Ellis used the occasion to state his personal views on censorship, arrived at after more than a generation of attacks by censors on his own writings.

Ellis, British criminologist and psychologist, in his scientific approach to problems of sexual behavior was the forerunner of Alfred Kinsey and later research workers. His *Studies in the Psychology of Sex* (seven volumes, 1898–1928) is a monumental contribution to the field, a source since extensively drawn upon by scholars and scientists. It paved the way for public acceptance of the work of Freud and Jung in psychology, and of writers like Joyce and Proust in literature. Despite general approval by the medical profession, legal proceedings charging obscenity brought against the first volume of *Studies in the Psychology of Sex,* when it was published in England, caused Ellis to issue the remaining volumes in the United States and Germany.

Havelock Ellis
OBSCENITY AND THE CENSOR

"To the Pure" is the title of a book—with the sub-title "A Study of Obscenity and the Censor"—just published in New York by the Viking Press. At the outset let me say that it is a title which, however useful as a label, contains implications we do not all accept. By this we mean no disrespect to St. Paul, for when he uttered the famous dictum, "To the pure all things are pure," he was not discussing literature or pictures or the kinema, but a matter to which they are hardly analogous. There are many things in books and art generally which the pure may be justified in not feeling to be pure, although there can never be any agreement as to which things these are. That indeed is one of the solid and permanent arguments against a censorship of "obscenity."

Fortunately it is only as a label that the authors of this book have chosen their title. They are two American lawyers, Morris Ernst and William Seagle, and between them they represent an active interest in both law and literature. Their collaboration has proved singularly fortunate. They are not only able to speak with authority of legal conditions in England and America—for the book is as much concerned with England as America—but they are extremely well informed in literature, and with a sufficiently adequate critical and æsthetic equipment for estimating literary values. The book is at once a competent history of the Anglo-Saxon censorship from the Victorian period until to-day, and at the same time a cogent and yet singularly temperate argument for freedom from censorship. It is not the first book which has taken this standpoint. There is, for instance, also from America, the substantial and powerful work of Theodore Schroeder, published some twenty years ago, on "Obscene Literature and Constitutional Law." But that book was hardly written for the general reader and it remains less well known than it deserves to be. "To the Pure . . ." is undoubtedly by far the best popular book—the best written as well as the most persuasive—that has yet appeared on this subject. And since it is a subject that concerns us here to-day at least as much as it concerns Americans, the sooner it is published here the better.

I have referred to the tone of the book as temperate. We have too often seen the slapdash hand exercising itself in this field. The foolish and extravagant rhetoric of those who fulminate against "obscenity" has been matched by the random and reckless smartness, sometimes scarcely less foolish, of those who took the other side. It was fully time to approach the question in a sane and serious spirit, which is not less so for allowing the play of wit and humour. Thus it is notable that these authors do not, as was not so long ago the fashion, howl over the supposed misdeeds of "Puritanism." They know that real Puritanism was on the side of liberty, and that it was the greatest of the Puritans who in the "Areopagitica" put forth the noblest denunciation of censorship that was ever uttered. It might be added that even in more recent days the most genuinely Puritanic of prominent publicists, W. T. Stead, was prepared to raise his voice for those haled before the courts for "obscenity," and was in fact himself once among them.

It is, indeed, well known that the Bible takes a high place among "obscene" books. There appears to be no definition of obscenity which will not condemn the Bible. Moreover, on the practical side, it is also known that the young find their chief source of information concerning sex—birth, masturbation, birth-control, rape, and perversion—from the Bible. This was, for instance, shown not long ago through a careful enquiry by a distinguished authority in social hygiene, Dr. Katharine Davis, among over a thousand unmarried women, all college graduates. The same women were also asked what they found most "sexually stimulating" (in the police courts it would be phrased "lewd, filthy, and disgusting"). The largest number replied "Man." The problem thus becomes of tragic consequence, for we see that if "obscenity" is to be suppressed it can only be done by the ex-

---

Havelock Ellis, "Obscenity and the Censor," London *Saturday Review*, 146:642–43 (November 17, 1928), copyright 1928 by the Saturday Review. Reprinted by permission of Mrs. F. Lafitte-Cyon, Literary Executrix, and the Society of Authors as the literary representative of the Estate of the late Havelock Ellis.

tinction of one-half of the human race. And as men, if asked the same question, would in an equal majority of cases undoubtedly answer: "Woman"—why, there goes the other half.

The authors of this book are not joking but they are concerned to show that the final refutation of the criminal obscenity laws lies in their futility. They are throughout dealing with the actual facts of life and of law in our own day; they marshal these facts with learning and with care (in spite of a few curious misprints); and their conclusions are logical, sober, and irresistible. They claim to have shown the necessity for *a revaluation of obscenity*. That is very far from meaning a justification of the things that most reasonable people find ugly and unpleasant. But it means a different attitude towards their suppression in practice. We know the results of the attitude which has prevailed in the past. We have all been the victims of it. A premium is put on things that are dirty and worthless. It is law alone which makes pornography both attractive and profitable. A simple-minded Home Secretary arises and declares that he feels it to be his duty to protect the young from the awful dangers that threaten them in books, postcards, and kinemas. Needless to say, the young of to-day are not in a mood to be preserved from these dangers, which can always be reached sooner or later, with a little trouble and money. And no doubt such things often give rise to some gloating, though in the absence of the alluring taboo they would call forth only indifference or dislike. The motive for producing them would then soon disappear. At the present time, thanks to the premium put on them, the production of obscene postcards and similar things is so large that even the number of those seized by the police soon mounts up to millions. All of us, it is probable, have once been stirred to gain access to such things simply because they were forbidden. For my own part, I remember how, long ago, in a quiet street of Seville, a furtive and shabby individual drew me aside and produced from beneath his long cloak a little book with coloured illustrations which curiosity induced me to spend several pesetas in buying. I found it pathetically crude and unpleasant, and I quickly destroyed it; my curiosity was once and for all satisfied. Such things are, of course, far away from art or science, which redeem all they touch, if it happens to need "redemption."

"The real obscenity lies in taboo"; that is the great truth on which Messrs. Ernst and Seagle have seized and sought to drive home in a world which is suffering from the ignorance of it. As they rightly point out, it is impossible to estimate the social damage which has thus been done. It is these taboos which have delayed until to-day the effort to combat venereal diseases and the discussion of the population question. The names of the evils were too "obscene" to mention and therefore the evils themselves were allowed to flourish unchecked, or else left to specialists and officials to discuss in technical terms. In another field the difficult problems raised by psycho-analysis have been dragged from the calm field of science to be perverted and distorted by the fascination or the repulsion of the taboo against obscenity. Even in the sphere of history and biography the taboo against obscenity has stood in the way of an accurate knowledge of personalities and events; while now that the taboo is losing its force there is naturally a movement to the other extreme, with a tendency to distortion in the opposite direction, and we magnify the importance of the facts that before we were not allowed to see. For it is not one of the least evils of taboos that even the inevitable reaction they lead to is evil.

It seems so simple, so innocent, so entirely praiseworthy, to put down indecent literature by laws against "obscenity." We are, none of us, in favour of what seems to us indecent. It is impossible we should be, for the word means, if we search into it, simply what is unfit. Yet the simpler and more fundamental the conception of decency is seen to be the more it eludes any prescription of positive law. It is determined by the nature of the individual himself, by the feelings of his social group, and very notably by fashion. Most of us are old enough to know that less than twenty years ago the whole young womanhood of to-day would have been held guilty of indecency in dress and liable to be conducted to the nearest police station. In literature fashion is even more uncertain and elusive than in life, for the good reason that it is not produced by mass action. Messrs. Ernst and Seagle constantly bring forward examples of such fluctuations of opinion regarding books condemned by law, as well as examples of books legally condemned as obscene in England and free in America, or legally condemned in America and free in England. "The obscenity of to-day will be the propriety of to-morrow."

Law is made ridiculous when it is thus prostituted to the fashion of the hour. It is made immoral when it is thus perverted to the supposed protection of children. It used to be "women and children" who were assumed to be in need of such protection from the dangers of "obscenity." It is now only children, for women have rightfully insisted that in this matter they are henceforth to be put on the level of men and not of children. The problem of the child remains, and one of the wisest chapters in this book is that on "Pornography and the Child." It ought to be clear that we are not entitled to protect children by laws which also extend to adults and thus tend (sometimes with too much success) to convert adults into children. It is for the parents and teachers to protect the children. Yet it is admitted that there is "a twilight zone of disputed control between parents and government." In the realm of economics it is rightly held that the forces against the child should be restrained by laws against long hours of work and similar hardships. But to protect the child against "obscenity" by legislation is not only more difficult but less necessary. Pornography has no meaning and no attraction for the healthy child who casually comes in contact with it; the reaction is one of indifference, if not of disgust. To-day if any harm is caused it is less likely to come from pornography than from the crudely exaggerated films of vice and disease, presented by virtuous propagandists of social hygiene, which are apt to cause a painful shock to the virginal mind, just as the tender skin of the infant is injured by the hot bath of a temperature wholesomely stimulating to the adult. There are many uncensored things in life far more injurious to the young than obscenity. "A minor's pornography law" is here suggested, but tentatively, with much doubt; "we have faith that education, through school and home, will prove the enduring solution." Parents and teachers alone can be trusted to guide the child safely through these risks without injury to the freedom of adults. To-day this is being recognized by parents and teachers alike, even if not yet always in ways that are according to knowledge.

"The modern counterpart of modern witchcraft"—it is so that in the Preface the authors of this book describe the superstition of "obscenity." It is, indeed, an analogy which might well be worked out in greater detail. The witch-finders of the seventeenth century are a close counterpart of the obscenity-finders of to-day. The lurid halo around the witch made her a really injurious influence, just as the glamour we now cast around obscenity imparts to it an influence it would not otherwise possess. Witchcraft, like obscenity, was not altogether the product of the witch-finder's imagination. But so far as it was real it could not be touched by the ducking-stool or the law court. It melted away under the influence of a more reasonably humane and civilized attitude.

It was precisely at the time when the development of science and civilization was leading to the proper estimate of witchcraft that ferocity in the persecution of witches reached its height. We may say the same to-day about obscenity. The old sex taboos are dissolving. We are beginning to face openly the facts of sex, with a degree of intelligence and frankness which even a quarter of a century ago was impossible. That new honesty and sincerity itself stirs up the persecutional fanaticism of the descendants of the witch-finders. Yet until the crime of "obscenity" goes the way of the crime of witchcraft, it is idle to talk of civilization.

D. H. Lawrence was almost constantly at odds with the censors from the time he began writing until his death in 1930. One of his first novels, *The Rainbow,* was withdrawn by the publisher when attacked by critics. This reaction was mild, however, in comparison to the reception accorded *Lady Chatterley's Lover,* which was widely damned as a piece of willful pornography. Unable to persuade any reputable publisher to accept it, Lawrence had to print it privately. Despite his difficulties, the book's influence on contemporary literature has been enormous. One of the most perceptive interpreters of Lawrence's work, Horace Gregory, wrote:

"No novelist or poet living today finds it necessary to continue the half-century fight for sexual liberation in English writing. After *Lady Chatterley's Lover* all subsequent uses of the sex symbol are anticlimactic. It has been a long fight from the publication of Whitman's 'Song of Myself' through the Oscar Wilde trial, through twenty years of

Freud to this last writing of a novel printed in Italy and Paris. The fight was won in 1928."

In "Pornography and Obscenity" Lawrence explains and defends his position. The essential point is his statement, "What is pornography to one man is the laughter of genius to another."

D. H. Lawrence
PORNOGRAPHY AND OBSCENITY

What they are depends, as usual, entirely on the individual. What is pornography to one man is the laughter of genius to another.

The word itself, we are told, means "pertaining to harlots"—the graph of the harlot. But nowadays, what is a harlot? If she was a woman who took money from a man in return for going to bed with him—really, most wives sold themselves, in the past, and plenty of harlots gave themselves, when they felt like it, for nothing. If a woman hasn't got a tiny streak of a harlot in her, she's a dry stick as a rule. And probably most harlots had somewhere a streak of womanly generosity. Why be so cut and dried? The law is a dreary thing, and its judgments have nothing to do with life.

The same with the word *obscene:* nobody knows what it means. Suppose it were derived from *obscena*: that which might not be represented on the stage; how much further are you? None! What is obscene to Tom is not obscene to Lucy or Joe, and really, the meaning of a word has to wait for majorities to decide it. If a play shocks ten people in an audience, and doesn't shock the remaining five hundred, then it is obscene to ten and innocuous to five hundred; hence, the play is not obscene, by majority. But *Hamlet* shocked all the Cromwellian Puritans, and shocks nobody to-day, and some of Aristophanes shocks everybody to-day, and didn't galvanise the later Greeks at all, apparently. Man is a changeable beast, and words change their meanings with him, and things are not what they seemed, and what's what becomes what isn't, and if we think we know where we are it's only because we are so rapidly being translated to somewhere else. We have to leave everything to the majority, everything to the majority, everything to the mob, the mob, the mob. They know what is obscene and what isn't, they do. If the lower ten million doesn't know better than the upper ten men, then there's something wrong with mathematics. Take a vote on it! Show hands, and prove it by count! *Vox populi, vox Dei. Odi profanum vulgus! Profanum vulgus.*

So it comes down to this: if you are talking to the mob, the meaning of your words is the mob-meaning, decided by majority. As somebody wrote to me: the American law on obscenity is very plain, and America is going to enforce the law. Quite, my dear, quite, quite, quite! The mob knows all about obscenity. Mild little words that rhyme with spit or farce are the height of obscenity. Supposing a printer put "h" in the place of "p," by mistake, in that mere word spit? Then the great American public knows that this man has committed an obscenity, an indecency, that his act was lewd, and as a compositor he was pornographical. You can't tamper with the great public, British or American. *Vox populi, vox Dei,* don't you know. If you don't we'll let you know it. At the same time, this *vox Dei* shouts with praise over moving-pictures and books and newspaper accounts that seem, to a sinful nature like mine, completely disgusting and obscene. Like a real prude and Puritan, I have to look the other way. When obscenity becomes mawkish, which is its palatable form for the public, and when the *Vox populi, vox Dei* is hoarse with sentimental indecency, then I have to steer away, like a Pharisee, afraid of being contaminated. There is a certain kind of sticky universal pitch that I refuse to touch.

So again, it comes down to this: you accept the majority, the mob, and its decisions, or you don't. You bow down before the *Vox populi, vox Dei,* or you plug your ears not to hear its obscene howl. You perform your antics to please the vast public, *Deus ex machina,* or you refuse to perform for the public at all, unless now and then to pull its elephantine and ignominious leg.

When it comes to the meaning of anything, even the simplest word, then you must pause. Because there are two great categories of meaning, for ever separate. There is mob-meaning, and there is individual meaning. Take even the word *bread*. The mob-meaning is merely: stuff made with white flour into loaves that you eat.

D. H. Lawrence, *Pornography and Obscenity* (New York: Alfred A. Knopf, 1930), copyright 1930 by Alfred A. Knopf, Inc. Reprinted by permission of the publisher and of the Executors of the Estate of the late Mrs. Frieda Lawrence.

But take the individual meaning of the word bread: the white, the brown, the corn-pone, the home-made, the smell of bread just out of the oven, the crust, the crumb, the unleavened bread, the shew-bread, the staff of life, sour-dough bread, cottage loaves, French bread, Viennese bread, black bread, a yesterday's loaf, rye, graham, barley, rolls, *Bretzeln, Kringeln*, scones, damper, matsen—there is no end to it all, and the word bread will take you to the ends of time and space, and far-off down avenues of memory. But this is individual. The word bread will take the individual off on his own journey, and its meaning will be his own meaning, based on his own genuine imagination reactions. And when a word comes to us in its individual character, and starts in us the individual responses, it is great pleasure to us. The American advertisers have discovered this, and some of the cunningest American literature is to be found in advertisements of soap-suds, for example. These advertisements are *almost* prose-poems. They give the word soap-suds a bubbly, shiny individual meaning, which is very skilfully poetic, would, perhaps, be quite poetic to the mind which could forget that the poetry was bait on a hook.

Business is discovering the individual, dynamic meaning of words, and poetry is losing it. Poetry more and more tends to far-fetch its word-meanings, and this results once again in mob-meanings, which arouse only a mob-reaction in the individual. For every man has a mob-self and an individual self, in varying proportions. Some men are almost all mob-self, incapable of imaginative individual responses. The worst specimens of mob-self are usually to be found in the professions, lawyers, professors, clergymen and so on. The business man, much maligned, has a tough outside mob-self, and a scared, floundering yet still alive individual self. The public, which is feeble-minded like an idiot, will never be able to preserve its individual reactions from the tricks of the exploiter. The public is always exploited and always will be exploited. The methods of exploitation merely vary. To-day the public is tickled into laying the golden egg. With imaginative words and individual meanings it is tricked into giving the great goose-cackle of mob-acquiescence. *Vox populi, vox Dei*. It has always been so, and will always be so. Why? Because the public has not enough wit to distinguish between mob-meanings and individual meanings. The mass is for ever vulgar, because it can't distinguish between its own original feelings and feelings which are diddled into existence by the exploiter. The public is always profane, because it is controlled from the outside, by the trickster, and never from the inside, by its own sincerity. The mob is always obscene, because it is always second-hand.

Which brings us back to our subject of pornography and obscenity. The reaction to any word may be, in any individual, either a mob-reaction or an individual reaction. It is up to the individual to ask himself: Is my reaction individual, or am I merely reacting from my mob-self?

When it comes to the so-called obscene words, I should say that hardly one person in a million escapes mob-reaction. The first reaction is almost sure to be mob-reaction, mob-indignation, mob-condemnation. And the mob gets no further. But the real individual has second thoughts and says: Am I *really* shocked? Do I *really* feel outraged and indignant? And the answer of any individual is bound to be: No, I am not shocked, not outraged, nor indignant. I know the word, and take it for what it is, and I am not going to be jockeyed into making a mountain out of a mole-hill, not for all the law in the world.

Now if the use of a few so-called obscene words will startle man or woman out of a mob-habit into an individual state, well and good. And word prudery is so universal a mob-habit that it is time we were startled out of it.

But still we have only tackled obscenity, and the problem of pornography goes even deeper. When a man is startled into his individual self, he still may not be able to know, inside himself, whether Rabelais is or is not pornographic: and over Aretino or even Boccaccio he may perhaps puzzle in vain, torn between different emotions.

One essay on pornography, I remember, comes to the conclusion that pornography in art is that which is calculated to arouse sexual desire, or sexual excitement. And stress is laid on the fact, whether the author or artist *intended* to arouse sexual feelings. It is the old vexed question of intention, become so dull to-day, when we know how strong and influential our unconscious intentions are. And why a man should be held guilty of his conscious intentions, and innocent of his unconscious intentions, I don't know, since every man is more made up of unconscious intentions than of conscious ones. I am what I am, not merely what I think I am.

However! We take it, I assume, that *pornography* is something base, something unpleasant. In short, we don't like it. And why don't we like it? Because it arouses sexual feelings?

I think not. No matter how hard we may pretend otherwise, most of us rather like a moderate rousing of our sex. It warms us, stimulates us like sunshine on a grey day. After a century or two of Puritanism, this is still true of most people. Only the mob-habit of condemning any form of sex is too strong to let us admit it naturally. And there are, of course, many people who are genuinely repelled by the simplest and most natural stirrings of sexual feeling. But these people are perverts who have fallen into hatred of their fellow-men: thwarted, disappointed, unfulfilled people, of whom, alas, our civilisation contains so many. And they nearly always enjoy some unsimple and unnatural form of sex excitement, secretly.

Even quite advanced art critics would try to make us believe that any picture or book which had "sex appeal" was *ipso facto* a bad book or picture. This is just canting hypocrisy. Half the great poems, pictures, music, stories of the whole world are great by virtue of the beauty of their sex appeal. Titian or Renoir, the Song of Solomon or *Jane Eyre*, Mozart or "Annie Laurie," the loveliness is all interwoven with sex appeal, sex stimulus, call it what you will. Even Michelangelo, who rather hated sex, can't help filling the Cornucopia with phallic acorns. Sex is a very powerful, beneficial and necessary stimulus in human life, and we are all grateful when we feel its warm, natural flow through us, like a form of sunshine.

So we can dismiss the idea that sex appeal in art is pornography. It may be so to the grey Puritan, but the grey Puritan is a sick man, soul and body sick, so why should we bother about his hallucinations? Sex appeal, of course, varies enormously. There are endless different kinds, and endless degrees of each kind. Perhaps it may be argued that a mild degree of sex appeal is not pornographical, whereas a high degree is. But this is a fallacy. Boccaccio at his hottest seems to me less pornographical than *Pamela* or *Clarissa Harlowe* or even *Jane Eyre,* or a host of modern books or films which pass uncensored.

At the same time Wagner's *Tristan and Isolde* seems to me very near to pornography, and so, even, do some quite popular Christian hymns.

What is it, then? It isn't a question of sex appeal, merely: nor even a question of deliberate intention on the part of the author or artist to arouse sexual excitement. Rabelais sometimes had a deliberate intention, so in a different way, did Boccaccio. And I'm sure poor Charlotte Brontë, or the authoress of *The Sheik,* did not have any deliberate intention to stimulate sex feelings in the reader. Yet I find *Jane Eyre* verging towards pornography and Boccaccio seems to me always fresh and wholesome.

The late British Home Secretary, who prides himself on being a very sincere Puritan, grey, grey in every fibre, said with indignant sorrow in one of his outbursts on improper books: "—and these two young people, who had been perfectly pure up till that time, after reading this book went and had sexual intercourse together! ! !" *One up to them!* is all we can answer. But the grey Guardian of British Morals seemed to think that if they had murdered one another, or worn each other to rags of nervous prostration, it would have been much better. The grey disease!

Then what is pornography, after all this? It isn't sex appeal or sex stimulus in art. It isn't even a deliberate intention on the part of the artist to arouse or excite sexual feelings. There's nothing wrong with sexual feelings in themselves, so long as they are straightforward and not sneaking or sly. The right sort of sex stimulus is invaluable to human daily life. Without it the world grows grey. I would give everybody the gay Renaissance stories to read, they would help to shake off a lot of grey self-importance, which is our modern civilised disease.

But even I would censor genuine pornography, rigorously. It would not be very difficult. In the first place, genuine pornography is almost always underworld, it doesn't come into the open. In the second, you can recognise it by the insult it offers, invariably, to sex, and to the human spirit.

Pornography is the attempt to insult sex, to do dirt on it. This is unpardonable. Take the very lowest instance, the picture postcard sold underhand, by the underworld, in most cities. What I have seen of them have been of an ugliness to make you cry. The insult to the human body, the insult to a vital human relationship! Ugly and cheap they make the human nudity, ugly and degraded they make the sexual act, trivial and cheap and nasty.

It is the same with the books they sell in the underworld. They are either so ugly they make you ill, or so fatuous you can't imagine anybody but a cretin or a moron reading them, or writing them.

It is the same with the dirty limericks that people tell after dinner, or the dirty stories one hears commercial travellers telling each other in a smoke-room. Occasionally there is a really funny one, that redeems a great deal. But usually they are just ugly and repellent, and the so-called "humour" is just a trick of doing dirt on sex.

Now the human nudity of a great many modern people is just ugly and degraded, and the sexual act between modern people is just the same, merely ugly and degrading. But this is nothing to be proud of. It is the catastrophe of our civilisation. I am sure no other civilisation, not even the Roman, has showed such a vast proportion of ignominious and degraded nudity, and ugly, squalid dirty sex. Because no other civilisation has driven sex into the underworld, and nudity to the w.c.

The intelligent young, thank heaven, seem determined to alter in these two respects. They are rescuing their young nudity from the stuffy pornographical hole-and-corner underworld of their elders, and they refuse to sneak about the sexual relation. This is a change the elderly grey ones of course deplore, but it is in fact a very great change for the better, and a real revolution.

But it is amazing how strong is the will in ordinary, vulgar people, to do dirt on sex. It was one of my fond illusions, when I was young, that the ordinary healthy-seeming sort of men in railway carriages, or the smoke-room of an hotel or a pullman, were healthy in their feelings, and had a wholesome rough devil-may-care attitude towards sex. All wrong! All wrong! Experience teaches that common individuals of this sort have a disgusting attitude towards sex, a disgusting contempt of it, a disgusting desire to insult it. If such fellows have intercourse with a woman, they triumphantly feel that they have done her dirt, and now she is lower, cheaper, more contemptible than she was before.

It is individuals of this sort that tell dirty stories, carry indecent picture postcards, and know the indecent books. This is the great pornographical class—the really common men-in-the-street and women-in-the-street. They have as great a hate and contempt of sex as the greyest Puritan, and when an appeal is made to them, they are always on the side of the angels. They insist that a film-heroine shall be a neuter, a sexless thing of washed-out purity. They insist that real sex-feeling shall only be shown by the villain or villainess, low lust. They find a Titian or a Renoir really indecent, and they don't want their wives and daughters to see it.

Why? Because they have the grey disease of sex-hatred, coupled with the yellow disease of dirt-lust. The sex functions and the excrementary functions in the human body work so close together, yet they are, so to speak, utterly different in direction. Sex is a creative flow, the excrementary flow is towards dissolution, de-creation, if we may use such a word. In the really healthy human being the distinction between the two is instant, our profoundest instincts are perhaps our instincts of opposition between the two flows.

But in the degraded human being the deep instincts have gone dead, and then the two flows become identical. *This* is the secret of really vulgar and of pornographical people: the sex flow and the excrement flow is the same to them. It happens when the psyche deteriorates, and the profound controlling instincts collapse. Then sex is dirt and dirt is sex, and sexual excitement becomes a playing with dirt, and any sign of sex in a woman becomes a show of her dirt. This is the condition of the common, vulgar human being whose name is legion, and who lifts his voice and it is the *Vox populi, vox Dei*. And this is the source of all pornography.

And for this reason we must admit that *Jane Eyre* or Wagner's *Tristan* are much nearer to pornography than is Boccaccio. Wagner and Charlotte Brontë were both in the state where the strongest instincts have collapsed, and sex has become something slightly obscene, to be wallowed in, but despised. Mr. Rochester's sex passion is not "respectable" till Mr. Rochester is burned, blinded, disfigured, and reduced to helpless dependence. Then, thoroughly humbled and humiliated, it may be merely admitted. All the previous titillations are slightly indecent, as in *Pamela* or *The Mill on the Floss* or *Anna Karenina*. As soon as there is sex excitement with a desire to spite the sexual feelings, to humiliate it and degrade it, the element of pornography enters.

For this reason, there is an element of pornography in nearly all nineteenth-century literature and very many so-called pure people have a nasty pornographical side to them, and never was the pornographical appetite stronger than it is to-day. It is a sign of a diseased condition of the body politic. But the way to treat the disease is to come out into the open with sex and sex stimulus. The real pornographer truly dislikes Boccaccio, because the fresh healthy naturalness of the Italian story-teller makes the modern pornographical shrimp feel the dirty worm he is. To-day Boccaccio should be given to everybody, young or old, to read if they like. Only a natural fresh openness about sex will do any good, now we are being swamped by secret or semi-secret pornography. And perhaps the Renaissance story-tellers, Boccaccio, Lasca, and the rest, are the best antidote we can find now, just as more plasters of Puritanism are the most harmful remedy we can resort to.

The whole question of pornography seems to me a question of secrecy. Without secrecy there would be no pornography. But secrecy and modesty are two utterly different things. Secrecy has always an element of fear in it, amounting very often to hate. Modesty is gentle and reserved. To-day, modesty is thrown to the winds, even in the presence of the grey guardians. But secrecy is hugged, being a vice in itself. And the attitude of the grey ones is: Dear young ladies, you may abandon all modesty, so long as you hug your dirty little secret.

This "dirty little secret" has become infinitely precious to the mob of people to-day. It is a kind of hidden sore or inflammation which, when rubbed or scratched, gives off sharp thrills that seem delicious. So the dirty little secret is rubbed and scratched more and more, till it becomes more and more secretly inflamed, and the nervous and psychic health of the individual is more and more impaired. One might easily say that half the love novels and half the love films to-day depend entirely for their success on the secret rubbing of the dirty little secret. You can call this sex excitement if you like, but it is sex excitement of a secretive, furtive sort, quite special. The plain and simple excitement, quite open and wholesome, which you find in some Boccaccio stories is not for a minute to be confused with the furtive excitement aroused by rubbing the dirty little secret in all secrecy in modern bestsellers. This furtive, sneaking, cunning rubbing of an inflamed spot in the imagination is the very quick of modern pornography, and it is a beastly and very dangerous thing. You can't so easily expose it, because of its very furtiveness and its sneaking cunning. So the cheap and popular modern love novel and love film flourishes and is even praised by moral guardians, because you get the sneaking thrill fumbling under all the purity of dainty underclothes, without one single gross word to let you know what is happening.

Without secrecy there would be no pornography. But if pornography is the result of sneaking secrecy, what is the result of pornography? What is the effect on the individual?

The effect on the individual is manifold, and always pernicious. But one effect is perhaps inevitable. The pornography of to-day, whether it be the pornography of the rubber-goods shop or the pornography of the popular novel, film, and play, is an invariable stimulant to the vice of self-abuse, onanism, masturbation, call it what you will. In young or old, man or woman, boy or girl, modern pornography is a direct provocative masturbation. It cannot be otherwise. When the grey ones wail that the young man and the young woman went and had sexual intercourse, they are bewailing the fact that the young man and the young woman didn't go separately and masturbate. Sex must go somewhere, especially in young people. So, in our glorious civilisation, it goes in masturbation. And the mass of our popular literature, the bulk of our popular amusements just exist to provoke masturbation. Masturbation is the one thoroughly secret act of the human being, more secret even than excrementation. It is the one functional result of sex-secrecy, and it is stimulated and provoked by our glorious popular literature of pretty pornography, which rubs on the dirty secret without letting you know what is happening.

Now I have heard men, teachers and clergymen, commend masturbation as the solution of an otherwise insoluble sex problem. This at least is honest. The sex problem is there, and you can't just will it away. There it is, and under the ban of secrecy and taboo in mother and father, teacher, friend, and foe, it has found its own solution, the solution of masturbation.

But what about the solution? Do we accept it? Do all the grey ones of this world accept it? If so, they must now accept it openly. We can none of us pretend any longer to be blind to the fact of masturbation, in young and old, man and woman. The moral guardians who are prepared to censor all open and plain portrayal of sex must now be made to give their only justification: We prefer that the people shall masturbate. If this preference is open and declared, then the existing forms of censorship are justified. If the moral guardians prefer that the people shall masturbate, then their present behaviour is correct, and popular amusements are as they should be. If sexual intercourse is deadly sin, and masturbation is comparatively pure and harmless, then all is well. Let things continue as they now are.

Is masturbation so harmless, though? Is it even comparatively pure and harmless? Not to my thinking. In the young, a certain amount of masturbation is inevitable, but not therefore natural. I think, there is no boy or girl who masturbates without feeling a sense of shame, anger, and futility. Following the excitement comes the shame, anger, humiliation, and the sense of futility. This sense of futility and humiliation deepens as the years go on, into a suppressed rage, because of the impossibility of escape. The one thing that it seems impossible to escape from, once the habit is formed, is masturbation. It goes on and on, on into old age, in spite of marriage or love affairs or anything else. And it always carries this secret feeling of futility and humiliation, futility and humiliation. And this is, perhaps, the deepest and most dangerous cancer of our civilisation. Instead of being a comparatively pure and harmless vice, masturbation is certainly the most dangerous sexual vice that a society can be afflicted with, in the long run. Comparatively pure it may be—purity being what it is. But harmless! ! !

The great danger of masturbation lies in its merely exhaustive nature. In sexual intercourse, there is a give and take. A new stimulus enters as the native stimulus departs. Something quite new is added as the old surcharge is removed. And this is so in all sexual intercourse where two creatures are concerned, even in the homosexual intercourse. But in masturbation there is nothing but loss. There is no reciprocity. There is merely the spending away of a certain force, and no return. The body remains, in a sense, a corpse, after the act of self-abuse. There is no change, only deadening. There is what we call dead loss. And this is not the case in any act of sexual intercourse between two people. Two people may destroy one another in sex. But they cannot just produce the null effect of masturbation.

The only positive effect of masturbation is that it seems to release a certain mental energy, in some people. But it is mental energy which manifests itself always in the same way, in a vicious circle of analysis and impotent criticism, or else a vicious circle of false and easy sympathy, sentimentalities. The sentimentalism and the niggling analysis, often self-analysis, of most of our modern literature, is a sign of self-abuse. It is the manifestation of masturbation, the sort of conscious activity stimulated by masturbation, whether male or female. The outstanding feature of such consciousness is that there is no real object, there is only subject. This is just the same whether it be a novel or a work of science. The author never escapes from himself, he pads along within the vicious circle of himself. There is hardly a writer living who gets out of the vicious circle of himself—or a painter either. Hence the lack of creation, and the stupendous amount of production. It is a masturbation result, within the vicious circle of the self. It is self-absorption made public.

And of course the process is exhaustive. The real masturbation of Englishmen began only in the nineteenth century. It has continued with an increasing emptying of the real vitality and the real *being* of men, till now people are little more than shells of people. Most of the responses are dead, most of the awareness is dead, nearly all the constructive activity is dead, and all that remains is a sort of shell, a half-empty creature fatally self-preoccupied and incapable of either giving or taking. Incapable either of giving or taking, in the vital self. And this is masturbation's result. Enclosed within the vicious circle of the self, with no vital contacts outside, the self becomes emptier and emptier, till it is almost a nullus, a nothingness.

But null or nothing as it may be, it still hangs on the dirty little secret, which it must still secretly rub, and inflame. For ever the vicious circle. And it has a weird, blind will of its own.

One of my most sympathetic critics wrote: "If Mr. Lawrence's attitude to sex were adopted, then two things would disappear, the love lyric and the smoking-room story." And this, I think, is true. But it depends on which love lyric he means. If it is the: *Who is Sylvia, what is she?*—then it may just as well disappear. All that pure and noble and heaven-blessed stuff is only the counterpart to the smoking-room story. *Du bist wie eine Blume!* Jawohl! One can see the elderly gentleman laying his hands on the head of the pure maiden and praying God to keep her for ever so pure, so clean and beautiful. Very nice for him! Just pornography! Tickling the dirty little secret and rolling his eyes to heaven! He knows perfectly well that if God keeps the maiden so clean and pure and beautiful—in his vulgar sense of clean and pure—for a few more years, then she'll be an unhappy old maid, and not pure nor beautiful at all, only stale and pathetic. Sentimentality is a sure sign of pornography. Why should "sadness strike through the heart" of the old gentleman, because the maid was pure and beautiful? Anybody but a masturbator would have been glad and would have thought: What a lovely bride for some lucky man!—But no, not the self-enclosed, pornographic masturbator. Sadness has to strike into his beastly heart!—Away with such love lyrics, we've had too much of their pornographic poison, tickling the dirty little secret and rolling the eyes to heaven.

But if it is a question of the sound love lyric, *My love is like a red, red rose——!* then we are on other ground. My love is like a red, red rose only when she's *not* like a pure, pure lily. And nowadays the pure, pure lilies are mostly festering, anyhow. Away with them and their lyrics. Away with the pure, pure lily lyric, along with the smoking-room story. They are counterparts, and the one is as pornographic as the other. *Du bist wie eine Blume* is really as pornographic as a dirty story: tickling the dirty little secret and rolling the eyes to heaven. But oh, if only Robert Burns had been accepted for what he is, then love might still have been like a red, red rose.

The vicious circle, the vicious circle! The vicious circle of masturbation! The vicious circle of self-consciousness that is never *fully* self-conscious, never fully and openly conscious, but always harping on the dirty little secret. The vicious circle of secrecy, in parents, teacher, friends—everybody. The specially vicious circle of family. The vast conspiracy of secrecy in the press, and at the same time, the endless tickling of the dirty little secret. The needless masturbation! and the endless purity! The vicious circle!

How to get out of it? There is only one way: Away with the secret! No more secrecy! The only way to stop the terrible mental itch about sex is to come out quite simply and naturally into the open with it. It is terribly difficult, for the secret is cunning as a crab. Yet the thing to do is to make a beginning. The man who said to his exasperating daughter: "My child, the only pleasure I ever had out of you was the pleasure I had in begetting you" has already done a great deal to release both himself and her from the dirty little secret.

How to get out of the dirty little secret! It is, as a matter of fact, extremely difficult for us secretive moderns. You can't do it by being wise and scientific about it, like Dr. Marie Stopes: though to be wise and scientific like Dr. Marie Stopes is better than to be utterly hypocritical, like the grey ones. But by being wise and scientific in the serious and earnest manner you only tend to disinfect the dirty little secret, and either kill sex altogether with too much seriousness and intellect, or else leave it a miserable disinfected secret. The unhappy "free and pure" love of so many people who have taken out the dirty little secret and thoroughly disinfected it with scientific words is apt to be more pathetic even than the common run of dirty-little-secret love. The danger is, that in killing the dirty little secret, you kill dynamic sex altogether, and leave only the scientific and deliberate mechanism.

This is what happens to many of those who become seriously "free" in their sex, free and pure. They have mentalised sex till it is nothing at all, nothing at all but a mental quantity. And the final result is disaster, every time.

The same is true, in an even greater proportion, of the emancipated Bohemians: and very many of the young are Bohemian to-day, whether they ever set foot in Bohemia or not. But the Bohemian is "sex free." The dirty little secret is no secret either to him or her. It is, indeed, a most blatantly open question. There is nothing they don't say: everything that can be revealed is revealed. And they do as they wish.

And then what? They have apparently killed the dirty little secret, but somehow, they have killed everything else too. Some of the dirt still sticks, perhaps; sex remains still dirty. But the thrill of secrecy is gone. Hence the terrible dreariness and depression of modern Bohemia, and the inward dreariness and emptiness of so many young people of to-day. They have killed, they imagine, the dirty little secret. The thrill of secrecy is gone. Some of the dirt remains. And for the rest, depression, inertia, lack of life. For sex is the fountain-head of our energetic life, and now the fountain ceases to flow.

Why? For two reasons. The idealists along the Marie Stopes line, and the young Bohemians of to-day have killed the dirty little secret as far as their personal self goes. But they are still under its dominion socially. In the social world, in the press, in literature, film, theatre, wireless, everywhere purity and the dirty little secret reign supreme. At home, at the dinner table, it is just the same. It is the same wherever you go. The young girl, and the young woman is by tacit assumption pure, virgin, sexless. *Du bist wie eine Blume.* She, poor thing, knows quite well that flowers, even lilies, have tippling yellow anthers and a sticky stigma, sex, rolling sex. But to the popular mind flowers are sexless things, and when a girl is told she is like a flower, it means she is sexless and ought to be sexless. She herself knows quite well she isn't sexless and she isn't merely like a flower. But how bear up against the great social life forced on her? She can't! She succumbs, and the dirty little secret triumphs. She loses her interest in sex, as far as men are concerned, but the vicious circle of masturbation and self-consciousness encloses her even still faster.

This is one of the disasters of young life to-day. Personally, and among themselves, a great many, perhaps a majority of the young people of to-day have come out into the open with sex and laid salt on the tail of the dirty little secret. And this is a very good thing. But in public, in the social world, the young are still entirely under the shadow of the grey elderly ones. The grey elderly ones belong to the last century, the eunuch century, the century of the mealy-mouthed lie, the century that has tried to destroy humanity, the nineteenth century. All our grey ones are left over from this century. And they rule us. They rule us with the grey, mealy-mouthed, canting lie of that great century of lies which, thank God, we are drifting away from. But they rule us still with the lie, for the lie, in the name of the lie. And they are too heavy and too numerous, the grey ones. It doesn't matter what government it is. They are all grey ones, left over from the last century, the century of mealy-mouthed liars, the century of purity and the dirty little secret.

So there is one cause for the depression of the young: the public reign of the mealy-mouthed lie, purity and the dirty little secret, which they themselves have privately overthrown. Having killed a good deal of the lie in their own private lives, the young are still enclosed and imprisoned within the great public lie of the grey ones. Hence the excess, the extravagance, the hysteria, and then the weakness, the feebleness, the pathetic silliness of the modern youth. They are all in a sort of prison, the prison of a great lie and a society of elderly liars. And this is one of the reasons, perhaps the main reason, why the sex-flow is dying out of the young, the real energy is dying away. They are enclosed within a lie, and the sex won't flow. For the length of a complete lie is never more than three generations, and the young are the fourth generation of the nineteenth-century lie.

The second reason why the sex-flow is dying is, of course, that the young, in spite of their emancipation, are still enclosed within the vicious circle of self-conscious masturbation. They are thrown back into it, when they try to escape, by the enclosure of the vast public lie of purity and the dirty little secret. The most emancipated Bohemians, who swank most about sex, are still utterly self-conscious and enclosed within the narcissus-masturbation circle. They have perhaps less sex even than the grey ones. The whole thing has been driven up into their heads. There isn't even the lurking hole of a dirty little secret. Their sex is more mental than their arithmetic; and as vital physical creatures they are more non-existent than ghosts. The modern Bohemian is indeed a kind of ghost, not even narcissus, only the image of narcissus reflected on the face of the audience. The dirty little secret is most difficult to kill. You may put it to death publicly a thousand times, and still it reappears, like a crab, stealthily from under the submerged rocks of the personality. The French, who are supposed to be so open about sex, will perhaps be the last to kill the dirty little secret. Perhaps they don't want to. Anyhow, mere publicity won't do it.

You may parade sex abroad, but you will **not**

kill the dirty little secret. You may read all the novels of Marcel Proust, with everything there in all detail. Yet you will not kill the dirty little secret. You will perhaps only make it more cunning. You may even bring about a state of utter indifference and sex-inertia, still without killing the dirty little secret. Or you may be the most wispy and enamoured little Don Juan of modern days, and still the core of your spirit merely be the dirty little secret. That is to say, you will still be in the narcissus-masturbation circle, the vicious circle of self-enclosure. For whenever the dirty little secret exists, it exists as the centre of the vicious circle of masturbation self-enclosure. And whenever you have the vicious circle of masturbation self-enclosure, you have at the core the dirty little secret. And the most highflown sex-emancipated young people to-day are perhaps the most fatally and nervously enclosed within the masturbation self-enclosure. Nor do they want to get out of it, for there would be nothing left to come out.

But some people surely do want to come out of the awful self-enclosure. To-day, practically everybody is self-conscious and imprisoned in self-consciousness. It is the joyful result of the dirty little secret. Vast numbers of people don't want to come out of the prison of their self-consciousness: they have so little left to come out with. But some people, surely, want to escape this doom of self-enclosure which is the doom of our civilisation. There is surely a proud minority that wants once and for all to be free of the dirty little secret.

And the way to do it is, first, to fight the sentimental lie of purity and the dirty little secret wherever you meet it, inside yourself or in the world outside. Fight the great lie of the nineteenth century, which has soaked through our sex and our bones. It means fighting with almost every breath, for the lie is ubiquitous.

Then secondly, in his adventure of self-consciousness a man must come to the limits of himself and become aware of something beyond him. A man must be self-conscious enough to know his own limits, and to be aware of that which surpasses him. What surpasses me is the very urge of life that is within me, and this life urges me to forget myself and to yield to the stirring half-born impulse to smash up the vast lie of the world, and make a new world. If my life is merely to go on in a vicious circle of self-enclosure, masturbating self-consciousness, it is worth nothing to me. If my individual life is to be enclosed within the huge corrupt lie of society to-day, purity and the dirty little secret, then it is worth not much to me. Freedom is a very great reality. But it means, above all things, freedom from lies. It is first, freedom from myself, from the lie of myself, from the lie of my all-importance, even to myself; it is freedom from the self-conscious masturbating thing I am, self-enclosed. And second, freedom from the vast lie of the social world, the lie of purity and the dirty little secret. All the other monstrous lies lurk under the cloak of this one primary lie. The monstrous lie of money lurks under the cloak of purity. Kill the purity-lie, and the money-lie will be defenceless.

We have to be sufficiently conscious, and self-conscious, to know our own limits and to be aware of the greater urge within us and beyond us. Then we cease to be primarily interested in ourselves. Then we learn to leave ourselves alone, in all the affective centres: not to force our feelings in any way, and never to force our sex. Then we make the great onslaught on to the outside lie, the inside lie being settled. And that is freedom and the fight for freedom.

The greatest of all lies in the modern world is the lie of purity and the dirty little secret. The grey ones left over from the nineteenth century are the embodiment of this lie. They dominate in society, in the press, in literature, everywhere. And, naturally, they lead the vast mob of the general public along with them.

Which means, of course, perpetual censorship of anything that would militate against the lie of purity and the dirty little secret, and perpetual encouragement of what may be called permissible pornography, pure, but tickling the dirty little secret under the delicate underclothing. The grey ones will pass and will commend floods of evasive pornography, and will suppress every outspoken word.

The law is a mere figment. In his article on the "Censorship of Books," in the *Nineteenth Century,* Viscount Brentford, the late Home Secretary, says: "Let it be remembered that the publishing of an obscene book, the issue of an obscene postcard or pornographic photograph— are all offences against the law of the land, and the Secretary of State who is the general authority for the maintenance of law and order most clearly and definitely cannot discriminate between one offence and another in discharge of his duty."

So he winds up, *ex cathedra* and infallible. But only ten lines above he has written: "I agree, that if the law were pushed to its logical conclusion, the printing and publication of such books as *The Decameron,* Benvenuto Cellini's *Life,* and Burton's *Arabian Nights* might form the subject of proceedings. But the ultimate sanction of all law is public opinion, and I do not believe for one moment that prosecution in respect of books that have been in circulation for many centuries would command public support."

Ooray then for public opinion! It only needs that a few more years shall roll. But now we see that the Secretary of State most clearly and definitely *does* discriminate between one offence and another in discharge of his duty. Simple and admitted discrimination on his part! Yet what is this public opinion? Just more lies on the part of the grey ones. They would suppress Benvenuto to-morrow, if they dared. But they would make laughing-stocks of themselves, because *tradition* backs up Benvenuto. It isn't public opinion at all. It is the grey ones afraid of making still bigger fools of themselves. But the case is simple. If the grey ones are going to be backed by a general public, then every new book that would smash the mealy-mouthed lie of the nineteenth century will be suppressed as it appears. Yet let the grey ones beware. The general public is nowadays a very unstable affair, and no longer loves its grey ones so dearly, with their old lie. And there is another public, the small public of the minority, which hates the lie and the grey ones that perpetuate the lie, and which has its own dynamic ideas about pornography and obscenity. You can't fool all the people all the time, even with purity and a dirty little secret.

And this minority public knows well that the books of many contemporary writers, both big and lesser fry, are far more pornographical than the liveliest story in *The Decameron:* because they tickle the dirty little secret and excite to private masturbation, which the wholesome Boccaccio never does. And the minority public knows full well that the most obscene painting on a Greek vase—*Thou still unravished bride of quietness*—is not as pornographical as the close-up kisses on the film, which excite men and women to secret and separate masturbation.

And perhaps one day even the general public will desire to look the thing in the face, and see for itself the difference between the sneaking masturbation pornography of the press, the film, and present-day popular literature, and then the creative portrayals of the sexual impulse that we have in Boccaccio or the Greek vase-paintings or some Pompeian art, and which are necessary for the fulfilment of our consciousness.

As it is, the public mind is to-day bewildered on this point, bewildered almost to idiocy. When the police raided my picture show, they did not in the least know what to take. So they took every picture where the smallest bit of the sex organ of either man or woman showed. Quite regardless of subject or meaning or anything else: they would allow anything, these dainty policemen in a picture show, except the actual sight of a fragment of the human *pudenda*. This was the police test. The dabbing on of a postage stamp—especially a green one that could be called a leaf—would in most cases have been quite sufficient to satisfy this "public opinion."

It is, we can only repeat, a condition of idiocy. And if the purity-with-a-dirty-little-secret lie is kept up much longer, the mass of society will really be an idiot, and a dangerous idiot at that. For the public is made up of individuals. And each individual has sex, and is pivoted on sex. And if, with purity and dirty little secrets, you drive every individual into the masturbation self-enclosure, and keep him there, then you will produce a state of general idiocy. For the masturbation self-enclosure produces idiots. Perhaps if we are all idiots, we shan't know it. But God preserve us.

▣ Another controversial writer who has had occasional brushes with censorship is Paul Blanshard. His *American Freedom and Catholic Power,* followed by his *Communism, Democracy, and Catholic Power,* brought him into conflict with ecclesiastical authorities and with public officials in localities sensitive to criticism of organized religious bodies. The *Nation,* as a result of its serialization of Blanshard's *American Freedom and Catholic Power,* was banned from the New York City public schools. This widely publicized case is discussed in the chapter, "The Schools under Attack."

Blanshard's varied career has taken him into

many fields. In recent years, however, he has devoted his time largely to writing. His *The Right To Read*, from which "Sex and Obscenity" is drawn, is perhaps the most readable, comprehensive, and generally satisfactory survey available of its field.

Paul Blanshard
SEX AND OBSCENITY

In March 1953, in Cleveland, during a police campaign against obscenity the submissive local booksellers withdrew from sale in their stores Sigmund Freud's *General Introduction to Psychoanalysis* "because it had a chapter on sex." Then, to show their moral concern with the classics, they banned *The Golden Ass* by Lucius Apuleius because, they said, "the title might be offensive."

No one knows where our present inhibitions about obscenity came from. The study of primitive culture does not supply a definite answer. If we consider the three supposedly unmentionable areas of reticence and evasion in the sexual field—copulation, the genitals and human excrement—and try to discover the historical origins of the embarrassments and silences surrounding them, we cannot find any clear and complete explanation. Although the practice of privacy in sexual intercourse is general among primitive tribes, it is not universal. Some Fiji Islanders have been discovered in public sexual orgies, participated in by the married and the unmarried without regard to marital ties. Many tribes permit complete exposure of the genitals without any consciousness of obscene conduct. It cannot be said that man's sense of shame about exposure is either instinctive or universal, nor is it possible to demonstrate that feminine modesty is any more instinctive or deeply rooted than masculine. Several primitive tribes have been discovered in which both men and women go entirely naked, and some have been found in which the men wear a thread girdle and the women wear nothing at all. Havelock Ellis pointed out that many naked tribes have "a highly developed sense of modesty," and that modesty is not necessarily dependent upon clothing.

Perhaps the nearest thing to an instinctive survival which we still retain in our present-day attitudes toward obscene literature is our general taboo of scatology. But even this may be an acquired characteristic, a reticence which has developed in the age of silent plumbing. Some animals share our aversion to scatological things, but we seem to have nothing else in common with the animals in the whole field of sexual censorship and taboo. No animal or bird thinks it necessary to surround sex with secrecy for fear of shocking the animal community. No animal or bird is ashamed of its genitals, or seeks to cover them up. Nor does any animal or bird dash for the shadows to conceal either the preliminaries or the finals of courtship. "Man," said Montaigne, "is the sole animal whose nudities offend his companions, and the only one who in his natural actions withdraws and hides himself from his own kind." Perhaps, Montaigne suggests, this is because we are really not pleasing to look at:

> In earnest, when I consider man stark naked, even in that sex which seems to have the greatest share of beauty, his defects, natural subjection, and imperfections, I find that we have more reason than any other animal to cover ourselves; and we are to be excused from borrowing of those to whom nature has in this been kinder than to us, to trick ourselves out with their beauties, and hide ourselves under their spoils, their wool, feathers, hair and silk.

It is quite possible that our acquired notions about what is decent and indecent in sex came originally from primitive man's fight against incest, and developed later into a whole system-pattern of censorship and taboo, more or less by accident. Malinowski, in his investigations of the sex life of the Trobriand Islanders, has revealed how severe were the restrictions on speech because of the incest taboo. He found that these island people would not permit a brother or sister to talk lightly of love or sex in the other's presence, or to engage in play with each other, or to live in the same house when they were grown up. Perhaps our primitive parents, determined to preserve the family against the destructive tendencies of incest, inaugurated special restraints that burgeoned out into our present code of decency, long after the original occasion for the restraints had lost significance. Unfortunately we cannot tell whether there is truth in these surmises, since the origin of sexual taboos is shrouded in the mists of pre-literary history.

Paul Blanshard, *The Right To Read* (Boston: Beacon Press, 1955), pp. 138–67, copyright 1955 by Paul Blanshard. Reprinted by permission of the publisher.

Of one thing we can be certain. Our present obscenity laws have no necessary instinctive basis in human behavior. They cannot be traced back to innate desires. Man, left to himself without social discipline or formal law, has no apparent antipathy to describing or using any of the acts or words of sexual life. His reticence seems to be wholly acquired. In fact, it is quite likely that he has an instinctive desire to confront as completely as possible the very facts of sex experience which are now buried under layers of silence and compulsive taboo.

The anthropologist Fison tells how some Fiji Islanders, while engaging at festival time in orgies of sexual license, also seem to gain a special kind of psychological release by shouting obscene words and descriptions at each other at the top of their lungs. The women seemed to enjoy this release fully as much as the men. The words which they drag up from the forbidden speech areas on such occasions are, of course, the very words which they are not permitted to use on ordinary occasions, and this departure from custom is the thing that seems to give the experience a special cathartic value.

The most specific thing that anthropology can teach us about sex and obscenity is that almost all standards in this field are relative. There is not even much correspondence in sexual patterns between nations and tribes. In one a woman's face must be covered and never mentioned, while her body is exposed; in another her face is uncovered but her body is clothed. And there are ironic paradoxes in human moral standards. Mohammed did not hesitate to adorn his heaven with hosts of concubines; the Puritan heaven had none. Seventeenth-century London permitted language on the stage and on the printed page which no burlesque comedian would venture to use in twentieth-century New York. Our Jewish ancestors practiced polygamy but stoned people for adultery.

THE RISE AND FALL OF PRUDERY

The change in American standards of literary decency in three hundred years has been truly astonishing. We have moved so far away from Puritan restrictions that most of the inhibitions of our grandfathers about sex seem to us utterly grotesque. It is only a hundred years since Browning's *Men and Women* was widely denounced as immoral; it is only about ninety years since an official of the Interior Department, snooping in Walt Whitman's desk in Washington, found an annotated copy of *Leaves of Grass* and discharged the poet for writing obscene literature. It is only about seventy years since the library of Concord banned *Huckleberry Finn,* after Louisa May Alcott had said: "If Mr. Clemens cannot think of something better to tell our pure-minded lads and lassies, he had best stop writing for them." When the book of Chesterfield's *Letters to His Son* was first circulated in America, it was thought necessary to eliminate his too-frank advice about relations with women. When Hawthorne's *Scarlet Letter* was first published, a reverend bishop protested against "any toleration to a popular and gifted writer when he perpetrates bad morals. Let this brokerage of lust be put down at the very beginning."

The attitude of the early nineteenth century concerning frankness in matters of sex was well expressed by the Boston *Ladies Visitor* in its first issue in 1806, when the editor declared that the pages of the magazine would be "closed against politics and obscenity" and also against "everything which might cause the crimson fluid to stain the cheek of unaffected modesty." At about that same time, in 1803, Harvard's principal commencement address was concerned with the indecencies and moral dangers of novel-reading.

Nevertheless, more and more people began to read more and more novels. While there was very little deliberate exploitation of pornography or indecency, the dialogue became franker and franker. The hem line of ladies' skirts began to go up, and corset ads began to appear. Some novels admitted that children could be born out of wedlock, and one novel, published in 1828, ran through thirty-one editions with a plot in which an illegitimate girl nearly married her own brother.

For almost the whole first century of our life as a nation we accepted English standards of literary decency and obscenity as good enough for America. Naturally enough, they were predominantly Protestant standards. When bewhiskered Anthony Comstock with his militant Puritanism and his YMCA vigilante committee, later to be known as the New York Society for the Suppression of Vice, inveigled Congress into passing with virtually no debate the first general law on obscenity in 1872, there were few dissenters. This sweeping statute, with its companion law of 1874, made it illegal to ship obscene literature and birth-control information in interstate commerce.

In New York, Comstock's anti-vice society was given the power of search and seizure, and gradually it made itself into a kind of semi-public national censor of all literature suspected of obscenity. It was followed by a new society in Boston, the New England Watch and Ward Society, which ultimately came under the leadership of the Rev. J. Franklin Chase. During the Comstock period, which lasted until World War I, states and cities throughout the country rushed to make "little Comstock laws" and other parallel ordinances banning any printed matter which was obscene, lewd or lascivious. Today almost every large city has an ordinance on the subject, and there is an anti-obscenity law on the books of every state except New Mexico.

At first the new Puritans had very little opposition. Even when the opposition began, it was not so much an organized resistance to Comstockery as a general change in the nation's moral climate. Life in the United States was undergoing a profound revolution in manners and mechanisms. The railroad, the electric light, the bicycle, the telephone and eventually the automobile changed the outlook of both men and women. It was women primarily who changed the fashions on sex and decency in print. They left the kitchen to enter offices and factories; they stripped off some of their petticoats and bought bicycles; they even went to college with men, and occasionally entered the professions. Pictures of the lower portions of their bodies began to appear in magazines, showing that they were actually bifurcated. Some time later pictures of the upper parts of their bodies began to appear, adorned with lace-trimmed Munsing underwear.

After 1900, the hero of a novel, in proposing to the heroine, sometimes kissed her mouth instead of her hand, and even asked her to marry him before he had spoken to her father. In 1906, Carrie Nation published in her little magazine, the *Hatchet*, a few simple and plain instructions about sex, designed for her growing sons, written in "scientifically chaste English." It was a startling idea to permit males to read about sex from a book written by a female, and Carrie Nation was put in jail. But she was soon released, and her idea marched on.

The transition from reticence to realism in our literature came very slowly, and the full meaning of the change was not apparent until well after World War I. Perhaps the returning soldiers had something to do with it. They learned to speak very frankly during the war, and they carried the habits of candid speech back home with them afterward. The clash between their standards and those of the civilian population was dramatized in the case of the most famous novel of World War I, Erich Maria Remarque's *All Quiet on the Western Front*. That novel was accepted in principle by the Book-of-the-Month Club, but the club's officers were not quite certain about the American reaction to certain realistic words and scenes. They suggested the elimination of two passages included in the European version, which were promptly dropped. The Boston publisher feared that the printing of these two passages might cause the work to be banned in that city.

The first banned episode described men sitting on toilet boxes in the open air, "square, neat boxes with wooden sides all around them," and having "unimpeachably satisfactory seats." "The soldier," said the offending passage, "is on friendlier terms than other men with the stomach and intestines. Three-fourths of his vocabulary is derived from these regions, and they give an intimate pleasure to expression of his greatest joy." The other deleted passage from this novel was a three-page episode which concerned an old man who had been in a hospital ten months without seeing his wife. When she came to the hospital to visit him, the other patients in the ward gathered at one end, made terrific diversionary noises, looked the other way, and permitted the old couple to exercise certain basic marital rights. The story was told with infinite delicacy and pathos; it was, as Edward Weeks of the *Atlantic* said, "one of the most tender and appealing in the book."

Contrast the deletion of these two incidents from *All Quiet on the Western Front* with the treatment of the greatest novel of World War II, *From Here to Eternity*, also a selection of the Book-of-the-Month Club. The latter novel freely uses forbidden four-letter words, and describes in considerable detail the processes which are associated with those words. Many of its vivid scenes are laid in Hawaiian whore-houses, and its chief female character is a professional. What is much more significant, the author does not attempt any general condemnation either of the ladies of the evening who entertain the troops or of their soldier clients.

An even more significant contrast in attitudes toward sexual frankness becomes apparent if we take as a current example the May 1955 selection of the Book-of-the-Month Club, Robert Ruark's *Something of Value*. Specific descriptions of rape and sexual orgies which in 1930 would have disqualified a work as a Book-of-the Month Club selection occur so frequently that it would be a long and tedious task merely to list them. . . .

Some critics will say that this change in the standards of decency since World War I is a calamity, and that it denotes a decline in the national moral fiber. Perhaps there is some truth in that charge, but we are interested here primarily in the shifting standards of frankness as they affect literary controls. The change in these standards is quite startling. Today, with few exceptions, American adults have the legal right to read almost anything about sex which is written with any faint trace of dignity or moral seriousness. And this shift has taken place since the 1920's.

The old laws are still on the statute books, but the words of prohibition have been given a new significance. The same Tariff Act of 1842 which, with the McKinley tariff law of 1890, banned from our ports a whole series of literary classics in the nineties has now been interpreted by the courts to permit the entrance of those very same works. The great change in standards in our law enforcement machinery came in the thirties. The year 1931 was a significant turning point, for it was then that the customs ban was lifted on Rabelais, Boccaccio's *Decameron,* Casanova's *Memoirs* and *The Golden Ass* of Apuleius.

Both Anthony Comstock in New York and J. Franklin Chase in Boston discovered in their anti-vice crusades that it was cheaper and easier to suppress books by unofficial collaboration with the police than by court trials. In most cases these vigilantes of the past found that they did not need the support of the literary community. For a long time the New York Society for the Suppression of Vice and the New England Watch and Ward Society were so powerful that they virtually dictated the New York and Boston arrests and convictions. In its first seventy-three years of existence the New York Society confiscated 397,000 books and brought about the arrest of 5,567 defendants. Although most of these books and defendants were underworld products, the victims included some authors and works of fame and merit. Theodore Dreiser's *The Genius* was suppressed in New York in 1916; James Branch Cabell's *Jurgen* was declared indecent in 1920. Of course both of these books are freely circulated today.

Boston was for many years the greatest center of literary suppression in America. Beginning with the banning of Walt Whitman in 1882, the unofficial censors in cooperation with public officials sometimes forced the withdrawal of as many as sixty books in a single year. Their victims included Sinclair Lewis' *Elmer Gantry,* Aldous Huxley's *Antic Hay,* Upton Sinclair's *Oil!,* Theodore Dreiser's *An American Tragedy,* Ernest Hemingway's *The Sun Also Rises,* H. G. Wells' *The World of William Clissold,* Michael Arlen's *Young Men in Love,* Carl Van Vechten's *Nigger Heaven,* Lion Feuchtwanger's *Power,* John Dos Passos' *Manhattan Transfer,* Sherwood Anderson's *Dark Laughter* and John Erskine's *The Private Life of Helen of Troy.* Most of these books were banned for obscenity by a private deal between the Watch and Ward Society and New England booksellers under which a book was withdrawn from circulation without prosecution or penalty if condemned by the society. Ironically, since most of these titles were never forbidden by the Post Office Department, proper Bostonians could get their copies through the mail if they wished.

The thing which finally discredited this kind of censorship was ridicule. H. L. Mencken journeyed to Boston in 1926 and peddled copies of the *American Mercury* on the Boston Common after an issue of the magazine had been banned because it contained a frank story, "Hatrack," about a prostitute. The *Mercury* had maintained a steady stream of caustic comment aimed at the Watch and Ward Society and allied puritans. In the glare of national publicity a judge dismissed the charge against Mencken and his magazine, and later a similar charge was dismissed in a federal court. From that moment Boston's puritans were on the defensive. Today, as we shall see below, Massachusetts has one of the more moderate and intelligent systems of literary censorship. In many ways its statutory handling of the problem is praiseworthy.

WHAT IS OBSCENITY?

The law in its lumbering majesty usually brings up the rear of any social-reform procession, and the legal story of obscenity is no exception to the rule. Defining the word "obscenity" in legal terms is something like estimating the number of angels that can dance on the point of a pin. It is a matter of imagination and surmise. Perhaps the best definition ever recorded in print is the one expressed by Judge Learned Hand in a 1913 case, *United States v. Kennerley,* in the form of a question: ". . . should not the word 'obscene' be allowed to indicate the present critical point in the compromise between candor and shame at which the community may have arrived here and now?"

When Judge Hand first expressed this thought, it was too far in advance of the moral thinking of most judges to win general acceptance. It smacked of Einstein's relativity in the world of morals, and all the preachers and priests had been assuring men for a long time that moral laws were built on less transient foundations. But in actual practice the courts have been compelled to use relative standards in appraising obscenity from the very beginning. They have defined obscenity in terms of other words equally vague in significance, and they have never been able to produce any more exact definition than Judge Hand's "critical point in the compromise between candor and shame."

The bewildered groping of policemen and judges for firm verbal footing in this field was demonstrated in the 1952 hearings of a House of Representatives committee, the Select Committee on Current Pornographic Materials, also known as the Gathings committee after its chairman, E. C. Gathings of Arkansas. A New York police captain testified before this committee about his bewilderment as follows:

> I took the trouble before coming down here of looking up the definitions of "obscene," and it says "lurid, lascivious, indecent."
>
> I looked up the word "indecent," and they referred back to "obscene," and so on. They could have simply just used the word "obscene," and left the other out.
>
> The thing is so nebulous that we, as law-enforcement officers, don't know whether we are coming or going.

The ablest lawyers also do not know whether they are coming or going in matters of obscene literature. As Judge Curtis Bok has put it, "to come to grips with the question of obscenity is like coming to grips with a greased pig." Blackstone's *Law Dictionary* has a 156-word definition of "obscene" which begins: "Offensive to chastity of mind or to modesty, expressing or presenting to the mind or view something that delicacy, purity, and decency forbids to be exposed . . ."

Unfortunately, the nineteenth century's leading opinion concerning the legal interpretation of the word "obscenity" was made by the wrong judge. His name was Cockburn (pronounced "Coburn") and he sat in England in the 1868 case of *Regina v. Hicklin*. It was a case in which he was asked to say whether a quarrelsome little tract reflecting upon the morals of Catholic priests in the confessional should be penalized as obscene libel. He voted against the tract, and said: "I think the test of obscenity is this, whether the tendency of the matter charged as obscenity is to deprave and corrupt those whose minds are open to such immoral influences, and into whose hands a publication of this sort may fall."

This innocent-sounding sentence plagued the literary world on both sides of the Atlantic for 165 years, and it still has a baleful effect on literary freedom in some localities. If "matter charged with obscenity" is interpreted in a narrow way, then individual words and descriptions can be taken out of the whole text and prosecuted for obscenity in isolation. The general tone of a whole book may be outbalanced by the tone of the condemned passages. Far worse, the Cockburn decision makes it possible to judge the effect of a book or passage by its effect on the mind of the immature, the neurotic and the unstable, since "those whose minds are open to such immoral influences" certainly include the immature, the neurotic and the unstable.

Victorian jurists on both sides of the ocean seized upon Justice Cockburn's ambiguous dictum to justify the punishment of books and authors for objectionable passages in otherwise unobjectionable books. They found in the decision an excuse for tempering literature to the most susceptible mind. Although the English suppressions did not parallel the Boston suppressions, they did include, temporarily at least, a great many famous works of fiction and non-fiction. Among them were Havelock Ellis' *Studies in the Psychology of Sex,* Radclyffe Hall's *The Well of Loneliness* and D. H. Lawrence's *Lady Chatterley's Lover.*

After more than sixty years of uncertain legal censorship under the rule in *Regina v. Hicklin,* American courts finally began to question its principles. The final break-through to a more tolerant and a more fair test of obscenity came in the famous 1933 case of James Joyce's *Ulysses.* Morris Ernst and Alexander Lindey served as defense counsel in this case, with Bennett Cerf and Random House as the defendants who had tried to import the book. Judge John M. Woolsey delivered the opinion of the federal court.

Ulysses had been a storm center on both sides of the ocean for a number of years. Some five hundred copies of a Paris edition in English had been burned by the authorities at Folkstone pier when a dealer tried to import them into England. In the United States in 1918 Margaret Anderson in her *Little Review* had started to publish the work in installments. When the chapter appeared in which Gertie raises her skirt a little and produces erotic fantasies in the mind of Leopold Bloom, Miss Anderson was arrested, tried and convicted in a New York court, and five issues of her magazine were banned by the Post Office Department as obscene.

Miss Anderson's experience during that trial reflected the mood of the public at that time. Writing later, she said:

> During the trial and afterwards, not a single New York newspaper came to our rescue; not a word was printed in defense of Joyce and his art; not a word about our courage in publishing what we considered the literary masterpiece of our generation.... We didn't have any proper publicity out of the trial, as every editor in the country was afraid to be identified with the "*Ulysses* scandal."

During the trial, says Miss Anderson, of the three presiding judges, "two were white-haired and went to sleep during most of the proceeding." But when the prosecuting attorney announced his intention of reading aloud the alleged obscene passages,

> ... the oldest of the two white-haired sleepers suddenly woke up and, regarding me with that protective paternity which is the outstanding characteristic of all American males, refused that such obscenity should be read in my hearing.
> "But she is the publisher," said Mr. Quinn [Miss Anderson's attorney].
> "Yes, but undoubtedly she didn't know the horrible significance of what she was publishing," responded the Judge, regarding me with tenderness and suffering.

Judge Woolsey was a judge of a different stripe, capable of believing that a woman could have a mature mind. He discarded the old English rule of "isolated-passage" obscenity, and declared that a book should be tested by its effect as a whole "on a person with average sex instincts." In spite of his personal conviction that many isolated passages in *Ulysses* might be considered obscene, he held that the book's purpose was not "to promote lust or portray filth for its own sake." He noted that Joyce did not have the "leer of the sensualist." *Ulysses* was admitted to America, and today it is a familiar landmark in college fiction courses.

Perhaps one factor in the defeat of the old isolated-passage rule was the knowledge that a strict application of that rule would result in the suppression of the Bible and much of Shakespeare. Many years before, in an English obscenity case, the famous theosophist Annie Besant, when charged with producing obscene literature, had compiled 150 allegedly indecent passages from the Bible to show that the isolated-passage principle could be used to condemn a good book as easily as a bad book. The 150 citations for these passages were reproduced in America in 1928 in a book by Morris Ernst and William Seagle, *To the Pure.* Many of the passages are both lurid and lascivious, and there is no doubt that if they were incorporated in modern English in a racy work of fiction with twentieth-century characters and a seductive cover, they would be immediately pounced upon by the vigilante committees.

The *Ulysses* victory gave new courage to writers and a new insight to judges. Even Boston began to be ashamed of its record, and a revision of the Massachusetts obscenity statute permitted a book to be judged as a whole even when it had obscene fragments. Aldous Huxley, writing in 1930, had expressed the new philosophy of frankness for authors when he said: "I cannot accept the Classicists' excommunication of the body. I think it is not only permissible, but necessary, that literature should take cognizance of physiology and should investigate the still obscure relations between the mind and the body."

Some judges began to show a sense of humor in dealing with decency and indecency. When James T. Farrell's *A World I Never Made* was brought before Magistrate Henry Curran in New York by the anti-vice raiders of 1937, the judge said:

> I don't think this book is pornographic. I think it is photographic . . . consider the young ladies in their bathing suits nowadays, how they toil not neither do they spin, but the Gibson girl in all her glory was not arrayed like one of these. If one of those lovely creatures of the far away nineties had really appeared in one of the little forget-me-not suits of today, I fancy there would have been a commotion on the beach—and the rockers on the summer hotel piazzas would have rocked hard and long.

Judge Curran was quite sound in his use of the bathing suit as a kind of decency yardstick for the judgment of current moral standards. One local legislator has actually tried to put that notion into law. As a member of the Nashville city council, he proposed a local ordinance which included the provision "That the word indecent used above shall include but not be limited to drawings or pictures of the female which show more of the nude body than bathing suits worn in the United States of America." Einstein himself could not have done better in defining a satisfactory standard for pellicular exposure.

The new contributions of psychology and anthropology to an understanding of sex finally bore fruit in 1948 in a mature and sophisticated court decision on obscenity. It was only a lower-court decision, but it was so wise and meaningful that it was approved unanimously by the appropriate upper courts, and it has set a new trend in American law. I refer to the decision of Judge Curtis Bok of Philadelphia in the case of *Commonwealth v. Gordon*.

The Philadelphia police had raided fifty-four bookstores and seized without warrants some two thousand allegedly obscene books. Undoubtedly some of them were deliberately and provocatively obscene, but others were first-rate examples of realistic literary art, produced by some of our best modern writers. The publishers wisely withdrew the less defensible books, and challenged the police in court with seven titles, including William Faulkner's *Sanctuary,* Erskine Caldwell's *God's Little Acre* and James T. Farrell's *A World I Never Made*. Judge Bok in dismissing the charge of obscenity against these books adopted the rule that they must be considered as a whole, and said:

> It is impossible to say just what his [the average modern reader's] reactions to a book actually are. . . . If he reads an obscene book when his sensuality is low, he will yawn over it. . . . If he reads the Mechanic's Lien Act while his sensuality is high, things will stand between him and the page that have no business there. How can anyone say that he will infallibly be affected one way or another? . . . The professional answer that is suggested is the one general compromise—that the appetite of sex is old, universal and unpredictable, and that the best we can do to keep it within reasonable bounds is to be our brother's keeper and censor, because we never know when his sensuality may be high. This does not satisfy me, for in a field where even reasonable precision is utterly impossible, I trust people more than I do the law.

Judge Bok's reasoning was supported by the superior courts in all except one particular. He attempted to establish the principle that no book should be suppressed unless it could be demonstrated that there was a clear and present danger of the commission of a crime as a result of its publication. On that point the state Supreme Court did not support him.

In spite of the fact that there is a new breadth of vision in some courts in interpreting our obscenity laws, the total legal picture is still very muddled. Because of our multiple jurisdictions, books legal in one state or city are illegal in others. The United States Supreme Court has not yet brought literary freedom in the field of sexual discussion squarely within the protection of the free-speech clauses of the First and Fourteenth Amendments. A Negro child, for example, is protected as an American against certain legal discriminations whether he lives in Alabama or Vermont, but a book is not so protected in all jurisdictions by one generally accepted obscenity test.

The Supreme Court has been asked to clear up this unequal protection under the law but, thus far, the only case to present this challenge squarely ended in a 4-to-4 draw—the case of Edmund Wilson's *Memoirs of Hecate County*. In that case the lower courts condemned the book as obscene, and when the Supreme Court split evenly on the question of obscenity, the adverse decision of the lower courts was automatically sustained. The long court battle redounded to the benefit of the author and publisher—the sales boomed from 5,000 to 70,000 during the controversy—but the central constitutional riddle remained unanswered.

Under our varying legal practices and statutes a less offensive book may earn a severe penalty while the more offensive work goes scot-free. Kathleen Winsor's *Forever Amber* was acquitted by the highest court of Massachusetts under a revised statute two years after Lillian Smith's *Strange Fruit* had been convicted under an antiquated statute. Although the decision of the Massachusetts court against *Strange Fruit* was a competent analysis of the issues, 99 per cent of today's literary critics would not agree with it. And, of these two works, the acquitted *Forever Amber* is cheap, provocative and vulgar; the convicted *Strange Fruit* is a searching and sensitive analysis of life. The acquitted book, according to the prosecutor, included 70 references to sexual intercourse, 7 to abortions, 33 to bedroom scenes which were more or less sexual, 39 to illegal pregnancies and 11 to venereal disease. But *Forever Amber* avoided the four-letter words, and it carried no message of social protest.

The Massachusetts Supreme Judicial Court, pointing out that *Strange Fruit* used something questionably erotic on the average of every fifth page, mentioned such phenomena as loosened blouses, bobbing breasts, masturbation by boys, bared male genitals, and assaults on little girls. But this was life in the raw as one perceptive writer saw it in a small town in Georgia, and the tragedy of Tracy Dean and Nonnie Anderson was as real and true as literary art could make it. Without these revealing details of sexual practice, normal and abnormal, the picture of Negro-white love in a Georgia town would have been less than the truth. And, as a dissenting judge declared in voting for acquittal, the evidence did not convince *him* that a finding of guilty was warranted. The same scenes which appealed to his confreres as indisputably obscene caused him to comment: "I can discover no erotic allurement such as the opinion makes necessary for conviction."

Twenty-six of America's leading publishers and many of its most noted critics joined him in protesting against the *Strange Fruit* conviction. Bernard De Voto, as a leading opponent of censorship, had been selected to get arrested for purchasing the book. The *Boston Herald* said that the decision put Massachusetts in the position of being "one forty-eighth of sane." The other states and even the post Office Department maintained their sanity and continued to regard *Strange Fruit* as permissible realism in matters of sex.

SYLVANUS STALL TO DR. KINSEY

The greatest gains in literary-sexual frankness in our time have been scored in the fields of sex education, birth control and venereal disease. Most of our grandfathers were denied the right to read about these vital aspects of personal life either by legal censorship or by religious taboo.

Theodore Schroeder tells how in 1892 Dodd, Mead and Company published a modest and reasonable little book of sex instruction, *Almost Fourteen,* written by a public-school teacher named Mortimer A. Warren. Mr. Mead, in order to be sure about the book's propriety, submitted it in advance of publication to his wife, to the pastors of the Broadway Tabernacle and the Church of Heavenly Rest, and to Dr. Lyman Abbott. They all endorsed its aim and tone. For five years after publication, no serious question was raised about the book. It was put in several Sunday-school libraries, and seemed to be well on the road to becoming a minor classic. Then in 1897, after an unpopular and aggressive reformer had started to give the work general circulation, the Watch and Ward Society of New England filed a complaint against it. The seller was arrested and convicted, and the author was driven from his position as principal of a public school.

Remember that this was only fifty years before Kinsey. Lest we feel too jubilant about the speed of the transition from Mortimer Warren to Alfred Kinsey we should remember that almost every step in that transition has involved a battle against suppression. Freud's realism was long considered too shocking for tender minds. The important pioneers in the fight for candid discussion of the "facts of life" have risked prison or ostracism, and some have been awarded both. In the beginning the great anti-vice societies were almost as hostile to serious descriptions of sexual processes as they were to deliberate pornography. Even in 1938 the publisher of *Life* had to fight for his liberty in a New York court for picturing some intimate aspects of the birth of a baby, although the treatment was dignified and the taboo against nudity carefully observed. A New Haven distributor was compelled to secure a court order against the local police before he could sell the magazine, and a Boston distributor was actually convicted and fined $500 for selling it.

Before World War I, American parents who wanted to tell their children about sex were allowed to read the "Self and Sex" series produced by a Baptist clergyman named Sylvanus Stall. The series began with *What a Young Girl Ought to Know* and ran clear through the life span of both sexes to *What a Man of 45 Ought to Know*. Although the sales of the books were prodigious, most readers felt defrauded. (I know, because I worked my way through college selling these books.) Dr. Stall omitted nearly all the facts about sexual techniques as too shocking for Christian eyes, and he recommended that husbands and wives should abstain from sex relations altogether throughout pregnancy.

Somehow America outgrew the "Self and Sex" books. Mary Ware Dennett was an important factor in the emancipation. About 1923 she had written a skillful and wholesome little pamphlet for her two growing sons, *The Sex Side of Life: An Explanation for Young People*. In 1929, after it had circulated quietly among informed parents for six years, she was arrested, charged with sending obscene literature through the mails, and convicted in a New York federal court. But the temper of the times would not permit punishment in such a case. The national uproar which greeted her conviction astonished even the vice crusaders, and a year later the circuit court of appeals reversed her conviction and held that "an accurate exposition of the relevant facts of the sex side of life in decent language and in manifestly serious and disinterested spirit cannot ordinarily be regarded as obscene."

This decision, written by Judge Augustus N. Hand, broke the log-jam of reticence and evasion surrounding the subject of sex education for young people. Next came adults. Books of sex instruction for them, as well as for children, soon began to appear in respectable shops. The language became more and more candid in describing sexual techniques. Religious and welfare leaders began to concede that engaged couples, in order to be happy in marriage, needed to know not only medical facts and physiological details but also details about positions, responses and adjustments.

There was a brief legal flurry in 1943 when a pamphlet, *Preparing for Marriage,* by Dr. Paul Popenoe of the American Institute of Family Relations, one of America's most respected specialists in this field, was banned from the mails by the Post Office Department. Dr. Popenoe took his case against Postmaster General Frank C. Walker to court and scored a complete victory. The obscenity law, said the court, does not intend that "we should reduce our treatment of sex to the standards of a child's library in the supposed interests of the salacious few." More recently, Edward Midgard's pamphlet of marriage instruction, *The Perfect Embrace*, ran afoul of a grand jury in Seattle, and the author was indicted for producing an obscene document; but with the help of the American Civil Liberties Union the indictment was dismissed.

Today we have almost complete freedom to buy and read books of sex instruction for both adults and children. Occasionally a book on sexual techniques, or a book on birth control addressed to a layman, may be declared unmailable; but this is rare. A work like Van de Velde's *Ideal Marriage* gives virtually all the facts which married people need to know about sexual adjustment. Some newspapers—the *New York Times* is one of them—still refuse to advertise sex books which feature the techniques of intercourse, but this refusal is due partly to the fact that the "sexology" field has been invaded by many publishers of doubtful standing whose publicity methods are not above reproach.

Today there is only one severely restricted area of importance in the whole field of sex education—the schools. Although progressive parent-teacher groups are attempting with some success to bring scientific sex instruction into the schools, they are meeting with determined resistance from conservative religious and political leaders.

Sometimes the opposition to sex education in the schools uses anti-Communism as an auxiliary weapon to stir up hysteria, implying that citizens who want scientific school instruction on sex matters are somehow associated with the Communist line. Such was the conclusion of the notorious Tenney legislative committee on un-American activities in California in 1946, when it was discovered that a high school in the town of Chico was using the progressive and intelligent book *Your Marriage* by Professor Norman E. Himes of Colgate not as a classroom text for children but as a reference book for teachers in sex education. Tenney issued garbled and twisted versions of the Himes text to the public, and then solemnly concluded that such things indicated "a carefully laid Communist plan for the corruption of America's coming generation."

The California press had enough sense of humor to laugh off the charge with headlines: "Tenney Fears Sex May Be Un-American." But the reactionary hysteria stirred up by Tenney's innuendoes later helped to defeat a legislative program for family-relations courses in California colleges and high schools. Because of such misrepresentation and pressure, progressive school principals and school-board members who dare to stand up for sex education in the schools against clerical and reactionary clamor are on the defensive today in many American localities.

Meanwhile, the final triumph of printed candor in the treatment of sex for adults came in 1948 and 1953 when Dr. Alfred C. Kinsey and his associates issued their famous studies, *Sexual Behavior in the Human Male* and *Sexual Behavior in the Human Female*. Whatever one may think about the meaning of these reports, it is clear that their circulation marked an enormous forward step in the development of candor. The publication of such material would have been unthinkable in the Victorian era. In fact, the report of the Chicago Vice Commission, a sober document revealing the evils of prostitution, was excluded from the mails as late as 1911. It was quite reticent compared with the Kinsey reports.

Of course the Kinsey reports did not receive unanimous and hearty welcome, or a uniform allotment of space, in the American newspapers. There were many critics who thought that the common people should not have the right to read such "scandalous rumor." The *New York Times* gave the first report a generous review but refused to advertise it. By the time the second report arrived five years later, the climate of American opinion had changed so much that the *Times* accepted advertising—this in spite of the fact that the conclusions of the second report were much more shocking to most Americans than those of the first. Both reports were circulated in the mails without hindrance, and offered for sale in most bookstores. Their sale was prodigious—the two together have sold more than half a million copies at $8 a copy—and there was a great supplementary sale of summaries and critical reviews of the Kinsey findings.

A few determined efforts were made to suppress the second report, with its revelations about sexual deviations from conformity among women. The United States Army banned it from army stands and post exchanges. New York Congressman Louis B. Heller, without reading it through, demanded that it be excluded from the mails, and denounced Kinsey for "hurling the insult of the century against our mothers, wives, daughters and sisters." The Indiana branch of a national Catholic women's organization demanded of the president of the University of Indiana that Dr. Kinsey be discharged. The resolution implied that if the demand was not heeded, the daughters of the members would be forbidden to attend the state university. On the day before the book's release, the Roman Catholic bishop of Western Kentucky caused a letter to be read at all masses in his diocese forbidding parishioners to read it. Since the book was so expensive, it was not difficult to persuade ordinary readers to refrain from buying it. The Post Office Department, remembering past defeats in free-speech cases, announced that its officials did not even have any plans for reading the Kinsey report.

In reply to the Catholic attack on Dr. Kinsey, President Herman B. Wells of Indiana University issued a public statement which said in part:

> The editor of the *Indiana Catholic* and Dr. Milner alike have failed to recognize that one of the differences between America and Communist Russia is that here a scientist is free to investigate in any field. They have further failed to recognize the responsibility of a scientist to investigate every phase of human activity. This freedom of human investigation is the democratic way as opposed to the way of Communism, which denies the right of individuals to follow the truth wherever it leads. The Communists not only prohibit such investigation but even eliminate people who do not follow the Party Line and they think that by destroying opposition they win.
>
> The University believes that the human race has been able to make some slow progress because individuals have been free to investigate all aspects of life. Knowledge so gained has contributed substantially in finding cures for social and emotional maladies of our society.

The two Kinsey reports raised in an acute form the question whether there should be any limitation upon the right of American newspaper readers to read about sex. About 75 per cent of

America's editors decided that their readers should have the right to read the second report in a rough summary, but there was strong opposition to this policy in some newspaper offices. *Editor and Publisher* said: "Our hearty congratulations to the twenty-five per cent of the nation's press which ignored the report and refused to publish its lurid details." This journal of the newspaper industry believed that "too much of the material was offensive to womanhood and harmful to the morals of youth."

In Philadelphia the only paper to publish a detailed newspaper account about "Kinsey on Women," as the second report came to be known, was the tabloid *Daily News*. The Philadelphia *Bulletin* explained that "an adequate summary would give unnecessary offense, and a censored account would be dishonest reporting." Some newspapers deleted particular words like "orgasm" and "prostitute" and ran short, doctored summaries. The *Raleigh Times* set up the story in type, then changed its mind about general circulation of such a story, and finally gave galley proofs free of charge to readers who sent in a stamped and addressed envelope. Most publishers rejected these compromises and printed a straightforward summary of the basic facts regardless of "offense." Most leading editors probably agreed with Gideon Seymour of the *Minneapolis Star-Tribune* that the report was the most important science story of 1953, with "deep meaning for millions."

The Kinsey story on women succeeded as a science story because it was written in the scientific spirit, without a word or an implication that could be branded as deliberately salacious. "Mr. Kinsey," said Bertrand Russell, "with consummate art, has succeeded in making his subject seem dull." "No book that we ever heard of," said the *New York News* in ridiculing the army's ban on Kinsey, "was better designed to take all the glamor out of sex."

PERVERSION, BIRTH CONTROL
AND NAKEDNESS

Dr. Kinsey's greatest contribution to literary freedom was in the field of the so-called abnormal sexual traits. These traits have been surrounded by silence and misunderstanding for centuries, and generally the law has treated them as obscene in themselves. Until the Kinsey reports were published, the words "masturbation" and "homosexuality" were not even allowed in book reviews. Kinsey talked so calmly about both of these subjects that he dispelled some of the hysteria surrounding them. He showed that "sex perversion" is much more "normal" than most people had supposed and that it is too widespread to be ignored as unimportant. In this report he carried forward the struggle for the right to read about homosexuality which had been going on since 1928, when Radclyffe Hall's famous novel on the subject, *The Well of Loneliness,* was cleared by the New York Court of Special Sessions.

In spite of Dr. Kinsey, the right to treat of homosexuality in print is still a very uncertain right in the United States. It is even uncertain in England, which has frequently been a trifle more liberal in such matters than the United States. The law permits sensitive and indirect treatments of the subject, such as Charles Jackson's *Fall of Valor,* but a more complete or direct analysis runs the risk of suppression. The general attitude toward all homosexuals is one of considerable horror and distaste, and discussion of the subject is tabooed in any organ of mass circulation. The English historian Geoffrey Gorer has pointed out that, in World War II, "Alone among the warring nations, America automatically rejected from the armed services all recognizable homosexuals; indeed almost the chief object of the psychiatric interview at induction was an attempt to segregate these. . . . Even when there was a real shortage of manpower there was no suggestion that these rejects should be reclassified."

The difficulties of a book dealing frankly with homosexuality in fiction may be illustrated by the case of Tereska Torres' *Women's Barracks,* a paperback novel about the French women's army corps stationed in London during World War II. It contains two incidents of unnatural relationships between women. After being banned in Canada, it met with both legal and extra-legal resistance in the United States. When it reached St. Paul, an aged anti-vice crusader who held the title of President of the National Council for Youth brought the book into court on a charge of obscenity. An English professor from the University of Minnesota and the book-review editor of the *Minneapolis Star-Tribune,* serving as witnesses for the defense, saved it from conviction. "It may not be a masterpiece," said Municipal Judge James C. Otis in dismissing the complaint, "but it gives us a glimpse of history not extensively dealt with by other authors, apparently, and as such may contribute to our general knowledge." But this legal clearance has not protected the book from renewed attacks by the National Organization of Decent Literature, the Gathings committee on pornography of the House of Representatives, and other agencies.

The right to read about birth control in the United States is more clearly established than the right to read about homosexuality. Originally the American ban on birth-control literature was a Protestant invention; today the remnants of the ban which still exist in the United States are sustained by Catholic power. The situation is anomalous because such an overwhelming majority of the American people believe in the right to read about birth control that, law or no law, literature on the subject is bound to be circulated. Even in the two states which still have anti–birth-control laws, Massachusetts and Connecticut, any public prosecutor who dared to enforce the statutes strictly against birth-control literature would have no political future.

When Anthony Comstock, in 1873, caused the ban on birth-control literature to be written into federal law, along with the general prohibition against obscenity, the law was passed with very little consideration by Congress. There was so little public discussion of or knowledge about birth control in those days that it is not certain that the Congressmen who voted for the bill knew exactly what they were voting for. Several states followed the national pattern quite blindly, and wrote similar statutes of their own without making clear in all cases where birth control stood in the general scheme of "obscene literature." It was simply assumed without discussion that birth control was an obscene subject. The McKinley tariff act of 1890 forbade the importation of birth-control literature, and both federal and state laws forbade its local distribution. When Margaret Sanger tried to distribute her pamphlet *Family Limitation* in New York in 1915, she was sent to jail.

Since then, surprisingly enough, the laws on birth control have changed very little. It is the judicial interpretations of those laws that have changed. Judges educated in the modern atmosphere of sexual realism will no longer treat contraceptive literature as per se obscene, and the specific prohibitions against it in some statutes have been watered down to nothingness by injections of judicial common sense. In 1930 Judge Woolsey admitted two books from England by the British birth-control leader, Marie Stopes. In 1937 the Consumers Union was permitted to distribute to qualified members through the mails its *Report on Contraceptive Materials*. In 1938, in the United States Court of Appeals, Norman Himes won the right to receive from abroad a copy of a magazine called *Marriage Hygiene,* containing material about contraception. That right now belongs to all "qualified" persons, and the courts have ruled that a qualified person may be a layman. In 1938 *Fortune* magazine published a detailed description of the contraceptive industry, with no attempt to omit specific facts about contraceptive techniques, and the Post Office Department did not venture to challenge it.

Today birth-control literature is usually carried through the mails, and it can be distributed directly to adults in every state of the Union except Massachusetts and Connecticut. Even in these states the literary features of the law are a dead letter. Magazines of general national circulation are unmolested when they discuss birth control. The final proof of the substantial victory for free speech in this area came when paperback books began to carry sound information about contraceptive techniques. Today, for example, city residents can buy at almost any newsstand or drugstore such a book as Maxine Davis' *Woman's Medical Problems,* published by Pocket Books and sold in huge quantities. Miss Davis speaks quite respectfully of the Roman Catholic opposition to contraception and notes that the "safe period" is alone permissible for good Catholics, but then goes on blandly to describe superior methods, and concludes: "All this means the dawn of a new day to mothers. Tried methods of contraception are available."

Two things about the birth-control victory should not be forgotten. It has been won only after forty years of ceaseless struggle by liberals like Margaret Sanger and her associates of the Planned Parenthood Federation of America; and the struggle for and against freedom in this area is still continuing. The statutes in several of our states are so vague and ambiguous that judges could conceivably reinterpret them to prevent the free circulation of birth-control literature if the courts fell into reactionary hands. Although Protestant and Jewish religious leaders now endorse birth control, America's largest and most powerful church, the Roman Catholic Church, still preaches that, as a matter of "faith and morals," literary freedom should not extend to birth-control literature. Scholarly journals and books now discuss contraception and overpopulation quite frankly, but religious pressure often prevents such discussion in newspapers and magazines of general circulation.

As far as legal birth-control rights are concerned, only one final technical battle remains to be fought. That is the battle to bring birth control within the protection of the First and Fourteenth Amendments. Oddly enough, in spite of many legal cases in this field, no one has ever clearly established the claim that the right to read about birth control in print is included in the free-speech guarantees of the Constitution. Until such a claim has been sanctioned by the United States Supreme Court, birth-control literature, particularly in such states as Massachusetts and Connecticut, will not be guaranteed free circulation.

Fortunately no such technicality obscures the people's right to read about the venereal diseases. These diseases, which were known as the "secret" diseases only a generation ago, have at last been dragged out into the open and plainly labeled. Although there is distressing undereducation on this subject in the schools, the barriers to candor in print are rapidly breaking down. "Is VD Coming Back?" is the title of an article in the September 1954 issue of *Reader's Digest*. Beneath the title runs a subhead: "Condensed from *Ladies Home Journal*." Those two lines epitomize the victory for free speech in the field of the "secret" diseases. The subject of syphilis and gonorrhea, whose mention once "caused the crimson fluid to stain the cheek of unaffected modesty," is now an entirely acceptable standard topic for America's leading family magazines.

Part of this new tolerance for frank discussion of venereal disease stems from a new attitude toward nakedness. Man is at last approaching the candor of the animal in regard to his own body. There are only a few square inches of his body still eligible to censorship, and even those may be exposed if a correct mood is maintained during the exposure. In May 1955, Postmaster General Summerfield lost his fight in the Supreme Court to ban from the mails future issues of a group of nudist magazines "which advocate and explain nudism and the nudist mode of living," and which print photographs of nude men and women. The lower courts had found that the magazines were not, by virtue of mere pictorial nakedness, obscene as a whole. The Supreme Court refused to disturb the interpretation. The *Washington Post,* commenting on the case, suggested that in view of current trends "especially in this warm weather" nudists scarcely needed to go to court to advance their cause. They could "just sit quietly back and await their seemingly inevitable triumph."

Eric Larrabee, one of the most brilliant young editors and writers in the United States today, presented his article, "The Cultural Context of Sex Censorship," at a symposium on "Obscenity and the Arts," sponsored by the Duke University School of Law.

Larrabee has served as associate editor of *Harper's Magazine* and has been a frequent contributor to this and other leading periodicals. In 1952 he was a member of the Carnegie Corporation's reconnaissance team to Africa. He is now executive editor of *American Heritage* and is also an associate in the Columbia University Seminar on American Civilization and secretary of the American Civilization Committee of the American Council of Learned Societies.

Eric Larrabee
THE CULTURAL CONTEXT OF SEX CENSORSHIP

I

In the United States today, no less than in other times and places, the subject of sex is charged with anxiety. In merely raising it, the writer must court suspicion—and consciously, for taboos surround him; immoderate interest would alert, though for different reasons, both the popular and professional mind. Sexual restrictions,

---

Eric Larrabee, "The Cultural Context of Sex Censorship," *Law and Contemporary Problems* (Durham, N. C.: Duke University School of Law, 1955), 20:672–88, copyright 1955 by Duke University. Reprinted (without amplifying footnotes) by permission of the author and of the publisher.

moreover, have this logic on their side: while customs vary, the maintenance of emotional tension between male and female—hence, of society's biological vigor—is characteristically associated with some form of social "censorship." The "natural" state of freedom from sexual inhibition is far more likely to be a fantasy of the sophisticated. Indeed, the rational background of restraint may be better understood by the primitive than by the modern mind. A young West African writer, for example, has explained with awareness and regret why his tribesmen surround with mystery the initiation ceremony of pre-adolescent males:

> Not only do they keep women and children in a state of uncertainty and terror, they also warn them to keep the doors of the huts firmly barred. . . . It is obvious that if the secret were to be given away, the ceremony would lose much of its power . . . [N]othing would remain of the trial by fear, that occasion when every boy has the opportunity to overcome his . . . own baser nature. . . . But, at the moment of writing this, does any part of the rite still survive? The secret. . . . Do we still have secrets?

Where sex is concerned, the imposition of partial curbs serves a double purpose: to stimulate and to hold back—never too much of either. A counterpoise to individual desires may also measure their intensity, in such an interlocked fashion as to become virtually a condition of their being. This is partly what the would-be censor means when he says that there has always been "censorship," or that the social structure depends on preserving it. In that sense, we all "censor," internally, our own actions and those of others whom we influence. We define in our heads, as a matter of course, the range between what our contemporaries will and will not tolerate. We play between these definitions, stretching them now one way, now another. We live in a state of permanent conflict between our daring and our decency; and, though few go out of their way to say as much, few would have it otherwise.

Yet, censorship, as we commonly know it, differs sharply from this internalized mechanism for enforcing communal assumptions. Of all forms of sex censorship, that of the individual psyche—which sees to it that some things simply cannot be said, even to oneself—is undoubtedly the most effective. It is truly effective, however, only for those tradition-bound societies in which sexual inhibitions are more or less uniformly shared. The modern world, where more than one set of assumptions exist about what is and is not to be allowed, can make sex censorship of literature and the arts a subject of heated dispute. Censorship as an issue, in other words, is almost by definition a by-product of class rivalry. It arises along the shared boundaries between two or more antagonistic schools of thought; and in societies like our own, where law has replaced the rule of universally accepted custom, it is inevitably (though not always successfully) dealt with by law.

Some forms of sexual behavior the law forbids outright: rape, "statutory" rape, incest, sodomy, prostitution, lewd acts with children, adultery, fornication, abduction, and miscegenation—all of which may be defined in terms of a concrete act. Sex censorship arises, however, not from what is done—at least, not hitherto—but from what is said, written, seen, heard, thought, or felt. The prohibited area in word or image is conveniently characterized by the terms "obscene" or "obscenity," and it falls under the "law" of obscenity—that is to say, an accumulation of statutes and precedent which reflect, but do not necessarily reveal, prevailing definitions of the sexually forbidden. The law underlines the vague sanctions of community disapproval with a tangible threat. It establishes certain minima of censorship, and maxima of license, and, therefore, the limits of acceptable variation in erotic tone. But it suffers severe criticism, even as law, both from its lack of grounding in the material or exact and from its exposed position between rival conceptions of the sexual and social—not to mention the esthetic—good.

Difficulties begin with the idea of "obscenity" itself. Not all that is obscene has to do with sex (*e.g.*, scatology), nor is everything sexually prohibited (*e.g.*, contraception) necessarily obscene. Typically, the word carries one or more of at least three distinct meanings: as (1) something which contravenes accepted standards of propriety, (2) something which tends to corrupt, and (3) something which provokes erotic thoughts or desires. The second and third are often thought to subsume the first, though not the other way around (as one Hemingway character might say to another, "I obscenity in the milk of thy mother's obscenity," without passion of any kind). The first is a common, if ill-defined, phenomenon, including the venerable four-letter Anglo-Saxon monosyllables as well as most of the improper anecdotes that are at any time considered proper to tell. The second and third have sometimes been regarded as identical, not only by censors, but by courts, as though the fact of sex were in fact obscene. Even when examined from a purely legal view, the law of obscenity is so hazy and illogical that it tends to disintegrate —to lead inevitably to a conclusion that "[n]o one seems to know what obscenity is."

In the forty-seven states where statutes relating to obscenity exist, all but six define it "by adding one or more of the following words: disgusting, filthy, indecent, immoral, improper, impure, lascivious, lewd, licentious, and vulgar." These words have no objective meaning. Dictionaries often define them circularly (as the young and curious are frustrated to discover), in terms of one another. They partake of reality only through shared judgments and largely through assumed standards of sexual behavior or assumed theories of social cause-and-effect. Even in the rare instances where a modern court has held obscenity to be a fact, determinable on examination by a judge or jury, the "true test" of this determination has been found in speculative social psychology—"whether the tendency of the matter charged as obscenity is to deprave and corrupt those whose minds are open to such immoral influences . . ."—the notorious *Hicklin* rule.

To the extent that the law of obscenity is the sum of the cases tried under it, the law deals with only a limited part of the relationship between sex censorship and the arts. Censorship may be highly effective, through coercion or consent, and yet be extralegal if not illegal. The study of the law, case by case, tends to reduce the "problem" of obscenity to the problems posed in a series of court proceedings of a rather specialized character, largely concerned with books and most often with books of a special kind—those that fall somewhere between the categories of obvious trash and of invulnerable classic— whose publishers are sufficiently tenacious or self-confident to sustain litigation. Since the law offers apparently endless possibilities for reinterpretation, both parties to an obscenity dispute tend to regard it as a critical test—a step, in whichever direction, along the linear scale between total censorship and total liberality. Thus, a lawyer may see in the *Ulysses* decision "a great stride forward, possibly a greater stride than in any previous single case," while a congressional committee can see it as "the basis for excuse to print and circulate the filthiest most obscene literature without concurrent literary value to support it, ever known in history." Both share the flattering illusion (for lawyers) that society takes its erotic cues from the bench; but the *Ulysses* decision, after all, followed a decade of sustained onslaught on social prudery of all kinds, and it was not, in its consequences, the mortal blow to the *Hicklin* rule that it seemed at the time to be.

The legal defense of literature against legal censorship, concurrently, has had a somewhat confusing effect on debates over obscenity. It has focussed attention on near-irrelevancies, such as the question of artistic merit or the number of equally objectionable elements in Shakespeare and the Bible, and distracted it from the conflicts more importantly at issue—"the fight between the literati and the philistines," as two scholars have put it, for jurisdiction over sexual manners and customs. Both adversaries have frequently found it advantageous, for their respective reasons, to conduct this battle in the courtroom: the censorious, because they see the shock value of bringing before the public selected passages of books that might privately be inoffensive to most literate adults; the defenders of such books, because they see that common sense and most of the law is on their side. The outcome is then in the lap of extremely whimsical deities, and both parties—in defeat—tend to be victimized by the eloquence of their briefs. The literati despairingly conclude that the victories of reason are seldom permanent; the philistines, that "the blackest mud"—the words are Anthony Comstock's—"is to be found behind the trees on which the sun shines brightest. In that shadow the slime lies thick."

II

Comstockery, as Shaw named the disease, is ever with us. No generation lacks for frightened witnesses to the power of obscenity to corrupt, even where such testimony must necessarily cast a curious light on the individual who offers it. The cause-and-effect relationship between obscenity and lowered morals, perversion, or crime is simply—for many—an article of faith which no evidence could disturb. Such evidence as there is, regrettably, would not disturb them anyhow since it is likely to be negative and prove mainly that no relationship can be proved—scholarly but superfluous support for Mayor Walker's dictum that no girl was ever ruined by a book. The very idea of literature having a tendency to corrupt can be amply shown to depend on assumptions about the affecting agent, the nature of the effect, the audience affected, and the arbiter of that effect which "are often inconsistent with each other, unprecise and confusing." But the censor marches serenely on.

To those concerned with the inadequacies of the obscenity laws, it has inevitably occurred that a reasonable way out would be to make the demonstration of obscenity contingent on the demonstration of a corrupting effect. One commentator has semiseriously suggested that "[i]t might be an interesting innovation if censorship laws operated only when a plaintiff could prove that he himself had been depraved for lack of proper public safeguards." Short of this, it might still be possible to require the prosecution of allegedly obscene works to produce at least one witness who would admit to being corrupted by it. Typically, such testimony is offered by the committed proponents of censorship or by law officers. The cases in which any objective effect of the work can be adduced are rare, however, and there would be grave obstacles, I should think, to requiring that individuals demean themselves in order to incriminate an object. If censorship is wrong in principle, as so many of its opponents believe, then they do ill to grapple with it in terms of tactical trivialities that may win them the engagement but lose the campaign.

Moreover, the so-called "advances" within the law can very quickly be cancelled by retrogressions outside it—a point less appreciated by the literati than by the philistines, who are not so bedazzled by legality. The past few years, in particular, have witnessed an extraordinary comeback among the believers in sex censorship—not simply among its traditional friends, but what can only be called their new intellectual allies. Even without the latter's help, however, the former have learned to mask their objectives and to seek them without putting the matter of methods to a legal test. In this they have been encouraged (and considerably instructed) by a committee of the Eighty-second Congress, the Select Committee of the House of Representatives on Current Pornographic Materials, known for short as the Gathings Committee, which tried to discover ways of achieving sex censorship without having to endorse it.

The Committee's report is a handy compendium of pro-censorship ammunition and a textbook in the techniques of local pressure, yet it obstinately avoids any overt defense (perish the thought!) of censorship. Aware that federal censorship would be unconstitutional—though its members and witnesses made veiled references to the possibility of one—the committee instead expressed approval of the "many splendid groups in existence throughout the Nation that devote their efforts assiduously toward eliminating the flood of pornographic material. . . ." It heard the testimony of such witnesses as the writer Margaret Culkin Banning, who had suggested that in order to avoid the need for censorship by law, the private citizen should "make his protests against printed obscenity felt through his business and professional clubs, his parent-teacher group, the lay association of his church"—that is, agitate and inflame, form posses, lynch books. The Committee's report, though its reading can hardly be recommended without qualms, merits attention as a fully developed example of Comstockery, genus 1952, at work.

The Gathings Committee seems genuinely not to have desired censorship; it merely desired censorship to be unnecessary. It would rather the whole equivocal business of obscenity were somebody else's problem. Aware that the Post Office is one of the few effective censors left, it asked to have lifted the last pretense of due process from the star-chamber methods by which an opinionated postal inspector can put a publisher out of business. Aware that no definition of obscenity is satisfactory, it tried to evade the word by diffusing it into a cloud of indefiniteness, recommending that the publishing business eliminate on its own initiative not only the conceivably obscene, but "that proportion of its output which may be classified as 'borderline' or 'objectionable' "—in other words, stop haggling about specific books and throw them all out wherever there is the slightest question. Aware that sex censorship is, at heart, a social and cultural issue, the Committee reserved its plainest words for a declaration of its social and cultural criteria: "The ascendancy of Puritanism in England promoted a pious reserve in language as in conduct. . . . The Victorian era was a time of literary restraint. . . . It may be that the time has come for the pendulum to swing back again toward decency, a consummation devoutly to be wished. . . ." Surely nothing could be more candid.

One of the many ironies of the obscenity issue is the way in which standards vary, in the eyes of both literati and philistines, among the media. What is permissible in one is forbidden in the next; what would be an outrageous limitation of freedom on one hand is tolerated on the other. The older or more established the medium, generally speaking, the greater the freedom from attack. When it is new, or exploiting a new audience, it must expect to be regarded as a potential outlet for the obscene. Like the Gathings Committee itself, the Victorian prudery that culminated in the *Hicklin* rule had been stimulated by the unprecedented extension of literature into previously untouched areas. The nineteenth-century novel, with its exposure of different classes to one another, was attracting new classes of readers through its serials and lending libraries. A similar impetus was lent to the Gathings Committee by the recent phenomenal development of the pocket-size, paperback book. The common element in each instance is the status rivalry between the lower-middle-class censor, who feels responsible for the morals of the class immediately below him, and the aristocrat, to whom the threat of literature is as nothing compared to the threat of censorship.

In comparison with Victorian times, the reading of books and periodicals by the lower-middle and lower classes (though not entirely free of concern) is today a less emotional issue; experience with mass literacy has increased our reluctance to generalize about literature's "tendencies." The burden of censorship now rests far more heavily on the new "mass media," which characteristically—to make matters worse—have a wider and more penetrating impact on the senses than their predecessors. The movies, radio, or television pose problems in censorship so unfamiliar that the upper-class defenders of freedom for the old-fashioned book hesitate to interfere with them. To cope with them at all, we have had to evolve and accept improvised regulations, like the self-policing "codes," which the old media of publishing, press, and stage would regard as unbearably restrictive. No one would dare ask of a newspaper that it observe the same restraints that are constantly being demanded of that current object of fashionable solicitude, the comic-book.

The nature of any censorship, in other words, is often a function of the anxieties generated by the medium or inherent in the milieu which the medium seeks to serve. At twenty-five to fifty cents, the pocket-size paperbacks are available not only to many adults who had not thought of themselves as book-buyers before, but to adolescents. Despite the overpowering incoherence and banality of its report, the Gathings Committee manages to make perfectly clear its desire to establish a connection between the corruption of the young, pornography, and the mass market enjoyed by the seven major paperback publishers then in operation. It denies to softcover books a degree of freedom it must allow to hard-cover ones, on the presumptive grounds that the increasing dissemination of the former constitutes a "menace to the moral structure of the Nation, particularly in the juvenile segment." The implication is that an adult who can afford to pay three dollars and fifty cents for obscenity can take care of himself. It is where the paperback book represents a penetration of "mature" attitudes from the minority bookstore class through to the majority newsstand class that the Committee is alarmed; it would like this process to be either halted or reversed. It sees its real enemies, as Comstock did, among the respectable, the partisans of the liberal enlightenment who insist upon unloosing evil—in the name of mere principle—on susceptible and unprotected youths.

Censorship and obscenity, as such, are not the real issues here—they are only camouflage for issues so embittered they cannot be openly posed. Nor are these, as they are often said to be, merely religious; one of the least sensible crochets of the anti-censorship school lies in attributing to Catholicism attitudes which are equally often, and often more vigorously, espoused by Protestants. In this respect, the Gathings Committee Report is especially instructive; it can representatively be described—like so much of the contemporary support for censorship—as a counterattack on an assumption of aristocratic invulnerability made by the forces that have been called the "discontented classes," vocal and dissident blocs formed by the intellectually dispossessed in the aftermath of the Roosevelt era. The Committee comes out against "modern" literature and "liberal" interpretations of the law in virtually the same breath, as though both had equally undermined the Republic. Often, views of this kind are called anti-intellectual, though they are, in many respects, not so much anti-intellectual as anti-chronological—part of a massive, integrated gripe against the passage of time. Clearly their holders are less antagonized by the work of the mind for its own sake than by the dominant literary and artistic style which has made them feel, for more than two decades, that they were esthetically out of fashion. Now that the wheel has turned, turned so far that the excesses of "liberalism" and "modernism" are deplored by those who once committed them, the day has come for revenge. A crusade against pornography, that most helpless of quarries, is made to order.

Thus it is that literature and its advocates find themselves so continually on the defensive, unprotected by the juridical triumphs of the past generation from the smut-hunters of the present one. The open competition among ideas cannot be relied on, where pornography is concerned, as long as no one will openly defend it. Like Communism or homosexuality, it can be attacked in the secure knowledge that no one will dare occupy its position. It then becomes the focal point for resentments less safe to assert, and everything suspect tends to be lumped together (not surprisingly, numerous citizens, loud in the pursuit of the dirty book, believe it to be somehow connected with the Communists). Often the "liberal" argument, as a way of touching base with respectability, has allowed that "smut for smut's sake" must be rigorously dealt with—forgetting that this is the only concession the would-be censor has ever needed to ask. As long as an exception is made for the indefensible or even the detestable—"Freedom for everybody, except Communists and pornographers"—then there will be people perfectly prepared to state that you or I are Communists and pornographers, or their dupes, until we prove to the contrary. It is at such times that one remembers why freedom has been said to be indivisible.

III

An equally serious objection to the treatment of obscenity as a largely legal problem arises from the distorting effect this has on any discussion of sexual morality. Concentration on what is forbidden, according to such arbitrary and variable rules, distracts attention from what is permitted—and from any perspective that might put the two in balance. It would surely seem desirable, where a subject is, by its nature, so delicate, to take into account the extraordinarily wide range of "normal" behavior, the fact that prudes are not the only ones entitled to reticence, and the universal human inability to draw a sharp line between lust and love. An adversary situation over obscenity reduces these factors to their ultimate fragility; it is the native environment of the neurotic, and Comstockery is its natural corollary. It renders the total effects of American sexuality even more ridiculous than they might naturally appear.

Yet, one cannot deal fairly with questions of obscenity without describing the context out of which they emerge—the muddle of preoccupations and prohibitions which define, at any given time, the standards each individual must reckon with long before the law does. On these, sex censorship by law has pronounced effects, but they must be regarded as pre-existing—as the raw material of experience in which the law works—rather than as exterior accidents or consequences. Otherwise, consideration in the courtroom of the social effects of obscenity is absurd. If the law cannot recognize the effects which would be found in the absence of a given work of putative obscenity, then it cannot very well determine the effect of that work. However haltingly, in a rough-and-ready fashion, it must operate on some kind of theory of the American sex life—of what it is, or ought to be.

Every disagreement over sex censorship is, by implication—and sometimes overtly, as in the Gathings Committee's endorsement of "pious reserve"—a discussion of the sexual state of the nation. The two sides are hardly to be distinguished by their degree of allegiance to the First Amendment or to Romans XIV: 14 as much as by their personal judgment of current standards as either too lax or too severe. Unless all forms of censorship come to be regarded with universal horror, or the law is removed by popular request from the field of obscenity, this state of affairs seems likely to continue for some time to come. That being the case, it devolves on those of us who view the combat from a distance—or from the relative security of other professions—to comment on the materials with a sexual purport which censorship presently lets pass, on the role played by cumulative repression in shaping the American Eros, and on the unintended and ambiguous effects of identifying obscenity with the stimulation of sensual desire. Until these topics can be documented from obiter dicta, however, they will have to stay in the domain of personal opinion which they occupy here.

American attitudes toward sex illustrate the inter-relationship between censorship and provocation in almost clinically pure form; to foreign critics, we offer the most striking example available of a society in which excitation and restraint have the continuous function of intensifying one another. Every censorship breeds evasion; it is in our highly developed techniques for evading our own censorship that the American culture fascinates the visitor—or the few local observers sufficiently alert to notice them. To the European eye, we give the impression of make an unwholesome fetish of the female breast, of overwhelming our adolescents with erotic stimuli, and of hiding behind a "puritan façade" the reality of "un des pays sexuellement les plus libres du monde." Confronted with the contrast between our preaching and our practice, we are hard put to refute the thesis propounded a decade ago by Philip Wylie: that the United States is "technically insane in the matter of sex."

The point need scarcely be labored that the American popular culture is saturated with sexual images, references, symbols, and exhortations; this is a conclusion that both literati and philistines might well agree on, and they might further agree that it reflects a condition of pervasive psychological disease. The difference would be in diagnosis. The censor sees a justification for intensified effort; his opponent sees the result of the censorship now in effect and a warning of disasters to come if more is applied. My own inclination is toward the latter view; and, though I appreciate the obligation to convince those who think differently, I can only fill it by inviting them to examine their own experience from this vantage-point before abandoning it entirely. It is my contention that the symptoms of the American sexual neurosis, if there is such a thing, are the reflected distortions of a moral perspective that diminishes the healthy and accentuates the sick.

To be sure, Americans overemphasize sex partly because they can afford the unique luxury of being able to. If we are the only nation to make love a problem, we are so in virtue of having emancipated women, reduced the burden of household routines, and offered both sexes an unrestricted vista of domestic bliss and self-fulfillment. "Their statesmen are intent on making democracy work," writes a Frenchman of us. "Everybody is trying to make love work, too." We demand a great deal of it. For modern man, sex has been called "the last frontier," to which he looks "for reassurance that he is alive." And while, in a mass-production society, it tends to become a consumption good like any other, it is a good whose enjoyment by others remains forever beyond the reach of comparison—an object of limitless potentialities for fantasy and envy. Our glamor figures, male and female, whose justification is, in other respects, obscure, serve to maintain an illusion that somewhere, for somebody, sex can be a full-time activity. The vast majority of us must live on in the knowledge that the indulgences of the glamorous are forbidden; and at times, the heavy Puritan hand descends even on a puzzled unfortunate (like Mr. Jelke, of New York) who was sure that he himself inhabited the charmed circle.

Expecting much of sex, but feeling as individuals that much is denied them, Americans, as a mass, create in the substance of suppressed desire the remarkable symbolic figures that are found here as in no other culture. The existence of "the great American love goddess" is more often noted than explained. It is apparent that she enjoys high status, that she is attended by elaborate ceremonials, and that the titular embodiment of the divinity (at this writing: Marilyn Monroe) is only the reigning head of a hierarchy of sub-divinities, all of whom possess similar attributes. She is most often a movie star, though her talents as an actress and the merits of the films in which she appears are plainly immaterial. Her primary function is widely understood but rarely mentioned—that is, to serve as the object of autoerotic reverie. She represents, in brief, the commercial exploitation of the assumption that the American public is composed largely of Peeping Toms.

The assumption would appear to be well founded. It draws sustenance from the approach to sex on similar principles institutionalized by the advertising business. Diverted from literature and the arts, the forces that underlie obscenity or pornography expend themselves in this characteristic American medium. Here sex may be treated as powerful motivation, but only by expressing it in warped and perverted forms—*e.g.*, the women's underwear that is advertised far beyond its proportion of the market, so that we are daily surrounded with pictures of the feminine bosom, leg, and abdomen tightly constrained by clothing (the difference in effect between these and the "bondage photos" confiscated by the police seems to me one of degree only). To serve the hunger for the unattainable, we have brought into existence an entire class of women whose profession is catering to voyeurs, not even in the flesh, but through photographs—namely, the models. At its top are found the handful who pose for the fashion magazines and set the pace in cosmetics, posture, style, and aura at the outer reaches of unreal sophistication, where their taut, nerveless langour stands unchallenged—for lack of more full-blooded substitutes—as an ideal of the sensual.

Then, there is the theme of homosexuality, which runs through American popular culture (as well as literature) like a thread of not-so-innocent deceit. What is deceitful about it is not the conspiratorial existence forced on, accepted by, or darkly attributed to homosexuals. It is the connivance of the public in something it wishes to be titillated by, but not name—in its approval of novelists whose major theme of hatred for women is rarely mentioned; of comedians whose stock-in-trade is the exhibitionism of spastic, semi-hysterical effeminacy; of Western and detective-story heroes who rigorously spurn their heroines in the search for sadomasochistic purification. All these are not only permitted, but profuse. Not a word of complaint about them comes from the self-appointed custodians of morality, who are far too busily occupied protecting teen-agers from de Maupassant. Censorship, official and unofficial, lets pass into the social mainstream countless images and innuendoes that could only be identified—if they were to be identified—as perverse. Of the normal, the lustful thoughts and desires of one sex for the other, it faithfully removes whatever trace it can.

This paradox has been the subject of a book, the most important study of Anglo-Saxon censorship yet to appear—Gershon Legman's *Love and Death*. Mr. Legman's subject is the literary sadism which is intensified by the censorship of sex; his motif is the shameful anomaly of American mores which make love, which is legal in fact, illegal on paper, while murder, which is illegal in fact, is not only legal on paper, but the basis of the greatest publishing successes of all time. To be sure, affection and hatred are opposite poles of human experience, and art necessarily concerns itself with each—the act in which life begins and that in which it ends. The highest skill need not morbidly exaggerate the physical details of either, but neither will be denied it. Deny one only, and the other takes its place. Mr. Legman overpoweringly documents his case that in contemporary America, this is what has substantially occurred.

Though we often speak of sex and sadism together—as two equally regrettable qualities in the novels of Mickey Spillane, for example—in actual practice, we tolerate blood and guts in a quantity and concreteness wholly denied to sexual love. The time-tested formula for the "sexed-up" cover of a paperback book is a near-naked girl with a revolver, and it is curious that critics should comment so often on the nudity and ignore the imminence of death. Within the letter of the law, as in the popular culture, sex and violence tend to be entangled—we label an atomic bomb with the title of a Rita Hayworth movie and call an abbreviated bathing suit a "Bikini"—but in the courts, it is exceptional that the two are prosecuted with equal emphasis. The typical law against obscenity prohibits it in company with other incitements to crime as well as lust, but we all take for granted the state of general acceptance for printed murdering, whipping, gouging, and wholesale blood-letting which makes half the law unenforceable.

And this is only part of the price we pay for prudery. Is it not too high?

IV

Needless to say, despite these distractions, society survives. The vanity of lawyers in assuming that the law has a significant effect on sexual habits is matched by the vanity of writers in assuming that literature has a comparable effect. Fortunately, there are other forces at work determining conduct. Almost by definition, such enjoyment of life as there is by the vast majority escapes observation and reporting. Young people, determined to explore the mysteries for themselves, continue to grow up without having been successfully convinced that sex is unclean; nor are they always unwilling to scandalize their elders. Throughout this society that resolutely pretends to the contrary, there remains a streak of amiable lewdness and bawdry that has nothing to do with literature and breaks through censorship of any kind at the most unexpected times and places. There is a shudder of outraged horror in each community where a "non-virgin club" is uncovered, but as far as I am aware, these remarkable institutions neither take their inspiration from books nor are in any way discouraged by censorship. They testify to the extent to which sex can be self-induced, self-sustaining, and ultimately self-justified.

But even the sophisticated objectors to pornography, who define it as "calculated to stimulate sex feelings independent of another loved and chosen human being," suppress or distort any suggestion that Eros has, in its own right, a civilizing and illuminating potential. They seem to regard its exclusive function as the continuation of the race, and they are somewhat arbitrarily cruel in their strictures on those whose desires fail to be co-ordinated with the propagative process. Mrs. Banning imagines the ads in "sexy magazines" to be directed at "frustrated men, who were too short or too fat or too friendless or too far from home to have a successful sex relationship"; while Margaret Mead defines the difference between bawdry and pornography as that between the music hall and the "strip tease, where lonely men, driven and haunted, go alone. . . ." Such views impress me as inadequately informed by an appreciation of sex, not simply as a genetic mechanism, but as one of the avenues through which reality is exposed to us. This blessing has been conferred on mankind impartially and is luckily not within anyone's province to allocate.

There is a sense in which every nation gets the pornography it deserves. If we forbid the writing of erotica to all but those who are willing to break the law, we have no fair complaint if the results are trivial, mean, and inartistic. We are little entitled to the conclusion that the subject matter of sex cannot be tastefully—or even beautifully—treated if we have never tried to treat it so. Least of all can we pride ourselves on our moral stature as a people until we have further progressed beyond the outhouse phase, manifested by the Gathings Committee and its numerous facsimiles, in which a sniggering shame is our characteristic approach to sex. The true obscenities of American life lie in our vicious public consumption of human suffering, in virtually every form and every media. By comparison, the literature of sexual love would seem to me vastly preferable, but in offering a personal opinion, I hasten to take counsel—while the chance remains—from the words of a distinguished jurist [Judge Curtis Bok].

> There will always be battle in the arena of free opinion; there always has been since Plato thought that Homer should be expurgated and said so. I believe in the constant working of these laws of natural censorship and am willing to work my own as a part of the process. . . . I know of no more important time for courageous good taste than when there is not much of it about. Liberty is easier to win than to deserve, and if it is treated as either a license or a vacuum, the police will come or the walls will fall.

Many liberal causes, not the least the freedom to read, lost a great champion in 1955 with the passing of Bernard De Voto. His hard-hitting, but amusing and civilized, anything-except-"Easy Chair" contributions to *Harper's Magazine* were eagerly anticipated each month. One of his favorite targets was the censor, especially the Boston variety.

De Voto's "Easy Chair" columns devoted to censorship issues, all highly readable and influential, were so numerous that a selection is difficult. Two of his best are included here, the first a frequently hilarious piece on the progress of sex education in our colleges, and the other an unmerciful lambasting of the notorious Gathings Committee, otherwise known as the Select Committee on Pornographic Materials. Representative Francis E. Walter of Pennsylvania thought so well of De Voto's "The Case of the Censorious Congressmen" that he had it inserted in the *Congressional Record*.

Bernard De Voto
THE EASY CHAIR

Before the world turned gray a superstition of the publishing business held that the summer

---
Bernard De Voto, "The Easy Chair," *Harper's Magazine,* 195:156–59 (August, 1947), copyright 1947 by Harper & Bros. Reprinted by permission of Mrs. Bernard De Voto.

months were no time for serious reading, that people put away brainwork with their woolen clothes and would read only light novels while dressed in seersuckers. The phrase "summer fiction" is a vestige of that belief and even today you will find few books listed at more than $2.75 in the summer lists of publishing houses. The magazines have discarded the notion entirely; their brows remain high and their chins firm throughout the hot weather; and as I write this the editors of *Harper's* are not, as they would have been ten years ago, sweating out the last week of June making up what we used to call the Midsummer Fiction Number.

In those days the Easy Chair piously observed the convention and every August turned away from the salvation of mankind to discuss matters of no importance whatever. I am moved to take up such a matter now because a few days ago while cleaning out an old file I found a manuscript which I was unable to find some years back when Henry Mencken asked me to write out for him what I remembered of the episode it was a part of. I wrote that reminiscence and Mr. Mencken filed it, I believe, with other documents in the New York Public Library to await a literary historian who may sometime be curious about the minor literary folkways of the 1920's. He has never found occasion to tell the story and it had no importance at all, so why not tell it now when old subscribers can read it between showers on the porch overlooking the golf course?

It takes us back to a year that seems never to have existed, 1926. Some two weeks after the April 1926 issue of the *American Mercury* reached the stands and was distributed through the mails, one of the finest gentlemen of Harvard Square sold a copy of the issue to an agent provocateur of the Watch and Ward Society. He was arrested for selling obscene literature and was found guilty and fined, as everyone was in those days when the Massachusetts courts regularly held that the presence of a single word in a book could make that book obscene. Later, someone came to his place of business by night and anonymously left there greenbacks to the exact amount of his fine. Those greenbacks may perhaps be evidence of the peculiar conscience of the then celebrated but now forgotten Jason Franklin Chase, who was by far the most expert detector of obscenity that the Watch and Ward Society has ever had.

Meanwhile two developments had occurred. The Postoffice Department had barred from the mails the April issue which it had finished distributing and Mr. Mencken had reacted with his usual vigor. He got an injunction against the Postoffice Department forbidding it to deny his magazine the use of the mails. He came to Boston, sold a copy of the April issue to the Rev. Mr. Chase himself (biting the half-dollar for soundness in the presence of reporters), was arrested for selling obscene literature, and was found not guilty. That verdict was the first check the Watch and Ward had ever received and marks the beginning of its slow decline, though the suffering was more severe four years later when Mr. Chase won the Dunster House Bookshop case but had his heart broken by a judicial bawling out.

Mr. Chase's attack on the *Mercury* was his way of replying to an article which it had previously published describing the all but incredible—quite incredible to people who did not live in Boston—methods that his organization used in what was then called vice crusading. The article in the April issue which he alleged to be obscene was an amusing piece by Herbert Asbury about rural manners in Missouri. It was called "Hatrack" after the small-town, part-time prostitute who appeared in the last part of it. I have just reread it and I am sure that the historian who finally gets round to it will seriously misconceive our culture, for he will read it with the knowledge that at least one person could say he thought it was obscene. I am sure that in 1926 no one, not even Mr. Chase, considered it obscene; it must have been cited as improving reading by at least metropolitan Sunday schools. The historian should take into account the fact that John S. Sumner, Chase's runner-up, did not proceed against it.

The inside back cover of that April *Mercury* announced as the lead article for May a piece called "Sex and the Co-ed." The announcement said, "For some time past the newspapers have been full of dark, smirking hints about the carnal doings going on in the great co-educational colleges, especially in the Christian Middle West. The *American Mercury* commissioned an intelligent and respectable professor to investigate the subject and report on it...." But when the May issue appeared it contained no such piece; instead the lead article was "On Learning to Play the 'Cello" by Doris Stevens. Ten days before it appeared the press services carried a story about a burst of excitement at the plant in Camden (or was it Newark?) that printed the *Mercury*. The AP and the UP said that several thousand copies of the May *Mercury* (one of them made it sixty thousand) had been burned there because it contained an obscene article. To this the INS added an account of how Alfred Knopf, the *Mercury's* publisher, had ordered this destruction without consulting the editor, Mr. Mencken, and how, smoking and flaming, Mencken had arrived at the printer's too late to prevent Mr. Knopf's orders from being carried out. And the managing editor of the Evanston, Illinois *News-Index,* of which my wife was the literary editor, was a good newspaperman, for when this story came over the wire he phoned me and told me about it. I said, how surprising but I don't know anything about it and it's none of my business.

Whether any copies of that May issue actually had been printed and were destroyed I don't know, for when I came to know Mr. Knopf and Mr. Mencken personally they were both a little reticent and all of us soon forgot about it. But the lead article was killed before publication—and for a very simple reason. The lawyer who was conducting Mr. Mencken's case in Boston and trying to get a restraining order against the Postoffice Department thought it imprudent, while the cases were going on, to feature a piece that had the word "sex" in the title. I have just reread that article too, for the first time in twenty-one years, and I am sure that the title is all he could have objected to.

For the news sense of my wife's editor was sound and the article that turned up in my files a few days ago was "Sex and the Co-ed," written by myself. (I was tolerably intelligent and phenomenally respectable but Mencken promoted me three full grades when he made me a professor. On the faculty of Northwestern University I ranked as an instructor in English.) I had been writing for the *Mercury* for a year or so and for this piece Mencken paid me either sixty-five or eight-five dollars, I can't remember which. I do remember that it bought me a dinner jacket, an elegance I had not previously been able to afford at Northwestern, and that when I wore it at a scholarly reception the most worldly of my colleagues asked me to dinner for the first time, having theretofore guessed that I lacked the ceremonial garments. Also, in order to keep my job, I had signed the article with a pen name. Since it wasn't published, John August made no public appearance till nearly twelve years later, when for reasons I cannot remember either I or someone else decided that the editor of the *Saturday Review* ought not to sign the mystery stories he was writing. I wish I could relieve the abdominal spasms of the literary thinker who has been so concerned about that name, but I honestly cannot remember what its provenance was. Maybe there was some association with the dinner jacket I proposed to buy. The Harvards will remember the name of a haberdashery in the Square.

In those days journals of opinion and of family life as well were obsessed with what they usually called the revolt of youth. Mostly they called it flaming youth, because there had been a silly novel of that title. The President of the United States himself, during the years when he was Vice President, had looked into things and told the circulation of a women's magazine that a hellish revolution was being preached and produced in the colleges, especially the women's colleges and most especially and most oddly Radcliffe. What had horrified Mr. Coolidge was some nameless threat to economic orthodoxies but there was nothing nameless about the horror of his fellow alarmists: they devoted themselves to morals, meaning sexual morals. Their fervor and a credulousness characteristic of the period sufficed to convince literary people, who in turn erected a cliché that nothing has been able to overturn. It is either Miss Skinner or Miss Kimbrough who has given us an affecting account of her failure to convince a niece born in the 1930's that she had not spent her college years drunk and in someone's bed. The fashion seems to have begun with *This Side of Paradise,* though I have never understood why that pleasant book shocked anyone. The hero formally asks his sweetie's permission before he kisses her and though he does indeed carry an intrigue farther than that at last it is a terrific climax and the girl is clearly shown to be not of His Class. But all publishers at once rushed out novels which showed that the colleges had kicked the moral code to pieces.

Mr. Mencken had commissioned me to inquire into the facts. Such an inquiry was easy. Far more students than members of the faculty came to my apartment and I had a wide acquaintance among Northwestern boys. I enlisted the services of my wife, who had been a Northwestern coed and had retained her sorority connections, and since she was a married woman was repeatedly consulted by undergraduate girls about the mysteries that most fascinated them. And I soon found out that they were mysteries. I began with the assumption that, like the mean annual rainfall, the amount of sexual intercourse had been one of the most dependable constants in the world since Eve's time. The assumption proved not to hold for Northwestern in 1926 or, by extension, for the other Midwestern universities. There was plenty of rumor about how debauched the coeds were but it nearly always turned out to be some other girl, some other group, some other college. The Kappas would confess that they were humiliatingly chaste and envy the glorious debauchery of the Gamma Phis, who in turn knew that it was the Tri-Delts who sinned. Wisconsin would report its own campus shamefully pure and hold that Michigan was a voluptuary's paradise.

My article hazarded no guesses about Northwestern men. It did make a numerical guess about the girls but I am not going to tell you what that guess was. My sense of history balks: this was a long and patient inquiry conducted by an experienced newspaperman who was also a trained researcher, who was trusted by the boys and whose wife was trusted by the girls, and still I cannot believe that the reality was so small as the figures John August arrived at after analyzing the evidence.

Rereading the article, however, has brought back a lot of that evidence to my mind and, whatever it may have indicated about chastity or unchastity, it demonstrated an altogether amazing ignorance of the physical, mechanical, and psychological facts of sex among Midwestern college girls in the mid-1920's. An ignorance, may I say, that had not characterized the girls of that age in Ogden, Utah, a few years before. There was the girl who understood that conception occurred during sleep, because there was that phrase about sleeping with a man. The girl who regularly gargled with Listerine after she had been kissed, as a contraceptive measure. The girl who, though she knew how women became pregnant in nature's way, thought there was also a way of achieving the same result verbally. And so on, dozens and scores of such girls and, through their reports of their friends and the reports of boys about them, hundreds all told. And there was the faculty woman who had been delegated to confer with all coeds who announced their engagements—a hundred or more every year—and lecture to them about what the professional jargon called sex education. She had an apartment on the floor below mine and by a happy coincidence she herself became engaged while my surreptitious inquiry was going on. So she sought out a neighbor, my wife in fact, and inquired just what happened, physically, when one got married. Later on I used that one in a novel.

John August's article is mostly concerned with this ignorance and with the ways in which a typical university dealt with it in the mid-twenties. It is quite true, on evidence repeatedly checked then and still attached to my copy of the article, that one dean of women regarded taxi drivers as habitual rapists, forbade her charges to wear red dresses when going out with boys since red would excite the male passions, cautioned them against crossing their legs, and warned them that their own eroticism would be aroused if they ate meat. That last meant a solid saving to undergraduate boys, if the girls did indeed confine themselves to lettuce sandwiches. More astonishing still was the annual lecture on sex that was compulsory for freshman girls. My wife had heard it as an undergraduate and went back and heard it again on my behalf. The woman physician who gave it was so handcuffed by restrictions that she never managed to talk realistically about anything except catamenia and could not discuss that very long. There was, however, a movie about reproduction. It showed a collie bitch frolicking with some puppies, a diagrammed sperm breaking the outline of a diagrammed ovum, and a bee entering a rose. Mr. August could not see that the lecture taught the coeds anything except possibly to avoid bees.

The colleges are conducting sex education very differently now. It is all frank, informative, white tile, and antiseptic. I wonder, though, whether these careful classes in the unpredictable get any farther than the idiocies that made John August so indignant in 1926. Dr. Marynia Farnham recently reported some results that have turned up in her consulting room and they show the well-informed undergoing painful embarrassments because experience proved to be unlike the rational science of the textbooks. Meanwhile the reports of other clinics in the colleges, those that investigate the mores of undergraduates, suggest that this is a field of education which they may now safely abandon altogether. Or are the clinics like the fiction that appalled people of my age during the 1920's? Whenever a public institution inquires by questionnaire how much I smoke and drink, I invariably reply a carton of cigarettes and four-fifths of a gallon of whiskey every twenty-four hours. Maybe the undergraduates don't like questionnaires, either.

At any rate in 1926 the press services found news in the fact that someone had written an article about sex at a temperature of 33° Fahrenheit and I would certainly have been fired if that article had appeared under my name. The eventual historian can triangulate something from those facts. Today nobody would be fired from a college for writing about sex, though of course it remains dangerous for a college teacher to write readably about anything. And what temperature about sex would, in 1947, start the bell ringing on a teletype?

Bernard De Voto
THE CASE OF THE CENSORIOUS CONGRESSMEN

Last May the House of Representatives became aware that there was one field at which it had not directed its investigatory power. So it appointed a Select Committee, with Congressman Gathings of Arkansas as chairman, to "conduct a study and investigation of current pornographic literature." The Committee has now published its report; it makes interesting reading.

Interesting but difficult, and some day Congress should investigate congressional prose.

Bernard De Voto, "The Case of the Censorious Congressmen," *Harper's Magazine*, 206:42–45 (April, 1953), copyright 1953 by Harper & Bros. Reprinted by permission of Mrs. Bernard De Voto.

This report is so ineptly written that in some places I cannot make out what the Committee is trying to say. Thus it declares that the First Amendment "was adopted only after a long and acrimonious debate." And "even as far back as 1789 the idea of granting unrestricted liberty of speech and publication was a moot question of no mean proportions. The founding fathers evidently realized that what was meant to be liberty could readily be transmuted by unscrupulous persons into license."

This drifts unattached in midair—how is it to be construed? Is the Committee saying that the fathers decided this "moot question" wrongly? Did they err when they wrote freedom of the press into the Constitution? I judge that this is what the Committee means. For the burden of what it goes on to say is that we had better put some restrictions on freedom of publication that the fathers refused to.

Does the Committee, then, favor censorship? It says repeatedly that it does not. Thus, p. 12, "a practical solution consistent with adequate safeguards against possible violation of the constitutional rights of free speech is the aim of the Committee and never has it entertained any thought of federal censorship of the press." Just as often, however, it entertains exactly such thoughts in the plain view of everyone. Page 17, "It follows logically that any effort by Congress . . . should be directed toward the publishers [of objectionable literature] either from the angle of statutory provisions or through self-imposed control if such is possible." Any effort of Congress from the angle of statutory provisions would be federal effort. Any statutory provisions directed at publishers would be censorship.

Or take this, which immediately precedes the denial I have quoted from p. 12. The Committee quotes Mr. Douglas M. Black as saying that the Publishers' Council believes there are enough federal and local laws on the books now to take care of obscene literature if they are properly enforced. Then the Committee says, "This seems to say in effect that if there is a law existing against the commission of a particular crime it is all right to commit the crime, if you can get away with it." I suppose that righteousness exempts the Committee from dealing intelligently with what Mr. Black has said, and even from characterizing it honestly; I suppose the gentlemen do not believe that it is all right to violate the Hatch Act while running for Congress if you can get away with the violation. But I read this as saying that we have not got enough laws to do the job and therefore need additional ones.

The Committee studied comic books, "cheesecake or girlie magazines," and "pocket-size paper-bound books." It heard testimony about the first two evils but devoted most of its attention to the third. Let me say right here that what the report says about pocket books spotlights an embarrassing dilemma: either the Committee is intolerably ignorant or else it is deliberately making intolerable misrepresentations. "This type of writing," the report says, "has now reached a stage where it has become a serious menace to the social structure of the nation." It may be news to you that the blonde in her underwear who adorns the cover of *Silas Marner* at the newsstand has undermined American society, but you have worse to learn. The Committee prints an unsigned letter from the combat zone in Korea which says that "most of the reading the Army provides us is filth and adultery." It appears to accept the statement, which must interest the Army, that this filth has "all but destroyed our first line of defense" and the further one, which should interest another House Committee, that it has "left us open to dangers far worse than communism."

The Committee says that publishers, meaning chiefly the reprint houses, "are resourceful public enemies, parasites on the free-press privilege." It regards such inflammatory language as justified by the speed with which the parasites have worked their will on us. Mrs. St. George, who lives in Tuxedo and represents the Twenty-ninth Congressional District of New York, "can remember very well that ten years ago so-called smutty literature was unknown in this country." One reason for this swift success is "a general lack of awareness of the problem in its modern form [presumably twenty-five cent books], its scope, magnitude, and techniques." There is a tendency to make light of the problem and to look on those who are disturbed by it as "professional reformists or bluenoses." But we are given leave to hope: various watchers on the walls have recognized the danger and the Committee acknowledges that the most heartening sign so far is the existence of the Committee itself.

But public apathy is not most to blame, we gather from the report; the courts are. The Committee says that they have developed "a new legal philosophy." It "serves as the basis for excuse to print and circulate the filthiest, most obscene literature without concurrent literary value to support it ever known in history." Be damned to such philosophy, and the Committee sets out to undermine the decisions that over the past thirty years have modernized the laws relating to obscenity. Decadence began with Judge Woolsey's decision in the *Ulysses* case, which on appeal was affirmed by Judge Hand. This double charter of obscenity "is as elastic as rubber in its interpretative susceptibility and supplies the purveyors of obscenity with an excuse regardless of what is the degree of obscenity involved, and requires every book to be judged separately, an almost impossible task."

Look at that wretched sentence again; its murkiness conceals the end to which all obscenity crusades come. To judge books separately is an almost impossible task. Then what? Then this: we must legally define a class of books, to-wit those that are pornographic, which shall be denied publication and circulation. How, without judging it, can we know that a book is pornographic? Apparently it will be enough if a cop, a district attorney, a "professional reformist," a Congressman, or (in one of the Committee's recommendations) a postmaster—if anyone says that it is. Whether or not the Committee knows it, that is how its thesis invariably works out—except under the court decisions it is trying to overthrow. Whether or not the Committee fully means to say it, that is what it says. But, mind you, no censorship.

The Committee moves on to Judge Curtis Bok's opinion in *Commonwealth v. Gordon et al.* In the Easy Chair for July 1949 I called it a great document in democracy and a great document in human freedom. The Committee disagrees. "To express it negatively, certainly such a decision contributed nothing whatsoever toward the reduction of the steadily increasing publication of and to [of?] the sales of pocket-sized books." It affects "all the elements of our social structure" and sanctions "by negative action the flow of salacious, scatological [no evidence of scatology cited in the report], and suggestive literature, reaching the degree of mass media." So the Committee must inquire into the background of the case—meaning Judge Bok's background.

Announcing that it would not dream of questioning his honesty or integrity, the Committee proceeds to slur them intolerably. His family has a large interest in the Curtis Publishing Company, which "owns 42½ per cent of the stock of Bantam Books, Inc." And Bantam Books, Inc., publishes the Committee's abomination, pocket-size paper-bound books. No reflection on Judge Bok—and yet: "It is, however, reasonably possible that having been associated so closely with the publishing business that he became inherently imbued [*sic*] with a liberal conception of the tradition founded upon the constitutional provision guaranteeing the freedom of the press."

Surely such half-illiterate writing is a greater danger to thought and morals than all the salacious literature ever printed in the United States. But what did it set out to say? This, I think: that we must narrow the First Amendment by repudiating a "liberal concept" and a dangerous "tradition" of freedom of the press. The Amendment says, "Congress shall make no law . . . abridging the freedom of speech, or of the press." The Committee appears to hold that this prohibition in itself does not cover pocket-size paper-bound books, that it has been extended to cover them only by an unjustified concept or a vicious tradition. It implies that Congress *can* make laws prohibiting their manufacture and sale and that it ought to. But, again, no censorship.

The Committee is preoccupied with that alarming phrase, "pocket-size paper-bound books." Would the same content be acceptable in royal octavo bound in cloth? Not necessarily, I judge, but it *would* be acceptable at three dollars. This does not mean that obscenity is a class prerogative. The offense is not that obscenity is offered for sale at a quarter, but that at that price it is offered for sale to so many people. The immature, meaning our children, can afford it.

The Committee faces away from the fact that almost all the two-bit books are reprints of more expensive ones that have had a pretty wide distribution in cloth. It conspicuously fails to remind us of another fact: that if twenty-five-cent books can be outlawed under the First Amendment, then so can books at any price. And, to make everything clear, the dissenting minority report reveals that the Committee read few, if indeed any, of the books which the majority describe as the filthiest, most obscene literature ever known in history. The hired help and some unpaid volunteers made extracts from various paper-backs, passages which contained "language of the streets" or episodes dealing "with sex and sexual relations." These extracts from a few books are what convinced the Committee that the reprint houses have brought our society to the verge of ruin.

The report ends with three recommendations. One would extend the federal statutes which now forbid common carriers to transport obscenity so that the same prohibition would cover transportation by private truck. The second would liberate the Post Office Department from two existing regulations which prevent it from dealing summarily with obscenity sent by mail. (These safeguards are to be removed because obscene material—the twenty-five-cent book—inflicts "swift and irreparable injury in such a comparatively short time.") Finally, the Committee recommends that publishers purify their output before the public demands *additional federal action*.

In their short but sharp minority report, Congressmen Celler of New York and Walter of Pennsylvania repudiate the methods, findings, and recommendations of their colleagues. They point out that the majority's objections are not confined to the obscenity they set out to investigate but extend to ideas, and that "this comes dangerously close to book burning." The objection to one book is that a passage in it advocates polygamy; to another, that its author does not seem to like law-enforcement officers or "the upper classes." The men who made these objections do not understand, the dissenters remark, that "these are, after all, matters of free speech and free expression."

"It is not the province of any congressional committee," Messrs. Celler and Walter say, "to determine what is good, bad, or indifferent literature." The majority on the Committee have set up their own personal taste as the criterion of what shall be published. Worse still, on the basis of some extracts from a few books, they have "made a sweeping indictment of current literature"—and they have neither official concern with current literature nor jurisdiction over it. The dissenters then move on to defend the reprint publishers, reviewing many facts which are known to everyone who buys books but which the Committee majority never took into account. They end by saying that if obscenity is a problem, there are state laws governing its distribution everywhere except in New Mexico, and Congress is not called upon to act.

The dissenters cover most of the points that must be made about this curious excursion by the House of Representatives. They do not, however, point out how obscurantist and untrue the Committee's report is. It is not true that today's magazines and paper-backs are the filthiest literature ever known in history. It is not true that cheap reprints are seriously menacing our social structure. It is not true that they are doing irreparable damage. Such statements are mendacious, ignorant, preposterous, and more dangerous in themselves than the sum total of obscenity printed since Gutenberg. Moreover, in all except a minute percentage of the paperbacks there is no more indecency, even casual verbal indecency, than in so many city directories. What does Congress mean by conducting so frivolous an inquiry, sanctioning so flagrant an attempt to frighten the public, and putting its seal on such a bulk of aggressive and irresponsible misrepresentation?

Such ignorance and prejudice as the Committee shows are routine in obscenity crusades, but also there is something new—and evil. The results it reaches are those of any police court smut-snooper; they come down to a wearily familiar demand, "This literature must be suppressed for we don't like it." The report alludes to lurid but entirely hypothetical dangers; not once does it produce or even mention any actual damage to anyone. It tells us that selected passages from some books have shocked it and that is all. A sense of shock is, of course, all that any crusade against obscene literature ever had. But this is not John S. Sumner. It is not a group of professional reformers expressing to a state legislature some professional horror which, they hope, will inspire the regular customers to throw another nickel on the drum. This is a Committee of the Congress of the United States, and it feels that the freedom guaranteed by the First Amendment ought to be abridged and believes that Congress has power to act. That is the dangerous novelty.

Are trashy novels, some of which may conceivably offend your taste and mine, a public problem? The occasional irresponsibility or exhibitionism of some Congressmen does not arouse us to crusade for the suppression of Congress. Because a child or an adolescent may buy for a quarter a book which we would just as soon he did not read until he is older and have therefore kept out of his hand at three dollars, we cannot let Congress make it unavailable to adults. We cannot, in fact, permit Congress in any way to censor our own reading or that of our children. What we may care to read is no concern of Congress. Congress has no power and no authority to control it. We are quite free to read anything we may choose to read and Congress can do nothing whatever about it. That's the way things stand now and we intend to keep them that way.

This particular investigation will produce no action, but it is a bad sign and it comes at a bad time. With amazing blitheness a House Committee has made another attack on the Bill of Rights that is the basic safeguard of our freedoms. It is no less dangerous an attack for being oblique. The gentlemen have been shocked by some passages in some books. (Though because gentlemen in Congress have stronger moral fibre than the rest of us, they were unharmed by what they feel sure must debauch us.) They propose that such books be heavily penalized. The plain bearing of what they say is that they must go on and forbid the publication of any paper-bound book they may happen not to like. And we have already slipped so far, impelled mostly by other committees of Congress, that no roar of anger mingled with laughter has rolled across the United States to silence them. The next step is clearly to forbid the publication of any books whatsoever that any Congressman may happen to dislike. In June 1949 Congressman John S. Wood called on some seventy colleges to submit to the Un-American Activities Committee all textbooks and supplementary reading used in all their courses in sociology, geography, economics, government, philosophy, history, political science, and American literature. His obvious intent was to determine what books Congress should permit colleges to use. His colleagues promptly called him off, but that was four years ago. This time Messrs. Velde and Jenner may try to make good on congressional proscription of reading matter.

The new Congress has been asked for an appropriation to continue the investigation begun by the Gathings Committee. Mr. Celler and Mr. Walter could perform no more valuable service than to appear before the Rules Committee and oppose continuation.

While Bernard De Voto was presiding over "The Easy Chair" department of *Harper's,* several of his most trenchant pieces were devoted to the suppression in Boston of Lillian Smith's novel, *Strange Fruit.* To test the extralegal processes under which the book was banned, De Voto bought a copy from a Cambridge bookseller. Both he and the bookseller were arrested, charged with dealing in obscene books. In the lower court, De Voto was found not guilty but the bookseller was convicted, and his conviction was subsequently sustained by the Massachusetts Supreme Judicial Court.

It is the *Strange Fruit* case with which Max Lerner is concerned in "On Lynching a Book." Lerner, one of America's most authoritative and respected commentators on government and public affairs, has had a varied career as author, editor, lecturer, university teacher, and radio news analyst. A number of his books have dealt with problems of intellectual freedom, e.g., *The Mind and Faith of Justice Holmes, Ideas Are Weapons, Ideas for the Ice Age,* and *America as a Civilization.*

Max Lerner
ON LYNCHING A BOOK

I keep asking myself: how would I go about explaining—in answer, let us say, to a barbed question by an intelligent foreigner—the whole messy effort to suppress Lillian Smith's novel, *Strange Fruit?* I would have to explain, first of all, that Lillian Smith is recognized as one of the most honest and courageous people writing in America today, a Southerner who knows her region and her home and her people, and a good craftsman in words. I would add that as a Southerner

---

Max Lerner, *Public Journal* (New York: Viking Press, 1945), pp. 131–34, copyright 1945 by Max Lerner. Reprinted by permission of the publisher.

and an American she regards the relation of whites and blacks in America as the toughest social problem, the most complex psychological problem, and the deepest moral problem we have to face in our country—and the failure to grapple with that problem as our most crying injustice. I would then say that out of this conviction, and out of what Rebecca West has called the "strange necessity" of an artist, she wrote a novel about whites and Negroes in a little town in Georgia that she calls Maxwell, and evidently knows with a terrible knowledge.

"Is it a good novel?" I hear my friend asking. Yes, would be my answer, it is. It is not a great novel—not Dostoevski nor Melville, not even E. M. Forster nor Faulkner nor Malraux. But the critics took it seriously as a novel of distinction. I have read it, and—reading it—I was absorbed with its story and moved by the anger and compassion behind the telling of it. Like many other novels it tells of a boy and a girl, of their star-crossed love, of parents and their unhappiness and demands, of a town and its life, of death and a hunt and violence, and of a final aching and numbed bewilderment. These are old and honored themes. But Lillian Smith has put them into a setting of a Southern town in which two races live side by side, with all the human in them drawing them together and all the tensions of caste and past pulling them violently apart.

And then, I would say to my friend, the silly thing happened. In one of our oldest cities (from which once our greatest writers and moral leaders came) the petty and the smutty, the ignorant and the bigoted, got busy. They found a short Anglo-Saxon word used in the book twice—a word that is tabooed in public print, although it has had a long and vigorous private career in our language. The word comes into the book casually and naturally, as part of the unfolding childhood memory of one of the characters, heard with innocence and remembered with repulsion. And they inflated that into a charge that the book is obscene, lewd, and calculated to corrupt the morals of the young. The booksellers in that city agreed not to stock the book. Then the police forbade its sale in Cambridge. A test case on the legality of this action has not yet been decided. About two weeks ago a minor official of the United States Post Office joined the hunt and banned the book from the mails. (The order has since been rescinded by a higher authority.)

Perhaps I should stop here, and set the whole thing down to the stupidity, the bigotry, and the prurience of the little men involved, and not try to probe more deeply. This is not the first case of book-burning by the Boston police, nor of silly censorship by the Post Office Department. The struggle for freedom from book-censorship stretches back for centuries, and John Milton once wrote a stirring defense of that freedom in his famous *Areopagitica*. To a reasonable person, the whole business of giving some little men the power of policing what shall be set down in books and sent through the mails is farcical.

Yet I doubt whether stupidity and bigotry and prurience are enough to explain the efforts to lynch Miss Smith's book. Bernard De Voto, who has had an honorable role in the test case of the book in Boston, writes that the people of Boston seem to be asking that sex be treated not with seriousness, but with a sickly leer and snigger. He is no doubt right. Yet I should guess that even deeper than this is a fear our self-appointed censors have—the fear that Americans will go probing too deeply into the nature of their society and its taboos. For if you read a book like this, which faces candidly some of the deepest issues of our time and place, you may get into the habit of facing other issues just as candidly.

To come back to my inquiring friend, that is what I should have to tell him in the end. Those who have power in America, whether in economic life or in political, know that once men begin understanding and fighting one form of injustice, the struggle is inevitably broadened. In an era of fascist terror, racism has become the great symbolic injustice. Better—they think—not to go too far in uncovering it. Here is an obscene word behind which we can hide that injustice, they think. And the sleight-of-hand and mumbo-jumbo begin.

My own concern about all this is not only that the people who write books should have freedom to say what they think, and that artists should have the freedom to create with integrity. My real concern is for an honest American culture, in which our children will be able to face squarely what we have done well and what we have done ill—and hold to the first, and mend the second.

You can't have that kind of America in an atmosphere of book-lynching. The police and Post Office censors say: "Do you want your children to be corrupted by this unprintable word?" And I answer: "I do not fear that a word will corrupt them, but a dishonest society, fearful of looking at itself in the mirror of art and truth."

I don't want my children to grow up without the knowledge that we have a system not only of economic class, but of racist caste in our country. I don't want to hide from them a Negro mother who, out of her great love for her child, whips him when he has mocked one of his white playmates—whips him so that the lesson will save his life. I don't want to hide from them the picture of how all the best natural drives of persons in both races—love and work and pride of craft—are frustrated and turned to hate and destruction because one race claims to be the master race. I want them to know about these things so that they will ask themselves how we get so tragically caught, so that they will fight the injustices with clear courage and resolve old and tangled problems with wisdom.

Courage and wisdom have to come from life itself. But books can point the way. And when a book is written that does, I don't intend to stand by and see it lynched.

Fashions in vulgarity are as variable as other changes in popular taste, Aldous Huxley points out in this essay. Expressions and ideas forbidden to writers in one era are accepted without question by the next. The essential criterion of what should be permissible, Huxley believes, is truth. "For those who are shocked by truth are not only stupid, but morally reprehensible as well . . . a familiar truth ceases to shock."

Aldous Huxley
**VULGARITY
IN LITERATURE**

It was vulgar at the beginning of the nineteenth century to mention the word "handkerchief" on the French tragic stage. An arbitrary convention

---

Aldous Huxley, *Vulgarity in Literature*, pp. 15–22, copyright 1930, 1931 by Aldous Huxley. Reprinted by permission of Chatto & Windus and Harper & Bros.

had decreed that tragic personages must inhabit a world, in which noses exist only to distinguish the noble Romans from the Greeks and Hebrews, never to be blown. Arbitrary conventions of one sort or another are essential to art. But as the sort of convention constantly varies, so does the corresponding vulgarity. We are back among the relativities.

In the case of the handkerchief we have a particular and rather absurd application of a very widely accepted artistic convention. This convention is justified by the ancient metaphysical doctrine, which distinguishes in the universe two principles, mind and matter, and which attributes to mind an immeasurable superiority. In the name of this principle many religions have demanded the sacrifice of the body; their devotees have responded by mortifying the flesh and, in extreme cases, by committing self-castration and even suicide. Literature has its Manichaeans as well as religion: men who on principle would exile the body and its functions from the world of their art, who condemn as vulgar all too particular and detailed accounts of physical actuality, as vulgar any attempt to relate mental or spiritual events to happenings in the body. The inhabitants of their universe are not human beings, but the tragical heroes and heroines who never blow their noses.

Artistically, the abolition of handkerchiefs and all that handkerchiefs directly or indirectly stand for has certain advantages. The handkerchiefless world of pure mind and spirit is, for an adult, the nearest approach to that infinitely comfortable Freudian womb, towards which, as towards a lost paradise, we are always nostalgically yearning. In the handkerchiefless mental world we are at liberty to work things out to their logical conclusions, we can guarantee the triumph of justice, we can control the weather and (in the words of those yearning popular songs which are the national anthems of Wombland) make our Dreams come True by living under Skies of Blue with You. Nature in the mental world is not that collection of tiresomely opaque and recalcitrant objects, so bewildering to the man of science, so malignantly hostile to the man of action; it is the luminously rational substance of a Hegelian nature-philosophy, a symbolic manifestation of the principles of dialectic. Artistically, such a Nature is much more satisfactory (because so much more easy to deal with) than the queer, rather sinister and finally quite incomprehensible monster, by which, when we venture out of our ivory towers, we are instantly swallowed. And man, than whom, as Sophocles long since remarked, nothing is more monstrous, more marvellous, more terrifyingly strange (it is hard to find a single word to render his *deinoteron*)—man, too, is a very unsatisfactory subject for literature. For this creature of inconsistencies can live on too many planes of existence. He is the inhabitant of a kind of psychological Woolworth Building; you never know—he never knows himself—which floor he'll step out at to-morrow, nor even whether, a minute from now, he won't take it into his head to jump into the elevator and shoot up a dozen or down perhaps twenty stories into some totally different mode of being. The effect of the Manichaean condemnation of the body is at once to reduce this impossible skyscraper to less than half its original height. Confined henceforward to the mental floors of his being, man becomes an almost easily manageable subject for the writer. In the French tragedies (the most completely Manichaean works of art ever created) lust itself has ceased to be corporeal and takes its place among the other abstract symbols, with which the authors write their strange algebraical equations of passion and conflict. The beauty of algebraical symbols lies in their universality; they stand not for one particular case, but for all cases. Manichaeans, the classical writers confined themselves exclusively to the study of man as a creature of pure reason and discarnate passions. Now the body particularizes and separates, the mind unites. By the very act of imposing limitations the classicists were enabled to achieve a certain universality of statement impossible to those who attempt to reproduce the particularities and incompletenesses of actual corporeal life. But what they gained in universality, they lost in vivacity and immediate truth. You cannot get something for nothing. Some people think that universality can be paid for too highly.

To enforce their ascetic code the classicists had to devise a system of critical sanctions. Chief among these was the stigma of vulgarity attached to all those who insisted too minutely on the physical side of man's existence. Speak of handkerchiefs in a tragedy? The solecism was as monstrous as picking teeth with a fork.

At a dinner party in Paris not long ago I found myself sitting next to a French Professor of English, who assured me in the course of an otherwise very agreeable conversation that I was a leading member of the Neo-Classic school and that it was as a leading member of the Neo-Classic school that I was lectured about to the advanced students of contemporary English literature under his tutelage. The news depressed me. Classified, like a museum specimen, and lectured about, I felt most dismally posthumous. But that was not all. The thought that I was a Neo-Classic preyed upon my mind—a Neo-Classic without knowing it, a Neo-Classic against all my desires and intentions. For I have never had the smallest ambition to be a Classic of any kind, whether Neo, Palaeo, Proto or Eo. Not at any price. For, to begin with, I have a taste for the lively, the mixed and the incomplete in art, preferring it to the universal and the chemically pure. In the second place, I regard the classical discipline, with its insistence on elimination, concentration, simplification, as being, for all the formal difficulties it imposes on the writer, essentially an escape from, a getting out of, the greatest difficulty—which is to render adequately, in terms of literature, that infinitely complex and mysterious thing, actual reality. The world of mind is a comfortable Wombland, a place to which we flee from the bewildering queerness and multiplicity of the actual world. Matter is incomparably subtler and more intricate than mind. Or, to put it a little more philosophically, the consciousness of events which we have immediately, through our senses and intuitions and feelings, is incomparably subtler than any idea we can subsequently form of that immediate consciousness. Our most refined theories, our most elaborate descriptions are but crude and barbarous simplifications of a reality that is, in every smallest sample, infinitely complex. Now, simplifications must, of course, be made; if they were not, it would be quite impossible to deal artistically (or, for that matter, scientifically) with reality at all. What is the smallest amount of simplification compatible with comprehensibility, compatible with the expression of a humanly significant meaning? It is the business of the non-classical naturalistic writer to discover. His ambition is to render, in literary terms, the quality of immediate experience—in other words, to express the finally inexpressible. To come anywhere near achieving this impossibility is much more difficult, it seems to me, than, by eliminating and simplifying, to achieve the perfectly realizable classical ideal. The cutting out of all the complex particularities of a situation (which means, as we have seen, the cutting out of all that is corporeal in it) strikes me as mere artistic shirking. But I disapprove of the shirking of artistic difficulties. Therefore I find myself disapproving of classicism.

Literature is also philosophy, is also science. In terms of beauty it enunciates truths. The beauty-truths of the best classical works possess, as we have seen, a certain algebraic universality of significance. Naturalistic works contain the more detailed beauty-truths of particular observation. These beauty-truths of art are truly scientific. All that modern psychologists, for example, have done is to systematize and de-beautify the vast treasures of knowledge about the human soul contained in novel, play, poem and essay. Writers like Blake and Shakespeare, like Stendhal and Dostoevsky, still have plenty to teach the modern scientific professional. There is a rich scientific harvest to be reaped in the works even of minor writers. By nature a natural historian, I am ambitious to add my quota to the sum of particularized beauty-truths about man and his relations with the world about him. (Incidentally, this world of relationships, this borderland between "subjective" and "objective" is one which literature is peculiarly, perhaps uniquely, well fitted to explore.) I do not want to be a Classical, or even a Neo-Classical, eliminator and generalizer.

This means, among other things, that I cannot accept the Classicists' excommunication of the body. I think it not only permissible, but necessary, that literature should take cognizance of physiology and should investigate the still obscure relations between the mind and its body. True, many people find the reports of such investigations, when not concealed in scientific text-books and couched in the decent obscurity of a Graeco-Latin jargon, extremely and inexcusably vulgar; and many more find them downright wicked. I myself have frequently been accused, by reviewers in public and by unprofessional readers in private correspondence, both of vulgarity and of wickedness—on the grounds, so far as I have ever been able to discover, that I reported my investigations into certain phenomena in plain English and in a novel. The fact that many people should be shocked by what he writes practically imposes it as a duty upon the writer to go on shocking them. For those who are shocked by truth are not only stupid, but morally reprehensible as well; the stupid should be educated, the wicked punished and reformed. All these praiseworthy ends can be attained by a course of shocking; retributive pain will be inflicted on the truth-haters by the first shocking truths, whose repetition will gradually build up in those who read them an immunity to pain and will end by reforming and educating the stupid criminals out of their truth-hating. For a familiar truth ceases to shock. To render it familiar is therefore a duty. It is also a pleasure. For, as Baudelaire says, *"ce qu'il y a d'enivrant dans le mauvais goût, c'est le plaisir aristocratique de déplaire."*

A novel point of view on censorship is introduced here by Ben Ray Redman. The basic question, he suggests, is not the rightness or wrongness of legislated morality, but the practicability of such censorship. "It is inconceivable," he concludes, "that any sex-censorship can ever be effective, for the simple reason that such censorship must seek to control an uncontrollable force by the futile expedient of eliminating external stimuli that are infinitely replaceable." His statement that "all normal persons, at one period or another of their development, experience a hunger for obscenity" will doubtless come as a shock to many, but Mr. Redman makes out a convincing case for his thesis.

Ben Ray Redman
IS CENSORSHIP POSSIBLE?

A great deal of ink has recently been poured out upon the subject of literary censorship, but it would seem that almost all of this ink has flowed around the fringes of the problem without reaching the heart of it. Secondary questions have been dwelt upon tediously and inconclusively, while a single primary question has been neglected. We have been asking "What is obscene?"

Ben Ray Redman, "Is Censorship Possible?" *Scribner's Magazine*, 87:515–17 (May, 1930), copyright 1930 by Charles Scribner's Sons. Reprinted by permission of the author.

and "Is censorship right or wrong?" when our first question, striking to the roots of the matter, should be: "Is censorship possible?" Simply that. Is censorship, as the censors themselves conceive it, possible; or are current censorial activities, however righteously inspired, based upon a fundamental misapprehension of the nature of the problem?

Briefly, I hold censorship to be impossible; I believe that the censorial organizations in this country, or any other, might be multiplied indefinitely, that they might be granted Czaristic powers, supported by the police, the full machinery of the law, and all good citizens, and that even then they would be incapable of accomplishing one jot or tittle of what they believe it their duty to accomplish. But, before moving on to argument and demonstration, let it be clear that we are here concerned only with the censor who would exterminate the corrupting influences of pornography and obscenity, not with the religious, political, or military censor. They are not within our scope; it is the "sex-censor" who is our quarry; and my purpose is to show that, although religious and political censorship can be moderately effective, and military censorship exceedingly effective, sex-censorship has never had and never will have a chance of accomplishing a fraction of its intention. It is conceivable that a religious censorship could ban from a community all writings that it deemed heretical and keep that community in ignorance of the fact that there was such a thing as heresy; it is history that many governments, for long periods, have been able to guard themselves quite effectively against subversive literature; and in our own day we have seen militaristic-patriotic propaganda flourish to the exclusion of enemy propaganda, and bear deadly fruit. But priest, statesman, and soldier are confronted by no such fundamental force as that against which the sex-censor levels his attack; and it is inconceivable that any sex-censorship can ever be effective, for the simple reason that such censorship must seek to control an uncontrollable force by the futile expedient of eliminating external stimuli that are infinitely replaceable. Its impotence resides in the fact that it can only do away with certain specific stimuli that it considers evil; it cannot diminish the desire for stimulation, and so long as that desire exists a dozen new stimuli can be found to take the place of every one that has been removed.

The sex-censor fights against the growing grass, and he can never number his enemies until the sands of the sea are counted grain by grain. His ideal could be realized only by destroying sex itself; in other words, by destroying life. But let us consider the matter more specifically.

Most thoughtful persons will agree, I think, that the gentlemen who frequented the bald-headed row of "The Black Crook" were excited in precisely the same way, and to the same degree, by the amply clothed ladies of the ensemble, as are the gentlemen who now pay speculators' prices for front-row seats by the "nude acts" in any of our current reviews. The thoughts and images that clustered behind those peering eyes of the day-before-yesterday were identical with the thoughts and images which obsessed the plump broker who was sitting on your left night before last. Today the contortion of a naked torso is called upon to do the work that was once accomplished by the twist of a padded hip. The stimulus has changed, but the satisfaction is the same, because the desire is the same, and it is a desire that will be satisfied willy-nilly. Turning to another familiar example, most male pedestrians must admit that the sight of a feminine ankle, seen beneath a lifted skirt, above a mud puddle, in 1908, was quite as stimulating to the questing masculine eye as were the bare female knees everywhere visible in 1928. Nor can there be any question that readers of "Three Weeks," which now seems almost mid-Victorian, once found the same vicarious carnal satisfaction that a newer generation discovers in the most erotic novels now falling from the press. The desire remains the same; the stimulus seized upon is any that happens to be at hand. And, in plain English, there is not a blooming thing that all the censors in the world can do about it.

But, some readers may protest, we must think of the welfare of the adolescent; even if we grant the adult the perilous right of self-censorship, even if we admit the impossibility of guarding the adult mind against its own baser desires, we are still charged with the duty of protecting our children from corruption. Their innocence must not be defiled. The faith upon which this argument rests is touching, but it is the faith of ignorance. No more than the adult can the child be protected against himself; whatever stimulation he seeks, he will find, despite a million censors. Parents shudder at the thought of obscene literature passing into the hands of their offspring, poisoning the springs of character and withering the tender shoots of personality; but even if they could destroy every obscene book on earth they would not have advanced one step nearer success in their protective efforts. The youngster who gets hold of a copy of "Only a Boy" may gloat over the series of obscene and erotic images that the tale evokes, and, as the spinster in "At Mrs. Beam's" was always remarking, "It's not a very nice thought, is it?" No, it is not a very nice thought, but the youngster who never encounters "Only a Boy," or any other classic of juvenile pornography, may get exactly the same thrill as his better-read contemporary by looking up recently learned and perfectly reputable words in the family dictionary. Such words as "harlot" and its good old Anglo-Saxon synonym will, when seen in print for the first time, prove quite as exciting to him as a whole chapter of "Mademoiselle de Maupin" may seem a few years later; and many an adolescent has found pages of "The Family Doctor," or some other medical work for household reference, sufficiently "corrupting" to satisfy him for months on end. Shall we, then, put all dictionaries, medical books, and encyclopædias on unreachable shelves? We may do so, but we shall gain nothing by the act. Growing boys get a great "kick" from obscene pictures, but if such pictures are unobtainable they will produce their own art work, based upon a fevered imagination and a knowledge that is often ludicrously inaccurate, and in the same way they write their own obscene literature on sidewalks, walls, and fences. Critical censorship must always be defeated by creative obscenity. Censorship, of any kind, is helpless because it is impotent to touch the root of the supposed evil that it would eradicate; so long as the obscene image is desired, an evocative and satisfying stimulus will be found.

The truth is that all normal persons, at one period or another of their development, experience a hunger for obscenity that is more or less intense, and whatever the intensity of the desire, great or little, the hunger is always satisfied in direct proportion to it, because it is a hunger that is capable of self-satisfaction. It feeds upon itself. External stimuli are fortuitous and their character is unimportant; the true stimulus is internal. In some persons this hunger, perhaps never troublesome, disappears at a comparatively early age; in others it makes itself intermittently felt throughout a lifetime; in still other, unfortunate, creatures it exercises a disastrous tyranny. It has been argued that censors, as a class, present an interesting case of arrested development when they are judged by their appetite for the obscene, but this is not the place for a repetition or elaboration of the argument. The point is that this hunger, whatever its degree of intensity, however short or long its span of influence, is beyond the reach of censorship. It will find food in the desert and satiety in a cell.

But, but, but—comes the protest, does this mean that you believe that any piece of writing, however lewd, lascivious, obscene, salacious and pornographic, within or without the meaning of any statute, might just as well be printed anywhere at any time? For all practical purposes, yes. Men will always seek, of course, to exercise some kind of censorship; communities will, according to their lights, always try to keep themselves "clean." But the apparent victories that are won on news-stands, in bookstores, and in theatres, must of necessity be inconsequential and satisfactory only to self-deluded persons. There is no real difference between a reader pruriently enjoying Frank Harris's "My Life and Loves," and a reader pruriently enjoying "Pamela," just as there is no real difference between the man who fixes a lascivious eye upon a chorus girl's naked thigh and a man who, with precisely the same emotions, lingers over some rotogravure photograph in which a comely pair of legs has been generously posed by a ship's cameraman. Obscenity does not reside in the stimulating object, but in the determined-to-be-stimulated subject; the sin, if sin there be, is not outside us, it is within. And that is the very simple explanation of why we can never arrive at a definition of obscenity: it assumes all forms, it is created by every individual for himself, from whatever materials may be available, according to the current dictates of his individual desire.

◻ In "Literature and Censorship," Father John Courtney Murray presents a deeply thoughtful discussion of problems involved in censoring so-called "obscene" literature. While written from the point of view of a liberal Catholic churchman, Father Murray's penetrating analysis considers fully the relationship of the state, of all types of private organizations, and of individuals to the philosophy and practice of censorship. His proposed four rules for the guidance of censoring bodies, if generally accepted and adhered to, would eliminate the major difficulties in this field. Certainly no believer in democratic government could question his fourth rule: "In a pluralist society no minority group has the right to impose its own religious or moral views on other groups, through the use of the methods of force, coercion, or violence."

John Courtney Murray
LITERATURE AND CENSORSHIP

In this difficult matter of censorship the casuistry is endless. Therefore, since this talk is supposed to have an end, it will be better to omit discussion of cases. Instead, I shall attempt to define certain central issues and to state some of the principles that bear upon their solution. We shall not be concerned with the problem of censorship in the areas of news or opinion, or of public morality in general, but only as it arises in the fields of literature and the arts. Here the perennial issue of obscenity has recently come to the fore.

The discipline of the Catholic Church in this matter is stated in canon 1399 of the Code of Canon Law. Among the eleven categories of books whose reading is *ipso iure* prohibited to Catholics the ninth is this: "Books which have for their principal purpose the description, narration, or teaching of matter lascivious or obscene." However, this canonical discipline is outside our present subject, which deals with the issue of censorship as it arises in the civil order.

An argument is sometimes set afoot about whether "the state," abstractly conceived, has or has not some right of censorship over the media of communications. And there is the complementary argument whether the individual writer or artist has or has not a right to absolute freedom of expression. These arguments I leave aside. We can start from a fact of political history, that every government has always claimed what is called police power, as an attribute of government.

John Courtney Murray, "Literature and Censorship," *Books on Trial* (now *The Critic*), 14:393–95+ (June–July, 1956), copyright 1956 by The Thomas More Association. Reprinted by permission of the author and of the publisher.

This power in itself is simply the principle of self-preservation and self-protection transferred to the body politic. It extends to the requirements of public morals, public health, public safety, public order, and the general comfort of society. The only question is, how far and in what circumstances does it extend to all these social values?

In virtue of the police power, society, acting through the agency of government, is entitled to impose restraints on property rights and on personal freedoms. The question is, what manner of restraints, under what conditions, is government thus empowered to impose, in restriction of rights and in restraint of freedom? These are the concrete questions that are relevant to censorship, which is, I take it, an exercise of the police power. It might, if you wish, be an exercise of what is called *patria potestas,* the emergency power which government is entitled to use, on occasion, to protect children and those who are *ad instar puerorum,* legally to be reckoned as children by reason of their helplessness. But the same concrete questions return: when and for what reasons and under what limitations is government empowered thus to act *in loco parentis?*

In addition to the problem of governmental or legal censorship there is the problem of censorship (at least in some wide sense of the word) as exercised by non-governmental bodies—by civic committees or voluntary associations of one sort or another. We shall also have to consider this aspect of the problem.

THE CENTRAL ISSUE

The issue that is central in the whole problem is the issue of social freedom. More exactly, it is the issue of striking a right balance between freedom and restraint in society. This is the most difficult problem of social science, to such an extent that all other difficulties are reducible to this one. No complete discussion is possible here; I shall simply make certain assertions, general in themselves, but relevant to our special problem.

First, in society constraint must be for the sake of freedom. It seems a paradox to assert that the imposition of a constraint must be justified by an increase in freedom, since every constraint is a decrease of freedom. What I mean, however, is that the constraint must create a freedom in another respect. Traffic regulations, for instance, are a constraint on freedom of movement on the streets; but they are justified because they create a freedom to move—at least, nowadays, in some minimal sense! Tax laws are a constraint on your freedom to do what you want with your money; but they create other freedoms—to live in security behind a national defense establishment, for instance. The whole texture of civilization is a web of restraints, which deliver man from a host of slaveries—to darkness, cold, and hunger; to ignorance and illness and wearisome labors. Delivered from these base slaveries man is free to be a man, to live the inner life of reason and love, the classic life of wisdom, the Christian life of faith.

The problem of constraint for the sake of freedom is difficult enough when it is only a question of organizing the material conditions of life. But it becomes even more inextricable when it is a question of organizing communications within society; for in this field religious and moral, intellectual and emotional values come into play. It is easy enough to see that the "press" (understood to mean all the media of communication) can be the vehicle both of corruptive and of beneficial influences. It is easy enough to say that corruptive influences ought to be put under reasonable restraints. And it is easy enough to define what you mean by corruptive influence; it is one which destroys or diminishes the rational freedom of man, either by damaging his power of personal reflection or by exciting his passions to the point where they interfere with his rational control of his thoughts and action. On these grounds you can certainly make a case against sexual propaganda of certain kinds as corruptive of human freedom. The influence of inordinate and unregulated sexual passion on the life of reason in man is a commonplace of human and historical experience. The susceptibility of youth to dominance by carnal desires, to the detriment of rational freedom, is particularly well documented—and hardly in need of documentation.

However, when you have made your case against these influences as socially corruptive, you have only reached the threshold of the problem of social freedom. Many questions remain. For instance, when and under what circumstances do these influences become so corruptive that they require animadversion by organized society itself? (It is presumed that the first solicitations of corruptive influences are resisted by the special resources of the family and the

Church.) Again, what agencies are to be enlisted against these influences—the public agencies of government and law, or the private agencies known as voluntary associations? Either or both? And to what extent each? Above all, what is the norm whose requirements are to be enforced, in one way or another, against influences that are corruptive? It is, of course, the norm of public order. But what requirements of public order can be made valid against the claims of freedom?

Even supposing these questions to have been satisfactorily answered, a further complicating consideration remains. The fact is that the imposition of constraints, the limitation of freedom, has consequences. They are numerous; but two require special notice.

First, if you impose a constraint on freedom in one domain, in order to increase freedom in another, you may take the risk of damaging freedom in a third domain, with consequences more dangerous to the community. Social freedom is a complex, whose constituent elements are closely interlocked. You may, for instance, wish to "clean up" political campaigns by limiting the freedom of the contestants to attack each other's personal integrity; but the means you take to this end may damage the freedom of the electoral process itself. Every constraint has multiple effects; it may impose restraints on a freedom which you would wish to see untouched.

There is, secondly, a consequent consideration. Because social freedoms interlock so tightly, it is not possible to know antecedently what the multiple effects of a regulation will be. At best, the effect you want can only be foreseen with probability, not certainty. And unforeseen effects may follow, with the result that a regulation, in itself sensible, may in the end do more harm than good.

For this reason, the social reformer whose only strength is a sense of logic may well be a menace. For instance, if drunkenness and alcoholism are social vices whose effect is to diminish and impair the free will of men (as indeed they are), the logical thing is to ban alcohol. Here in America we learned by experience the disastrous effects of that type of mad logic. In contrast, the illogicality of the liquor law in Belgium commends itself. The retail sale of liquor in public bars is forbidden, but you can get liquor if you go to a store and buy two quarts at once! When you unravel its seeming lack of logic, you find that the Belgian liquor law protects the citizen against his own reckless impulses, but permits him the freedom to act deliberately. This, of course, is his essential human freedom.

I should call attention here to the somewhat unique difficulties presented by the problem of the public enforcement of standards of sexual morality. Jacques Leclercq, of the Catholic University of Louvain, who is no slight authority, concludes a brief advertence to this subject with this remark: "In short, it may be said that no government has ever succeeded in finding a balanced policy of combating unhealthy sexual propaganda without injuring legitimate freedom or provoking other equally grave or worse disorders."

Everybody agrees that debauchery of the sexual faculty is morally wrong, and that incitement to such debauchery should be legally forbidden. On the other hand, in the case of incitement as open as houses of debauchery, a view that goes back to St. Augustine's treatise, *De ordine,* warns against the dangers of attempting a total coercive repression of this particular incitement.

The strictness of traditional Catholic doctrine in regard to sexual lust appalls the libertarian; the laxness of the many Catholic governments in the same regard equally appalls the Puritan. In 1517 the number of prostitutes in the city of Rome considerably surpassed the number of married women. And in 1592, under a Pope of formidable strictness, Sixtus V, there were more than 9,000 prostitutes amid a population of 70,000. This was in the capital of the papal states. The figures are not indeed edifying; but perhaps they are interesting, not least when one considers that during the same era the newly constituted Index of Forbidden Books was being used with extreme severity by successive Pontiffs (Paul IV, Pius IV, Pius V) against heretical propaganda. To this day the Italian who is merely amused by the obscene *pasquinade* is deeply offended by the earnest inanities of a Baptist minister from Texas.

To the proper Bostonian all this is profoundly shocking. Just as to the Continental European, especially if he is a Latin, the spectacle of the U.S.A. is infinitely puzzling. A man is free to call error truth, and truth error, if he likes; but he is not free to use the notorious four-letter word which, in direct French monosyllabic translation, is alleged to have escaped from the lips of Napoleon when he heard of the debacle of the sunken road at Waterloo. Again, the Supreme Court declares that the category of the sacrilegious is altogether indefinable, while the Post Office rules that Aristophanes' *Lysistrata* is an obscene book. This is indeed puzzling.

Considerations such as these would seem to indicate that the problem of social freedom is insoluble, if by solution is meant a simple formula that is applicable to all cases and similar for all countries. However, a community can do one important thing: it can decide on the general orientation it wishes to give to its particular solution. We have done this in the United States. We have constitutionally decided that the presumption is in favor of freedom, and that the advocate of constraint must make a convincing argument for its necessity or utility in the particular case.

I would only add that the presumption in favor of freedom does not rest on doctrinaire grounds. Its basis was not the philosophic rationalism that called itself Enlightenment, but only a political pragmatism more enlightened than the Enlightenment ever was, because it looked to the light of experience to illuminate the prudential norms necessary to guide it in handling a concrete social reality that is vastly complicated. In this light the option was made for the civil freedom of the citizen under a government whose powers are limited, and under a rule of the law whose reach is likewise limited, chiefly by the axiom that the constraints of law must serve the cause of essential human freedom.

In our case, the consequence of this fundamental option which gives a basic orientation to our constitutional law, is that freedom of expression is the rule, and censorship the exception. A more particular further consequence is the ban laid by the First Amendment (exceptional cases apart) on all prior restraint of communications, at the same time the government reserves the right to punish, subsequently, communications that offend against law. The freedom toward which the American people are fundamentally orientated is a freedom under God, a freedom that knows itself to be bound by the imperatives of the moral law. Antecedently it is presumed that a man will make morally and socially responsible use of his freedom of expression, hence there is to be no prior restraint on it. However, if his use of freedom is irresponsible, he is summoned after the fact to responsibility before the judgment of the law. There are indeed other reasons why prior restraint on communications is outlawed; but none are more fundamental than this.

CENSORSHIP AS A JURIDICAL PROCESS

After this brief discussion of the central issue involved in censorship I come to my proposition. It may be briefly stated thus: censorship in the civil order must be a juridical process. In using the word "juridical" I mean that the premises and objectives of the program should be defined in accord with the norms of good jurisprudence; that the forms of procedure should be properly judicial; and that the structure and workings of the process should be sustained by the consent of the community. I should maintain that this concept of a juridical process should be verified, *mutatis mutandis,* in every form of censorship, whether governmental or non-governmental.

GOVERNMENTAL OR LEGAL CENSORSHIP

Censorship exercised by public authority is obliged to be literally juridical, in the sense described. As a legal process this censorship is controlled by the canons of necessity or utility for the common good. That some degree of punitive censorship is necessary is sufficiently evident. Pornography, for instance, the kind of obscenity that is a perverse and vicious profanation of the sacredness of sex, seems to hold a permanent attraction for a portion of humanity. That it is a corruptive social influence is not to be denied; consequently, few would deny that its repression is necessary. Beyond this, how much more censorship is useful, and how useful is it? That seems to be the central question.

A preliminary answer is furnished by the principle, basic to jurisprudence, that morals and law are differentiated in character, and not coextensive in their functions. It is not the function of the legislator to forbid everything that the moral law forbids, or to enjoin everything that the moral law enjoins. The moral law governs the entire order of human conduct, personal and social; it extends even to motivations and interior acts. Law, on the other hand, looks only to the public order of human society; it touches only external acts, and regards only values that are formally social. For this reason the scope of law is limited. Moreover, though law is indeed a moral force, directive of human society to the common good, it relies ultimately for its observance on coercion. And men can be coerced only into a minimal amount of moral action. Again from this point of view the scope of law is limited.

Therefore the moral aspirations of law are minimal. Law seeks to establish and maintain only that minimum of actualized morality that is necessary for the healthy functioning of the social order. It does not look to what is morally desirable, or attempt to remove every moral taint from the atmosphere of society. It enforces only what is minimally acceptable, and in this sense socially necessary. Beyond this, society must look to other institutions for the elevation and maintenance of its moral standards—that is, to the Church, the home, the school, and the whole network of voluntary associations that concern themselves with public morality in one or other aspect.

Law and morality are indeed related, even though differentiated. That is, the premises of law are ultimately found in the moral law. And human legislation does look to the moralization of society. But, mindful of its own nature and mode of action, it must not moralize excessively; otherwise it tends to defeat even its own more modest aims, by bringing itself into contempt.

Therefore the law, mindful of its nature, is required to be tolerant of many evils that morality condemns. A moral condemnation regards only the evil itself, in itself. A legal ban on an evil must consider what St. Thomas calls its own "possibility." That is, will the ban be obeyed, at least by the generality? Is it enforceable against the disobedient? Is it prudent to undertake the enforcement of this or that ban, in view of the possibility of harmful effects in other areas of social life? Is the instrumentality of coercive law a good means for the eradication of this or that social vice? And, since a means is not a good means if it fails to work in most cases, what are the lessons of experience in the matter? What is the prudent view of results—the long view or the short view? These are the questions that jurisprudence must answer, in order that legislation may be drawn with requisite craftsmanship.

It is, in fact, the differentiated character of law and morals that justifies the lawyer or judge when he insists that punitive censorship statutes should be clearly drawn, with the margin of uncertainty as narrow as possible.

The net of all this is that no society should expect very much in the way of moral uplift from its censorship statutes. Indeed the whole criminal code is only a minimal moral force. Particularly in the field of sexual morality the expectations are small; as I have suggested, they are smaller here than anywhere else. It is a sort of paradox, though an understandable one, that the greater the social evil, the less effective against it is the instrument of coercive law. Philip Wylie may have been right in saying that American society "is technically insane in the matter of sex." If so, it cannot be coerced into sanity by the force of law. In proportion as literary obscenity is a major social evil, the power of the police against it is severely limited.

This brings up the matter of consent. Law is indeed a coercive force; it compels obedience by the fear of penalty. However, a human society is inhumanly ruled when it is ruled only, or mostly, by fear. Good laws are obeyed by the generality because they are good laws; they merit and receive the consent of the community, as valid legal expressions of the community's own convictions as to what is just or unjust, good or evil. In the absence of this consent law either withers away or becomes tyrannical.

The problem of popular consent to the order of law and to its manifold coercions becomes critical in a pluralist society, such as ours. Basic religious divisions lead to conflict of moral views; certain asserted "rights" clash with other "rights" no less strongly asserted. And the divergences are often irreducible. Nevertheless, despite all the pluralism, some manner of consensus must support the order of law to which the whole community and all its groups are commonly subject. This consensus must include, in addition to other agreements, an agreement on certain rules which regulate the relations of the divergent groups among one another, and their common relation to the order of law. In what concerns our present subject of censorship, I suggest that there are four such rules. Before stating them I would note that in the United States at present all the religious groups are—from the sociological, even if not from the statistical, point of view—minority groups.

First, within the larger pluralist society each minority group has the right to censor for its own members, if it so chooses, the content of the various media of communication, and to protect them, by means of its own choosing, from materials considered harmful according to its own standards.

Second, in a pluralist society no minority group has the right to demand that government should impose a general censorship, affecting all the citizenry, upon any medium of communication, with a view to punishing the communication of materials that are judged to be harmful according to the special standards held within one group.

Third, any minority group has the right to work toward the elevation of standards of public morality in the pluralist society, through the use of the methods of persuasion and pacific argument.

Fourth, in a pluralist society no minority group has the right to impose its own religious or moral views on other groups, through the use of the methods of force, coercion, or violence.

I cannot pause here to demonstrate the reasonableness and justice of these four rules. I would only note that they are not put forth as rules that were made in heaven, necessarily inherent in the constitution of an "ideal" society. On the contrary, they are to be considered as rules made on earth, by the practical reason of man, for application in the conditions—by no means "ideal"—of a religiously and morally divided society. Agreement on them would seem to be necessary in the common interests of social peace. Their supposition is the jurisprudential proposition that what is commonly imposed by law on all our citizens must be supported by general public opinion, by a reasonable consensus of the whole community. At the same time they suppose that within a pluralist society the minority groups have certain definite, if limited, rights to influence the standards and content of public morality. The statement of these rules leads to the next subject.

NON-GOVERNMENTAL CENSORSHIP

In the United States there are a multitude of voluntary agencies which exercise some measure of surveillance, judgment, and even control of various media of communication. For the most part they shy away from the idea of being called "censoring" agencies. We need not quibble over the word; the frequent fact is that many of them achieve the results of censorship, even when they refuse the name. With regard to these agencies I should maintain the general proposition stated above—that their censoring should also be a juridical process, if not literally, certainly in spirit.

The juridical premise of their action is not in doubt. In the United States it is generally acknowledged that the voluntary association is entitled to concern itself actively with matters that relate to the public welfare. It is invidious to stigmatize all such associations as "pressure-groups," pursuing "private interests." The fact is that, in their own way, they can perform a public function.

The more difficult question concerns the methods used by these associations or committees. There can be no slightest quarrel when they use simply the methods of persuasion; that is, when they appeal for voluntary cooperation on the grounds of a common moral and social responsibility. Thus, for instance, many associations interested in decent literature and movies (surely a public interest) seek the responsible cooperation of producers and theater-owners, of publishers and distributors, with a view at least to diminishing the volume of obscenity, or other objectionable features, in these media. Surely here all is entirely rightful and prudent.

Other methods—at the other end of the spectrum, so to speak—seem to have at least the appearance of coercion. As an example one might take the organized boycott, against a merchant, a theater, etc. It is a sort of "consumers' strike"; it is sometimes accompanied by picketing; it normally involves some form of economic sanctions invoked against the offending party. What is to be thought of such methods?

It will be agreed that the use of formal coercion in society is reserved to public authority and its agencies of law. Coercion of a more informal kind—through economic pressures, etc.—is also employed by various associations that do not hesitate to identify themselves as "power-groups." Such for instance, is a trade union. It does indeed seem a bit incongruous that other types of voluntary association, concerned with values that are spiritual and moral, aesthetic and cultural, should pursue their ends by what appear to be the methods of power rather than of persuasion. On the other hand, it is not possible to prove the position, taken by some, that an action like the boycott of a moving-picture is somehow "unrightful," or "unconstitutional," or "undemocratic." No one can show that such an action lies beyond the limits of a primeval American right to protest and object. The action may indeed be strenuous; but the American right to protest and object is permitted to run to some pretty strenuous extremes.

This said, against the doctrinaire, it remains true that methods of action which verge upon the coercive exhibit some incongruity when used by citizen-groups in the interests of morality in literature or on the screen. Even if they raise no issue of abstract right, they do raise the concrete issue of prudence, which, equally with justice, is one of the cardinal virtues. The issue rises most sharply in the case of Catholic associations. The chief danger is lest the Church itself be identified in the public mind as a power-association. The identification is injurious; it turns unto a hatred of the faith. And it has the disastrous effect of obscuring from the public view the true visage of the Church as God's kingdom of truth and freedom, justice and love. Our purpose is to stand before the world as men and women of faith, and therefore of reason too, whose reliance is on the methods of reason and not of force. We would wish always to be men and women of courage, ready to face any issue; but also men and women of prudence, who understand the art of procedure, and understand too that we are morally bound, by the virtue of prudence, to a concrete rightness of method in the pursuit of moral aims.

It should be noted too that prudence is an intellectual virtue, a refinement of intelligence. It may therefore properly be asked, how intelligent is it to have recourse to methods that approach coercion in this delicate field of censorship? Few things are worse than to make oneself ridiculous. And when an effort to coerce is made at the dictates of stupidity, the result arouses ridicule as well as resentment.

This brings up the question, who is competent to censor, even in some extralegal fashion? To say that all censorship should be a juridical process is to say by implication that it ought to be intelligently done. This means close attention to the qualifications of the censor. Here the example of the Church is instructive. In his reform of the discipline of censorship Benedict XIV laid great stress on the rule that the censor is to possess professional competence in the particular field in which he is called upon to pass judgment. Censorship is no job for the amateur. Like stress is placed on the censor's obligation to perform his task impartially, in the fullness of the judicial spirit that forbids the intrusion of any private likes or dislikes. In the process of censorship there is no room for the personal, the arbitrary, the passionate. The censor is not called upon for a display of moral indignation; he is asked only for a judgment, calm and cool, objective and unemotional. So too in the civil sphere, the less we have of moral indignation, and the more we have of professional competence and an unclouded faculty of judgment, the better it will be for the juridical nature of the censorship process.

In what concerns the problem of obscenity I would not discount the value of what is called the "common estimation" of men. People in general have a fairly clear notion of what obscenity is. And people in general can make, for themselves, a pretty good judgment on whether a particular work is obscene. Certainly the Code of Canon Law seems to suppose that the ordinary Catholic can make this concrete judgment for himself. I repeat, for himself. The question is, who can make it for others, i.e., as a censor.

Here a distinction is in order. Certainly the ordinary father and mother ought to be qualified to act as censors within the family. And to decide what their children may or may not be prudently exposed to, in the way of reading, movies, etc. But I should not think that the ordinary father or mother, *qua* such, are qualified to act as censor within society at large, or to decide what literature and movies may be displayed before the general public. Society has an interest in the artist's freedom of expression which is not necessarily shared by the family. If adult standards of literature would be dangerous for children, a child's standard of literature is rather appalling to an adult. If therefore any censorship is to be administered in the interest of society, the professional competence of the literary critic must play a role in the process.

Here perhaps the characteristic Catholic care for the welfare of children (often coupled with the typically American cult of the child-centered home) ought to be aware of a danger. The contemporary argument about censorship is sometimes described as a "battle between the literati and the philistines." The description is snobbish, if you will. But it would be lamentable if Catholics were to go over to the camp of the philistines. After all, we do stand, not only within the oldest religious tradition of the Western world, but also within its most venerable tradition of intellect, literature, and art. The tradition has produced great achievements in writing, painting, and the plastic arts. Not all of them are fit for children indeed—not even the Bible in all its parts. But that is no justification for any form of philistinism.

In one further and final respect the process of extralegal censorship ought to be juridical, pursued in the spirit of law—that is, in its adoption of minimal aims. Fussiness is out of order. There ought to be a few, only a few, areas of concentration, in which a little bit (if not much) can be done. I suggest that the chief area is the "pornography of violence," as it has been called. Mischief enough is done by the obscenities that occur in the portrayal of illicit love (by literary hacks who never learned what the genuine artist knows instinctively—that, though art may "say all," there are certain things it is never allowed to say explicitly). But here sex is at least rescued from full profanation by its tenuous connection with love, as love is still resident in lust. However, when sex is associated with, and becomes symbolic of, the hatreds and hostilities, the angers and cruelties, that lie deep in men and women, the profanation of the most sacred thing in sex—its relation to love and to the hope of human life—is almost complete. It could move perhaps only one step deeper into the diabolical—in that association of sex and blasphemy that pervades the Black Mass.

The image of the truly evil thing in the obscenities of our day is seen on the typical cover of the "tough" kind of pocket-book—the semi-nude woman, with a smoking gun in her hand. The scene is one of impurity, but that is its lesser evil. The real evil is the violence in the impure scene. There is the perversion. If some restraint could be imposed upon this pornography of violence—so damning in its revelation of a vice in our culture—it would indeed be a moral achievement.

CONCLUSION

It is a good thing to keep our problems in perspective. Our chief problem, of course, is not literary censorship, but literary creation. This is true in the Church. She has no trouble in finding censors; but she prays continually that God may give her men of learning who can write the works that need to be written. The American Catholic community particularly needs to attend seriously to this problem of literary creation. Leo XIII is indeed remembered for his revision of the Index of Forbidden Books. But he was not the first Pope to point to the dangers of reading bad books. It is his great glory that he was the first Pope to say, in substance and effect, in a multitude of discourses, that today there is great danger in not reading good books. This is why I think it is a fine thing for the Thomas More Association to sponsor a lecture on censorship—once every seventeen years! Now it may resume the high apostolic function which it has been splendidly performing.

Published with ecclesiastical approval.

Chapter VI
Political subversion and censorship

Since the end of World War II no issue has split the American people more profoundly or caused more unfortunate international repercussions than the question of subversion. When is subversion real and when merely imagined? What is the difference between legitimate criticism of governmental actions and procedures and giving aid and comfort to the enemy? Are charges of subversion, so freely thrown about in recent years by officials in high and low places, solidly based or simply devices to gain political advantage?

The American form of government, and the English from which it evolved, are founded on freedom of expression. Only in this way, is our assumption, can the citizens of a country be fully informed about public affairs and be qualified to exercise their democratic prerogatives. No official is presumed to be above criticism. As Judge Learned Hand wrote in the case of *United States v. Dennis* in 1950, freedom of speech "rests upon a skepticism as to all political orthodoxy, upon a belief that there are no impregnable political absolutes, and that a flux of tentative doctrines is preferable to any authoritative creed."

This point was further clarified and emphasized by David Fellman in his *The Censorship of Books:*

"Our political system recognizes the essentially contingent character of ideas and institutions. It is, basically, a methodology for making and unmaking and remaking political decisions.

But in addition, as the Continental Congress noted so many years ago, freedom to discuss is built upon apprehensions concerning the use of power by those who have in their hands that enormous leviathan, the state machinery. It is rooted in a profound skepticism about the nature of human nature, and therefore exposes the men of power to ceaseless criticism and political opposition. Our system denies the legitimacy of either permanent or absolute power, and rejects the assumptions concerning human infallibility which lie at the base of a closed society."

Thus does the democratic form of government differ in its fundamental concepts from the communistic, the fascist, the monarchial, the oligarchic, or any other founded on authoritarian principles. The American system and structure of government are inconceivable without almost unlimited freedom of speech and press, for, as Woodrow Wilson stated in his *Constitutional Government in the United States,* "Nothing chills nonsense like exposure to the air; nothing dispels folly like its publication; nothing so eases the machine as the safety valve."

There are sincere and earnest, but doubtless misguided, citizens who maintain that the troubled era through which we are now living is different and consequently we can no longer afford the luxury of free expression. The survival of the race appears to many to be at stake. As man has perfected instruments of warfare capable of destroying the world, fear and tension have become constant factors in everyday life. How natural it is, therefore, to demand that books dealing with disliked political ideologies be suppressed, that libraries be purged of Communist literature, that extreme precautions be taken against radicals in government service and in universities. These are perfectly normal reactions to suspicion and hatred of an enemy. Nevertheless, the clear-thinking political scientist, looking back at history, would insist that we cannot emulate the methods of our enemies without becoming like them. Further, he would maintain that much of our strength as a nation lies in the basic rights and protections enumerated in the U.S. Constitution, particularly in the First Amendment, relating to freedom of speech, press, and assembly.

These are some of the momentous issues analyzed by the group of distinguished commentators whose papers are included in the present chapter.

Julian P. Boyd, historian and editor, and head of the Princeton University Library, 1940–52, is firmly convinced that Americans have the strength of mind and of character to reject unsound doctrines when they see them in print. Since 1950, Boyd has been editor of Thomas Jefferson's papers, ultimately expected to fill fifty printed volumes. In "Subversive of What?" he considers some lessons learned from Jefferson as to the nature of subversion and loyalty, especially in relation to our own time.

Julian P. Boyd
SUBVERSIVE OF WHAT?

In 1813 a native of France by the name of Regnault de Bécourt published a book entitled *Sur la Création du Monde, ou Système d'Organisation Primitive.* He and his book would have been forgotten long since if he had not written a letter to the one person in America who, more than any other, was in the habit of buying, reading, and appraising the literature of the past and present—Thomas Jefferson. The title of the forthcoming work intrigued Jefferson. A book on the creation of the world seemed to the great scholar-statesman at Monticello to give promise of being either a geological or an astronomical treatise. He thereupon subscribed for the work, received it in due course, and authorized payment of the two dollars that the book cost.

Authorization of payment involved another Frenchman, a well-known bookseller of Philadelphia by the name of Nicholas Dufief, an ardent bibliophile who had been selling books to Jefferson for more than a decade. Dufief promptly paid Bécourt the two dollars. The transaction was apparently at an end, save only for the fact that Jefferson could not avoid being disappointed in so trivial a work as that of Bécourt, which turned out to be neither a geological nor an astronomical work, but merely an infantile attack on the system of philosophy of Sir Isaac Newton.

But this simple book purchase was very far from being at an end. A few months after Dufief

---

Julian P. Boyd, "Subversive of What?" *Atlantic Monthly,* 182:19–23 (August, 1948), copyright 1948 by the Atlantic Monthly Co. Reprinted by permission of the author and of the publisher.

had paid Bécourt the two dollars, the Philadelphia constabulary visited the bookshop and hailed him into court on the charge of vending subversive if not blasphemous literature. Whereupon Dufief in great anxiety and distress appealed to Jefferson, urging him to set the minions of the law right by informing them that he, Dufief, had not actually sold the book but had merely acted as Jefferson's agent in a financial transaction.

Jefferson of course immediately complied with the urgent request of the bookseller. He stated the facts succinctly and accurately, no doubt satisfying both Dufief and the Philadelphia magistrates. But while this may have been enough for Mr. Dufief, who was interested only in keeping out of the toils of the law, or for the Philadelphia magistrates, who were determined only to safeguard American institutions, it was very far from being enough to satisfy the author of the American philosophy of government.

Jefferson thereupon stated in his own incomparable way the true nature of the issue involved. The issue, as he presented it, was one that made the fact of Dufief's arrest a trivial and irrelevant circumstance. It was an issue as great as the cause of America itself, involving one of the fundamental precepts upon which the philosophy of Jefferson and of his country rested. It was the same issue, indeed, that had earlier called forth the unforgettable declaration that now stands carved upon one of the three great monuments of our national capital: "I have sworn upon the altar of God eternal hostility against every form of tyranny over the mind of man." It was the issue to which Jefferson devoted his entire life, invariably upholding the oath he had taken in defense of free inquiry.

"I really am mortified," he declared in his letter to Dufief, "to be told that, *in the United States of America,* a fact like this can become a subject of inquiry, and of criminal inquiry too, as an offense against religion: that a question about the sale of a book can be carried before the civil magistrate. Is this then our freedom of religion? And are we to have a censor whose imprimatur shall say what books may be sold, and what we may buy? And who is thus to dogmatize religious opinions for our citizens? Whose foot is to be the measure to which ours are all to be cut or stretched? Is a priest to be our inquisitor? Or shall a layman, simple as ourselves, set up his reason as the rule for what we are to read, and what we must believe?

"It is an insult to our citizens to question whether they are rational beings or not; and blasphemy against religion to suppose it cannot stand a test of truth and reason. If M. de Bécourt's book be false in its facts, disprove them; if false in its reasoning, refute it. But, for God's sake, let us freely hear both sides, if we choose. I know little of its contents, having barely glanced over here and there a passage and over the table of contents. From this the Newtonian philosophy seemed the chief object of attack, the issue of which might be trusted to the strength of the two combatants; Newton certainly not needing the auxiliary arm of the government, and still less the holy author of our religion as to what in it concerns him. I thought the work would be very innocent and one which might be confided to the reason of any man; not likely to be much read, if let alone, but if persecuted it will be generally read. Every man in the United States will think it a duty to buy a copy, in vindication of his right to buy, and to read what he pleases. . . .

"But," Jefferson concluded, "it is impossible that the laws of Pennsylvania, which set us the first example of the wholesome and happy effects of religious freedom, can permit these inquisitorial functions to be proposed to their courts. Under them you are surely safe."

Impossible? Dufief was safe, for he had a stalwart champion and the generation that had fought for the great cause of American liberties in the Revolution was still on the scene, still determined to admit no failure of the proposition to which they had dedicated their lives and sacred honor. That proposition was grounded upon the belief that man was innately good rather than evil; that he was endowed by nature with certain indefeasible rights; that, if the yoke of tyranny in every form were removed, man's natural reason and humane instincts would lead him to prefer justice to injustice, equality to privilege, independence of mind to servile obedience to authority, rational judgments to superstition, ignorance, and bigotry; and that, finally, in order to achieve this end and to give mankind full freedom to pursue this course and to govern himself in accordance with its high ideals, it was absolutely essential that every man should have free access to knowledge, unopposed by any barriers that might be erected by any authority.

This was not a new ideal or a new faith. It was what Milton called "the good old cause" and its lineage could be traced through many countries and many ages. But old as it was as an ideal, no government in history had adopted it as a philosophy until Jefferson and his compatriots brought forth a union indissolubly linked with the cause of liberty.

This philosophy sustained and informed all of Jefferson's private thinking and public acts. But he was too much a realist not to know that mankind had a peculiar susceptibility to folly, superstition, and the easy and comfortable inclination of yielding obedience to authority. He believed mankind capable of progress, but only if men were free to know their rights and privileges. The people must be free to form their own opinions and to exercise their native reason untrammeled by authority.

Jefferson's devotion to the Union and his belief in the people required courage as well as faith. For the issue of liberty versus authority arbitrarily exercised was one that he was obliged to face in the arena of practical politics. In 1798 the party in power, fearful of the threat of foreign ideas and their subversive tendencies, enacted the Alien and Sedition Acts which made it a criminal offense for "brawlers against government" to voice opinions considered dangerous or revolutionary.

Jefferson declared these acts to be as palpably unconstitutional in their infringement of the right of free speech as if Congress had ordered the citizens of the United States to bow down and worship a golden calf. More, he brought forth the Virginia-Kentucky Resolutions, a weapon that he used reluctantly and with caution, for the doctrine of nullification on which these resolutions rested pointed straight toward disunion. But, he must have reasoned, since liberty and the Union were one cause, of what value was the Union if its powers were used to destroy those liberties guaranteed by the Declaration of Independence and the Bill of Rights?

Fortunately, the ultimate recourse to disunion was not necessary. The verdict of the people whose rights Jefferson was defending was an overwhelming verdict. In 1800 those who had attempted to suppress dissent were dispossessed of their offices and their legislative authority. Aiming their blows directly at Jefferson and his supposedly dangerous following, the Federalists succeeded only in committing political suicide and in elevating their most conspicuous enemy to the chief magistracy. A self-confident nation, inspired by the steadfast faith of one who had not separated himself by fear or distrust from the bulk of his countrymen, had taken heart from his example.

Jefferson recognized the implications of this verdict in his First Inaugural. Many, he knew, had doubted the permanence of the Union and had questioned the ability of the nation to survive such a political revolution as it had just experienced. "I know indeed," he declared, "that some honest men have feared that a republican government cannot be strong; that this government is not strong enough. . . . I believe this, on the contrary, the strongest government on earth." It was strongest, Jefferson meant, in its reliance upon a great ideal lying in the hearts and minds of its people, without which armies and economic power and even constitutions would be valueless.

Nowhere in American annals has this spirit of tolerance of dissent received a more transcendent expression than in these words from Jefferson's great First Inaugural: *"If there be any among us who wish to dissolve this union or to change its republican form, let them stand undisturbed as monuments of the safety with which error of opinion may be tolerated where reason is left free to combat it."*

II

The discoveries of the nineteenth and twentieth centuries have made it philosophically and historically impossible for us to cling to the absolutes that Jefferson accepted as self-evident. There are no absolutes in the twentieth century —at least we think there are none—and the concept of natural law is no longer accepted as fixed and unchallengeable. Yet, even though we think ourselves justified in discarding as untenable the basic assumption upon which the Jeffersonian philosophy rested, the gravest question that we can ask ourselves is whether we are justified in discarding the system along with its premises. Do we dare discard the rights of man along with the concept of natural law?

The least we can do in attempting to answer this grave question, reaching to the roots of all organized society and its institutions, is to know what it is that we propose to do if we discard both the premise and the conclusion. The least we can do if we engage now in what Jefferson would have regarded as a palpable violation of individual rights of opinion and conscience is to be conscious of what we are doing and to do it with a full realization of the consequences that may flow from our actions. Have we done this much?

Have we consciously and deliberately come to the conclusion that Jefferson's tolerance of subversive ideas and of disloyal dissent can no longer be justified? If so, on what grounds have we reached that conclusion? Are we doing it in the name of liberty if not of natural law? If so, what kind of liberty? Jefferson would scarcely have understood our use of the term liberty if in its name we attempt to control the way in which men speak or the thoughts which they express or the intellectual investigations which they undertake. He would have called it tyranny and he would have fought it with every resource at his command.

Let us return to Dufief, the bookseller who was anxious to keep out of jail. Jefferson, you will recall, felt that Dufief had nothing to fear under the liberal laws of Pennsylvania. He felt that it was impossible that in the United States of America, founded upon confidence in man's reason and ability to choose the truth, a citizen could be denied the right to purchase a book because of its ideas or arguments, however erroneous, or that a bookseller could be hailed before the magistrates because he had sold such a book. But is it impossible for us?

It is not only not impossible or improbable but is indeed an actual and sickening fact. Today, at this moment, both civil and criminal causes are being tried in the city in which Dufief lived. These causes arise largely because of the instigation of an ecclesiastical hierarchy and also of some of those who are supposed to be the direct heirs of that Reformation which established the right of men to judge for themselves in matters of conscience. At this instigation police officers arrested booksellers and seized not one book but two thousand, without compensation, because in the opinion of these self-appointed censors some books were subversive of morals or institutions or were dangerous for other men to read.

The seizure of books, some of them used in college instruction, is only one incident in a mounting demand for conformity. The House of Representatives passed by an overwhelming majority a bill which would have made Thomas Jefferson liable to imprisonment and fine if he had voiced the opinion in the First Inaugural that I have just quoted—a bill establishing so firmly the dangerous principle of "guilt by association" that it may limit the right to publish books because of the author's politics or because of the political views expressed.

The preamble of this so-called Subversive Activities Control Act declares its justification to be that of protecting American institutions and the nation itself from infiltration by those who would establish a totalitarian dictatorship. How can we justify so far-reaching a piece of legislation except on the fundamental assumption that the people cannot be trusted to distinguish truth and error?

This bill was sponsored by the House Committee on Un-American Activities. Though it pays lip service to the First Amendment, it is comparable only to the Alien and Sedition Acts of 1798, acts which Thomas Jefferson regarded as so subversive, so destructive of everything that the American Union stood for, that he was driven along the pathway toward disunion in his attempt to defeat so gross a violation of individual right.

But this bill and its sponsoring committee are only the larger symptoms of a disease that is epidemic throughout the country. The public press, the great instrument for the protection of our liberties which Jefferson preferred to government itself, has shamefully acquiesced. Not only acquiesced; but, shaken by the fear of a common foe, distrustful of the ability of the people to distinguish between right and wrong, has actually helped to produce the hysteria that would compel uniformity.

Editors have approved tacitly or explicitly the withdrawal of textbooks and the expulsion of teachers whose ideas do not conform to the established economic or political views; they have aided in compelling educators, school boards, trustees, and others to yield to the pressures of unofficial groups that object to dissenting opinion in the realm of economics, politics, or religion. They have committed the ultimate disloyalty to their trust by attempting to command loyalty, overlooking the simple fact that loyalty cannot be commanded but can only be deserved. Educators, editors, librarians, even those scholars who hold, or at least have the responsibility of defending, the last citadel of civil rights, have all but capitulated to the wave of fear and distrust that is now sweeping over us. Too many have acted the part of Dufief, putting themselves first; too few the part of Jefferson, defending his country's principles at all costs.

III

Just where will this demand for conformity, for unquestioning loyalty, lead? Thomas Jefferson, for one, was certain that it would not lead to human enlightenment, to progress, or to the fullest expressions of reason, justice, and equity toward which our nation directed its early course.

"I join you therefore," he wrote to one of his young protégés after the passage of the Alien and Sedition Acts, "in branding as cowardly the idea that the human mind is incapable of further advances. This is precisely the doctrine that the present despots of the earth are inculcating, and their friends are re-echoing: and applying especially to religion and politics; that it is not probable anything better will be discovered than what was known to our fathers. We are to look backward then and not forward for the improvement of science, and to find it amidst feudal barbarisms and the fires of Spitalfields. But thank heaven the American mind is already too much opened, to listen to these impostures; and while the art of printing is left to us, science can never be retrograde; what is once acquired of real knowledge can never be lost."

But to what advantage, we may ask Jefferson, is the art of printing if what is printed must conform to the established pattern? Of what value is the vaunted public press or our institutions of higher learning, dedicated to the progress of the mind in all fields, when the trustees of the University of Wyoming appoint a committee to examine textbooks for "subversive" material? Of what value is our professed ideal of free education, of the untrammeled pursuit of knowledge, when we acquiesce in the action of the Newark Board of Education which removed certain periodicals from school libraries? What precisely do we mean by liberty as we contemplate the magnates of Hollywood who, in trembling haste, toss sacrifices to a clamoring committee of Congress and beat their breasts in loud protestation of their innocence of a charge that none but the Un-American Activities Committee could bring against them with a straight face—the charge that they employ revolutionists to prepare their mediocre art?

These are only a few specific incidents and they are taken at random. Every day's news adds to the list and the most thoughtful educators are becoming increasingly concerned with this growing threat to a basic concept of American institutions. It is not without significance that large numbers of professors in our institutions of higher learning have signed petition after petition throughout the country, protesting against the proposed Act of Congress sponsored by the Committee on Un-American Activities. Their petitions have uniformly condemned both the bill and the activities of the committee itself as being subversive of the ideals for which this country has traditionally stood. I think such testimonials cannot be dismissed as the statements of paid hirelings of a foreign totalitarianism. These men have fought Milton's "good old cause" on too many fronts and they have sacrificed too much in the cause of education to be charged with such a calumny. Nor can they be dismissed as theorists, visionaries, and crackpots, unrealistic in their views and out of touch with the world of affairs: for these are the men—some of them at least—who formed the chief reliance of this nation in the scientific knowledge which shortened World War II and brought success to American arms.

Responsible heads of the public press who point in commendation to the Committee on Un-American Activities in its shameless pillorying of American citizens and in its flagrant disregard of rights and liberties are either ignorant of the nature and the extent of the protest that is beginning to swell or they value suppression more than they value our freedom or they are deliberately misleading their public. In any event, history has proved time and again that the cause they espouse is a shameful and a futile cause. They lack the vision and the courage that led Jefferson in the infancy of our nation to defy any threat in the realm of ideas, not by suppression but by tolerance. They have little faith and in its place they offer what Jefferson declared to be an insult to the American citizenry—the insult of saying in effect that Americans cannot be trusted to read or to understand or to discriminate. They fear a foreign ideology, unaware of the fact that here at home the liberty that they profess to cherish is in danger of being done to death in the house of friends and with their aid.

I do not impugn the motives of those legislators, editors, educators, and others who have adopted this mistaken course. I do not doubt their devotion to this nation. I do not question their loyalty to the high ideals of a free press. But I do affirm that the methods they have supported in this present issue put them on the side of the enemies of the "good old cause" of Milton and of Jefferson. Those who have adopted this course of compulsory loyalty, though they might disagree with me on everything else, would I think join me in saying that Thomas Jefferson, more than any other single American, can rightfully be regarded as the great spokesman for our ideals and our liberties.

IV

All this, it may very properly be said, is beside the point. Jefferson's agricultural economy, for this nation at least, is a thing of the past, however realistic his philosophy may have been for such an economy at the time he lived. The twentieth century is a century of science and industry and technological power. Under such circumstances, is it not likely that Jefferson would have changed his views, would have given up his eternal values and absolutes as we have given them up, would have recognized the necessity of opposing evil to the utmost limits, however much an individual here and there might suffer?

I think it is undoubtedly true that Jefferson, always a realist and a man of practical statesmanship, would have viewed our problems in the light of our knowledge. Since he was a relativist in a world of absolutes, he would probably be more so in a relativistic world. Though he knew history as few in his generation did, he looked to it for perspective, not for dogmatic authority. He would very likely have regarded it as cowardly of us to look to him as our sole guidance. The earth, he declared, belongs to the living. "Can one generation bind another and all others in succession forever?" he asked. "I think not. The Creator has made the earth for the living not the dead. . . . A generation may bind itself as long as its majority continues in life; when that has disappeared, another majority is in place, holds all the rights and powers their predecessors once held and may change their laws and institutions to suit themselves. Nothing then is unchangeable but the inherent and inalienable rights of man." But he also declared that justice is the fundamental law of society and that "the majority, oppressing an individual, is guilty of a crime, abuses its strength, and by acting on the law of the strongest breaks up the foundations of society."

It may be that today, because we have achieved such an excess of power and knowledge beyond our ability to manage, we cannot afford the tolerance and the free flow and interchange and clash of ideas that he advocated. I do not think so. At least, if this is so, the alternative evil to which we must turn in our dilemma is worse than the evil from which we fly, simply because of the vast power now in our hands. But even if this were true, let us be honest. Let us not exercise this power of the majority to suppress the rights of individuals and call it the honored name by which our liberties have come down to us. Let us not call it a free republic whose principles we deny while we commit acts that desecrate its name. Let us frankly, solemnly, and with a full realization of what we are doing and what consequences we may draw from our actions, admit that we no longer believe in the ideals that made us great.

I for one do not fear the outcome. The verdict in the twentieth century will, I believe, be what it was in 1800 and what it was in the Age of the Reformation. I believe with Jefferson that "in every country where man is free to think and speak, differences of opinion will arise from differences of perception, and the imperfection of reason; that these differences when permitted, as in this happy country, to purify themselves by free discussion, are but as passing clouds overspreading our land transiently and leaving our horizon more bright and serene."

But I believe also that we cannot wait complacently on the calm assumption that this will come about through acquiescence or through temporary yielding to pressures of authority or through letting the storm spend itself. It will come about only when, as Jefferson said, "to preserve the freedom of the human mind and freedom of the press every spirit should be ready to devote itself to martyrdom; for as long as we may think as we will and speak as we think, the condition of man will proceed in improvement."

The alternative that he implied was obvious: deny this freedom, acquiesce in this abridgment of our liberties—and the promise of improvement of the human race would diminish or cease. If, then, the power that we have achieved in the twentieth century, which is nothing less than the power of planetary destruction, is so great as to deny us the rights that have been achieved over the centuries, let us frankly acknowledge that the price of this denial is the loss of our promise of moral and intellectual improvement. It is a price so fearfully exacting as to make man's future one of mere existence and not of destiny. It is a price that mankind has steadfastly refused to pay.

With the possible exception of Allan Nevins, a colleague at Columbia, Henry Steele Commager is the most prolific American historian functioning today. Indeed, as one biographer noted, "it is difficult to locate the man behind the works." From 1926 to 1938, Commager was a member of the New York University history faculty. He then joined and has remained in the Columbia University faculty.

Among Commager's numerous books are several pertaining directly to freedom, including *Majority Rule and Minority Rights, The American Mind, Living Ideas in America,* and *Freedom, Loyalty, Dissent.* Commager has frequently been characterized as a Jeffersonian Democrat, and he himself has stated that the American historian he most admires is Vernon Parrington, who was also a Jeffersonian with a liberal slant of mind.

No one has more vigorously and honestly presented the case for freedom of speech and for adherence to the liberties which made America great than does Commager in "Free Enterprise in Ideas." Elsewhere in *Freedom, Loyalty, Dissent,* from which this essay is taken, Commager concludes: "The great danger that threatens us is neither heterodox thought nor orthodox thought, but the absence of thought."

Henry Steele Commager
FREE ENTERPRISE IN IDEAS

"I sometimes think that when folks talk about things they've begun to lose them already," says Stark Young's Hugh McGehee to his son after an evening of Southern rodomontade. It would be an exaggeration to say that we have begun to lose liberty in America, but it is sobering that there should be so much talk about it, just as it is sobering that there should be so much talk about Americanism and about loyalty. It was a happier time when these things could be taken for granted instead of being soiled and worn by every sunshine patriot eager for cheap applause. Nor is much of the talk itself reassuring. Liberty is enlisted in strange armies, pressed into service for curious causes, and as we listen to some of the arguments for censorship or exclusion or suppression, all in the name of liberty, we are reminded irresistibly of Madame Roland's cry on the scaffold, "Liberty, what crimes are done in thy name."

Nor is the difficulty wholly with those who, in a sort of vindication of Orwell's *1984,* invoke liberty for oppression. Some of the difficulty comes from well-intentioned idealists who are content with familiar formulas, or who would interpret liberty as wholly a personal and individual affair—a matter of abstract principle rather than of conduct, of private rights rather than of general social responsibilities.

When we consider civil and political liberties we must avoid the pleasant illusions of abstractions and get down to cases. We must look to the meaning of our freedoms in their present-day context, and in their operation. And when we do this we must remember what Harold Laski so insistently urged upon us (in *Reflections on the Revolution of Our Time*), that rights and liberties do not mean the same thing to all of us:

The rule of law is a principle with a fairly long history behind it. And if the burden of that history has one outstanding lesson it is that, over the social process as a whole, the rule of law is only equally applied as between persons . . . whose claim on the state power is broadly recognized as equal. The rule of law is not an automatic principle of action which operates indifferently as to time and place and the persons to whom, as judges, its application is entrusted. It is very likely to be one thing for a Negro in Georgia and another thing for a white man in Georgia.

The function of freedom—let us say of the guarantee of due process or of the right to vote—for

---

Henry Steele Commager, *Freedom, Loyalty, Dissent* (New York: Oxford University Press, 1954), pp. 72–92, copyright 1954 by Oxford University Press. Reprinted (without footnotes) by permission of the publisher.

the Negro and the white in the South is one very obvious example of why we have to look to the operation of the principle rather than to its mere formulation. Others come readily to mind: the difference in guarantees of freedom to white and to Oriental during World War II, for example, or the different treatment afforded the vagrant and the respectable citizen, or that difference in the attitude toward corporate crime and individual crime which Professor Sutherland has explored in his study of *White Collar Crime*.

We must recognize, too, at the outset that there are two very broad categories of violations of liberty: the political and the nonpolitical, or perhaps we should say the official and the unofficial. Only the first has received adequate attention—invasion of personal rights by the federal or state governments or by some administrative body. These are the impairments of liberty that are dramatized in the press and challenged in the courts—a flag-salute law, a segregation law, a white primary law, the censorship of a film, or the administrative seizure of an industry. Yet the second category of invasion and impairment, the unofficial, is more widespread and more effective than the first. It is invasion by social or community pressure, by the pressure of public opinion or of public customs and habits—the kind of invasion that Tocqueville described and warned against over a century ago. It is very difficult to get at this by law. Fair Employment Practice Acts may prevent a Negro or a Jew from getting fired for racial reasons, but they will not go far toward getting him a job in the first place. A teacher who has been guilty of dangerous thoughts can take a broken contract to court, but she cannot deal with community pressure that makes it advisable for her to move on, nor can she force other school boards to give her a job. We have only to read Norman Cousins' description of the interplay of social and economic pressures in Peoria, Illinois, to realize how enormously effective these are and how difficult it is to do anything about them. As John Stuart Mill observed a century ago, "The immense mass of mankind are, in regard to their usages, in a state of social slavery; each man being bound under heavy penalties to conform to the standard of life common to his own class."

Our basic freedoms, in short, are not as basic as we like to think, just as our passion for individualism is not as passionate as we suppose. If we content ourselves with abstractions we may go seriously astray; as Professor Denis Brogan has remarked in his recent book on revolutions, the American claim to—and hope for—a special place in the affections of Asian peoples is frustrated by the elementary fact that of all the powers of the world "America is the most color conscious." We may believe that our words—which we assume to express our principles—represent us more truly even than our actions, but to outsiders it is the actions that are more eloquent than the words.

Now it will be granted at once that our traditional liberties are not absolute—not in a mathematical sense, anyway. All of them are qualified by the rights of society, or of the state. There are limits on liberty, as there are limits on authority. The broad principle of those limits is generally recognized and accepted; no liberties may be exercised so as to injure others, or injure the community.

Needless to say, this does not get us very far. That liberty is not absolute is one of those truisms that is almost always brought out and put to work whenever somebody wants to censor a book or a film that he doesn't like, or to throw a teacher or a librarian or a radio performer out of his job. Actually it is worth stating only as an introduction to the real problems. How do we determine the limits on liberty and the rights and interests of the community? And who are the "we" who determine? It is easy to fall back on the generalization that the freedom of the individual must not be used to injure the community, and easy enough to say that in the last analysis it is society which determines. But these vague answers are of no practical help. To draw the line between the exercise of freedom and the limitations on freedom is one of the most delicate tasks of statesmanship and philosophy. And the power of drawing the line is one of the most complex and sobering exercises of political authority.

It is in the drawing of lines, the setting of boundaries, the fixing of limits, the reconciliation of claims that the problems rise. Look where we will, in our own society we will find that problems of freedom or of rights revolve around this matter of fixing limits and drawing lines. Thus in the conflicting claims of a free press and a responsible press, or of freedom and license in the press. Thus in the conflicting claims of liberty and security in diplomacy, or in science. Thus in the conflicting claims of artistic freedom and of the protection of the morals of the community, or of religious freedom and protection against blasphemy or the stirring up of religious hatreds. Thus in the conflicting claims of the right to public entertainment and the right to privacy. Thus in the conflicting claims of the right to private organization and the interest of society in protecting itself against dangerous organizations. Thus in the conflicting claims of conscience—let us say of conscientious objectors to military service or a flag salute—and of national defense or of patriotism. Thus in the conflicting claims of academic freedom and of the right of a democracy to determine what should be taught in its schools—and how.

Now we have been using the word "conflicting" somewhat uncritically. But is not the conflict exaggerated, and have we searched intensively enough for the reconciliation? We must keep in mind that the community has a paramount interest in the rights of the individual, and the individual a paramount interest in the welfare of the community of which he is a part. The community cannot prosper without permitting, nay encouraging, the far-reaching exercise of individual freedom; the individual cannot be safe without permitting, nay supporting, the far-reaching exercise of authority by the state.

There is, in short, too much emphasis on independence and not enough on interdependence; too much emphasis on division and not enough on unity. Actually it is only to the superficial view that there is any genuine conflict between liberty and security, for example, or between academic freedom and social freedom.

For what is clear on closer examination is that we cannot have any one of these alleged goods without the other. There is no real choice between freedom and security. Only those societies that actively encourage freedom—that encourage, for example, scientific and scholarly research, the questioning of scientific and social orthodoxies and the discovery of new truths—only such societies can hope to solve the problems that assail them and preserve their security. The experience of Nazi Germany is all but conclusive on this (we are still required to wait until all the returns are in from Russia, but it is a reasonable prophecy that Russia will fall behind on scientific and social research just as Germany did). A nation that silences or intimidates original minds is left only with unoriginal minds and cannot hope to hold its own in the competition of peace or of war. As John Stuart Mill said in that essay on "Liberty" to which we cannot too often repair, "A state which dwarfs its men, in order that they may be more docile instruments in its hands . . . will find that with small men no great thing can really be accomplished."

It is probable that other alleged alternatives so vehemently urged upon us are equally fictitious. Take, for example, the matter of the claims of "academic freedom" and of a society concerned with the teaching of truth—as is every sound society. Clearly there is no genuine conflict here. All but the most thoughtless or the most ignorant know that unless education is free the minds of the next generation will be enslaved. Even in American Legion halls it is probably a bust of Socrates that stands in the niche—Socrates who was condemned because he was a corruptor of youth—rather than of those forgotten members of the tribunal who put him to death. We have always known that academic freedom, like other freedoms, was subject to abuse, but we have also known (up to now, in any event) that the abuse was part of the price paid for the use, and that it was not in fact a high price. The simple fact is that the kind of society that cherishes academic freedom is the kind that gets the best teachers and scholars and students, and the kind that tries to control what teachers may teach or students learn is the kind that ends up with mediocre teachers and mediocre students. A comparison of German science and scholarship in the generation before the First World War and the generation of Nazism should be conclusive on this.

So, too, with the problem of freedom of the press as against the right of the community to protect itself against libel or obscenity or sedition or against similar dangers. Granted that there is no absolute freedom of the press—no right to proclaim blasphemy to church-goers or to distribute obscene literature to children—the alleged conflict is still largely fictitious. The hypothetical dangers linger in the realm of hypothesis; when they emerge from this to reality they can be dealt with by ordinary nuisance or libel or criminal laws, not by censorship laws. We are all familiar with Justice Holmes's graphic illustration of the man who cries "fire" in a crowded theater, but the fact is that no sane man ever does this, and our ordinary laws should not be made for the hypothetical insane. The fact is that censorship always defeats its own purpose, for it creates, in the end, the kind of society that is incapable of exercising real discretion, incapable, that is, of doing an honest or intelligent job, and thus guarantees a steady intellectual decline.

We must, then, keep in mind that we are dealing with realities, not abstractions. We must learn to think things, not words; we must fasten our attention on consequences, not on theories. We must keep ever in mind the warning of William James that meaningful discussion will "hinge as soon as possible upon some practical or particular issue."

The importance of this becomes clear when we realize that almost everyone agrees on the principles that should govern our conduct. At least almost all say and probably think that they agree. It is the application that is different. Southerners who deny Negroes a fair trial purport to be enthusiastic for the Bill of Rights but do not apply it in the same way to whites and Negroes. The Legislature of Texas which passed a resolution outlawing any party that "entertained any thought or principle" contrary to the Constitution of the United States was doubtless sincere enough, but it did not intend to outlaw the Democratic party because that party "entertains" a thought contrary to the Fifteenth Amendment. Senator McCarthy doubtless thinks of himself as a paladin of Constitutional liberties and so does Senator McCarran; Merwin K. Hart of the National Economic Council and Allen Zook of the notorious National Council for American Education invoke the Constitution, as do the editors of *Counterattack* and of *Red Channels*. All this is too obvious for rehearsal. We must get beyond the principles to their application in order to discover where the difficulty is, and to discover how to resolve it.

When we approach the problem this way we can see that the most compelling argument for freedom is not the argument from theory or principle, but the argument of necessity. To put the issue as simply as possible: we maintain freedom not in order to indulge error but in order to discover truth, and we know no other way of discovering truth. It is difficult to think of any situation where this principle does not apply.

This does not mean for a moment that the principles are unimportant. They are enormously important. They provide the framework of our thinking. They provide us with a common vocabulary. They crystallize for us the values we cherish. If we did not have a body of principles of freedom, we should not be discussing this matter at all. The principles are important, then, and essential. But it is in the application that we discover their meaning. It is the application that is the test. If we are to solve our problems, it must be by traveling the road of conduct and consequences. Theory may mislead us; experience must be our guide.

Let us note three or four examples. Here, for instance, is perhaps the most important of all at the moment—the conflicting claims of scientific freedom and national security. To talk in abstract terms of the freedom of the scientist does not get us very far, for that is not an abstract freedom; it is a freedom whose effective exercise requires a good deal of co-operation from the community. Nor does it get us very far to talk in abstract terms about national security. Everyone is in favor of national security, but Senators Morse and McCarthy have different notions about how it is to be achieved. The meaningful approach is that of consequences. What happens when you adopt a policy of freedom for research—freedom with commonsense regulations that any sensible man may be expected to observe? What happens when you permit the Government or the military to control the research? Fortunately, we need not speculate here; Walter Gellhorn's remarkable study of *Security, Loyalty, and Science* has covered the ground and furnished the moral.

The costs of secrecy [he says] are high. When the freedom of scientific exchange is curtailed, an unfavorable reaction upon further scientific development is inevitable. We pay for secrecy by slowing the rate of our scientific progress, now and in the future. This loss of momentum may conceivably be disastrous, for even from the strictly military point of view "it is just as important for us to have some new secrets to keep as it is for us to hold on to the old ones." If it is unsound to suppress scientific knowledge during the long years of a cold war, the American people may one day discover that they have been crouching behind a protective wall of blueprints and formulas whose impregnability is an utter illusion.

Or let us look to an equally familiar field—the effort to rid our school system of alleged "subversives." Ignore for the moment all questions about the definition of subversive (a term that has not yet been legally defined) or about the rights of teachers. Look solely to the social interest, the community interest, in the matter, and apply the test of consequences. What happens when a state tries to purge its state universities or a community tries to purge its public schools of alleged subversives?

We have a good deal of evidence on this matter by now, for the campaign against subversives has gone on for some time. We can therefore speak here with some assurance. What happens is not that the state or city gets rid of hordes of Communists. Not at all. It very rarely finds any, and it rarely finds any subversives unless it wants to stretch that term to embrace anyone who rejoiced in Russian victories in 1943 or who reads *The Nation* or who favors socialized medicine. What happens is the demoralization and the eventual corruption of the school system. This is not a momentary or even a temporary affair; it is something the consequences of which may be felt for years. The search for subversives results in the intimidation of the independent, the original, the imaginative, and the experimental-minded. It discourages independence of thought in teachers and students alike. It discourages the joining of organizations that may turn out to be considered subversive. It discourages the reading of books that may excite the suspicion of some investigator or some Legionnaire. It discourages criticism of educational or of Governmental policies. It discourages the discussion of controversial matters in the classroom, for such discussion may be reported, or misreported, and cause trouble. It creates a situation where first-rate minds will not go into teaching or into administration and where students therefore get poor teaching. In the long run it will create a generation incapable of appreciating the difference between independence of thought and subservience. In the long run it will create a generation not only deprived of liberty but incapable of enjoying liberty.

Turn where we will to apply the test of consequences, we discover that we must insist on freedom because we cannot do without it, because we cannot afford the price of its denial. Thus the most powerful argument against Congressional programs of investigation of Foundations ("To determine if they are using their resources for un-American and subversive activities or for purposes not in the interest or tradition of the United States") is that if it is put into effect it will endanger existing foundations and discourage philanthropists from setting up others and discourage that boldness and independence which foundations can provide more freely than almost any other institution. The most powerful argument against the censorship of textbooks and the elimination of "un-American" ideas or of anything critical of the "American spirit of private enterprise" is that such censorship will guarantee the elimination of textbooks with any ideas at all. The compelling argument against the purging of libraries is that if the kind of people who believe in purges have their way and work their will, our libraries will cease to be centers of light and learning and become instead instruments of party or church or class, or depositories of literature whose only merit is its innocuousness. The compelling argument against denying passports or visas on the grounds of unpopular political or economic ideas is that by silencing criticism in those who expect to travel from country to country we deprive ourselves of the value of what foreigners might have to tell us, discourage criticism in our own citizens, and deny to foreigners living evidence that the United States encourages intellectual independence. The decisive argument against the kind of censorship of radio and motion-picture performers that we are now witnessing is that it will leave us, in the end, with programs devoid of ideas and performers devoid of originality or of courage to apply originality.

In every case it is society that is the loser. Our society can doubtless afford to lose the benefits of ideas or character in any one instance, but the cumulative costs of the intimidation of thoughtful and critical men and women is something no society can afford.

A society that applies doctrinaire notions to social conduct will find itself in the end the prisoner of its own doctrines. A society that takes refuge in shibboleths like "subversive" or "un-American" will find itself unable to recognize reality when it appears—even the reality of danger. A society that discourages experiment will find that without experiment there can be no progress, and that without progress, there is regress. A society that attempts to put education and science and scholarship in strait jackets will find that in strait jackets there can be no movement, and that the result will be intellectual atrophy. A society that repudiates free enterprise in the intellectual arena under the deluded notion that it can flourish in the economic alone will find that without intellectual enterprise, economic enterprise dries up. A society that encourages state intervention in the realm of ideas will find itself an easy prey to state intervention in other realms as well.

That government which most scrupulously protects and encourages complete freedom of thought, expression, communication, investigation, criticism is the one which has the best chance of achieving security and progress. "They that can give up essential liberty to obtain a little temporary safety deserve neither liberty nor safety," wrote Benjamin Franklin two centuries ago, and what he said is as valid now as it was then. Government and society have a paramount interest in independence, originality, heterodoxy, criticism, nonconformity, because all experience teaches that it is out of these that come new ideas, and because every society needs a continuous re-examination of old ideas and a continuous flow of new ideas. And it is relevant to remember, too, that it is nonconformity that needs encouragement. As William Ellery Channing said over a century ago, "We have conservatives enough."

Three centuries ago John Milton addressed himself to the problem that now confronts us, and what he said in *Areopagitica* is still valid:

> Believe it, Lords and Commons, they who counsel ye to such a suppressing do as good as bid ye suppress yourselves. . . . Ye cannot make us now less capable, less knowing, less eagerly pursuing of the truth, unless ye first make yourselves, that made us so, less the lovers, less the founders of our true liberty.

Harold D. Lasswell is probably the foremost American authority on propaganda techniques and mass communication. Since 1946 he has been a professor of law at Yale University. Previously, from 1922 to 1938, he was on the political science faculty at the University of Chicago. Other assignments have included a lectureship at the New School for Social Research, directorship of War Communications Research for the Library of Congress, and membership on the Commission on Freedom of the Press. Numerous books from his pen include several directly pertinent to the study of censorship, e.g., *Propaganda Technique in the World War, Psychopathology and Politics, World Politics and Personal Insecurity, World Revolutionary Propaganda, Democracy through Public Opinion,* and *National Security and Individual Freedom.*

The essay on "Politics and Subversion" was presented by Professor Lasswell in 1953 at the Second Conference on Intellectual Freedom at Whittier, California, sponsored by the American Library Association.

Harold D. Lasswell
POLITICS AND SUBVERSION

There is no doubting the gravity of the national security crisis in which we live and hold this conference. As the principal arsenal of the Free World we are in the midst of an armament race against the Soviet Union. The race is the direct outcome of a world civil war precipitated by the rulers of the Soviet fortress; and this race will not be halted until the top elite of the Soviet domain are unwilling or unable to continue it.

By recognizing the seriousness of the crisis, we do not imply that the only thinkable outcome is World War III. Soviet leaders undoubtedly prefer the cheapest and the least dangerous path to power. They will go ahead with the tactics of piecemeal expansion at the periphery of the Soviet system of garrison-prison states. The program of partial and peripheral expansion has widened the area under the control of the Soviets to include several states in Europe and the whole of continental China. Between the pincers of pressure from without and of subversion from within many states have crumbled into submission. Soviet policy is at work today preparing the way for another ring of possible acquisitions, particularly in Asia.

If the strategy of piecemeal and peripheral expansion continues to bring success, the Soviet fortress will eventually encircle the deadliest enemy of all, from their point of view, which is

---

Harold D. Lasswell, "Politics and Subversion," in *Freedom of Book Selection* (Chicago: American Library Association, 1954), pp. 42–55. Reprinted by permission of the author.

the United States. As they see the present posture of world affairs, Soviet leaders look upon themselves as the encircled, not the encircling, power. When they try to account for the ring of states that stands in the way of Soviet imperial expansion, they are made aware of the extraordinary role of the industrial and military strength, actual and potential, of the United States. Through the grand strategy of global encirclement the Soviet elite hopes one day to succeed in detaching the United States from the rest of the world. If this day approaches, the Soviet expectation is that the United States in turn will weaken and fall into their hands without a major war. They believe that the mothers and wives of our nation will sink into a mood of desperate despondency and that the whole community will fall into political apathy. It is prophesied that industrial and military production will lag, that dissatisfaction will corrode the loyalties that unite the American people and reduce the nation to a rubble of quarrelling factions. In this crisis they predict that a hard corps of Sovietized Americans will seize the initiative to stage the final subversion that brings the United States into the Soviet orbit.

What place do Soviet leaders assign to ideas, to persuasion, to propaganda, to communication in all this? What is the role of reading, of authorship, of publication, of the dissemination of ideas?

It is true that in a deep sense the elite of the Soviet system has little respect for ideas. At the root of Soviet policy is a doctrine that teaches the subordination of ideas to material factors. Hence it is taken for granted that it is necessary to transform the material facts of society before the "superstructure" of ideas can be transformed. In the mint of material fact the Soviet leaders expect to stamp the raw stuff of the mind in a material image.

Now this doctrine does not wholly deny that ideas are influential in social and historical processes. But from the Soviet point of view it does deprive the ideas of the majority of any claim to be taken seriously, since the doctrine holds that once a system of material facts has imprinted the minds of a people with a pattern of ideas, the ideas will persist after the material stamp has changed. Thus ideas are supposed to display inertia, which is one of the properties of material objects. Any widespread system of pre-Soviet ideas is regarded as a reflection of *past* material relationships. While the ideas of old majorities are denied validity, the doctrine assigns extraordinary potency to some ideas. These ideas belong to a minority. This minority is believed to be sufficiently alert to expose itself to a true picture of the newly emerging material facts, the new facts, that will eventually reshape society.

In the light of these basic doctrines, it is apparent why Soviet leaders are not trying to convince the majority of the American people, or indeed of any free people, that their basic ideas are true. They are under no illusions whatsoever about winning a majority vote. On the contrary, they are convinced that they cannot win by majority consent. And why? Because, they say, the control of the material instruments of communication reflects old material relations. *After* the alleged triumph of Soviet power, *after* a new set of material facts has been brought into being, the majority will then be indoctrinated with Soviet ideas by exposure to the monopolized instruments of the press, the school, and all other significant means of communication.

Well! How can an acknowledged minority hope to carry a self-declared world civil war to a victorious conclusion? They have a ready answer: by pursuing the same strategy that enabled a tiny minority to seize power in Moscow in 1917, and subsequently elsewhere. As with many fundamental ideas, the strategy can be quite simply stated: keep your enemies distracted and fighting among themselves until you gather a sufficiently strong material force to take an advantage of an opportune moment for the seizure of total power.

Hence the role of propaganda—the dissemination of ideas—in Soviet strategy is: (1) divide and weaken, and (2) recruit and indoctrinate the hard corps of the Party for an ultimate *coup d'état*. The detailed tactics vary according to the relative strength of Soviet power in the various countries outside the Soviet fortress, with: (1) those nations where there's no significant penetration; (2) nations where Soviet-controlled groups are available to enter coalitions; (3) nations where a Soviet group can betray a coalition and seize power. Italy and France are, of course, of the second group; Czechoslovakia was in the third; our own country is obviously in the first.

In these various countries the media of mass

communication are used to accomplish the same mission: to divide and weaken actual or potential opponents. It is not the mission of the mass channels of communication to recruit and train the hard corps of professional revolutionaries who are supposed to seize power one day. This is sought by the tactics of localized material supremacy. During the early penetration phase in a given country the available material factors of limited personnel, limited books and other publications, are to be managed according to the principle of the primacy of material factors. A localized predominance is possible, for example, in a study group organized and run by trained Party workers. This is not a question of study groups run under scholarly or politically diverse auspices. I'm referring to small groups dominated by the Party, as when such meetings are held in private homes. Individuals with no initial intention of succumbing to the Party are drawn into the web at such meetings, where they're in a minority of numbers, conviction, and knowledge.

Now it is not to be supposed that such primary occasions use only the instrumentalities of teaching and persuasion. The Party knows of many unobtrusive ways by which an individual can be made dependent upon the Party. The practical operations of such traps for the unwary have been many times described—nowhere better than in the report of the Commission of the Canadian Government that tried to describe and explain the astonishing and disturbing fact that scientists of undoubted competence, education, and character were drawn into the Soviet espionage network. Trading initially upon curiosity, idealism, and resentment, the Party began early to prepare the way for eventual blackmail. Individuals in no need of money were given unexpected gifts and payments. Having accepted these presents, the individual was open to the threat of being denounced to his own government if at any time he faltered in the execution of Party requests, which eventually became Party orders.

The fact is that the organizations controlled by Moscow are falsely labeling themselves when they claim to be political parties. Political scientists quite properly reserve the term "political party" for a group that lives up to the democratic rules of give and take, coercing neither its members nor other parties. Functionally speaking, Soviet-controlled organizations, whatever their labels, are political orders, not political parties. Their members become members of a state within a state. Their task is to prepare the day for the eventual seizure of power. The political order is part of a vast program, devoted to espionage—indeed every form of subversion designed to bring the world civil war to a victorious conclusion from the Moscow point of view.

After this brief glance at the Soviet program, let's have a look at our own position. The outstanding fact appears to be that our national security, and the security of others outside the Soviet orbit, depends in great part upon our present supremacy in the industrial and technical capacity necessary to produce weapons of atomic warfare. We are likely to retain our advantage in this area for at least a time. A second fact is less satisfactory. The non-Soviet world is only partly united in objective, in outlook, or in method. We are divided in independent national units, many of which are fearful of acknowledging the dominant role that our industrial strength has given us. Flowing across the political divisions of our world are the residual animosities originally directed against the empires of Europe. These hostilities are often justified and guided in terms of "color." In the non-Soviet world are the industrialized democracies of Western Europe (and of Western European origin). In many non-Soviet states, however, the ruling class is composed of feudal landlords who display many degrees of stubbornness in adapting to the rising currents of nationalism, land reform, industrialization, and democracy.

If our national security is to be maintained under these circumstances, a vast and continuing effort is obviously essential. One of our minimum objectives has been, and must continue to be, the deterrence of Soviet leaders from all-out or limited aggression. In the former we have been successful; in the latter we have frequently failed. Another objective is more far-reaching. We want to bring about a fundamental change in the policies of the Soviet leadership, whatever individuals may be involved at any given moment. We want a change so that the Soviet world enters candidly into the effective liquidation of the arms race, and engages in cooperative activities with the world community as a whole. We desire to obtain these basic transformations, so indispensable for genuine security, by persuasion if possible. However, if aggression continues, it will eventually reach a point where we will find it necessary to pursue these ends by every means at our disposal.

In our turn, how do we conceive of the role of ideas in this quest for national security? In accord with our tradition we look at the influence of ideas in individual and social development in a perspective that differs markedly from Soviet doctrine. We reject the conception that ideas are nothing more than a developed film of yesterday's material facts. For us perhaps the most decisive function of ideas is in shaping the course of future events. It is true that our ideas about the future may include the forecast that past trends will be prolonged. But this does not exhaust our ideas. We can imagine new potentialities, whether we're speaking of the processes of society or of nature. In originating and choosing among future alternatives, our clarified conceptions of social values play a most decisive part.

We escape from the repetitive compulsion of old habits and old social institutions by employing the goal-clarifying, projective, inventive, and evaluative functions of the mind. The act of insight into the occurrence of a repetition may result in breaking the connection upon which the very repetition depends, enlarging the scope of effective choice and variation in the future. Freed from automatic, unconscious, uncritical submission to habit and custom, we are able to use the higher integrative functions of the human being, as individuals, as members of society. Information relating to events in the present is transformed into raw material, raw material for a map of future goals and pathways of achievement.

To sum it up in one proposition: From our point of view the basic Soviet doctrine is obsolete and superficial. To an inquiring mind with access to available knowledge, the supposed dichotomy between fact and idea (the material and the subjective) has dissolved into a much more differentiated pattern of events. We think in terms of psychosomatic systems whose parts (when operationally described) are perceived as interacting, and whose external connections are with other similarly complex systems that function on a local, regional, global or historical scale. The chain of interdependence is at once too vast and too refined to admit of the early-nineteenth-century conception of a "material" fact stamping its heel on an inert screen and creating an "idea."

When we apply this perspective of ours to world affairs, we find that the very successes of the Soviet cause give the lie to their own theory of ideas and support our own. Sovietism has no foothold in the advanced industrial nations, where Marx and Engels thought the proletariat would rise to power. It is among the non-industrialized peoples that the response to Soviet agitation and propaganda has been so very impressive. The appeal of ideas far outruns material facts. It is the appearance of a new image of the future that gives expression to the yearnings and hopes of simple people for a better life. According to this image men are prosperous and safe; they are treated with respect and freed of discriminative shackles. Hence the formidable strength of whatever social movements attach themselves to the expectation of future felicity.

When we remind ourselves of the past, when we consider the place of Western European civilization in giving articulate form to the doctrine of human dignity, when we recall how ingenious Western countries have been in devising institutions in which income, safety, and deference values have been more widely shared by more people than at any time in human history, we may well marvel why there is any appeal whatsoever in the blandishments of a system of garrison-prison states in which the ideals of the Western tradition are disseminated as a cover-up for a gigantic program of forced industrialization and militarization. This is truly puzzling. There must have been, and there must continue to be, something inept about the way in which our policies have been presented through the years to the people of this world. It may be that our difficulties stem from the spontaneous way in which images of the future were stimulated and exaggerated by America's very success in the nineteenth century. Possibly the lowly and the suppressed came to think of us as limitlessly rich, so that if we have left them in misery it is because we are hostile, arrogant, or indifferent to them.

If we think that the outlook of foreign peoples toward the United States and the Soviet world is baffling, we may perhaps remember that our fellow citizens are full of inconsistencies that affect national security. Some American policies appear to be veritable masterpieces of prevision, exhibiting statecraft of the highest order, drawing mankind toward confidence in the future of the Free World. At the same time our public life is full of words and deeds that belie these policies, dividing Americans from one another and from other free peoples.

Apparently there is something insufficient about the image of the future that prevails among us. American leaders, governmental or private, seem insufficiently unified in a common conception of our goal values, or in the understanding of world conditions affecting our security, or upon the grand strategy at home and abroad by which our basic values can be made more secure. Inconsistency and vacillation among the leaders are reflected in, and sustained by, a similar vagueness among the various constituencies, public or private, comprising the American nation.

The anxieties and uncertainties widespread among us imply at least partial recognition that all is not well. Under these circumstances of chronic tension it is not surprising to see more Americans demanding and using coercion against whatever they imagine to be connected with the enemy, and which is near at hand. Since Soviet-controlled organizations are relatively scarce in the United States, and operate to a large extent out of sight, there are too few unimpeachable targets to supply the current demand. Since evidences of Soviet affiliation are largely absent, rumor easily takes the place of the missing evidence. As a result targets are often chosen to pay off old scores and to damage rivals. The hand of one politician is raised against another, of one publisher against another, one union leader against another, one teacher against another, and so on through the innumerable elements that compose our complex and highly competitive society.

Now the targets are not only individuals and groups; they are ideas. Every book that is supposed to originate in the Soviet world, or to be written by a person friendly to the Soviet cause—or who has been assumed to be friendly—or any book that contains anything deemed friendly becomes subject to coercive attack. As among the individual targets, the idea targets are likewise generalized, tending to include all books, periodicals, programs, and other expressions of ideas that are disagreeable to the initiators and promoters of the attack.

Under these conditions the tension of the group is heightened by the promotional zeal of destructive personality types. In every group there are likely to be relatively compulsive and obsessional individuals who live in a perpetual state of inner conflict generated by the effort to hold their destructive impulses in check. By seizing upon an external target internal tension is somehow alleviated. This displacement of private needs upon such public objects as individuals or ideas does not of course assuage the difficulties of the community as a whole, however contributory it may be to the therapy of the individual. Nor does it contribute to the rational discovery and execution of policies that are compatible with the nation's security. Adding to the din then of the general tension are the hysterical types, who increase the general confusion, intensified by the obsessives and the compulsives.

But the spreading of hatred and suspicion among Americans, and between Americans and other peoples of the Free World, is plainly a menace to national security. If scientists, engineers, executives, civil servants, workers, and other specialized groups develop a sense of grievance as coerciveness spreads, the nation is endangered in many ways. If American officials abroad grow timid about reporting what they see, because of fear of how the facts will be received at home, the eyes of national security policy are put out. This is not only true of diplomatic, military, air, naval, and other attachés stationed in foreign countries. It extends to the correspondents and the editors of our newspapers and periodicals, to the authors of books concerned with international relations, to the teachers and lecturers on world politics and world affairs. Advertisers become apprehensive of the slightest whiff of suspicion, and inaugurate a reign of pre- and post-censorship. In choosing who shall be given scholarships, research facilities, professorships, college presidencies, librarianships, and the like, colorless timidity seems to be a better bet than outspokenness. Looking into the future, it is obvious that such paralytic processes endanger our survival as free men in a free world. For if in the act of seeking to out-arm and out-produce the Soviet world, we unconsciously imitate Soviet hatred of the free play of ideas, it will become progressively difficult for the peoples of the globe to distinguish between the two worlds. The basic self-assurance of our own community will be undermined, and without conscious subversion there can occur a withdrawal of motivation that robs the nation of the devoted energy and skill essential to survival.

The heart of our difficulty is an insufficient image of America's place in the world. In coping with this situation, we must invoke the principle that the most important cure of insufficient ideas is better ideas. And in our world the only effective way to spread ideas is competitive and not coercive. If our national inadequacy is to be overcome, it will be done by confronting ideas with ideas, not by trying to kill rival ideas by using coercion.

For the next few years at least we shall need a program devoted to voluntary enlightenment in all that concerns national security. This study of national security has three major divisions: self-knowledge; knowledge of the Soviets; knowledge of the intermediate world. Committees on National Security Studies need to be organized at all of our institutions of learning at every level from the university down. Committees on National Security Studies are needed in our civic associations, bar associations, medical societies, trade unions, and trade associations. They are in harmony with the present needs of all professional organizations connected with the physical or biological sciences, or with the social sciences and the humanities. These committees are within the scope of all who touch the media of dissemination: the publishers, the editors, librarians, journalists, radio-TV station owners and operators, program managers—just to name a few examples. Programs of National Security Studies are most emphatically within the competence of the tradition of librarians and libraries.

For adequate self-knowledge, that is, knowledge of American history and institutions, will convincingly demonstrate the importance of national security studies now. When the colonies seceded from the British Empire we were exceedingly well-informed about our antagonist, and this knowledge enabled our agents to take advantage of friendly elements in governmental and popular circles in Great Britain. We were well-informed about the leading nations of Europe, and our leaders recognized the importance of obtaining diplomatic, military, economic and psychological support from elements hostile to British power. The fact that we did obtain support from France and from other Continental powers eager to weaken the British by strengthening our secession proved decisive in the Revolutionary struggle. Similarly, when we fought Germany in both the First and Second World Wars we were extremely well-acquainted with our enemy, and with every nation that played a role in those struggles. Millions of our fellow citizens were of German origin and kept German connections, and millions more had traded, studied, or traveled in Germany and elsewhere.

Now we are by no means so well off in the current world civil war. Our connections with Russia have been severely impaired for many years, so that there are no longer millions of Americans possessing up-to-date knowledge of the core country of the Soviet world. The situation is much better so far as some of the recent victims of Soviet aggression are concerned. But it is extraordinarily difficult to keep reliably informed on Soviet capabilities and intentions, and to arrive at any sound basis for judging the public policies that we are called upon to evaluate and sustain in this country. Fortunately we are fairly well equipped with a body of scholars who are sufficiently unfettered by the muzzle of military secrecy to contribute basic information and comment for the understanding of the Soviet world. The institutes at Harvard and Columbia, for example, publish monographs of the first importance for anyone who purports to have a disciplined understanding of Soviet theory and practice at home and abroad. The new institutes devoted to the study of other areas provide a fundamental map of knowledge for all the intermediate cultures, nations, and peoples upon whom our national security must, in varying degree, depend.

Our programs of self-knowledge can provide indispensable guidance for the present emergency by acquainting us with what Americans have done in the past. In every tense period there have been citizens who adhered firmly to the basic principles of American life. At the same time there have always been individuals who betrayed our fundamental principles. Apparently the latter have been under the impression that their fellow citizens are a weak-minded lot. Hence they have approved or used coercion against ideas for the sake of protecting Americans "for their own good." They have sought by means of intimidation and deprivation to interfere with the free circulation of ideas, and to deny public access to anything of which they did not approve.

In the present crisis, many Americans are standing firm in support of the American principle of relying upon good ideas to drive out the bad. They believe, for instance, that freedom to read is a cornerstone of American democracy. They understand freedom to read to mean that we should know of controversial opinions, and that we should know how they are justified, without allowing government officials or private individuals to keep us in ignorance on either point. They see that freedom to read also means that we should have access to all pertinent facts, without being subject to the censorship of persons who try to impose their own notions of pertinence upon us. Furthermore, they see that freedom to read includes the idea that questions of taste are to be settled without being blindfolded by governmental or private individuals who try to foist their tastes upon everyone else.

In this crisis, too, some Americans, it must be conceded, are disloyal to fundamental principles. Some of them belong to organizations that work directly under the control of Moscow on the task of subversion. Others, who have no subversive intentions, have subversive effects. They do the work of Moscow from ignorance, from the ruthless and careless pursuit of private individual or special group advantage. In such a crisis we can evaluate the effectiveness of our past practice of civic education in the homes, schools, churches, and neighborhoods of our country. And we find many failures. In past crises our nation has been strong enough to survive its previous failures of civic education, and we confidently expect to pull through once again. But the present struggle is only beginning. And if we are to protect freedom in America it will be necessary to put enormous energy behind such programs as the fostering of enlightenment on questions of national security.

To the extent that the history of the past is a guide to the present, we can say that one of the gravest enemies of our national security is the reputable citizen who is not genuinely convinced of the soundness of the American legal and moral principle of respecting the freedom of the mind. These specific instances of defective civic education are not suffering from mental disorder. They are not operating "rackets" in the name of patriotism, party loyalty, religion, or race. They are honestly misguided. They lack the intellectual tools to attain the secuirty of mind enabling them to preform the obligations of citizenship in a crisis period. Lacking enlightened and intense conviction they crawl and concede where principles are at stake. For instance, they are likely to be squeamish about letting other people read what the Communists have published, or what's been published explaining the theories and practices of Sovietism. They are excessively "tactful," much given to wobbling in the face of pressure from the fanatics who want to fight ideas with censorship and suppression. The idea of book-burning is likely to shock them. But they are queasy enough to think that controversial items ought to be taken off the accessible shelves of the library, and put in the back room. They are impressed by glib analogies between material objects and ideas, and fall into the trap of supposing that an authoritative label, like that applied to a material object, can be permanently and authoritatively affixed to an idea. They have adopted the materialistic conception of ideas, without knowing it, and failed to recognize that ideas are subject to unending diversities of interpretation, as contexts change.

How can we cope with the unintended subversive effects created by faltering Americans of good local reputation? The first step, I suppose, is to find men and women of true civic integrity. Fortunately, American civic training has by no means been a total loss everywhere. Rugged citizens are to be found who are able and eager to uphold the hands of courageous librarians—for instance—who have a fight on their hands in fending off hysterics and compulsives, self-seekers, racketeers, and the misguided. They are willing to stop the creeping subversion of thought control wherever it occurs, especially in connection with the local library.

The present crisis differs in one important particular from previous crises: it is likely to continue for many years to come. We have been slow to awaken to the nature of the problem because it is largely without precedent in American experience. Hence the urgent need of enlightenment on national security issues. The continuing study of national security problems calls for self-knowledge, knowledge of the Soviets, knowledge of the peoples in between. And in place of the present outlook, our conception of America's future can become sharp and realistic. By clarifying our images we can unify the resources of the Free World and put a term to the partial and peripheral expansion of Sovietism. By outproducing, out-arming, and out-thinking the Soviet world we can eventually obtain a more secure world order in which the stupendous potentialities of human energy can be put to creative use. However imposing the global strategy may be, we cannot wisely forget that the front lines in this struggle are in strange places. They are in distant geographical areas. And they are also close at home. Decisive engagements are being fought out day by day in the choices that occur in the board rooms and the staff offices of our libraries and publishers. Every American, and indeed every member of the human race, has a profound stake in our tenacity and our skill, and I trust in our ultimate success.

Charles G. Bolte was executive secretary of the American Book Publishers Council, 1952–56, and is a director of the American Civil Liberties Union. He was formerly a member of the United States Mission to the United Nations; organizer and chairman of the American Veterans Committee; special writer for the Office of War Information; and newspaper correspondent. Since 1956 he has been vice-president of the Viking Press. Not unexpectedly, with such a background, he concludes that "For us, there can be no security through book burning: only the rigid crust of conformity."

Charles G. Bolte
SECURITY THROUGH BOOK BURNING

I looked for a text from the American humorists, because they so often illuminate our follies better than the sobersided do, and because if we laughed more often at the pygmies who are trying to take us prisoner, instead of treating and

---

Charles G. Bolte, "Security through Book Burning," *Annals of the American Academy of Political and Social Science*, 300: 87–93 (July, 1955), copyright 1955 by the American Academy of Political and Social Science. Reprinted (without footnotes) by permission of the publisher.

entreating them so earnestly, we might the better blow them away. I found two texts.

Mark Twain, of course, first:

> It is by the goodness of God that in our country we have those three unspeakably precious things: freedom of speech, freedom of conscience, and the prudence never to practice either of them.

Then Walt Kelly, whose "Pogo" recently featured an exchange between a blameless owl and an inquisitorial badger, the latter supported by two junketeering crows:

> BADGER: I won't *threaten* you, Mr. Owl. But here is a book that says: Owls migrate north about April first. . . . You got a day to pack.
> OWL: Why, *you* jes' writ *that* you' ownself. . . . Where is Captain Wimby's Bird Atlas?
> BADGER: *Discredited.* It didn't agree with *our* observations. . . . Did it, men?
> FIRST CROW: No sir, it's out of date.
> SECOND CROW: *And* on fire.
> BADGER: There's nothing quite so lovely as a brightly burning book.

CLASHING SYMBOLS

My theory is that we had all better be a little less prudential in exercising our precious freedom of speech and freedom of conscience, if we want to keep them. Like other rights, they grow weak when not used. This makes life too easy for those who enjoy the sight of brightly burning books.

The title assigned me is "Security Through Book Burning." A dear old lady I know asked a while ago, "What is all this bother about book burning? Why, I always dispose of my old books that way. How else does anyone get rid of books he doesn't want any more?" Well, ours is an age of symbols. The shortage of shelf space bothers us all, I hope. We shall simply have to get used to sending books we can no longer keep to the veterans' hospitals and the Merchant Marine Library. Offensive books can be buried. But burning is out.

This is now pretty generally realized. The Boy Scouts in Portsmouth, Rhode Island, decided to celebrate Lincoln's Birthday this year by burning "objectionable" books on the grounds of Fort Butts, a shrine of the Revolution. They ended by withholding the torch and consigning the offensive matter to the town dump instead, when the announcement of their proposed celebration received what the sponsors mildly called "adverse publicity."

This outcome supports my theory that we need to exercise our freedoms, and bellow and laugh more often and more loudly at those who have forgotten what country they are living in. Nobody denies a man's, or a Boy Scout's, right to junk a piece of printing which he decides, after reading it, that he does not like. But form counts for a lot. In any society, ideas without procedure are a mess; in our society, which has staked everything on the principle of government by laws not men, a breakdown in method means an unholy mess, and points to the end of our society as we have known it. Book burning is a symbol which denies the validity of the symbols of Lincoln, the Revolution, or, one would have thought, the Boy Scouts.

However, American history can be read as a long succession of clashing symbols (spell it either way). We no sooner resolve one tension in our dark continent than we generate another. There are always enough of us sure enough that we are right to guarantee constant prayers to God to make our neighbors see the right as we have given Him to see it. "I'll make that fellow feel brotherly love if I have to kill him" is an old story with us.

The drive to achieve security through book burning has consequently never lacked supporters, nor is it likely to. A royal governor of Virginia wrote in 1671:

> I thank God there are no free schools nor printing, and I hope we shall not have any these hundred years; for learning has brought disobedience, and heresy, and sects into the world.

Holmes

Two and a half centuries later the Supreme Court was still dealing with the problems caused by this view of the world. Holmes, with distaste but with understanding, wrote:

> Persecution for the expression of opinion seems to me perfectly logical. If you have no doubt of your premises or your power and want a certain result with all your heart you naturally express your wishes in law and sweep away all opposition. To allow opposition by speech seems to indicate that you think the speech impotent, as when a man says that he has squared the circle, or that you do not care wholeheartedly for the result, or that you doubt either your power or your premises.

I ration myself to one paragraph only of Holmes—this would not be a paper on my subject without at least that much—but I know you will all remember that it is the next paragraph which goes on to say that "time has upset many fighting faiths," that "ultimate good desired is better reached by free trade in ideas," and that "the best test of truth is the power of the thought to get itself accepted in the competition of the market."

Holmes's was a dissenting opinion; it is not always clear that the majority of the country is with him even now. This need not shake our belief in the validity of his conclusion, since we have Thoreau's word for it that any man more right than his neighbors is a majority of one already. It only means that we need to be diligent in challenging the power and questioning the premises of all those, in or out of office, who want a certain result with all their hearts, even if it means destroying what is in ours.

Lenin

A year after Holmes's dissent in the Abrams case, Lenin set forth the Communist view:

> Why should freedom of speech and freedom of the press be allowed? Why should a government which is doing what it believes to be right allow itself to be criticized? It would not allow opposition by lethal weapons. Ideas are much more fatal things than guns. Why should any man be allowed to buy a printing press and disseminate pernicious opinions calculated to embarrass the government?

This quotation, to be found in Alan Barth's new book, *Government by Investigation,* which I commend to you all, is offered free of charge to those who still want proof that any American who favors book burning is guilty of Communism by association.

If we could be sure that we were right, that the complex of our national policies and accepted truths added up to the truth for all time, then I suppose we could find security through book burning. Lenin was surely right in this, that "ideas are much more fatal things than guns" (if we can admit that there are degrees of fatality). Ideas *are* dangerous; and in a perfectly regulated world, new ones would not be admitted, to turn over the existing order.

But it is not in the cards for us to have this kind of certainty, this faith *à la russe*. We shall need to make do with what we have: a tough-minded faith, which accepts a pluralistic society, moving through trial, unafraid of error, receptive to new ideas.

Embarrassing the government is an old American tradition. For my part, surveying the press of national problems, I sense an absolute need for fresh thought. I am not persuaded that every one of our national policies is beyond all doubt the wisest for us in our present time and place and situation. I fear more harm from everybody thinking alike than from some people thinking otherwise. The nation needs more men who march to a different drummer, not fewer. We can dare to disagree even with decisions of the Supreme Court. After all, four of nine justices often do.

Safeguarding the Republic

The saddest thing about our censors is the evidence they give that they mistrust their neighbors and doubt the validity of American ideas. Is our own cause really so frail that we must be safeguarded from reading attacks on it? Is a textbook by a politically unpopular writer really going to turn the kids from little Republicans into little Comrades?

Are United Nations documents in the San Antonio library really going to undermine the Texas constitution? Are *Pravda* and *Izvestia* really going to provide ammunition for scholars to blow up bridges with? Is the Communist Manifesto in the Boston Public Library really going to supplant the Mayflower Compact in the affections of the next Massachusetts generation? Did it really safeguard the Republic when a security check was run on a private citizen who had written a pamphlet advocating more ground forces, before the pamphlet was circulated in the Pentagon?

Apparently so, in the view of the aroused citizens who have been attacking textbooks all over the country, the patriotic Texans who cried out against the United Nations documents, the Post Office officials who denied the mails to *Pravda* and *Izvestia* except to "authorized" addresses, the Bostonians—including two of five trustees of the library—who favored the removal of Communist literature from the stacks, and the officers who ran the security check on the professor before using his arguments on their side.

TEXTBOOKS FOR BOOK BURNERS

This kind of activity does, I believe, deserve that ugly epithet "un-American." Who are these un-American characters, seeking to tell us what we may not read and judging a book by its author's history instead of by reading the book? Some of them are dangerous pyromaniacs, who feel with the badger that there's nothing quite so lovely as a brightly burning book. Mostly, though, they are honest and worthy, if temporarily frightened, souls, who have just forgotten their history, and what America is all about. They perhaps need to be reminded, as Murray Kempton said a while ago, that the Bill of Rights was written by a revolutionary to protect bad literature and undesirable people.

Let us, therefore, not denounce their ignorance or condemn their motives: let us seek to improve their understanding. Lead them gently to the Constitution; introduce them to Socrates, Milton, Voltaire, Jefferson, Mill, Holmes, and Hand; show them the passage beginning "Don't join the book burners" from Eisenhower's Dartmouth Commencement speech; remind them that, although the Devil can quote Scripture and make a profit at it, these are still the American scriptures, and must be lived by if we are to remain Americans. The price of our liberty is the free grant of it to those we suspect may be seeking to destroy it.

THE NEED TO KNOW

Aside from the Constitution and the American scriptures—what might be called the needs of the American psyche—there is the obvious pragmatic reason for this. The need to know is not less intense in this generation than it was in the last. A knowledge of Communism is obviously essential to any American who wants to be able to combat it effectively. A university president, challenged by an alumnus that they were teaching Communism in the college, is said to have replied, "Yes, and we teach cancer in the medical school." Yet the Post Office now intercepts mail from the Iron Curtain countries and destroys periodicals addressed to subscribers here, excepting only those institutions and individuals "authorized" by the Post Office Department. (Imagine being authorized by the Post Office Department.) It would be in the national interest if the Post Office, instead of suppressing *Pravda* and *Izvestia,* were to carry them free, and perhaps even make their reading compulsory (although this, on second thought, would be an infringement of that equally valuable freedom, the freedom not to read).

At a deeper level than this is the need for new thought about our own society and our conduct in the world. Salvation tomorrow may lie in the unpopular today. In the words of the Freedom to Read Statement issued a couple of years ago by the librarians and publishers, "No society of free men can flourish which draws up lists of writers to whom it will not listen, whatever they may have to say."

Yet this kind of listing, or blacklisting, is now widespread, especially in the field of textbooks. Texas requires authors of textbooks to declare that they are not and never have been members of the Communist party, and are not and have not for ten years been members of any organization on the Attorney General's list. Other communities, denied such helpful and clear-cut legislation, have had to content themselves with informal lists or the dropping of works whose writers are locally unpopular.

One thing about lists: it saves people the trouble of reading the books.

Melville puts a footnote on a fresh thought at the end of *Billy Budd:* "An irruption of heretic thought hard to suppress." I suspect most of us have been suppressing our heretical thoughts lately. It is precisely here, I believe, that there lies a danger far more grave than the circulation of the most insidiously concealed Communist doctrines. If thoughts heretical of the current official orthodoxy are suppressed, where are the new and saving ideas to come from?

PRUDENT AFTERMATH

There is not, in fact, much official suppression of political ideas in the country today. The crisis of that particular folly seems to have been at least temporarily passed two years ago, when those two young men made everyone laugh at their antic raid on our overseas libraries. Freedom of expression stands high in our courts. Most libraries and schools have withstood the open assaults on their collections and texts from the local vigilantes and the would-be brainwashers.

But these battles leave their scars. Our present danger, I say, is here: that the school superintendent, having fought off an American Legion raid on his textbooks, may limit his selections afterwards to books by writers who never joined anything; that the librarian, having maintained her right to have pamphlets of the United Nations Educational, Scientific and Cultural Organization on the shelves, may not exercise that right on the next lot; that the publisher, having weathered the storm over a book by a writer who gave ten dollars to Spanish War relief in 1938, may decide his next book does not fit into the list; that the scholar, having observed the drawing and quartering of his colleague for a dispassionate study of recent Chinese history, may defer his own book on contemporary problems of the Far East and start revising his monograph on court customs of the Ming Dynasty; that the book-review editor, having received the document from the United States Atomic Energy Commission attacking the Alsops' book on the Oppenheimer case, may not review the book at all.

I do not say that any of these things have happened; although I am told that only three newspapers in the country have reviewed *We Accuse,* there were other factors involved in this case. I say only that it would be in human nature for things like this to happen. I do not believe that we are, as a nation, terrified; but I think some of us have got pretty cautious. If we have, so much the worse for us, and so much the worse for our country, which needs depth of insight, and boldness in speaking out, just as much today as it ever did.

Books—all kinds of books, expressing all kinds of views—are not a luxury but a necessity. They contribute to the strength of America. The best of them challenge our convictions and our settled ways of thought and make us learn not only what we believe but why we believe it. They cannot serve their most important social function if caution and prudence, even without censorship and suppression, serve to limit the range of ideas and of expression. Censorship, one student of the subject remarked recently, is like the common cold: it is a mild irritant, always with us, and there is nothing much to be done about it. If this is so, those who believe in free expression will at least avoid having the self-induced, or psychosomatic, sniffles when there are no germs about.

CENSORSHIP ON MORAL GROUNDS

They will also, if they are wise, take steps to combat the germs wherever they appear. At the moment, the chief censorship activity in this country is directed against publications not on political but on moral grounds. This seems, but is in fact not, remote from our topic. The local ordinance that is drawn to prevent the sale of horror and crime comics to children can be stretched to suppress *The Brothers Karamazov,* or the newspaper that gives the details of the latest love-nest killing. Aware of the latter possibility, but apparently unconcerned by the former, some legislative bodies have put language in their bills specifically exempting newspaper accounts of crime; a curious provision, considering that the First Amendment was drawn to protect not so much newspapers as books and pamphlets, and considering further that children are apparently affected more by what they believe to be the truth than by what they know to be fiction. The current morals laws do extend, either explicitly or implicitly, to magazines and books.

More serious than these laws, most of them of dubious constitutionality, is the current rash of extralegal censorship by citizens' groups. The technique here is to use lists of "objectionable" publications—often the list compiled monthly by the National Organization of Decent Literature, a Catholic lay group—to purge the neighborhood newsstands and drugstores. Dealers are asked to "co-operate" with the citizens' groups by withdrawing from sale the books and magazines on the lists. The consequence of non-co-operation is nontrade. Most dealers go along.

The seamless web

These drives are avowedly aimed at protecting the morals of the young. However, some cities have banned the works of Freud and other writers on psychoanalysis. Begin with morals, and suppression on doctrinal or political grounds soon becomes too tempting. No one will contest the right of a church to prescribe what its followers shall read. But is it also to prescribe what its nonfollowers shall read? And shall adults be limited to what is thought suitable for adolescents?

Everybody understands that you can demand the protection of due process of law for a man accused of murder without condoning murder. But it is not always easy to make it clear that you can insist on due process for books accused of obscenity without harboring any sympathy for obscenity. Despite the risk of misunderstanding and consequent denunciation, I am suggesting that those who believe in free expression must take this position. A breakdown in due process for the publication we abhor makes it that much more likely that there will follow a breakdown in due process for the publication we esteem. There is no such thing as a little censorship. This is one web that really is seamless. The citizens who boycott the dealer for selling crime comics or William Faulkner may be around next week to demand the removal of *The Age of Jackson* because they do not like Americans for Democratic Action or of *American Diplomacy* because they do not trust State Department officials even when they have resigned.

Law enforcement and censorship

The distinction that needs to be made, I think, is between law enforcement and censorship. The police department fobs off its duty when it sets up a citizens' committee to advise it on what books are "objectionable." It moves away from law and into taste. The principle is the same for politics as for morals. Support of rigorous enforcement of the laws, and opposition to extralegal efforts, is the way to guard ourselves against those so sure they are right that they are prepared to take the law into their own hands. If a book is unlawful, this is to be established in a court. If it is not unlawful, it is improper for the state or for any group within the state to attempt to suppress by coercion what cannot be suppressed by law.

The observance of due process, so central to our society, is being overlooked today in the quite natural revulsion against the horrors of some of the comics and the quite natural concern about exposing the young to books their parents do not want them to read. People who would cry out against any effort to censor on political grounds are silent about the censorship of morals because it is difficult to develop much enthusiasm for anyone's right to publish some of the things that have lately been displayed. The danger here is that precedents will be established and that censorship will spread. This is not fanciful. A congressional committee set up to investigate "pornography" issued a report in which one book was criticized because the author appeared to advocate polygamy; another because the author did not seem to have the properly respectful attitude toward law-enforcement officers; another because the "author is obviously trying to cash in on the Scottsboro pro-Negro agitation which was Communist-inspired."

New York City Bar Association

The Committee on the Bill of Rights of the Association of the Bar of the City of New York recently considered the suppression of books on political or moral grounds and concluded that, as a result of private censorship actions:

... one group within the community is compelling the balance of the community to conform to its standards of what it thinks should or should not be read. The censorship thus exercised, since it is that of a private group, is without the benefit of the procedural safeguards established by law as necessary to insure the proper application of the proscriptive standard. . . .

The wrong is basically public not private. What is involved is the infringement of a keystone of a democratic society: the preserving of a political system which permits the greatest possible freedom in the exchange of ideas.

The committee proposed a remedy:

Legislation penalizing organized private action which interferes, as described above, with the distribution of reading material would cure this danger. Legislation such as this would compel private groups which wish to prohibit the distribution, or the maintenance on a library shelf, of a particular book or magazine to invoke action under the applicable local ordinance.

The Bar Association accepted this report last month and approved unanimously a resolution by which it

... deplores and condemns the attempts of any individual or group, private or public, to interfere in any manner with the publication, circulation, or reading of any published matter, other than by means of regular applicable statutory procedures and standards; this resolution does not purport to limit the expression of views by any individual or group concerning any published matter.

THE RIGHT TO DECIDE

Our freedoms are involved: our right to decide for ourselves what we shall read. For us, there can be no security through book burning: only the rigid crust of conformity, and the end of that great conversation about who we are, what we are doing, and where we are going that is the essence of our national life. Let us see to it that the conversation continues.

In 1954–55 the U.S. Information Agency purchased and sent abroad 29,811 copies of Emily Davie's *Profile of America: An Autobiography of the U.S.A.*, with a foreword by Charles A. Lindbergh and an introduction by Louis Bromfield. A popular anthology made up of documents and selections covering American history from the beginnings to 1953 and containing numerous photographs, *Profile* soon became the USIA's most requested book. When the Agency sought an appropriation for the purchase and distribution of a large number of additional copies, however, the request was denied by Congress. Charging that the book did not fairly represent America and was therefore undesirable for use in the information program, several Congressmen objected to pictures of a 1750 schoolhouse, a dust storm, and Negro dancers, and to the inclusion of a scene from Eugene O'Neill's *Ah, Wilderness!* and the passage, "The mass of men lead lives of quiet desperation," from Thoreau's *Walden*.

Emily Davie
"PROFILE" AND THE CONGRESSIONAL CENSORS

"Defend me from my friends; I can take care of my enemies," was the comment of Maréchal Villars as he took leave of Louis XIV. Many must echo this sentiment today as they observe the peculiar way Americans bicker over how to tell the American story abroad.

In discussing America's overseas information program in "Can Propaganda Make Friends?" Victor Lasky made the astonishing statement that "Obviously the reason the U.S. has been unable to sell itself abroad is we have little to sell."

This is the kind of hair-shirt philosophy that gives such despair to those who are trying to present a balanced picture of our country to the peoples of the world. Unhappily, Mr. Lasky's lack of confidence seems to be shared by a small but potent group in Congress who faced with decisions of how to present our story abroad become so fearful and confused that they create havoc where none really exists. The antics of this group are having a lethal effect on the programs of the USIA, whose job it is "to promote the bet-

---

Emily Davie, " 'Profile' and the Congressional Censors," *Saturday Review*, 38:11+ (November 5, 1955), copyright 1955 by the Saturday Review Associates, Inc. Reprinted by permission of the author and of the publisher.

ter understanding of the United States among the peoples of the world and to strengthen cooperative international understanding."

An example of such Congressional confusion was the recent censorship of my book "Profile of America." Here was a source history telling the story of our country from its discovery by Leif Ericsson to President Eisenhower's "Atoms for Peace" proposals. With a foreword by Charles A. Lindbergh and introduction by Louis Bromfield, the book contains most of the nation's great documents, excerpts from the writings of our Presidents, pioneers, inventors, artists, and leaders in all fields. The story is told in words of the people who made our history and the text is dramatized with authentic pictures. For reasons never really made clear a House Subcommittee on Appropriations placed a ban on its future use by the government. As this case points up the need for better understanding of our information program, I think it is worth recording.

The USIA every year selects books it feels will best represent and explain America. Trial copies are then sent to our overseas libraries. These libraries then re-order according to each book's usefulness and demand in their area. In other words, no one man or group of men in Washington decides haphazardly how many copies shall be distributed; rather, the book's own success determines the numbers needed and its continued use. From trial copies sent last year the USIA received re-orders for over 300,000 copies of "Profile of America." This re-order of "Profile" is the largest request for a single volume in the history of the department. In spite of this, when the USIA asked for funds to meet the order two members of the House Subcommittee on Appropriations decided against the book. Though funds were granted for other books on the program the House report specified none could be used for "Profile." When asked at a press conference the reasons for this censorship John J. Rooney [D., Brooklyn], chairman of the Subcommittee and the man directly responsible for the ban, said: "All the members of the Subcommittee thought it was a fine book for American consumption. But when it comes to showing foreigners what foul balls we are that is something different." A glance at the Table of Contents makes one wonder who Mr. Rooney had in mind, and does he mean we should tell a different story abroad?

I then came across the following comment in the April 14 *Congressional Record* by a Congressman not on the Subcommittee: "I am mindful that the Committee eliminated all funds for the use of reproduction of 'Profile of America,' which I have had an opportunity to review and which I found to be objectionable, even obnoxious in parts.... I can well understand the position of the Committee and compliment them for stopping immediately any further reproduction and dissemination of this ill-conceived and damaging book. Obviously, I do not have in mind this type of book when I promote the Nonprofit Book Corporation."

In the May 11 *Congressional Record* it was with some relief that I read the following statement by Mrs. Katharine St. George [R., N.Y.], "I have been deeply concerned at the virtual banning of the book 'Profile of America' by a Subcommittee of the Appropriations Committee. This book has received the highest praise from everyone who has read and studied it. Of course, I am well aware that the Subcommittee has not had the time to do either with the tremendous volume of work before them. Some of us have said so often, and so loudly, that we disapproved of book burning, censorship, and all other evils that would shackle the human mind and spirit. Now we are taking a history of our country, carefully edited, taking all facets of that history from the beginning to the present ... we say it cannot be sent abroad. This would be funny if it were not tragic.... That such a book should be banned is at worst great comfort to our enemies and will be food for their propaganda specialists. At best it shows we are not yet adult in our thinking."

Though they had censored it nobody had yet given a specific reason for objecting to "Profile," but I realized that the stigma of Government rejection of a history book could seriously damage its domestic use in schools and libraries, as well as its overseas distribution, so I went to Washington to try to discover why my book had received such treatment and here is what I learned:

Mr. Rooney and his colleague Frank Bow [R., Ohio] had the following objections to the book. A photograph of a 1750 little red schoolhouse, used to illustrate the text of a McGuffey reader, they felt might give the Russians the idea this was typical of our school system, though following pages showed a modern high-school, state university, Harvard, William and Mary, Annapolis, West Point, and Mt. Holyoke; Thoreau's "Walden" they considered "damaging," and Eugene O'Neill's "Ah, Wilderness!" they thought "obscene"; pictures of a dust-storm and arid land they felt might lead foreigners to believe America was a wasteland, though they approved photos of the TVA, which showed how we controlled such conditions; a picture of a rural schoolteacher in a classroom was objected to on the grounds that someone had seen a Russian propaganda book with a better-looking teacher!

In an effort to get the ban on "Profile" lifted I testified before a Senate Subcommittee. Looking at a photograph of two Negro dancers used to illustrate an article by Agnes de Mille on the history of the dance Senator Harley M. Kilgore [D., W.Va.] said: "This dance in the picture is not a typical American dance . . . I can see how this would show foreigners a very distorted picture of our native life. They would think we were looking at the wrong things." He repeated this puzzling idea later when he said: "I question anything that is not typically American." And then he objected to the picture of the little red schoolhouse! After lengthy discussion with me on the contents of the book Senator Kilgore wound up his remarks with the comment: "I want to say that this is the first time I have seen the book. . . . Probably if I read the entire text I would get a different viewpoint." There's a kind of underwater quality in trying to talk to somebody about a book they haven't read, especially if it's yours. I do not know what the Senator's final viewpoint was, but the full Senate reinstated the book by writing an amendment into the Bill authorizing funds for American books "including 'Profile of America,'" and on June 7 Senator Kilgore released a press statement announcing he would support this amendment. What actually took place next is best told in the words of Rep. Frederic R. Coudert, Jr. [R., N.Y.], a member of the Conference Committee: "There was no controversy over that provision (*i.e.,* the 'Profile' amendment). The Voice of America got $85,000,000, which is about as much money as they expected to get, and in return the Senate yielded on these little things including the book. . . . When you have different things in dispute the two chairmen (Rooney and Kilgore) just traded them off back and forth. In this instance the Senate side yielded to Rooney on the book immediately without a fight."

After the conference action I wired the committees to try to discover whether or not "Profile" was still banned. I received the following reply from the Senate: "There is no legislative ban on your book 'Profile of America.' The USIA is charged by law with the responsibility of selecting and procuring books for their program and their actions are of course subject to Congressional review. Harley M. Kilgore." No reply came from Mr. Rooney, the House Chairman, but John Taber [R., N.Y.] wrote me the following letter: "I have your telegram of July 3. I expect that if the USIA decided to that the so-called 'Profile' might be printed by the United States Information setup. However, the appropriation that was passed was passed after the Committee had been advised that you had withdrawn the book and that the Administration did not intend to use it. Under these circumstances I think you might very readily expect considerable criticism from Congressional sources if they should use the book. I have looked over the book myself and it is impossible for me to see how the printing of the book could possibly be justified by the Administration. But that the best solution would be for the Administration not to print it. It is such things as this that have brought the Agency in the past into disrepute. Very sincerely yours, John Taber." I, of course, did not withdraw the book. Indeed, it was with considerable frustration that I was sitting in the Gallery when I heard Mr. Rooney state from the floor of the House that "the Director of the Agency, Mr. Streibert, withdrew the request *after* the committee had already acted." Such, then, were the reasons and methods that blocked further distribution of "Profile of America," the USIA's most requested book.

Ironically, in his article Mr. Lasky said of "Profile": "It is doubtful whether any book so laudatory of U.S. life would find ready acceptance among suspicious foreign intellectuals, particularly when distributed by the USIA." Mr. Lasky certainly has the right to his opinion, and it is a refreshing contrast to that of the Congressmen! But in criticizing the USIA's use of this book what seems to have been overlooked is that "Profile of America" is a source history, a factual record of events as they happened, and history cannot be rewritten to suit the tastes of "suspicious foreign intellectuals" or anybody else. To disavow dust-storms, a little red schoolhouse, and the writings of Thoreau, to call the same book both "damaging" and "too laudatory" is to suggest the need not for censorship but for common sense.

Unfortunately, the case of "Profile of America" is far from unique. It merely illustrates an unwise use of Congressional power, and the urgent need for better liaison between Congress and the USIA if that Agency is not to be rendered useless by the devastating effects of yanking books off shelves and the scuttling of carefully-planned projects by reckless individuals in Congress who haven't the qualifications to pass sound judgment on its many programs.

In 1953 President Eisenhower said: "It is not enough for us to have sound policies, dedicated to goals of universal peace, freedom, and progress. These policies must be made known to and understood by all peoples throughout the world. That is the responsibility of the new United States Information Agency."

This is a tremendous job and it can be done only if the Government and the people support our Information Agency. . . . One thing is certain: If we truly hope to "win the struggle for men's minds" abroad we must find a way to circumvent small minds at home.

Chapter VII

The writers fight back

No one, of course, has a greater stake in the freedom to write and to read than the professional author. It is not, in most cases, merely a question of his livelihood. He may quite likely have other means of earning a living. The true literary artist, however, has something to say and is deeply frustrated if not permitted freely to express himself. His devotion to his craft, the innate urge to convey the truth as he sees it, to derive some meaning from life—these he can exercise fully only through the written word. The writer is constantly driven by his inner compulsions to pass on—through novels, short stories, poetry, plays, essays—his thoughts and dreams. Language is his prime mode of expression, and the printed page furnishes his standard transmission belt.

Out of a population of more than 200,000,000 people in the United States and Great Britain today, it is doubtful that more than a few score writers have been endowed with this sublime gift.

Given this set of conditions, the writer naturally has a strongly adverse reaction to censorship in any shape or form, seeing in it a strait jacket to restrict his freedom, a prison for his thoughts and inspirations. In his own defense, or when rallying to the aid of beleaguered fellow-authors, therefore, he speaks out with courage and conviction against the evils of censorship. There are few issues over the centuries which have stirred writers so deeply, and to their unyielding stand we are indebted for some of the most eloquent and moving statements in the

English language, before and since John Milton's *Areopagitica*.

The essays included in the present chapter span the last half-century. They are limited to the work of British and American writers, and are necessarily highly selective from among a mass of important and stimulating literature on the subject.

Complementing the librarians' and publishers' manifesto, "The Freedom To Read," the Authors League of America, at its first national convention in 1957, adopted a strongly worded "Freedom To Write" declaration. The League, with about 3,500 members, is the principal organization of professional writers in the United States.

Authors League of America
FREEDOM TO WRITE

I.

The United States of America was born in the belief that freedom is the essence of life, and that freedom to write is the essence of the life of the mind. Our nation has grown and prospered in that belief.

While the ideal, and the governing principle, is complete freedom, the American people have considered that the public welfare requires safeguards of the principle in three general ways; and our laws contain penalties for the following, when proved by due legal process:

1. Corruption of public morals by unrestrained obscenity and depravity.
2. Direct and perilous incitement to such crimes as treason, murder, and civil violence.
3. Defamation of character through slander and libel.

Courts of law have been called on, as times have changed and standards of taste evolved, to define and redefine these terms. But for nearly two centuries the application even of these restrictions has been limited by the will of a free people resolved to stay free.

II.

In a large part of the world today, the freedom to write does not exist.

The Soviet Union, and the great block of countries under its control, have set above this freedom the absolute sway of the state. Writing must conform, in such lands, to what is called the true interests of the state; and these interests are defined by despots and enforced by the police.

The doctrine that society cannot with safety allow men to write freely is not new. Plato stated it in the Republic. Hobbes affirmed it in the Leviathan. The bloody regimes of Fascism were built on that doctrine. Every tyranny in history, every oligarchy, every theocracy, every absolute monarchy, every dictatorship—in short, every authoritarian government, ruling by force rather than by consent of the governed—has denied to its people the freedom of the written word. Depending on the whim of the ruler or the pressures of the time, censorship has been sometimes more drastic, sometimes less so; but censorship as a principle, in such lands, has dominated the life of the mind.

III.

The Authors League of America, representing the main body of writers in the United States, has noted with increasing concern, in the decade since the Second World War, a drift in our own national life toward censorship.

The impetus in this authoritarian drift is coming mainly from groups who above all should hold totalitarianism in abhorrence: a few religious organizations, and a few patriotic organizations, where zeal has overcome wisdom.

It is a grave development in our country's life that the vital forces of religion and patriotism should have been diverted, in however small a measure, toward Soviet methods. The Authors League holds that this development rises out of the international crisis; that it is the product of unreasoned hate and fear; that it defeats its avowed purposes; and that it should and must be stopped in the traditional American way, by an awakening of the public conscience to the facts of the situation, and to its dangers.

IV.

The censorship drift follows a consistent pattern.

Individuals and organized groups take on

A declaration by the Authors League of America presented at the National Assembly of Authors and Dramatists at New York on May 8, 1957.

themselves the right to decide what is obscene, what is depraved, what is treasonous, what is seditious, what is libelous. Ignoring the state laws and state courts, the federal laws and federal courts, which have defined criminal abuses of the freedom to write, and which exist to punish violators, the self-appointed censors take direct action against schools, libraries, booksellers, and even private individuals. Intimidation is the method. Ostracism and economic vengeance are threatened, and are carried out. Sometimes these self-appointed censors have no official standing at all; sometimes they hold municipal or county status.

The aim, and often the effect, of these censorship actions is to expunge certain writings and writers from the life of the community by denying the public any access to them. The public has no voice in the decision. The censors impose their own notions as to what the people shall not read, or hear, or see.

V.

The League holds that any individual or group has the right to disapprove of a writing or a writer and to state publicly that disapproval.

It further holds that any group has a right to recommend to its own members not to read certain writings or attend certain performances. The League in principle disagrees with such curtailment of individual free judgment of literature; but it is aware of conflicting views on this question, and the right of others to live by their views, provided that those views are not imposed on the entire community.

Authoritarian Fascism was destroyed in a war of terrible cost. The free nations of the world, including the United States, are engaged in a struggle with authoritarian communism for the leadership of the human race. Any trend to authoritarianism within our borders is a betrayal of what we stand for.

VI.

The Authors League of America declares that the preservation of freedom to write is necessary to our nation's survival as a free republic.

The Authors League of America denies the right of any individual or group in the United States to set limits on the freedom to write, which includes the freedom of publication, distribution, and performance of writings; and it declares that the right to define legal abuses of the freedom to write, and to punish violators, must be limited to the national and state legislatures and law courts, subject to the basic guarantees of the Constitution as interpreted by the Supreme Court of the United States.

Any other body, official or unofficial, which attempts to define these abuses and to impose its definitions on the community at large, invades the American freedom to write, and commits an act of authoritarian suppression.

Officials of a municipality, a county, or any other local civic body below the level of a state government, do not have the right to abridge or limit the freedom to write. Where they have done so, the action has been against the law and the spirit of the American system.

VII.

The Authors League calls on all those to whom the freedom of the written word is sacred —the press, the universities, the clergy of every denomination, and all thinking patriots—to join in the battle against authoritarian censorship. Where honest error has caused hasty action, let the errors be uncovered and the action corrected. Where there has been deliberate subversion of our heritage of freedom, let the subversives be unmasked, and the un-American weapon of censorship stricken from their hands.

The Authors League calls for continuing vigilance in this vital arena of American life until the drift to censorship is stopped. We cannot compete with the communists in the use of censorship; it is their traditional weapon.

Our hope must be, as it has always been, in freedom under law. In freedom under law we have become the strongest and most prosperous nation on earth. In freedom under law—and the freedom to write is a central part of that freedom —we will win the friendship and the trust of mankind.

The emergence of George Bernard Shaw on the English stage introduced what his biographer Archibald Henderson has called "troublesome new ideas in the theatre," and the shocked censors lost no time in attempting to suppress them. It seems probable that on more than one occasion Shaw deliberately baited the authorities. In part this was done because of his desire to change the licensing system, which enabled the censor to ban a play before its production, and in part to his inborn flair for controversy.

"The Rejected Statement" grew out of the contretemps over Shaw's "religious" play, *The Shewing-Up of Blanco Posnet,* described by the playwright as "a crude melodrama in one act—the crudity and melodrama both intentional." A license was refused by the Lord Chamberlain on grounds of blasphemy. Out of the furor came appointment of the Joint Select Committee of the House of Lords and the House of Commons on Stage Plays for the investigation of censorship. In order to have his views on the matter fully set forth, Shaw placed in the hands of the committee his privately printed *Statement of the Evidence in Chief of George Bernard Shaw Before the Joint Committee on Stage Plays (Censorship and Theatre Licensing).* This strong indictment of the theory and practice of censorship with arguments for its abolition was, by vote of the committee, omitted from the evidence included in its printed report. Shaw thereupon reproduced his statement as a preface to the published version of *Blanco Posnet.*

George Bernard Shaw
THE REJECTED STATEMENT

THE WITNESS'S QUALIFICATIONS

I am by profession a playwright. I have been in practice since 1892. I am a member of the Managing Committee of the Society of Authors and of the Dramatic Sub-Committee of that body. I have written nineteen plays, some of which have been translated and performed in all European countries except Turkey, Greece, and Portugal. They have been performed extensively in America. Three of them have been refused licences by the Lord Chamberlain. In one case a licence has since been granted. The other two are still unlicensed. I have suffered both in pocket and reputation by the action of the Lord Chamberlain. In other countries I have not come into conflict with the censorship except in Austria, where the production of a comedy of mine was postponed for a year because it alluded to the part taken by Austria in the Servo-Bulgarian war. This comedy was not one of the plays suppressed in England by the Lord Chamberlain. One of the plays so suppressed was prosecuted in America by the police in consequence of an immense crowd of disorderly persons having been attracted to the first performance by the Lord Chamberlain's condemnation of it; but on appeal to a higher court it was decided that the representation was lawful and the intention innocent, since when it has been repeatedly performed.

I am not an ordinary playwright in general practice. I am a specialist in immoral and heretical plays. My reputation has been gained by my persistent struggle to force the public to reconsider its morals. In particular, I regard much current morality as to economic and sexual relations as disastrously wrong; and I regard certain doctrines of the Christian religion as understood in England today with abhorrence. I write plays with the deliberate object of converting the nation to my opinions in these matters. I have no other effectual incentive to write plays, as I am not dependent on the theatre for my livelihood. If I were prevented from producing immoral and heretical plays, I should cease to write for the theatre, and propagate my views from the platform and through books. I mention these facts to shew that I have a special interest in the achievement by my profession of those rights of liberty of speech and conscience which are matters of course in other professions. I object to censorship not merely because the existing form of it grievously injures and hinders me individually, but on public grounds.

THE DEFINITION OF IMMORALITY

In dealing with the question of the censorship, everything depends on the correct use of the word immorality, and a careful discrimination between the powers of a magistrate or judge to administer a code, and those of a censor to please himself.

Whatever is contrary to established manners and customs is immoral. An immoral act or doctrine is not necessarily a sinful one: on the contrary, every advance in thought and conduct is by definition immoral until it has converted the majority. For this reason it is of the most enormous importance that immorality should be protected jealously against the attacks of those who have no standard except the standard of custom, and who regard any attack on custom—that is,

---

George Bernard Shaw, *Prefaces* (London: Constable, 1934), pp. 408–22, copyright 1934 by Constable & Co. Ltd. Reprinted by permission of the Public Trustee and the Society of Authors.

on morals—as an attack on society, on religion, and on virtue.

A censor is never intentionally a protector of immorality. He always aims at the protection of morality. Now morality is extremely valuable to society. It imposes conventional conduct on the great mass of persons who are incapable of original ethical judgment, and who would be quite lost if they were not in leading-strings devized by lawgivers, philosophers, prophets, and poets for their guidance. But morality is not dependent on censorship for protection. It is already powerfully fortified by the magistracy and the whole body of law. Blasphemy, indecency, libel, treason, sedition, obscenity, profanity, and all the other evils which a censorship is supposed to avert, are punishable by the civil magistrate with all the severity of vehement prejudice. Morality has not only every engine that lawgivers can devize in full operation for its protection, but also that enormous weight of public opinion enforced by social ostracism which is stronger than all the statutes. A censor pretending to protect morality is like a child pushing the cushions of a railway carriage to give itself the sensation of making the train travel at sixty miles an hour. It is immorality, not morality, that needs protection: it is morality, not immorality, that needs restraint; for morality, with all the dead weight of human inertia and superstition to hang on the back of the pioneer, and all the malice of vulgarity and prejudice to threaten him, is responsible for many persecutions and many martyrdoms.

Persecutions and martyrdoms, however, are trifles compared to the mischief done by censorships in delaying the general march of enlightenment. This can be brought home to us by imagining what would have been the effect of applying to all literature the censorship we still apply to the stage. The works of Linnæus and the evolutionists of 1790–1830, of Darwin, Wallace, Huxley, Helmholtz, Tyndall, Spencer, Carlyle, Ruskin, and Samuel Butler, would not have been published, as they were all immoral and heretical in the very highest degree, and gave pain to many worthy and pious people. They are at present condemned by the Greek and Roman Catholic censorships as unfit for general reading. A censorship of conduct would have been equally disastrous. The disloyalty of Hampden and of Washington; the revolting immorality of Luther in not only marrying when he was a priest, but actually marrying a nun; the heterodoxy of Galileo; the shocking blasphemies and sacrileges of Mahomet against the idols whom he dethroned to make way for his conception of one god; the still more startling blasphemy of Jesus when He declared God to be the son of man and Himself to be the son of God, are all examples of shocking immoralities (every immorality shocks somebody), the suppression and extinction of which would have been more disastrous than the utmost mischief that can be conceived as ensuing from the toleration of vice.

These facts, glaring as they are, are disguised by the promotion of immoralities into moralities which is constantly going on. Christianity and Mahometanism, once thought of and dealt with exactly as Anarchism is thought of and dealt with today, have become established religions; and fresh immoralities are persecuted in their name. The truth is that the vast majority of persons professing these religions have never been anything but simple moralists. The respectable Englishman who is a Christian because he was born in Clapham would be a Mahometan for the cognate reason if he had been born in Constantinople. He has never willingly tolerated immorality. He did not adopt any innovation until it had become moral; and then he adopted it, not on its merits, but solely because it had become moral. In doing so he never realized that it had ever been immoral: consequently its early struggles taught him no lesson; and he has opposed the next step in human progress as indignantly as if neither manners, customs, nor thought had ever changed since the beginning of the world. Toleration must be imposed on him as a mystic and painful duty by his spiritual and political leaders, or he will condemn the world to stagnation, which is the penalty of an inflexible morality.

WHAT TOLERATION MEANS

This must be done all the more arbitrarily because it is not possible to make the ordinary moral man understand what toleration and liberty really mean. He will accept them verbally with alacrity, even with enthusiasm, because the word toleration has been moralized by eminent Whigs; but what he means by toleration is toleration of doctrines that he considers enlightened, and, by liberty, liberty to do what he considers right: that is, he does not mean toleration or liberty at all; for there is no need to tolerate what appears enlightened or to claim liberty to do what most people consider right. Toleration and liberty have no sense or use except as toleration of opinions that are considered damnable, and liberty to do what seems wrong. Setting Englishmen free to marry their deceased wife's sisters is not tolerated by the people who approve it, but by the people who regard it as incestuous. Catholic Emancipation and the admission of Jews to parliament needed no toleration from Catholics and Jews: the toleration they needed was that of the people who regarded the one measure as a facilitation of idolatry, and the other as a condonation of the crucifixion. Clearly such toleration is not clamored for by the multitude or by the press which reflects its prejudices. It is essentially one of those abnegations of passion and prejudice which the common man submits to because uncommon men whom he respects as wiser than himself assure him that it must be so, or the higher affairs of human destiny will suffer.

Such submission is the more difficult because the arguments against tolerating immorality are the same as the arguments against tolerating murder and theft; and this is why the Censor seems to the inconsiderate as obviously desirable a functionary as the police magistrate. But there is this simple and tremendous difference between the cases: that whereas no evil can conceivably result from the total suppression of murder and theft, and all communities prosper in direct proportion to such suppression, the total suppression of immorality, especially in matters of religion and sex, would stop enlightenment, and produce what used to be called a Chinese civilization until the Chinese lately took to immoral courses by permitting railway contractors to desecrate the graves of their ancestors, and their soldiers to wear clothes which indecently revealed the fact that they had legs and waists and even posteriors. At about the same moment a few bold Englishwomen ventured on the immorality of riding astride their horses, a practice that has since established itself so successfully that before another generation has passed away there may not be a new sidesaddle in England, or a woman who could use it if there was.

THE CASE FOR TOLERATION

Accordingly, there has risen among wise and far-sighted men a perception of the need for setting certain departments of human activity entirely free from legal interference. This has nothing to do with any sympathy these liberators may themselves have with immoral views. A man with the strongest conviction of the Divine ordering of the universe and of the superiority of monarchy to all forms of government may nevertheless quite consistently and conscientiously be ready to lay down his life for the right of every man to advocate Atheism or Republicanism if he believes in them. An attack on morals may turn out to be the salvation of the race. A hundred years ago nobody foresaw that Tom Paine's centenary would be the subject of a laudatory special article in The Times; and only a few understood that the persecution of his works and the transportation of men for the felony of reading them was a mischievous mistake. Even less, perhaps, could they have guessed that Proudhon, who became notorious by his essay entitled "What is Property? It is Theft," would have received, on the like occasion and in the same paper, a respectful consideration which nobody would now dream of according to Lord Liverpool or Lord Brougham. Nevertheless there was a mass of evidence to shew that such a development was not only possible but fairly probable, and that the risks of suppressing liberty of propaganda were far graver than the risk of Paine's or Proudhon's writings wrecking civilization. Now there was no such evidence in favor of tolerating the cutting of throats and the robbing of tills. No case whatever can be made out for the statement that a nation cannot do without common thieves and homicidal ruffians. But an overwhelming case can be made out for the statement that no nation can prosper or even continue to exist without heretics and advocates of shockingly immoral doctrines. The Inquisition and the Star Chamber, which were nothing but censorships, made ruthless war on impiety and immorality. The result was once familiar to Englishmen, though of late years it seems to have been forgotten. It cost England a revolution to get rid of the Star Chamber. Spain did not get rid of the Inquisition, and paid for that omission by becoming a barely third-rate power politically, and intellectually no power at all, in the Europe she had once dominated as the mightiest of the Christian empires.

THE LIMITS TO TOLERATION

But the large toleration these considerations dictate has limits. For example, though we tolerate, and rightly tolerate, the propaganda of Anarchism as a political theory which embraces all that is valuable in the doctrine of Laisser-Faire and the method of Free Trade as well as all that is shocking in the views of Bakounine, we clearly cannot, or at all events will not, tolerate assassination of rulers on the ground that it is "propaganda by deed" or sociological experiment. A play inciting to such an assassination cannot claim the privileges of heresy or immorality, because no case can be made out in support of assassination as an indispensable instrument of progress. Now it happens that we have in the Julius Cæsar of Shakespear a play which the Tsar of Russia or the Governor-General of India would hardly care to see performed in their capitals just now. It is an artistic treasure; but it glorifies a murder which Goethe described as the silliest crime ever committed. It may quite possibly have helped the regicides of 1649 to see themselves, as it certainly helped generations of Whig statesmen to see them, in a heroic light; and it unquestionably vindicates and ennobles a conspirator who assassinated the head of the Roman State not because he abused his position but solely because he occupied it, thus affirming the extreme republican principle that all kings, good or bad, should be killed because kingship and freedom cannot live together. Under certain circumstances this vindication and ennoblement might act as an incitement to an actual assassination as well as to Plutarchian republicanism; for it is one thing to advocate republicanism or royalism: it is quite another to make a hero of Brutus or Ravaillac, or a heroine of Charlotte Corday. Assassination is the extreme form of censorship; and it seems hard to justify an incitement to it on anti-censorial principles. The very people who would have scouted the notion of prohibiting the performances of Julius Cæsar at His Majesty's Theatre in London last year, might now entertain very seriously a proposal to exclude Indians from them, and to suppress the play completely in Calcutta and Dublin; for if the assassin of Cæsar was a hero, why not the assassins of Lord Frederick Cavendish, Presidents Lincoln and McKinley, and Sir Curzon Wyllie? Here is a strong case for some constitutional means of preventing the performance of a play. True, it is an equally strong case for preventing the circulation of the Bible, which was always in the hands of our regicides; but as the Roman Catholic Church does not hesitate to accept that consequence of the censorial principle, it does not invalidate the argument.

Take another actual case. A modern comedy, Arms and The Man, though not a comedy of politics, is nevertheless so far historical that it reveals the unacknowledged fact that as the Servo-Bulgarian War of 1885 was much more than a struggle between the Servians and Bulgarians, the troops engaged were officered by two European Powers of the first magnitude. In consequence, the performance of the play was for some time forbidden in Vienna, and more recently it gave offence in Rome at a moment when popular feeling was excited as to the relations of Austria with the Balkan States. Now if a comedy so remote from political passion as Arms and The Man can, merely because it refers to political facts, become so inconvenient and inopportune that Foreign Offices take the trouble to have its production postponed, what may not be the effect of what is called a patriotic drama produced at a moment when the balance is quivering between peace and war? Is there not something to be said for a political censorship, if not for a moral one? May not those continental governments who leave the stage practically free in every other respect, but muzzle it politically, be justified by the practical exigencies of the situation?

THE DIFFERENCE BETWEEN LAW AND CENSORSHIP

The answer is that a pamphlet, a newspaper article, or a resolution moved at a political meeting can do all the mischief that a play can, and often more; yet we do not set up a permanent censorship of the press or of political meetings. Any journalist may publish an article, any demagogue may deliver a speech without giving notice to the government or obtaining its licence. The risk of such freedom is great; but as it is the price of our political liberty, we think it worth paying. We may abrogate it in emergencies by a Coercion Act, a suspension of the Habeas Corpus Act, or a proclamation of martial law, just as we stop the traffic in a street during a fire, or shoot thieves at sight if they loot after an earthquake.

258 *The writers fight back*

But when the emergency is past, liberty is restored everywhere except in the theatre. The Act of 1843 is a permanent Coercion Act for the theatre, a permanent suspension of the Habeas Corpus Act as far as plays are concerned, a permanent proclamation of martial law with a single official substituted for a court martial. It is, in fact, assumed that actors, playwrights, and theatre managers are dangerous and dissolute characters whose existence creates a chronic state of emergency, and who must be treated as earthquake looters are treated. It is not necessary now to discredit this assumption. It was broken down by the late Sir Henry Irving when he finally shamed the Government into extending to his profession the official recognition enjoyed by the other branches of fine art. Today we have on the roll of knighthood actors, authors, and managers. The rogue and vagabond theory of the depravity of the theatre is as dead officially as it is in general society; and with it has perished the sole excuse for the Act of 1843 and for the denial to the theatre of the liberties secured, at far greater social risk, to the press and the platform.

There is no question here of giving the theatre any larger liberties than the press and the platform, or of claiming larger powers for Shakespear to eulogize Brutus than Lord Rosebery has to eulogize Cromwell. The abolition of the censorship does not involve the abolition of the magistrate and of the whole civil and criminal code. On the contrary, it would make the theatre more effectually subject to them than it is at present; for once a play now runs the gauntlet of the censorship, it is practically placed above the law. It is almost humiliating to have to demonstrate the essential difference between a censor and a magistrate or a sanitary inspector; but it is impossible to ignore the carelessness with which even distinguished critics of the theatre assume that all the arguments proper to the support of a magistracy and body of jurisprudence apply equally to a censorship.

A magistrate has laws to administer: a censor has nothing but his own opinion. A judge leaves the question of guilt to the jury: the Censor is jury and judge as well as lawgiver. A magistrate may be strongly prejudiced against an atheist or an anti-vaccinator, just as a sanitary inspector may have formed a careful opinion that drains are less healthy than cesspools; but the magistrate must allow the atheist to affirm instead of to swear, and must grant the anti-vaccinator an exemption certificate, when their demands are lawfully made; and in cities the inspector must compel the builder to make drains and must prosecute him if he makes cesspools. The law may be only the intolerance of the community; but it is a defined and limited intolerance. The limitation is sometimes carried so far that a judge cannot inflict the penalty for housebreaking on a burglar who can prove that he found the door open and therefore made only an unlawful entry. On the other hand, it is sometimes so vague, as for example in the case of the American law against obscenity, that it makes the magistrate virtually a censor. But in the main a citizen can ascertain what he may do and what he may not do; and, though no one knows better than a magistrate that a single ill-conducted family may demoralize a whole street, no magistrate can imprison or otherwise restrain its members on the ground that their immorality may corrupt their neighbors. He can prevent any citizen from carrying certain specified weapons, but not from handling pokers, table-knives, bricks, or bottles of corrosive fluid, on the ground that he might use them to commit murder or inflict malicious injury. He has no general power to prevent citizens from selling unhealthy or poisonous substances, or judging for themselves what substances are unhealthy and what wholesome, what poisonous and what innocuous: what he *can* do is to prevent anybody who has not a specific qualification from selling certain specified poisons of which a schedule is kept. Nobody is forbidden to sell minerals without a licence; but everybody is forbidden to sell silver without a licence. When the law has forgotten some atrocious sin—for instance, contracting marriage whilst suffering from contagious disease—the magistrate cannot arrest or punish the wrongdoer, however he may abhor his wickedness. In short, no man is lawfully at the mercy of the magistrate's personal caprice, prejudice, ignorance, superstition, temper, stupidity, resentment, timidity, ambition, or private conviction. But a playwright's livelihood, his reputation, and his inspiration and mission are at the personal mercy of the Censor. The two do not stand, as the criminal and the judge stand, in the presence of a law that binds them both equally, and was made by neither of them, but by the deliberate collective wisdom of the community. The only law that affects them is the Act of 1843, which empowers one of them to do absolutely and finally what he likes with the other's work. And when it is remembered that the slave in this case is the man whose profession is that of Eschylus and Euripides, of Shakespear and Goethe, of Tolstoy and Ibsen, and the master the holder of a party appointment which by the nature of its duties practically excludes the possibility of its acceptance by a serious statesman or great lawyer, it will be seen that the playwrights are justified in reproaching the framers of that Act for having failed not only to appreciate the immense importance of the theatre as a most powerful instrument for teaching the nation how and what to think and feel, but even to conceive that those who make their living by the theatre are normal human beings with the common rights of English citizens. In this extremity of inconsiderateness it is not surprising that they also did not trouble themselves to study the difference between a censor and a magistrate. And it will be found that almost all the people who disinterestedly defend the censorship today are defending him on the assumption that there is no constitutional difference between him and any other functionary whose duty it is to restrain crime and disorder.

One further difference remains to be noted. As a magistrate grows old his mind may change or decay; but the law remains the same. The censorship of the theatre fluctuates with every change in the views and character of the man who exercises it. And what this implies can only be appreciated by those who can imagine what the effect on the mind must be of the duty of reading through every play that is produced in the kingdom year in, year out.

WHY THE LORD CHAMBERLAIN?

What may be called the high political case against censorship as a principle is now complete. The pleadings are those which have already freed books and pulpits and political platforms in England from censorship, if not from occasional legal persecution. The stage alone remains under a censorship of a grotesquely unsuitable kind. No play can be performed if the Lord Chamberlain happens to disapprove of it. And the Lord Chamberlain's functions have no sort of relationship to dramatic literature. A great judge of literature, a far-seeing statesman, a born champion of liberty of conscience and intellectual integrity—say a Milton, a Chesterfield, a Bentham—would be a very bad Lord Chamberlain: so bad, in fact, that his exclusion from such a post may be regarded as decreed by natural law. On the other hand, a good Lord Chamberlain would be a stickler for morals in the narrowest sense, a busy-body, a man to whom a matter of two inches in the length of a gentleman's sword or the absence of a feather from a lady's head-dress would be a graver matter than the Habeas Corpus Act. The Lord Chamberlain, as Censor of the theatre, is a direct descendant of the King's Master of the Revels, appointed in 1544 by Henry VIII to keep order among the players and musicians of that day when they performed at Court. This first appearance of the theatrical censor in politics as the whipper-in of the player, with its conception of the player as a rich man's servant hired to amuse him, and, outside his professional duties, as a gay, disorderly, anarchic spoilt child, half privileged, half outlawed, probably as much vagabond as actor, is the real foundation of the subjection of the whole profession, actors, managers, authors and all, to the despotic authority of an officer whose business it is to preserve decorum among menials. It must be remembered that it was not until a hundred years later, in the reaction against the Puritans, that a woman could appear on the English stage without being pelted off as the Italian actresses were. The theatrical profession was regarded as a shameless one; and it is only of late years that actresses have at last succeeded in living down the assumption that actress and prostitute are synonymous terms, and made good their position in respectable society. This makes the survival of the old ostracism in the Act of 1843 intolerably galling; and though it explains the apparently unaccountable absurdity of choosing as Censor of dramatic literature an official whose functions and qualifications have nothing whatever to do with literature, it also explains why the present arrangement is not only criticized as an institution, but resented as an insult.

THE DIPLOMATIC OBJECTION TO THE LORD CHAMBERLAIN

There is another reason, quite unconnected with the susceptibilities of authors, which makes it undesirable that a member of the King's Household should be responsible for the character and tendency of plays. The drama, dealing with all departments of human life, is necessarily political. Recent events have shewn—what indeed needed no demonstration—that it is impossible to prevent inferences being made, both at home and abroad, from the action of the Lord Chamberlain. The most talked-about play of the present year (1909), An Englishman's Home, has for its main interest an invasion of England by a fictitious power which is understood, as it is meant to be understood, to represent Germany. The lesson taught by the play is the danger of invasion and the need for every English citizen to be a soldier. The Lord Chamberlain licensed this play, but refused to license a parody of it. Shortly afterwards he refused to license another play in which the fear of a German invasion was ridiculed. The German press drew the inevitable inference that the Lord Chamberlain was an anti-German alarmist, and that his opinions were a reflection of those prevailing in St James's Palace. Immediately after this, the Lord Chamberlain licensed the play. Whether the inference, as far as the Lord Chamberlain was concerned, was justified, is of no consequence. What is important is that it was sure to be made, justly or unjustly, and extended from the Lord Chamberlain to the Throne.

THE OBJECTION OF COURT ETIQUET

There is another objection to the Lord Chamberlain's censorship which affects the author's choice of subject. Formerly very little heed was given in England to the susceptibilities of foreign courts. For instance, the notion that the Mikado of Japan should be as sacred to the English playwright as he is to the Japanese Lord Chamberlain would have seemed grotesque a generation ago. Now that the maintenance of *entente cordiale* between nations is one of the most prominent and most useful functions of the Crown, the freedom of authors to deal with political subjects, even historically, is seriously threatened by the way in which the censorship makes the King responsible for the contents of every play. One author—the writer of these lines, in fact—has long desired to dramatize the life of Mahomet. But the possibility of a protest from the Turkish Ambassador—or the fear of it—causing the Lord Chamberlain to refuse to license such a play has prevented the play from being written. Now, if the censorship were abolished, nobody but the author could be held responsible for the play. The Turkish Ambassador does not now protest against the publication of Carlyle's essay on the prophet, or of the English translations of the Koran in the prefaces to which Mahomet is criticized as an impostor, or of the older books in which he is reviled as Mahound and classed with the devil himself. But if these publications had to be licensed by the Lord Chamberlain it would be impossible for the King to allow the licence to be issued, as he would thereby be made responsible for the opinions expressed. This restriction of the historical drama is an unmixed evil. Great religious leaders are more interesting and more important subjects for the dramatist than great conquerors. It is a misfortune that public opinion would not tolerate a dramatization of Mahomet in Constantinople. But to prohibit it here, where public opinion would tolerate it, is an absurdity which, if applied in all directions, would make it impossible for the Queen to receive a Turkish ambassador without veiling herself, or the Dean and Chapter of St Paul's to display a cross on the summit of their Cathedral in a city occupied largely and influentially by Jews. Court etiquet is no doubt an excellent thing for court ceremonies; but to attempt to impose it on the drama is about as sensible as an attempt to make everybody in London wear court dress.

WHY NOT AN ENLIGHTENED CENSORSHIP?

In the above cases the general question of censorship is separable from the question of the present form of it. Everyone who condemns the principle of censorship must also condemn the Lord Chamberlain's control of the drama; but those who approve of the principle do not necessarily approve of the Lord Chamberlain being the Censor *ex officio*. They may, however, be entirely opposed to popular liberties, and may conclude from what has been said, not that the stage should be made as free as the church, press, or platform, but that these institutions should be censored as strictly as the stage. It will seem obvious to them that nothing is needed to remove all objections to a censorship except the placing of its powers in better hands.

Now though the transfer of the censorship to, say, the Lord Chancellor, or the Primate, or a Cabinet Minister, would be much less humiliating to the persons immediately concerned, the inherent vices of the institution would not be appreciably less disastrous. They would even be aggravated, for reasons which do not appear on the surface, and therefore need to be followed with some attention.

It is often said that the public is the real censor. That this is to some extent true is proved by the fact that plays which are licensed and produced in London have to be expurgated for the provinces. This does not mean that the provinces are more strait-laced, but simply that in many provincial towns there is only one theatre for all classes and all tastes, whereas in London there are separate theatres for separate sections of playgoers: so that, for example, Sir Herbert Beerbohm Tree can conduct His Majesty's Theatre without the slightest regard to the tastes of the frequenters of the Gaiety Theatre; and Mr George Edwardes can conduct the Gaiety Theatre without catering in any way for lovers of Shakespear. Thus the farcical comedy which has scandalized the critics in London by the libertinage of its jests is played to the respectable dress circle of Northampton with these same jests slurred over so as to be imperceptible by even the most prurient spectator. The public, in short, takes care that nobody shall outrage it.

But the public also takes care that nobody shall starve it, or regulate its dramatic diet as a schoolmistress regulates the reading of her pupils. Even when it wishes to be debauched, no censor can—or at least no censor does—stand out against it. If a play is irresistibly amusing, it gets licensed no matter what its moral aspect may be. A brilliant instance is the Divorçons of the late Victorien Sardou, which may not have been the naughtiest play of the 19th century, but was certainly the very naughtiest that any English manager in his senses would have ventured to produce. Nevertheless, being a very amusing play, it passed the licenser with the exception of a reference to impotence as a ground for divorce which no English actress would have ventured on in any case. Within the last few months a very amusing comedy with a strongly polygamous moral was found irresistible by the Lord Chamberlain. Plenty of fun and a happy ending will get anything licensed, because the public will have it so, and the Examiner of Plays, as the holder of the office testified before the Commission of 1892 (Report, page 330), feels with the public, and knows that his office could not survive a widespread unpopularity. In short, the support of the mob—that is, of the unreasoning, unorganized, uninstructed mass of popular sentiment—is indispensable to the censorship as it exists today in England. This is the explanation of the toleration by the Lord Chamberlain of coarse and vicious plays. It is not long since a judge before whom a licensed play came in the course of a lawsuit expressed his scandalized astonishment at the licensing of such a work. Eminent churchmen have made similar protests. In some plays the simulation of criminal assaults on the stage has been carried to a point at which a step further would have involved the interference of the police. Provided the treatment of the theme is gaily or hypocritically popular, and the ending happy, the indulgence of the Lord Chamberlain can be counted on. On the other hand, anything unpleasing and unpopular is rigorously censored. Adultery and prostitution are tolerated and even encouraged to such an extent that plays which do not deal with them are commonly said not to be plays at all. But if any of the unpleasing consequences of adultery and prostitution—for instance, an *unsuccessful* illegal operation (successful ones are tolerated) or venereal disease—are mentioned, the play is prohibited. This principle of shielding the playgoer from unpleasant reflections is carried so far that when a play was submitted for licence in which the relations of a prostitute with all the male characters in the piece was described as "immoral," the Examiner of Plays objected to that passage, though he made no objection to the relations themselves. The Lord Chamberlain dare not, in short, attempt to exclude from the stage the tragedies of murder and lust, or the farces of mendacity, adultery, and dissolute gaiety in which vulgar people delight. But when these same vulgar people are threatened with an unpopular play in which dissoluteness is shewn to be no laughing matter, it is prohibited at once amid the vulgar applause, the net result being that vice is made delightful and virtue banned by the very institution which is supported on the understanding that it produces exactly the opposite result.

THE WEAKNESS OF THE
LORD CHAMBERLAIN'S DEPARTMENT

Now comes the question, Why is our censorship, armed as it is with apparently autocratic powers, so scandalously timid in the face of the mob? Why is it not as autocratic in dealing with playwrights below the average as with those above it? The answer is that its position is really a very weak one. It has no direct coercive forces, no funds to institute prosecutions and recover the legal penalties of defying it, no powers of arrest or imprisonment, in short, none of the guarantees of autocracy. What it can do is to refuse to renew the licence of a theatre at which its orders are disobeyed. When it happens that a theatre is about to be demolished, as was the case recently with the Imperial Theatre after it had passed into the hands of the Wesleyan Methodists, unlicensed plays can be performed, technically in private, but really in full publicity, without risk. The prohibited plays of Brieux and Ibsen have been performed in London in this way with complete impunity. But the impunity is not confined to condemned theatres. Not long ago a West End manager allowed a prohibited play to be performed at his theatre, taking his chance of losing his licence in consequence. The event proved that the manager was justified in regarding the risk as negligible; for the Lord Chamberlain's remedy—the closing of a popular and well-conducted theatre—was far too extreme to be practicable. Unless the play had so outraged public opinion as to make the manager odious and provoke a clamor for his exemplary punishment, the Lord Chamberlain could only have had his revenge at the risk of having his powers abolished as unsupportably tyrannical.

The Lord Chamberlain then has his powers so adjusted that he is tyrannical just where it is important that he should be tolerant, and tolerant just where he could screw up the standard a little by being tyrannical. His plea that there are unmentionable depths to which managers and authors would descend if he did not prevent them is disproved by the plain fact that his indulgence goes as far as the police, and sometimes further than the public, will let it. If our judges had so little power there would be no law in England. If our churches had so much, there would be no theatre, no literature, no science, no art, possibly no England. The institution is at once absurdly despotic and abjectly weak.

AN ENLIGHTENED CENSORSHIP STILL WORSE THAN THE LORD CHAMBERLAIN'S

Clearly a censorship of judges, bishops, or statesmen would not be in this abject condition. It would no doubt make short work of the coarse and vicious pieces which now enjoy the protection of the Lord Chamberlain, or at least of those of them in which the vulgarity and vice are discoverable by merely reading the prompt copy. But it would certainly disappoint the main hope of its advocates: the hope that it would protect and foster the higher drama. It would do nothing of the sort. On the contrary, it would inevitably suppress it more completely than the Lord Chamberlain does, because it would understand it better. The one play of Ibsen's which is prohibited on the English stage, Ghosts, is far less subversive than A Doll's House. But the Lord Chamberlain does not meddle with such far-reaching matters as the tendency of a play. He refuses to license Ghosts exactly as he would refuse to license Hamlet if it were submitted to him as a new play. He would license even Hamlet if certain alterations were made in it. He would disallow the incestuous relationship between the King and Queen. He would probably insist on the substitution of some fictitious country for Denmark in deference to the near relations of our reigning house with that realm. He would certainly make it an absolute condition that the closet scene, in which a son, in an agony of shame and revulsion, reproaches his mother for her relations with his uncle, should be struck out as unbearably horrifying and improper. But compliance with these conditions would satisfy him. He would raise no speculative objections to the tendency of the play.

This indifference to the larger issues of a theatrical performance could not be safely predicated of an enlightened censorship. Such a censorship might be more liberal in its toleration of matters which are only objected to on the ground that they are not usually discussed in general social conversation or in the presence of children; but it would presumably have a far deeper insight to and concern for the real ethical tendency of the play. For instance, had it been in existence during the last quarter of a century, it would have perceived that those plays of Ibsen's which have been licensed without question are fundamentally immoral to an altogether extraordinary degree. Every one of them is a deliberate act of war on society as at present constituted. Religion, marriage, ordinary respectability, are subjected to a destructive exposure and criticism which seems to mere moralists—that is, to persons of no more than average depth of mind—to be diabolical. It is no exaggeration to say that Ibsen gained his overwhelming reputation by undertaking a task of no less magnitude than changing the mind of Europe with the view of changing its morals. Now you cannot license work of that sort without making yourself responsible for it. The Lord Chamberlain accepted the responsibility because he did not understand it or concern himself about it. But what really enlightened and conscientious official dare take such a responsibility? The strength of character and range of vision which made Ibsen capable of it are not to be expected from any official, however eminent. It is true that an enlightened censor might, whilst shrinking even with horror from Ibsen's views, perceive that any nation which suppressed Ibsen would presently find itself falling behind the nations which tolerated him just as Spain fell behind England; but the proper action to take on such a conviction is the abdication of censorship, not the practice of it. As long as a censor is a censor, he cannot endorse by his licence opinions which seem to him dangerously heretical.

We may, therefore, conclude that the more enlightened a censorship is, the worse it would serve us. The Lord Chamberlain, an obviously unenlightened Censor, prohibits Ghosts and licenses all the rest of Ibsen's plays. An enlightened censorship would possibly license Ghosts; but it would certainly suppress many of the other plays. It would suppress subversiveness as well as what is called bad taste. The Lord Chamberlain prohibits one play by Sophocles because, like Hamlet, it mentions the subject of incest; but an enlightened censorship might suppress all the plays of Euripides because Euripides, like Ibsen, was a revolutionary Freethinker. Under the Lord Chamberlain, we can smuggle a good deal of immoral drama and almost as much coarsely vulgar and furtively lascivious drama as we like. Under a college of cardinals, or bishops, or judges, or any other conceivable form of experts in morals, philosophy, religion, or politics, we should get little except stagnant mediocrity.

THE PRACTICAL IMPOSSIBILITIES
OF CENSORSHIP

There is, besides, a crushing material difficulty in the way of an enlightened censorship. It is not too much to say that the work involved would drive a man of any intellectual rank mad. Consider, for example, the Christmas pantomimes. Imagine a judge of the High Court, or an archbishop, or a Cabinet Minister, or an eminent man of letters, earning his living by reading through the mass of trivial doggerel represented by all the pantomimes which are put into rehearsal simultaneously at the end of every year. The proposal to put such mind-destroying drudgery upon an official of the class implied by the demand for an enlightened censorship falls through the moment we realize what it implies in practice.

Another material difficulty is that no play can be judged by merely reading the dialogue. To be fully effective a censor should witness the performance. The *mise-en-scène* of a play is as much a part of it as the words spoken on the stage. No censor could possibly object to such a speech as "Might I speak to you for a moment, miss?" yet that apparently innocent phrase has often been made offensively improper on the stage by popular low comedians, with the effect of changing the whole character and meaning of the play as understood by the official Examiner. In one of the plays of the present season, the dialogue was that of a crude melodrama dealing in the most conventionally correct manner with the fortunes of a good-hearted and virtuous girl. Its morality was that of the Sunday school. But the principal actress, between two speeches which contained no reference to her action, changed her under-clothing on the stage! It is true that in this case the actress was so much better than her part that she succeeded in turning what was meant as an impropriety into an inoffensive stroke of realism; yet it is none the less clear that stage business of this character, on which there can be no check except the actual presence of a censor in the theatre, might convert any dialogue, however innocent, into just the sort of entertainment against which the Censor is supposed to protect the public.

It was this practical impossibility that prevented the London County Council from attempting to apply a censorship of the Lord Chamberlain's pattern to the London music halls. A proposal to examine all entertainments before permitting their performance was actually made; and it was abandoned, not in the least as contrary to the liberty of the stage, but because the executive problem of how to do it at once reduced the proposal to absurdity. Even if the Council devoted all its time to witnessing rehearsals of variety performances, and putting each item to the vote, possibly after a prolonged discussion followed by a division, the work would still fall into arrear. No committee could be induced to undertake such a task. The attachment of an inspector of morals to each music hall would have meant an appreciable addition to the rate-payers' burden. In the face of such difficulties the proposal melted away. Had it been pushed through, and the inspectors appointed, each of them would have become a censor, and the whole body of inspectors would have become a *police des mœurs*. Those who know the history of such police forces on the Continent will understand how impossible it would be to procure inspectors whose characters would stand the strain of their opportunities of corruption, both pecuniary and personal, at such salaries as a local authority could be persuaded to offer.

It has been suggested that the present censorship should be supplemented by a board of experts, who should deal, not with the whole mass of plays sent up for licence, but only those which the Examiner of Plays refuses to pass. As the number of plays which the Examiner refuses to pass is never great enough to occupy a Board in permanent session with regular salaries, and as casual employment is not compatible with public responsibility, this proposal would work out in practice as an addition to the duties of some existing functionary. A Secretary of State would be objectionable as likely to be biased politically. An ecclesiastical referee might be biased against the theatre altogether. A judge in chambers would be the proper authority. This plan would combine the inevitable intolerance of an enlightened censorship with the popular laxity of the Lord Chamberlain. The judge would suppress the pioneers, whilst the Examiner of Plays issued two guinea certificates for the vulgar and vicious plays. For this reason the plan would no doubt be popular; but it would be very much as a relaxation of the administration of the Public Health Acts accompanied by the cheapening of gin would be popular.

THE ARBITRATION PROPOSAL

On the occasion of a recent deputation of playwrights to the Prime Minister it was suggested that if a censorship be inevitable, provision should be made for an appeal from the Lord Chamberlain in cases of refusal of licence. The authors of this suggestion propose that the Lord Chamberlain shall choose one umpire and the author another. The two umpires shall then elect a referee, whose decision shall be final.

This proposal is not likely to be entertained by constitutional lawyers. It is a naïve offer to accept the method of arbitration in what is essentially a matter, not between one private individual or body and another, but between a public offender and the State. It will presumably be ruled out as a proposal to refer a case of manslaughter to arbitration would be ruled out. But even if it were constitutionally sound, it bears all the marks of that practical inexperience which leads men to believe that arbitration either costs nothing or is at least cheaper than law. Who is to pay for the time of the three arbitrators, presumably men of high professional standing? The author may not be able: the manager may not be willing: neither of them should be called upon to pay for a public service otherwise than by their contributions to the revenue. Clearly the State should pay. But even so, the difficulties are only beginning. A licence is seldom refused except on grounds which are controversial. The two arbitrators selected by the opposed parties to the controversy are to agree to leave the decision to a third party unanimously chosen by themselves. That is very far from being a simple solution. An attempt to shorten and simplify the passing of the Finance Bill by referring it to an arbitrator chosen unanimously by Mr Asquith and Mr Balfour might not improbably cost more and last longer than a civil war. And why should the chosen referee—if he ever succeeded in getting chosen—be assumed to be a safer authority than the Examiner of Plays? He would certainly be a less responsible one: in fact, being (however eminent) a casual person called in to settle a single case, he would be virtually irresponsible. Worse still, he would take all responsibility away from the Lord Chamberlain, who is at least an official of the King's Household and a nominee of the Government. The Lord Chamberlain, with all his short-comings, thinks twice before he refuses a licence, knowing that his refusal is final and may promptly be made public. But if he could transfer his responsibility to an arbitrator, he would naturally do so whenever he felt the slightest misgiving, or whenever, for diplomatic reasons, the licence would come more gracefully from an authority unconnected with the court. These considerations, added to the general objection to the principle of censorship, seem sufficient to put the arbitration expedient quite out of the question.

▱ In this gently satirical, tongue-in-cheek "justification" of the censorship of plays, John Galsworthy maintains that the activities of such a beneficent institution should not be confined to the stage, but ought to be extended to literature in general, art, science, religion, and politics.

Later in the same year in which this essay was published, 1909, Galsworthy appeared as a witness before the Joint Committee of Parliament concerned with censorship of the theater. His statement to the committee, in part, went as follows:

"I have read the following plays, which have either been censored or in whose cases verbal or written intimation has been given by the Censor that they had better not be presented for license: The *Oedipus Rex* (Sophocles); *The Cenci* (Shelley); *Monna Vanna* (Maeterlinck); *Ghosts* (Ibsen); *Maternité* (Brieux); *The Three Daughters of Monsieur Dupont* (Brieux); *Mrs. Warren's Profession* (Shaw); *Waste* (Barker); *The Breaking Point* (Garnett); *Bethlehem* (Housman). I consider that all these plays are essentially moral, and some of great dramatic and artistic merit, and I do not see why any single one of them should not have been presented here . . . those persons who deliberately go to theatres from prurient motives would be most disagreeably disappointed by witnessing a performance of any of these plays."

Two years before, in 1907, Galsworthy had drafted a circular letter, protesting against censorship of the drama. This letter, signed by seventy-one leading British authors, appeared in the London *Times* and other newspapers, receiving wide attention and comment.

John Galsworthy
ABOUT CENSORSHIP

Since, time and again, it has been proved, in this country of free institutions, that the great majority of our fellow-countrymen consider the only Censorship that now obtains amongst us, namely the Censorship of Plays, a bulwark for the preservation of their comfort and sensibility against the spiritual researches and speculations of bolder and too active spirits—it has become time to consider whether we should not seriously extend a principle, so grateful to the majority, to all our institutions.

For no one can deny that in practice the Censorship of Drama works with a smooth swiftness—a lack of delay and friction unexampled in any public office. No troublesome publicity and tedious postponement for the purpose of appeal mar its efficiency. It is neither hampered by the Law nor by the slow process of popular election. Welcomed by the overwhelming majority of the public; objected to only by such persons as suffer from it, and a negligible faction, who, wedded pedantically to liberty of the subject, are resentful of summary powers vested in a single person responsible only to his own conscience—it is amazingly, triumphantly, successful.

Why, then, in a democratic State, is so valuable a protector of the will, the interests, and pleasure of the majority not bestowed on other branches of the public being? Opponents of the Censorship of Plays have been led by the absence of such other Censorships to conclude that this Office is an archaic survival, persisting into times that have outgrown it. They have been known to allege that the reason of its survival is simply the fact that Dramatic Authors, whose reputation and means of livelihood it threatens, have ever been few in number and poorly organized—that the reason, in short, is the helplessness and weakness of the interests concerned. We must all combat with force such an aspersion on our Legislature. Can it even for a second be supposed that a State which gives trial by Jury to the meanest, poorest, most helpless of its citizens, and concedes to the greatest criminals the right of appeal, could have debarred a body of reputable men from the ordinary rights of citizenship for so cynical a reason as that their numbers were small, their interests unjoined, their protests feeble? Such a supposition were intolerable! We do not in this country deprive a class of citizens of their ordinary rights, we do not place their produce under the irresponsible control of one not amenable to Law, by any sort

---

John Galsworthy, *The Inn of Tranquility*, pp. 236–53, copyright 1912 Charles Scribner's Sons; renewal copyright 1940 Ada Galsworthy. Reprinted by permission of Charles Scribner's Sons and William Heinemann Ltd.

of political accident! That would indeed be to laugh at Justice in this Kingdom! That would indeed be cynical and unsound! We must never admit that there is no basic Justice controlling the edifice of our Civic Rights. We do, we must, conclude that a just and well-considered principle underlies this despotic Institution; for surely, else, it would not be suffered to survive for a single moment! Pom! Pom!

If, then, the Censorship of Plays be just, beneficent, and based on a well-considered principle, we must rightly inquire what good and logical reason there is for the absence of Censorship in other departments of the national life. If Censorship of the Drama be in the real interests of the people, or at all events in what the Censor for the time being conceives to be their interest—then Censorships of Art, Literature, Religion, Science, and Politics are in the interests of the people, unless it can be proved that there exists essential difference between the Drama and these other branches of the public being. Let us consider whether there is any such essential difference.

It is fact, beyond dispute, that every year numbers of books appear which strain the average reader's intelligence and sensibilities to an unendurable extent; books whose speculations are totally unsuited to normal thinking powers; books which contain views of morality divergent from the customary, and discussions of themes unsuited to the young person; books which, in fine, provide the greater Public with no pleasure whatsoever, and, either by harrowing their feelings or offending their good taste, cause them real pain.

It is true that, precisely as in the case of Plays, the Public are protected by a vigilant and critical Press from works of this description; that, further, they are protected by the commercial instinct of the Libraries, who will not stock an article which may offend their customers—just as, in the case of Plays, the Public are protected by the common-sense of theatrical Managers; that, finally, they are protected by the Police and the Common Law of the land. But despite all these protections, it is no uncommon thing for an average citizen to purchase one of these disturbing or dubious books. Has he, on discovering its true nature, the right to call on the bookseller to refund its value? He has not. And thus he runs a danger obviated in the case of the Drama which has the protection of a prudential Censorship. For this reason alone, how much better, then, that there should exist a paternal authority (some, no doubt, will call it grand-maternal—but sneers must not be confounded with argument) to suppress these books before appearance, and safeguard us from the danger of buying and possibly reading undesirable or painful literature!

A specious reason, however, is advanced for exempting Literature from the Censorship accorded to Plays. He—it is said—who attends the performance of a play, attends it in public, where his feelings may be harrowed and his taste offended, cheek by jowl with boys, or women of all ages; it may even chance that he has taken to this entertainment his wife, or the young persons of his household. He—on the other hand—who reads a book, reads it in privacy. True; but the wielder of this argument has clasped his fingers round a two-edged blade. The very fact that the book has no mixed audience removes from Literature an element which is ever the greatest check on licentiousness in Drama. No manager of a theatre,—a man of the world engaged in the acquisition of his livelihood,—unless guaranteed by the license of the Censor, dare risk the presentment before a mixed audience of that which might cause an *émeute* among his clients. It has, indeed, always been observed that the theatrical manager, almost without exception, thoughtfully recoils from the responsibility that would be thrust on him by the abolition of the Censorship. The fear of the mixed audience is ever suspended above his head. No such fear threatens the publisher, who displays his wares to one man at a time. And for this very reason of the mixed audience, perpetually and perversely cited to the contrary by such as have no firm grasp of this matter, there is a greater necessity for a Censorship on Literature than for one on Plays.

Further, if there were but a Censorship of Literature, no matter how dubious the books that were allowed to pass, the conscience of no reader need ever be troubled. For, that the perfect rest of the public conscience is the first result of Censorship, is proved to certainty by the protected Drama, since many dubious plays are yearly put before the play-going Public without tending in any way to disturb a complacency engendered by the security from harm guaranteed by this beneficent, if despotic, Institution. Pundits who, to the discomfort of the populace, foster this exemption of Literature from discipline, cling to the old-fashioned notion that ulcers should be encouraged to discharge themselves upon the surface, instead of being quietly and decently driven into the system and allowed to fester there.

The remaining plea for exempting Literature from Censorship, put forward by unreflecting persons: That it would require too many Censors—besides being unworthy, is, on the face of it, erroneous. Special tests have never been thought necessary in appointing Examiners of Plays. They would, indeed, not only be unnecessary, but positively dangerous, seeing that the essential function of Censorship is protection of the ordinary prejudices and forms of thought. There would, then, be no difficulty in securing tomorrow as many Censors of Literature as might be necessary (say twenty or thirty); since all that would be required of each one of them would be that he should secretly exercise, in his uncontrolled discretion, his individual taste. In a word, this Free Literature of ours protects advancing thought and speculation; and those who believe in civic freedom subject only to Common Law, and espouse the cause of free literature, are championing a system which is essentially undemocratic, essentially inimical to the will of the majority, who have certainly no desire for any such things as advancing thought and speculation. Such persons, indeed, merely hold the faith that the *People, as a whole, unprotected by the despotic judgments of single persons, have enough strength and wisdom to know what is and what is not harmful to themselves. They put their trust in a Public Press and a Common Law, which deriving from the Conscience of the Country, is openly administered and within the reach of all.* How absurd, how inadequate this all is we see from the existence of the Censorship on Drama.

Having observed that there is no reason whatever for the exemption of Literature, let us now turn to the case of Art. Every picture hung in a gallery, every statue placed on a pedestal, is exposed to the public stare of a mixed company. Why, then, have we no Censorship to protect us from the possibility of encountering works that bring blushes to the cheek of the young person? The reason cannot be that the proprietors of Galleries are more worthy of trust than the managers of Theatres; this would be to make an odious distinction which those very Managers who uphold the Censorship of Plays would be the first to resent. It is true that Societies of artists and the proprietors of Galleries are subject to the prosecution of the Law if they offend against the ordinary standards of public decency; but precisely the same liability attaches to theatrical managers and proprietors of Theatres, in whose case it has been found necessary and beneficial to add the Censorship. And in this connection let it once more be noted how much more easily the ordinary standards of public decency can be assessed by a single person responsible to no one, than by the clumsy (if more open) process of public protest.

What, then, in the light of the proved justice and efficiency of the Censorship of Drama, *is* the reason for the absence of the Censorship of Art? The more closely the matter is regarded, the more plain it is, that *there is none!* At any moment we may have to look upon some painting, or contemplate some statue, as tragic, heart-rending, and dubiously delicate in theme as that censured play "The Cenci," by one Shelley; as dangerous to prejudice, and suggestive of new thought as the censured "Ghosts," by one Ibsen. Let us protest against this peril suspended over our heads, and demand the immediate appointment of a single person not selected for any pretentiously artistic feelings, but endowed with summary powers of prohibiting the exhibition, in public galleries or places, of such works as he shall deem, in his uncontrolled discretion, unsuited to average intelligence or sensibility. Let us demand it in the interest, not only of the young person, but of those whole sections of the community which cannot be expected to take an interest in Art, and to whom the purpose, speculations, and achievements of great artists, working not only for to-day but for to-morrow, must naturally be dark riddles. Let us even require that this official should be empowered to order the destruction of the works which he has deemed unsuited to average intelligence and sensibility, lest their creators should, by private sale, make a profit out of them, such as, in the nature of the case, Dramatic Authors are debarred from making out of plays which, having been censured, cannot be played for money. Let us ask this with confidence; for it is not compatible with common justice that there should be any favouring of Painter over Playwright. They are both artists—let them both be measured by the same last!

But let us now consider the case of Science. It will not, indeed cannot, be contended that the investigations of scientific men, whether committed to writing or to speech, are always suited to the taste and capacities of our general public. There was, for example, the well-known doctrine of Evolution, the teachings of Charles Darwin and Alfred Russel Wallace, who gathered up certain facts, hitherto but vaguely known, into presentments, irreverent and startling, which, at the time, profoundly disturbed every normal mind. Not only did religion, as then accepted, suffer in this cataclysm, but our taste and feeling were inexpressibly shocked by the discovery, so emphasised by Thomas Henry Huxley, of Man's descent from Apes. It was felt, and is felt by many to this day, that the advancement of that theory grossly and dangerously violated every canon of decency. What pain, then, might have been averted, what far-reaching consequences and incalculable subversion of primitive faiths checked, if some judicious Censor of scientific thought had existed in those days to demand, in accordance with his private estimate of the will and temper of the majority, the suppression of the doctrine of Evolution.

Innumerable investigations of scientists on subjects such as the date of the world's creation, have from time to time been summarised and inconsiderately sprung on a Public shocked and startled by the revelation that facts which they were accustomed to revere were conspicuously at fault. So, too, in the range of medicine, it would be difficult to cite any radical discovery (such as the preventive power of vaccination), whose unchecked publication has not violated the prejudices and disturbed the immediate comfort of the common mind. Had these discoveries been judiciously suppressed, or pared away to suit what a Censorship conceived to be the popular palate of the time, all this disturbance and discomfort might have been avoided.

It will doubtless be contended (for there are no such violent opponents of Censorship as those who are threatened with the same) that to compare a momentous disclosure, such as the doctrine of Evolution, to a mere drama, were unprofitable. The answer to this ungenerous contention is fortunately plain. Had a judicious Censorship existed over our scientific matters, such as for two hundred years has existed over our Drama, scientific discoveries *would have been no more disturbing and momentous than those which we are accustomed to see made on our nicely pruned and tutored stage.* For not only would the more dangerous and penetrating scientific truths have been carefully destroyed at birth, but scientists, aware that the results of investigations offensive to accepted notions would be suppressed, would long have ceased to waste their time in search of a knowledge repugnant to average intelligence, and thus foredoomed, and have occupied themselves with services more agreeable to the public taste, such as the rediscovery of truths already known and published.

Indissolubly connected with the desirability of a Censorship of Science, is the need for Religious Censorship. For in this, assuredly not the least important department of the nation's life, we are witnessing week by week and year by year, what in the light of the security guaranteed by the Censorship of Drama, we are justified in terming an alarming spectacle. Thousands of men are licensed to proclaim from their pulpits, Sunday after Sunday, their individual beliefs, quite regardless of the settled convictions of the masses of their congregations. It is true, indeed, that the vast majority of sermons (like the vast majority of plays) are, and will always be, harmonious with the feelings of the average citizen; for neither priest nor playwright have customarily any such peculiar gift of spiritual daring as might render them unsafe mentors of their fellows; and there is not wanting the deterrent of common-sense to keep them in bounds. Yet it can hardly be denied that there spring up at times men—like John Wesley or General Booth —of such incurable temperament as to be capable of abusing their freedom by the promulgation of doctrine or procedure, divergent from the current traditions of religion. Nor must it be forgotten that sermons, like plays, are addressed to a mixed audience of families, and that the spiritual teachings of a lifetime may be destroyed by ten minutes of uncensored pronouncement from a pulpit, the while parents are sitting, not, as in a theatre vested with the right of protest, but dumb and excoriated to the soul, watching their children, perhaps of tender age, eagerly drinking in words at variance with that which they themselves have been at such pains to instil.

If a set of Censors—for it would, as in the case of Literature, indubitably require more than one (perhaps one hundred and eighty, but, for reasons already given, there should be no difficulty whatever in procuring them) endowed with the swift powers conferred by freedom from the dull tedium of responsibility, and not remarkable for religious temperament, were appointed, to whom all sermons and public addresses on religious subjects must be submitted before delivery, and whose duty after perusal should be to excise all portions not conformable to their private ideas of what was at the moment suitable to the Public's ears, we should be far on the road toward that proper preservation of the *status quo* so desirable if the faiths and ethical standards of the less exuberantly spiritual masses are to be maintained in their full bloom. As things now stand, the nation has absolutely nothing to safeguard it against religious progress.

We have seen, then, that Censorship is at least as necessary over Literature, Art, Science, and Religion as it is over our Drama. We have now to call attention to the crowning need—the want of a Censorship in Politics.

If Censorship be based on justice, if it be proved to serve the Public and to be successful in its lonely vigil over Drama, it should, *and logically must be,* extended to all parallel cases; it cannot, it dare not, stop short at Politics. For, precisely in this supreme branch of the public life are we most menaced by the rule and license of the leading spirit. To appreciate this fact, we need only examine the Constitution of the House of Commons. Six hundred and seventy persons chosen from a population numbering four and forty millions, must necessarily, whatever their individual defects, be citizens of *more than average* enterprise, resource, and resolution. They are elected for a period that may last five years. Many of them are ambitious; some uncompromising; not a few enthusiastically eager to do something for their country; filled with designs and aspirations for national or social betterment, with which the masses, sunk in the immediate pursuits of life, can in the nature of things have little sympathy. And yet we find these men licensed to pour forth at pleasure, before mixed audiences, checked only by Common Law and Common-Sense political utterances which may have the gravest, the most terrific consequences; utterances which may at any moment let loose revolution, or plunge the country into war; which often, as a fact, excite an utter detestation, terror, and mistrust; or shock the most sacred domestic and proprietary convictions in the breasts of vast majorities of their fellow-countrymen! And we incur this appalling risk for the want of a single, or at the most, a handful of Censors, invested with a simple but limitless discretion to excise or to suppress entirely such political utterances as may seem to their private judgments calculated to cause pain or moral disturbance in the average man. The masses, it is true, have their protection and remedy against injudicious or inflammatory politicians in the Law and the so-called democratic process of election; but we have seen that theatre audiences have also the protection of the Law, and the remedy of boycott, and that in their case this protection and this remedy are not deemed enough. What, then, shall we say of the case of Politics, where the dangers attending inflammatory or subversive utterance are greater a million fold, and the remedy a thousand times less expeditious?

Our Legislators have laid down Censorship as the basic principle of Justice underlying the civic rights of dramatists. Then, let "Censorship for all" be their motto, and this country no longer be ridden and destroyed by free Institutions! Let them not only establish forthwith Censorships of Literature, Art, Science, and Religion, but also *place themselves* beneath the regimen with which they have calmly fettered Dramatic Authors. They cannot deem it becoming to their regard for justice, to their honour, to their sense of humour, to recoil from a restriction which, in a parallel case they have imposed on others. It is an old and homely saying that good officers never place their men in positions they would not themselves be willing to fill. And we are not entitled to believe that our Legislators, having set Dramatic Authors where they have been set, will—now that their duty is made plain—for a moment hesitate to step down and stand alongside.

But if by any chance they should recoil, and thus make answer: "We are ready at all times to submit to the Law and the People's will, and to bow to their demands, but we cannot and must not be asked to place our calling, our duty, and our honour beneath the irresponsible rule of an arbitrary autocrat, however sympathetic with the generality he may chance to be!" Then, we would ask: "Sirs, did you ever hear of that great saying: 'Do unto others as ye would they should do unto you!'" For it is but fair presumption that the Dramatists, whom our Legislators have placed in bondage to a despot, are, no less than those Legislators, proud of their calling, conscious of their duty, and jealous of their honour.

With his gift for irony and understatement, Sir Osbert Sitwell views the pleasures and emotional releases provided by the burning of books. Formerly "unorganized and sporadic," book burning under the Nazis, with true Teutonic thoroughness, entered "an era of organization and efficiency." As a consequence, Sir Osbert suggests, the world may never be the same again.

Osbert Sitwell
ON THE BURNING OF BOOKS AS PRIVATE PASTIME AND NATIONAL RECREATION

Comparatively few persons, we have just prophesied, will read printed matter in the future; but I doubt whether this need inevitably affect the production of books. Because reading it is not the only thing you can do with a book—you can also burn it. Newspapers are already used in the majority of houses to light fires, and the book of the future may serve a similar but more general purpose.

In a sense, the burning of one's books is a gesture similar to that of burning one's boats. It marks a definite step. Moreover it affords relief, both to the private individual and to the general public. The unliterary mind, it may be, finds more pleasure in the smashing of a plate; but, to those who know and hate literature, there is no satisfaction comparable to that of poking some special volume's glowing ashes.

We have been treated to a good deal of the sport in the past few decades. My first experience of it was when I saw those responsible for the education of my sister warming their hands at the embers of Swinburne's *Poems and Ballads*. Thirty or forty years earlier, no doubt, it would have been Shelley rather than Swinburne. But, though up to the close of King Edward's lifetime books were still burnt as part of the normal upbringing of any intelligent child, it was not until the war years that the setting alight of printed matter became a national recreation. . . . Who can ever forget those enjoyable bouts of newspaper-burning? The circulation of the condemned journals must have risen by thousands; for in order to burn a newspaper one has first to buy it. And any paper which did not suggest that the war was the best possible war, that the lads loved it, and that it would swiftly be brought to a glorious conclusion, was publicly burnt as a matter of course.

Nevertheless, newspapers are, by their very nature, ephemeral, and therefore their destruction does not offer to a cultured person the feeling of release afforded him by the burning of a *book*. Alas! only latterly has book-burning attained to national proportions. At one time it was unorganized and sporadic; and thus unsuitable to an era of organization and efficiency. But the matter has now been remedied. With the rise to power of the Nazi Government, book-burning, in Germany at least, has once for all assumed its proper place. All books that were un-German have been consigned to the stake, and in so doing, who knows but that the Nazis may have lighted such a candle as shall never be put out? Moreover, should a similar situation arise here, where literature is taken less heavily than on the Continent, would it not be the authors, rather than their works, who would be sacrificed?

The reasons for the widespread hatred of literature are to be sought in many morbid complexes. There is the gnawing and continual fear, which the most uninteresting people perpetually entertain, that they may be "put into a book"; a fear which fortunately in some cases makes them nervous of meeting authors, though in others it leads to an irritating amount of rudeness. (Many, it is true, are too shy to be rude individually and alone. These unfortunates are compelled to form themselves into lecture-associations, luncheon-clubs and the like; to which they invite the author to come without payment, and then, having got him there, pro-

---

Osbert Sitwell, *Penny Foolish* (London: Macmillan & Co. Ltd., 1935), pp. 328–33, copyright 1935 by Macmillan & Co. Ltd. Reprinted by permission of the author and of the publisher.

ceed in mass to insult him.) For any author, more especially a novelist, is regarded by these persons as a collector of specimens, who stalks through life catching the poor creatures unaware and imprisoning them in those curious cubes which he manufactures.... (If only a character could know the degree of touching up and of toning down which he requires if he is to appear even as the most humble auxiliary!) ... Then, too, there is the fact that, since an author is often endowed with the gift of words, he can, when challenged, crush his specimen with ease. ... It is singular, therefore, that fears thus engendered should incline the character to be rude to the author from the beginning. Surely it would be better to propitiate him?

Again, there is much chagrin at the miserliness which authors display in the giving of their time for advice. They exist to be consulted on every subject, and it is well known that they have at their disposal hours unlimited; but are they willing to bestow it on every worthy cause? No! This is responsible for much annoyance, and I well remember an old lady, unknown to my sister, who wrote to her inquiring if she could explain the secret of how to keep a hot-water bottle *really* hot during the night? Apparently, however boiling the water might be when put into the bottle, it would never remain at the right temperature for more than five or six hours. This occurred during the lifetime of Mr Arnold Bennett, and my sister replied that she happened to be rather busy at the moment, and therefore regretfully found herself unable to devote as much time as she would have liked to the solution of the problem, but that, since both Mr H. G. Wells and Mr Arnold Bennett were proverbially idle, she advised the old lady to write to them instead. They, she was sure, would be delighted to give their advice on a subject of such concern to humanity.

Upon another occasion a rather stout lady, wearing a sombrero hat, and clad in a sensible coat and skirt, appeared at my house and, when I opened the door, quickly threw her foot into the gap, and asked me to take down in coloured silks the embroideries which she would sing to me. She indicated that she had taught this remarkable accomplishment to an Indian student, whom she had specially trained for the purpose. She used to sing: and from her singing he would seize the appropriate design and colour. Unfortunately he had died, and she had concluded, from my writings, that I would serve instead. I assured her that this was not the case, and supplied her with the addresses of various friends whom I thought more suitable for her purpose. ...

Whether the root of such incidents is in a conscious desire to waste the time of authors and thus prevent their working, or whether it is merely a matter of instinct, will, I suppose, never be scientifically decided: but book-burnings are their outcome. Speaking for my own part, as long as the book is bought, I do not mind its being burnt; but the end which I fear is that the book will be borrowed, and then burnt: for just as it is known that authors have this infinite time upon their hands, so the public believes them to have an unlimited supply of books; to be, in fact, a sort of lending library of their own works. More than this, nobody who is proposing to organize a bazaar ever thinks twice before asking an author to give his works, and, in addition, to sign them. ...

It may be worth while now to conjecture which English books would meet the same fate in England as that of the un-German books in Germany, should the government of the day be in the happy position of being able to enforce these decrees? Some authors would be spared because they are not read, and others would be burnt for the same reason. Shakespeare would be spared, one presumes, because he is so little read: though were he a German writer, and had he written of Germans in the same way that he wrote of Bottom, Snout and Starveling, he would most certainly have been burnt. ... I suppose no writer earlier than the nineteenth century would be consigned to the flames? Shelley is presumably safe: but nearly all modern poets would be burnt, and the works of all such philosophers as Bertrand Russell. D. H. Lawrence would similarly be a favourite for fiery treatment, because perhaps full enjoyment of an *auto-da-fé* is only to be obtained when there is also the support of a fanatical minority.

Which books should be chosen would, I imagine, be decided by the readers of the newspapers; and I venture to suggest that Mr James Douglas, of the *Sunday Express,* would make a suitable executioner; for in him the moral sense seems to be developed to its finest form and most acute degree.

> In this review of Bernard Causton and G. Gordon Young's *Keeping It Dark, or The Censor's Handbook,* Aldous Huxley makes a convincing appeal for a civilized attitude toward censorship. At the same time, he effectively demolishes the notion that adult reading should be determined by what is proper and fit for young girls.

Aldous Huxley
CENSORSHIP

Keeping It Dark is informative, amusing and very sensible. Its descriptions of the methods of modern censorship serve to round off the more considerable historical work of Seagle and his collaborator, *To the Pure.* These two books, together with *Le Mythe Vertuiste* by the great sociologist, Vilfredo Pareto, and the two pamphlets of D. H. Lawrence, on pornography and in defence of *Lady Chatterley's Lover* respectively, contain, so far as I know, all the significant facts about censorship in England, America and the Latin countries, together with all the relevant arguments in its disfavour. No rational being could read these five books and pamphlets and still remain a believer in censorship—or so, at least, it seems to me. For, so far as I am concerned, the arguments which they state and imply are perfectly convincing. But then, I must admit, I do not need to be convinced. Those who start with other temperamental and educational major premises than mine will doubtless find that these same arguments are wholly without cogency and will marvel how any rational being could be taken in by such palpable sophistry. Between Nature's censors and Nature's non-censors there can only be war.

Being one of Nature's non-censors, I simply cannot understand why any human being should want to prevent other responsible human beings from writing or reading what they like; or why literature should be debarred from taking cognizance of any fact whatsoever. That we should never be allowed to write (except in a Graeco-Latin jargon and in the decent obscurity of a scientific text-book) about experiences which all of us have had seems to me simply incomprehensible. This native incomprehension of mine is, of course, impervious to any of the arguments in favour of censorship. In my eyes they are all equally bad. Let us consider a few of them.

There is, to begin with, the religious argument. We ought not to write or read of certain subjects because, by doing so, we displease the Almighty. Hobbes dealt with this contention in words which are so beautifully to the point that I cannot forebear from quoting them in full. "If a man pretend to me that God hath spoken to him immediately and supernaturally, and I make doubt of it, I cannot easily perceive what argument he can produce to oblige me to believe it. It is true that, if he be my Sovereign, he may oblige me to obedience, so as not by act or word to *declare* I believe him not; but not to *think* any otherwise than my reason persuades me. But if one that hath not such authority over me shall pretend the same, there is nothing that exacteth either belief or obedience." The cautious literary man, when he finds himself under a "Sovereign" of the stamp of Lord Brentford, refrains from "declaring" by censorable act and word his disbelief in the divine nature of censorship. But even a Home Secretary cannot compel his thoughts.

Systems of morality have a way of outliving the religious dogmas, upon which they were based. But men feel uncomfortable when their prejudices are not supported. Unbelieving censors have therefore found it necessary to invent several new, non-religious arguments to justify their persecuting zeal. Of these the prime favourite is what I may call the *argumentum ad puellam.* We must not allow anything to be published which might in any way offend the least of these little flappers. In a word *la jeune fille des éditeurs, la jeune fille des rédacteurs en chef, la jeune fille épouvantail, monstre, assassin de l'art* must be the final judge of literature. This notion that children are more important than adults is, of course, completely preposterous. Preventing adults from thinking in a grown-up way about the truth does incomparably more harm to society than allowing an occasional child to think about it precociously. The Infantile Man was a dangerous monstrosity invented during the nineteenth century; he is still with us. Compare Dickens's aged infants (all his virtuous men and women suffer from retarded development), compare the later Pickwick, and Mr. Garland,

---
Aldous Huxley, "Censorship," *Fortnightly,* 134:415–16 (September, 1930), copyright 1930 by Chapman and Hall, Ltd. Reprinted by permission of the publisher.

and the Cheerybles with the thoroughly manly, realistic and intelligent good men of Fielding's novels. It is the difference between deformity and perversity on the one hand and health on the other. Dickens's ghoulish old Peter Pans were the product of Victorian censorship; those noble eighteenth-century men were the grown-up and fully human sons of truth-telling.

Censorship has many other deleterious effects on adults and their literature; but I have no time to enumerate them here. I must return to the *jeune fille monstre, assassin de l'art*. It is obviously important that the precocious sexual interests of children should be sublimated and canalized in the interests of education. Children who live like the Trobriand boys and girls described by Malinowski cannot find the time or energy to acquire culture. The difficulty of reconciling precocious sexual activity with higher education is insisted on by Gandhi in the chapter of his autobiography dealing with his own schoolboy marriage. Again, there is reason to believe that the "necking" so common at present among American boys and girls is not doing much good to the cause of learning. But it is quite easy so to organize society that its young people do not live like Trobrianders, Hindus or even little Americans. Mere knowledge, and even emotional stimulation, can do very little harm to any reasonably well-brought-up child—particularly to the modern child who, if he has been educated at an up-to-date school, already at the age of ten knows much more about ova, spermatozoa, cell division and all the processes of reproduction than most of the adults by whom he is surrounded.

The censors extend the *argumentum ad puellam* to the world at large. They promote themselves to be the fathers of a humanity too childish to look after itself, too imbecile to assume its own responsibilities. Men and women (this is what their arguments boil down to) are so feeble-minded and so naturally depraved that if censorship were removed and if, as an inevitable consequence, floods of pornography were let loose upon the world, they would all lose their heads and plunge into debauchery. But men and women are not quite such criminal imbeciles as the censors seem to imagine. Consider the facts. In countries where pornographical literature is sold almost freely, as in France, people continue to behave with all desirable decorum and in spite of the laxity of the censorship, floods of pornography do *not* flood the market. Moreover, what in fact is the reaction to pornography of the great majority of men and women leading a normal sexual life? To the very rare specimens of this branch of literature which are well written and therefore convincing they may react positively—that is to say, they may be temporarily excited by the reading of artistically good pornography. There is nothing very criminal in this. Practically all our amusements, from dancing to the watching of dancing are admittedly more or less aphrodisiac. Artistically written pornography is more, not less, aphrodisiac, that is all. As to inartistic pornography (and practically all pornographic books are written atrociously)—the reaction to that is generally negative. Its vulgarity and stupidity are not exciting, but shocking and repellant. In its extreme form pornography is emotionally distressing. Nobody who is not temperamentally akin to the Marquis de Sade can possibly read *Justine* without being horrified. But why should I continue? The remedy against pornography is in the hands of everyone who chooses to use it. If you do not like a book, all you have to do is not to read it. Let every man be his own censor.

Following the death of Anthony Comstock in 1915, the New York Society for the Suppression of Vice, of which he was one of the creators, continued to flourish for some years under the direction of John S. Sumner. During this period, when it was the chief instrument for literary censorship in New York City, the Society's most relentless gadfly was the widely read columnist, Heywood Broun. The countercrusades of such critics as Broun and Mencken no doubt account for the gradual decline of the Society into its present state of innocuous desuetude.

Broun's *Anthony Comstock, Roundsman of the Lord* is the standard biography of his subject.

Heywood Broun
CENSORING THE CENSOR

Mice and canaries were sometimes employed in France to detect the presence of gas. When these

---

Heywood Broun, *Collected Edition of Heywood Broun* (New York: Harcourt, Brace, 1941), pp. 118-22, copyright 1941 by Heywood Hale Broun. Reprinted by permission of the publisher.

little things began to die in their cages the soldiers knew that the air had become dangerous. Some such system should be devised for censorship to make it practical. Even with the weight of authority behind him no bland person, with virtue obviously unruffled, is altogether convincing when he announces that the book he has just read or the moving picture he has seen is so hideously immoral that it constitutes a danger to the community. For my part I always feel that if he can stand it so can I. To the best of my knowledge and belief, Mr. Sumner was not swayed from his usual course of life by so much as a single peccadillo for all of *Jurgen*. His indignation was altogether altruistic. He feared for the fate of weaker men and women.

Every theatrical manager, every motion picture producer, and every publisher knows, to his sorrow, that the business of estimating the effect of any piece of imaginative work upon others is precarious and uncertain. Genius would be required to predict accurately the reaction of the general public to any set piece which seems immoral to the censor. For instance, why was Mr. Sumner so certain that *Jurgen,* which inspired him with horror and loathing, would prove a persuasive temptation to all the rest of the world? Censorship is serious and drastic business; it should never rest merely upon guesswork and more particularly not upon the guesses of men so staunch in morals that they are obviously of distant kin to the rest of humanity.

The censor should be a person of a type capable of being blasted for the sins of the people. His job can be elevated to dignity only when the world realizes that he runs horrid risks. If we should choose our censors from fallible folk we might have proof instead of opinions. Suppose the censor of *Jurgen* had been someone other than Mr. Sumner, someone so unlike the head of the vice society that after reading Mr. Cabell's book he had come out of his room, not quivering with rage, but leering and wearing vine leaves. In such case the rest would be easy. It would merely be necessary to shadow the censor until he met his first dryad. His wink would be sufficient evidence and might serve as a cue for the rescuers to rush forward and save him. Of course there would then be no necessity for legal proceedings in regard to the book. Expert testimony as to its possible effects would be irrelevant. We would know and we could all join cheerfully in the bonfire.

To my mind there are three possible positions which may logically be taken concerning censorship. It might be entrusted to the wisest man in the world, to a series of average men,—or be abolished. Unfortunately it has been our experience that there is a distinct affinity between fools and censorship. It seems to be one of those treading grounds where they rush in. To be sure, we ought to admit a prejudice at the outset and acknowledge that we were a reporter in France during the war at a time when censors seemed a little more ridiculous than usual. We still remember the young American lieutenant who held up a story of a boxing match in Saint-Nazaire because the reporter wrote, "In the fourth round MacBeth landed a nice right on the Irishman's nose and the claret began to flow." "I'm sorry," said the censor, "but we have strict orders from Major Palmer that no mention of wine or liquor is to be allowed in any story about the American army."

Nor have we forgotten the story of General Pétain's mustache. "Why," asked Junius Wood of the *Globe,* "have you held up my story? All the rest have gone."

"Unfortunately," answered the courteous Frenchman, "you have twice used the expression General Pétain's 'white mustache.' I might stretch a point and let you say 'gray mustache,' but I should much prefer to have you say 'blond mustache.'"

"Oh, make it green with purple spots," said Junius.

The use of average men in censorship would necessitate sacrifices to the persuasive seduction of immorality, as I have suggested, and moreover there are very few average men. Accordingly, I am prepared to abandon that plan of censorship. The wisest man in the world is too old and too busy with his plays and has announced that he will never come to America. Accordingly we venture to suggest that in time of peace we try to get along without any censorship of plays or books or moving pictures. I have no desire, of course, to leave Mr. Sumner unemployed—it would perhaps be only fair to allow him to slosh around among the picture postcards.

Once official censorship had been officially abolished, a strong and able censorship would immediately arise consisting of the playgoing and reading public. It is a rather offensive error to assume that the vast majority of folk in America are rarin' to get to dirty books and dirty plays. It is the experience of New York managers that the run of the merely salacious play is generally short. The success which a few nasty books have had has been largely because of the fact that they came close to the line of things which are forbidden. Without the prohibition there would be little popularity.

To save myself from the charge of hypocrisy I should add that personally I believe there ought to be a certain amount of what we now know as immoral writing. It would do no harm in a community brought up to take it or let it alone. It is well enough for the reading public and the critic to use terms such as moral or immoral, but they hardly belong in the vocabulary of an artist. I have heard it said that before Lucifer left Heaven there were no such things as virtues and vices. The world was equipped with a certain number of traits which were qualities without distinction or shame. But when Lucifer and the heavenly hosts drifted into their eternal warfare it was agreed that each side should recruit an equal number of these human, and at that time unclassified, qualities. A coin was tossed and, whether by fair chance or sharp miracle, Heaven won.

"I choose Blessedness," said the Captain of the Angels. It should be explained that the selection was made without previous medical examination, and Blessedness seemed at that time a much more robust recruit than he has since turned out to be. A tendency to flat foot is always hard to detect.

"Give me Beauty," said Lucifer, and from that day to this the artists of the world have been divided into two camps—those who wished to achieve beauty and those who wished to achieve blessedness, those who wanted to make the world better and those who were indifferent to its salvation if they could only succeed in making it a little more personable.

However, the conflict is not quite so simple as that. Late in the afternoon when the Captain of the Angels had picked Unselfishness and Moderation and Faith and Hope and Abstinence, and Lucifer had called to his side Pride and Gluttony and Anger and Lust and Tactlessness, there remained only two more qualities to be apportioned to the contending sides. One of them was Sloth, who was obviously overweight, and the other was a furtive little fellow with his cap down over his eyes.

"What's your name?" said the Captain of the Angels.

"Truth," stammered the little fellow.

"Speak up," said the Captain of the Angels so sharply that Lucifer remonstrated, saying, "Hold on there; Anger's on my side."

"Truth," said the little fellow again but with the same somewhat indistinct utterance which has always been so puzzling to the world.

"I don't understand you," said the Captain of the Angels, "but if it's between you and Sloth I'll take a chance with you. Stop at the locker room and get your harp and halo."

Now today even Lucifer will admit, if you get him in a corner, that Truth is the mightiest warrior of them all. The only trouble is his truancy. Sometimes he can't be found for centuries. Then he will bob up unexpectedly, break a few heads, and skip away. Nothing can stand against him. Lucifer's best ally, Beauty, is no match for him. Truth holds every decision. But the trouble is that he still keeps his cap down over his eyes, and he still mumbles his words, and nobody knows him until he is at least fifty years away and moving fast. At that distance he seems to grow bigger, and he invariably reaches into his back pocket and puts on his halo so that people can recognize him. Still, when he comes along the next time and is face to face with any man of this world, the mortal is pretty sure to say, "Your face is familiar but I can't seem to place you."

There is no denying that he isn't a good mixer. But for that he would be an excellent censor.

Henry Louis Mencken, "the sage of Baltimore," was never happier than when exposing the absurdities of such movements as "Comstockery" —a term which he coined. Mencken's own brush with the censors in the "Hatrack" case, in the mid-twenties, amused and edified the whole country.

As an influential literary critic, Mencken contributed immeasurably to public acceptance and recognition of such controversial figures as James Branch Cabell, Theodore Dreiser, and Sinclair Lewis, staunchly defending them against attacks by censors and ultraconservative critics.

H. L. Mencken
COMSTOCKERY

In 1873, when the late Anthony Comstock began his great Christian work, the American flapper, or, as she was then called, the young lady, read *Godey's Lady's Book*. To-day she reads—but if you want to find out what she reads simply take a look at the cheap fiction magazines which rise mountain-high from every newsstand. It is an amusing and at the same time highly instructive commentary upon the effectiveness of moral legislation. The net result of fifty years of Comstockery is complete and ignominious failure. All its gaudy raids and alarms have simply gone for naught.

Comstock, of course, was an imbecile; his sayings and doings were of such sort that they inevitably excited the public mirth, and so injured the cause he labored for. But it would be inaccurate, I believe, to put all the blame for its failure upon his imbecility. His successor, in New York, John S. Sumner, is by no means another such unwitting comedian; on the contrary, he shows discretion and even a certain wistful dignity. Nevertheless, he has failed just as miserably. When he took office "Three Weeks" was still regarded as a very salacious book. The wives of Babbitts read it in the kitchen, with the blinds down; it was hidden under every pillow in every finishing-school in the land. To-day "Three Weeks" is dismissed as intolerably banal by school girls of thirteen. To make a genuine sensation it is not sufficient that a new book be naughty; it must be downright pathological.

I have been reviewing current American fiction pretty steadily since 1908. The change that I note is immense. When I began, a new novel dealing frankly with the physiology and pathology of sex was still something of a novelty. It was, indeed, so rare that I always called attention to it. To-day it is a commonplace. The surprise now comes when a new novel turns out to be chemically pure. Try to imagine an American publisher, in these days, getting alarmed about Dreiser's "Sister Carrie" and suppressing it before publication! The oldest and most dignified houses would print it without question; they print far worse every day. Yet in 1900 it seemed so lewd and lascivious that the publisher who put it into type got into a panic of fright, and hid the whole edition in the cellar. To-day that same publisher is advertising a new edition of Walt Whitman's "Leaves of Grass," with "A Woman Waits for Me" printed in full!

What ruined the cause of the Comstocks, I believe, was the campaign of their brethren of sex hygiene. The whole Comstockian case, as good Anthony himself used to explain frankly, was grounded upon the doctrine that virtue and ignorance were identical—that the slightest knowledge of sin was fatal to virtue. Comstock believed and argued that the only way to keep girls pure was to forbid them to think about sex at all. He expounded that doctrine often and at great length. No woman, he was convinced, could be trusted. The instant she was allowed to peek over the fence she was off to the Bad Lands. This notion he supported with many texts from Holy Writ, chiefly from the Old Testament. He was a Puritan of the old school, and had no belief whatever in virtue *per se*. A good woman, to him, was simply one who was efficiently policed. Unfortunately for him, there rose up, within the bounds of his own sect, a school of uplifters who began to merchant quite contrary ideas. They believed that sin was often caused by ignorance—that many a virtuous girl was undone simply because she didn't know what she was doing. These uplifters held that unchastity was not the product of a congenital tendency to it in the female, but of the sinister enterprise of the male, flowing out of his superior knowledge and sophistication. So they set out to spread the enlightenment. If all girls of sixteen, they argued not unplausibly, knew as much about the dreadful consequences of sin as the average police lieutenant or midwife, there would be no more seductions, and in accordance with that theory, they began printing books describing the discomforts of parturition and the terminal symptoms of lues. These books they broadcasted in numerous and immense editions. Comstock, of course, was bitterly against the scheme. He had no faith in the solemn warnings; he saw only the new and startling frankness, and he believed firmly that its one effect would be to "arouse a libidinous passion . . . in the mind of a modest woman." But he was spiked and hamstrung by the impeccable re-

---

H. L. Mencken, *Prejudices, Fifth Series* (New York: Alfred A. Knopf, 1926), pp. 15–21, copyright 1926 by Alfred A. Knopf, Inc. Reprinted by permission of the publisher.

spectability of the sex hygienists. Most of them were Puritans like himself; some were towering giants of Christian rectitude. One of the most active, the Rev. Dr. Sylvanus Stall, was a clergyman of the first chop—a sorcerer who had notoriously saved thousands of immortal souls. To raid such men, to cast them into jail and denounce them as scoundrels, was palpably impossible. Comstock fretted and fumed, but the thing got beyond him. Of Pastor Stall's books alone, millions were sold. Others were almost as successful; the country was flooded from coast to coast.

Whether Comstock was right or wrong I don't know—that is, whether these sex hygiene books increased or diminished loose living in the Republic I don't know. Some say one thing and some another. But this I *do* know; they had a quick and tremendous influence upon the content of American fiction. In the old-time novel what are now called the Facts of Life were glossed over mellifluously, and no one complained about it, for the great majority of fiction readers, being young and female, had no notion of what they were missing. But after they had read the sex hygiene books they began to observe that what was set out in novels was very evasive, and that much of it was downright untrue. So they began to murmur, to snicker, to boo. One by one the old-time novelists went on the shelf. I could make up a long and melancholy roll of them. Their sales dropped off; they began to be laughed at. In place of them rose a new school, and its aim was to tell it all. With this new school Comstock and his heirs have been wrestling ever since, and with steadily increasing bad fortune. Every year they make raids, perform in the newspapers and predict the end of the world, but every year the average is worse than the worst of the year before. As a practicing reviewer, I have got so used to lewd and lascivious books that I no longer notice them. They pour in from all directions. The most virtuous lady novelists write things that would have made a bartender blush to death two decades ago. If I open a new novel and find nothing about Freudian suppressions in it, I suspect at once that it is simply a reprint of some forgotten novel of 1885, with a new name. When I began reviewing I used to send my review copies, after I had sweated through them, to the Y.M.C.A. Now I send them to a medical college.

The Comstocks labor against this stream gallantly, but, it seems to me, very ineptly. They can't, of course, proceed against every naughty book that comes out, for there are far too many, but they could at least choose their marks far more sagaciously than they do. Instead of tackling the books that are frankly pornographic and have no other excuse for being, they almost always tackle books that have obvious literary merit, and are thus relatively easily defended. In consequence, they lose most of their cases. They lost with "Jurgen," they lost with "The Genius," they lost with "Mlle. de Maupin," and they have lost countless other times. And every time they lose they grow more impotent and absurd. Why do they pick out such books? Simply because raiding them gets more publicity than raiding more obscure stuff. The Comstock Society, like all other such pious organizations, is chronically short of money, and the way to raise it is to make a noise in the newspapers. A raid on "Night Life in Chicago," or "Confessions of an Escaped Nun" would get but a few lines; an attack on "Jurgen" is first-page stuff for days on end. Christian virtuosi, their libido aroused, send in their money, and so the society is saved. But when the trial is called and the case is lost, contributions fall off again, and another conspicuous victim must be found.

Well, what is the Comstocks' own remedy for this difficulty? It is to be found in what they call the Clean Books Bill. The aim of this bill is to make it impossible for a publisher accused of publishing an immoral book to make any defense at all. If it ever becomes a law the Comstocks will be able to pick out a single sentence from a Dreiser novel of 10,000 pages and base their whole case upon it; the author and publisher will be forbidden to offer the rest of the book as evidence that the whole has no pornographic purpose. Under such a law anyone printing or selling the Bible will run dreadful risks. One typographical error of a stimulating character will suffice to send a publisher to jail. But will the law actually achieve its purpose? I doubt it. Such extravagant and palpably unjust statutes never accomplish anything. Juries revolt against them; even judges punch holes in them. The Volstead Act is an excellent specimen. Has it made the Republic dry?

In his characteristically urbane, witty style, George Jean Nathan on several occasions loosed sharp barbs at the inanities and mischievous activities of censors. His brief essays "On Censorship" and "A Programme for Censorship" appeared in the heyday of the *American Mercury,* when he and H. L. Mencken were jointly editing that lively and irreverent journal.

George Jean Nathan
ON CENSORSHIP

The plain trouble lies not with censorship, but with censors. There isn't one of us, once his loud talk has died down, but believes in censorship in one degree or another. I should like to inquire of the stoutest foe of all censorship just what his attitude would be were a French peep-show, to which minors were freely admitted, to be opened on either side of his home. I should, further, like to make a similar inquiry of the staunchest opponent of theatrical censorship in the event that, let us say, the curtain to the dramatization of Dreiser's *An American Tragedy* were at one point kept aloft a few moments longer and the seduction episode in which Clyde and Roberta figure pursued with a Zolaesque realism. And I should like to continue the inquiry in the case of the loudest howler against literary censorship in the event that copies of John Cleland's immortal tome were published at a nickel each and sold freely to school-children. The way to beat censorship is not to deny all sense to it and all justification, but to give ground where ground must be given and then, when the enemy oversteps its bounds, to let fly with the full artillery of calm intelligence. The last way in the world in which to win a battle is to try to convince one's self that the enemy has no guns. To contend that the cause of art is in danger because the censors edit or condemn and suppress a lot of dirty postcards, pornographic pamphlets, cheap moving pictures and equally cheap plays, to say nothing of a second-rate novel or so, is to make one's self and one's convictions ridiculous. Now and again, of course, a good piece of work suffers along with the contemptible because of the ignorance of the censors, but art is a poor and pitiable thing if it cannot survive such an occasional calamity. It has stood it in the past, and often enough. A relatively few years pass, the suppressed work duly comes into its own again, and all is as tranquil as before. True art simply can not be suppressed for long; history proves that much. If it can be suppressed and stay suppressed, you may rest assured that it isn't art. In all the centuries, not one genuinely fine piece of work has been suppressed by censorship for more than a little while. Art crushed to earth soon rises again. Only the spurious in art remains lying in the dirt.

I am against censorship not because it is censorship, but because it is generally ignorant. I am against censors because, all the time, they disgrace the theory of censorship in its soundest sense and make it objectionable even to men who may be willing to grant its periodic integrity. I have before me two documents in illustration. One is a copy of an address, made recently on the floor of the House of Representatives by a Congressman from a Southern State, advocating a general censorship of magazines. After denouncing a certain magazine as immoral and corruptive, this would-be censor quoted at length, in chief and eloquent support of his case, an article which I myself had written, carefully omitting the name of the magazine in which it had appeared. Who among his hearers was to know that the article was published in the very magazine that he was denouncing? What is one to say of such open-and-shut hypocrisy and double-dealing? A second illustration is to be had in a letter lying on my desk as I write this. It comes to me from a gentleman of God and one of the two leading champions of censorship in New York State. This holy gentleman, mistaking my attitude toward censors and censorship, observes that it is his opinion that the stage of New York City is unutterably filthy, that the law should promptly and forcibly be brought down upon it, and then asks me to supply him with the names of any plays that are dirty, confessing that he has not seen any of them himself! In other words, what we engage here is a censor who is certain that censorship is called for but who doesn't know what it is that should be censored. It is men like these—and they are typical

---

George Jean Nathan, "On Censorship," *American Mercury,* 11:243-44 (June, 1927), copyright 1927 by the American Mercury. Reprinted by permission of the publisher and of the Executor and Trustee of the Estate of the late George Jean Nathan.

of the tong—who bring censorship into vile disrepute and who cause all fair-minded and upright men and women to hold their noses. But let us get on our knees and thank God for them. It is they who are ruining irrevocably the cause of censorship amongst even censorship's more rational proponents.

George Jean Nathan
A PROGRAMME FOR CENSORSHIP

Since all the railing at censorship, whether on the part of intelligent men or the gaseous gentry, doesn't seem to have accomplished anything, it may be a good idea to look at the situation as it still stands and to attempt a suggestion that may, perhaps, have a bit of practicability to it. One thing, at the outset, appears to be certain, and that is that we are as bound to have censorship in one form or another as we are to have Socialists and fleas, that we may as well face the fact and, facing it, see what we can best do about it. Censorship, whether external or self-imposed, has been in evidence since the grandson of the first Yahoo momentarily left off pulling his squaw around by the hair in order to hew the picture of a bird in the hillside rock, and it will doubtless persist until the earth disintegrates into its original constituent chemicals. If an Anthony Comstock objected to the anatomical indelicacy of the "September Morn" chromo, the Greeks objected no less to a certain biological realism in sculpture and, by force of their neo-puritanical opinion, brought their greatest sculptors so to figleaf or to astringe the physiological emblem of Siva as to cause a gaping perplexity among hordes of future Cook's tourists.

Censorship is found to have been and to be not peculiar to a certain time and a certain people; in this way or in that it has exercised itself to its own odd end the world over century upon century. An outline of the history of censorship by one of our Wellses, Van Loons, Durants or some other such chauffeur of data would bring considerable embarrassment to all the Greenwich Village rebels who currently single out the Sumners and Fords of the Republic for their especial catcalls and derisions, for the world has never been without its Sumners and Fords and its Comstocks and the fact remains that neither ridicule nor the courts of law have effectively succeeded in ridding the scene of them and of their opprobrious shenanigans. At one time they have taken one shape, at another time some other, but they and the doctrines they stand for have none the less been unmistakably in evidence. Censorship drove Æschylus from Athens to spend his last remaining days in Sicily. It was censorship, after the introduction of Christianity into Europe in the Middle Ages, that caused the setting aside of Greek and Roman plays, partly —I quote Schlegel—because the moralists observed them to have "reference to heathen ideas and partly because they had degenerated into the most shameless immorality." Philosophy and politics, suffering the stings of censorship, have seen the undoing of Socrates, "the corrupter of youth," the excommunication of Spinoza, the imprisonment of Voltaire, "the poisoner of youth," and the kicking of a Scott Nearing out of the University of Pennsylvania. Literature, goosed by censorship, has witnessed the squirmings and jumpings of Swifts and Zolas, Byrons and Whitmans, Smolletts and Balzacs. Music, horned into by censorship, has seen its waltz time banned by the Methodist Church and its Wagnerian treasures barred for several years from American opera houses. Sculpture has been censored from the American chautauquas and from American public squares and drinking fountains, terpsichore in one of its phases has been censored off the stages of France, and everything from "Androcles and the Lion" to "Gentlemen Prefer Blondes" has been censored in whole or in part from British platforms and book-stalls.

Censorship, we find, is as deeply rooted in human social pathology and as deplorably unavoidable as endoenteritis. If the America of the moment is caught in its grip, so, too, are the England and the Germany, the Italy and the Russia and the France. If Ellis and Bourdet are attacked by the current mudlarks in America, Ellis and Bourdet suffer much the same attack in England. If Cabell is attacked here, Marguéritte is attacked in France. If Schnitzler is on occasion banned here, so also is he banned in Austria and

---

George Jean Nathan, "A Programme for Censorship," *American Mercury*, 13:369–71 (March, 1928), copyright 1928 by the American Mercury. Reprinted by permission of the publisher and of the Executor and Trustee of the Estate of the late George Jean Nathan.

Germany. If it is forbidden to play the Black Bottom in certain American locales, so is it also forbidden in Italy. If Emma Goldman's views are offensive to the United States and she is because of them barred out of the country, we may speculate as to how many gala cocktail parties Mr. J. P. Morgan would be tendered were he to visit Russia.

But I wander from the point. Leaving censorship in its general aspects to the care of other professors, I bring myself back to a consideration of it as it has to do in America with the arts alone. Granting that we cannot get rid of the nuisance altogether, what, then, is the most workable scheme that we can evoke to handle it, at least in a measure,—a scheme that may possibly be satisfactory to both sides? Since arguments pro and con have got us nowhere—and by us I mean the smutsers on the one hand and the liberals on the other—since the nose-fingerings on both sides have accomplished nothing but hard feelings and some snappy *mots,* I propose a way out of the *impasse* by suggesting a slight and very simple alteration in the present statute. As the law now reads, it is one-sided and unfair; the artists get the dirty end of the stick. They are condemned not *after* the commission of a misdemeanor or crime, but *before* it, and, what is more, for a misdemeanor or crime purely hypothetical. To condemn a man for corrupting morals without actual proof that the morals of a single person have been corrupted is to sentence a man for arson because he is caught carrying a match. Yet that is exactly the situation that confronts the littérateur in America at this moment. He is prosecuted on and convicted of the charge of inciting lewd and lascivious thoughts in purely theoretical crania and of corrupting the morals of purely imaginary young folk. If he were to be haled into court for having written a book on safe-cracking and were thereupon to be sentenced to Dannemora as the potential accomplice of the next yegg to crack a safe, the picture would not be more ridiculous. As with all other criminals, the littérateur should be properly tried and convicted upon the evidence and the evidence alone. Today, he is tried and convicted by *gratis dictum.* If "Jurgen" has actually filled someone's head with dirty thoughts and impaired someone's morals, let us have the witness in the box and let him swear on the Bible to his ruin. Then let Cabell be put in stripes and lodged on the stone-pile if need be. If Mr. Justice Ford's daughter has been contaminated by reading Dreiser or any other such literary devil, let her papa put her on the stand and let's all have a look, and then, if we blush, let Theodore be put on the first New York Central express to Ossining.

Deponent, being an aged and hence reputable bachelor, not knowing, he cannot say whether girls are or are not ruined by reading a book, but if they are let us have them testify openly to the sad fact and then let the law deal with the guilty gent. If a play corrupts the public morals, let us have some fair, open testimony on the point—a single high-school girl, if she be moderately comely, will do. Let us have at least *one plain fact.* It is unfair to prosecute or convict a man for theoretical malfeasance. He at least has a right to be convicted on circumstantial evidence, and even such evidence is presently not offered against the artist. If he is a corrupter of decency he has a right to see and to hear his victim. Arbitrarily to assert, as the ordinance now asserts, that he is guilty of a criminal act *in vacuo* is like sending to the electric chair every man with murder in his heart. The hope of an intelligent and decent peace between the moralist and artist camps lies in the just and honorable recasting of a presently unjust, unfounded and highly equivocal statute.

The ebullient, effervescent, highly imaginative quality of William Saroyan's writings has attracted a host of readers to his short stories and novels and of theater-goers to view his plays. A cascade of books has poured from his fertile mind since he first broke into print twenty-five years ago. The "fresh, original, and imaginative talent he has brought to our American Theatre" was cited some years ago by the New York Critics Circle in choosing Saroyan's *The Time of Your Life* as the best play of the season.

"A Cold Day" appeared in Saroyan's first book of short stories, *The Daring Young Man on the Flying Trapeze, and Other Stories.* Possibly autobiographical in nature, the description of the writer's revulsion at the thought of burning books —any books—is, at any rate, a powerful expression of John Steinbeck's statement, "A book is somehow sacred."

William Saroyan
A COLD DAY

Dear M—,

I want you to know that it is very cold in San Francisco today, and that I am freezing. It is so cold in my room that every time I start to write a short story the cold stops me and I have to get up and do bending exercises. It means, I think, that something's got to be done about keeping short story writers warm. Sometimes when it is very cold I am able to do very good writing, but at other times I am not. It is the same when the weather is excessively pleasant. I very much dislike letting a day go by without writing a short story and that is why I am writing this letter: to let you know that I am very angry about the weather. Do not think that I am sitting in a nice warm room in sunny California, as they call it, and making up all this stuff about the cold. I am sitting in a very cold room and there is no sun anywhere, and the only thing I can talk about is the cold because it is the only thing going on today. I am freezing and my teeth are chattering. I would like to know what the Democratic party ever did for freezing short story writers. Everybody else gets heat. We've got to depend on the sun and in the winter the sun is undependable. That's the fix I am in: wanting to write and not being able to, because of the cold.

One winter day last year the sun came out and its light came into my room and fell across my table, warming my table and my room and warming me. So I did some brisk bending exercises and then sat down and began to write a short story. But it was a winter day and before I had written the first paragraph of the story the sun had fallen back behind clouds and there I was in my room, sitting in the cold, writing a story. It was such a good story that even though I knew it would never be printed I had to go on writing it, and as a result I was frozen stiff by the time I finished writing it. My face was blue and I could barely move my limbs, they were so cold and stiff. And my room was full of the smoke of a package of Chesterfield cigarettes, but even the smoke was frozen. There were clouds of it in my room, but my room was very cold just the same.

Once, while I was writing, I thought of getting a tub and making a fire in it. What I intended to do was to burn a half dozen of my books and keep warm, so that I could write my story. I found an old tub and I brought it to my room, but when I looked around for books to burn I couldn't find any. All of my books are old and cheap. I have about five hundred of them and I paid a nickel each for most of them, but when I looked around for titles to burn, I couldn't find any. There was a large heavy book in German on anatomy that would have made a swell fire, but when I opened it and read a line of that beautiful language, *sie bestehen aus zwei Hüftgelenkbeugemuskeln des Oberschenkels, von denen der eine breitere,* and so on, I couldn't do it. It was asking too much. I couldn't understand the language, I couldn't understand a word in the whole book, but it was somehow too eloquent to use for a fire. The book had cost me five cents two or three years ago, and it weighed about six pounds, so you see that even as fire wood it had been a bargain and I should have been able to tear out its pages and make a fire.

But I couldn't do it. There were over a thousand pages in the book and I planned to burn one page at a time and see the fire of each page, but when I thought of all that print being effaced by fire and all that accurate language being removed from my library, I couldn't do it, and I still have the book. When I get tired of reading great writers, I go to this book and read language that I cannot understand, *während der Kindheit ist sie von birnförmiger Gestalt und liegt vorzugsweise in der Bauchhöhle.* It is simply blasphemous to think of burning a thousand pages of such language. And of course I haven't so much as mentioned the marvelous illustrations.

Then I began to look around for cheap fiction. And you know the world is chock full of such stuff. Nine books out of ten are cheap worthless fiction, inorganic stuff. I thought, well, there are at least a half dozen of those books in my library and I can burn them and be warm and write my story. So I picked out six books and together they weighed about as much as the German anatomy book. The first was *Tom Brown at Oxford: A Sequel to School Days at Rugby,* Two Volumes in One. The first book had 378 pages, and the second 430, and all these pages would have made a small fire that would have lasted a pretty long time, but I had never read the book

---

William Saroyan, *The Daring Young Man on the Flying Trapeze* (New York: Random House, 1934), pp. 153–63, copyright 1934 by the Modern Library, Inc. Reprinted by permission of the publisher.

and it seemed to me that I had no right to burn a book I hadn't even read. It looked as if it ought to be a book of cheap prose, one worthy of being burned, but I couldn't do it. I read, *The belfry-tower rocked and reeled, as that peal rang out, now merry, now scornful, now plaintive, from those narrow belfry windows, into the bosom of the soft southwest wind, which was playing round the old gray tower of Englebourn church.* Now that isn't exactly tremendous prose, but it isn't such very bad prose either. So I put the book back on the shelf.

The next book was *Inez: A Tale of the Alamo*, and it was dedicated to The Texan Patriots. It was by the author of another book called *Beulah*, and yet another called *St. Elmo*. The only thing I knew about this writer or her books was that one day a girl at school had been severely reprimanded for bringing to class a book called *St. Elmo*. It was said to be the sort of book that would corrupt the morals of a young girl. Well, I opened the book and read, *I am dying; and, feeling as I do, that few hours are allotted me, I shall not hesitate to speak freely and candidly. Some might think me deviating from the delicacy of my sex; but, under the circumstances, I feel that I am not. I have loved you long, and to know that my love is returned, is a source of deep and unutterable joy to me.* And so on.

This was such bad writing that it was good, and I decided to read the whole book at my first opportunity. There is much for a young writer to learn from our poorest writers. It is very destructive to burn bad books, almost more destructive than to burn good ones.

The next book was *Ten Nights in a Bar Room, and What I Saw There* by T. S. Arthur. Well, even this book was too good to burn. The other three books were by Hall Caine, Brander Matthews, and Upton Sinclair. I had read only Mr. Sinclair's book, and while I didn't like it a lot as a piece of writing, I couldn't burn it because the print was so fine and the binding so good. Typographically it was one of my best books.

Anyway, I didn't burn a single page of a single book, and I went on freezing and writing. Every now and then I burned a match just to remind myself what a flame looked like, just to keep in touch with the idea of heat and warmth. It would be when I wanted to light another cigarette and instead of blowing out the flame I would let it burn all the way down to my fingers.

It is simply this: that if you have any respect for the mere idea of books, what they stand for in life, if you believe in paper and print, you cannot burn any page of any book. Even if you are freezing. Even if you are trying to do a bit of writing yourself. You can't do it. It is asking too much.

Today it is as cold in my room as the day I wanted to make a fire of books. I am sitting in the cold, smoking cigarettes, and trying to get this coldness onto paper so that when it becomes warm again in San Francisco I won't forget how it was on the cold days.

I have a small phonograph in my room and I play it when I want to exercise in order to keep warm. Well, when it gets to be very cold in my room this phonograph won't work. Something goes wrong inside, the grease freezes and the wheels won't turn, and I can't have music while I am bending and swinging my arms. I've got to do it without music. It is much more pleasant to exercise with jazz, but when it is very cold the phonograph won't work and I am in a hell of a fix. I have been in here since eight o'clock this morning and it is now a quarter to five, and I am in a hell of a mess. I hate to let a day go by without doing something about it, without saying something, and all day I have been in here with my books that I never read, trying to get started and I haven't gotten anywhere. Most of the time I have been walking up and down the room (two steps in any direction brings you to a wall) and bending and kicking and swinging my arms. That's practically all I have been doing. I tried the phonograph a half dozen times to see if the temperature hadn't gone up a little, but it hadn't, and the phonograph wouldn't play music.

I thought I ought to tell you about this. It's nothing important. It's sort of silly, making so much of a little cold weather, but at the same time the cold is a fact today and it is the big thing right now and I am speaking of it. The thing that amazes and pleases me is that my typewriter hasn't once clogged today. Around Christmas when we had a very cold spell out here it was always clogging, and the more I oiled it the more it clogged. I couldn't do a thing with it. The reason was that I had been using the wrong kind of oil. But all this time that I have been writing about the cold my typewriter has been doing its work excellently, and this amazes and pleases me. To think that in spite of the cold this machine can go right on making the language I use is very fine. It encourages me to stick with it, whatever happens. If the machine will work, I tell myself, then you've got to work with it. That's what it amounts to. If you can't write a decent short story because of the cold, write something else. Write anything. Write a long letter to somebody. Tell them how cold you are. By the time the letter is received the sun will be out again and you will be warm again, but the letter will be there mentioning the cold. If it is so cold that you can't make up a little ordinary Tuesday prose, why, what the hell, say anything that comes along, just so it's the truth. Talk about your toes freezing, about the time you actually wanted to burn books to keep warm but couldn't do it, about the phonograph. Speak of the little unimportant things on a cold day, when your mind is numb and your feet and hands frozen. Mention the things you wanted to write but couldn't. This is what I have been telling myself.

After coffee this morning, I came here to write an important story. I was warm with the coffee and I didn't realize how really cold it was. I brought out paper and started to line up what I was going to say in this important story that will never be written because once I lose a thing I lose it forever, this story that is forever lost because of the cold that got into me and silenced me and made me jump up from my chair and do bending exercises. Well, I can tell you about it. I can give you an idea what it was to have been like. I remember that much about it, but I didn't write it and it is lost. It will give you something of an idea as to how I write.

I will tell you the things I was telling myself this morning while I was getting this story lined up in my mind:

Think of America, I told myself this morning. The whole thing. The cities, all the houses, all the people, the coming and going, the coming of children, the going of them, the coming and going of men and death, and life, the movement, the talk, the sound of machinery, the oratory, think of the pain in America and the fear and the deep inward longing of all things alive in America. Remember the great machines, wheels turning, smoke and fire, the mines and the men working them, the noise, the confusion. Remember the newspapers and the moving picture theatres and everything that is a part of this life. Let this be your purpose: to suggest this great country.

Then turn to the specific. Go out to some single person and dwell with him, within him, lovingly, seeking to understand the miracle of his being, and utter the truth of his existence and reveal the splendor of the mere fact of his being alive, and say it in great prose, simply, show that he is of the time, of the machines and the fire and smoke, the newspapers and the noise. Go with him to his secret and speak of it gently, showing that it is the secret of man. Do not deceive. Do not make up lies for the sake of pleasing anyone. No one need be killed in your story. Simply relate what is the great event of all history, of all time, the humble, artless truth of mere being. There is no greater theme: no one need be violent to help you with your art. There *is* violence. Mention it of course when it is time to mention it. Mention the war. Mention all ugliness, all waste. Do even this lovingly. But emphasize the glorious truth of mere being. It is the major theme. You do not have to create a triumphant climax. The man you write of need not perform some heroic or monstrous deed in order to make your prose great. Let him do what he has always done, day in and day out, continuing to live. Let him walk and talk and think and sleep and dream and awaken and walk again and talk again and move and be alive. It is enough. There is nothing else to write about. You have never seen a short story in life. The events of life have never fallen into the form of the short story or the form of the poem, or into any other form. Your own consciousness is the only form you need. Your own awareness is the only action you need. Speak of this man, recognize his existence. Speak of man.

Well, this is a poor idea of what the story was to have been like. I was warm with coffee when I was telling myself what and how to write, but now I am freezing, and this is the closest I can come to what I had in mind. It was to have been something fine, but now all that I have is this vague remembrance of the story. The least I can do is put into words this remembrance. Tomorrow I will write another story, a different story. I will look at the picture from a different viewpoint. I don't know for sure, but I may feel cocky and I may mock this country and the life that is lived here. It is possible. I can do it. I have done it before, and sometimes when I get mad about political parties and political graft I sit down and mock this great country of ours. I get mean and I

284 The writers fight back

make man out to be a rotten, worthless, unclean thing. It isn't man, but I make out as if it is. It's something else, something less tangible, but for mockery it is more convenient to make out that it is man. It's my business to get at the truth, but when you start to mock, you say to hell with the truth. Nobody's telling the truth, why should I? Everybody's telling nice lies, writing nice stories and novels, why should I worry about the truth. There is no truth. Only grammar, punctuation, and all that rot. But I know better. I can get mad at things and start to mock, but I know better. At its best, the whole business is pretty sad, pretty pathetic.

All day I have been in this room freezing, wanting to say something solid and clean about all of us who are alive. But it was so cold I couldn't do it. All I could do was swing my arms and smoke cigarettes and feel rotten.

Early this morning when I was warm with coffee I had this great story in my mind, ready to get into print, but it got away from me.

The most I can say now is that it is very cold in San Francisco today, and I am freezing.

A sharer of William Saroyan's reverence for the book and his horror at the idea of its willful destruction is John Steinbeck. Not infrequently a target for censors, himself, Steinbeck has, notwithstanding, established himself as one of the most significant American novelists of this generation, with an international following exceeding that of any of his contemporaries, except perhaps Ernest Hemingway.

The brief gem from Steinbeck's pen included here is an excerpt from a longer essay on the author's attitude toward the format of books.

John Steinbeck
**SOME RANDOM AND
RANDY THOUGHTS ON BOOKS**

The book itself took on its magical, sacrosanct and authoritative character at a time when there were very few books and those possessed by the very rich or the very learned. Then the book was the only release of the mind into distant places and into golden thinking. There was no other way of going outside one's self except through the talesman of the book. And it is wonderful that even today with all competition of records, of radio, of television, of motion pictures, the book has kept its precious character. A book is somehow sacred. A dictator can kill and maim people, can sink to any kind of tyranny and only be hated, but when books are burned, the ultimate in tyranny has happened. This we cannot forgive. The use of the book as propaganda is more powerful and effective than any other medium. A broadcast has little authority but a book does not lie. People automatically distrust newspapers. They automatically believe in books. This is strange but it is so. Messages come from behind the controlled and censored areas of the world and they do not ask for radios, for papers and pamphlets. They invariably ask for books. They believe books when they believe nothing else. This being true, I wonder that governments do not use books more often than they do. A book is protected and passed on. It is the rarest of things for a man to destroy a book unless he truly hates it. Book destruction is a kind of murder. And in the growing tendency to censor and control for the problematical good of the people, books have escaped more than any form. A picture can be cut to ribbons, but any restraint laid on a book is fought to a finish.

"Note: Last November the grand jury of Whitley county, in the hill country of Kentucky, discovered that *The Big Sky* was available to borrowers in the public library at the town of Corbin.

"On the complaint of a missionary whom news stories identified only as a Mr. Davis, the grand jury read passages which Mr. Davis had underscored as examples of 'lust' and thereupon decided that neither adults nor children should be allowed to read the book. It asked the librarian why it was being circulated. It recommended that the next panel investigate further.

"The state Library Extension Division naturally was upset. It feared that its whole program might suffer as a consequence of this one instance. And so it asked A. B. (Bud) Guthrie, Jr., the author, for a statement that might widen understanding.

John Steinbeck, "Some Random and Randy Thoughts on Books," in *The Author Looks at Format*, edited by Ray Freiman (New York: The American Institute of Graphic Arts, 1951), pp. 31–32, copyright 1951 by The American Institute of Graphic Arts. Reprinted by permission of the author, the editor, The Viking Press, and The American Institute of Graphic Arts.

"For the sake of the program and its participants—and with what good nature he could summon—Bud made the following reply." (*Nieman Reports,* April, 1958)

A. B. Guthrie, Jr.
THE PETER RABBIT LIBRARY?

To each, his opinion.

On that principle we Americans have operated and do operate well, indeed at least as well as people anywhere.

But the principle does not imply that uninformed and bigoted opinion should weigh equally with that which is informed and dispassionate. Quite the contrary! Out of the conflict of sentiments, foolish and narrow and thoughtful and broad and in-between, we believe that our people can and largely do choose courses that are wise and good. Our history, our legislation, our judicial decisions all support us, if not wholly, in that belief. The censors, the book-burners, the people who would impose their own fears and faiths on all of us—we put them eventually in their places, for there exists a hard sense in the American people. They like the climate of freedom. They know, if not always consciously, that censorship is indoctrination. Each cherishes the right to do his own thinking, to choose his own reading, to defy the extremists who, in their exclusive wisdom, would make him a copy of themselves.

All this is by way of preface to some reflections on my own work and the Whitley county grand jury's criticism of *The Big Sky* and its presence in the Corbin Public Library.

I am not writing for my own sake. The Whitley jury has done me a favor. Its report means increased sales. But other people are involved; and the issue is important aside from personalities and personal advantage.

The writer of fiction, if he is serious and conscientious, strives to re-create and illuminate experience. It is not his right to falsify. He has to be honest to his materials. He has to be honest to himself. He operates in the conviction that if anything is important it is truth as he has been led to see it.

Critics, like the missionary Davis who brought the complaint to the Whitley grand jury, disagree. They would have authors prettify experience. They would have the writer make a doll house out of life, though by Mr. Davis' very calling he acknowledges it is not a doll house but a house, so to speak, of hovels as well as mansions. With no understanding of the office of serious fiction, these critics ask the fictionists to be dishonest—as if morality were promoted by misrepresentation! Mr. Davis obviously does not believe, with The Book, that the truth will set you free.

I can defend *The Big Sky* as an accurate representation of a time and a place. There is not a word in it that cannot be supported by reference to sources. Fifteen years of thinking and study went into it. I believe I can say that all the prime as well as many secondary sources were consulted. My notes fill half a dozen drawers. Authorities on the fur trade are virtually unanimous in acclaiming it. It has been translated into I don't know how many languages, a dozen at least. The library is rare in which it is not available.

I am embarrassed to recite these facts, for the recital smells of immodesty. Yet the facts are important to a judgment that I wrote the book in the conviction that an honest novel of the fur trade never had been told.

With these points behind us, I would ask the jury: Was anyone, man or child, ever corrupted by a word? A word, after all, is only a sound on the tongue or symbols on paper. To the vulgar and profane ones, most of us have been and are exposed, and without apparent ruination.

Then if words don't corrupt people, what in writing does? Attitudes perhaps, just perhaps. The false. The cheap. The trashy. The deliberately mischievous. *The Big Sky* never has been accused of these, never at least until now if it is now so accused. It is almost embarrassingly moral. Through it runs the theme of atonement. It is the story of a man who reaps what he sows. If anyone can find in it any profit in evil, let him speak! But if any defender asserts the converse, that it shows virtue always rewarded, let him think twice!

The news stories report that Mr. Davis underscored what he thought were objectionable pas-

---

A. B. Guthrie, Jr., "The Peter Rabbit Library?" *Nieman Reports,* 12:17–18 (April, 1958), copyright 1958 by Alumni Council. Reprinted by permission of the publisher.

sages in my book and that the grand jury based its criticism on his samples. It ought not to be necessary to remind anyone that expressions taken out of context carry no authority. It is the blunder of the ignoramus and the trick of the cheat to characterize a man or his work by divorcing words from those that precede and follow. By this device almost any writer and almost any speaker can be damned. So I would ask members of the next Whitley grand jury to examine all the evidence—that is, to read the book in its entirety—before reaching a decision.

An adverse decision, even then, would be wide open to attack, for it is a part of our system that judgments like these need be supported by evidence. *The Big Sky* has been in print for more than ten years. I don't know how long the Corbin Library has carried it, but long enough surely for numbers of people to have read it. Has any single one of them been corrupted as a consequence? Until, under rules of evidence, such an instance is proven, the book stands clear. Without such enforcement any judgment against it is and would be subjective and infirm.

If *The Big Sky* is to be banned for what is called its "lust," what is the library to stock? I ask the names as they pop into my head. The Bible? It chronicles some sinful doings. Shakespeare? He isn't always what Mr. Davis would term wholesome. Voltaire? Dreiser? Sinclair Lewis? Hemingway? De Voto? Steinbeck? Cozzens? Who? This random scattering of questions represents but a fraction of a list far too long to enumerate. Remove from the shelves all volumes that can be so listed, and Corbin will have no library, or at best one that might appropriately be named "The Tale of Peter Rabbit" Library.

Finally, it is the business of librarians to operate libraries. They qualify by experience, training, special education, study of function and so are above the crowd, as the banker or mechanic or accountant or farmer is above the crowd in his specialty. Thus it not only appears brash, it *is* brash for people who have no particular qualifications to challenge the book selections of those who do have.

Of contemporary American writers none, with the possible exception of Erskine Caldwell, has been so frequently under fire from the censors as James T. Farrell. Since his first novel *Young Lonigan* appeared in 1932, Farrell has been the center of numerous literary controversies. Called "the last of the *natural* writers," in the tradition of Norris and Dreiser, his depiction of the seamy side of life has kept him almost continuously involved in disputes with critics and legal authorities.

Farrell's realism has an authentic base among his own people, the Irish of Chicago's South Side, the favorite milieu of his prolific crop of novels and short stories.

In 1948, after the Philadelphia police had interfered with the sale of *Young Lonigan, The Young Manhood of Studs Lonigan,* and *Judgment Day,* Farrell and his publisher, the Vanguard Press, decided that the best defense was to attack, and brought successful proceedings for an injunction against the police department. Presented here is a transcript of the testimony heard by the court on that occasion. Presiding was Guy K. Bard, Judge of the U.S. District Court for the Eastern District of Pennsylvania.

As Farrell expressed his philosophy in the course of the hearing, he aims in his books to present "as complete a picture of the story of America as I knew it, of the hopes, the shames, the aspirations, of everything that it was possible for me to use as the legitimate material of literature . . . So my effort has been to present life as it is, in so far as I can see it, to present it in terms of the patterns of destiny, the patterns of language, and the patterns of thought and consciousness, which I can grasp and open, or which I imagine with the conviction that this is the way it is."

James T. Farrell
THE AUTHOR AS PLAINTIFF: TESTIMONY IN A CENSORSHIP CASE

Testimony (examination and cross-examination) May 17, 1948, of James T. Farrell in successful proceedings brought by James T. Farrell and the Vanguard Press, Inc., his publishers, to restrain the police of Philadelphia from interfering with the sale of Young Lonigan, The Young Manhood of Studs Lonigan, *and* Judgment Day.

James T. Farrell, *Reflections at Fifty* (New York: Vanguard Press, 1954), pp. 188–223, copyright 1954 by James T. Farrell. Reprinted by permission of the author and of the publisher.

Messrs. Arthur E. Farmer and Charles E. Kenworthey were the attorneys for Mr. Farrell and Vanguard Press; Norman R. Bradley represented Craig Ellis; Hyman A. Guth represented John R. McCarthy; and James Francis Ryan, as attorney for the city of Philadelphia, appeared for James H. Malone and also for Messrs. Ellis and McCarthy. The presiding judge was Guy K. Bard, Judge of the United States District Court for the Eastern District of Pennsylvania.

MR. FARMER: Mr. James T. Farrell.

JAMES T. FARRELL; having been duly sworn, was examined and testified as follows:

DIRECT EXAMINATION

by Mr. Farmer:

Q. Mr. Farrell, what is your occupation?
A. I am a novelist and literary critic.
Q. Did you write three works entitled, respectively, *Young Lonigan, The Young Manhood of Studs Lonigan,* and *Judgment Day?*
A. I did.
Q. Have you written other works?
A. A number of them.
Q. And have those works been published?
A. They have.
Q. Will you tell the Court the titles of your published writings?
A. I have published twenty-one books; there are ten novels in addition to *Lonigan*. The novels are titled: *Gas-House McGinty; A World I Never Made; No Star Is Lost; Father and Son; My Days of Anger; Ellen Rogers;* and *Bernard Clare.*

I published one novelette entitled *Tommy Gallagher's Crusade.*

I have published the following books of short stories: *Calico Shoes, and Other Stories; Guillotine Party, and Other Stories; Can All This Grandeur Perish? and Other Stories; $1000 a Week, and Other Stories; To Whom It May Concern, and Other Stories; When Boyhood Dreams Come True, and Other Stories; The Life Adventurous, and Other Stories.*

I have published the following works of literary criticism: *A Note on Literary Criticism; The League of Frightened Philistines and Other Papers;* and *Literature and Morality,* a collection of a number of essays.

Q. In addition to these published writings, have you written other articles on literary subjects and book reviews?
A. Yes, I have written at least several hundred of them.
Q. Would you name some of the newspapers and periodicals in which your reviews and articles are published?
A. Yes, sir: the *New York Times,* the *New York Herald Tribune,* the *New York Sun,* the *New York Post,* the *Philadelphia Bulletin,* the *Chicago Daily News,* the *Atlantic Monthly,* the *Chicago Post,* which is now defunct. Did I mention *The Saturday Review of Literature? The Saturday Review of Literature,* the *National Journal of Books,* the *Technical Journal—College English,* a technical journal, *Scribner's Magazine,* now defunct, the *American Mercury,* and endless others, both in the United States and abroad.
Q. Have you ever lectured on literary subjects?
A. I have, fairly frequently.
Q. Have you lectured at any colleges and universities?
A. I have. Last week I lectured on Theodore Dreiser at Temple University. In this area I have also lectured at Swarthmore University; Princeton; Connecticut College for Women; Bennington College; University of Minnesota; University of Iowa; University of Indiana; University of Chicago; Columbia University; City College; New York University.
Q. Are you a member of any honorary literary group?
A. Yes, the National Institute of Arts and Letters.
Q. How does one become a member of that group?
A. One is elected by members. It is an American version, I presume, of what they call the Academy in France.
Q. Where were you born?
A. Chicago, Illinois.
Q. How many years did you live in Chicago?
A. I lived there permanently, with the exception of eight months, from my birth on February 27, 1904, to April 16, 1931.
Q. Your novels, *Young Lonigan, Young Manhood of Studs Lonigan,* and *Judgment Day,* are set in Chicago, are they not?
A. They are.

Q. Are they set in a part of Chicago where you lived?

A. Yes, sir.

Q. Will you give the Court a very brief outline of the story of that trilogy?

A. Yes.

The time of the novel runs from 1916 to 1931. The novel is the attempt to give what I would call, if I may, a life history of an American boy.

It begins when he is graduated from parochial school, and it ends with his death from pneumonia, from deprivation, when he has suffered economic losses.

It attempts to deal directly, as frankly as I was able, as truthfully as I could, with his dreams, his thoughts, his hopes, his aspirations, his shames, his sufferings, his failures, his experiences with other boys, his experiences on the street and in the home, at work, in the poolroom, his experiences while sober, his experiences while drunk, his dreams. I have included in it a number of his dreams.

The novel is written mainly from the standpoint of immediate experiences. By that I mean this: any event which appears in the book is presented in terms of how it immediately happens, how it registers upon the consciousness of one or more of the characters, how it happens directly.

The first novel takes him through the period from June to November of 1916, when he is graduated from school; I mean, from grammar school, and his first period in high school. In that period in his dream of himself he looks forward.

Gradually, and particularly through the second volume, that dream of himself, that image of himself, tends to become a dream in which he looks backward.

At the end of the second novel his life is really over, and he has not realized it, and then he starts [word missing]—the third novel, *Judgment Day,* shows this slow and steady decline. It is a biological decline and a social decline.

The book is intended to illustrate in terms of the condition of youth what I would call aspects of the biological and the social tragedy which many men face besides Studs Lonigan.

The book is written with directness and with frankness, and it attempts to present an image of the world as this boy sees it and as this boy feels it.

His ideal, as stated in his own language, is to become strong and tough and the real stuff. By that I mean this: He has an image of himself as tough, and as hard, and represses his feelings, so that there is a division in his nature, and his dreams are not consistent with each other. In his dreams he is, in terms of his own level of intelligence and experience, apathetic and dreamy, and he finds in his [word or words missing]—I mean his consciousness, there is this contrast that is often sadistic, even his aggressive action. The elements of the book which go to make the tragedy of Studs Lonigan, as I conceive it, are the aggressiveness, an intense, an undue, and a super-aggressiveness. That aggressiveness leads mainly to the formation of a concept of sex. It is not complete in his mind, it is the way he looks at it, and acts in which he is aggressive toward the girls, and he condemns them, and has contempt for them, an attitude, a competitive attitude toward other boys, which is expressed in the idea of fighting.

I would mention one more point, that this can be confirmed or noted by anyone who reads it, if they will take things like this, if they will take his dream life, the flow of his consciousness, and the compensations, and the times when he sees himself as a hero in his own mind. He becomes a hero in his own mind by thinking of beating somebody up.

That, in substance, is, I hope, a sufficient explanation of what I see in *Studs Lonigan* for these purposes.

Q. You say *Studs Lonigan* was placed in Chicago. What part of Chicago?

A. The South Side.

Q. What kind of district is the South Side—or was it, at the time you lived there?

A. It was a district racially composed largely of Irish and Irish-Americans, with a considerable proportion of Jewish families, and on the fringes of it some colored and some Polish and other Slavic families. The neighborhood had no clearly defined composition, it was a neighborhood of homeowners, of small businessmen, of workingmen, part of the workingmen who were considered to be the labor aristocracy, and then a number of poor families. It was also a neighborhood in which you had a number of first- and second-generation American boys. You had a sufficient composition on the basis of race and of color and of creed to have an exacerbation based upon senses of differences, which is a very common American phenomenon, and for years it has been talked about, the rivalries based upon race, religion, and color, and you had sufficient of them to have an intensification of hostility, to have gang fights and so on. Furthermore, a number of people who had lived in this neighborhood, say, as far back as 1916, when *Studs Lonigan* began, felt that they had become settled for life, and they did not realize that under their feet the growth of Chicago, the change of Chicago, was going on, and this whole neighborhood was going to change, and all that they felt secure was going to crumble.

Q. You mentioned a change. Do you portray the change in the reaction of individuals to that?

A. Yes, I do; for instance, in one section of the book I use a soapbox speaker to do it, but he even states it in terms of sociological formulations which have been made by the University of Chicago sociologists, and I attempted to register that change more directly in terms of the reactions of the characters to it. Those reactions were not exactly correct in terms of any clear analysis of why the change was, but it was their ideas. For instance, the most common view in white neighborhoods is that Jewish people and colored people caused the change, so that it exacerbated prejudice. So that is put down plainly and directly in the book.

Q. In the book, Studs Lonigan goes to parochial school, does he not?

A. Yes.

Q. Did you go to parochial school?

A. Yes.

Q. In the book Studs Lonigan goes downtown on the celebration of Armistice Day. Were you in Chicago at that time?

A. I was in town. I did not go downtown, but I took that scene from newspaper accounts and from stories I have been told.

Q. To what extent is that work, and I refer to these three novels as a single work, autobiographical, and to what extent is it imaginary?

A. I would say this: It is like the life I saw as a boy. It is like it in terms of the attitudes, the types, the thoughts, the types and patterns of language, the patterns of destiny. I mean, there is a high incidence of early death in the book, and a number of the characters literally drink and dissipate themselves to death. Now, as to all of those factors, it is like it in that sense, and autobiographically I would say this, other than passing incidents perhaps it would only connect with me in this sense, that it is all I decided I would not be and I did not want to be, and in that sense it is a criticism of the conditions of youth in the city and in the neighborhood and in the times in which I grew up.

Q. Did you see in your youth characters of the kind portrayed in *Studs Lonigan?*

A. I can say that I literally saw hundreds.

Q. Did you live among many of them?

A. I did.

Q. Did you afterward write the Danny O'Neill series, which contrasted the protagonist there with the protagonist here?

A. I did.

Q. What was your purpose in writing that?

A. I conceive the Danny O'Neill series, consisting of these four books, I repeat them, *A World I Never Made, No Star Is Lost, Father and Son,* and *My Days of Anger,* as I considered the characters of Danny O'Neill and of Studs Lonigan as diametrical opposites. In the case of Studs Lonigan it is a character who goes down. In the case of Danny O'Neill it is a character who is not submissive, and who revolts and goes out into the world. At the end of [the] Danny O'Neill [books] he states what I consider, and it is my view, a mature struggle against what he thinks is going to be harmful, that he is going to be self-responsible, that he is going to be a writer, and as a writer he is going out to tell the truth.

That contrast was conceived, and at the time I was writing *Studs Lonigan* I conceived, and I stated it many times in conversation, and it was mentioned occasionally in writings and so on, that I proposed to write a series of works of fiction, of novelettes, novels, sketches, a series, which at that time I conceived to run to twenty-five books, and which now will run more, and which would contain, to the best of my ability, as complete a picture of the story of America as I knew it, of the hopes, the shames, the aspirations, of everything that it was possible for me to use as the legitimate material of literature.

Q. In writing the works comprising the *Studs Lonigan* trilogy, what particular literary technique did you use? Is it a recognized school today?

A. Yes, it is referred to as "realism" or "naturalism." The tradition of naturalism goes back many decades. It is associated with French writers, such as Flaubert and Zola. It is really connected with the Russian writers, such as Tolstoi and Dostoevski. Many things can be said about it, but I would prefer to just state what I tried to do, and I would say this: That realism to me, as I have attempted [it], is to attempt an exploration of the nature of experience, to see experience directly, to see it unflinchingly. I have often quoted a motto from Spinoza, which I like very much: "It is not to weep, not to laugh, but to understand." And the second one, a sentence from the Notebooks of Anton Chekhov, a Russian writer: "Man will only become better when you make him see what he is like."

So my effort has been to present life as it is, in so far as I can see it, to present it in terms of the patterns of destiny, the patterns of language, and the patterns of thought and consciousness, which I can grasp and open, or which I imagine with the conviction that this is the way it is.

Q. When did you start writing *Young Lonigan?*

A. In June, 1929.

Q. When did you finish *Young Lonigan?*

A. I finished *Young Lonigan* and the greater part of what became *The Young Manhood of Studs Lonigan* by February, 1931. I published *Young Lonigan* and set the rest of it aside, and wrote a book which is somewhat connected with it, in that there is recurrence of some of the characters, called *Gas-House McGinty;* then I completed *The Young Manhood of Studs Lonigan* in 1933; it was published in 1934. I almost immediately began *Judgment Day,* which was the final volume, and completed that in February, 1935.

Q. Did you do any rewriting after you had written the first draft?

A. Yes, some of the scenes of *Young Lonigan* —one scene, there is a scene of the boy Studs and the girl Lucy in the tree—was rewritten twenty-five times.

Q. Not all of the work?

A. No, but every part of the book was written at least three times.

MR. FARMER: Your witness.

MR. BRADLEY: If the Court please, it seems to me that this has been a very interesting lecture on literature, but I do not think it is probative. The issue is whether these particular books have violated Section 524 of the Penal Code, and there is at least one Circuit Court of Appeals case that holds that what is in the mind of the author is not important. We have a book before us, and it is not important, although, if we had a jury, we would have objected sooner, but since there was not one we permitted the Court to have a nice lecture, but I still believe that the testimony should be stricken from the record as being improper.

THE COURT: You make that motion?

MR. BRADLEY: Yes, I do, I so move.

THE COURT: Motion denied.

MR. BRADLEY: Exception.

CROSS-EXAMINATION

by Mr. Ryan:

Q. Mr. Farrell, you say the Danny O'Neill series, of which *A World I Never Made* is the first one, was supposed to show the opposite to this Studs Lonigan series?

A. That is correct.

Q. Yet in both of them you use the same incident of a sister trying to get her young brother to get in bed with her to do something naughty because it might be fun, don't you?

A. May I talk about that?

THE COURT: Just answer that.

THE WITNESS: Yes.

THE COURT: Now you can make any explanation you want.

THE WITNESS: All right, may I explain it?

MR. RYAN: Yes.

THE WITNESS: Number 1, in neither instance does it happen.

by Mr. Ryan:

Q. That is not the girl's fault in either instance, is it?

A. The Judge said I might make a comment.

MR. KENWORTHEY: He is answering your question in two parts.

MR. RYAN: It is another lecture under any circumstances.

THE WITNESS: It is the case of a boy who is aged seven and a girl who is aged five, and it is obvious on its face that it is very innocent; they do not understand it. And in the second case, in the case of Studs Lonigan, the boy and the girl do not do it.

It is a common fact that this kind of tension exists in many families, and it is often the case that it goes no further.

by the Court:

Q. I want to interrupt you. Do you want the Court to understand that that was the general rule in the families of the South Side of Chicago?

A. I would say this, that that situation can happen in any family.

Q. That is not my question. My question was, if you think that was typical of the families in the South Side of Chicago.

A. In one form or another it was typical. By that I mean this, that there would be some expression of curiosity, some expression of attraction which would possibly, shyly, guiltily, without any awareness of what it all meant, be started and not finished. It was not [an] experience in the book, it does not happen that there would be actual relationships.

by Mr. Ryan:

Q. In your *Studs Lonigan,* which we are speaking about, you have him and his sister, they are both graduated from grammar school, that evening—

A. Yes.

Q. —and in a game of Post Office at the party, where there are a number of children, you have this one boy kissing a girl and tightening up against her—

He kissed her again, and she powerlessly tightened against him. He forced her to the bed.

"Stop touching me there. Stop!" she whispered.

When he paused, breathless, she demanded an apology. "Shut up!" he muttered.

He bent down and kissed her.

"Unhand me, you cur. Take your hands off!" she whispered. "Take your hands off there, or I'll scream!"

And they continued kissing.

And then the sister brings that to the attention of the brother:

". . . Do you think they did anything in the post office?"

"What do you mean?" he asked.

This is after the family has gone to bed, and she is in a nightgown; she wore a thin nightgown, he could almost see right through it.

You said:

"You know. Do you think they did anything that was fun . . . or that the Sisters wouldn't want them to do . . . or that's bad?"

"I don't know," he answers.

Dirty thoughts rushed to his head like hot blood.

He told himself he was a bastard because . . . she was his sister.

"I don't know," he said, confused.

"You think maybe they did something bad, and it was fun?"

He shrugged his shoulders and looked out the window so she couldn't see his face.

"I feel funny," she said.

Without reading all that conversation, after he refused to get up, the sister calls him:

Fran called him. She was lying in bed without the sheets over her.

"It's hot here. Awful hot. Please put the window up higher."

"It's as high as it'll go."

"I thought it wasn't."

He looked at Fran. He couldn't help it.

"And please get me some real cold water."

He got the water. It wasn't cold enough. She asked him to let the water run more. He did. He handed the water to her. As she rose to drink, she bumped her small breast against him.

She drank the water. He started out of the room. She called him to get her handkerchief.

"I'm not at all tired," she said.

Now, that, do you say, is necessary to bring out the fact that there exists such things in all the families out there, or any of the families out there?

A. That is a necessary part of the whole story of Studs Lonigan.

Q. Necessary—

MR. KENWORTHEY: Let him finish.

THE WITNESS: It is a necessary part in the sense that Studs in the course of the three volumes is exposed to a very wide series of temptations, a very wide series of experiences, and Studs' relationships to a number of people are presented directly and completely.

Now, I would say this, I do not think that you can take a work that it took six years to write, a work that is composed of 1100 pages, and tear one scene out of context, and take that by itself. It just does not make sense.

MR. BRADLEY: There are many such scenes.

THE COURT: Just one moment. I will give you an opportunity. We must have one at a time.

by Mr. Ryan:

Q. You gave us in the record quite a summary of these books, his relations with this and that, but you did not mention the fact that there were continuously through the books his relations with girls, and his sexual relations with girls, did you?

A. You know, sex is a primary fact of life.

THE COURT: The question now is whether it recurs through this book, whether it is primary or not.

THE WITNESS: It does recur through the book

THE COURT: That answers the question.

THE WITNESS: It recurs—

THE COURT: That is responsive to his question.

THE WITNESS: Surely.

THE COURT: Ask the next question.

by Mr. Ryan:

Q. You made a point there, or you showed that part of your idea was to show this racial situation, the racial change and that you emphasized that, or you brought that out by this socialist out in the park to the crowd?

A. He was just a soapbox speaker, he was unidentified.

Q. Yes, a soapbox speaker. In order to bring that out was it necessary to bring in there the line where the man yelled out at him:

"And I tell you I'm the traveling salesman that made Mary heavy with Christ. Yah."

You have that in your book.

A. I set out in *Studs Lonigan* to describe and present the way many different types of people talk; the fact that people have said that, the fact that this kind of joke has been made is, I say, sufficient justification for its inclusion. It is part of a general scene in which there is misunderstanding on both sides, in which there are a number of insults of different kinds, in which there is a near riot, and in which there is a character who is an atheist; there is an old man who is a Catholic. Various opinions are expressed and they are set forth in this particular scene.

Q. You do not identify who says that particular line, do you?

A. If I see the book. Very frequently in the book two people are talking, and I do not identify them each time, because as you read you can see it is a conversation, and it may be that; in the other instances, where there are crowds, it does not particularly matter who says something.

Q. In delineating this character was it necessary for you to bring out, and then refer to again and again and again, the gang shags given by Iris, where she took a half a dozen boys up in the afternoon and had intercourse with them, and they shot craps for turns?

MR. KENWORTHEY: I wonder if the form of that question is fair?

MR. RYAN: I think it is more than fair.

THE COURT: Just a minute. Are you objecting?

MR. KENWORTHEY: I am objecting.

THE COURT: Will you read it?

(The last question was repeated by the reporter as follows:)

"Q. In delineating this character was it necessary for you to bring out, and then refer to again and again and again, the gang shags given by Iris, where she took a half a dozen boys up in the afternoon and had intercourse with them, and they shot craps for turns?"

THE COURT: I will overrule the objection. I will let him answer that.

THE WITNESS: On the question of the gang shags, that is where the boy has his first sexual experience. This I may say—I might make a general statement: In this particular youth, and particularly in the case of these boys, there is an intense aggressiveness, and the values which are lived by, rather than talked about, of these boys on the street are related to sexual conquests and physical aggressiveness. Now, this particular scene was for these boys one which they talked about a lot.

Now, secondly, it is contrasted through the boy by the confused memory in his nostalgia for his pure love of his childhood sweetheart, Lucy. All through the book there are these counter currents, this nostalgia for the pure love, his memory of the time when the girl sat in the twilight and blew him a kiss, and his memory of this other type of relationship with girls.

It seems to me that that exists all through the book, that there is revealed that there is a double standard, on the one hand the girls of your own family, and the girls whom you might want to marry, are good, are pure, are superior to you, and all other girls are no good; they are depersonalized; they are looked at in a condemning fashion, and they are considered to be objects of aggression.

I did not invent them, in the sense that I did not think up something that did not exist in life; it is not only my experience, but it is in the experience of many people, many people who have been in courts, many people who have been sociologists, criminologists, and so on, and I did attempt to present those phases of human experience.

You may or may not like them, but I do not think that you are really trying to come to any understanding of anything by tearing out one aspect of the book and not the other, asking me questions, but not seeing these contrasts where Studs also is ashamed of himself, where Studs also dreams of his lost purity, these contrasts run right through the whole volume.

by Mr. Ryan:

Q. The lost purity is the last paragraph of two pages about the gang shag, is it not?

A. No, you are incorrect, it is not so, it ran all through.

Q. He decides he won't do it again?

A. No, it runs all through. No, you are factually incorrect.

Q. Mr. Farrell, in the delineation of your character, which you say is the reason for the book, is it really necessary for you to put in from Page 336 to the end of the *Young Manhood of Studs Lonigan,* which is 349, this drunken New Year's party in a hotel, in which one girl gets raped and beaten so badly that she is crippled for life; another one is a virgin, but she is not any more, and they sent another man in after her; the girls stripped—I think His Honor can read it for himself—and another one going to jump out of a window because she has been raped, and has to be stopped; is there any reason that that has to go in?

A. Yes, sir.

Q. Except for the fact that you have to get him drunk and have him catch a cold that night?

A. Yes, one of the frontispiece quotations from *Young Lonigan* is taken from John Dewey's *Human Nature and Conduct,* it reads:

> The poignancy of situations that evoke reflections lies in the fact that we really do not know the meaning of the tendencies that are pressing for action.

Now, these tendencies which press for action are focused dramatically in a terrible sense in this New Year's Eve scene. One of the characters in this book is Weary Reilley. We have the situation of these boys growing up, you have their intensive aggressiveness. That boy who is most mean, that boy who is most vicious, that boy who is most neurotic will tend to set the pattern of conduct. Now, that is the role of the character Weary Reilley in this book. He commits this terrible rape, in which he paralyzes the girl. Here are some of the possibilities of some of these tendencies that are present for action, here are the consequences of undue aggression, undue sadism, here is part of the condition of youth as I have seen it in my own lifetime.

THE COURT: If that theory is correct, then I do not think there is much hope for the human race, if the most neurotic boy is the one who governs all the rest and who is going to attract everybody toward him. I do not follow you on that. Then we are on the downgrade.

THE WITNESS: May I clarify what I mean?

THE COURT: Yes.

THE WITNESS: If you have the unchecked expression of values in these terms, that is the significance; I mean, all of the boys in this book do not rape a girl, this one boy does. In serious literature you sharply and dramatically focus.

THE COURT: I was thinking of your statement that you said that he is the one that sets the pattern of conduct.

THE WITNESS: I should correct myself. I should say *tends to,* unless there is some check on these tendencies, and that the function of Weary Reilley is to dramatize that tendency. You can see that all of the boys do not do what he does. He is the one that does this terrible rape.

THE COURT: Another thing that struck me while you were testifying—I have not read these books—that has been running through my mind for a number of years; I do not know if it has anything particularly to do with this case, and I do not know if it has anything to do with the law, but you said that you are one of the authors that belongs to the school of realism, and then you mentioned many of these dreams. I have been observing in a lot of these books of the authors that you say belong to this school of realism, that practically all, if not all, most, of the objectionable parts the authors seem to set forth in dreams, as though those dreams conveyed the realism of the world. I do not quite understand that.

That has been running through my mind for several years, just as a matter of literature, aside from being a judge, but it recurred here several times again, and your remarks just brought it to my mind. I do not quite understand it.

THE WITNESS: I can comment on it and I would be glad to.

THE COURT: I would be glad to have you comment, and if the other side has any objection to my remarks I want it noted on the record.

THE WITNESS: What is relevant to that is that in *Studs Lonigan* the dreams are drifting. I would say this, at the present time, and particularly as a result of the influence of a Czech writer called Franz Kafka, there is the presentation of writing which is presented from the standpoint of a hallucination. Kafka was a small government clerk in the Austrian Empire, and what he intensely wanted was security. He was a man who felt that he had no identity. In his dreams he presented a true character in the terms of hallucinations, he seeks identity, influence with people, a name, and belonging. Kafka, while he is a genius, presented his own desire and his own anxiety for security. In the United States today, where we have more normal experience, where more normal experience involves that we have not been overwhelmed by any great tyranny, and we have not been overwhelmed by any catastrophic war, with true social relationships, that Kafka pattern has been taken over by newer writers. I think it is very unhealthy. It does not come to reality with American experience, it is not warranted in American experience. It is the idea that the reality is a hallucination.

In that sense I think I agree with you, and it is a psychologically unhealthy tendency to present what is not a hallucination as a hallucination.

I would say that that has nothing to do with the presentation of dreams here.

THE COURT: I find it myself in talking with my acquaintances. I think it is the experience of the human race that we have some horrible and terrible dreams, but the nice part about it is that, when we go about our business, by noon we have forgotten most of it, and we can get on with the realistic things in the world. I get a little tired sometimes with authors always clarifying dreams in books, it spoils the books for me, but that may not have anything to do with this case.

Proceed.

by Mr. Ryan:

Q. Mr. Farrell, we will take up where I left off.

THE COURT: I will try not to interrupt.

MR. RYAN: I do not mean it that way, sir.

by Mr. Ryan:

Q. (*Continuing*) With this beating of the girl, and her screams, the kicking her here and punching her there; that is described in great detail in your book on Page 347 of the *Young Manhood of Studs Lonigan*. Would you say this sadism is more in the author or in the character?

A. Why, of course, it isn't in me. Why do you think it is?

Q. You wrote this part out at great length, covering page after page, about everything that is done to each one of these girls; one is drunk, on Page 344:

"I got mine from that broad," said Mahoney.
"I thought she was a virgin," said Fluke.
"She was!"
"Well, how did you do it?"
"I got her blind. She's out."
"Where is she?"
"She's in the second bedroom. She passed out, and I carried her there. She's out like a light."
"Mind if I try my luck?"
"Go to it, Fluke," said Mahoney.

You have the girl trying to jump out of a window because she has been raped, and you finish it with this other one.

Don't you think there were sadistic tendencies in the author of the book?

A. You must take the book as a whole. You must understand this, that when Studs Lonigan dies and receives extreme unction there is a complete and total picture; there is attempted a complete picture of his illness; when Studs Lonigan plays football there is a long presentation of the football game. The picture is built up, the accumulation of details, the details relative to the sequence are put in. When you have a scene such as this scene, and it is motivated, and I assert that in terms of my view of this matter it is definitely motivated, you cannot do anything but present the thing directly. Now, the mere directness of the presentation should cause you not to have the kind of thoughts implied in the questions asked me, but it should cause you to be revolted and repulsed, you should be shocked by it; those things shock me.

Q. They did not shock you, Mr. Farrell, so much but that you can put them on paper and get a good royalty out of it, did they?

MR. FARMER: I object to that. You should ask the question and let the witness answer it.

THE COURT: Read the question.

(The last question was repeated by the reporter as follows:)

"Q. They did not shock you, Mr. Farrell, so much but that you can put them on paper and get a good royalty out of it, did they?"

THE COURT: I think the royalty part is objectionable at this time.

by Mr. Ryan:

Q. They did not shock you so much but that you put them down for everybody to read, did you?

A. Of course, I want everybody to know about the conditions of life as I have seen them. I think people should know the facts of life.

Q. Yes, they should know the facts of life. Coming back to the question of royalties, do you think they should know them just to your profit just by putting them in books?

MR. FARMER: I object to this.

THE WITNESS: I have not done this for my profit.

by Mr. Ryan:

Q. You are getting royalties out of these books?

A. Yes, sir.

Q. Practically all the books you have ever written are pretty much in the same fashion, are they not?

A. Incorrect. Will you read them and find out?

THE COURT: There is nothing wrong in an author getting paid for what he writes, nor is there anything wrong in a lawyer getting paid for trying a case. The question is whether it is a proper book, or whether it is proper to seize the book.

by Mr. Ryan:

Q. He did know a rather decent girl named Lucy, didn't he?

A. Yes, sir.

Q. And you say you rewrote a number of times the story of their going out to the park, when they sat up on the limb of a tree?

A. Correct.

Q. You rewrote that twenty-five times?

A. Yes, sir.

Q. Each one of the twenty-five times did you put in the part—oh, it occurs five, or six, or seven times through there—that having seen her bloomers he then thought he would like to feel her?

A. It ran through the organization of the whole thing.

Q. It ran right through it several times?

A. Yes, sir, and he was too shy to do it.

Q. He was too shy to try to feel her?

A. Also, he was too worshipful of her and too fearful.

Q. Later on he takes her to the dance, at Page 253 of the *Young Manhood of Studs Lonigan*, and they are coming home in a taxicab; do you remember that incident?

A. Yes, I do.

[He] was french-kissing her. He dug through her dress and touched her breast. She froze up, turned her face away.

"I'm not that kind of a girl."

He tried, crudely, determined, unthinking, to pull her to him again.

"Please be careful," she said cuttingly.

He looked out the window. He saw the lake. He grabbed her hand. He kissed her. She opened her mouth on the next kiss. He felt under her dress.

And, by the way, at this time he has gonorrhea, does he not?

A. Yes.

Q. "I won't hurt you. Come on," he said huskily. He didn't even think of his dose, all he had in mind was Lucy.

"I can't . . . no . . . not here. If mother isn't home, maybe. . . ."

"Why not?" he said.

"I can't . . . It'll be awful . . . I'll ruin my clothes: Please wait till we get home," she begged.

He believed her. They kissed, and he felt her all the way home. She got out of the car rumpled, and rushed into the hallway. He paid the bill.

She opened the inside door and stood holding it, blocking his entrance. She pursed her lips for him. They kissed. He tried to push open the door.

"No," she said.

She pushed his hat off, and when he turned, closed the door on him. He watched her go upstairs. She didn't look back.

Is that all necessary, this french-kissing, and the breast feeling, and feeling her all the way home, to bring out something that you think is important to show the relationships between the races, and the people in the neighborhood in Chicago there?

A. No, just a minute, I didn't say it was just the races. We are mixing up different things.

Q. Your first analysis was based on the sociological importance of the book?

A. My first analysis also said it was an attempt to give the life history of a boy. It was an attempt to give a picture of one human life. In terms of the total picture it is necessary to present those aspects of his life which have a bearing on his full psychology, on his full nature. Now, I said before, and I might repeat again, that sex is one of the primary facts of life. I would add that in this particular case the time was 1923 and 1924, and if you will refresh your memory, that was the Prohibition Era, with talks of the jazz age, and if you will look through old newspaper files, you will find that there were a great many things, just as I have described them, appearing in many newspapers all over the country.

Q. Weren't there a great many decent people, and decent girls, living around in these United States of America, that did not do it?

A. I didn't say there weren't.

Q. But it is necessary for you to put that in your book to make it the proper book, in your opinion?

A. For this particular story, the story of the disintegration of this boy.

Q. I am jumping around on these parts. Let us take *Judgment Day*. He [Studs] goes to his brother-in-law's horse-race betting establishment. He sees a lady who loses her money. You wrote up there all the details of her taking four men from that place to her home, where her baby is living, and having them go to the drugstore—she makes them go to the drugstore for protection, on the way, and after they draw cards for turns, she goes in the bedroom with them one after another, while her baby is crying.

Is that a necessary thing?

A. Isn't that a revelation of the evils of gambling?

Q. A revelation of the evils of gambling?

A. The woman by gambling loses her money to take care of her family. She is so desperate, she is so afraid of her husband, that she does not know what she does. She turns herself into a prostitute to get back the money.

Q. Is that an impeachment of gambling?

A. Isn't it?

Q. I think it is more than—

THE COURT: You ask him questions, and do not argue.

by Mr. Ryan:

Q. To come to this end of this very splendid history of, I think you said, an American boy, when he finally gets himself engaged to a decent girl, you have him, the first night they are alone in her home, take her clothes off, ruin her, and then keep on with her in the park, until he gets her pregnant, and then dies leaving her that way. That is the end of the book, is it not?

A. Yes; it is a tragic story.

THE COURT: I just want to caution the audience that I do not want any outbursts. I want counsel on both sides and the witnesses to feel free. We are here in a serious matter and I do not want to have any expressions of disapproval from the audience. Now, let that caution be taken by everybody.

You may proceed, Mr. Ryan.

MR. RYAN: Your Honor is going to look at the books yourself, and I was going to ask him about some of these incidents.

by Mr. Ryan:

Q. By the way, Mr. Farrell, you were asked about your schooling, and you said you went to parochial school.

A. I did.

Q. And what further schooling did you have?

A. I went to high school, where the Carmelite Fathers taught. I attended De Paul University evenings for nine months; I attended the University of Chicago for almost three years; and then seven years later I went back to New York University to take one course.

Q. Were you ever a student in a seminary?

A. No.

Q. Referring to Page 265, that is the page I called your attention to before.

A. Yes.

Q. Asking you if there was any reason or excuse for that to appear in there:

"And I tell you I'm the traveling salesman that made Mary heavy with Christ. Yah."

A. Yes, I will tell you, the sense of that is this—I am sorry if I interrupt you. You finish.

Q. Since it appears in a group in the park, where there were soapbox orators, and right ahead of it someone says: "Friend, I shall explain the basic principle of relativity in one sentence that even you can understand," and it does not reiterate about that; is there any connection there?

A. Yes; there used to be a place in Chicago quite like what I have described. It was called the Bug Club; a number of men and women used to go over there of an evening, and in summer, and on Sundays, and they used to talk all day. There used to be intense arguments, there used to be sharp conflicts, insults, there used to be strong religious arguments; there were militant atheists who would go there and insult people, and there were religious people who would go there and insult atheists; and there was talk of that character.

Q. And that to you was sufficient justification for you to put it in the book?

A. Life is a sufficient justification. I am trying to write about life.

Q. You think that anything that happens, or anything that is said by anybody, is proper to put in a book?

A. No.

Q. Where do you draw a line?

A. It is proper if it is put into a total structure. It is a structure of 1100 pages, and you must take it in its context.

Q. What in relation to any part of your structure has the Nativity of Christ to do with this portion here?

A. I explained to you, there were people there who used to insult religious people, and there were religious people who used to insult atheists, and they talked that way.

Q. And therefore because they said those things there you think it is proper to put it in your book?

A. Yes.

Q. And anything that is said by anybody at any time under any circumstances, since it is life—

A. I didn't say that.

Q. —in your mind is proper to appear?

THE COURT: He did not say that.

THE WITNESS: I explained the context.

THE COURT: He said it helps to erect the structure.

THE WITNESS: I explained the context of the thing to you and then you just turned it around and said something else.

by the Court:

Q. Mr. Farrell, I think I understand your answer, but could you not always fashion any structure you felt like there and put almost anything in it?

A. Well, that is a very general question, this is a very specific structure.

Q. I know it is a general question, but you gave a general answer, when he asked you specifically if you thought it was proper, your answer was that perhaps not by itself, but to fit into your entire structure.

Let me ask you this then: Do you think it is perfectly proper to fashion any kind of structure into a book?

A. Not any kind of structure. I think it is perfectly proper to take the material facts of life, and take the language of people, and take the attitudes of people, and take their contacts, and to present them in a serious and tragic way. I think particularly it is proper to do that with youth. If I may say one thing in reference to the way I looked at my books. When I was a boy I felt that many things only I felt, that all of these feelings and problems were only mine. I felt totally isolated. I did not realize that many boys felt the same way. In writing these books I felt if you can show the conduct and conditions of youth, the patterns of his experience can be treated in a serious, tragic way, you indicate that you are not alone in this, that these things that bother you are things that are more common than you think, and in doing that you actually tell youth that the problems and even the shames, and the humiliations, and the difficulties you go through, are things worthy of the serious attention of the literate public of America.

Now, that is part of the feeling that I had in writing *Studs Lonigan* and many other works of mine. I think in terms of that feeling and the total structure of the book, and I think everything in the book is justified.

Q. You speak of other books of yours?

A. Yes, sir.

Q. What would be the justification in *A World I Never Made* for having the eleven-year-old brother for a nickel tell a seven-year-old brother in the most vulgar terms possible how babies are made?

A. It is [a] very common thing, that is, curiosity about procreation and about birth. It is very common. That curiosity occurs in children; when it is not explained to them, when they are not told about it, they seek to find it out in other ways, and that is one instance of that.

Q. You wrote *Studs Lonigan* because, you say—or I understood you to say a moment ago that you think that your clearing up of the troubles of the youth of today, if they will read this, then they will understand all about these problems?

A. I would not be so foolish as to say that one book can do that. I would say it is part of my contribution toward these problems, and I would say that many penologists and many criminologists, judges among others, have felt and they have said, and I hope I am not immodest, that it was. They have encouraged students and others to read it. Besides being required reading in literary courses, it is required reading in sociology and criminology in many universities in this country. I would say it is my attempted contribution and I would like anybody to judge it for what it is worth. I do not want them to take my word for it. They can read it.

Q. Are you run down?

A. I beg your pardon?

Q. Every time I start a question—

THE COURT: Just go ahead and ask a question.

by Mr. Ryan:

Q. You consider that the effect on a young man, or not a young man, take a boy, fourteen, fifteen, sixteen, seventeen years old, of reading this book, with all the sex in it, where every other page he watches a girl come along, and notices how her bubs bounce, and wonders whether she is made, or whether he can make her—do you think that would have a nice effect on him?

A. The total picture of it, the consequences of the book, what happens to Studs because of the consequences of the values that he accepts, the serious end to which he comes as a result of this exaggerated, he-man psychology; there are many other things, and if you take the total picture I would say it is very likely that in the greater number of instances it is likely to have a very helpful effect, not a harmful one.

Q. Let us talk for a second about *A World I Never Made*. Do you think that that would be helpful to children by having you put that in the book to let them know, to satisfy this healthful curiosity as to sex?

A. I did not write the book to satisfy a healthful curiosity.

MR. FARMER: I object to that.

THE COURT: Read the question.

(The last question was repeated by the reporter as follows:)

"Q. Let us talk for a second about *A World I Never Made*. Do you think that that would be helpful to children by having you put that in the book to let them know, to satisfy this healthful curiosity as to sex?"

THE COURT: I will sustain the objection because I think it is too long and too involved.

MR. RYAN: All right.

by Mr. Ryan:

Q. Mr. Farrell, admittedly the question of sex, which you say is a primary, basic question, runs all through the Lonigan books, does it not, from beginning to end?

A. It occurs again and again, yes. I mean Studs is at the age when it is a strong impulse, and Studs also has defective values and does not find a road to peace, health, and prosperity; he finds a road to tragic deterioration.

Q. I am still seeking to get in my own mind your explanation for most of the book.

For instance, toward the end he has got the girl to whom he is engaged pregnant. He is out looking for a job, it is a rainy day. So you have him go into a burlesque show, and get sex aggravation watching the girls in the burlesque show bounce around there and strip, and he stays there until he has a sex action himself.

A. What happens there to Lonigan, he is in a state of incipient delirium and fever, and he is becoming very sick with a sickness that brings him down, and he goes in there by accident, if I recall it correctly, and when he is in there it is a very boring and disgusting type of performance; it was the type of performance which the authorities of Chicago permitted, which the authorities of many cities permit. It was a common feature of the world in which he lived, the values to be found in *Studs Lonigan*.

Q. You do not say anything about it being a disgusting or nasty exhibition, you have him saying, "Take them off," and enjoying himself quite thoroughly.

A. Mr. Ryan, I try to be an artist, I try to present life accurately, vividly, and directly. When I wrote *Studs Lonigan* I did not know that on May 17, 1948, you were going to ask me questions of this kind, which were isolated, I could not anticipate that. I was trying to recreate a picture of life, and that picture of life obviously does not please you, but it is a true, and it is a valid picture of one pattern of destiny in our life.

Q. This is not an autobiography and, therefore, the events in it were put in there from your imagination, based upon some facts that occurred in various lives?

A. Based upon some facts; nobody has ever challenged the validity of that book.

Q. I am not challenging it.

THE COURT: Ask a question.

by Mr. Ryan:

Q. Let us take the succession of them. It was under your control entirely, was it not?

A. In the sense that anything is under the writer's control.

Q. Whether or not you put in anything about a burlesque show was entirely at your option, was it not?

A. Yes.

Q. You could have left it out, could you not?

A. Yes.

Q. Therefore, what I am going to ask on this, as I did on the other things, where is the necessity for telling a story and for bringing in now on Page 313 of *Judgment Day,* "The urinal smell of the 10-cent burlesque show made Studs feel as if he would become diseased or contaminated just by sitting in it."

THE COURT: I do not want to interrupt you. I think you have asked that same question in five different ways, and he has answered them all the same way. I suppose he will answer this the same way as he did the others. I do not see any merit in just repeating: Why did you put this particular thing in, or why that? I do not want to interrupt. Perhaps both sides think it is necessary, but I do not think it adds much to it one way or the other. I think he has given us an explanation of it. If there are a good many instances like that you can later call them to the attention of the Court.

MR. RYAN: Your Honor, as I did in the case before, I have prepared a list of pages on which there are matters to which attention is directed.

THE COURT: I do not think this matter is any different from what the others were, and I think he has given his explanation of it. What I mean is that I think it just adds repetition to it, and it does not help us one way or the other.

MR. RYAN: Yes, sir. The answer will be the same, I presume.

by Mr. Ryan:

Q. May I only, Mr. Farrell, go back to a question that was brought up a while before: is there any place at which you draw the line of what should be put into a book, when, as you say, you are attempting to be realistic and to depict a thing which happened or might happen in life?

A. The artistic pattern, the scenes, the characters, the pattern of the language, they determine the line. I would say this, I do not think that anything human is foreign to me. I think that we must look at anything that exists in life and not blink our eyes at it, but try to understand it.

I would again repeat what I said, a motto I am very fond of, what the Russian writer Chekhov says: "Man will only become better when you make him see what he is like."

Now, man often acts in a way that is not of the best, and a man in court is familiar with that, because he comes in contact with it every day. I would say that the material of life which a lawyer, a doctor, a psychiatrist handles is also the valid material of life for the artist. I have always held that position, it is not a question of drawing any line. I draw a line on anything that I consider bad taste, too, but I do not see anything of bad taste here.

by the Court:

Q. Is it your theory then that the more filth and muck a youth is exposed to the stronger he will be as a man?

A. No, the whole sense of this book is that here is a condition of youth that is bad, that is alarming, and it is intended as a tragic story.

I did not say that. I have been, in my life, in every possible way opposed to such things. Mr. Ryan brought in the question of *A World I Never Made.* One of the questions I asked myself, when I wrote that book—

Q. What I understand you said is that because he was not strong enough to resist this, there was decay in his life, both physical and moral, but, as I understand, if you carried it to its logical conclusion, then, a youth who was brought up without being exposed to a lot of these vile things, you think, would not have the strength and the fortitude to resist them?

A. No, I would not say that at all. The thing is that this is one pattern of American destiny I have contrasted with another pattern in my other series of books, and I intend to contrast it with additional ones in future books.

THE COURT: I see.

MR. RYAN: I think that is all.

THE COURT: Now, Mr. Bradley.

by Mr. Bradley:

Q. Mr. Farrell, the Court here has overruled defense's objections to your literary lecture, and has borne with you very generously.

THE COURT: Do not go over that. I allowed Mr. Ryan to cross-examine a lot longer than the direct examination. If you are so sure of your standpoint that I was wrong in that, then, if I were you, I would not cross-examine at all on the defendants' side. I have ruled on that, and if I am wrong I will hear it on argument.

Go ahead and ask a question.

MR. BRADLEY: I was making a point that this testimony—

THE COURT: You were delivering a lecture. Ask a question.

by Mr. Bradley:

Q. Your testimony has been along the lines of the purpose in writing this book, but did you ever consider the effect on the readers?

A. Yes, I did. I said that I think that in the greater number of instances the effect has been good.

Studs Lonigan was completed in February, 1935; it has been in circulation as a completed work for thirteen years, and the American Republic continues to stand. It has been studied in colleges. It was very popular among soldiers in the army. It has been recommended by figures from many walks of life, including one Assistant Secretary of State, and America continues to stand. There are students, there has been more than one generation of students brought up on it, and many of them are writers, many of them are teachers, and they go along in their walks of life, and that would be an empirical question, and, if I may say it, I would think that some burden of proof would be on you.

Q. Your answer is yes?

A. I think the effects are generally to stimulate a rejection of this. This book, as I stated, has the effect of saying these are the consequences, this is what I did not want to be, and I believe that in the great number of instances it has the same effect on youth.

Q. I did not ask you what the effect was, I ask whether you considered the effect.

A. The answer is obvious, that I have.

Q. Do you know that the effect of such writings is governed by law in various states, and the Penal Code, as in this case, in Pennsylvania, governs that?

MR. FARMER: I object to that.

THE COURT: Objection sustained. He does not need to know what the law is. We are only interested in whether this is a proper or an improper book, or whether the police did the proper or the improper thing. Unfortunately that is my responsibility. I would like to pass it to somebody else.

It does not help us; you asked him if he knows there is a law. That does not excuse him if he does not.

by Mr. Bradley:

Q. Let me put it this way: Do you think that the effect would be the opposite, that it would have a stimulating and aphrodisiac effect on the readers, too, more or less?

A. No, I was sure it would not.

MR. BRADLEY: That is all.

THE WITNESS: I was positive it would not.

REDIRECT EXAMINATION

by Mr. Farmer:

Q. Do you feel it would be fair to say that the effect of the book was an emetic rather than an aphrodisiac?

A. I would prefer my own statement to Judge Woolsey's. I would say the effect of the thing was this: I would say the effect of the book would be to take a reader and carry him through a series of rejections, where he feels this is wrong, this is not humane, this is not what I want to be. I think that would be the effect.

Q. Do you regard Studs Lonigan as a typical American boy?

A. I would say that he is a normal American boy, and by saying that I would have to define what it is. It is this: That all American boys do not die like Studs Lonigan, do not end like Studs Lonigan, but the pattern of emotions, the pattern of temptations, the type of attitude, the type of things to which they are exposed, in that sense it is normal.

Q. You mean that the problems are normal?

A. The problems are common, and the language is common. All through *Studs Lonigan,* scene after scene, it is the most common type of scenes, and in that sense it is normal, and in that sense Studs is a normal American boy.

Q. Is the resolution of the problem that you bring about in Studs' life a normal resolution?

A. It is a tragic resolution.

Q. It is a special resolution?

A. I mean the end. After all, we have always considered—and I do not want to say that other than this is an intention, I would have others judge—that the highest form of literature is tragic. Now, my aim, my intention, was tragic.

Q. Did you anywhere in *Studs Lonigan* describe a sexual act?

A. I don't recall a direct description of it as such.

Q. Do you recall?

A. I do not recall. I would have to refresh my memory. I mean, that is a factual question which the Court can decide when it reads it.

MR. RYAN: Page 217 in *Judgment Day.*

He said he would have to be reminded. I am pointing it out to him.

THE WITNESS: The thing is to what degree it is a description.

Yes, I would presume you would call it directly such a description.

by Mr. Farmer:

Q. That was one instance of it, is that correct?

A. That is correct.

MR. RYAN: Do you want me to call some others to his attention?

THE COURT: Just a moment, Mr. Ryan.

by Mr. Farmer:

Q. Did you write that scene or any other scene for the purpose of arousing sexual desire?

A. No.

Q. Did you write that scene for the purpose of portraying a part of a pattern in a man's life?

A. I did. The whole is a pattern of a man's life.

Q. Do you portray any so-called—and I say so-called because of Mr. Ryan's terminology—decent people in your book?

A. Surely, the mother and father are decent; they do not have a great deal of understanding. At the end of the book the father is in a desperate condition and he drinks, but he is decent. The sisters are decent. Many of the characters in the book are decent.

I mean, some of the things the boys do, particularly at the age of fourteen and fifteen, you cannot interpret them in the same way you can interpret a man's conduct. I mean, it is a type of mischief that can result in one or another consequence, but most of the parents in the book I should say are decent. For instance, the father takes care of his family, he tries to be a good provider, and definitely he is a decent person.

MR. FARMER: That is all.

RECROSS-EXAMINATION

by Mr. Ryan:

Q. This very decent father ends up the book, comes out drunk, when Studs, his son, is dying, does he not?

A. Yes; he is very desperate.

THE COURT: He said he becomes very desperate and drinks.

THE WITNESS: Yes, many decent men become desperate and they drink.

by Mr. Ryan:

Q. Before he knows that his son is dying he gets so drunk that somebody else has to bring him home.

A. Yes, he does it, he comes back to the scene of his childhood.

THE COURT: He said he drinks. I will let you inform the Court later what the significance of that is.

MR. FARMER: I have no further questions.

MR. RYAN: Your Honor will read the books.

THE COURT: Mr. Bradley, have you any further questions?

MR. BRADLEY: No.

THE COURT: Have you, Mr. Guth?

MR. GUTH: No.

This concluded Mr. Farrell's testimony. As stated in the introductory note, the injunction requested by him and his publishers, the Vanguard Press, Inc., was granted by Judge Bard.

Chapter VIII
The librarians take a stand

MATTERS of intellectual freedom have often been in the forefront of American librarians' attention. They have vigorously opposed censorship in any form, ranging from such comparatively innocuous acts as book labeling and loyalty oaths to shocking examples of book burning. Among the high lights of the past twenty years, it would be pertinent to mention the American Library Association's reaffirmation in 1948 of the Library Bill of Rights, a document stating certain fundamental principles which has been widely accepted as a guide by librarians and library trustees of the country.

The 1950's produced some of the most violent assaults on freedom of information in American history and simultaneously inspired the most unyielding defense of such freedoms by the library profession. Among actions by the national association that stand out are a strong resolution, in 1951, against labeling of books in libraries; a fighting statement on the American information libraries overseas, adopted in the midst of the McCarthy investigations in 1953; and a resounding manifesto on the freedom to read, adopted jointly by the American Library Association and the American Book Publishers Council, also in 1953. The courageous stand of the librarians won the support of no less a figure than President Eisenhower, whose letter addressed to the A.L.A. conference in Los Angeles received wide publicity. Further backing came from another influential source, the American Bar Association's House of Delegates, meeting at Boston in August, 1953. These basic documents in the librarians' battle for intellectual freedom are reproduced at the end of this chapter.

◖ Wherever libraries and librarians have come under attack, loyal friends have rallied to their defense. Among the able publicists who have spoken out effectively on various occasions James Rorty is outstanding. His article, "The Attack on Our Libraries," which appeared first in *Commentary,* reviews several notorious censorship cases that were troubling the nation during the 1950's.

James Rorty
THE ATTACK ON OUR LIBRARIES

Traditionally, American libraries have been quiet little sanctuaries, untroubled islands of repose far removed from the swirling tides of political strife. Their custodians have tended to be gentle and scholarly non-combatants, vowed to poverty by the meager rewards of their profession, and to impartiality as the stewards of the cultural heritage.

All this was changed by the cold war, the Congressional investigations of Communist subversion, and the resulting concern of citizens—often exaggerated and fanned by local demagogues and publicity seekers—lest libraries be used as channels for the distribution of Communist propaganda, especially to school children. Fear collided with fear: the public's fear of underhand, Communist-inspired books, and the librarians' fear of hysterical, intolerant "book-burners."

In scores of American communities these fears made headlines in the local newspapers and heated the atmosphere of packed town meetings. In the nation, apprehensions began to be voiced that a wholesale attack on the libraries was being mounted which might result in a purge of all controversial books from their shelves and go far toward destroying America's "freedom to read." The case histories that follow span the period 1950–54; they show the essential pattern of these controversies, which, in 1953, were heightened and multiplied by the McCarthy hearings on the United States International Information Administration, with its televised parade of Communist authors whose books had been found in the State Department's overseas libraries. It was at this point that national solicitude found its strongest expression in President Eisenhower's declaration at Dartmouth College on June 14, 1953: "Don't join the book-burners," he warned. "Don't think you're going to conceal faults by concealing evidence that they ever existed. Don't be afraid to go to your library and read every book, as long as any document does not offend your own ideas of decency. That should be your only censorship."

A month after the Communists invaded South Korea, Ruth Brown lost her job as librarian of the Bartlesville, Oklahoma, public library. The two events were not wholly unconnected. With American young men fighting in Korea, American mothers and fathers all across the nation had become increasingly concerned about Communist subversion on the home front.

Miss Brown was never a Communist, nor was she ever charged with being one. The complaint, voiced by a citizens' committee, and investigated by the City Commission, was that she had given library shelf space to the *New Republic,* the *Nation,* and *Soviet Russia Today*. It was also alleged that she had participated in group discussions of race relations—always a highly charged subject in a border state. Later, when the City Commission recommended Miss Brown's discharge by the Library Board, it added *Consumer's Research* and the *Negro Digest* to the list of publications it considered objectionable.

Miss Brown fought back. A city ordinance provided that the librarian could be dismissed only for misconduct or neglect of duty, neither of which was charged. Moreover, Miss Brown had the confidence of the Bartlesville Library Board, which ruled that, while *Soviet Russia Today* might well be discontinued as unnecessary, the *New Republic* and *Nation* might be retained.

Her victory was short-lived. Although the Library Board was an autonomous body, appointed by the City Commission under state

---

James Rorty, "The Attack on Our Libraries," *Commentary,* 19:541–49 (June, 1955), copyright 1955 by American Jewish Committee. Reprinted (without amplifying footnotes) by permission of the author and of the publisher.

statute, there existed a home rule charter under whose authority the City Commission repealed the ordinance which had seemingly made Miss Brown's job secure. The Commission then passed a new ordinance, gave itself control of the library, dismissed Miss Brown, and appointed a new librarian.

With the support of a member of the old Library Board, Miss Brown appealed her case to the Oklahoma Supreme Court, contending that the action of the Commission was contrary to state statutes, to "state interest in library matters," and to the "general welfare." Two years later the court ruled against Miss Brown, holding that "the operation and administration of a city library is a matter of strictly municipal concern."

The Boston Public Library is the oldest tax-supported library in America and one of the finest. Its Research Division is the ally and educational collaborator of Harvard, the Massachusetts Institute of Technology, and a dozen other colleges and universities in and around the hub of New England culture. Professional librarians have the highest respect for the competence of its staff. Yet during the summer and fall of 1952, the year before it celebrated its hundredth anniversary, the library had to fight, as never before in its history, for its integrity and freedom.

For that ordeal, the library is indebted, if indirectly, to Senator Joseph McCarthy, whose book *McCarthyism and the Fight for America* was not available on its shelves when, on September 22, the Boston *Post* started serializing it. In its September 25 issue the *Post* deplored this fact, but also noted that the book had been ordered and would be made available for circulation.

In subsequent issues of the newspaper the library was charged, not with having pro-Soviet material on its open shelves, but merely with having available, on request, files of the *New World Review, Pravda,* and *Izvestia;* also with having included, in a lobby display arranged by the Great Books Foundation, a copy of Karl Marx's *Communist Manifesto;* and with having in its reference collection Vishinsky's *Law of the Soviet State* and "thousands of other Communist publications."

All counts in the indictment were true and admitted. As the director of the library, Milton E. Lord, pointed out, "It is essential that information on all aspects of political, international, and other questions be available for information purposes in order that citizens of Boston may be informed about the friends and enemies of their country."

This did not satisfy the Boston *Post,* which declaimed: "WE BELIEVE that pro-Soviet literature should be suppressed in our public libraries. . . . WE BELIEVE that to permit pro-Communists to circulate their poison among our people is sheer stupidity." The *Post* was answered editorially by its conservative Republican contemporary, the Boston *Herald:* "The basic question is whether we still have confidence in the average American's ability to separate bad ideas from good by his own unaided effort. When we lose that confidence, we shall have lost our faith in democracy itself."

Among those who rallied to the library's support was Herbert Philbrick, former undercover agent for the FBI and author of *I Led Three Lives.* He disconcerted the local McCarthyites by telegraphing: "Shocked to hear that the Boston Public Library has under consideration the suppression of vital information concerning the methods, nature, and extent of the Soviet conspiracy against the United States. Such suppression would be directly in line with the current policy of the Communist party in the United States to conceal the true aims of the party from all except its trusted members. The Boston Public Library should have more, and not less information available to the American people to aid them in their fight against Communism."

Communist literature that the library didn't have, but should have had, in Mr. Philbrick's opinion, included the *Daily Worker,* the Cominform bulletin *For a Lasting Peace, for a People's Democracy,* and J. Peters' *Manual on Party Organization,* which the party has tried to suppress.

The library's Board of Trustees split three to two on the issue. Frank W. Buxton, a retired newspaper editor, Lee M. Friedman, a lawyer and noted book collector, and the Rt. Reverend Robert H. Lord, a Catholic priest and former Harvard professor, supported the director. Frank J. Donahue, a judge of the Superior Court, and Patrick F. MacDonald, a steel merchant, said that the library should not purchase or make available Communist materials. Two local American Legion commanders, the president of the City Council, and one councilman joined the attack on the library, while the *Herald,* the *Christian Science Monitor,* and the *Pilot,* a Catholic diocesan paper, continued to defend it. Two-thirds of the library's staff signed a petition asking the trustees to defend the principle of free inquiry.

At an open meeting of the library trustees with four councilmen, Trustee MacDonald contended that Communist literature should not be bought by the library, but the next day the trustees, by a three to two vote, passed a resolution declaring that material presenting all points of view concerning the problems and issues of our times, international, national, and local, should be made available to the public; that the library authorities had no right to prescribe what the public was and was not to read; but that the library "should not be misused for wrongful propaganda purposes to the injury of our country."

It was a narrow victory, probably helped by the fact that, years before, Library Director Milton Lord had helped in the cataloguing of the Vatican Library in Rome. At a subsequent election, the Catholic archbishop of the diocese became a member of the five-man library board; since then opposition to the library's continued provision of Communist materials has subsided.

After a brief, uncomfortable appearance in newspapers all over the country, Galion, Ohio, has probably had its fill of book censorship. The town is an overgrown crossroads village, now industrialized and spread across the tracks of the New York Central fifty miles north of Columbus. A century and a half ago the region was settled by German immigrants whose descendants still dominate the business and social life of the town. Seventy-five years ago a Negro, later proved innocent of the charge of rape, was dragged through the main street of Galion and lynched; since then no Negro has lived in Galion.

The town's principal industry is the United States Steel Grave Vault Company, whose secretary-treasurer is Mr. Charles Cunningham, son of the founder of the company and one of the town's leading citizens. It was Mr. Cunningham's election to the School Board, along with a conservative and economy-minded majority, that precipitated the library censorship fight. In the background was a long-standing con[flict] over school bond issues; also an ancient feu[d] between Mr. Cunningham and the liberal school superintendent, who cherished modern ideas like the employment of remedial teachers and a school psychologist. Mr. Cunningham's original program on taking office had included a review by the School Board of the qualifications of the teaching staff, and a requirement that all teachers sign a loyalty oath.

In February 1954, the Board heard the complaint of a Galion father whose daughter had obtained from the school library copies of Richard Wright's *Native Son* and two books by Hervey Allen: *Anthony Adverse* and *Toward Morning.* A month later the Board voted three to two to remove the school library's meager collection of about 2,000 volumes and turn them over to a committee of the ministerial association for "screening" during the summer vacation; previously, Miss Elizabeth Allwardt, librarian of the Galion public library, had declined the request of the School Board that she censor the school library.

Immediately after the March meeting, reporters poured into Galion from Columbus and Toledo. *Life* magazine sent its usual formidable task force. Galion winced under the glare of the national spotlight, and Mr. Cunningham secluded himself from *Life's* photographers. This undoubtedly helped the minority on the board, led by Robert Ricksecker, a local attorney, to stage a successful counter-offensive. Two weeks after the first Board meeting, Mr. Ricksecker published a paid advertisement in the Galion *Inquirer* setting forth his position. Subsequently the *Inquirer* editorialized against book censorship and published the text of Ricksecker's opposition statement before the Board, arguing that the net result of the censorship resolution would be to remove all books except the Pollyanna series; also, that what the library needed was more, not fewer books, and a professional librarian to select them.

Within a week of the March meeting a grassfire of public protest was racing through the community; Mr. Cunningham's telephone lines were choked with calls and his supporting majority began to beat a retreat. The idea of a loyalty oath was abandoned. The Board met again and voted unanimously to restore the books to the library, with the exception of the sioned the original complaint. [...] not without its casualties, [...] of his badly needed remedial [...] erwise frustrated by the [...] hool Board, Galion's liberal [...] superintendent resigned to [...] teaching job in another Ohio city.

Mt. Lebanon, Pennsylvania, is one of the smartest suburbs in the Pittsburgh area. In the 1952 Republican primary it voted 90 per cent for Taft. The town was somewhat disconcerted, therefore, when in September of 1953 Mrs. Katharine Mitchell, a local resident—and the possessor of a Ph.D. degree—wrote the board of directors of the Mt. Lebanon Public Library that she had found it contained many books by allegedly pro-Communist or fellow-traveling writers, but none by John Flynn or Joseph McCarthy. Moreover, Mrs. Mitchell said, when she attempted to right the balance by presenting the library with seven books by reputable anti-Communist authors (one of them being McCarthy), her gift was declined by the librarian on the ground that only the official Library Board was competent and authorized to accept it.

After a tumultuous public meeting, which got full-page reporting in the Pittsburgh *Press,* the Board appointed a committee of prominent citizens to investigate Mrs. Mitchell's charges. Chairman of the committee was John D. Paulus, public relations director of the Jones and McLaughlin Steel Company, and formerly book editor of the Pittsburgh *Press.* Three months later the committee reported that they had found no planned effort to foist Communist or Socialist propaganda on the citizens of Mt. Lebanon. It did, however, criticize certain of the librarian's selections, including *Two Years with the Chinese Communists,* by William and Claire Band, noting that, unlike most of the earlier selections about which Mrs. Mitchell had complained, this book had been purchased within the current year. The committee remarked, further, that "there is a very serious doubt as to how far a public library of our size should go in presenting controversial books which attack our form of government and mode of life."

The report took exception to the passage in the "Freedom to Read" statement adopted in May 1953 by the Westchester Conference of the American Library Association and the American Book Publishers Council, which says: "It is the responsibility of publishers and librarians, as guardians of the people's freedom to read, to contest encroachments upon that freedom by individuals or groups seeking to impose their own standards or tastes upon the community at large."

In conclusion, the report observed that if the controversy led to the creation of an adequate and well-housed library, the whole episode would have been worthwhile—the sort of observation which in a number of similar cases has signified the relief of the embattled librarian by the mobilized common sense of the community.

Thus far no American city has actually burned any books. But San Antonio, Texas, came rather close. A month before the President's "book-burning" speech in 1953, the heat engendered by critics of the San Antonio library system reached the scorching point. The controversy exploded in the press when Mrs. Mildred G. Hance, organizer of the San Antonio Minute Women, presented to the City Council a list of six hundred books, allegedly by Communist sympathizers, with the recommendation that these books "be stamped on the inside cover with a red stamp, large enough to be seen immediately, showing that the author has Communist front affiliations, and the number of the citations."

Included on Mrs. Hance's list were Einstein's *Theory of Relativity,* Thomas Mann's *Joseph in Egypt* and *The Magic Mountain,* Dorothy Canfield Fisher's *Fables for Parents,* and Norbert Wiener's *Cybernetics;* also various anthologies of poetry and folk songs, also books on sculpture, the mentally ill, alcoholics, child care, architecture, and mystery novels. Adoption of Mrs. Hance's proposal was urged by Mayor Jack White, whose wife was a Minute Woman. Wylie Johnson, San Antonio's acting City Manager, went Mrs. Hance one better and declared that the books on her list should be burned, rather than labeled.

San Antonio's chief librarian, Julia Grothaus, has held her post for over twenty years. Calmly, she acknowledged that the library did indeed have books on Communism, as well as books by alleged or known Communists. "These books," said Miss Grothaus, "are carefully chosen so that the reader may learn all that should be known about Communism. . . . After all, you cannot remain ignorant about a thing and fight it."

Promptly, San Antonio's liberals rallied to the support of their library system. M. H. Harris, veteran San Antonio editor and for over thirty years chairman of the Library Board declared: "I do not propose to preside over the degradation of San Antonio's library system." Under the leadership of former Congressman Maury Maverick and Mrs. Marie Sien Halpenny, a local writer, various civic groups organized the American Activities Committee, pledged to the defense of "Freedom of religion, thought, press and publication, assembly, individual liberty, dissemination of information, and the promotion of American holidays and the traditional American sense of humor."

Unamused, the Minute Women and their allies pressed on. The city administration replaced the liberal Library Board with a new board more to its liking and slashed the library budget. Six months after the publication of Mrs. Hance's list the San Antonio *News* reported that the library was far behind in its purchase of books. In January, 1954, the *News* declared editorially that "the pro-administration majority faction of the San Antonio Library Board of Trustees appears determined to surrender the system to city hall political domination in clear violation of the spirit, if not the letter, of the council-managed charter." The liberals refused to admit defeat, however. A month later the Board adopted, although by a bare majority, the American Library Association's "Bill of Rights" as its official policy of book selection; subsequently, under pressure from Mr. Harris, every member of the Board went on record against either book-burning or book-branding.

Meanwhile, however, adaptations of Mrs. Hance's little list were being used by Minute Women and other volunteer censors to harass school and library authorities in many communities, including San Francisco. There Mrs. Anne Smart, leader of the local crusade, declared that she favored "voluntary book-burning —the only kind we will ever have in the United States."

The peak of the library controversy was reached and passed with President Eisenhower's "book-burning" speech in 1953. That year the ALA's Intellectual Freedom Committee reported over a hundred library controversies of greater or less intensity.

The President, of course, was speaking metaphorically, using the most extreme symbol of the thing he objected to. But his provocation was extreme: when he spoke, no books had been burned in America since Colonial times, but for weeks on end Senator McCarthy had been bludgeoning the heads of the United States International Information Administration and its foreign libraries, and in the resulting panic one librarian actually burned eleven books.

Of course, these libraries have always been recognized as "special purpose" institutions whose collections, since they serve the American information and propaganda effort abroad, answer to different requirements and must be appraised by criteria quite different from those applicable to public libraries and school libraries in this country. The question of "freedom to read" was therefore not so directly involved here; but the spirit with which Senator McCarthy "investigated" the overseas libraries was clearly inquisitorial and repressive. And there was legitimate fear that this extremist approach would help spur vigilantism against libraries at home.

From the beginning it was apparent that the State Department was anxious to placate its Congressional critics and settle the controversy, if possible, off the television screen—if only because Senator McCarthy's inquiry, which was widely publicized abroad, was providing welcome grist for the Communist propaganda mill. The USIIA's information centers were popular and effective precisely because they provided a genuine sample of the freedom to write, to publish, and to read that prevails in the United States, and an agreeable contrast to the dull and censored reading matter available in the sparsely visited Soviet propaganda centers.

The immediate result of the McCarthy inquiry, and even more, of the State Department's frantic efforts to appease its Senatorial inquisitor, was that the overseas libraries lost face and favor with their patrons and American prestige abroad suffered a setback.

The directive under which the libraries had been operating was based on the recommendations of an advisory committee of distinguished editors and publishers. It provided that "in the selection of materials it would be possible as a general rule to draw upon the great body of resources available, produced by persons whose ideological position is unquestioned." The directive added, however, that in exceptional cases books by ideologically questionable persons might be used if their content served the objectives of the information administration.

When these mild and patently reasonable provisions were challenged by Senator McCarthy and other members of his committee, Bradley Connors, then Assistant General Administrator for Policy and Plans of the IIA, announced that the directive had been withdrawn and replaced by a memorandum ordering that "no material by any controversial persons, Communists, fellow-travelers," etc. will be used under any circumstances in any IIA media. (It was during the confusion that followed the issuance of this fantastic order that America's unique contribution to the modern history of book-burning occurred.) The order was almost immediately superseded by a succession of ten somewhat less inept directives or supplementary instructions on the subject of books in the overseas libraries.

Meanwhile Senator McCarthy continued to exhibit to his television audience a parade of well-known Communist authors, a few of whose books had been found in a few overseas libraries. Most of these books had been inherited from army overstock, purchased during the honeymoon of the wartime Grand Alliance. Their number was insignificant. On July 15, 1953, on the eve of his resignation as administrator of the IIA, Dr. Robert L. Johnson reported that the books objected to by Senator McCarthy constituted a minute fraction of one per cent of the 3,000,000 in the overseas libraries; that since 1948 the State Department had purchased over 16,000 copies of anti-Communist books for use in these libraries; and that apart from library use more than 6,000,000 copies of 44 anti-Communist titles were distributed through commercial channels in addition to some 84,000 copies of government documents on Communism.

In his swan song, Dr. Johnson issued a final directive for the libraries which is still in effect at this writing. With minor modifications, it restores the policy which had been in effect before the McCarthy inquiry.

Thus the effects of Senator McCarthy's investigation of the overseas libraries were chiefly negative. Abroad, the investigation resulted in a lowering of American prestige and a setback of the American propaganda effort. In this country it undoubtedly had the effect of reviving the apprehensions of the patriotic organizations, with the result that in 1953 the pressure for censorship of American public libraries, and especially school libraries, rose to an all-time high, noted above, of over a hundred reported cases, with as many more, in all probability, that were never brought to the attention of the Intellectual Freedom Committee.

In all these library battles the alignment of forces is usually the same. On one side we see the librarian, whose professional rights, interests, and obligations are represented and defended by the American Library Association, its official journal, and its Intellectual Freedom Committee. On the other, we have the librarian's lay critics, represented usually by the patriotic organizations, especially local posts of the American Legion, which in turn are stimulated, armed, guided, and to some extent restrained by the Legion's National Americanism Commission and its bulletin *The Firing Line*.

In between is the Library Board, which is the community's instrument for implementing, extending, and safeguarding the freedom to read. Usually the Board is an appointive body; its members are chosen by the mayor or the City Council and serve without salary. The Board determines the library's budget and raises its funds, in which public support is usually supplemented by private donations; it directs the library's expenditures, appoints the librarian, and delegates to him the responsibility for selecting the library's book collections, either wholly or subject to the supervision of a reading committee. When the librarian is attacked the Board provides, in its public meetings, the arena in which he confronts his critics.

But the Board is seldom neutral in these contests; usually the majority of its members is against censorship. In the Fund for the Republic's recent survey of current American opinion, the chairman of the local Library Board was one of the fourteen community leaders who were interviewed. On all issues, but especially on issues involving freedom to read, the Library

Board chairmen proved to be considerably more tolerant than the average of all the leaders sampled, and far more tolerant than the national cross-section of opinion.

When asked whether they favored removing from the library a book by a socialist advocating government ownership, 86 per cent of the library chairmen were against it, as compared with 79 per cent of all the community leaders and 52 per cent of the national cross-section.

On the question: "Would you favor removing from the library a book by a man who wrote against religion and the churches?" 74 per cent of the Library Board chairmen answered no, as compared with 64 per cent of all leaders and 35 per cent of the sample of the national cross-section.

Eighty-nine per cent of the Library Board chairmen were against removing from the library a book by a person whose loyalty had been questioned before a Congressional committee, but who had sworn he was not a Communist, as compared with 88 per cent of all leaders and 71 per cent of the national cross-section.

Even in the case of a book by an admitted Communist, 67 per cent of the Library Board chairmen were against removing it from the library, whereas at this point the tolerance of the community dropped precipitously to 42 per cent for all community leaders and 27 per cent for the national cross-section.

Of the fourteen community leaders selected for sampling (a total of 1,500 interviews were reported) the Library Board chairmen ranked highest in tolerance, with the possible exception of the local newspaper publishers—who in many communities are likely to be found serving on the Library Board as member or chairman.

It is important to note that the Gallup and Roper interviewers who conducted this survey were asking *hypothetical* questions, seldom currently posed by the local situation. When the chips are down in a library fight, the level of tolerance, interestingly, tends to rise rather than drop, both inside the Library Board and in the community as a whole. Hence when a librarian chooses to resist censorship pressure and make a public fight of it, he usually wins, as we have seen.

On the other hand, his victory is seldom an unqualified one. Book selection, in the view of the typical American community, is not solely or exclusively the librarian's business, nor does the freedom to read imply any professional right, enjoyed by the librarian, to maintain shelves overbalanced with disguised party-line books. The citizens of Mt. Lebanon, Pennsylvania, acquitted their librarian of any such malfeasance, but they also criticized certain book selections, and ended by asking, with a certain acerbity: "Who made the publishers and librarians the guardians of the people's freedom to read?"

By implication, Mt. Lebanon's answer, like that of most American communities, is that the power to determine what a community may or may not read in its library is not an absolute professional right enjoyed by the librarian, but a responsibility delegated by the community, which must remain the final judge of how well that responsibility is exercised.

The verdict is not always a liberal one, in which case the librarian may appeal beyond the community—successfully, or vainly as in the case of Ruth Brown of Bartlesville, Oklahoma—to the law and the higher courts. But in the overwhelming majority of these library fights the librarian's appeal to the community has been successful; fears have been dissipated, and the conflicts out of which they arose have been clarified, if not wholly resolved.

On the one hand, the librarians have been obliged, both as individuals and as an organized profession, to reexamine their legal and moral obligations to their patrons; to review their policies of book selection and classification; to redefine and defend both their professional rights and their delegated responsibilities. That librarians were usually able to command the support of their boards and the press, and most frequently emerged with the confidence of their communities unimpaired, is largely due to the integrity and conscientiousness they showed in this double task of reexamination and defense.

On the other hand, the librarians' critics have been obliged to reread the Bill of Rights; to examine more closely the books of the authors whom they would proscribe, and thereby to sharpen and sophisticate their categories of what is and is not disguised Communist propaganda. As they acquainted themselves with the librarian and his problems, they discovered that he was not, as they had frequently supposed, a Communist or fellow-traveler; and that while vigorously resisting censorship of his selections or the removal of books from his shelves, he was prepared to buy as many good anti-Communist books as his meager funds permitted. Sometimes a violent controversy has blown over when it came to be realized that the librarian was scarcely to be blamed because his more or less unbalanced collection reflected the ignorance and illusions of writers, publishers, critics, and also librarians—indeed, of much of the country—during an earlier era, or because, now that the political climate had changed, his inadequate budget made it difficult to restore the balance.

In a subsequent article I shall report on how the librarians, responding to the criticisms of the patriotic organizations, have attempted to deal with the problems of unbalanced collections and the identification of books of Communist propaganda, while maintaining the traditions of tolerance essential to their profession.

More than a hundred years ago Tocqueville pointed out the strong pressures at work in America attempting to force an intolerant conformity on the nation. Professor Stouffer's book is one more piece of evidence for this. But it also shows that almost invariably the American system entrusts decisions to leaders far more tolerant than the general populace; it is as if the people, distrusting themselves, make sure to select leaders who will oppose their own worst tendencies.

The ordeal of the library gives grounds for believing that the procedures of American democracy can work on the library front of freedom; not perfectly, but better than any other way we are presently prepared to consider. But the fight to safeguard freedom to read from vigilante censorship is by no means over.

◐ At the height of the McCarthy investigations and "book-burning" controversy in 1953, Robert B. Downs, retiring president, American Library Association, and Director of Libraries and Library School, University of Illinois, was invited to contribute to Robert S. Allen's nationally syndicated column. The accompanying article stated the current issues from the point of view of the library world.

Robert B. Downs
THE BOOK BURNERS CANNOT WIN

At home and abroad, books are under attack. Book-burning, real and symbolic, has become a common spectacle. A phenomenon commonly associated with medievalism, the Inquisition, Nazi Germany, Communist Russia, and other authoritarian regimes has suddenly appeared to menace certain basic freedoms in the United States.

Repressive action takes various forms:

(1) Inquiries by congressional committees, state legislation, local ordinances, extra-legal steps by police officials, movements by sectarian interests, veterans' organizations, and other private pressure groups to ban books of which they disapprove; (2) the withdrawal by school boards of liberal textbooks (mainly in the social sciences); (3) attempts to force libraries to remove from their shelves or to label controversial books and magazines; and (4) boycotts and legal measures against booksellers and publishers.

Incited by these activities, our lunatic fringe has proposed such absurdities as the formation of a vigilante committee to purge a great Midwestern university library of Communist literature, the labeling of "all subversive material" in the Library of Congress, the removal of publications of the United Nations and UNESCO from school libraries, and the branding in red ink in letters an inch high all Communist or "subversive" material kept in libraries for research purposes.

According to a recent estimate, over one hundred communities in the country are feeling the impact of censorship, and there are signs in every direction that the drive is gaining momentum.

This wave of obscurantism is easily explainable psychologically in terms of the period in which we live.

The people are reacting in a perfectly normal fashion to fear and hatred of an enemy. They are responding to demagogic statements by headline-seeking politicians, to the inflammatory and violently-prejudiced writings of a few sensa-

---

Robert B. Downs, "The Book Burners Cannot Win," in "Robert S. Allen Reports," distributed by The Hall Syndicate, Inc. All Rights Reserved. Reprinted by permission of The Hall Syndicate.

tional columnists, to growing antagonism to the United Nations and internationalism in general, and to other emotional appeals.

In every critical era of our history there have been similar attempts to suppress unpopular points of view, but probably none comparable to the present in virulence and intensity, because our very survival as a nation appears to many to be at stake.

Another factor is that more books, magazines, and newspapers are being read than ever before, and the rise of American literacy has made reading more suspect among the anti-intellectuals. Legitimate scholarship and creative literature in the United States are therefore being threatened in ways unmatched in our time, except during the Hitler reign in Germany and in Communist Russia.

An object lesson in the rapidity with which an important operation can be undermined, sabotaged, and partially destroyed may be observed in what has happened to the U.S. information libraries abroad in the past six months.

Here was an excellent system of 194 centers in sixty-one countries, standing high in prestige and influence, among the most effective ambassadors any country could have, with 30,000,000 visitors passing through their doors last year. The information libraries were engaged in presenting a broad, fair picture of life in the United States, helping to correct the too-prevalent conviction that Americans are barbarians, with no genuine culture or civilization of their own. The book collections were representative of our best writings in science, technology, fine arts, literature, history, philosophy, religion, and the social sciences.

Within a few short months, through violent attacks from various sources, largely uninformed, the State Department's confused and confusing directives, the bad judgment of several librarians in the field, who, lacking proper guidance, had the incredibly bad judgment to burn some books, and the accompanying unfavorable publicity throughout the world, there was a quick reversal of sentiment toward the information libraries.

Because of the presence of a few hundred controversial books among a total of more than two million volumes, the library staffs have been demoralized, the reputation for objectivity of the libraries has been seriously damaged among the people they are designed to reach, reduced congressional appropriations may force the closing of about one-half the centers, and the impression has spread around the world that freedom of speech and of the press no longer exists in the United States.

This is a high price to pay for the removal of a handful of questionable books—books which, if they did not belong, should have been quietly taken off the shelves without fanfare.

What can be salvaged from the wreckage by the now-independent International Information Administration remains to be seen.

How to combat and to counteract the current reactionary trend against books, reading, and other things of the mind is a complex problem.

No doubt our difficulties will continue until the end of the cold war and international turmoil, for it is in such an atmosphere that fear and hysteria flourish. We need also a revival of confidence in the rightness of American traditions, in particular those fundamental guarantees enumerated in the First Amendment to the United States Constitution.

Most of all, we need courage on the part of influential citizens, following President Eisenhower's precedent, to speak out against those forces which, often plausibly and with good intentions, are trying to destroy freedoms essential to our form of government.

In one locality after another, it has been found that where citizens' committees or other organizations are willing to take a strong stand against censorship, it has been possible to defeat pending legislation, to have municipal ordinances declared unconstitutional, to stop illegal police activities, to frustrate self-appointed private groups, and to awaken the people to the dangers inherent in repressing free expression.

There are two basic facts about censorship which would-be censors apparently will never learn.

First, banning a book, given the contrary-streak characteristic of human nature, automatically creates a universal desire to read it, and frequently has been responsible for making best-sellers out of what would otherwise remain mediocre failures. (For an analogy in another field, note our "noble experiment" of the twenties and thirties.)

Second, ideas cannot be killed by suppression. There is scarcely any record of a book's total disappearance being caused by censor's fires. Somewhere, almost invariably, a copy has survived which can be multiplied and passed on to succeeding generations. Only when the ideas expressed in books have lost their interest do the books vanish.

The most certain way to breathe life into a book and to insure its longevity is to prohibit its being read.

Leon Carnovsky, editor of the *Library Quarterly* since 1942 and a member of the University of Chicago Graduate Library School faculty since 1932, is a long-time leader in the never ending fight for intellectual freedom. His liberal, but sane and judicious, treatment of the problem of censorship in libraries, presented here, has already become a classic on the subject.

Leon Carnovsky
THE OBLIGATIONS AND RESPONSIBILITIES OF THE LIBRARIAN CONCERNING CENSORSHIP

I have never met a public librarian who approved of censorship or one who failed to practice it in some measure. In some cases the practice was resented and adopted only in response to assumed or actual pressure; in others, it was accepted as proper and was justified on the score that no library can provide all books and that, just as most books which have been published cannot be found in any single library, so a library is forced to practice censorship in effect, if not in name, by failing to acquire the thousands and millions of books which it passes up for reasons of money, space, community interest, or whatever cause.

First of all, I should like to clear up the confusion behind this conception; it is a confusion between book selection and censorship. Though the result may be the same in both—nonprovision of a book—the *reasons* are different and should be clearly recognized. Assume a typical public library in a middle western town of ten thousand, run by a librarian doing the best he can to provide a wide assortment of literature. The librarian sees a review of a history of Persian art, priced at $25.00, but he quickly concludes that this book is not for him, a decision obviously based on sound reasoning. The elements in his reasoning are lack of potential interest, cost, possession of other books on the same general subject, and the relative importance to the accomplishment of his objectives of this book as compared with half-a-dozen others that he can buy for $25.00. Then he sees an announcement in *Publishers' Weekly* of a new book by Faith Baldwin, but he has always felt that the literary standards of his collection required a better quality of fiction; therefore he does not even seriously consider the book, much less order it. Next he reads about a book entitled *Studs Lonigan*. It is well reviewed, widely publicized, inexpensive, and a lot of people ask for it. Yet the librarian decides not to buy it. Though all three books are thus denied the potential borrower, one would have to employ a highly specious logic to conclude that a censorship was operative in all three cases. We must clearly distinguish between identical effects that result from altogether different causes, and we shall never face the censorship problem squarely and honestly until we see that book selection (which implies book rejection) and censorship are not identical.

Censorship is defined in the *Encyclopaedia of the Social Sciences* as "the policy of restricting the public expression of ideas, opinions, conceptions and impulses which have or are believed to have the capacity to undermine the governing authority or the social and moral order which that authority considers itself bound to protect." It is a conscious policy and may be enforced without the assent of the majority; indeed, it may be instituted by a small group or even by an individual who feels strongly concerning a certain issue. Though such issues may fall in any sphere of human interest, the practice of censorship has been most frequently invoked in three areas, namely, politics, religion, and morals, and therefore it is in these areas that the problems of censorship as they impinge on library administration are most often encountered.

The theory of free speech in the political realm has been so thoroughly discussed that it

---

Leon Carnovsky, "The Obligations and Responsibilities of the Librarian concerning Censorship," *Library Quarterly*, 20: 21–32 (January, 1950), copyright 1950 by the University of Chicago Press. Reprinted (without footnotes) by permission of the author and of the publisher.

seems a little strange that it should need a defense in 1949. Clearly and forthrightly expressed in the First Amendment to the Constitution, copied and incorporated in some form in our state constitutions, strongly supported by court decisions of the most respected and honored members of our judiciary, it still remains an ever present issue to plague and puzzle us. The reason is that freedom is not and can never be an absolute. My freedom to make noise is directly contrary to your freedom to enjoy quiet. Nor can there be absolute freedom of speech; society itself imposes limits upon it, and it becomes the business of the courts to determine whether the limits have been transgressed in individual cases.

Perhaps the clearest expression concerning free speech appears in our Bill of Rights: "Congress shall make no law . . . abridging the freedom of speech or of the press"; and the finest explication of the free-speech doctrine is to be found in John Stuart Mill's essay *On Liberty*. Little that has been written since adds much to his cogent argument. His primary object in writing his essay was to establish the principle that "the sole end for which mankind are warranted . . . in interfering with the liberty of action of any of their number, is self-protection. That the only purpose for which power can be rightfully exercised over any member of a civilised community, against his will, is to prevent harm to others." Included in the sphere of liberty of action is "the liberty of expressing and publishing opinions," even though such expression goes beyond strictly individual concern and extends to other persons. However, says Mill, since expression of thought is so closely allied to freedom of thought itself, it is practically inseparable from it.

The champions of free speech, from Milton through Mill to Justice Holmes in our own day, have all been much more concerned with the preservation of the right of free speech for the individual—even though he be the only person in the nation who believes what he believes. Indeed, this is no more than the recognition of the fact that all progress in human affairs is possible only in an atmosphere which permits the unusual person, who is frequently the unpopular person, to get himself heard. The harm in silencing such a person is only incidentally the harm to him; the greater harm is to society, which may be thus deprived of the opportunity to learn a possible truth of which only he may be the master. The truth or wisdom of any issue, like the nature of the good and the beautiful, is never discerned by taking a vote; majorities as such have force on their side but little else. To silence a dissident is to solidify a position and thus to make less likely the possibility of change. Listen to Mill on this point:

> The peculiar evil of silencing the expression of an opinion is, that it is robbing the human race: posterity as well as the existing generation; those who dissent from the opinion still more than those who hold it. If the opinion is right, they are deprived of the opportunity of exchanging error for truth; if wrong, they lose, what is almost as great a benefit, the clearer perception and livelier impression of truth, produced by its collision with error.

And again, with even greater force:

> I insist thus emphatically on the importance of genius, and the necessity of allowing it to unfold itself freely both in thought and in practice, being well aware that no one will deny the position in theory, but knowing also that almost everyone, in reality, is totally indifferent to it. People think genius a fine thing if it enables a man to write an exciting poem, or paint a picture. But in its true sense, that of originality in thought and action, though no one says that it is not a thing to be admired, nearly all, at heart, think that they can do very well without it. . . . Originality is the one thing which unoriginal minds cannot feel the use of.

This, however, is only one argument for free speech; others are equally cogent. Mill mentions three: first, a suppressed opinion, though false on the whole, may yet contain certain elements of truth. Accepted or "prevailing opinion on any subject is rarely or never the whole truth; it is only by collision of adverse opinions that the remainder of the truth has any chance of being supplied." Again, even in the unlikely event that on any given issue the opinion we hold is the complete truth, our confidence in it becomes more strongly intrenched as we see it in the light of lesser truths or even of false doctrines. And finally, says Mill, the meaning of the doctrine itself, if it is never challenged, may be lost and become a mere formal profession accepted from habit and not from conviction.

Since the case for free speech is so solid in our historic tradition, in our constitutional guaranties, and in its logical persuasiveness, it seems odd that the principle is continually being challenged and has been fought several times all the way up to the Supreme Court. And yet it is not so odd, for, as we have said, the concept of free speech is not an absolute, and it is continually necessary for the courts to determine where free speech may become a menace to society or even to the achievement of short-term goals which society, through its legislatures, may envisage. The single most important case involving free speech is the famous Schenck case, heard before the Supreme Court. Here the decision of the Supreme Court was written by Justice Holmes—not a dissent but presenting the unanimous opinion of the Court.

In June, 1917, and May, 1918, Congress enacted legislation aimed at controlling speech which might be construed as disloyal or seditious. The defendants, Schenck and his associates, had been found guilty in the lower courts of mailing circulars calculated to cause insubordination in the military forces; the circulars declared conscription to be despotism and urged the conscriptees to obstruct its operation. The defense invoked the free-speech clause of the Constitution, and it is this aspect that makes the case important for us. The statement of Justice Holmes in ruling on this point has been often quoted, because it laid down a rule that comes close to furnishing a yardstick, to drawing the line where the constitutional protection of free speech no longer applies. Said Holmes:

> We admit that in many places and in ordinary times the defendants in saying all that was said in the circular would have been within their constitutional rights. But the character of every act depends upon the circumstances in which it is done. . . . The most stringent protection of free speech would not protect a man in falsely shouting fire in a theater and causing a panic. . . . The question in every case is whether the words used are used in such circumstances and are of such a nature as to create a clear and present danger that they will bring about the substantive evils that Congress has a right to prevent. It is a question of proximity and degree. When a nation is at war many things that might be said in time of peace are such a hindrance to its effort that their utterance will not be endured so long as men fight and that no court could regard them as protected by any constitutional right.

The key phrase in this decision is "clear and present danger." The problem still remains to determine when a publication or an act constitutes a danger to the state or to society, but at least we have the right question, even if we cannot always provide the right answer. Indeed, even the Supreme Court was unable, in applying the test, to come out with a consistent answer. This is most clearly shown in the Abrams case, also decided in 1919, the year of the Schenck decision. Abrams and his associates had strewed some leaflets from the roof of a building in New York. These leaflets were not aimed at interfering with the war against Germany but protested against American intervention in the Russian Revolution. Included in the protest was a call for a general strike; this could be construed as interfering with the war against Germany, therefore the group was indicted. No strike was actually called, and there was no evidence that a single person had been moved to stop any kind of war work as a result of the leaflets. Nevertheless, the defendants were found guilty in the District Court, and the sentence imposed was upheld by a 7–2 vote of the Supreme Court. The great importance of this case for us lies in the dissenting opinion of Justice Holmes, concurred in by Justice Brandeis; in this opinion Holmes further develops the "clear and present danger" principle. He strikingly shows how strongly he has been influenced by both Milton and Mill; his statement has been said to be the greatest utterance on intellectual freedom by an American and ranking with *The Areopagitica* and the essay *On Liberty*.

> Persecution for the expression of opinions seems to me perfectly logical. If you have no doubt of your premises or your power and want a certain result with all your heart you naturally express your wishes in law and sweep away all opposition. To allow opposition by speech seems to indicate that you think the speech impotent, as when a man says that he has squared the circle, or that you do not care wholeheartedly for the result, or that you doubt either your power or your premises. But when men have realized that time has upset many fighting faiths, they may come to believe even more than they believe the very foundations of their own conduct that the ultimate good desired is better reached by free trade in ideas—that the best test of truth is the power of the thought to get itself accepted in the competition of the market, and that truth is the only ground upon which their wishes safely can be carried out. That, at any rate, is the theory of our Constitution. It is an experiment, as all life is an experiment. Every year if not every day we have to wager our salvation upon some prophecy based upon imperfect knowledge. While that experiment is part of our system I think that we should be eternally vigilant against attempts to check the expression of opinions that we loathe and believe to be fraught with death, unless they so imminently threaten immediate interference with the lawful and pressing purposes of the law that an immediate check is required to save the country. . . . Only the emergency that makes it immediately dangerous to leave the correction of evil counsels to time warrants making any exception to the sweeping command, "Congress shall make no law . . . abridging the freedom of speech."

I hope the implications for libraries of what I have said have not been lost. If there is one agency above all which has the power to put teeth into the principle of free speech, it is the public library. I know of no nobler function which it has to perform than this: the presenting of all points of view, however unpopular, even loathsome, some of them may seem; by the same token, I know of no greater evil, no surer betrayal of that function, than the denial of the expression of certain viewpoints through a deliberate or contrived censorship. This, you may say, is all very well in theory; does it really have any application today? Today the great competing political doctrines are, of course, democracy and communism. Within the framework of democracy itself there is room for dissension: the social welfare state versus an uncontrolled laissez faire, to name but one conflict. No library is likely to quibble over the presentation of these two points of view, or variations of them. The serious problem does arise over the presentation of the literature of communism. Here is material the publication of which is clearly sanctioned by the First Amendment; it is altogether legal by any test we may apply. The understanding of communism is as important as the understanding of democracy, capitalism, or the divine right of kings. No court, as far as I know, has ruled that the distribution of the literature of communism represents a "clear and present danger" to the security of our civilization. It is clearly up to us to give the widest possible latitude to free speech within the political realm.

It is sometimes convenient to forget this principle in the face of certain pressures against a given position. An overzealous American Legion post, a D.A.R. chapter, a religious or national group, or even an individual may feel so antagonistic toward another country or toward another faith or philosophy that it would deprive everyone else of the opportunity to read about them. They do not apply the "clear and present danger" principle; in fact, they apply no rational principle at all but act from a deeply felt emotion. Disagree with them, and you are labeled "un-American"—a strange transvaluation of values when a position espoused by the greatest American of our generation is called "un-American."

Numerous presentations in support of free speech might readily be cited; they are brilliantly summarized in a great dissenting opinion by Justice Brandeis, concurred in by Holmes. The case was that of *Pierce* v. *United States* and consisted of the prosecution of three Socialists for distributing a pamphlet denouncing war. Said Brandeis:

> The fundamental right of free men to strive for better conditions through new legislation and new institutions will not be preserved if efforts to secure it by argument to fellow citizens may be construed as criminal incitement to disobey the existing law—merely, because the argument presented seems to those exercising judicial power to be unfair in its portrayal of existing evils, mistaken in its assumptions, unsound in reasoning or intemperate in language.

We do well to remember with Chafee, the author of *Free Speech in the United States,* that the First Amendment was designed to protect two kinds of interest in free speech: the freedom of the individual to express himself and the freedom of society to listen, to weigh arguments, to balance claims. The boundary to free speech "is fixed close to the point where words will give rise to unlawful acts," and "the great interest in free speech should be sacrificed only when the interest in public safety is really imperiled, and not . . . when it is barely conceivable that it may be slightly affected." This is especially true in peacetime.

We next turn to free speech as it applies to religion, a subject on which we tend to be more sensitive than on any other. Criticism of one's most personal spiritual beliefs is bad manners at the least. It may become a serious nuisance, as it was when Jehovah's Witnesses hired loudspeakers to condemn publicly the members or tenets of other faiths. As a result many communities passed ordinances requiring licenses for the use of sound trucks. Jehovah's Witnesses, however, ignored this legislation and continued berating other creeds; they were arrested, prosecuted, and eventually appealed their case to the Supreme Court on the grounds that such licensing requirement constituted an abridgment of free speech. The Court, by a 5–4 vote, sustained the Witnesses, and the ordinance designed to curb the overexuberant preachings of this sect was declared unconstitutional. An even clearer case is that of *Lovell* (a Jehovah's Witness) v. *Griffin* (Ga.), where it was held by Justice Hughes, speaking for a unanimous Court, that an ordinance requiring written permission from the city manager for the distribution of literature of any kind was unconstitutional. "Whatever the motive which induced its adoption," said Hughes, "its character is such that it strikes at the very foundation of the freedom of the press by subjecting it to license and censorship." It should be noted that free speech was the issue in both these cases, not criticism of religion. *This* issue was not even raised. Just as it is legally proper to criticize agnosticism, paganism, atheism, or any other negative form of religion, so it is proper to criticize its positive forms—Judaism, Catholicism, or any of the branches of Protestantism.

Interference with the right to criticize religions has been a serious library problem only sporadically in a few localities. Christian Scientists objected to Edward Dakin's biography of Mary Baker Eddy, published by Scribner's in the 1920's; and you are undoubtedly familiar with the strenuous objection raised in New York and a few other places to the *Nation's* series of articles by Paul Blanshard in which he criticized certain aspects of the Catholic church. In neither case did the issue reach the courts, for the right of publication guaranteed in the Constitution was too patent. Yet in both cases pressures were brought against libraries, and some censorship resulted. Censorship of the Blanshard articles in the *Nation* took a particularly serious form in New York, for not only were the issues containing the offensive articles removed from school-library shelves but subscriptions to the periodical were canceled at the direction of the superintendent of schools. We find here an implied threat against any periodical that may contemplate the publication of any article to which some powerful and numerous group might take exception.

It seems unnecessary to stress the library's responsibilities in this delicate area. The right to criticize religion must not be abrogated any more than the parallel right to criticize social or political beliefs. We plainly have the right to look critically at any religion, and members of a religious group lay themselves open to suspicion if they attempt to deny to anyone this right. The answer to free speech is *more* free speech, not its obliteration. Serious discussion of the beliefs or operations of any established church is surely proper material for a public library.

In spite of the dangers of censorship of political and social ideas, it is in the area of morals that librarians have experienced the greatest difficulty, both from external interference and from the nature of the decision concerning the line between morality and immorality. Strictly speaking, it is not morality that introduces the problem but such concepts as obscenity, pornography, filth, or whatever other synonyms one prefers. Here too, as in political censorship, the First Amendment is invariably invoked by the publisher or author whose book is objected to. He may claim that the book is not obscene, or, less frequently, he may argue that the free-speech principle confers an unlimited right and that considerations of obscenity are irrelevant. However, we clearly have the right to legislate against the distribution of filth, and in one notable case, *United States* v. *Limehouse,* the Supreme Court upheld such a right. One Limehouse had written letters which the Court characterized as coarse, vulgar, disgusting, indecent, and unquestionably filthy within the popular meaning of that term. Does this type of thing create "a clear and present danger"? It would be difficult to prove this, yet Justice Brandeis took the position that Congress had the right to punish the distribution of filth.

It will be recognized that this was not the sort of "free speech" the Founding Fathers had in mind when drawing up the First Amendment. It has nothing to do with arriving at truth or rational decisions on the basis of conflicting ideas, of presenting evidence for a point of view, or even of propagandizing for or against action construed in the public interest. The suppression of such speech harms no one but the individual suppressed. His right to be obscene is curbed in the interest of a larger right—that of the rest of us to be saved from his obscenities. Chafee has likened this to the curb we place on an individual to prevent his smoking in streetcars. The injury in both cases is immediate, in the discomfort caused the nonsmokers and in the shock to the sensitive listener and reader. Free speech does not include license or licentiousness; the "clear and present danger" test cannot here be invoked to draw the line between the permissible and the proscribed.

This, however, is only the beginning and the simplest part of the problem. The major question remains that of an operational rather than of a dictionary definition of obscenity. This has turned out to be a matter of extraordinary difficulty, and it has been treated with little consistency from one court to another; frequently the decision seems to have been based on hunch or intuition—at any rate, without the spelling-out of definition acceptable to other judges, to publishers, or to librarians. We speak glibly about ours being a nation governed by laws; but laws are not only made by men, they are also interpreted by men, and one man's interpretation is different from another's. Hence the vast number of dissenting opinions, in obscenity cases as well as in others.

Historically, American and British law has tended to rely on the definition provided by Lord Chief Justice Cockburn, in 1868, in ruling against a pamphlet entitled *The Confessional Unmasked:* "I think the test of obscenity is this, whether the tendency of the matter charged as obscenity is to deprave and corrupt those whose minds are open to such immoral influences, and into whose hands a publication of this sort may fall." By this definition we must determine for any one publication whether its effect is likely to be that envisaged by Judge Cockburn, and such decision is reserved to the courts. Usually, objection to certain books is raised by local police, perhaps at the instigation of private individuals or groups, and is disposed of by local courts. Federal courts have been involved far less frequently.

Lord Cockburn's formulation, continually cited as a guide, has recently been considered quite unsatisfactory because it goes much too far. It tacitly accepts as the boundary line the lowest common denominator of human intelligence. Any book might conceivably fall into the hands of a child or of a pathological adult who might thereby be corrupted. As Justice Qua, in the Massachusetts *Strange Fruit* case, observed: "A book placed in general circulation is not to be condemned merely because it might have an unfortunate effect upon some few members of the community who might be peculiarly susceptible." (Even so, Justice Qua joined the majority of the Massachusetts Supreme Court in upholding the right of the lower court to find the book obscene.)

In general, the recent tendency has been—outside Boston—to permit considerable latitude to the author, though most commentators agree that a line must be drawn somewhere. Liberal and intelligent commentators—like Chafee and Huntington Cairns, who as former assistant general counsel to the Treasury Department was charged with ruling on literary importations—believe the line should be drawn at pornography, and on this point Cairns has written as follows:

> Art . . . has its own morality, its own integrity, which those who would limit its treatment of sexual detail would do well to recognize. . . . We have to recognize, however, that this principle of justification covers only half, or less than half, the case. Not all writing is literature, not all information is science. There is . . . that class of material which is put forward with no other purpose in view than the stimulation of the sexual impulse. . . . In their bulk, these photographs and drawings, these miserably printed pamphlets and books, are as far removed from art as they could well be. . . . The principle which accords complete freedom to the artist and scientist in the treatment of sexual detail plainly does not justify pornography.

He then goes on to say: "There is no difficulty in distinguishing between those books the impulse behind which is literary and those whose impulse is pornographic. Any man with a modicum of literary knowledge can do so without hesitation." I wonder if Mr. Cairns would be quite so confident today. Consider the interesting case of Edmund Wilson's *Memoirs of Hecate County*. The book raised a storm of protest throughout the country, and the publisher, Doubleday, was brought before the New York Court of Special Sessions on the grounds of the book's alleged obscenity. Here it was judged obscene, with one justice dissenting. He held that the prosecution's interpretation of the law was "grossly inadequate," and he stated:

> The writer of the story is evidently and honestly concerned with the complex influences of sex and of class consciousness and man's relentless search for happiness. That is a problem which also is of deep concern to the matured reading public. That public is entitled to the benefit of the writer's insight and that right may not lightly be disregarded by excluding from consideration all interests but those of the young and immature.

Nevertheless the book was held obscene, the judgment appealed successively to the Appellate Court, the Appeals Court, and the United States Supreme Court, and all upheld the ruling of the lower court. In the Supreme Court the vote was a 4-4 tie. Clearly the line between honest writing and obscenity is not easy to draw, even by persons with considerably more than Mr. Cairns's suggested "modicum of literary knowledge."

Perhaps the most widely publicized censorship case in recent years is that of James Joyce's *Ulysses*. This book, published abroad, was held up in customs on the charge of obscenity, and the case was heard before Judge Woolsey in the United States District Court. Judge Woolsey first raised the question of author's intent and concluded that the book was not written "for the purpose of exploiting obscenity." "I do not detect anywhere," he wrote, "the leer of the sensualist." But a second question arises: in spite of the author's sincerity, in spite of the book's quality, is it likely to harm the reader? Or, in line with the somewhat lurid language of the statute, did the book tend "to stir the sex impulses or to lead to sexually impure and lustful thoughts"? In short, what would be its effect upon the average man—*l'homme moyen sensuel?*

To answer this question, Judge Woolsey depended not only upon his own reading but also upon the opinions of two friends. Their conclusion was that the book did not tend to excite sexual impulses but instead served as "a somewhat tragic and very powerful commentary on the inner lives of men and women." Judge Woolsey said in his decision: "I am quite aware that owing to some of its scenes *Ulysses* is a rather strong draught to ask some sensitive, though normal, persons to take. But my considered opinion, after long reflection, is that, whilst in many places the effect of *Ulysses* on the reader undoubtedly is somewhat emetic, nowhere does it tend to be an aphrodisiac."

Three elements in this case are worth noting. The first is the consideration of the author's intent; the second, the possible effect on the reader; and the third, the method used to arrive at a decision—that of inviting others to join in judging the book. In a sense this method is the same as dependence on a jury but with this difference: that here the friends of the judge were selected deliberately for their ability to make a mature judgment on a difficult work of literary craftsmanship.

Thus far we have seen how the objection to obscene literature revolves around a question of definition, a definition not contained in the statutes enacted against obscenity but, rather, left to the courts. First, we have seen that in some instances pornography is readily identified and is beyond the protection of the First Amendment. Second, we have seen that the "clear and present danger" test is difficult to apply when the issue is obscenity. Who can say where the danger lies in being exposed to dirty language or unconventional situations? If we were to apply this test to literature, we might as well give up any attempt to bar filth. If a book is not obviously pornographic and if the "clear and present danger" test cannot be invoked, how shall the line be drawn? Here the answer has been the standards of the community, or, as Chafee suggests, how much frankness the community will stand. This I frankly do not like; it seems to substitute one difficulty for another, without solving the basic problem. The "community" itself is difficult to define; is it a region, a city, or a neighborhood? Is it the majority of adults, and, if so, how do we know what they will accept? If we cannot depend on majorities, whose level shall be accepted as representing the community—that of a well-read minority or of a poorly read, superficial majority, or something in between? Under the circumstances, our best solution is probably the one Judge Woolsey hit upon: to rely upon the judgment of intelligent readers and to expect them to be as liberal as possible in making their decision. There is far less danger to the community, however defined, in permitting questionable literature to be published and read than there is in a strict definition of "obscenity" that would deny access to such literature. After all, what is the real objection? Are the censors afraid that we will be offended by books like *Studs Lonigan?* If there be any among us who would be offended, the solution is simple and readily at hand: we can close the book. Happily the freedom to read implies the freedom to desist from reading. But many of us will not desist, and that is what the censor truly fears: not that we will be offended but that we will be pleased.

Where does this leave the library? Shall the library provide books which some courts—notably in Massachusetts—have ruled obscene? Shall it consider as unacceptable books that have actually been cleared by the courts? And what about the large mass of books that never come to the courts at all? In fact, it is this group that may cause the library the most heart-searching and even embarrassment. The library cannot wait for a test case to be brought to trial, yet it must make its decision shortly after publication. My answer would be that in the first case, where the courts have ruled a book obscene, it all depends on *which* court. If it is a state or municipal court, we need take its ruling seriously *only* when our library is within the jurisdiction of the ordinance on which the court acts. There is no reason for a library in Ohio to remove *Strange Fruit* from its collection merely because a Massachusetts court considered it obscene. In the second case, where a book has been cleared by the courts, that is a point in its favor, although there may be other good and sufficient reasons why it may be rejected by the library. A book should have more to commend it than the mere absence of dirt before it is judged legitimate library bookstock.

As for the third case, where we cannot look to the courts for guidance, I believe we must depend on some such test as that which Judge Woolsey applied. Here the librarian himself must be the judge, and he should apply his best efforts toward determining whether the book in question, taken as a whole, is to be considered obscene. In making his decision he should give the benefit of the doubt to the book. Presumably, it is not "dirt for dirt's sake"; like most books, it is not likely to lead the reader to sexual excesses or immorality; it is not likely to give offense to the normal reader because of its language or frank descriptions. If the librarian, like Judge Woolsey, wishes to check his judgment against that of others, he may call on literate citizens at large, whose judgment he trusts, for an opinion. They too should be very slow to rule against a book, and in judging its possible effect on the library's readers they should certainly not take as the norm the adolescent or immature adult, nor should they give undue weight to the probability that the book will offend some people. Most important of all, they should never lose sight of the fact of which Chafee reminds us, "that stamping on a fire often spreads the sparks, that many past suppressions are now considered ridiculous, that the communication of ideas is just as important in this field as in any other, and that healthy human minds have a strong natural resistance to emotional poisons." Remember that Whitman's *Leaves of Grass* was at one time considered unfit to be read; remember, too, that books like *The Naked and the Dead* and *The Young Lions* would probably not have found a publisher twenty years ago but are today listed among the notable books of 1948.

Yet even with all these precautions some people will protest. They may be a church group, a superpatriotic society, or even one or two individuals. The protest may be lodged against books in the political or social realm or against a novel. It may take the form of mere objection, or it may become an ugly threat against the library or its librarian. Even more important, perhaps, is the fear of such objection, a fear that, oftener than we think, may lead a librarian or library board to rule out certain books to avoid an embarrassing situation which *may* develop—in short, to deprive the potential and interested reader rather than take a chance on someone's objection. Such objection is thought to create bad public relations, though we should remember that equally bad public relations may develop by failing to provide certain books.

Let us analyze this situation for a moment, taking the matter of a potential objection first. We might as well recognize that this is an ever present possibility; we can never escape the chance that someone may feel unhappy about a particular book. Yet I think that in an overwhelming number of cases, where a library has actually obtained the book, no protest developed at all. Fear of protest usually turns out to be a straw man. But suppose that a protest is lodged: should it be taken seriously enough to withdraw the book? We must consider the nature of the book and the nature of the protestant. If the book was seriously weighed in the light of its quality and of library policy and was acquired because it met the standards imposed by the library, I see no reason for its withdrawal. As for the protestant, does he represent a sufficiently numerous citizenry, or is he speaking solely for himself or for a special group? Even if the librarian were to decide on the basis of numbers, why should he assume that more people would object to the book than would welcome it or would at least be indifferent to its provision?

We hear a great deal these days about the need to protect minorities, particularly their right to free speech and assembly. But in protecting minority rights we must be careful to distinguish between the right to express and the right to dominate. Majorities also have their rights: no minority should abuse its privilege so as to shackle the majority. What "right" permits any minority—racial, national, or religious—tacitly to say to the rest of the community: "You shall not read this book"? In assuring minorities their right to self-expression, their right to object, let us not extend to them the privilege of dictating to the rest of us what we may or may not read. As the philosopher F. H. Bradley has written: "What is not tolerable is that stunted natures should set up their defects as a standard. It is an outrage, it is sheer blasphemy, when they bring the divine creations of literature and art to the touchstone of their own impotence, their own animalism, and their own immorality."

Censorship is an evil thing. In accepting it, in compromising, in "playing it safe," the librarian is false to the highest obligations of his profession. In resisting it, he retains his self-respect, he takes his stand with the great champions of free speech, and he reaffirms his fundamental faith in the dignity of man.

Another aspect of the librarian's relation to the question of censorship is Margaret Culkin Banning's condemnation of "restricted shelves" as presently administered in many libraries. Her constructive suggestions have influenced progressive librarians toward reform of the system. Mrs. Banning, prolific novelist and essayist, is a contributor to many of the large-circulation magazines.

Margaret Culkin Banning
THE RESTRICTED SHELF: CENSORSHIP'S LAST STAND

Sometimes it means a locked bookcase. Or it may be a row of books which stands in the backroom of a library, a row composed of volumes that are not admitted to the open shelves nor even listed in the usual catalogues. Sometimes it is only an informal place under the librarian's desk, where books which are never put into general circulation must wait until borrowers ask for them. Sometimes they wear out quickly and sometimes they gather dust. To borrow these books you must make a definite request, and though they would not be denied to any respectable adult, since permission is involved so is

censorship. The device of such restriction may be one thing or another, but the interesting fact is that the administrators of most public libraries still think it is wise, or at least expedient, to have a hideaway for some of the books which they buy.

The closed or restricted shelf is usually a short one and almost always contains a confused, heterogeneous group of books. Most of them will be books which pertain to sex. They may be manuals of sex instruction, or serious theses on abnormal sex, or modern novels which are unrestrained in dialogue or plot. Very occasionally there may be a political book. At one time one library did not put "Mein Kampf" on the open shelves because of the very great objection of Jewish taxpayers, and Catholic citizens have sometimes within my own knowledge objected to certain studies of the Jesuit priesthood, which were therefore put on the restricted shelves.

There are some books in such collections which seem so namby-pamby that it would seem that nobody could object to them. But there they are because someone has objected. If you take a look at the restricted shelf in almost any library it is bewildering and informing. There is no consistency discernible in the practice of restriction, says one librarian, nor is any very high degree of common sense evident in its application. The restricted shelf as a rule looks like what it is, a pie in which there have been too many fingers.

It shows, too, that the public may strain at a gnat while we know it swallows a camel. I have seen Dorothy Canfield's "Her Son's Wife" tucked away on a restricted shelf, and "God's Little Acre" (which was probably taken for a work on agriculture by the same censor-minded patron who objected to Miss Canfield's novel) loose in the same library. "Europa" may be on the restricted shelves and Ernest Hemingway's "To Have and Have Not" on the open shelves. "The Decameron" or Havelock Ellis's books on sex may rub covers with James Gray's "Shoulder the Sky." "Raffles" was once taboo in our own library because the objection had been made that it glorified the criminal. This was a long time ago, but once on the restricted shelf you serve a long term, and it is only recently that "Raffles" was released for general circulation. Bromfield's "A Good Woman" was held out of circulation because it ridiculed the church "sister." Down

---

Margaret Culkin Banning, "The Restricted Shelf: Censorship's Last Stand," *Saturday Review*, 19:3-4+ (October 29, 1938), copyright 1938 by the Saturday Review Associates, Inc. Reprinted by permission of the author and of the publisher.

through the years there has been objection to "The Green Hat," "Strange Interlude," "Ann Vickers," and, lately, to "Imperial City." There is no telling where censorship will strike. It is a twister.

But nine times out of ten it hits a book which presents, in fiction or otherwise, some phase of sex conduct. If the restricted shelf included all the books in a library, to say nothing of the pieces in magazines, which deal with sex in a manner which would have been objectionable twenty years ago, it would certainly have to enlarge its quarters. Every librarian knows this. Every trustee who reads many of the books in his own library knows it. But, in spite of what seems to be a very palpable absurdity in inclusion and exclusion, the restricted shelf survives.

We hear less and less of censorship of publications. The number of prigs and bigots and self-appointed guardians of public morals seems to have pleasantly diminished. The publicity value of censorship has also been so completely demonstrated that there is considerable hesitation among sensible people about helping out the sale of a book whose content may be deplorable by attracting a perverse attention or curiosity to it. If you want to spend your money on morbid books or erotica, probably no one will prevent you today.

This is not mere public callousness. There has been a steady progress on the part of readers, writers, publishers, and distributors toward toleration of frankness in print, as well as a growing willingness to study the abnormal in character and situation. This seems by actual test to be progress and not degeneration. For though delicacy has suffered, salaciousness has had the worst of it. Sex absorption has apparently passed its peak in current fiction at least. Most of its manifestations, pathological, neurotic, phallic, bawdy, sadistic, and the rest are now so familiar that their shock power has diminished with a great body of readers. We may be less modest of mind than we used to be, but we are less easily provoked or tempted by whispers of evil, if we are reasonably well-read.

But censorship of publication is one thing and the existence of a restricted shelf is another. If you are interested in libraries, and particularly in public libraries, you know that the question of this second sort of censorship is never dead, though it may sleep for months while purchases and borrowing of books go on in uninterrupted stream.

Then some citizen comes into the library with a copy of "Eyeless in Gaza" in his hands, which he borrowed yesterday. He is both irate and horrified at having the abortion description and discussion in it on the shelves where anyone can read about it. He is stirred up and threatens to make trouble for the library. That book, he says, it not one that "kids" should read. The taxpayers' money should not be spent for books like that. Such an angry complaint cannot be disregarded. The person who talks like that can make librarians and trustees tremble in their boots, not because of his literary judgment but because he may do damage to the library.

I have a personal nightmare about this. It is a nightmare in which I am arguing for a book budget before the city council of my own city, or your city, or any city, and especially making a plea for the book fund. And, as I work up to a climax, some taxpayer objects and begins to read passages from some of the books on the shelves in the library, saying public money should not be spent on books like that. He might read, for example, the night scene in bed between Morgan and his wife in "To Have and Have Not," or he might read the chapter of "Imperial City" when the society girl turns prostitute for pin-money.

This has never happened to me and it is a predicament which I hope will never happen, but it is one reason—and so most librarians would agree—for a restricted shelf. The matter cannot be dismissed by poking fun at the aldermen and saying that they are a narrow-minded lot. How are you going to make your alderman, who is a good citizen and a family man, believe that it is right to pay out the taxpayers' money for scenes of fornication and prostitution? He simply wouldn't follow your argument. I doubt if he should.

None the less, it is not right for a modern library not to have a complete collection of Mr. Hemingway's works. They are modern literature. So is Mr. Rice's "Imperial City." Any public library which has taste and pride wants to house good contemporary literature, strong human stuff though it may be. Fiction collections in a library, far more than in the drug-store or rental library of a department store, should be "representative of the spirit of the age and of the most stimulating and significant tendencies and development of literary art." I am quoting Miss Helen Haines of Pasadena, who lectures at library schools and says it better than I could.

The problem is to do this so that the public money is spent for a collection that will be interesting in the immediate present and valuable in the future, and at the same time not to affront the man who is paying the taxes and footing the bills. Library budgets do not come out of income taxes. They come from real estate taxes, and those press much too heavily on many poor people to increase them more than is necessary. But the public library is supported because it is educational. The taxpayers may sometimes growl at its cost, but they regard it as a good influence and one which will not betray their ideals of a good community life. They believe in sexual privacy, in closing up disorderly houses so young people will not be attracted by any false glamor, in monogamy, in decent living. To find books which do not uphold their ideals on their library shelves, paid for out of taxes, seems to them quite wrong.

Why, a man asked me once, should even a mill of the public money be spent for books which either defend or present as attractive acts and practices which are prohibited by the city ordinances, which set down in print the matters which decent people will not even discuss with one another? We pay policemen to stop people from doing the very things that are described in some books as being romantic or justified, and we pay them out of the very same tax dollar with which we buy the books. Isn't it a paradox to encourage reading about the very kind of things that the law is trying to stamp out?

There is a point there, but it carries with it an assumption which experience denies. It is that reading carries over swiftly into conduct, and that we do or are tempted to do many of the things of which we read. Normally that is not true. One may read, wrote Claude Washburn, the conversation between Jurgen and the Hamadryad, without having any desire to go downstairs and assault the cook. A wish for romance, for travel, even for lust may come into the mind which is affected by a book. But it is usually only in stories that the influence of a story actually directs conduct. Against the few times when this happens to the extent of misfortune, we must balance the great benefit of the extension of human knowledge, even a knowledge of bad habits. For wide reading makes less ingenuous, less bigoted, ultimately more tolerant and kind people. That is the proper result of reading on conduct. Also we must remember that all those who obey city ordinances willingly do not share a point of view on what is obscene. Lawrence said that well. "What is pornography to one man is the laughter of genius to another."

This argues the case a little but does not dispose of the problem. The book disputed by the taxpayer would probably go on a restricted shelf where it may be a gesture, or simply an "out" for librarian and trustee. Books of equal power of suggestion would undoubtedly remain on open shelves, unnoticed, creating no quarrel. If the restricted shelf is to be more than a hideout for books that are scapegoats, we must consider it further.

The reasons for its continued existence are usually two, when they come up for discussion, as was true recently at a meeting of trustees in my own state. The first was the reason of caution, having a refuge for books that belonged in the collection and that someone might find objectionable. The second was the important one, also voiced by many taxpayers, that some books should not be read by those who were not prepared for such reading by experience, education, or a proper age. This was the reason of conscience, dictated only by the fear of harming young and sensitive minds, and of preventing normal growth, a very real fear with most parents.

There happened to be inherited books on sexual inversion and erotic symbolism and cognate subjects on my bookshelves while my children were growing up and while their friends were going in and out of the study. The books had a good deal of wear but I didn't hide them. The better thing to do seemed to me to give the children under my care a sufficiently broad reading so that the knowledge which came from those books—or from such stories as "Sanctuary" later on—would be in proper proportion. One can always make other reading a prerequisite for books which might throw the thoughts out of balance, if a given situation can be given enough attention.

This, it seems to me, is the place at which the restricted shelf could really function instead of merely hide. Here is the chance of censorship not to close the gates of reading but to open them, instead of making people peer through the cracks in the fence and get a limited view. The restricted shelf should be a definite part of book selection.

Reading may not carry over into conduct, but it often does carry over into fixations, into prejudices, and into definite limitations of knowledge. From a story of sex adventure like "Serenade" a young reader may, unless he extends his knowledge, get the idea that most young people are impious, that they drink all the time, that they are never shy of approach. From "Imperial City," which is undoubtedly a true picture of part of New York, the provincial reader gets no idea of the thousands of New York people who go home on trains to the simplest of suburban lives every night. From "Appointment in Samarra" the New Yorker, on the other hand, gets no proper notion of the Middle West Country Club. He ought to begin his knowledge of Middle West life by reading "What People Said," or "The Great American Novel."

All educators know that if the mind is not to be jumbled, it must take its knowledge in a certain order. Anyone familiar with college catalogues knows that in the great universities the closest attention is given to the prerequisites for each course. You cannot understand higher mathematics without a preliminary course. You cannot take an advanced course in history without a number of precedent studies. This principle should extend to fiction, to stories of sex, descriptions of intricate human passion. Some people, because of youth and inexperience, or because of lack of education, may not be ready for them.

"It is not literature that confuses but the fact that the easily confused are able to read," writes Jonathan Daniels, and a statement was never made that was more applicable to the problems of a public library and the actual opportunity of a restricted shelf. If the restricted shelf cannot be abandoned, and fear of aldermen will take care of that for a while, the shelf should be made useful. It should not be a patchwork of prejudices but a shelf containing books for which some prerequisite of reading is necessary. This is done for people who are lucky enough to have care given to their private education. It should be done for those dependent on public education in so far as it is possible.

Any librarian knows what this means. It means having a restricted shelf that isn't an untidy mess. It means training readers' guides among the librarians. It means many branches of libraries, so that the librarians may know the patrons. It means advancing toward the end to which good libraries work, making librarians not custodians but public educators.

And if censorship would properly defend this last stand, it might have a chance to lose its harsh name and blend with education. We might take the bad name from the dog and not have to hang him.

An eloquent spokesman for liberalism and democracy is the author of this strong affirmation of the librarians' obligation "to despise objectivity when objectivity means neutrality and neutrality when neutrality interferes with the performance of their duties as librarians." Archibald MacLeish, former Librarian of Congress, Pulitzer Prize Winner in poetry, is now Boylston Professor of Rhetoric and Oratory, Harvard University. His address, "A Tower Which Will Not Yield," was given at the dedication of the Carleton College Library, September 22, 1956.

Archibald MacLeish
A TOWER WHICH WILL NOT YIELD

There may be, indeed there are certain to be, men and women in this audience who will consider the ceremony performed here today nothing but ceremony: the kind of academic occasion which academic people are always thinking up to justify the dragooning of yet another audience to sit uncomfortably through yet another hour to listen respectfully (more or less) to yet another academic speaker making yet another academic speech. Why dedicate a library—even a library as impressive as this— even a library built to serve the needs of a college as notable in its past as Carleton and as hopeful in its future? Libraries are undoubtedly respectable institutions and necessary parts of colleges and universities. Their construction

---

Archibald MacLeish, "A Tower Which Will Not Yield," *ALA Bulletin*, 50:649–54 (November, 1956). Reprinted courtesy Carleton College.

should be an occasion for congratulation all around. But why make more of it than that? Why *dedicate* a building full of books?

But the students of this college, having heard their distinguished president on the subject, will have little difficulty with the answer to that question. One dedicates a new library in the United States today because the building of a new library in the United States today is itself an act of dedication. It commits a man or an institution or a community to one side rather than the other side of the profound spiritual struggle in which our generation is engaged—the spiritual civil war, if I may call it that, which quietly but bitterly divides the country.

The reason will be obvious to anyone who considers what a library actually is—or, rather, what the word has come to mean on our continent over the past half century or so. We can no longer use it to designate those towering rooms, lined from floor to ceiling with yellow leather, which our houses used to contain because our houses no longer contain them, and no one would think of using it to describe the four foot shelf behind the television screen where six best sellers, still in their dust jackets, lean against a pair of roller skates. A library to us is something more and something different. It is many books, but it is also many *kinds* of books: as many books of as many kinds as can be gathered. Where the private library of the eighteenth and nineteenth centuries was a *se*lection, the library as we think of it, the academic or public library of the twentieth century, is a *col*lection. Where once the criterion of choice was one man's preference of the books which interested him or with which he felt comfortable, today the criterion of choice is a disinterested completeness within the limits of a practicable relevance. Where once a library admitted only those books of which its owner approved, excluding all those whose language offended him or whose doctrines contradicted his own, today a library—what we call a library—includes every book which falls within the limits of the library's concern, and the library's means, whether it pleases the librarian or not and whether or not its conclusions agree with his.

A library's subject field may be limited: some of the finest libraries in the United States today are what librarians call special libraries. But to no aggregation of books, no matter what its scope, do we wholeheartedly accord that proud title, which determines its content by other criteria than those of substance and relevance. The honor of the modern American librarian is the completeness as well as the worth of his collection. He would no more suppress a relevant and substantial book because it was offensive to himself personally or to his employer or to those who attempt to influence his employer than a college scientist would suppress a part of the evidence of his laboratory because it disappointed his preconceptions or disturbed the board of overseers or outraged the convictions of the loudest alumni. A modern American librarian regards himself as a trustee of the printed record of his civilization, or of so much of it as his means and his mission permit him to collect, and he would regard any exclusion from his collection of a relevant book or class of books as a falsification of the record and a breach of trust.

The consequence is that any American library —any institution we would call a library—any institution called a library whose opening decent men would solemnize—will inevitably contain books with whose arguments and conclusions many Americans, even, conceivably, all Americans, will violently disagree, as well as books whose language and whose observations of human conduct millions of us will find offensive. There will be books on political theory, all kinds of political theory including the political theory of Karl Marx. There will be books on religion, all kinds of religion including the religion of cannibals and of Protestants like myself. There will be books on art, all kinds of art including the art which produces apoplexy among Senators. There will be books in which the observation of life includes the observation of love, and books in which the observation of love keeps the eyelid open long after most of us would modestly have let it fall. There will be all sorts and kinds of books having nothing whatever in common with each other but the fact that it is these books— these and the others that could be added to them if means permitted—which contain among themselves the vast and various record of human perception, human speculation, human questioning, human doubt, human wonder, human creativeness which constitutes the memory and the fact of our human civilization.

To open a library, a modern American library, to its public of students or citizens is therefore to open a kind of Pandora's box, a box of variety. Hope is here, beauty is here, wisdom is here, but there are other stinging buzzing things beside. There are doubts which may not have been felt before. There are questions which may never before have been asked. There are old errors long since recognized as such and new errors which might conceivably be truths. There are windows into corridors of the soul which have not yet been entered and glimpses into miraculous labyrinths of the body which have not been guessed at. There are shadows and shinings of emotions never sensed or seen. And all these whirling, humming things, moreover, even the best of them, even beauty, even wisdom, may be dangerous. Men have been driven mad by too much truth. Men have been debauched by beauty. And as for the power of error, no one doubts that it exists and that mankind is wonderfully vulnerable to it. Have we not the spectacle in our own day of half the world persuaded by error to accept the slavery of the self?

So that the opening of a library is, in the most literal sense of the term, an invitation to danger. But it is also something more than that, and it is the something more I wish to speak of. Carleton College does not merely invite its students to risk themselves in this new building. It assures them at the same time—and it assures the world as well—that it believes the risks thus taken is the road to life. It affirms by this stone and steel and glass that it is a good and desirable thing for men and women, young as well as old, to have access to books of all kinds and of all opinions and to come to their own conclusions; that it is a good and desirable thing for men and women, young as well as old, to examine heretical arguments as well as orthodox arguments and to decide for themselves which is right and which is wrong; that it is a good and desirable thing for men and women, young as well as old, to learn how life has looked to all kinds and conditions of observers of life, the despairing as well as the hopeful, the sensuous as well as the ascetic, and to determine for themselves which aspect of life is truth and which aspect of life is misconception: which is abhorrent and which is beautiful.

And it is precisely in this affirmation that the dedication we are seeking here consists. For to affirm what the structure of this library affirms is to commit oneself to one of the deepest and most courageous of all human beliefs. It is to commit oneself to a belief in the intelligence and the power to discriminate of the human mind. If you assert that all the opinions, all the perceptions, all the visions, all the arguments, all the images, are to be made available, insofar as you can gather them, to any mind which wishes to search them out, you are asserting at the same time that you believe the mind which searches them out is capable of judging among them and arriving at sensible conclusions. You are putting your trust, that is to say, not in indoctrination and dogma—not in the conclusions of other and earlier men which have now achieved the authority of accepted doctrine—but in the mind itself which is the instrument of all conclusions, and in the act of mind, which is also an act of spirit, by which the image of the world, generation after generation, is recreated.

Stated in the usual commonplaces of philosophic discourse such a dedication may seem neither particularly daring nor particularly new. Belief in the freedom of the mind—for this, I suppose, is what the philosophers would call it—is something of a platitude in Western dialectic. Theoretically we all of us believe in the freedom of the mind, if for no other reason than that the Communists don't believe in it. Theoretically, also, we are all of us aware that our Republic was founded upon a belief in the freedom of the mind and that the fundamental law which holds our Republic together guarantees that freedom. All this, however, is theory only. There is also fact. And fact tells a very different story. The fact is that the official philosophic agreement of all Americans on the principle of freedom of the mind covers a profound and bitter disagreement which, since the Second War, has divided us far more deeply than most of us are willing to admit. There are few Americans as yet who are willing openly to attack the Constitution and the tradition of individual liberty which it incorporates. But there have been increasing numbers of our fellow citizens who have questioned in recent years the specific Constitutional guarantees of individual freedom established in the Bill of Rights. And a surprising proportion of our people are today engaged in activities, such as the attempted suppression of books and opinions by boycott and by economic pressures of various kinds, which openly violate the spirit if not the letter of the Constitutions of the Federal Government and the several States.

In this situation the affirmation of belief in the freedom of the inquiring mind which the opening of a new library implies is anything but an affirmation of the obvious. On the contrary it is an affirmation which some Americans would regard, if they spelled its implications out, as an impudent affront. Here is a city, here is a college, which says to its citizens or its students: you may read what you please even if what you choose to read is *Das Kapital* or Ernest Hemingway or D. H. Lawrence or the *Ulysses* of Joyce. You may know whatever you choose to know; even the facts of Soviet life; even the reveries of Molly Bloom. You may read and you may know because you have a right as a free man to read and know—because your intelligence depends on your reading and knowing—because the safety of the Republic depends on your intelligence. This, to the boycotter and suppresser, is dangerous and subversive talk. He does not believe in intelligence; what he believes in is the Truth and the Truth he knows already. As for the Republic, if the Republic needs to be saved the Marines will save it or the FBI or a Congressional Committee. There is no need for the citizens, young or old, to read opinions other than the accepted opinions, or to imagine life in terms other than the accepted terms, and the institution which invites them to do either is un-American.

One wonders, incidentally, what these people think, if they ever do think, of the seal and symbol of the country for which they claim to speak. The eagle is a bird chiefly notable for the catholicity of its vision. It hangs at a great height in clear air where a whole valley, a whole mountain, is spread out beneath it, and nothing stirs in all that country-side which it does not see. Its passion is to see. Its life is to see. That other, clumsy, grounded bird which deals with every new experience of the world by covering its eyes with sand and exposing its nude enormous anatomy to the weapons and the wind was never considered worthy of a place on the great seal of the United States until our time. Today it has become the symbol of the selectors of text books in a number of American states and the emblem of most veterans' committees. But the eagle is still aloft there in the federal air. Will it stay, one wonders, when it sees these other clumsy frightened creatures burrowing with their beaks and chins to hide the actualities of the earth?

But this, as I say, is an incidental matter. What concerns us here—and we may thank God for it—is not the folly of the frightened but the meaning of the act of faith. The frightened are important to us only because they make the act of faith come clear. And how clear they make it come! One has only to consider what is really in issue between the offerers of books and the withholders of books to see what the offering of books, the making available of books, means to this Republic and to the free civilization in which this Republic exists. To withhold books, to suppress books, to censor books, to deny the people of a town or of a state or of the country the right to read books as they choose to read them, is to question the basic assumption of all self-government which is the assumption that the people are capable of governing themselves: that the people, that is to say, are capable of examining the evidence for themselves and making up their own minds and coming to their own conclusions. The unstated pretension of all those who undertake to withhold books is the pretension that someone else knows better than the people: that the Chicago Archdiocesan Council of Catholic Women with its monthly blacklist of books knows better than the people; that the police chiefs of various towns and cities with their extra-legal threats to booksellers and libraries know better than the people; that the Attorney General of Massachusetts, should a bill pass directing him to establish a code "regulating and defining the permissive content of books, pamphlets etc." would know better than the people. It is the nerve-center, the heart, of democracy which is struck at by these practices and measures, for the heart of democracy is the right of a people to make up their minds for themselves. And, by the same sign, it is democracy itself, at its heart, at its center, which is strengthened whenever a free choice of books is made available to the people—whenever the people are told in their towns, in their colleges: Here are the books! Read them as you please! Make up your own minds! Determine your own destiny! Be free!

It is for this reason that the opening of a new library is no longer the merely architectural event which it would have been in the days when Andrew Carnegie was dotting the American landscapes with those placid domes of his. What were once peaceful establishments secluding themselves behind their marble animals and their metal mottoes and the enormous names of those happy authors whom they chose for more or less eternal remembrance, have become strong points and pill boxes along the extended and dangerous frontier where the future of free institutions is being fought out, day after day, in minor skirmishes rarely noticed in the public press and tactfully deprecated, when they are recorded at all, in the various professional publications. It would be difficult, I think, to overestimate the debt owed by the party of freedom in the United States today to the unknown and unsung librarians who, with little backing from their fellow citizens, and with less economic security than would encourage most of the rest of us to be brave, have held an exposed and vulnerable front through ten of the most dangerous years in the history of American liberty.

The changed situation is reflected in nothing more dramatically than in the changed status of the men and women who work in libraries. Fifty years ago no one would have questioned the assertion that the fundamental qualification of the librarian is objectivity: fifty years ago most librarians were objective—and looked it. But when, in February of this year, Mr. Quincy Mumford, the Librarian of Congress, laid down objectivity as the prime requirement of a Library employee, there was an immediate and sharp reaction which, because of the circumstances surrounding the statement, had repercussions in the press. Dr. Albert Sprague Coolidge, son of the Library's greatest private benefactor, Mrs. Elizabeth Sprague Coolidge, had been invited by the Library to serve on the advisory committee for the Coolidge Foundation but had subsequently been passed over. In explaining the reasons for this curious sequence of events, the official *Information Bulletin* of the Library of Congress stated in its issue of February 6 that "The Librarian felt that Dr. Coolidge's past associations and activities, entirely aside from the 'loyalty' or 'security' issue, would impair that objectivity in the fulfillment of his duties that one has a right to expect of a public employee, even in an advisory capacity on cultural matters."

Made by a less distinguished librarian than Mr. Mumford and in a case of less importance than that of Dr. Coolidge, this would not perhaps have been regarded by anyone as a particularly remarkable statement. Made in the circumstances in which it was made and by the man who made it, it was felt to be remarkable indeed. And obviously it was, for what it clearly implied was that a man is not suitable for work in a library who has taken sides on controversial issues. There was, as Mr. Mumford went out of his way to state, and as those who have been associated with Dr. Coolidge well knew, no question whatever of disloyalty. Dr. Coolidge had been an effective and outspoken anti-Communist and anti-authoritarian all his life and Mr. Mumford was fully aware of that fact: "Dr. Coolidge," the *Bulletin* says, "has not been labelled a security risk by the Library of Congress either in private or in public." What was wrong was merely that Dr. Coolidge had joined organizations and taken positions which lined him up to be counted on one side—what men who love freedom would generally regard as the right side —of controversial public issues.

Now I have the greatest respect for Mr. Mumford. He came to the Library of Congress originally on my invitation: to head the new Processing Department following the reorganization of the Library in 1940 and 1941. I know at first hand his devotion, his intelligence and his professional skill. I have not the slightest doubt that he acted reluctantly in the Coolidge matter and that the step he took was the step he believed right. Nevertheless I cannot help wondering whether he fully considered the implications of his reasoning and above all whether he related it to the actual, present situation of the profession he leads. That his ruling would automatically exclude at least one former Librarian of Congress from the Library's service in the future is doubtless irrelevant and in any event immaterial since that Librarian is very fully and happily employed elsewhere. But it is not irrelevant and it is not immaterial that the statement as it stands would exclude a great many others including many of the most respected librarians in the country. No librarian who believes in the freedom guaranteed by the Constitution, and who detests authoritarianism, can avoid taking positions on controversial issues—indeed on the most controversial of all issues: for the issue of the freedom of the mind in America today is precisely that. He must believe in that freedom or he cannot be an honest librarian, and, if he believes in it, and acts on his belief, he can hardly hope to avoid contention. He may avoid such associations as Dr. Coolidge seems to have engaged in but he cannot avoid decision. And whenever he decides that a book which somebody wants suppressed shall not be suppressed, whenever he decides that a magazine which somebody wants discontinued shall not be discontinued, he will have ceased to be "objective." He will have taken sides. He will have become a controversial figure, and as such will no longer be a desirable employee under the Librarian's rule.

I am completely certain that Mr. Mumford intended no such consequence. He knows, as any man must know who has that great institution in his charge, that the Library of Congress is the custodian of something more than a large number of books and pamphlets, maps and manuscripts. It is the custodian also of the cultural conscience of the federal government, and its actions, though they may be little noticed at the time, have enduring consequences. Had Herbert Putnam and his predecessors not accomplished the still inexplicable miracle of turning a modest legislative library into the national library of the United States, Washington would be a very different city and the federal government a very different government. Had Elizabeth Sprague Coolidge never given the Library of Congress its Coolidge Auditorium and made possible the magnificent concerts of music, new as well as old, which the Auditorium provides—had the Archives of American Folksong never been established in the Library's Music Division—the history of American music would have been a very different history. It is quite inconceivable that such an institution should now revert to a doctrine of library management, and therefore of library function, which seeks to neutralize belief and courage. The gelded librarian is a sacrifice which only McCarthyism demands and McCarthyism in decay need not now be handed its dearest victim.

Rather, the whole energy of the profession should be directed in the opposite sense. Librarians should be encouraged to despise objectivity when objectivity means neutrality and neutrality when neutrality interferes with the performance of their duties as librarians. They should be encouraged to believe positively and combatively in those principles of a free society in which they must believe to keep their libraries whole and sane. They should be brought to see that you cannot keep an even hand, a neutral hand, between right and wrong in the running of a library in a country and a time like ours. There are certain issues as to which objectivity, if objectivity means unwillingness to take a positive position, to stand up and be counted, is impossible to a decent man in a critical period, and the issue of human freedom is one of them. You cannot be neutral on that issue anywhere in the world we live in and least of all can you be neutral on it in a library. You are for it or you are against it and if you are silent you are against. The test of a man's fitness for service in a library in the United States today is not, therefore, his lack of opinions or his failure to declare them. It is the *kind* of opinions he holds and the courage with which he makes them known. If you believe in the use of books to indoctrinate—which is to say, in the suppression of certain books in order to leave available only the views expressed in certain others—you have no place in an American library however well fitted you may be for service in a library in Czechoslovakia or Spain. If you believe in free and equal access to all substantial books regardless of their views, and if you are willing to assert your belief in words and to defend it in action, the profession, if you are otherwise qualified, should welcome you.

And it is my conviction that it will. I do not believe that American libraries will adopt the rule laid down, or seemingly laid down, in the Coolidge case. The word, "objectivity," is, of course, a tempting word. It seems to offer a respectable way of disposing of a troublesome problem without quite facing it. "Objectivity" is one of the *good* words of our contemporary vocabulary. Scientists are objective about their findings. Judges are objective in their opinions. Great newspapers are distinguished from newspapers which call themselves great by the objectivity of their presentation of the news. When we are referred to as objective we are pleased and when we refer to others in the same terms we mean to compliment them. The word raises a standard to which our scientifically minded generation can repair as the men of the Nineties repaired to "passion" and the men of the Eighteenth Century to "sensibility." But like all *good* words "objectivity" has another side and American librarians know it. It connotes a quality—a suppression of personal commitment and personal feeling—which is admirable in a journalist reporting the news or a scientist observing an experiment or a judge judging a case, but which is anything but admirable when there is a cause to defend or a battle to be fought. A general who was objective about the outcome of a campaign might be a great military technician but he would be a soldier of limited usefulness. And a librarian who was objective about the survival of the tradition of free inquiry on which western civilization is founded might be an admirable administrator but his services to the human spirit in a place and time like ours would be negligible or worse.

The great American libraries have given courageous proof over the past few years that this kind of objectivity does not tempt them. And the Library of Congress itself, I feel certain, has no real intention of deserting the principle. Indeed, I have good reasons for believing that the Library of Congress regards itself as still standing firm in the faith despite the unfortunate language of its statement of policy in the Coolidge case. The Library of Congress, I am reliably informed, used the word "objectivity" in that ruling as a synonym for "good judgment" (a tribute to the influence of the scientists in our society) meaning no more than that a man who would join the organizations Sprague Coolidge had joined could not be counted on to exercise discrimination in advising the Library on the music to be played at Sprague Coolidge's mother's concerts and similar matters. If this is so the position should perhaps be clarified. Good judgment is a desirable characteristic in a library employee as in any one else—though it may well be doubted whether the soundness of a man's aesthetic sense can be determined by the orthodoxy of his political affiliations: if it could, few of the great artists and writers and musicians who have provided the contents of our libraries and museums would be employable in their management. But sound judgment as a euphuism for an unwillingness to take sides on fundamental moral and intellectual issues is not desirable anywhere in a free society and least of all in the libraries which house its memory and its conscience.

One cannot be objective in that sense and be the champion of a cause, and every American librarian worthy of the name is today the champion of a cause. It is, to my mind, the noblest of all causes for it is the cause of man, or more precisely the cause of the inquiring mind by which man has come to be. But noblest or not, it is nevertheless a cause—a struggle—not yet won: a struggle which can never perhaps be won for good and all. There are always in any society, even a society founded in the love of freedom, men and women who do not wish to be free themselves and who fear the practice of freedom by others—men and women who long for the comfort of a spiritual and intellectual authority in their own lives and who would feel more comfortable still if they could also impose such an authority on the lives of their neighbors. As long as such people exist—and they show no sign of disappearing from the earth, even the American earth—the fight to subvert freedom will continue. And as long as the fight to subvert freedom continues, libraries must be strong points of defense.

It is not as a strong point that we regard this peaceful building on the day of its dedication. But it is one notwithstanding, and will continue to be one for a long, long time to come. Young men and women will find defenses for the freedom of the mind in this place by finding here what freedom of the mind can mean. And a whole countryside will know that one more tower has been raised against ignorance and bigotry and fear: a tower which will not yield. That dedication is in the stones themselves. We do no more than name it.

The point of view of an enlightened public official is presented by John Anson Ford, a member of the Los Angeles County Board of Supervisors since 1934. Herein, Mr. Ford expresses deep faith in the ability of the average American, provided with uncensored sources of information, to arrive at the truth on controversial questions.

John Anson Ford
WE WILL GAMBLE ON THE AMERICAN

Perhaps it would be a healthy thing if every American generation were confronted with the

John Anson Ford, "We Will Gamble on the American," *Library Journal,* 74:917–19 (June 15, 1949), copyright 1949 by R. R. Bowker Co. Reprinted by permission of the author and of the publisher.

proposal to banish "undesirable" books from all public library shelves. It sets a lot of folks to thinking—should I say, for the first time? Such a proposal—or demand—at once creates a new and acute awareness of things which most people have been taking for granted.

"Who selects the books for our libraries, anyway?" asks the newly aroused Pilgrim who has been enjoying a sojourn in the Land of the Free, lo, these many years. "I have read a lot of things about communism and I know it's bad," says the Pilgrim. "Yes, everybody, or practically everybody, knows it's bad. I have rejected it. 'Most everybody else with a sense of loyalty has rejected it. So what are we waiting for? Isn't it perfectly logical to reject—or eject—communism from our public libraries?"

But this line of reasoning leads to a dilemma. The average person can't qualify to select books for a public library. So the alternative is considered of setting up the right kind of a committee to check on the library's books. Committees often are good, and library boards certainly can be good, usually are. But likewise they can be a headache for him or her on whom falls the technical task of book selecting. But that's another story. Proper book selecting, like book-writing, is a highly specialized job, carrying a lot of responsibility. Like marriage or surgery, it's not undertaken lightly.

THE FARTHER ONE FOLLOWS . . . .

The sincere critic of communistic literature can bewail the presence of material which he and all his friends recognize as advocating the wrong principles, as advocating many evil things "which we all know must be condemned." But that person may not think the censorship problem through to its conclusion. The path of apparent patriotism which he has begun to tread so firmly in the interest of truth as he sees it and truth in general, quickly leads over the Hill of Distinction (if I may continue a Bunyan-esque phraseology) and into a Slough—if not of Despond, at least of Confusion. For that is right where censorship leads.

The farther one follows this path of censorship the more terrible are the obstacles and dangers met with. If one steps into this slough to ban communism, then what about other un-American political philosophies, including "Mein Kampf"? And traveling a little farther on (the while getting somewhat more into a mire), one has to make up his mind about religion and then about sex. By this time he is far from firm ground and knoweth not how to escape.

Of course, all this Bunyan-esque talk of mine is in one sense begging the question. Our librarians do not intend to censor our public library shelves, but they certainly must accept some books and reject others. Obviously he would be no librarian who would buy books as they came to him until his book fund was exhausted. What then is the difference, from a layman's point of view, between book selecting and book censoring?

INTEGRITY AND OPEN MINDEDNESS

I think these factors help determine the right attitude toward books good and bad, toward controversial literature, if you please: (1) a realization that perfect and complete truth has never yet been attained, hence, we should be slow to condemn new ideas. (2) that different minds will see different facets of truth. (3) that proven principles can afford to be challenged. (4) that history proves: what is gospel truth for one generation may be heresy for another generation. (5) that civilization is a process of growth, not a state of "perfect" coma, and growth means change. (6) that the best proof of the validity of our beliefs is its ability to withstand the attack of unbelievers.

I am not one who would propose that for every book advocating democracy we should have an opposing book advocating communism. Let me illustrate from a field in which I am somewhat familiar—news reporting. A skilled and conscientious editor does not fail to select his news material with due recognition of the tastes and standards of his readers. And while giving space to "both sides" he does not attempt a perfect for-and-against balance of all questions. He believes he knows what is right in some controversial fields and does not hesitate to give emphasis to his convictions.

While the parallel is not complete, the able librarian gives substantial recognition to the accepted and prevailing standards of his time. With that principle supplying the core or heart of his book selecting, in controversial fields he then sets about with integrity and open mindedness to select literature truly representative of the opposite or heretical views. This he does for the sake of the inquiring minds which so often are the most promising and most valuable minds in a community. By such as they, thought progresses and humanity marches forward. Thus each oncoming generation is given a chance anew to re-shift the old and match it against the new, rejecting some and retaining some.

Perhaps in 10 years—certainly in any 25 years in the Twentieth Century—what I call "the prevailing standards of one's public" will change. That will be reflected in the books on the shelves of the expert and conscientious librarian. Indeed, what was political or religious heresy may some day become orthodox, and vice versa. It has happened that way in the past. Witness Walter Wanger's vast and colorful presentation of *Joan of Arc*.

GIVEN ALL SIDES

All of this generalization might leave one very much up in the air if one did not add the conviction that some things abide—in books and in thought as well as in the realm of physical nature. Within the span of our knowledge and imagination we cannot conceive, for example, of the principle of the supreme value of the human individual being supplanted. The degree to which he should submerge himself for the good of the State may be a proper subject for controversy—but we as citizens and librarians still use as a working base of our philosophy the supremacy of the individual in the scale of values.

That is why we want to make knowledge available to the individual. That is why we want each library reader to learn to stand firmly on his own "intellectual feet"—not because we "told him so," but because in his own way and by his own sincere, even if imperfect, mental processes he has come to his own conclusions.

A. Gilmore Flues, president of the Friends of Toledo, Ohio, Public Library, has expressed the whole idea so well: "I believe absolutely that public libraries do *not* have an obligation to censor material on their shelves, other than to guard against the merely salacious and immoral. But the issue here is not such material and its restriction. The issue here is whether or not a public library is to remain a repository for the free expressions of free men, where others, equally free, may come to study a question from all possible sides, to evaluate them, and to seek the truth out of such study. Freedom in the public library is the corollary of freedom of speech by the First Amendment to our Constitution. . . . We will still gamble on the average American—that given access to all sides of a question, and being allowed to pursue without hindrance the answer to that question, he will come reasonably close to the conception that his forefathers had of him. We have traveled far and to glory on the freedom train: who would be base enough to desert or derail it?"

In this address, originally delivered at the opening of the New Haven, Connecticut, State Teachers College Library, February 21, 1954, David H. Clift, Executive Director of the American Library Association, takes a long view of censorship problems in relation to libraries. Without adequate support, Mr. Clift emphasizes, libraries will hardly be in a position to promote freedom of inquiry and other "enduring rights."

David H. Clift
ENDURING RIGHTS

When one considers the times—and the occasion that brings together this assemblage of persons—it would be hard to conceive a more appropriate and timely subject than the one around which this new library has planned its opening—"Man's Right to Knowledge and the Free Use Thereof." For these two great rights are enduring rights, embracing as they do both the political and the social.

These are rights that existed before the advent of libraries as we know them today. And they will exist beyond the life of present physical structures, however well planned and lastingly built. But they will not exist beyond the idea of a library.

For while libraries serve the immediate needs of the day as one of their most important functions their existence rests upon man's insistence that there be dissemination of knowledge. Libraries must, indeed, shoulder the belief of Socrates that there is "one only good, namely

---

David H. Clift, "Enduring Rights," *Wilson Library Bulletin*, 28, no. 10:851–54+ (June, 1954), copyright 1954 by H. W. Wilson Co. Reprinted by permission of the author and of the publisher.

knowledge; and one only evil, namely ignorance."

Lately we have witnessed a number of instances in this country in which man's right to knowledge has been challenged. These efforts have been aimed at schools and at libraries. The freedom to read has been under attack. Private groups and public authorities in various parts of the country have tried to remove books from sale; they have sought to censor textbooks; they have tried to label "controversial" books; they have distributed lists of books and authors objectionable to them. And they have tried to control libraries.

We must be deeply concerned over these efforts. It is contrary to the democratic tradition to allow individuals or groups to determine what is good and what is bad for their fellow citizens. The ordinary citizen has, for a long time, done a pretty good job in accepting the good and rejecting the bad; I think that my faith is in him and in his slow but wise judgment rather than in the self-appointed arbiter who thinks he must act for us by taking unnecessary action through means which are an affront in order to provide a protection which is not needed.

It is not strange that books and the ideas to be found in them come under attack in these uneasy times. So many of our apprehensions are directed against an ideology. The expression of a dissident idea becomes then a thing feared, in itself, and there is a tendency to react against it as against a hostile deed.

But suppression of ideas serves us no better than the ostrich is served by the sand into which he sticks his head. President Eisenhower went straight to the heart of the matter in his Dartmouth speech when he asked:

> How will we defeat communism unless we know what it is? What it teaches—why does it have such an appeal for men? Why are so many people swearing allegiance to it? It's almost a religion, albeit one of the nether regions.

In a later and memorable statement to the American Library Association, the President said further:

> ... any who act as if freedom's defenses are to be found in suppression and suspicion and fear confess a doctrine that is alien to America.

The solution is not by the suppression of dissident ideas but by the very widest exposure, accompanied by thoughtful analysis. And for this to become wholly true, libraries have a clear and unalterable responsibility; a responsibility for the dissemination of knowledge—a responsibility above and beyond that which the library owes, as an agency of service to its particular community of users.

The political and moral censors have not, of late, felt this way about libraries. The list of attempts against the freedom to read is lengthy and not restricted to any particular section of the country.

There have been many attempts by local authorities to exert pressure through extra-legal efforts to restrict the sale and circulation of materials deemed objectionable. Citizens committees have been set up in communities as far apart as Texas and Washington. Lodge members, pharmacists, the American Legion, textbook boards of review—all have felt it incumbent upon themselves to institute community action against books considered by them to be objectionable and unfit either to be disseminated or read.

The roll call of incidents has not been without instances that have brought amused smiles to the faces of many—and headlines in the foreign press. Witness that state where a member of the textbook commission argued for the removal of all references to Robin Hood and the Quaker religion because each tended to support communism. The member insisted that when Robin Hood robbed the rich and gave to the poor he was advancing the communist line; and as for Quakers, they do not believe in fighting wars.

In another state, a mother set off a chain reaction. She complained to the sheriff about the immorality of a library book brought home by her daughter. The sheriff wrote to the governor. The governor asked the secretary of state, who is also state librarian, to look into the matter. The secretary of state issued a directive to the library staff forbidding the circulation of all books of a salacious, vulgar, or obscene character. The library staff was also notified not to purchase books of this nature in the future. The library staff went to work and culled about eight thousand volumes representing four to five hundred titles from the shelves.

The final effect of such a blanket order, if it operated to meet the complaint for which it was issued, would be to restrict adults to reading deemed suitable for adolescents.

Public opinion was immediate and forceful. The books are now back but the decision of the secretary of state to "tighten up supervision" of adult books has resulted in some strange happenings.

One other instance—recently a story by Sherwood Anderson, appearing in a collection of stories, was objected to for use in the public schools because of a feeling that it helped children learn to play hooky. Of this, the Louisville, Kentucky, *Times* opined:

> It comes down to this. . . . Kids who read books, even Sherwood Anderson's, are usually too busy with their literary pursuits to find time to play hooky. The truants, on the other hand, are too busy with their truancy to read books.

It is interesting to study the history of banned books. Last December, the University of North Carolina offered such a study to its readers. It put on an exhibit of banned books which, before or after censorship, "became milestones in man's struggle for freedom of thought and of the press."

What, among other things, did the exhibit demonstrate? It showed that one of the "most censored" and "most frequently banned books" has been the Bible, in all its various translations and editions. American authors in the display included Nathaniel Hawthorne's *Scarlet Letter*, banned by Nicholas I of Russia; Walt Whitman's *Leaves of Grass,* which so shocked some people that Whitman lost his job in the Department of the Interior; Mark Twain's *The Adventures of Tom Sawyer,* which was excluded temporarily from the shelves of several public libraries; and Theodore Dreiser's *An American Tragedy,* which enjoys the somewhat dubious distinction of having been banned in Boston.

A great deal of recent censorship activity has been in the area of alleged obscenity. And here we come into a field of especial sensitivity, for individual tastes are involved, as well as reading to which children are exposed.

It is true that much of modern literature is shocking to some. It is also true that much of life is shocking. Should we, because it is shocking, prevent serious writers from dealing with the stuff of life?

Librarians would be the first to admit that responsibility must go along with opportunity in providing reading materials for the young. No parent and no teacher would, however, accept the idea that the total responsibility rests within the library.

In the words of the recent thoughtful analysis, the Freedom to Read Statement:

> Parents and teachers have a responsibility to prepare the young to meet the diversity of experience to which they will be exposed in life, as they have a responsibility to help them learn to think critically for themselves. These are affirmative responsibilities not to be discharged simply by preventing them from reading works for which they are not yet prepared.

"We (all) deplore catering to the immature (and) the retarded or maladjusted taste." But if violations exist here, these must be dealt with according to due process of law. There are Federal statutes dealing with the dissemination of obscene and pornographic materials. Such statutes exist in every state in the Union except one and even the Congressional committee which investigated the subject feels that the statutes are adequate.

Most persons would find themselves in agreement with the view expressed in the Freedom to Read Statement issued jointly by the American Library Association and the American Book Publishers Council and since endorsed widely by national and state groups. Among other propositions, this statement affirmed that:

> The present laws dealing with obscenity should be vigorously enforced. Beyond that there is no place in our society for extra-legal efforts to coerce the taste of others, to confine adults to the reading matter deemed suitable for adolescents, or to inhibit the efforts of writers to achieve artistic expression.

Why then, if there be adequate laws, is there this continuing sound and fury? Dealing with both aspects of the censorship turmoil, Congressman Emanuel Celler offered this view:

> This is not the first nor will it be in history, the last attempt to prescribe a mold into which to pour the human mind. Along with every battle for freedom has been fought the battle against censorship. There will always be people who must play God. But when people stop being fighting mad at those who would put them in a mental straitjacket, fighting mad at those who would reduce the life of imagination, the vigor and multiplicity of creativeness, to two-by-nothing dimensions, then they have lost their souls to the dead weight of tyranny.

The American citizen, thank goodness, is pretty touchy about his rights. He is particularly unwilling to be told what he can do and what he cannot do. Lately, he has been more quick to see that what happens to books and to the library happens also to him in a very important and critical kind of way. Consequently, in recent attacks we have witnessed a quick and firm defense of the job of the library. In fact, it is not spoken of as the job of the library, but the *right* of the people—which is what the library has said all along.

I suspect, too, that the average citizen is pretty fond of his library. More fond, perhaps, than his limited acquaintance renders proper. The library is just as much a part of the American scene and the American heritage as is the little red schoolhouse. And if the little red schoolhouse is more and more only a figure of speech, so is the old-fashioned library.

There are many healthy and encouraging signs that local and self-appointed pressure groups are coming to be recognized for what they are—the expression of a willful opinion without regard for the rights of others; the imposition of a self-created authority; exponents of submission through intimidation.

It is happily clear that the score for 1953 is very much in favor of those who believe in America's traditional freedom to speak and read as it wishes. Speaking of events of the past year, the Chicago *Sun-Times* commented:

In almost every incident, public opinion forced public officials to back away from book burning [conducted] under the excuse of protecting public morals.

But Man's Right to Knowledge and the Freedom to Read are more than political rights, they are social needs. The freedom to read will continue to exist, safe in the long run, from the snipings of the censor. But this freedom to read assumes that there are books and other materials available to be read.

The political right of access to books on all subjects is better met today than is the provision of books to meet the social need. There can be no freedom to read, save in the abstract and only the right to knowledge without the free use thereof for those 30,000,000 Americans who are without libraries to which they can turn for education, for practical information, for recreation.

While I, for one, can think of no better name for it than the American *free* public library, I do wish the connotation of "free" were better understood. As in a college or university, the services and the books are freely available to all who constitute the body of legal users. But libraries cost money and so they do not come free and without charge to the taxpayers' pocketbook—whether it be a public library or the New Haven State Teachers College Library. And I wish that fact could become more a matter of exact knowledge to all users of libraries. I wish that the borrower's library card might show the portion of his tax dollar that goes to keep the doors open to all. Librarians would then, I think, welcome the indignant, "I'm a taxpayer!" when a book cannot be supplied. And the greater awareness that the community is spending, for each individual 10c or 65c or 75c or $1 or more per year, might reconcile the reader to library conditions through reminding him of the extent of his investment; better still, it might cause him to wish to increase his support.

A very recent survey of present conditions in the libraries of the country, sponsored by the New York State Library, reached the conclusion that "the American public library is facing a major crisis." The study revealed insufficient reading materials and inadequate staffs in most of the 7,500 public library systems of the country. Nearly 53,000,000 persons do not have easy access to books and, while estimates vary, it is safe to place the number of persons with no library service of any kind at about 30,000,000. There are about 3,000 counties in the United States; 464 of these counties—or one out of every six—have no public library service.

It seems clear that communities and states are not meeting, for one reason or another, the obligation to provide acceptable and needed library service. The inadequate amounts of money appropriated for this purpose fail more and more to do the job as inflation combines with an increasing population to be served.

If you will allow me to mention just a few figures, the implications of the situation become more clear. Recently compiled figures set the 1950–1951 expenditures, excluding capital outlay, for public library systems in cities with a population of 100,000 or more at $58,000,000. The same figure for 1944–1945 was $32,000,000, so the favorable per-cent change is about eighty per cent. If, however, you convert the 1944–1945 dollars to dollars with 1950–1951 purchasing power, you find exactly the same thing you discover when you relate the purchasing power of your own personal income for 1950–1951 to the income you had in 1944–

1945. For the increase in purchasing power of these libraries to which I have referred is not eighty per cent; it is only thirty per cent with which to meet increased costs of all sorts and serve a growing population.

One other statistic: In 1952, the 106 cities in this country with a population of 100,000 or more spent just over $8,000,000 for books and periodicals for the people of those cities. This is an impressive figure until you relate it to the population of those cities. You might expect, with *Publishers' Weekly,*

> that the cities' annual per capita expenditure for public library reading matter should be at least as much as retail cost of a 25c book. It isn't, though, it's not quite 18c.

If the free public library is to remain an important factor in citizenship training and education for all the people of the country, this can only come about through increased local support and interest and recognition and the states must have the equalizing interest and support of the Federal Government. The worth of the investment is clear, for the library is a firm bulwark against ignorance and prejudice; it is no summer soldier in the battle for truth and for the freedom of ideas.

Almost seventy years ago, James Russell Lowell in speaking at the opening of the Free Public Library in Chelsea, Massachusetts, sorrowed with his audience that there was so much to read about. The speech of the scholar of old, he said,

> was noble because they lunched with Plutarch and supped with Plato. . . . Instead of communing with the choice thoughts of choice spirits . . . we diligently inform ourselves, and cover the continent with a cobweb of telegraph wires to inform us, of such inspiring facts as that a horse belonging to Mr. Smith ran away on Wednesday, seriously damaging a valuable carryall; that a son of Mr. Brown swallowed a hickory nut on Thursday; and that a gravel bank caved in and buried Mr. Robinson alive on Friday. Alas it is we ourselves that are being buried alive under this avalanche of earthy impertinence.

If the telegraph wires constitute an earthy impertinence, one wonders with what language Mr. Lowell would describe today's twin bearers of news—the radio and TV.

Mr. Lowell would, I think, be pleased with some of our progressive libraries of today, that have done so much in the field of adult education. He would, I'm certain, appreciate the advances in information techniques and advisory assistance by which the reader is helped through the bewildering output of today's welter of printed and audio-visual materials.

Mr. Lowell's remarks and his fears remind us that there was a time when the library's role, in man's search for knowledge and information, was a passive one, a time when librarians and communities as well felt that of libraries it was sufficient to allow that "they also serve who only stand and wait." Milton said that of the blind, and Peter B. Kyne said it of horses. It is no longer sufficient for libraries; libraries no longer are content to stand and wait. They are rapidly losing the passive character that marked them a generation or more ago. The times are complex and the needs of our society for information and knowledge reflect that complexity. Libraries have moved to meet the need.

If I have seemed to talk overmuch about public libraries and too little about the type of libraries exemplified by the facilities in this splendid new building, it is certainly from no lack of respect for the important responsibilities accepted and discharged by the college and university library. Rather, it is to suggest that Man's Right to Knowledge and the Free Use Thereof faces practical and immediate difficulties in the arena of public life and public opinion. Here, within these walls—and the walls of all colleges and universities—a large part of the eventual decision is being forged.

I used to be a practicing librarian, and at one time had the opportunity to read many books—an opportunity which, strangely enough, too many librarians are denied by other duties incident to serving their public. Consequently, when I today say I wish there were a book on this or that, I more often than not find that it does exist and I have simply not known of it. Let me say it in a different way this time: Sometime I would like to read a collection of inscriptions over libraries. Some are given in Mr. Van Doren's brochure on Columbia's celebration. Not given is one that I have cherished for over twenty years for its rolling phrase and its proud faith. It is over the entrance to Low Memorial Library at Columbia University and it reads:

> King's College founded in the Province of New York by Royal Charter in the reign of George II perpetuated as Columbia College by the people of the State of New York when they became free and independent—main-

tained and cherished from generation to generation for the advancement of the public good and the glory of Almighty God.

Yale's Sterling Memorial Library proclaims over its High Street entrance that a library is the heart of the university.

The use to which a library is put, as Plutarch observed, is more magnificent than its collection or its facilities. President Eisenhower's words of last summer to the librarians of the country provide an inscription for some future library that is eloquently expressive of that idea. Compounded of the fears and the faiths of our times, looking into the past and future alike with calmness and certainty, he stated an enduring charter for libraries for these times, and for all times, when he said:

The libraries of America are and must ever remain the homes of free, inquiring minds. To them, our citizens—of all ages and races, of all creeds and political persuasions—must ever be able to turn with clear confidence that there they can freely seek the whole truth, unwarped by fashion and uncompromised by expediency.

American Library Association
LIBRARY BILL OF RIGHTS

The Council of the American Library Association reaffirms its belief in the following basic principles which should govern the services of all libraries:

1

As a responsibility of library service, books and other reading matter selected should be chosen for values of interest, information, and enlightenment of all the people of the community. In no case should any book be excluded because of the race or nationality, or the political or religious views of the writer.

2

There should be the fullest practicable provision of material presenting all points of view concerning the problems and issues of our times, international, national, and local; and books or other reading matter of sound factual authority should not be proscribed or removed from library shelves because of partisan or doctrinal disapproval.

3

Censorship of books, urged or practiced by volunteer arbiters of morals or political opinion or by organizations that would establish a coercive concept of Americanism, must be challenged by libraries in maintenance of their responsibility to provide public information and enlightenment through the printed word.

4

Libraries should enlist the cooperation of allied groups in the fields of science, of education, and of book publishing in resisting all abridgment of the free access to ideas and full freedom of expression that are the tradition and heritage of Americans.

5

As an institution of education for democratic living, the library should welcome the use of its meeting rooms for socially useful and cultural activities and discussion of current public questions. Such meeting places should be available on equal terms to all groups in the community regardless of the beliefs and affiliations of their members.

Adopted by the Council of the American Library Association at Atlantic City, June 18, 1948. By official action of the ALA Council, February 3, 1951, the Library Bill of Rights shall be interpreted to apply to all materials and media of communication used or collected by libraries.

American Library Association
STATEMENT ON LABELING

In view of our own convictions and those of other practicing librarians whose counsel we sought, the Committee on Intellectual Freedom recommends to the ALA Council the following policy with respect to labeling library materials:

Librarians should not use the technique of labeling as a means of predisposing readers against library materials for the following reasons:

1

Although totalitarian states find it easy and even proper, according to their ethics, to estab-

---

Recommendations unanimously adopted by the American Library Association Council, July 13, 1951.

lish criteria for judging publications as "subversive," injustice and ignorance rather than justice and enlightenment result from such practices, and the American Library Association has a responsibility to take a stand against the establishment of such criteria in a democratic state.

2

Libraries do not advocate the ideas found in their collections. The presence of a magazine or book in a library does not indicate an endorsement of its contents by the library.

3

No one person should take the responsibility of labeling publications. No sizable group of persons would be likely to agree either on the types of material which should be labeled or the sources of information which should be regarded with suspicion. As a practical consideration, a librarian who labeled a book or magazine pro-communist might be sued for libel.

4

Labeling is an attempt to prejudice the reader, and as such, it is a censor's tool.

5

Labeling violates the spirit of the Library Bill of Rights.

6

Although we are all agreed that communism is a threat to the free world, if materials are labeled to pacify one group, there is no excuse for refusing to label any item in the library's collection. Because communism, fascism, or other authoritarianisms tend to suppress ideas and attempt to coerce individuals to conform to a specific ideology, American librarians must be opposed to such "isms." We are, then, anti-communist, but we are also opposed to any other group which aims at closing any path to knowledge.

American Library Association and American Book Publishers Council
THE FREEDOM TO READ

The freedom to read is essential to our democracy. It is under attack. Private groups and public authorities in various parts of the country are working to remove books from sale, to censor textbooks, to label "controversial" books, to distribute lists of "objectionable" books or authors, and to purge libraries.

These actions apparently rise from a view that our national tradition of free expression is no longer valid; that censorship and suppression are needed to avoid the subversion of politics and the corruption of morals. We, as citizens devoted to the use of books and as librarians and publishers responsible for disseminating them, wish to assert the public interest in the preservation of the freedom to read.

We are deeply concerned about these attempts at suppression. Most such attempts rest on a denial of the fundamental premise of democracy: that the ordinary citizen, by exercising his critical judgment, will accept the good and reject the bad. The censors, public and private, assume that they should determine what is good and what is bad for their fellow citizens.

We trust Americans to recognize propaganda, and to reject obscenity. We do not believe they need the help of censors to assist them in this task. We do not believe they are prepared to sacrifice their heritage of a free press in order to be "protected" against what others think may be bad for them. We believe they still favor free enterprise in ideas and expression.

We are aware, of course, that books are not alone in being subjected to efforts at suppression. We are aware that these efforts are related to a larger pattern of pressures being brought against education, the press, films, radio, and television. The problem is not only one of actual censorship. The shadow of fear cast by these pressures leads, we suspect, to an even larger voluntary curtailment of expression by those who seek to avoid controversy.

Such pressure toward conformity is perhaps natural to a time of uneasy change and pervading fear. Especially when so many of our apprehensions are directed against an ideology, the expression of a dissident idea becomes a thing

---

A statement prepared by the Westchester Conference of the American Library Association and the American Book Publishers Council—May 2 and 3, 1953. The statement has been endorsed by the American Book Publishers Council, Board of Directors; the American Library Association Council; the American Booksellers Association Board of Directors; the National Commission for the Defense of Democracy through Education, appointed by the National Education Association of the U.S.A.; the Book Manufacturers' Institute.

feared in itself, and we tend to move against it as against a hostile deed, with suppression.

And yet suppression is never more dangerous than in such a time of social tension. Freedom has given the United States the elasticity to endure strain. Freedom keeps open the path of novel and creative solutions, and enables change to come by choice. Every silencing of a heresy, every enforcement of an orthodoxy, diminishes the toughness and resilience of our society and leaves it the less able to deal with stress.

Now as always in our history, books are among our greatest instruments of freedom. They are almost the only means for making generally available ideas or manners of expression that can initially command only a small audience. They are the natural medium for the new idea and the untried voice, from which come the original contributions to social growth. They are essential to the extended discussion which serious thought requires, and to the accumulation of knowledge and ideas into organized collections.

We believe that free communication is essential to the preservation of a free society and a creative culture. We believe that these pressures toward conformity present the danger of limiting the range and variety of inquiry and expression on which our democracy and our culture depend. We believe that every American community must jealously guard the freedom to publish and to circulate, in order to preserve its own freedom to read. We believe that publishers and librarians have a profound responsibility to give validity to that freedom to read by making it possible for the reader to choose freely from a variety of offerings.

The freedom to read is guaranteed by the Constitution. Those with faith in free men will stand firm on these constitutional guarantees of essential rights and will exercise the responsibilities that accompany these rights.

THE PROPOSITIONS

We therefore affirm these propositions:

1. *It is in the public interest for publishers and librarians to make available the widest diversity of views and expressions, including those which are unorthodox or unpopular with the majority.*

Creative thought is by definition new, and what is new is different. The bearer of every new thought is a rebel until his idea is refined and tested. Totalitarian systems attempt to maintain themselves in power by the ruthless suppression of any concept which challenges the established orthodoxy. The power of a democratic system to adapt to change is vastly strengthened by the freedom of its citizens to choose widely from among conflicting opinions offered freely to them. To stifle every nonconformist idea at birth would mark the end of the democratic process. Furthermore, only through the constant activity of weighing and selecting can the democratic mind attain the strength demanded by times like these. We need to know not only what we believe but why we believe it.

2. *Publishers and librarians do not need to endorse every idea or presentation contained in the books they make available. It would conflict with the public interest for them to establish their own political, moral, or aesthetic views as the sole standard for determining what books should be published or circulated.*

Publishers and librarians serve the educational process by helping to make available knowledge and ideas required for the growth of the mind and the increase of learning. They do not foster education by imposing as mentors the patterns of their own thought. The people should have the freedom to read and consider a broader range of ideas than those that may be held by any single librarian or publisher or government or church. It is wrong that what one man can read should be confined to what another thinks proper.

3. *It is contrary to the public interest for publishers or librarians to determine the acceptability of a book solely on the basis of the personal history or political affiliations of the author.*

A book should be judged as a book. No art or literature can flourish if it is to be measured by the political views of private lives of its creators. No society of free men can flourish which draws up lists of writers to whom it will not listen, whatever they may have to say.

4. *The present laws dealing with obscenity should be vigorously enforced. Beyond that, there is no place in our society for extralegal efforts to coerce the taste of others, to confine adults to the reading matter deemed suitable for adolescents, or to inhibit the efforts of writers to achieve artistic expression.*

To some, much of modern literature is shocking. But is not much of life itself shocking? We cut off literature at the source if we prevent serious artists from dealing with the stuff of life. Parents and teachers have a responsibility to prepare the young to meet the diversity of experiences in life to which they will be exposed, as they have a responsibility to help them learn to think critically for themselves. These are affirmative responsibilities, not discharged simply by preventing them from reading works for which they are not yet prepared. In these matters taste differs, and taste cannot be legislated; nor can machinery be devised which will suit the demands of one group without limiting the freedom of others. We deplore the catering to the immature, the retarded, or the maladjusted taste. But those concerned with freedom have the responsibility of seeing to it that each individual book or publication, whatever its contents, price, or method of distribution, is dealt with in accordance with due process of law.

5. *It is not in the public interest to force a reader to accept with any book the prejudgment of a label characterizing the book or author as subversive or dangerous.*

The idea of labeling supposes the existence of individuals or groups with wisdom to determine by authority what is good or bad for the citizen. It supposes that each individual must be directed in making up his mind about the ideas he examines. But Americans do not need others to do their thinking for them.

6. *It is the responsibility of publishers and librarians, as guardians of the people's freedom to read, to contest encroachments upon that freedom by individuals or groups seeking to impose their own standards or tastes upon the community at large.*

It is inevitable in the give and take of the democratic process that the political, the moral, or the aesthetic concepts of an individual or group will occasionally collide with those of another individual or group. In a free society each individual is free to determine for himself what he wishes to read, and each group is free to determine what it will recommend to its freely associated members. But no group has the right to take the law into its own hands, and to impose its own concepts of politics or morality upon other members of a democratic society. Freedom is no freedom if it is accorded only to the accepted and the inoffensive.

7. *It is the responsibility of publishers and librarians to give full meaning to the freedom to read by providing books that enrich the quality of thought and expression. By the exercise of this affirmative responsibility, bookmen can demonstrate that the answer to a bad book is a good one, the answer to a bad idea is a good one.*

The freedom to read is of little consequence when expended on the trivial; it is frustrated when the reader cannot obtain matter fit for his purpose. What is needed is not only the absence of restraint, but the positive provision of opportunity for the people to read the best that has been thought and said. Books are the major channel by which the intellectual inheritance is handed down, and the principal means of its testing and growth. The defense of their freedom and integrity, and the enlargement of their service to society, requires of all bookmen the utmost of their faculties, and deserves of all citizens the fullest of their support.

* * *

We state these propositions neither lightly nor as easy generalizations. We here stake out a lofty claim for the value of books. We do so because we believe that they are good, possessed of enormous variety and usefulness, worthy of cherishing and keeping free. We realize that the application of these propositions may mean the dissemination of ideas and manners of expression that are repugnant to many persons. We do not state these propositions in the comfortable belief that what people read is unimportant. We believe rather that what people read is deeply important; that ideas can be dangerous; but that the suppression of ideas is fatal to a democratic society. Freedom itself is a dangerous way of life, but it is ours.

American Library Association
OVERSEAS LIBRARIES STATEMENT

The American Library Association has been intimately associated with the overseas library

---

Approved by the American Library Association Council, June 25, 1953.

program of the United States Government from its initiation. Under contract from the Government it established and operated in Latin America the first libraries opened under this program. Most of the librarians overseas and the professional staff of the program in the United States have been members of this Association. The Association has been represented regularly on advisory committees and consultants' groups established to give guidance to the program. All told, hundreds of our members over the last ten years have had opportunity in one way or another to observe the operation of the overseas libraries at first hand and to make detailed professional judgments of their holdings, their services, and their effectiveness with foreign audiences.

We know that these libraries have been operated throughout the years with a single-minded devotion to the interests of the United States. With many impartial observers, we believe that they are among the most effective weapons possessed by the United States in the battle to preserve free men and free minds from the enslavement of Communist political and intellectual tyranny. We know that their effectiveness has depended on the conviction among foreign users that here was a free and open source of truth to which they could turn with confidence for information and enlightenment.

We have been dismayed by the confused and fearful response of the State Department to recent attacks upon this program. The hastily changed directives, the delays in the purchase of books, the charges of book-burning, the fear to buy any books at all have presented a shocking picture abroad and have seriously damaged the effectiveness of the program.

We are therefore enormously heartened by the President's recent vigorous attack on book-burning. We support this position fully.

We reaffirm our conviction of the indispensable value of free libraries as the enemy of enslaved minds abroad as at home and our confidence in the professional administration of the overseas libraries. We welcome the opportunity given the new administrator of the proposed independent International Information Administration to reassert the integrity and effectiveness of this program. A decade of world-wide experience makes it clear that that integrity and effectiveness require four things:

1. The libraries must express in themselves and in their services the ideas of freedom for which they speak.
2. They must provide a service of uncompromising integrity. Their usefulness to the United States rests on the assurance of their users that they are places in which to learn the truth.
3. The Information Administration must be free to use in its libraries what books soever its responsible professional judgment determines are necessary or useful to the provision of such a service. To deny itself the tools it needs to serve the United States for irrelevant reasons of the past associations of authors and in fear of domestic criticism is indefensible.
4. Though no one could justify or would seek to justify the use of the overseas libraries to disseminate material harmful to the United States, it is unworkable to abandon the simple criterion of whether a book is useful to the purpose of the libraries and to substitute elaborate, irrelevant, and offensive schemes of "clearance" of authors.

The American overseas libraries do not belong to a Congressional Committee or to the State Department. They belong to the whole American people, who are entitled to have them express their finest ideals of responsible freedom. In no other way can the libraries effectively serve their purpose, and in no other pattern can this Association aid their progress.

Dwight Eisenhower
LETTER ON INTELLECTUAL FREEDOM

The White House
Washington
June 24, 1953

Dear Dr. Downs:

Thank you for your letter of June fifteenth. I am glad to know of the annual conference of the American Library Association convening this week, and of the spirit of conscientious citizenship ruling its deliberations.

Our librarians serve the precious liberties of our nation: freedom of inquiry, freedom of the spoken and the written word, freedom of exchange of ideas.

Upon these clear principles, democracy depends for its very life, for they are the great sources of knowledge and enlightenment. And knowledge—full, unfettered knowledge of its own heritage, of freedom's enemies, of the whole world of men and ideas—this knowledge is a free people's surest strength.

The converse is just as surely true. A democracy smugly disdainful of new ideas would be a sick democracy. A democracy chronically fearful of new ideas would be a dying democracy.

For all these reasons, we must in these times be intelligently alert not only to the fanatic cunning of Communist conspiracy—but also to the grave dangers in meeting fanaticism with ignorance. For, in order to fight totalitarians who exploit the ways of freedom to serve their own ends, there are some zealots who—with more wrath than wisdom—would adopt a strangely unintelligent course. They would try to defend freedom by denying freedom's friends the opportunity of studying Communism in its entirety—its plausibilities, its falsities, its weaknesses.

But we know that freedom cannot be served by the devices of the tyrant. As it is an ancient truth that freedom cannot be legislated into existence, so it is no less obvious that freedom cannot be censored into existence. And any who act as if freedom's defenses are to be found in suppression and suspicion and fear confess a doctrine that is alien to America.

The libraries of America are and must ever remain the homes of free, inquiring minds. To them, our citizens—of all ages and races, of all creeds and political persuasions—must ever be able to turn with clear confidence that there they can freely seek the whole truth, unwarped by fashion and uncompromised by expediency. For in such whole and healthy knowledge alone are to be found and understood those majestic truths of man's nature and destiny that prove, to each succeeding generation, the validity of freedom.

Sincerely,
(Signed)
DWIGHT EISENHOWER

Dr. R. B. Downs, President,
American Library Association,
Statler Hotel,
Los Angeles, California.

American Bar Association
STATEMENT ON THE FREEDOM TO READ

"Resolved that the freedom to read is a corollary of the constitutional guarantee of freedom of the press and American lawyers should oppose efforts to restrict it."

There has lately been considerable discussion about so-called "book burning," a phrase which has come to be used to describe recent removals or suppression of books primarily because of the views of their authors, some of which did not appear in the books. Such activities have included removal of books from Government libraries abroad and an increasing variety of attacks on the contents of libraries at home. These attacks are often made by zealous and well-meaning people, in the name of national security. Because of the Bar's interest in balancing the true needs of national security with individual freedom, it is right that we should speak plainly now about these developments before they spread further.

As to libraries maintained by our Government abroad, there should be no doubt that the Government may properly restrict their contents to those which, in the judgment of the responsible officials, fairly and effectively present American life and culture, the presentation of which is the purpose of such libraries. There is no good reason why such libraries should include propaganda against the United States. In this matter we are not dealing with a facet of a constitutional problem but only with the practical administration of a governmental program. Of course, in the interest of maintaining a national reputation for cool-headedness, some judgment must be used in determining what books should be included or excluded and ordinarily their actual contents would seem to be the best criterion.

But when we come to libraries at home, we are dealing with a policy involving the rights of our own people and we should oppose efforts to suppress or deny access which are not based upon accepted bans against obscenity or other illegality of contents. The reasonable judgment of librarians and others charged with selection of books should not be put in a strait jacket. The

---
Adopted by the House of Delegates, Boston, August, 1953.

"Freedom to Read" is naturally a corollary of the great constitutional guarantee of a free press. While that guarantee protects the writer or publisher against interference, it is obviously not for their benefit alone. Also, while it applies in terms only to governmental restrictions, its spirit applies to all sources of restriction. That spirit is that our people should not be denied the right to read anything, not obscene or otherwise illegal, which may be published. This is because we, like our forefathers, believe that truth can be counted on to prevail in a free competition of ideas. Any fear that our people have become so soft-headed that they must now be protected against an opportunity to examine the books of authors whose personal views or conduct are obnoxious is unfounded.

It does not advance the interest of national security to surrender any of our freedoms at home unless necessary to survival. Instead, weakening those freedoms actually causes injury to our national security. If our people are not allowed to judge the truth for themselves or if they cannot learn the nature of our enemy or his propaganda, it will be harder for them to develop the cool and informed heads and stout hearts needed to combat that enemy. The mind like the body should have every opportunity to develop the anti-toxins necessary to sound health. Furthermore, if we supinely accept unnecessary restrictions on freedom, we shall dull our best weapon against our enemy. We cannot burn books at home and object effectively to tyranny over the human mind by our enemy abroad.

The insidious part of all such efforts is that they are usually based upon some premise which most of us accept. Thus today one of the attacks is upon books written or illustrated by people who have refused to testify before Congressional Committees because of possible self-incrimination. No group could oppose more vigorously than lawyers do the activities or views which have led these people to take that position. No group deplores more than we do conduct which prevents a citizen from candidly revealing his activities and views affecting the possible safety of his country when interrogated by proper authority. But if today we ban books on these grounds, tomorrow there will be others. The smoke of burning books, like the smell of midnight oil in the rewriting of history by Nazi or Soviet historians to make it more palatable to their regimes, offends American nostrils. The place to stop is before the process begins. American lawyers have sufficient confidence in the common sense of our people and the stability of our institutions to urge that we can and should keep them free.

It is, therefore, desirable that the Bar be alert to discourage efforts to restrict the freedom to read. At every opportunity, lawyers should emphasize the importance to national security of keeping our freedoms intact and the dangers to national security of surrendering them except when required for survival. A learned profession like ours is peculiarly aware that books contain the core of the great traditions of our history and civilization. No one should be allowed to tamper with them without sharp reaction from the Bar.

Chapter ix

The schools under attack

No institutions in our society are more vulnerable to pressures from every direction than the public schools. Close to the grass-roots level, their affairs constantly in the center of community attention, and dependent for support upon public tax funds—it is perhaps surprising that the schools retain any large degree of freedom. Pressure groups—economic, nationalistic, political, religious, and the like—intent upon shaping the educational system to fit their particular ideologies, have sought to dictate to the schools what may or may not be taught.

Legislatures in a number of states also, sensitive to lobbies and other forms of organized pressure, have enacted statutes highly arbitrary and restrictive in nature to control textbook selection and curricula.

An extreme example of the activities in this field of a private organization was the program of the Conference of American Small Business Organizations which, in the early 1950's, became so flagrant that it came under investigation by the U.S. House of Representatives Select Committee on Lobbying Activities. CASBO's pressure tactics included establishment of the *Educational Reviewer,* "a quarterly review of educational materials," the function of which was to examine textbooks from the point of view of their attachment to the principles of "personal liberty and economic liberty" and their freedom from "concealed theories of collectivism." As stated in the Congressional Committee's report, "The long-run aim of this program is obvious, and this is nothing less than the establishment of CASBO's philosophy as the standard of educational orthodoxy in the schools of the Nation."

In a statement applicable not only to this, but to all other narrowly conceived and selfish special interests attempting to shape public education in their own image, the Committee concluded:

"We all agree, of course, that our textbooks should be American, that they should not be the vehicle for the propagation of obnoxious doctrines. Yet the review of textbooks by self-appointed experts, especially when undertaken under the aegis of an organization having a distinct legislative ax to grind, smacks too much of the book-burning orgies of Nuremberg to be accepted by thoughtful Americans without foreboding and alarm. It suggests, too that the reviewers distrust the integrity, good faith, and plain common sense of the school boards and teachers of the country. If these educators are so utterly naïve and untrained as to need help from a lobbying organization in selecting proper classroom materials, then our educational system has decayed beyond all help. This proposition we cannot accept."

A frequent target for attacks by textbook censors, Harold Rugg, Professor Emeritus of Education, Teachers College, Columbia University, author of a widely used series of social science texts, writes from painful firsthand experience. This article is based upon Dr. Rugg's book, *That Men May Understand*, which, he states, "analyzes . . . the recurring cycles of social hysteria and witch-hunting in the schools; it presents the story of my own twenty-year attempt to bring into the schools a full account of modern civilization, an analysis of the psychology of consent as the basis of democratic government, and the ordeal of distinguished Americans who have explored various creative frontiers."

Harold Rugg
**A STUDY
IN CENSORSHIP:
GOOD CONCEPTS
AND BAD WORDS**

I have read Dr. Anderson's article in the January, 1941, issue of this magazine [*Social Education*], with great interest and agreement. Since my own work has been one of the chief targets for the attack of the self-appointed censors in the schools I should like to generalize and extend Dr. Anderson's discussion a bit, supplying some additional factual details. But first I wish to join him in a categorical denial of the ridiculous charges made against teachers and writers in the social studies. There is not the slightest vestige of truth in them. It is to be regretted that a situation can be built up in our country in which it becomes necessary to deny charges of this kind. I do so only after years of silence and at the urgent request of teachers, colleagues, and friends. Those who know me and those who *have* read and understood my books—and these include tens of thousands of students and teachers and parents who have used them for almost twenty years—know that the statements made against them do not describe my philosophy or my work.

The present attack on liberalism in education is not the first of its kind. It is true that this one is nation-wide, more virulent, and promises to last longer and to set back the work of the schools more than any previous one. But it *has* happened before. Five times since the World War a wave of censorship has rolled up on the schools.

As I write there stands behind me a four-foot shelf of manufactured conflict about "un-Americanism" in the schools. It is a twenty-year documentary record—newspaper clippings . . . articles and cartoons from national magazines . . . scrapbooks and folders . . . pamphlets, bulletins, and official reports . . . chapters clipped from books . . . transcriptions of records of hearings and court actions . . . stenographic records of Hearst newspaper interviews . . . and whatnot.

Does it indicate nation-wide popular protest? It does not. Although six to eight million Americans have buzzed with questions about Rugg and his books since 1939, the entire phenomenon is a record of controversies initiated and kept alive by a few hitherto unknown persons standing in strategic places and with access to powerful national means of communication and community action.

Harold Rugg, "A Study in Censorship: Good Concepts and Bad Words," *Social Education*, 5:176–81 (March, 1941), copyright 1941 by the National Council for the Social Studies. Reprinted by permission of the publisher.

Let there be no doubt about the general staff of the patrioteers now invading education. Eight hitherto unknown persons of almost no prestige or influence have made the attack and are artificially keeping it alive:

1. Merwin K. Hart, of Utica, New York, and New York City; executive of his personally organized New York State Economic Council.
2. Bertie C. Forbes, of Englewood, New Jersey, and New York City; for many years a columnist for the Hearst newspapers, and publisher of his own magazine, *Forbes.*
3. Major Augustin G. Rudd, of Garden City, Long Island, New York, former U.S. Army man, business executive, and active in the American Legion.
4. E. H. West, of Haworth, New Jersey, and New York City; business executive; active in the American Legion; zealot for rooting out "un-Americanism" in the schools.
5. Major General Amos A. Fries, of Washington, D.C.; retired U.S. Army man; editor of *Friends of the Public Schools,* a periodic bulletin frequently attacking the work of certain public schools.
6. Elizabeth Dilling, of Kenilworth, Illinois; wealthy author and publisher of *The Red Network;* lecturer on "Un-Americanism" and the danger of communistic tendencies in America; one of the chief "stirrer-uppers" of tension and suspicion.

These few persons make up the spearhead of the present attack on the schools. To them must be added at least two professional writers who have written and published articles against the schools in national mass-circulation magazines:

1. George E. Sokolsky, of New York City; wrote three articles in *Liberty* in 1940, reaching millions of readers and causing unrest and suspicion about the schools.
2. O. K. Armstrong, of Springfield, Missouri; active in the American Legion; writer of "Treason in the Textbooks," which appeared in the *American Legion Magazine,* in September, 1940.

The influence of these persistent enemies of liberalism working alone as individuals would no doubt have been insufficient to stir up suspicion the country over. But their present success is due in large part to the fact that they have had access to the facilities of national agencies, the principal ones being:

1. The Hearst newspapers with their affiliated syndicated features, reaching many millions of readers, daily and weekly.
2. National patriotic organizations with memberships totalling several millions.
3. Several of the largest and most powerful national business organizations with vast sums of money set aside to carry on such kind of "reform" work.
4. The American Parents Committee on Education formed by Hart, Rudd, *et al.* in the spring of 1940. Their office distributes reprints of articles and other materials dealing with liberalism in the schools.

In spite of the provincial nature and influence of these individuals—I suspect nobody regards them as competent students of American civilization or public opinion—they have succeeded in stirring up unrest in hundreds of communities and fear in thousands of teachers and administrators. I have explicit proof of this—from actual personal participation in several community controversies; from the written and spoken statements of teachers, administrators, and citizens interested in the schools; from histories back of the elimination of the Rugg and other books and of *Scholastic* and other magazines; and from school administrators' and teachers' confidential communications—"they must sit tight" until "things blow over" and "get less hysterical."

GOOD CONCEPTS AND BAD WORDS

Almost from the beginning of my work in preparing school materials it was evident that to get a sound and clear description of society into the school required more than my own capacity to understand that society myself and to write it clearly and with the greatest possible objectivity. It required parents' cooperation in helping to build understanding in our young people. Would they give it? Would other citizens, especially those of the community who have prestige and leadership go along with us on the idea? Could they be brought to see the importance of young people confronting social conditions and issues squarely and digging to the very roots of our changing culture?

As the years passed, I became more and more convinced that democracy could not survive the attacks upon it unless young Americans came to a thorough understanding of the world in which they were living. The democratic process in America, I was sure, could not be guaranteed unless our youth were introduced to the full story—the deficiencies as well as the achievements of our society, the problems and issues as well as the narrative of adventure. Would adults in the community share this view?

It was not long before we found out. Throughout the years thousands of parents have read the books along with their children. Reports from them have come continuously, and these show that they themselves have become aware of the urgency of having a real description of society in the schools. It is not these who have voiced the protest against the ideas presented. It is the small group of self-appointed censors, to whom I have referred. They took it upon themselves to criticize the content, approving some ideas and some words and condemning others, all in terms of their own interests, prejudices, and philosophy. Increasingly we saw that certain indispensable ideas came to be the nub of the attack. These ideas I have called "the good concepts" and "the bad words." The table on the following page illustrates some of them.

Were these ideas, these concepts, dangerous to youth, as the critics said? In the light of twenty years of documentation these are my conclusions concerning them:

First, every concept in both lists is indispensable to a real understanding of American life—the country's magnificent achievements, its vast potentiality for an abundant physical and spiritual life, certainly; but also its deficiencies and problems. All are needed that men may understand.

Second, the ideas listed on the left called "Good Concepts" arouse no opposition at all. The patrioteers as well as the merchants of conflict think they are grand; in fact they constitute the bulk of their own verbal stock-in-trade. America to them is portrayed only in these terms.

Third, the concepts listed on the right, called "Bad Words," simply can not be introduced into the school, in any form, without arousing the bitter opposition of certain special-interest groups—persons like Miller of the 1921–1926 witch-hunt and the Forbes-Hart-Rudd-West combination of today. It can be seen from my story that although these persons are very few in number and inconsiderable in prestige, they are powerful in influence. They can and do try to prevent materials that speak "the bad words" from being used. Furthermore, the ideas are such that they can not be camouflaged with "good words." The ideas must be made clear, and as soon as they are, no matter how phrased, they become "bad"—"subversive," "un-American," "poisonous," "treason"—or what-not.

Fourth, the evidence is clear that the preponderance of our thinking citizens who do not have personal axes to grind by censoring the schools are actually well-disposed toward having all of the indispensable ideas for understanding presented to their children. Indeed, after studying the problem, they welcome—no, insist on—it. I draw a clear line, therefore, between the vast body of reasonable and well-intentioned citizens and the little corporal's guard of self-appointed censors of the schools.

"YOU CAN'T SAY THAT!"

The lists deserve careful study. Note that one can talk about the "free play of private enterprise," but not about "controlling the free play of private enterprise in the public interest."

One can describe the founding fathers as "brilliant and devout patriots" but not as "the founding fathers, brilliant and devout patriots, men of property who made the Constitution difficult to change."

One can praise the Constitution as "one of the world's greatest state papers," but one can not say or imply any "economic determination of the Constitution," even though the monographs of Charles A. Beard and others are now accepted as valid documentary evidence.

One can teach "America—a land of opportunity," but not "America—a land of opportunity for many, but not a land of equal opportunity for all"—even though proof that it isn't glares at us from 10,000 communities and 10,000,000 poverty-stricken families.

One can speak of "scientific management in industry"; but "technological unemployment"—that's bad! I need not go on; the reader can multiply the examples many-fold.

It becomes clearer and clearer, then, just what the liberal-baiters will not have in the schools. They will not have (1) anything that even approaches a questioning of the complete purity

Harold Rugg 347

SOME "GOOD CONCEPTS"	SOME "BAD WORDS"
American life—a high standard of living.	America, highest standard of living in the world and potentially a land of plenty, is, compared to its potentialities, a depressed society.
The individual should have full liberty of action to make the most of himself.	"My freedom stops where my neighbor's, or the public's, good begins."
America—a land of opportunity with a ladder of opportunity for those who compete, work hard, and persist.	America, a land of great opportunity for many, but—today not of equal opportunity for all.
The American system of free enterprise.	Free competition balanced by government controls over economic enterprise for the general welfare.
The Founding Fathers—brilliant and devout patriots.	The Founding Fathers, brilliant and devout patriots—men of property who made the Constitution difficult to change.
The free play of private ownership.	Private ownership except where public ownership is necessary to guarantee public welfare.
Unrestricted freedom to develop natural resources.	In parts of America land and people were exploited, eroded, and wasted by too uncontrolled freedom.
Scientific management in industry.	Accelerating technological unemployment.
The American constitution one of the world's greatest state papers of democratic government.	The "economic determination of the Constitution."
Democracy as the American way of life. Initial swift development of the continent a magnificent achievement, but necessarily not planned.	The characteristics of socialism, communism, and fascism compared with those of democracy. To prevent the recurring break-down of the economic system it must be planned.
Resourceful people, each looking out for himself. A sense of equality, absence of class lines among the people. "I'm as good as you."	Our people exhibit vast individual differences, energy, intelligence, ambition, and other traits.

of motives and behavior of the founders of our country or the leaders of the past; (2) anything that questions contemporary American life; (3) anything that presents negative aspects of American history or development; (4) anything that portrays social change; and (5) anything that deals with controversy. "Such things must not be brought into the school!" they say. These guardians of "everything rosy" know well, of course, that our young people are confronted with striking examples of social change every day of their lives. They themselves engage in the discussion of matters of controversy in public and private life. As for the deficiencies in American life, it is hardly necessary to remind ourselves of the fact that youth's eyes and minds are open to evidences of them on every side—in their homes, on the streets, in the playgrounds, in the movies, where-not; they read and hear about them in the newspapers and magazines, and over the radio. But, say the attackers, our young people may not talk about such things in the classroom, shouldn't even think about them. They must not question American life, its heroes of the past or present. The function of education is to build in youth an admiration for things-as-they-are. The school is to be used to buttress the *status quo*.

The first lesson that I learned, then, from the self-appointed censors in our schools was that in dealing with the materials of education one must distinguish sharply between the Good Concepts and the Bad Words. Even the good concepts become bad words, of course, in the minds of the attackers.

HOW TO INTRODUCE THE "BAD WORDS"?

The second lesson deals with the question which then faced us: How shall we handle the ideas called "The Bad Words"? They can not be camouflaged; they must be clarified. One step in this direction is the launching of a vigorous campaign of adult education. The local community leaders, along with superintendents, principals, and teachers, must take the chief responsibility and carry the community along in advance of the use of controversial issues in the schools. If the study of the ideas underlying the culture is undertaken by the adult population there will be no fears about them or rebellion against them, because the people will have come to understand.

The other step must be taken by the teachers, curriculum organizers, and writers of the materials. They must make meticulous distinction between "history" and "hypothesis." Some concepts are so firmly established and so fully documented by research data that they can be taught as history. On the soundness of these the total body of historians stand, a solid phalanx of support. Other concepts and generalizations, while confirmed by some buttressing evidence, still do not command the full support of all the competent students of society. Where there is still some doubt about their validity, the tentative conclusions must be recognized and deliberately pointed out in the text of the materials. Those which have been established by history should have all the supporting evidence in place.

With regard to the hypothetical concepts, they too must be brought into the school, but must be presented as hypotheses, with all evidence for and against included. They must be introduced as questions and treated as problems for investigation and thorough discussion of all sides. These are the concepts which frighten the timid soul and enrage the representatives of special interest groups which feel that they are being attacked.

Thus it seems to us that the distinction between fact and theory, history and hypothesis, becomes increasingly clear to young people if so presented in the materials for study.

SHALL WE HAVE CONTROVERSIAL ISSUES IN THE SCHOOLS?

Another example of the content that the patrioteers will not permit in the schools is that which deals with controversial issues and problems. It is my thesis that if we are to have consent in a democratic people it must be built upon the study of controversial issues, because such study is the intellectual foundation of the schools. One of the chief planks of my program is that the young people shall be urged constantly to *take thought before they take sides,* but it is obvious that to "take thought," to make choices, they must confront the alternatives set out clearly before them. How else can human beings practice decision-making than by confronting issues! *To keep issues out of the school program is to keep thought out of it.* Issues are the very nub of the psychology of consent. Indeed, the psychology of learning inevitably leads to the conclusion that the whole intellectual program of the school must be organized around issues if the school itself is to be a practicing democracy.

Of course, I am not unmindful of the fact that most human events are to a certain extent episodes in censorship. The very nature of the development of personality in social groups tends to bring that about. The culture itself, by virtue of the child's membership in certain face-to-face groups (such as being born into a family of given political-economical-social-religious orientation, and growing up in similarly "censored" play groups, school and church groups, what-not)— the culture itself, I say, presents to him a definitely censored world. But this is naïve censorship, the kind of limitation which in inherent in heterogeneous groups of multitudinous and varied pressures.

We recognize also that there is a kind of conscious, deliberate censorship in times of crisis, which can be justified as being "in the public interest." It is imposed for the public good by officials elected for the purpose. They are subject to recall by the general body of electors whenever the need disappears. This kind of deliberate censorship is not opposed to democratic government in action, though its constructive usefulness does depend upon the wisdom, competence, and honesty and personal disinterestedness of the censors.

CENSORSHIP AND SOCIAL DANGER

Finally a brief word about the question of censorship. Let us not fail to discriminate clearly between censorship and the proper expression of the opinions of any group of our people concerning what shall be taught in the schools. There is no opposition to the latter; in fact, active interest and expression on the part of all citizens in the education of their children should be encouraged. I hold that true democracy can not be carried on unless such expression is actually heard from all sectors of the population. From *all sectors,* I repeat. Throughout twenty years of making new social science materials for the schools this has been my guiding principle.

But to censor is to withhold. It is for one sector of the population, by virtue of its prestige and power, and hence its control over the agencies of communication, to withhold data needed for the total group to carry on social life efficiently and cooperatively. Whereas to propagandize is positively to *distort* the data that are necessary for group decisions and the enhancement of social welfare, to censor is to withhold such data altogether. As Lippmann has well phrased it: it is to erect a barrier between the event and the public. It is to transform a public event into a private one. It is the artificial creation of privacy.

THE TRULY SUBVERSIVE ENEMIES OF DEMOCRACY

But for minority groups to attempt to censor the citizen's world in a democratic society, and particularly in a time of crisis, is a matter fraught with great danger. It is to destroy the only instrument which can make democracy work. So I say to the self-appointed censors of education: Censor the schools and you convict yourselves by your very acts as the most subversive enemies of democracy. Censor education and you destroy understanding . . . you instate bias . . . you give free reign to prejudice . . . finally, you create fascism. Nothing but an education in the whole of American life will build tolerant understanding in our people and guarantee the perpetuation of democracy.

In over twenty years' service as reporter and editor of education news for the *New York Times,* Benjamin Fine had an extraordinary opportunity to observe the ebb and flow of censorship activities in the nation's school system. In touch with the leading American educators, a participant in innumerable educational conferences, and fully informed of educational trends, Dr. Fine was in an almost unique position to analyze and evaluate the motives of the censors, public and private, individual and organized. Here he sums up his observations.

Benjamin Fine
THE TRUTH
ABOUT SCHOOLBOOK
CENSORSHIP

Our school and college textbooks are under fire. In all parts of the land, widespread attacks are being made on books and other classroom materials.

Books that have been used for a quarter of a century or more suddenly become "subversive." Books written by men or women who are on so-called "un-American" lists are tossed from the public libraries. Superpatriotic groups, professional agitators, opportunists and those who hate our democratic way of life are smearing scholarly books by below-the-belt name-calling.

What is "subversive"? One critic objects to a text because it praises the Tennessee Valley Authority; another says all economics books favor the New Deal. A third dissenter opposes the use of the term "free public schools" and still another finds a text objectionable because the nation is described as a democracy instead of a republic.

Label all books, the censors urge. Not long ago the Montclair, N. J., Chapter of the Sons of the American Revolution put pressure on the libraries of New Jersey to place a label on publications which advocate communism or are issued by "un-American" groups. These books would not be available for general circulation. Last fall the president of Fairmont, W. Va., State College met with the Marion County Antisubversive League. The Committee demanded that he label all periodicals received by the college library which were listed in the House Committee on un-American Activities' "Guide to Subversive Organizations and Publications."

Self-appointed committees are being organized to serve as censors. You and your children are at the mercy of these book vigilantes. Timid school board members or superintendents often run for cover at the least sign of trouble. Call a

---

Benjamin Fine, "The Truth about Schoolbook Censorship," *Parents' Magazine,* 27:46+ (December, 1952), copyright 1952 by The Parents' Institute, Inc. Reprinted by permission of the author and of the publisher.

book subversive, communistic, socialistic or un-American long enough and honest citizens will become confused, too.

Take the case of "American Government" written thirty-five years ago by Frank Magruder, the most widely used history text for three decades. On July 15, 1949, a review appeared in *The Educational Reviewer,* published by the Committee on Education of the Conference of American Small Business Organizations. The reviewer said the book had socialistic and communistic overtones. Passages were taken out of context and distorted to prove how "dangerous" the book was.

After radio commentators picked up the review, things began to happen fast. The state of Georgia dropped the book—but agreed to sell the 30,000 copies it had on hand to the highest bidder. Houston, Texas, banned the book; Little Rock, Arkansas, dropped it as a text but retained it for reference. New Haven, Conn.; Council Bluffs, Iowa; Washington, D. C.; Jackson, Mich., and Trumbull County, Ohio, to name just a few communities, felt the lash of the Magruder critics. Probably not one in a hundred actually read the book, or had even seen a copy. But all the same, the smell of blood was scented, and the wolf pack sought out its victims.

Many communities fought back. New Haven's Board of Education appointed a committee of twenty teachers to examine the Magruder text—and gave it a clean bill of health. Council Bluffs recommended that the book be retained. So did Trumbull County. The Florida department of education found the book "objective, accurate and fair." But despite the appraisals by numerous lay and professional committees, Magruder is in for continuing attacks.

Other books are getting the poison-smear treatment, too. Consider what happened to "Basic Economics," written by four reputable Rutgers University professors. This book was first condemned by a corporal in an anonymous letter to the Phoenix, Arizona, *Gazette.* The letter writer demanded that it be dropped from Phoenix College. A committee of the local American Legion post examined the book and agreed that it was "socialistically and communistically inclined." The Legion urged that the book be dropped.

An Alice-in-Wonderland struggle took place. The book was approved by the Phoenix Board of Education and upheld by the college president and the school superintendent. A public meeting was held to discuss the merits of the book. So heated had the issue become that the public auditorium was filled. At the hearing a letter signed by the four "Basic Economics" authors—Anatol Murad, Monroe Berkowitz, William C. Bagley and Broadus Mitchell—was read. The writers said, in part:

"The author (of the anonymous letter) accuses himself by admitting that he had not read the book; he merely 'glanced through' a text of 500 pages which was prepared to be studied for a semester. Are we to be discredited by the rash complaint of an anonymous person who had 'glanced' at the pages that required years of training and experience, and months of composition, on our part?"

You can't blame the Rutgers professors for being distressed. Their book, in its first year, had been adopted by forty colleges and universities. It was considered educationally sound, academically scholarly. But one poison-pen smear was enough to label it "subversive."

It seems incredible that we, American citizens, can be swept away by this hysteria. We are afraid to trust our good judgment, and some people do not trust the democratic way. It is not often that a community engages in actual book-burning, à la Hitler or Stalin, but Sapulpa, Oklahoma, proved what fear could do to us. A woman's civic group picked out a number of books from the Sapulpa High School library and tossed them into a blazing fire. The books, the ladies said, were bad because they "used improper language in the presentation of ideas." Besides, they sounded pretty socialistic.

The growth of textbook censorship is causing our leading educators serious concern. School librarians, school principals and superintendents are intimidated. Unwilling to risk their jobs or risk a public controversy, they quietly fold their tents and sneak away from their own ideals. The self-appointed censors often are able to win without firing a shot.

It's not easy when you are on the firing line. School boards are constantly attacked for being "soft" toward communism, for permitting books written by fellow travelers into the classroom. To show the community they are on the job, they start a campaign of their own or follow the lead of the censors. That's the serious problem we now face. The anti-intellectual campaign is a major threat to our democratic society.

In the words of Dr. David K. Berninghausen, for many years chairman of the American Library Association's Committee on Intellectual Freedom, "Copying the Nazis or the Communists in thought control techniques in communications and education is not the way to meet our problem. The antidote to authoritarianism is not some form of American authoritarianism. The antidote is free inquiry."

In a democratic land, all of us have the right to voice our opinion, to criticize a book or anything else, if we so desire. But that criticism should be honest and informed.

You may wonder what assurance you have that the textbooks your child uses are not subversive? Be reassured; hardly a product in the land is so carefully scrutinized as are textbooks. Publishers, editors, textbook selection committees, the teachers who use the books and those who review them, all go over them carefully. Is it reasonable to believe that this cumulative screening would miss subversive, communistic or un-American passages in our textbooks?

Textbook censorship is poisoning America's free spirit, warns Dr. Luther H. Evans, Librarian of Congress. "The experts in vituperation, the sadists of freedom, are abroad in the land, and are having a heyday. We must learn not to fear them. We must show them up for what they are. They are cowards who are unwilling to live the American dream."

Who are these cowards referred to by Dr. Evans? Some are the superpatriots who get excited about books they have never read—but that someone else has charged with being dangerous or subversive. Or they may be organized complainers eager to exploit the present tension for financial or political gains. They may even be professional agitators, who do not like America, and would make it over in their own unwholesome image.

Yet there are many conscientious, honest, decent parents and citizens in the country who are concerned, too. They have heard much wrangling, and have seen mud fly. And they are wondering what is happening, and if they can be certain that the charges are based on fact. They are genuinely puzzled.

It should reassure them to know that every community has some form of screening plan. Half the states have uniform textbook commissions, while the rest have local committees that examine all textbooks. Since the books are usually used by all the states, if one community would miss a "subversive" passage, another would catch it soon enough.

Here are examples of the way textbook commissions operate:

Oklahoma—The State Textbook Committee is composed of nine active members, none of whom may succeed themselves, appointed for four year terms by the governor. Each member of the committee has an advisory group which reviews the books. Not more than five books may be chosen in any one subject; the list goes to local textbook committees in each school district in the state. These local committees are composed of not less than five nor more than nine teachers; they may adopt the book they want for a period of six years.

Mississippi—The State Superintendent of Education appoints a professional committee to evaluate textbooks. The committee recommends at least three textbooks to the State Textbook Purchasing Board. The board then selects one of the three books receiving the highest evaluation. Both the committee and the textbook purchasing board analyze the books thoroughly.

Texas—A 21-member State Board of Education, elected by popular vote, appoints a 15-member State Textbook Committee. The committee is composed of educators actively engaged in teaching in the Texas public schools. The committee makes its recommendations to the commissioner.

About half the states have local screening boards. In Ohio the selection of textbooks is the function of the local boards of education. In Montana the textbooks in the local schools are selected by the school board and the administrators. In Massachusetts the selection of books is left to the local school boards. The New Jersey State Board of Education recommends that local school boards approve all textbooks before they are put in the classrooms.

Whether the textbooks are screened by state or local committees, the job is unusually thorough. But that is not enough to satisfy the professional agitators, the superpatriots. They see a communist plot on every page.

What can be done about it? New York State is supplying one answer. Recent resolutions by state groups such as the D.A.R., the American Legion and the Federation of Women's Clubs charged that the schools were using textbooks containing subversive, socialistic and un-American material. By action of the State Board of Regents, Commissioner Lewis A. Wilson appointed a three-man commission, consisting of himself, as Commissioner of Education, and two lay persons of considerable prestige, educational background and respect in the community. Now any person can send whatever complaints he may have to the Commission. Established last January, the textbook commission has been widely publicized. Yet at this writing, *not a single complaint has been filed.*

Remember, freedom of thought has always been the landmark of the American way of life. We should not accept the rantings of insecure agitators. You can help keep our country free by being alert and well informed. Freedom from arbitrary censorship is one of our basic freedoms.

In its usual gently satirical vein, the *New Yorker* "Notes and Comments" department goes to the heart of the textbook-selection controversy. Only a few short paragraphs are needed to expose the fallacious, specious reasoning upon which the New York City Board of Education's censorship policies are based.

The "New Yorker" COMMENTS ON NEW YORK TEXTBOOK CENSORSHIP

The Board of Education has twenty-three criteria for selecting textbooks, library books, and magazines for use in the public schools. We learned this by reading a fourteen-page pamphlet published by the Board explaining how it makes its choice. One criterion is: "Is it [the book or magazine] free from subject matter that tends to irreverence for things held sacred?" Another

"Comments on New York Textbook Censorship," Editorial "Notes and Comments," *New Yorker,* 25:19 (October 9, 1949), copyright © 1949 The New Yorker Magazine, Inc. Reprinted by permission of the publisher.

criterion is: "Are both sides of controversial issues presented with fairness?" Another: "Is it free from objectionable slang expressions which will interfere with the building of good language habits?"

These three criteria by themselves are enough to keep a lot of good books from the schools. Irreverence for things held sacred has started many a writer on his way, and will again. An author so little moved by a controversy that he can present both sides fairly is not likely to burn any holes in the paper. We think the way for school children to get both sides of a controversy is to read several books on the subject, not one. In other words, we think the Board should strive for a well-balanced library, not a well-balanced book. The greatest books are heavily slanted, by the nature of greatness.

As for "the building of good language habits," we have gone carefully through the pamphlet to see what habits, if any, the Board itself has formed. They appear to be the usual ones—the habit of untidiness, the habit of ambiguity, the habit of saying everything the hard way. The clumsy phrase, the impenetrable sentence, the cliché, the misspelled word. The Board has, we gather, no strong convictions about the use of the serial comma, no grip on "that" and "which," no opinion about whether a textbook is a "text book," a "text-book," or a "textbook." (The score at the end of the fourteenth was "text book" 5, "text-book" 11, "textbook" 5.) It sees nothing comical, or challenging, in the sentence "Materials should be provided for boys and girls who vary greatly in attitudes, abilities, interests, and mental age." It sees no need for transposition in "Phrases should not be split in captions under pictures." It sees no bugs in "The number of lines should be most conducive to readability." And you should excuse the expression "bugs"—a slang word, interfering with the building of good language habits.

We still have high hopes of getting *The New Yorker* accepted in the schools, but our hopes are less high than they were when we picked up the pamphlet. We're bucking some stiff criteria —criteria that are, shall we say, time-tested?

Illustrative of the application in practice of the rules adopted by the New York City Board of Education—and so tellingly stripped bare by the

New Yorker's comments—was "'The Nation' Case." Here Professor Archibald W. Anderson, of the University of Illinois, traces the history of one of the most widely publicized instances of censorship in the public schools.

Archibald W. Anderson
"THE NATION" CASE

On June 8, 1948, the Board of Superintendents of the New York City school system eliminated *The Nation* from the official list of periodicals approved for libraries in the public high schools of the city. This action precipitated a controversy, not yet settled, which has been marked by a considerable amount of bitterness and confusion.

The educator who lives away from the scene of conflict, and who is dependent upon occasional and partial accounts in newspapers and magazines for information, frequently has had difficulty in learning what the exact nature of the controversy is. The judgment which the individual educator ultimately makes about the action of the Board of Superintendents will, of course, be colored by many things: the facts in the case, the interpretation and relative weight he attaches to the facts, his social philosophy, the functions he considers appropriate or essential for education to carry on, and others. These various matters will have significance in affecting ultimate judgment only as they are brought to bear upon the basic issues at stake. Clarity about such issues, therefore, is a primary requisite for intelligent judgment. Unfortunately, just what these basic issues are is itself a matter of controversy.

The issues as seen by the Board of Superintendents are presented in a printed pamphlet, *Should Religious Beliefs Be Studied and Criticized in an American Public High School?*, written by William Jansen, Superintendent of Schools, City of New York, and issued by the Board of Superintendents on October 1, 1948. The intent of this pamphlet is "to do away with the misrepresentations and evasions that have prevented the friends of public education from seeing the real issue."

The issues as seen by those on the other side of the controversy are presented in a *Brief Amicus Curiae,* submitted to the Commissioner of Education of New York State by Archibald MacLeish on behalf of "a Number of Individuals and Organizations Who Have Protested the Action of the Board of Superintendents in This Case." This statement also is intended to clarify the "real issue" and to counter efforts to confuse it or to raise false issues.

These two documents are in fundamental disagreement as to what issues are raised by the action of the Board of Superintendents in banning *The Nation*. The teaching profession, however, cannot afford to let the matter thus rest in confusion. It is obvious that when reading materials are excluded from school libraries fundamental questions of educational and public policy are involved. These questions go deeper than the specific incident and have wider implications than the selection of library materials. They are questions having to do with the role of education in a democracy, the methods and materials for carrying on that education, the bases for selecting such methods and materials, and the agencies of selection. These questions are of vital importance to the teaching profession because the answers to them define the function of the profession in our society. In an effort to throw light upon these more fundamental questions, as well as upon the specific issues in the present case, the remainder of this article is devoted to an analysis of the points of disagreement in the two documents containing the statements of the parties to the controversy.

THE GENESIS OF THE CONTROVERSY.

Between November 1, 1947, and June 5, 1948, *The Nation* published a series of articles on the Catholic Church written by Paul Blanshard. Because one factor in the controversy is the charge that opponents to the banning of *The Nation* have suppressed the titles of some articles in describing the series, the complete lists of titles is given here: 1. "The Roman Catholic Church in Medicine"; 2. "The Sexual Code of the Roman Catholic Church"; 3. "The Roman Catholic Church and the Schools"; 4. "The Roman Catholic Church and Fascism"; 5. "The Roman Catholic Church and Fascism";

Archibald W. Anderson, "'The Nation' Case," *Progressive Education,* 26:151–57 (March, 1949), copyright 1949 by American Education Fellowship. Reprinted (without footnotes) by permission of the author and of the publisher.

354 The schools under attack

6. "The Roman Catholic Church and Fascism"; 7. "Roman Catholic Censorship"; 8. "Roman Catholic Censorship"; 9. "Roman Catholic Science I. Relics, Saints, and Miracles"; 10. "Roman Catholic Science II. Apparitions and Evolution"; 11. "The Catholic Church and American Democracy"; 12. "The Catholic Church and American Democracy."

On April 20, 1948, the Board of Superintendents discussed the articles which had appeared by that date. Because it felt that Blanshard had gone beyond the discussion of the topics indicated by the titles to articles 1 through 5 and had "introduced a discussion of religious questions," the Board authorized high school principals "to withdraw from circulation any issue containing criticism of religious practices." After another discussion on June 1, the Board voted, on June 8, to eliminate *The Nation* from the list of approved publications on the grounds that articles 9 and 10 ". . . did *not* deal with the policies of the Roman Catholic Church with respect to public questions. Those two articles are devoted to a criticism of Catholic beliefs, dogmas, and religious practices. Catholic beliefs and religious practices are not only criticized but are ridiculed by innuendo."

When the Board's action became publicly known, a temporary "Ad Hoc Committee" was established for the purpose of opposing the ban. This committee which represented 34 organizations and 72 individuals, issued a statement of its position entitled *An Appeal to Reason and Conscience*. One hundred and seven persons authorized the use of their names as signers of the *Appeal* and 56 others later endorsed it. The total group has been characterized as follows:

> Included are a former President of the New York Board of Education who is also one of the leaders of the New York Bar; eight of the country's leading lawyers: among them the acknowledged American authority on freedom of the press; five Professors of Law; the country's foremost theologian; a former Under-Secretary of State; twenty-one presidents of universities and institutions of higher learning; seventeen Professors, including four historians; twenty-one religious leaders of various denominations including six Bishops; nineteen writers of established reputation; seven educators; seventeen editors and publishers.

In reply, the Superintendent of Schools submitted the statement already mentioned to the signers on the grounds that the case had been misrepresented and that they had signed the *Appeal* in ignorance of the facts or under a misapprehension. He invited them to read his justification and to communicate with him. The temporary committee seconded this invitation and assisted in circulating the Superintendent's statement. So far as is known, none of the signers or endorsers of the protest altered his view as a result of the Superintendent's statement, and of the 33 who are known to have communicated with him, all reaffirmed their previous position. It was after these events that MacLeish prepared his *Brief Amicus Curiae* for submission to the New York State Commissioner of Education in support of the appeal which the publishers of *The Nation* had made to that official.

CONFLICTING STATEMENTS OF THE BASIC ISSUE.

The basic issue as seen by the Superintendent of Schools apparently is indicated by the title of his statement:

"Should Religious Beliefs Be Studied and Criticized in an American Public High School?"

The basic issue as seen in the *Brief Amicus Curiae* is presented as follows:

> The issue in this case is unusually clear and simple. It is: whether the action of the Board of Superintendents in excluding *The Nation* in the future from the high school libraries of the City of New York because *The Nation* had published in the past certain statements critical of the Catholic Church is or is not justifiable.

It seems clear that these two statements of the issue are not focussed on the same question. Which, if either, of the two statements lies closer to the heart of the controversy can be determined only after a fuller exploration of the positions presented in the two documents with which this article is concerned. It may be helpful, as a step in the direction of greater clarity about the basic issue, to see what the controversy is not about.

THE ISSUE IS NOT ONE BETWEEN CATHOLICS AND NON-CATHOLICS.

There is a clear implication in Jansen's statement that he feels that at least part of the protest was due to the mistaken belief that the Board's action was Catholic-inspired and was intended to protect the Catholic Church from all types of criticism. MacLeish's *Brief,* on the other hand, agrees that the Catholic Church did not take a part in the banning of *The Nation;* but he is equally insistent that the opposition to the ban was not inspired by hostility to the Catholic faith. There is, therefore, a general agreement between the two documents that, whatever else the controversy may be about, it is not over the question of Catholicism versus Anti-Catholicism. Pertinent quotations from both documents are presented below.

From the statement by the Superintendent of Schools:

> Readers of *The Nation* know that for years there have appeared in *The Nation* criticisms of the Catholic Church or the Catholic hierarchy for its stand or policy with respect to a number of problems. . . .
> *During all the years that these criticisms appeared in the columns of* The Nation *the Board of Superintendents took no action whatsoever concerning them, nor were* The Nation's *editorial policies so much as discussed by the Board of Superintendents.*
> It is obvious that these facts have an important bearing on the present controversy. *They constitute a prima-facie case for the pronouncement of the Board of Superintendents that* The Nation *was not eliminated because it criticized the political and social policies of the Roman Catholic Church.* It is taken for granted that when the Catholic hierarchy or any other organization takes a stand on public issues, its policies and points of view are open to legitimate criticism. . . .
> *Throughout all the years in which criticism of Catholic policies appeared in* The Nation, *the Catholic hierarchy did not try to influence the Board of Superintendents. It is a fact that neither directly nor indirectly has a single member of the Board of Superintendents been asked by anyone representing or pretending to represent the hierarchy, to eliminate* The Nation.

From the *Brief Amicus Curiae*:

> Clear and simple as the issue is, however, efforts have been made to confuse it. One, and the most unworthy, is the effort to suggest or imply that the issue is really one between Catholics and non-Catholics. It is not—as *The Appeal to Reason and Conscience* makes clear. There are Catholics among those who have protested the action of the Board, and none of the signers, as the *Appeal* declares, "have been moved to protest by reason of hostility to the Catholic faith." The Superintendent has insisted, and certainly with reason, that the Catholic Church took no part in the imposition of the ban on *The Nation*. There is no reason to suppose that representatives of that Church approve the ban any more than representatives of other churches.

IS THE STUDY OF RELIGIOUS
CONTROVERSY AN ISSUE?

The statement by Superintendent Jansen gives grounds for believing that the Board of Superintendents feels that the question of whether religious controversy should be studied in school is one of the issues in the controversy. This is implied by the title of the Superintendent's statement. It is more explicitly stated in the sentence, "The Board of Superintendents is of the opinion that it is contrary to the American public-school tradition to bring religious controversies into the classrooms of the public schools."

MacLeish and those associated with him reject this as a valid issue. The *Brief* states:

> The second effort to cloud the issue has been made by those who have attempted to confuse the real question in litigation with the wholly unrelated question of the teaching of religious controversy in schools. The Superintendent himself has been primarily responsible for this distortion. This effort to substitute a straw man for the real figure in the controversy was sharply challenged by three of those who accepted the Superintendent's invitation to comment on his defense of the Board's action.

MacLeish quotes from a letter by Lewis Mumford, who after quoting the title of Jansen's statement, says:

> That is possibly a very important question; but it has nothing whatever to do with *The Nation* articles or with school libraries. *The Nation* is not a textbook; nor were the articles on the Roman Catholic Church required reading in any public school classes; nor did Mr. Blanshard, the author of these articles, propose that religious beliefs should be studied and criticized in our public schools. Hence your question is worse than irrelevant: for it can serve no other purpose than to mislead the casual reader on the question at issue.

IS CENSORSHIP OF THE
PRESS AN ISSUE?

The quotation from Jansen's statement already presented in the section of this article entitled, "The Genesis of the Controversy," indicated that *The Nation* was banned because of the two articles dealing with "Roman Catholic Science." The statement quoted a number of passages from the articles in support of the contention that they were critical of religious beliefs and practices. It is on the basis of this contention that the Board claims justification for banning the magazine rather than withdrawing the particular issues in which the articles appeared:

> The question of whether or not to adhere to this policy was discussed in the Board of Superintendents. It was decided that this policy of withdrawing single issues could no longer apply in the case of *The Nation*. It was obvious that, with the publication of the two articles referred to, the editorial policy of *The Nation*

had been modified to permit the publication of articles that are an attack on the Catholic religion.

If, after the publication of these two articles, *The Nation* were continued on the list of authorized publications, the Board of Superintendents would have to direct the principal of each school subscribing to have each issue of *The Nation* reviewed before permitting its circulation in the library. The Board of Superintendents does not care to list publications that require a scrutiny of this kind.

Jansen defended this action of the Board from the charge of censorship on the grounds that the Board was exercising its right and duty to supervise the reading material of pupils:

It was to be expected that the cry of censorship would be raised. The term is useful for name-calling purposes. But obviously, the Board of Superintendents does not want to censor *The Nation*. As far as the Board is concerned, the editor of *The Nation must not permit herself to believe that* she will determine what shall be read in the high schools of New York City. It is the Board of Superintendents that has the legal responsibility and duty to determine what books and magazines are to be used. If this is censorship, then well and good.

Every responsible citizen realizes that somewhere in a school system, large or small, there must be placed squarely on the shoulders of an individual or of members of a board, the difficult business of selecting reading material for the students. The only fair demand the public can make is that the responsible individual state what standards he applies in making his decisions. Such standards were promulgated some time ago by the Board of Superintendents. Two of these standards stated in question form read as follows:

Does the book contain any derogatory statements concerning racial or religious groups? Does the book contain matter which is so interwoven into the text as to give rise to misunderstanding and prejudice?

These statements by Jansen deal with two major questions: (1) Whether the elimination of a magazine from school libraries constitutes censorship of the press; and (2) whether the printing of religious criticism is an adequate basis for such elimination. The statements from MacLeish's *Brief* dealing with the first question will be presented in this section of the present article. Those dealing with the second question will be presented in the next section.

MacLeish regards the action of the Board as an unjustifiable act of censorship and sees in it a threat to freedom of the press. Because of space limitations, it is impossible to present his statements in its entirety but the following paragraphs give the gist of his position:

In his defense of the Board's action, the Superintendent of Schools attempts to justify the exclusion from high school libraries of future issues of *The Nation* on the ground that *The Nation* published twenty-one sentences which he finds objectionable and which he quotes. *The Nation* was founded in 1865. It has been published continuously ever since. It has a long record of serious, and, most of us think, responsible and distinguished journalism. It has been available to students in the high school libraries of New York City since 1937. But because twenty-one sentences which the Board finds objectionable were published in two articles it is now stigmatized as no longer fit to be read by high school students, and future issues are ordered excluded. It is a serious thing to stigmatize a publication as unfit for use by students in public schools. A precedent which would permit public officials, in their wholly extra-judicial discretion, thus to punish a periodical, a newspaper or a publishing house for a specific past publication involves, as we declared in our *Appeal,* a grant of "a power of intimidation and possible blackmail . . . which no free society can tolerate and which a free press could not long survive." From the suppression of *The Nation* for publishing twenty-one sentences which the Board finds objectionable, to the suppression of the *New York Times* or the *New York Mirror* or the *New York Star* for the publication of twenty-one sentences—or nineteen, or twelve or seven or one—is not a long step.

There is no reason why so dangerous a rule should have been adopted by the Board in the first place, and even less why it should be now approved. Nothing is more firmly established by the courts than the contrary rule that the suppression of a publication, for whatever reason, can only be justified on the basis of *a consideration of the publication as a whole.* The fact that the standards of selection for high school libraries differ in certain ways from the standards of selection for general libraries does not mean that civil rights can be disregarded in high school libraries, that the rights of authors and publishers cease to exist, that the rights of readers may be disregarded or that capricious and arbitrary action can be justified. It is as important to preserve the institutions of a free society in the schools as elsewhere. . . .

IS THE CRITICISM OF RELIGIOUS BELIEFS AN ISSUE?

The quotations from Jansen's statement already presented make clear that he and the Board of Superintendents regard the question of whether religious beliefs have been questioned as one of the fundamental issues in the controversy. Furthermore, they have explicitly stated that the publishing of such criticism is a valid basis for keeping periodicals or other materials out of the schools.

MacLeish and others whom he quotes in his *Brief* have approached this question of the place, or lack of place, of religious criticism in schools in several ways. MacLeish, himself, has taken the position that the basis of the exclusion, as stated, is too sweeping and would have undesirable and unexpected effects:

> Since the word "criticism" is not qualified, the intention must be understood to be to exclude from New York City school libraries henceforward all books, periodicals and newspapers which contain criticism of religious beliefs of any kind, whether true or false, whether responsible or irresponsible, whether honest or partisan.

It is difficult to believe that this threatening and intemperate statement was carefully weighed or fully understood by its author. We have indicated in our *Appeal to Reason and Conscience* what the effect of such a ruling would be in the fields of literature and history. Not only would the whole American Puritan tradition vanish from the shelves of high school libraries but the founders of the Republic themselves would be bowdlerized or silenced.

Some of those whose letters are quoted by MacLeish raise the questions of (1) just how "criticism of religious beliefs" is to be defined, and (2) whether the examination of such criticism is not, after all, a part of the educative process. The following two quotations are typical of this approach:

Alexander Meiklejohn, former President of Amherst College, philosopher and educator:

> I fully agree with your contention that exclusion of a book from a reading list may not be an act of censorship.... But your action against The Nation, taken on the grounds which you give is, I, am sure, censorship in an objectionable sense....
> First, in the field of education, the fact that reading contains "derogatory statements concerning racial or religious groups" does not give proper ground for exclusion. The purpose of education is not served by keeping such groups free from legitimate and reasonable criticism. The meeting of such criticism, whether of one's own beliefs or those of others, is an essential feature of the education of a young American.
> Second, education requires not that pupils be kept safe from statements which "give rise to misunderstanding and prejudice," but that they learn how to deal with those statements fearlessly and reasonably.

The Right Reverend Edward L. Parsons, Retired Bishop of California:

> One must recognize that on the surface there would seem to be a distinction between the articles in The Nation which discussed the Roman Catholic Church's position on political questions and the like, and those dealing with science.
> The distinction is however not fundamentally valid. It is quite proper as a matter of public policy to keep out of the school libraries journals or books which are frankly denominational, or those which make a business of attacking other religious faiths, but if we are to have educated and intelligent citizens it is of first importance that they should learn to think for themselves. In order to think for themselves they must know something of the way in which their particular religious beliefs cut across and make impact upon the ordinary culture of the society in which they live. Science plays too large a part in modern life to be left out as a part of that culture. If high school boys and girls are old enough and intelligent enough to use journals like The Nation for help in political or economic questions they ought to know what a competent writer may have to say about the relation of their religion to such questions as Mr. Blanshard discussed, or to any others. I should myself be sorry to think that any young people of my own Church were to be protected from knowing what other people might think of the position of that Church upon any question, whether social, political, economic or scientific. In one sense there is here an issue of freedom, but in my judgment it is primarily a question of what kind of American citizens we want.

IS THE STUDY OF ANY CONTROVERSIAL PROBLEM AN ISSUE?

Other than to state that as long as *The Nation* confined itself to political, economic and social criticism it was admitted to the approved list, Jansen's pamphlet did not deal with the implications of the ban on *The Nation* for other subjects of study. A number of those quoted in the MacLeish brief, however, were concerned with those implications. These writers felt that a logical application of the principle upon which this particular magazine was excluded would jeopardize not only the study of our most important historical traditions but also any consideration of the most vital contemporary problems, many of which are admittedly of a controversial nature. In a sense, the point raised is similar to that raised by the quotations in the preceding section, namely, the question of the difficulty of drawing a line between religious and non-religious controversy. This position is brought out in the following statements quoted in MacLeish's *Brief:*

Mr. Nathan Frankel, in his reply to the Superintendent:

> If you really wanted to apply this principle in practice, you would have to eliminate all courses in the history of medieval and modern Europe. This history abounds in highly controversial facts and faiths, creeds and opinions, all pertaining to religion. What is the sale of indulgences, Luther's theses at Wittenberg, Galileo, Savonarola, the Inquisition? Is a discussion of the sale of relics in the Twentieth Century less a fact of life and history than the sale of indulgences in the Sixteenth Century? Or is it the current educational standard of your Board that pupils are scrupulously to be kept in ignorance of the facts and doctrines, beliefs and opinions of their own generation?

358 The schools under attack

Walter Gellhorn, Professor of Law, Columbia University:

In the final analysis I suppose that it is one of education's chief aims to stimulate reexamination and reevaluation of ideas and beliefs which we might otherwise never appraise. In this connection I am troubled by your concluding assertion that "the Board will continue to see to it that there shall be no criticism of the religious beliefs of any groups in the schools of New York City." If this statement be taken at face value, you seem to suggest that criticism of any view which its holders choose to describe as "religious" is to be forbidden, without reference to its reasonableness, thoughtfulness, or purpose.

Professor H. Gordon Hullfish, The Ohio State University:

We live in a world of controversy and will continue to do so so long as we remain true to our heritage. Our educational task is to help young people live within that world with a maximum of independence. This task cannot be accomplished by withdrawing them from the presence of controversy. Quite the contrary is the case. A school is the one place in this culture where controversy may be met head-on under educative conditions. If this opportunity is denied in connection with religion, it may then be denied in connection with every issue on the horizon. Our schools will then have gone out of business so far as preparing young people to live as citizens in a free world is concerned.

IS THE NATURE OF DEMOCRATIC EDUCATION AN ISSUE?

One of the principal defenses advanced by Jansen is that the Board's action upholds the American tradition of the proper role of public education. He states:

> Every responsible school superintendent and every responsible Board of Education will state that criticism of religious beliefs should not be carried on by our teachers or pupils because the American public school is and always must be a unifying factor in American life.

The concluding paragraph in the pamphlet reiterates this allegiance to the traditions of the function of American education in American life:

> The Board of Superintendents issues this statement because it is necessary to do away with the misrepresentations and evasions that have prevented the friends of public education from seeing the real issue. Once the facts are known, the action taken by the Board of Superintendents must be considered not only right but necessary. That action is in accord with the highest traditions of public education in America. Guided by those traditions, the Board will continue to see to it that there shall be no criticism of the religious beliefs of any groups in the schools of New York City.

These paragraphs must be regarded as significant because they attempt to ground the Board's specific action not in a specific set of circumstances but upon a fundamental conception of the nature, purpose, and function of education in American democracy. They move, therefore, toward a revelation of those fundamental questions which, as indicated in the introductory section of this article, seem to be beneath the more obvious issues.

The whole tenor of the *Brief Amicus Curiae* indicates that MacLeish and his associates are equally willing to ground a judgment of the Board's action upon American tradition and upon a fundamental conception of the role of American education. Their reading of that tradition and their conception of that role, however, are markedly different from that contained in the Jansen statement. MacLeish's own position is:

> As we stated at the beginning of this Brief, what gives us concern in this whole matter is not so much the arbitrary and unconscionable banning of *The Nation*, as it is the general practice of the Board which the banning of *The Nation* reveals. Even if it is granted, for the purposes of argument, that the twenty-one sentences to which the Superintendent takes exception were sentences so insidiously corrupting in their effect on immature minds that immature minds could not be trusted to judge them for themselves—an assumption difficult to defend—it would hardly follow that the proper method of dealing with such a situation was to put *The Nation* on an index expurgatorius of publications which the school libraries are forbidden to contain.
>
> Lists of forbidden books, whether established affirmatively or negatively, are wholly foreign to the American tradition of individual responsibility and individual dignity, resting as it does on freedom of mind and freedom in inquiry.

The conception of education which seems in keeping with general thought of the *Brief* has been indicated by some of the quotations already presented. The relation of that conception to the American tradition is brought out in the following quotation from the statement of the Executive Committee of the National Society of College Teachers of Education:

> The action of the Board is an attack upon democratic education, a primary obligation of which is the right of the individual to learn. It is an established and fundamental principle that only as boys and girls have an opportunity to study all aspects of controversial issues and thus come to their own conclusions on

the basis of fact and logic can they become responsible men and women in a free society. The long accepted and cherished ideal of the American people is that the way to defeat a wrong idea is to have a sounder and better one, but not to suppress those ideas with which we disagree, even though they may be questionable or debatable. Abandonment of this principle is a first step on the path to the suppression of academic freedom, and toward thought-control, and finally the denial of all types of democratic freedom.

In concluding the *Brief,* MacLeish dealt with the question, raised by Jansen, of making the school a unifying force in American life. MacLeish's statement is:

There remains, of the Superintendent's argument, therefore, only the defense that the duty of the schools to unify American life justifies the exclusion from school libraries of periodicals which contain "criticism of the religious beliefs of any groups." . . . The Superintendent is to be congratulated on his concern for unification. But he should recall that the reason most commonly given for infringement of individual liberties in totalitarian states is precisely the argument that it is necessary to silence certain opinions in order to unify the people. In a free society the freedom of the individual, and the responsibility for individual inquiry and individual decision which accompanies that freedom, come *first.* They can never be sacrificed to other considerations, however worthy, without endangering the essential character of the society itself.

Mr. Lewis Mumford, in his letter to the Superintendent which has been cited above, replies to this argument of the overriding importance of unification in the following words:

"Before you irrevocably commit yourself to this kind of censorship, I beg you to consider the full implications of your policy. There are two methods of achieving unity in any society: one is by suppression of differences; the other is by the cooperative pursuit of common goals, which transcend the partialities and particularities of special interests. Precisely because the separation of Church and State rules out any kind of religious teaching in our schools, it is important that this great realm of human life should be open to the student's independent exploration. High religion need fear no form of open inquiry: the baser forms of religion, irrational dogma, superstition, empty taboo should in the interests of a healthy democracy be subject to fearless examination, if not in the classroom, then at least in the student's private study in the library. To have access to truth and reasonable opinion, even when established institutions are opposed to its expression, is the essential right of every citizen living under the Constitution of the United States of America; and to ensure this access is a duty of every public school in our land. There is no higher obligation in public education."

Robert Shaplen
SCARSDALE'S BATTLE OF THE BOOKS: HOW ONE COMMUNITY DEALT WITH "SUBVERSIVE LITERATURE"

"If one were to nominate the American community least likely to succumb to Communism, Westchester County's Scarsdale—affluent, Republican, sedate—would be a strong candidate. Indeed, one might expect that if—as many think—this country is infected with hysteria on the question of Communism, Scarsdale would be a quick victim. Here, however, is the story of what happened when a group of zealots tried to purge the school libraries of the works of Mr. Howard Fast, an acknowledged Communist—a case study from which our readers may be prompted to discover in what respect Scarsdale's experience and Scarsdale's pattern of community action contain a lesson for American communities. Robert Shaplen was formerly *Newsweek* correspondent in the Far East, and has written for the *New Yorker,* the *Progressive,* and other periodicals. His novel, *A Corner of the World,* was published in 1949 by Knopf." [Editorial note in *Commentator.*]

The community of Scarsdale, which lies approximately forty minutes north of New York City in fashionable Westchester County, likes to refer to itself, somewhat coyly, as "just a dormitory to Manhattan." As denizens of the wealthiest county in the State of New York, one of the richest per capita in the country, the 14,500 occupants of the dormitory voted five to one Republican in the last national election and pridefully claim the highest proportion of *Who's Who* listings of any incorporated locality in the United States. They are even prouder of their public school system, which, with those of neighboring Bronxville and Winnetka, Illinois, is rated the nation's best.

During the past two years, the chief topic in Scarsdale homes and on the trains to and from

---

Robert Shaplen, "Scarsdale's Battle of the Books: How One Community Dealt with 'Subversive Literature,'" *Commentary,* 10:530–40 (December, 1950), copyright 1950 by American Jewish Committee. Reprinted by permission of the author and of the publisher.

360 The schools under attack

Grand Central Terminal in New York has been the persevering, and hitherto unsuccessful, attempt of a small and indefatigable group to remove from the high school library and selected reading shelves a variety of works—novels, biographies, anthologies, and texts—declared to be subversive because they were written or edited by persons either known or alleged to have Communist leanings. This frenzied battle of the books has had several "climaxes." Probably the most significant occurred early this past summer when, at its final school-year meeting, the board of education, composed of prominent New York business and professional men and some wives, unanimously voted down the request of the village minority for a full-dress investigation of Communist infiltration of the entire Scarsdale school system. Previously, one bitter phase of the lengthy battle culminated last May in the annual election for school board members; more than ten times the usual number of voters turned out and in formal secret ballot registered their nearly 100 per cent disapproval of those who had questioned the board's handling of the book matter. Lately, as recently as October, the board has had occasion to reaffirm its position, in the face of a vocal and determined opposition.

Scarsdale's reaction to its crisis is in large part the result of the unique way in which the village administers all local affairs—including operation of the schools. The initial phase of the book battle, for example, had to do with the novels of Howard Fast, a man who had not denied his Communist party affiliations and who has a long record of supporting Communist front organizations. Despite a universal distaste for Communism, and with no particular affection for Fast or his books, the Scarsdalians nevertheless were prompted to keep eight of his works in the library not only because they deeply opposed any kind of book-burning, even in the coldest of cold wars, but chiefly because of a sense of outrage that anyone should have impugned their proven system of governing themselves; this includes the manner in which teachers, and hence books, have been selected, and the consequent way students have been taught to read and study.

The "Scarsdale system" goes back two decades, to the time when a group of local commuters decided to take full advantage of the fact that some of the nation's most skilful executives lived in their midst. What has since evolved is akin to the concept of the old New England town meeting, at which men were "tapped" for office after being deemed worthy by their peers. Both the Scarsdale village board and the school board are so chosen. Each consists of seven persons called "trustees," and while the former makes a political point of including two known Democrats, the non-partisan school board is made up strictly on the basis of professional capabilities. Whatever is needed—lawyer, doctor, engineer, or banker—Scarsdale dips into its reservoir of talent and comes up with it.

Being exceptionally civic-minded, perhaps because they are away all day earning their living in the noisome metropolis, the men of Scarsdale feel a special obligation to keep in touch with village life. Nine hundred of them belong to the Town Club, which has nineteen standing committees for the furtherance of everything from boy scout and girl scout programs to reading, swimming, safety, the gathering of regional lore, the affairs of local, county, and state government, and, above all, those having to do with Scarsdale's main concern—education. It is not unusual for a single subject—such as "Shall Scarsdale High School Offer a Course in Driver Education and Training?"—to occupy a committee of a dozen high-powered corporation officials over a period of months. The distaff counterpart of the Town Club is the Scarsdale Woman's Club. The heads of these two clubs, and of the Parent-Teacher Association Council, form the nucleus of a citizens' committee of fifteen which every year taps the men and women it wants for the school board. As with those similarly selected for mayor and other village posts, "no" is not taken for an answer; the designated persons are simply told their services are required by the community. The annual May election always administers a public stamp of approval.

About a year and a half ago a group calling itself the "Committee of Ten" addressed a private memorandum to the school board. The committee, which at that time listed only seven members, spoke fervently of the need for greater spiritual awareness in the classroom and implied, by the force of its appeal, that Scarsdale's schools were morally neglectful.

While this was the first declaration of the Committee of Ten, the man everyone in Scarsdale believed to be its organizer had been heard from before. He is Otto Dohrenwend, bespectacled Manhattan broker and father of four children; according to his wife, he has devoted much if not most of his time in the past four years to a meticulous study of Communist front organizations in America. Among his particular aids and guides, on the basis of what he has said and written, have been the Fourth Report on Un-American Activities in California, printed and submitted in 1948 to the California legislature by the so-called Tenney committee; the publications of the United States Chamber of Commerce, especially one called "A Program for Community Anti-Communist Action"; and the files of *Counterattack,* a bitter and frequently indiscriminate anti-Communist magazine partly written and edited by former FBI agents.

Even before the book battle-royal began, in the fall of 1948, Dohrenwend made a commotion because in a speech by the high school principal, Lester W. Nelson, a passing nonpolitical reference was made to the Harvard astronomer Harlow Shapley, who has supported many Communist front organizations and admittedly voted for Henry Wallace for President. (Nelson had spoken on "Current Trends in Higher Education" and had noted that Shapley was among those who favored more liberal arts training for scientists and technicians.) About the same time, at a fathers' meeting of the Fox Meadow elementary school PTA, Dohrenwend violently objected to the appearance on a class bulletin board of the cut-out mounted figure of a knight, pasted up by one of the children, because it had been taken from a popular magazine spread depicting how the Italian Communists made use of the Crusades as a subject for propaganda.

It was also in the fall of 1948 that Dohrenwend first brought up the question of books in the high school library. He asked for information on the available works of Howard Fast and of Anna Louise Strong, who at that time had not yet fallen from Moscow grace. There were then ten Fast books on the shelves, he was told, and one by Strong. In the months that followed, Principal Nelson, Superintendent Smith, and Assistant Superintendent Archibald B. Shaw (later Acting Superintendent and now Superintendent) engaged in a series of communications and conferences with Dohrenwend, without achieving a meeting of minds on the question of what kinds of books Scarsdale's youth should find in their school libraries.

By the summer of 1949 word had got around of the Committee of Ten's existence, but nothing had come out in the open and it was hoped nothing would. The Scarsdale *Inquirer,* an excellent and profitable weekly of 4,700 circulation, owned by the Woman's Club and edited for the last twenty years by Mrs. Ruth Nash Chalmers, ran no news about it. The paper knew about Dohrenwend, however, through his previous letters to the editor, including one about the perils of over-secularized schooling. It was not until last year's first fall meeting of the school board—held each September in a room adjacent to Shaw's office in the high school, which itself occupies an attractive 25-acre tract in the Fox Meadow area—that the question of the books was publicly raised.

This was the first meeting Shaw attended as Acting Superintendent and he has since described it as "a whang-doodle." Shaw is a large, handsome, energetic, graying man just under forty. A navy radar lieutenant during the war, he knew, when he took over administration of the Scarsdale schools (enrollment 2,500, half in the high school and the rest in three elementary schools), that he was inheriting one of the best such jobs in the country, in a sophisticated, harmonious community where politics had been miraculously wished away. Accordingly, when Dohrenwend appeared, unprecedentedly bringing with him his New York lawyer, and began sharply questioning the new Acting Superintendent about the method of selecting high school books, Shaw was taken aback.

During the meeting, Dohrenwend wanted to know in detail how both texts and library books were selected, if there was an attempt made to reject books by "left-wing" authors (he referred specifically to Howard Fast's novels and Louis Untermeyer's poetry anthologies), and asked if the school board and superintendent knew the contents of books chosen. Shaw explained that the four schools used 150 texts and had 25,000 volumes in their libraries, and that with 2,500 to 3,000 books being added yearly it was impossible for him to read every one. The board decided, only partly because of Dohrenwend's criticism, to appoint a committee to study procedures for combating subversive influence under the new state law known as the Feinberg Act.

At the monthly meetings that followed, the issue really began to boil. This was chiefly due to the appearance of a local clergyman, the Reverend William C. Kernan, thenceforth to play as significant a role in the book battle as Dohrenwend.

Father Kernan, as he prefers to be called (he is a High Church Episcopalian), recently became a full-time assistant at the fashionable Church of St. James the Less in Scarsdale. However, he has lived in the village, which is predominantly a Protestant community, for ten years, during which he was a part-time St. James assistant, devoting the bulk of his time to outside secular affairs.

Now fifty years of age, Kernan was ordained a priest in 1929. For twelve years he was vicar of a church in Palms, California, and then moved to Trinity Church, in Bayonne, New Jersey. Early in 1939 he appeared one day at the offices of radio station WEVD in Manhattan and said he wanted to make a radio address against Mayor Frank Hague of Jersey City. He was persuaded instead to speak out against Father Charles E. Coughlin. The speech went over so well that the station received one hundred telephone calls and fifteen hundred letters. *Time* magazine called Kernan "exciting—but more important . . . sane," and the program became a WEVD fixture as the Free Speech Forum. On the first anniversary of his debut, the station printed a book of his talks called *The Ghost of Royal Oak,* to which Kernan appended such quotations as Voltaire's "I disapprove of what you say but I will defend to the death your right to say it."

Kernan's broadcasts were kept up until last year. He acquired, after Coughlin subsided, a wider reputation as a liberal anti-fascist and anti-Communist cleric. Starting in 1940 he branched out as a columnist and lecturer, under the aegis of the Institute for American Democracy. He quit his Bayonne parish for this new work, which was concentrated on anti-Hitler propaganda with religious overtones. But a year later, arrangements were made for Kernan to become a two-day-a-week assistant at St. James the Less, and he moved to Scarsdale with his wife and six children.

Dark and ascetic-looking, with a high forehead above deep-set eyes and a vibrant voice, Kernan quickly established a local reputation as a spellbinder in the pulpit. Increasingly, after the war ended and Communism became the new chief threat to liberty, he would stigmatize it as the antithesis of Christianity and comment despairingly on the inroads he saw it making. By last year, it was apparent to the friends with whom Kernan had worked as a radio propagandist and columnist in New York that he had not only decided to devote his full time once again to the church, but that his general approach had changed a good deal. But even they were surprised at the priest's bitterness when, commenting on his permanent appointment to St. James after his long sortie into the secular world, he wrote, in the April 1950 issue of the St. James "Parish Register": "I come to this work with an experience which, perhaps, few parish priests have had, in that, having been active for ten years in the secular world, I have learned that there is no recognition of Christ there. So, there is no effort in the secular world, however noble in purpose it may seem or is intended to be, which is without selfishness, envy or uncharitableness."

Kernan's appearance on the matter of the books inevitably lent stature to Otto Dohrenwend's campaign, since, whether everyone approved of him or not, Kernan bore listening to. Surrounded by Dohrenwend's plentiful files, the two men have invariably sat side by side at school board meetings. At the October 1949 session, Kernan made his first attack on the books. He protested against the inclusion in the high school library of works by "Communist and fascist apologists," and named four specific writers, Fast, Strong, Untermeyer, and Shirley Graham, author of a sympathetic biography of Paul Robeson. The Fast books, Kernan said, singling out *The American* and *Haym Salomon, Son of Liberty,* falsified history because they portrayed the revolution as "a revolt of the masses" instead of as "a revolt against the mother country." All books practicing hate should be banned, he added, and in the light of the anti-Semitism created by the Nazis even Dickens's *Oliver Twist* and Shakespeare's *The Merchant of Venice* could be considered undesirable.

The immediate reaction to Kernan that night was a swelling murmur of disapproval among the fifty-odd persons in the room. Board President A. Chauncey Newlin, a New York lawyer, was applauded when he said, "I don't care a hoot what a man's politics or religion are if he writes a good book." Kernan accused Newlin of "trying to throw a lot of dust in the air," and declared, "I'm surprised that I have to come here, sir, to give you a lecture on Communism." When Dohrenwend made the general charge that "the whole textbook industry has been infiltrated by Communists," he got a cold stare from S. Spencer Scott, president of the publishing house of Harcourt, Brace and Company, who earlier in the evening had presented to Kernan a copy of the Untermeyer anthology published by his firm.

Several other people attending the meeting spoke heatedly in support of the traditional procedure of the teachers' picking books in the light of their best judgment. Thenceforth under the persistent hammering of Dohrenwend and his cohorts, the board and the apparent majority of citizens were to permit themselves to be maneuvered into a position where they defended selections from specific books in a manner that was sometimes naive and even played into the hands of the vocal minority. The fundamental principle of permitting teachers whose loyalty was unquestioned to choose and recommend books in such a way that pupils would be helped to draw their own conclusions, after "free inquiry," became subverted by this bitter and emotional argument over content, during which both sides undoubtedly did considerable quoting out of context. As a matter of fact, the longer the battle raged over various "lifted" passages and loosely prepared "case histories" of certain authors who may have been Communists or fellow-travelers, the wider became the chasm between the two sides and the more first principles were forgotten. Ultimately, Dohrenwend himself denied that content *was* the issue and said the character, reputation, and loyalty record of teacher or author was the vital element—thus at once implying that his chief and privately selected sources of determining these factors, such as the widely discredited Tenney report and the highly dubious files of *Counterattack,* were basic and legitimate guides. On the other hand, and despite some excellent statements that did stress the important principle of untrammeled inquiry, the board—as will subsequently be noted—lamely defended such items as the Fast books on the basis of specific content.

Two days after the meeting Kernan spoke to the Scarsdale Post 52, American Legion, which adopted a resolution that books by "leftists" be banned from the community's schools. That same week, the names of the Committee of Ten's by-then nine members were made public for the first time by the New York *Herald Tribune's* school reporter, Mrs. Judith Crist. In addition to Dohrenwend and Kernan, the committee was composed of I. H. Schaumber, a Manhattan investment specialist and prolific writer of letters to the editor; Dr. Henry C. Link, head of the Psychological Corporation and author of *The Return to Religion* and other books; Professor Oscar Halecki, a Polish refugee who teaches at Fordham University; Ellis H. Carson, a British-born insurance executive; Sylvan Gotshal, a lawyer active in the United Jewish Appeal; Henry C. Koch, a contractor; Thomas E. O'Donnell, a lawyer.

The day this story appeared, Robert Gordon, president of the Town Club and a lawyer for the National Dairy Products Corporation, asked three other key club members to come to his house that evening to discuss the matter of the books. The four men debated for two hours whether to issue any statement in support of the board or do nothing and hope the affair would blow over. It was decided it had already gone too far for that and was further deemed a civic matter that concerned not only the Town Club but all of Scarsdale. Before they went home the men telephoned nine other persons, representing several village organizations, and another meeting was called at the Gordon home for the following Tuesday, at which those summoned were to appear as individuals. That meeting, also held at the Gordon home, began about eight o'clock and lasted until two in the morning. The consensus, according to one person at the meeting, was that since Dohrenwend and Kernan "had persuasive tongues and insidious arguments, we had better get our position across before people start to think there really might be some Communists in our schools." It was decided to issue a statement, signed by prominent members of the community, and at that point five of those attending began, somewhat sheepishly, to pull sheets of paper out of their pockets, confessing that they had by coincidence already written out a little something at home. A committee of three, Mrs. Burnham Finney, wife of a magazine executive, Dr. Warren Weaver, who is director of the natural sciences at the Rockefeller Foundation, and Dr. Courtney C. Brown, an economic consultant for the Chase Bank, went into the dining room to work over the various drafts.

"They closed us in with a quart of scotch and told us if we needed any more we could have it but not to come out without a statement," Dr. Weaver says.

The remaining nine men and women meanwhile drew up a list of names of potential signers, trying to confine themselves to persons who were active in Scarsdale. The list got up to eighty-one. In about an hour the triumvirate from inside reappeared and more time was spent by the whole group going over the amalgam pronouncement. It was now quite late. The eighty-one names were divided up among the thirteen, one of whom took the finished statement home and brought back copies to the Gordon place at eight in the morning of the next day, Columbus Day. By eight-thirty each of the thirteen had, somewhat sleepily, called for his or her copy and set off on a Paul Reverish round of signature-gathering. The task had to be completed before the following morning in order to get the statement into Friday's *Inquirer*.

All except a few of the eighty-one were handed a copy of the statement and personally read it before signing. There were no demurrals. Among the last to sign, simply because they were hard to track down, were Charles E. Wilson, president of the General Electric Company; Harry E. Humphreys, Jr., president of the United States Rubber Company, who had been out all afternoon playing golf; and Sigurd S. Larmon, president of the advertising agency of Young and Rubicam, who returned from out of town on a late train. The list of signers included several former Scarsdale mayors, and a cross section of the prominent business and professional leaders who live in Scarsdale. Among them were Jacob Aronson, a vice-president of the New York Central System; John M. Hancock, investment banker and atomic control expert; Allan Sproul, president of the Federal Reserve Bank of New York; Alexander C. Nagle, president of the First National Bank of New York City; Sidney J. Weinberg, president of Goldman, Sachs and Company, investment brokers; and Arthur S. Meyer, retiring chairman of the New York Mediation Board. Quite a few active wives signed, not only for themselves, but also for husbands who were away on business trips.

The statement, which appeared on the first page of the *Inquirer* of October 14, proclaimed in part: "We do not minimize the dangers of Communist and fascist indoctrination, but we want to meet these dangers in the American way.

"We live in a democratic state. We are the inheritors of a tradition that has encouraged a dynamic development in our intellectual as well as our material life. That tradition has been based on a tolerance that has not feared to permit independent thought. A state that fears to permit the expression of views alternative to those held by the majority is a state that does not trust itself. . . .

"Any sensible person would agree that there are risks involved in allowing young persons relatively free access to a wide range of reading material. Of course there are risks. But we believe there are greater risks in any alternative procedure. Surely we have not, as a people, lost the courage to take the risks that are necessary for the preservation of freedom."

The columns of the *Inquirer* that week began to be filled with much relevant and some irrelevant data about the battle of the books. There was an editorial entitled "Cool Heads Needed," which advocated careful and not over-hasty decisions, and the first salvo of what was to prove a long barrage of letters. There were seven letters in the issue, and the longest represented the formal bow of the so-called Committee of Ten. It was signed by Dohrenwend for all nine members, whose names were attached, and was a stated effort to explain the committee's purposes in the light of the "unsought publicity" arising out of the board meeting. Dohrenwend still maintained that "anything smacking of witch-hunting is farthest from the committee's plan," and said: "We are primarily interested in a positive approach. For example, we should like a statement by the Board of Education as to what its policy is with regard to educating Scarsdale children in the principles of Americanism."

The other six letters were five to one in support of the board's position. The following week the ratio was almost exactly reversed. A high proportion of all letters received were from mothers, who invariably introduced themselves by announcing their maternal box scores. Mrs. Chalmers, editor and mother herself, calculated that she probably established a modern newspaper record for references per square inch of space to the Bill of Rights. There is also little doubt that a principal effect of the issue's airing was a quick race for the bookshelves. "About this time," Mrs. Chalmers recalls, "you couldn't get a book of Fast's anywhere, either in the public library or in White Plains. There were waiting lists two weeks long and you couldn't buy a pocket edition either." By then, too, the book battle had become the main topic of conversation over cocktails, dinner tables, and the New York Central's Harlem Division.

The next meeting of the Scarsdale school board, in November, was attended by so many persons, about 250, that it had to be held in the high school gym. This meeting has been described as "a real wild one," in the sense that "everyone screamed at everyone else." Many hoped the issue would be resolved, however, by a six-page report of the committee that had been appointed to examine the book situation in the light of the new Feinberg law. The committee recommended, and the board in executive session afterward approved, that the existing method of selecting books be maintained. The report declared that "protection against subversive influences can best be achieved by the positive approach of vigorous teaching rather than by negative methods of repressive censorship," and added: "The latter ensures undue attention to the censored items and substitutes fear of ideas for freedom of inquiry. Truth is to be found through open doors."

It was soon apparent that the Committee of Ten, led by Father Kernan, was not ready to give up the fight. Although the report was heartily applauded, Kernan got up and at once began reading selections from Fast's novels. He quoted passages and juxtaposed them against something said in the *Daily Worker* or by some Communist leader. After each Fast quotation, he would assert, "That, gentlemen, is Communism."

In addition to Kernan, several other members of the Committee of Ten spoke; Professor Halecki drew a distinction between burning books and recommending them and complained that Miss Strong's book gave an entirely false picture of his native Poland (which is undoubtedly the case); and Mr. Schaumber contributed quotations from Paul Robeson's writings and did not endear himself to the ladies present by sweeping a hand toward the audience and shouting, "And here, too, we even have the women knitting."

It may have been the Christmas season that kept the next two meetings relatively peaceful. In the interim, however, the battle of the books waged fast and furious in the letters column of the *Inquirer* and spread over into the newspapers of Yonkers and White Plains. Dohrenwend and Schaumber were the most ardent correspondents, combining continued attacks on Fast, whose considerable activities on behalf of Communism and Communist causes were effectively outlined, with new and wider thrusts at progressive education. Schaumber, in replying to an editorial in the White Plains *Reporter-Dispatch,* said: "We have long recognized that God has been outlawed in the classroom, and as 'nature hates a vacuum,' a new 'being' of adoration has arisen, called 'society.' Its apostles are proponents of the John Dewey philosophy known as 'progressivism,' which denies the religious nature of man. . . ."

The letter-writing marathon was presently joined, in January, by Howard Fast himself. A Scarsdale importer, J. Anthony Marcus, had written to the *Inquirer* quoting Fast as having said, "There is no nobler, no finer product of man's existence on this earth than the Communist party." Fast, in decrying Marcus's "fishcalling," insisted that "in fifteen years of consistent service to my country, I have never written a book or story outside of my concept of love and reverence for the United States of America." The *Inquirer* appended a note to the letter, pointing out, for the record, that Fast had not denied making the statement attributed to him by Marcus. Fast replied that although the quote had not been quite correct, "there is enough validity in it for me to choose not to deny it." So far as is known, this ended the only participation in the battle of Scarsdale of any of the authors whose books were mentioned.

A week after the Fast exchange, the *Inquirer* printed a letter that was to provide the ammunition for round two of the book battle. It came from a nonmember of the Committee of Ten, C. S. Treacy, a civil engineer, whose ancestors, according to a letter he had sent in earlier, "landed at Plymouth Rock from a little vessel called the Mayflower...." Treacy's charge was clearly documented. "I have just read the Bantam [twenty-five cents] edition published in 1946 of Howard Fast's *Citizen Tom Paine*," he wrote. "I would like to explain why I believe this book should not be recommended reading for minors in Scarsdale schools.... Cursing occurs on pages 31, 52, 56, 82, 124, 131, 138, 139, 156, 176, 177, 183, 233, 245, and 315. I believe this should be offensive to Protestant, Catholic, or Jew. Personally, the continued cursing in this book nauseated me. I feel that it is an offense against God and a bad example to the young.... Perhaps I am old-fashioned in my belief. However, the ten commandments are also old-fashioned.... What I think to be one of the greatest dangers to the young in this book occurs on pages 26, 27, and 28. These pages describe the auction sale of what are described as breeding wenches. The Negresses are shown naked to the buyers, and the effect on Tom Paine is described as one which made him both eager and ashamed. The description of the slave auction itself and of the auctioneer is quite vivid. It is the boast of the latter that all pregnant slaves, when sold, are pregnant by him. The description of one of the individual slaves would seem to me certainly to be quite broad, especially when the slave's usefulness is described as one which would make her suitable to take to bed or into a hayloft.... I do not believe that the young people of Scarsdale are undersexed, and I do not believe that this is the kind of reading matter to recommend to normally sexed adolescents...."

At the school board meeting February 6, 1950, Treacy appeared, along with Kernan and Dohrenwend, who had been absent from the two previous meetings, and asked Board President Newlin why *Citizen Tom Paine* was in the high school library in view of its blasphemy and immorality. Treacy said he was raising the issue on specific content, but Newlin would not allow him to read what he called "the spiciest sections" and he was told to refer the matter to the professional staff that had chosen the book. The board subsequently agreed to consider Treacy's *Inquirer* letter as a formal written complaint, and a close study of *Citizen Tom Paine* was ordered. A nine-page, single-spaced report was prepared by the heads of the English and social studies departments of the high school and the librarian, who together spent thirty-three hours on it. They noted that it is "the only current novel which centers around the figure of Tom Paine and his contributions to the founding of our democracy." The three judges deplored "the presence of so much profanity," but said there were historical and literary reasons for it. To ban books because they contain objectionable words or depict such things as adultery would do away with the Bible and other eminent works, it was added.

On the issue of Fast's Communism, the judges demonstrated a certain naive oversimplification. "We did not find him following the party line in this book," said the judges, and they cited as proof of their point Fast's apparent attitude toward dictatorship, atheism, and the doctrine that the end justifies the means. "All references to Washington, the Jacobins, and Napoleon, and all the implications are against dictatorship," the report declared. Far from showing Paine believing that the end justifies the means, the report added, the doctrine "is shown as repugnant to Paine and to all the 'good' characters. Specifically, in dealing with the use of force, the episode concerning Napoleon is unmistakably against cloaking force as a means to a good end...."

At the April meeting of the board, which was again held in the high school gym when 300 persons attended, only Superintendent Shaw's summary approval of the report was read, but this was enough to touch off the most boisterous session of the entire controversy. (The board itself also approved of retaining *Citizen Tom Paine,* although there was not complete agreement on all phases of the matter; it was, incidentally, about this time that the book mysteriously vanished from the high school library shelves, to which it has not yet been restored.) Treacy still insisted the biography was "filthy," suggested it would be a good text for a course in "advanced blasphemy," and pointed out that it had been banned in New York City schools for not giving a true account of Paine's life, being poorly written, and containing objectionable passages: one woman replied that she hoped Scarsdale would not emulate New York. Treacy again asked for permission to read aloud from the book, prefacing his request by saying, "I don't want to shock the ladies...." He was told by Newlin that if it made him feel any better, he could go ahead and read. Amid considerable tittering, he thereupon read aloud the three-page slave-auction scene, and a briefer one where, as a staymaker's apprentice at thirteen, Paine is undone by a two-hundred-pound woman come to have her corset fitted.

The reaction of Father Kernan to the *Citizen Tom Paine* ruling was to declare that "the board has gone on record in direct contradiction to the teachings of the church." He added that he would see to it "that word of this is spread beyond Scarsdale"—something he had actually already done. By now a great deal of what was said was repetitious, if more barbed, but there was a certain sharpening of issues which bore directly on the vital balloting that took place the following month. The sentiment gained ground that the Committee of Ten was impugning the whole school system and that it was seeking specific scapegoats. Newlin, at one point, emphasized that the morale of the entire school staff and Scarsdale's fine educational reputation were being undermined.

At another point, the direct issue of secularism versus religion in the schools was brought into the open by Mrs. Martin J. Brennan, wife of a noise-abatement specialist and mother of four children in the Scarsdale schools. Mrs. Brennan, hitherto silent, began by reiterating that there were few in Scarsdale who held any brief for Howard Fast and his books or who really cared if his works were in or out of the library. But, continued Mrs. Brennan, "Suppose we ban *Citizen Tom Paine*? Suppose we ban all the Fast books, the Untermeyer anthology? Will they stop there? What comes next?" She alluded to the several letters that had dealt with the question of secularism versus spiritual and moral training and asked, with a certain finality, "I want to know what's behind all this." Kernan had his reply prepared. "What's behind this is to keep Communism out of the Scarsdale school system," he snapped. "It's already there and you don't know Communism when you see it."

Several of the letters that followed were critical of Kernan's contention that the board had flouted the church in the battle of the books. The one that drew the most attention came from the Reverend Edward C. Boynton, popular minister of the Congregational Church in Scarsdale, who wrote: "It is not clear from Mr. Kernan's use of the words 'the church' exactly for whom he speaks authoritatively. To avoid any misunderstanding because of my profession as a Minister, I state simply, Mr. Kernan does not speak for me." Kernan nevertheless continued to speak, at least for himself. Twice in the month that followed, once to the Peekskill Rotary Club and once to three hundred delegates of State Exchange Clubs at the Westchester Country Club in Rye, he severely criticized the Scarsdale school board for its allegedly lax attitude toward Communism. Dohrenwend and other members of the Committee of Ten meanwhile complained that the board and Newlin especially had been discourteous to them and had not given them a fair hearing.

The annual election for school board members took place on the first Tuesday in May. Because of the stir created by the months-long dispute, the election was bound to receive more than the usual attention. But it is doubtful whether anyone expected 1,400 persons to crowd into the high school gymnasium on the night of May 2, and that 1,090 of them would cast ballots. (This, compared to a total of only 59 votes cast the year before.) Chiefly as a result of the stormy April meeting, word got around that there might be additional nominations from the floor or an opposition write-in vote. Once more, Bob Gordon of the Town Club got together a small group of Scarsdale's active citizens—this, by the way, marking the only other organized effort to counteract the Committee of Ten—and it was decided to urge everyone's attendance at the election meeting on the simple grounds that the tested non-partisan method might be threatened. "A lot of people did a lot of telephoning," one woman later admitted, "and, as usual, a dirty job like that was handed over to the ladies." Several persons disclosed they were called three or four times, and one man rushed home from an Atlantic City Convention just to vote.

The fears of those who had suspected an opposition slate proved unfounded. Because there were so many present, the balloting lasted an hour and a half, but when it was over the results showed that the three incumbent members up for re-election, Newlin, George Rutherford, a vice-president of National Dairy Products, and G. Stanley McAllister, a vice-president of Lord and Taylor, New York City department store, had received respectively 1,081, 1,085, and

1,084 votes. There were sixteen blanks and one write-in vote apiece for Kernan, Dohrenwend, Treacy, and a man named E. W. Berlin whom no one was able immediately to identify.

Scarsdale felt, after the election, that the issue of the books had been properly disposed of. The villagers, however, failed to reckon with the persistence of its minority watchmen. Prior to the June meeting of the school board, the Committee of Ten gave way to a new unnamed group that included, in addition to Kernan, two other local ministers, the Reverend August W. Brustat, pastor of the Trinity Lutheran Church, and the Reverend Hugh J. Rooney, an assistant at the Roman Catholic Church of the Immaculate Heart of Mary; several previous members dropped out but were replaced by others. Dohrenwend remained a key figure. On the night of June 5, Edward O. McConahay, an assistant vice-president of the Metropolitan Life Insurance Company in New York and spokesman for the new group, requested the school board to meet with it to consider further evidence that subversive influences were infiltrating the school system. For the first time, openly, the charge was made that some of the teaching staff might have connections with a Communist front seeking to get certain textbooks into the public schools. (There was never, however, any accusation made against a specific teacher, nor was the "front" ever defined or identified; the nearest approach to an attack on any one teacher was a fruitless effort on the part of the minority led by Dohrenwend to obtain the name of the individual who signed the requisitions for certain books—a demand that was refused by the board on the perfectly sound ground that such a signature meant nothing since it was purely the normal product of the whole book-selection process outlined in painful detail at one of the earlier board meetings.)

A special meeting was called for the nineteenth of June with the stipulation that only new information would be brought forth. The case against the schools that night was presented for two and a half hours by ten speakers who sought to describe how the general pattern of Communist influence had been brought to bear in Scarsdale. Four well-known and widely used textbooks were cited. These included *World History,* by Boak, Slosson, and Anderson, edited by Harvard Professor William Langer, and used in the tenth grade; it was submitted to be prejudiced because it had frequent pictures of Marx, Lenin, and Trotsky to the exclusion of portraits of American heroes and Founding Fathers, because it described as "a stupendous achievement" the "transformation of the Russian peasant into a serious, highly trained industrial worker," and because it allegedly dismissed the Chinese Communists as "rarely anything but hungry peasants, whose chief interest was in getting more land rather than in political or economic theories." The other three books—each cited, with selections read aloud, by a different speaker—were *Story of America,* by Ralph V. Harlow, declared to picture America as being at the mercy of big corporations and utilities; *Our World Today,* allegedly a pro-Russian geography textbook; and *American Democracy Today and Tomorrow,* by Goslin, Goslin, and Storen, alleged to be subtly subversive in several places.

Pamphlets used as reference material, including those of the Foreign Policy Association, were declared to be equally subversive. Dohrenwend listed the names of several men and women who had spoken in Scarsdale schools under the auspices of the Parent-Teacher Association or conducted special off-campus courses for teachers under the aegis of New York University and Sarah Lawrence College. These included a number of sponsors or speakers who, he said, had attended the Communist front World Peace Conference held in March 1949 at the Waldorf-Astoria Hotel in New York. Among them were Professor Bert James Loewenberg, of Sarah Lawrence; Shirley Graham, the Robeson biographer; Louis Untermeyer, Dorothy Parker, Langston Hughes, the poet; Vera Micheles Dean, author of several books on foreign affairs and an officer of the Foreign Policy Association, and Anna Louise Strong. Dohrenwend, making what was perhaps his strongest point of the whole lengthy investigation, urged the school board to determine whether, over a four-year period, there had been a preponderant number of speakers at Scarsdale PTA meetings or at off-campus course sessions whose opinions might be questioned as exemplifying an objectionable "educational philosophy."

The Reverend Dr. Brustat summed up the charges by referring to Louis F. Budenz's *Men Without Faces,* in which that ex-Communist author speaks of a Communist plot to influence citizens of Westchester County, directly or indirectly, through wealthy party members and leftist lecturers. When Dr. Brustat had finished, Board President Newlin asked him if he believed the evidence offered during the lengthy session warranted an investigation aimed at "rooting out" teachers suspected of promoting the use of subversive material. The pastor promptly answered, "I most assuredly do."

Superintendent Shaw thereupon arose and read a report on "The Loyalty of Our Teachers." He referred to the "understandable uneasiness" Scarsdale families had come to feel as a result of "the repetition over the months of charges implied and overt," now capped by "new and grave, if hitherto unsupported, accusations involving our staff." After reviewing the standards which govern the selection of the 133 teachers in the Scarsdale school system, Mr. Shaw said: "I want to state positively, without reservation, that every teacher in our schools is a loyal American. . . ." He added that he couldn't say they were alike in their religious, economic, social, or political beliefs, nor did he know what they read, but "I do know that they are good people for our children to be with." In teaching various subjects as well as "the acts of citizenship in a democracy," Mr. Shaw emphasized, "a good teacher, alert and imaginative, calls on many sources, many references," using books "as tools, no more, to be picked up and laid down as useful."

On July 5, at the next regular board meeting, Mr. McAllister, the new president, made the climactic announcement that the board had voted 7–0 against conducting an investigation. He said: "In the two years or more since this subject has been under discussion, no one has presented any evidence to indicate that our teachers, by the use of books or pamphlets or otherwise, have been inculcating subversive ideas in our school children." Superintendent Shaw read selections from the four textbooks that had been cited to deny the charge that they were slanted.

The Scarsdale citizens' group that demanded the investigation, after condemning the "whitewash" by the board, has indicated it regards the whole affair as a continuing one, although at the second 1950 fall meeting, in October, the board finally announced that it would hear no more verbal attacks at the monthly public sessions; this led at once to a barrage of letters to the *Inquirer* charging a "gag." At the same time, however, not as a result of the lengthy battle but because Superintendent Shaw has wanted to do it for some time, a committee to study citizenship education in Scarsdale was established, composed of eight lay members and three from the school staff.

Under the circumstances of mounting tension between the Communist and non-Communist world, as exemplified by the Far Eastern crisis and other probable crises to come, the Scarsdale affair will undoubtedly be repeated in communities throughout the nation. It may be too much to expect every town and village involved in a similar conflict to treat it as patiently as did Scarsdale and with such a cool collective head (one woman explained, "You know, this is a community of executives, and they just don't like to be told what to do"). It is not even inconceivable that in the days to come Scarsdale's citizens themselves might suffer a failure of poise. Given the present dynamics of Communist expansionism, with its attendant tactics of disruption everywhere, it will inevitably become harder and harder to define what is subversive and to distinguish between healthy exposure of false and subtle propaganda on the one hand and blind fear of anything less than "100 per cent Americanism" on the other.

There are few in Scarsdale who would not admit today (if indeed they ever had doubts) that Communists in the United States do seek to "infiltrate" our schools, communities, organizations, etc. Most villagers also acknowledge that a good, thoroughly indoctrinated Communist will try to bring the party line into what he says or writes (although this does not necessarily hold good of a Communist sympathizer). Further, those Scarsdalians who sat through the endless school board sessions and then went home and read the "subversive" books were undoubtedly aware that some of them came from the pens of persons not especially reticent in their praise of Soviet Russia. Yet the decision was made that any form of censorship represented a much worse sort of risk. In the last analysis, Scarsdale affirmed its faith in its children as well as its teachers; Superintendent Shaw at one point reminded everyone that there hasn't been a fellow-traveler in a carload of high school graduates, a good proportion of whom have distinguished themselves in the ultra-respectable halls of Princeton, Yale, and Harvard.

Finally, and perhaps of most import in the long run, Scarsdale's handling of its crisis set back—or at least gave no aid or comfort to—a nationally spreading hysteria; invariably, elsewhere as here, this has found expression in guardians whose bland assumption that they and they alone have the blessing and vision of God leads them into the belief that others ostensibly less clairvoyant and omniscient are incapable of recognizing and appraising a "clear and present danger." Many a Scarsdalian who has voted the straight Republican ticket since he came of age was surprised, in the last two years, to hear himself called a "soft liberal" by the nervous watchmen in his midst. Presaging, it may be hoped, a broader development, much needed, the proud Scarsdalian simply reared back and asserted his "enlightened conservatism."

Another victim of arbitrary school-board censorship action and often under fire by ultraconservative groups, Mark Van Doren, poet, critic, novelist, and Professor of English at Columbia University since 1920, replied to his critics in this speech to the Hudson County Chapter of Americans for Democratic Action in Jersey City, New Jersey, on February 20, 1951.

Mark Van Doren
IF ANYBODY WANTS TO KNOW

I understand that I am here tonight, not to be investigated or tried, or to speak in defense of anything I have ever done or said, but to assist in the discussion of an important principle. I hope that none of you came with the expectation that anything would be proved, either about me or about the Board of Education of this city, one or more of whose members have seen fit to order the removal of four of my books from the library of Jersey City Junior College. It appears that they did so without knowledge of what was in those books. All my books are about literature, or else they try to be literature themselves, and so it is safe to assume that the four in question may be so described. It further appears that the Board of Education was soon made aware of this; but that it decided not to alter its original position, alleging opinions and associations of mine as evidence that in any case I was an undesirable person who should be listened to on no subject whatsoever.

A few anonymous letters that I have received express agreement with the Board. But the great majority of those who have written or spoken to me have expressed emphatic disagreement, and have gone on to say that the action of the Board was either ridiculous or outrageous. I myself make neither charge. I am more interested in the principles and procedures that seem to be involved, and in the question whether Americanism and democracy have been well served in Jersey City. I come entirely alone to discuss this question. I represent nobody but myself; though I recognize how many friends of mine, some of whom I never knew before, hope that some degree of clarification will result. I gather that the issue is as important to them as it is to me; and, frankly, it is in their interest as well as mine that I am here, against my own natural inclination to live without trouble in the country I love.

Some of these friends have pointed out to me that the incident which inspired this meeting is already in some measure out of date. A rapidly growing number of citizens, from President Truman on down, have in recent weeks and days indicated their doubt that our program of security—in itself an absolutely necessary thing—is being handled to the best advantage: to the advantage, that is, of our own health and strength at a time when we need health and strength as never perhaps before. A religious leader in New York, for example, was all but stating a commonplace when in the newspapers for February 11 he said: "That American security is endangered is undeniable; but the greatest threat to our security is the fear that drives us to limit the very freedoms that have made us strong. Investigations and oaths and complex security laws—which in effect censor opinion rather than control conduct—are not providing the strength we need to meet the challenge of the inter-

---

Mark Van Doren, "If Anybody Wants To Know," *American Scholar*, 20, no. 4:396–405 (Autumn, 1951), copyright 1951 by the United Chapters of Phi Beta Kappa. Reprinted by permission of the author and of the publisher.

national situation. . . . Scholars are becoming suspect, distinguished thinkers are discouraged from government service, and the spirit of free inquiry at great universities is in danger of being curtailed. . . . By making one's associations the test of loyalty, by identifying any unorthodox viewpoints with communism, we put a premium on conformity and stifle the spirit of freedom, the right to criticize, by which democracy lives and grows." The statement, however, is still not commonplace enough; that is why we are here tonight.

By a coincidence more pertinent yet to the reason for our meeting, I received only week before last, from the American Library Association, a copy of its Library Bill of Rights. This document is a welcome sign that groups of Americans are taking their own steps these days to safeguard their existence. I quote its third paragraph: "Censorship of books, urged or practiced by volunteer arbiters of morals or political opinion or by organizations that would establish a coercive concept of Americanism, must be challenged by libraries in maintenance of their responsibility to provide public information and enlightenment through the printed word." The application of these excellent words to the Board of Education's act in removing my books from one of the libraries for which it is responsible may not appear on one count to be perfect, and indeed by my own judgment is not. I happen to believe, and I have often said, that the right of school authorities to select the books their students shall read is not to be infringed. But on another count the application is clear. The Jersey City Board of Education, after conceding that my books are unobjectionable, still call their author objectionable—do so publicly—and still presume to protect the students of at least one college from contact with his mind.

They do this to me, it might appear, because they disagree with some of my opinions and disapprove of some of my associations. I say "it might appear," for I am not at all certain that they know any more about my opinions than they do about my books; though it is clear that they jump to conclusions, and want others to do so, from the associations they list and allege. I do not propose to challenge their list, though to the best of my knowledge it is sometimes erroneous, and at other times, if not erroneous, misleading. I am not here to repudiate anything I ever said, or to deny that I joined others in saying it—often through organizations which at the time were objectionable to nobody. An example would be the Independent Citizens' Committee of the Arts, Sciences and Professions, which I joined with many others in 1944 to assist in the election of Franklin D. Roosevelt as President of the United States, and from which I subsequently resigned. Nor is there time to argue the merits of my beliefs—either their present merits or their merits in the context (sometimes five, sometimes ten, sometimes twenty years old) which produced them. I am here to consider with you the inference which the Board of Education has publicly drawn from them—whether or not to my personal damage may not for the moment matter; or whether to the damage of the Board of Education's prestige, which might be supposed to depend upon its conduct of any affair involving logic and justice.

The one thing the Board did not do—indeed, by saying that the case was "closed" it showed it did not want to do it—was to discover what my opinions actually were and are, to consider their truth or untruth, and if they seemed untrue, to refute them by fair means. The Board seems not to be interested in the good old institution of argument. If I have ever been wrong in anything I publicly said or joined others in saying, I deserve to be proved wrong and in fact should welcome it. I could have been wrong; I can be wrong now; and certain of my friends who disagreed with me about particular matters have told me so, and given their reasons why, and sometimes I have found these to be good reasons. This, I take it, is the process of civilization. By the same token it is not, I take it, the process of civilization to say of someone with whom you disagree either that he is your personal enemy—which does not follow at all—or that he is the enemy of his country and of civilization itself. To be called irrelevant and erroneous names in argument is not agreeable, and it does not settle the argument. It is a dangerous method even for those who use it, since it can be turned against them. If I am your enemy then you are mine, and I may be forced to question your motives for thinking and saying what you do. I do not call in question the motives of the Board of Education in doing what it has done; I do not insist on knowing why they exaggerate and insinuate as in my case they do; I do not accuse them of joining with others in some sinister cause. I merely point out that they have not proceeded in what I am old-fashioned enough to believe is the American fashion—has been, still is, and always must be the American fashion if our oldest tradition is to keep its meaning.

My faith in the American people and their government—even though some members of that government have shown signs of panic—is still so great that I say this here and now: Whenever I shall be asked my opinion on any crucial matter, and when I have an opinion that I feel deeply, I will express it and join others in expressing it; and I will never bring pressure to bear, by prejudicial publicity, on anybody who disagrees with me, though I will argue with him as capably as I can, and if he is more capable, or proves that he is better informed, I will change my mind and admit that I have done so.

This for me is the essence of Americanism. But there seem to be Americans (I do not know how many) who are so bent upon having everybody agree with them (I don't know exactly about what) that they take another line. If they cannot have agreement in fact, they want it in the form of silence. Nobody must say anything or belong to anything. For the penalty, if he does, is that they will accuse him of supporting a foreign force. That force, it goes without saying, is communism; or it is Russia, which gives communism today whatever force it has. But there is an astonishing similarity between the two dogmatisms. In Russia also there is no third alternative to agreement or silence. I still believe with all my heart that for us this third alternative exists—and not only exists, but is necessary to our survival. I still maintain that it is obligatory for all Americans to speak their minds on matters of common importance, with the understanding that the proper penalty for their being wrong, if they are wrong, is that someone prove them so.

Whether they are right or wrong is infinitely more important, I think, than whom they happen to agree with. The current assumption sometimes seems to be that no man ever thinks for himself; he thinks only with a group, or as a group dictates. But it is American, as it is democratic, for men to make up their own minds. I for one can say that it is nobody's business why I ever said what I said, but that I am willing to say why. I meant what I said, and believed it to be true. If I sound naïve, it is perhaps because many have grown cynical. And I am sorry to say that I must include among the cynical not only those members of the Board of Education who assume an alien source for my ideas, but certain very well-meaning friends of mine who talk as if there were nothing to be done in this situation, which they themselves deplore. I thought there was something to be done. I came here tonight, and I did not think it was useless to do so. Nor was I in the least afraid to come. The Board says it is afraid of me, and the friends in question act as if they were afraid of the Board. So far as I know, I have no fear, and I see no reason why I should have any. Some of the letters I got were letters of condolence, as if I had died. I feel very much alive, and furthermore I am confident. I know I am not alone in my confidence; though even if I were, I should have to act as I am acting now. In the America of Lincoln and Thoreau there is no good reason for fear.

Yet many Americans are afraid today. And if enough more become so, we shall have lost our freedom. Freedom and courage come and go together, like liberty and argument. It has been insinuated that I "support the proponents of a change of government by force." Nothing could be more absurd. If I believe anything, I believe that the only force that can change or destroy our common life is the force of fear, which by its very ability to operate among us would seem to indicate a doubt that we really do have (as I am sure we have) the best way of life in the world—if we only stick to it with free minds and pure hearts. The last thing we should fear is communism itself, which some Americans denounce in one breath as contemptible and then in the next breath honor by trembling before its supposed power. It would have no power if they believed in themselves. It could not dominate them if they knew it couldn't. An American poet—poets sometimes do speak of serious matters—recently published his opinion that we as a people are already dominated by communism. He meant, by fear of communism, and by an obsession with it that prevents us from thinking of any other subject. I do not like to think that this is true. There is still time, I trust, for us to come back to the business of being ourselves, and of making our own life as free and strong as men can make it. This means, of course, preparing ourselves against our enemies. It also means remembering who and what we are. We have been the admiration of the world; but the world shows signs of distrusting us because we do not trust our own tradition.

Courage, said Socrates, is the knowledge of what is to be feared and what is not to be feared. Some things, therefore, are to be feared. One thing we can fear is that we should go the way of Germany, our former enemy, or of Russia, our potential present and future enemy, or of both combined, in the suppression of thought and discussion, and of political action harmonious with these. We are not so hard up that we need to do that. We are not hard up at all. There may be those who think we are, but they have already despaired. They think there is nothing left except for us to become indistinguishable from our foes. They are already beaten. For if they mean this, and if the rest of us come to agree with them, there will indeed be nothing left. The shortest way to weaken ourselves for any struggle we may have with Russia is to throw away the one imperishable strength we have, our faith in individual liberty and dignity, and our faith that the life of any democratic society is measured by the number of its members who believe it to be necessary, for the common good and for their own, that they think as well as they are able, and speak as sensibly as they can.

A letter to me last week assured me that I would have perpetual immunity from such challenges as the present one if I became forever silent. In such a case the silence would not be greatly noticeable. I do not flatter myself that I have been a person of public importance. I have actually said very little; and if the list of organizations with which I have been associated seems long to others, it does not seem long to me, particularly since the association has been for the most part slight and in almost no case active—I signed something I wanted to sign, or I sympathized with certain objectives when I thought all Americans should. But I have no intention, even within these modest limits, of becoming silent. Silence in democracy is death, and I do not want democracy to die. Whenever I believe something I will say it, without any other illusion, if illusion it be, than that in difficult times it is good for thinking to go on.

I have never forgotten the face of a Connecticut farmer I know, a Republican of course, as he turned to me from the radio where he had been listening to a transcription of the latest proceedings of the Un-American Activities Committee. It was a face filled with fear. And fear of what? Of the Committee.

"I've never heard anything like that in this country," he said. "I wouldn't want them to be asking me questions."

"Why not?" I asked.

"Because they were bullying that fellow. He may have done something bad, but I think they were worse. Can't anything be done?"

Perhaps there was nothing for him to do, but with him in mind I protested—like thousands of others—against the method and spirit of the investigation then going on. Communists protested too, doubtless for a different reason. I had my own reasons, which were as American as those of the Connecticut Yankee who was scared. If I also was scared, it was only lest nobody think it safe to object. When thousands did I was reassured—not for myself, but for a country that had still not lost its reason.

Such and so would be my record if I wanted to present it at this time and place. I have no such desire, partly because my record has not been kept, at least by me. I did not think I lived in a police state. The somewhat dreary list of organizations which the Board of Education has drawn up is in my own mind, I confess, an unreal and academic thing. The emphasis it places on membership and association seems merely technical, or else fanatical. My interest, as I have said, has never been in organizations as such; my connection with them has usually been short lived; and I am aware at this moment of belonging to none that should cause worry in any mind. The simple fact is that I never did knowingly join any Communist or Communist-front organization.

But I did not come here to say precisely this, and certainly I did not come to minimize my record, such as it is. It is the record of one who never hesitated to agree with others that the good life is worth talking about and fighting for in so far as words can fight. Most of my effort has been spent in the area where artists, intellectuals and teachers have to stand up for their freedom. It is of the utmost importance to me that those whose business it is to use their minds and imaginations should not be paralyzed, either by cynicism or by fear, or by attempts on the part of others to control them, until they lose their function in the world of men. They fared badly in Hitler's Germany, where their books were burned. They fare badly in Stalin's Russia, where musicians and novelists, not to say scientists and philosophers, must work under constant supervision from above. No great work can be done that way, and eventually, perhaps, no work at all. I should hate to see the same blunder made in America, and I shall continue to do whatever I can to prevent it. It was in this spirit that I protested when the Un-American Activities Committee turned its attention to the movie industry as a producing center of art, and when the industry itself made no effort to protect its legitimate interests. The result has been, as many foresaw, a lowering of movie standards and a lessening of the movie audience. This could be an accident, or it could be television; I think it is the chilling and numbing effect of a force felt from the outside, a force than can strangle the imagination even before it is born.

I am opposed to communism, both as a theory and in the form it now takes before the world; but I should like to distinguish between my opposition to it and that of certain anti-Communists who think they need to be nothing else. The good life is both negative and positive; it is against what would hurt it, but at the same time that it makes itself safe it considers what it wants to be safe for, and what it could build if it were free.

The American people may be moving into a period of unprecedented power and responsibility. If this is true, as I think it is, they cannot have too much help from within. They must hold their own, in peace or in war, and toward this end the services of no citizen may be insignificant. The services, or the ideas—or both, for they can be the same thing. The time to recruit these services is now, and the best atmosphere for the purpose is the atmosphere of confidence and faith. If all we have is the fear that communism can destroy us, we are already destroyed; for we have lost our self-respect. Democracy that believes in itself and remembers its great origins need have no fear of competition with any system in the world, least of all a system that distrusts individuals. The true opposite of communism is not anti-communism as it is preached by those in panic; it is democracy, which, when it knows itself, is never afraid. We ought to be not only against communism but above it, as justice is above despair. The Communists are promising to save the world, but we can really do it. Equality is a better thing than uniformity, liberty than the enforced love of law, and fraternity than the domination of one class. The question is how deeply and simply we understand this. If the world is hesitating to follow us away from communism, the reason may be that it sees signs in us of fear and doubt. We cannot convince others if we are not convinced.

My own position would be funny if it were not fairly serious. It is, of course, not unique. I have remained the liberal I was in the beginning, with the result that I have never been in what you would call the fashion. In the 1930's I was unconvinced by communism, and today I am uncontaminated by the fear of it that makes many Americans forget how much they naturally believe in the good heart and the just mind. By never fluctuating in my love of these things I have become, as appearances now go, suspect. But only, I am sure, as appearances go. It cannot be true—most of my friends persuade me of this—that any considerable body of Americans seriously doubts its obligation to be for those better things which Communists only pretend to be for. Communists can say what they do not mean, for purposes of their own; but we must mean, for no purpose beyond our integrity, whatever we say. And we must not stop talking. We may or may not arrive at the truth; but we shall utterly fail if we desist from the attempt.

In Plato's *Republic,* which is a dialogue about justice, there is a speaker named Thrasymachus who suddenly denies that justice exists. It is only the name, he says, we give to the right of the strong. Last year in New York, lecturing on Karl Marx, I called him the Thrasymachus of the modern world. He said, as communism still says, that justice is merely the will of the strongest class. Marx wanted a new class to prevail, and therefore a new justice. But justice is neither new or old. It is not one will, whether of a tyrant or of a class. It is itself, and it is the thing that all men love when they are serious. That, if you still care to know, is the politics I have.

State legislatures have frequently made it their business to place restrictions on what may be read and taught in schools and colleges. Such legislation reached a *reductio ad absurdum* in an act passed by the Alabama legislature on September 19, 1953. As anticipated by its critics, the law proved unworkable. Renwick C. Kennedy is an Alabama Presbyterian minister.

Renwick C. Kennedy
ALABAMA BOOK-TOASTERS

Anti-communist hysteria has reached a point of pure but not simple imbecility in Alabama, whose three million people probably do not include as many as a dozen Communists. State Legislator James B. Morgan, hitherto relatively unknown, is a business man from the redoubtable city of Birmingham. In 1953 this member of the Alabama house of representatives secured the passage of Act 888, now more notoriously known as the "poison label bill." The preface to the law states that its purpose is "to prohibit the use of certain textbooks and writings in public schools, institutions of higher learning and trade schools" in the state of Alabama. A more fantastic scheme for regulating the instruction of youth has probably never occurred to the mind of man than is contained in this ineffable law. The body of Act 888 reads:

Section 1. Neither the state textbook committee nor the state board of education nor any other public body or official shall consider for adoption or approval, or adopt or approve for use in the public schools or trade schools or institutions of higher learning of this state, any textbook or other written instructional material (not including periodical newspapers and magazines nor legal opinions by courts of record) which does not contain a statement by the publisher or author thereof indicating clearly and with particularity that the author of the book or other writing and the author of any book or writings cited therein as parallel or additional reading is or is not a known advocate of communism or Marxist socialism, is or is not a member or ex-member of the Communist party, and is or is not a member or ex-member of a communist-front organization.

Section 2. The use of any book or other writing which is prohibited by this act may be enjoined upon the application of any resident taxpayer.

Section 3. This act shall become effective January 1, 1954. However, this act shall not affect the use of any textbook heretofore adopted or approved for use in this state until one year from the date the act becomes law.

This act means that every book used in the colleges, the public schools and the trade schools of the state must be labeled. The label must indicate that the author is or is not an advocate of communism or socialism, is or is not a member of a Communist party, is or is not a member of any communist-front organization. It also must give the same information about the author of any writing cited in the book. The bill also provides that any citizen may take court action to prohibit the use of any book he thinks violates its provisions.

It is significant that this bill originated in Birmingham. The citizens of the brawling city are divided into two groups, the bourgeoisie and the workers. The latter yearn to be bourgeoisie, the former yearn for culture and do their best to buy it. In this melting pot of former farmers and of outsiders, the Dixiecrat mentality of the owners and the aspirations of the proletarian workers wage a continual and fierce battle. The rest of the state expects strange and unaccountable antics from its uncivilized big city. It does not fail to get them. Birmingham is a haven for superpatriots. Recently a Birmingham real estate association tried to ban the use of a public school textbook, *The Challenge of Democracy*. The charge was that it discouraged the purchase of homes by low income families; the real purpose was probably something else.

ANYTHING TO FIGHT COMMUNISM

Act 888 was passed by the Alabama legislature on September 19, 1953, in the closing days of its session. Undoubtedly most members did not know what they were voting on. The bill was against communism; therefore they voted for it. Probably a majority of them today regard it as a bad law.

The state superintendent of education has placed his approval upon the law and has said that he intends to see that it is obeyed. He has also stated that he hopes other states will adopt similar laws. The proponents of the bill must by now have realized, however, that they have espoused an issue that may explode in their hands. The *Montgomery Advertiser* has attacked the law with a series of devastating editorials. The publisher of the *Anniston Star* has declared it "outrageous, illegal and intolerable." Other newspapers have made similar attacks.

On February 18 the state department of education sent out a letter to county and city super-

---

Renwick C. Kennedy, "Alabama Book-Toasters," *Christian Century*, 71:428–29 (April 7, 1954), copyright 1954 Christian Century Foundation. Reprinted by permission of the publisher.

intendents explaining what they must do to bring their practices in line with the new act. Each principal was instructed to prepare a list of every book in his school, giving title, copyright date, author and publisher; then to apply to the publisher for an appropriate label for the book; then to paste the label in the book. Label B, for instance, states that the publisher has been unable to secure information. Principles have been warned that use of a book carrying Label B may involve a teacher in serious trouble if the book is later found to have a communist taint.

WATCH THOSE LABELS!

The law applies to all textbooks used in classes from the first grade to the graduate division of state schools. It applies to all library books that may be assigned for reading or reference. It applies to books owned by teachers and pupils if such books are used in the schools. It even applies to publications of the state department of education and other departments of government that may be used in any way in the public schools. It applies to all books in print and to those out of print.

Presumably Shakespeare's plays will have to be labeled. Was John Milton tainted with communism? Who knows? Who shall say? A strict interpretation of the law would almost certainly eliminate the Bible as a socialist document. Many people already so regard it. Who wrote the Mother Goose rhymes? How safe are they? There are scholars who do not regard them as simple rhymes but as veiled social and political lampoons. Who shall certify them as sound?

The University of Alabama has about a half million books in its library. Other colleges in the state have thousands of books, and there are other thousands in the public schools. Each must be labeled with a safety brand lest youth may be contaminated. In Act 888, Mr. Morgan failed to make provision for any money for the tremendous task of certifying and labeling the books.

BLOCK THOSE FOOTNOTES!

Some aspects of this insane law are amusing. Not only must the author of the book be cleared of leftish taint, but *the author of every citation in the book* must also be cleared! The writer talked with a history professor who stated that the American history tome he uses as a textbook in his college classes has more than 1,000 references to other books and authors in the text, the footnotes and the bibliography. The author of each of these citations must be certified as pure before the book can be safely and legally used.

One might expect propaganda, perhaps, in a social science book. But an algebra textbook or a treatise on atomic physics must also be cleared or it is unsafe to use. Probably no college physics department could remain open, for some scholars who have done important work in physics live behind the iron curtain.

No provision is made in the law for books whose authors are dead or whose publishing firms have gone out of business. The law requires that the firm or the author supply the statement that the book is pure. Books whose publisher and author are no longer extant will perhaps be burned. Books like the Bible and Shakespeare can presumably be cleared, since present day publishers have an interest in their continued circulation.

The law makes it possible for any crackpot, screwball or sorehead to challenge any book he dislikes. By so doing he could attack a teacher, principal or superintendent he happened to dislike by challenging a book used in his school. He need not even be able to read.

ANTI-AMERICAN RESTRICTIONS

Presumably a tainted book can be legally used if correctly labeled as such. Actually, schools would not buy such books and teachers would be fearful to use them. It will no longer be possible to read the works of Marx, Engels or even Norman Thomas in Alabama, except in private colleges.

This law is obviously un-American. It denies youth the right of free inquiry their parents have had and deprives them of the opportunity to seek the truth unhampered. The present danger in Alabama is not communism but raw fascism, of which this foolish law is an expression. Realizing this fact, school people in Alabama are becoming possessed by a great wrath. Their hope is that when the general public becomes aware of what Act 888 means, it will be repudiated. Meanwhile, the law seems likely to be ignored and unenforced. It is obviously unworkable. The next legislature will no doubt abolish it, but it may pass a substitute.

In the meantime, however, the law makes

Alabama a laughingstock. It presents an impossible problem for publishers, libraries and school people in general. It is Hitlerian in its implications. It is the kind of thing that is attempted and done in communist-controlled countries. It is an expression of the McCarthy mentality, an act of hysteria.

An editorial writer on the *Montgomery Advertiser* coined a neat term. He said of a supporter of the law that he "seems but one degree removed from a book-burner—which, we suppose, is a book-toaster."

Chapter x

Censorship in Ireland

An editorial writer for the *Commonweal,* liberal Catholic journal of opinion, recently commented:

"For some years now Ireland has maintained a tradition of dubious distinction. It has produced and suppressed more literary works of genuine merit than any other country this side of the Iron Curtain. The riots over John Synge's 'The Playboy of the Western World,' for instance, were the occasion for W. B. Yeats' fiery condemnation of the provincial, puritanical attitudes from which such suppressions derived. But the latest word from Ireland indicates the tradition is far from weakening, that the same attitudes are still flourishing." [1]

---

[1] Editorial, *Commonweal,* 67:556 (February 28, 1958).

Ireland offers an instructive case study of the workings of arbitrary and rigid censorship laws in a democratic nation. As soon as the Irish government established its independence from Great Britain, censorship of publications was proposed by the Catholic Church and by such lay bodies as the Catholic Truth Society. There is every indication, however, as Margaret Barrington stresses, that what Ireland has had for the past thirty years "is a national, not a religious censorship."

The "Censorship of Publications Bill," first enacted by the Irish Free State in 1929, functions through a Board of Censorship. Its five members, chosen by the government, are expected to read the books and then to recommend banning actions to the Minister of Justice. Since the members are people busy with other occupations, it appears that they depend chiefly upon informers to detect questionable books. The results are appalling.

Seán O'Faoláin, who describes himself as "an Irishman and a Catholic," and who is also a distinguished novelist, historian, biographer, critic, and playwright, a few years ago contributed a widely discussed article, "Love among the Irish," to *Life* magazine. Seeking an explanation of Ireland's declining birth rate, Mr. O'Faoláin concluded that the root cause was the Irish fear of sex. "Our censorship of books and publications, instigated by the clergy and submitted to, willy-nilly, by everybody," he asserted, "is a symbol of this fear of sex." Mr. O'Faoláin continued:

"In the 150 close-packed pages of the official register of books and periodicals banned by the Irish Censorship Board we find the name of almost every single Irish writer of note, some for one book, some for several. The banning is done in secret. There is no appeal to the courts of law, apart from a possible indictment of the Minister for Justice on the grounds of unconstitutional behavior, a process beyond the means of any writer and not very likely, in the present state of public opinion, to be fruitful. After 20 years of agitation, headed originally by such writers as the late AE and W. B. Yeats, an appeal board was established, also giving its decisions in secret conclave, and without right of appeal therefrom to the courts of law. It has debanned a minute fraction of banned books and periodicals, by which time the books are often out of print and the writer's name irretrievably smeared.

"Among authors who, for one book or several, have been considered indecent and obscene are George Bernard Shaw, William Faulkner, Hervey Allen, Graham Greene, F. Scott Fitzgerald, Eric Linklater, Lucius Apuleius, Ernest Hemingway, Erskine Caldwell, Thomas Wolfe, John Dos Passos, Somerset Maugham, Aldous Huxley, James T. Farrell, Jean Paul Sartre, Albert Camus, Arthur Koestler, André Malraux, Charles Morgan, Anatole France, John Steinbeck, Joyce Cary, Sean O'Casey, Liam O'Flaherty, Frank O'Connor, George Moore, Sinclair Lewis. . . . Really, the roster is so lengthy with its thousands of names, that one might be done with it by saying that the motto of the Censorship Board could be, 'If it's good we've got it!'

"Nor is this all. Under the influence of this official censorship a widespread censorship-rabies has developed throughout the country. If any old woman, of either sex, utters an objection to a library book (as they do early and often) the librarian must withdraw it from his shelves unless he is prepared to live like a hunted beast for the rest of his life. I have before me several private lists, exchanged between librarians, of books considered unsuitable within their bailiwicks. A list issued by the Dublin County Libraries Committee, headed 'Books Considered Unsuitable for General Circulation,' includes among other astonishing titles: George Borrow's *Lavengro,* Thomas Hardy's *Tess of the D'Urbervilles,* Feodor Dostoevski's *Crime and Punishment,* Leo Tolstoi's *Anna Karenina,* Victor Hugo's *The Hunchback of Notre Dame,* Willa Cather's *Death Comes for the Archbishop* and the complete works of John Galsworthy.

"Any reader with a gram of imagination will be able to imagine that young people in a country which sees dangers to chastity in *Death Comes for the Archbishop* are not living in an atmosphere favorable to a sane or healthy attitude to sex. The only ray of light is that of farce. Some time ago a priest objected to a performance of *Othello.* And when O'Casey's *The Shadow of a Gunman* visited Cork the local dean decided to do some censoring. (He has since gone to his reward where all men and women are angels and Irish men and women, of course, the most angelic angels of the lot.) In this play a volley of shots evokes from one of the characters the terrified cry, 'Jesus, Mary an' Joseph!' The line was cut on the ground that no proper Irish person would utter such a cry. The play went on, and the shots went off, evoking a terrified cry of 'Jesus, Mary an' Joseph!' in the first row of the pit—from a lady.

"One novel banned as indecent was written—the censors discovered too late—over a pen name by Count Michael de la Bedoyère, the respected editor of *The Catholic Herald*."[2]

The heavy hand of censorship nowhere falls more heavily than on the Irish librarians. Their dilemma was posed in an editorial in *An Leabharlann, Journal of the Library Association of*

---

[2] Seán O'Faoláin, "Love among the Irish," *Life,* 34:152–54 (March 16, 1953), © 1953 Time, Inc.

Ireland. In part, the editor's lament went as follows:

"Although we have had a Censorship of Publications Act for over quarter of a century, the end of public controversy on the subject is nowhere in sight. In private argument it must rank second in popularity to politics or the cost of living; but of all three, the Censorship Act must stand first as to the vastness of ignorance it is possible for the average person to possess on a topic of major public interest.

"The librarian is frequently obliged to temper this ignorance in his readers, especially those who stand amazed at the exclusion of certain books and writers from the libraries. He has to explain how the selection of fiction is affected by the Censorship Board's misapplication and misinterpretation of the 1946 Act, and by the censoriousness of the local reader whose recent assumption of power over The Book is the least known of the phenomena created by legal prohibition.

"Let us set down a few facts. No reputable bookseller in this country will traffic in obscenity or indecency, and neither will any librarian. Not so long ago, eighty per cent of the books on prohibited lists had never been seen in an Irish bookshop or on library shelves. In the list of November last there was a book which is said to be a classic, by a classic writer, of which not much more than a dozen copies were sold before the prohibition. It was revoked, and sales went up. The January list has a popular adventure story first published twelve years ago and forgotten (until the ban) by most people.

"Public libraries are the largest buyers of books in this country, and the majority of people who read books get them from the libraries, which make great efforts to select the best publications in every subject and to avoid giving offence to any kind of person. Principles of selection based on long experience, on demand and on prudence, have been evolved and work successfully. There is, for instance, a section in the 1946 Act which enjoins on the Board of Censors the necessity for considering the literary, artistic, scientific or historic merit or importance of the books before it; sensible advice that might very well be found in any textbook of Book Selection for student librarians. But it is ignored by the Board, and the consequences for libraries and for literature in Ireland are lamentable.

"Books being now prohibited by the sackful, it is impossible to say in advance what is likely to be banned, or when. The librarian has three courses left to him. He can try to cast off the spectre of censorship which stalks this land, and buy according to his judgment, knowing that some of his selections will be banned. He can buy 'on approval' for selected readers, provided books are kept in mint condition in preparation for a return to the bookseller when the first (or second? or third?) banned list appears. Or he selects nothing but light romance, cowboy stories and possibly a few shockers. The first scheme presupposes throwing out public money; the second is bad, undemocratic, and creates a class of privileged readers; the third is treachery to the whole idea and purpose of the public library movement.

"The Censorship Board does not know what 'obscene' and 'indecent' mean in literature; nor does the Appeal Board know how these words have attached themselves to certain banned books, for it has revoked orders in something like eighty per cent of the appeals made to it last year. Unfortunately for libraries, the damage has been done before the revocation; it is not easy to get a branded book accepted by a local committee. Further, the unbanning of a book stimulates an unhealthy demand that ignores its literary quality.

"What can the librarian do? There was a time when great reliance was placed on reviews (of novels in particular) appearing in Catholic periodicals. That day has gone, for too many recommended books are being prohibited. Who then is he to rely on? Is he totally wrong in his attitude towards current literature, and especially towards the operations of the Censorship Board? There is not much he can object to in the Act as written . . .

"The dilemma of the Irish librarian is serious. An eminent theologian has written that 'Catholic authors are under no obligation to cater to the prejudices of a sanctimonious bourgeoisie.' This dictum also applies to the librarian, but he must bow to the civil law in regard to censorship, even when he realises that the censorship may be ill-applied, and not in accord with the advice of theologians whom he dare not follow." [3]

Actually, the first fierce onslaughts on litera-

---

[3] *An Leabharlann, Journal of the Library Association of Ireland,* 14:3–4 (March, 1956).

ture in Ireland date back more than half a century. As Robert Hogan commented in the *New Republic:*

"The Irish dramatic resurgence of the past 60 years has been as blotted by censorship, suppression, vilification and riot as it has been illuminated by masterpieces and genius. The celebrated riot impelled by the use of the word 'shift' in J. M. Synge's *The Playboy of the Western World* in 1907 was merely an overture to the symphony of vituperation of the ensuing decades. Sean O'Casey's second great play, *The Plough and the Stars,* was greeted with as enthusiastic a riot as was enjoyed by *The Playboy.* The audience screamed, roared, wrenched up seats from the auditorium floor, threw shoes and other handy missiles. One man climbed onto the stage and was smartly dispatched back into the stalls by a clip on the jaw by Barry Fitzgerald. W. B. Yeats, in long white hair and evening dress, stormed onto the stage and bawled his infuriated contempt unheard into the uproar. Constables flooded into the theatre to restore order." [4]

That the situation has not improved appreciably during the intervening fifty years was demonstrated in May, 1958, at the Dublin International Theatre Festival. The Dublic Tostal Council's festival committee decided to drop production of Allan McClelland's play, *Bloomsday,* a dramatization of James Joyce's *Ulysses,* while Sean O'Casey withdrew his latest play, *The Drums of Father Ned,* because he was unwilling to grant the producer's demand that he be given authority to make such alterations as he might require.

Since the writers under heaviest attack are highly literate and, like all good Irishmen, never run away from a fight, the prolonged controversy over censorship in Ireland has produced some powerful polemics. An excellent historical study, with William Butler Yeats as the central figure, is Professor Marion Witt's "'Great Art Beaten Down': Yeats on Censorship."

Yeats himself, then serving as a senator in the Dáil Éireann, eloquently expressed his opposition to the censorship bill when it was first introduced in 1928. These views are stated in the *Spectator* for September 29, 1928, from which his "The Irish Censorship" is taken.

Another stalwart fighter against the bill was "AE," George William Russell, one of Yeats' lifelong friends. AE, the pen name under which Russell always wrote, was active in the Irish literary renaissance, one of the founders of the famous Abbey Theatre, and through his editorship of the *Irish Statesman* an influential journalist. His "The Censorship in Ireland" appeared in the London *Nation* at the height of the controversy over the censorship bill.

Francis Hackett, Irish-American critic, biographer, and novelist, author of "A Muzzle Made in Ireland," was still another native son who experienced at first hand the rigors of the Irish censorship. His novel, *The Green Lion,* and his wife's *Eve's Doctor* were prohibited by government censors in Ireland, causing the Hacketts to shake the dust of the island off their feet and go to reside in Mrs. Hackett's native Denmark.

The distaff side is heard from in Margaret Barrington's "The Censorship in Eire." An Irish writer who has been published extensively in the United States, Miss Barrington in private life is married to Liam O'Flaherty, novelist and short-story writer, also a notable figure in the Irish literary revival. Naturally, many of her husband's works are on the Irish index of banned books.

An Irish historian of note, Brian Inglis, views his country's problem in "Smuggled Culture." Inglis' *The Story of Ireland,* issued in 1958, is regarded as one of the most adequate and readable general histories of Ireland to date. In an earlier work, *The Freedom of the Press in Ireland, 1784–1841,* Inglis examines in historical perspective some of the questions that continue to trouble his native land.

The concluding selection is by a writer who was for a number of years New York's most popular newspaper columnist. Heywood Broun's "It Seems to Me" column, first in the *New York Tribune,* and later in the *New York World* and *New York Telegram,* was widely read and quoted. His department, "It Seems to Heywood Broun," ran in the *Nation* from 1925 to 1931. The piece reproduced here makes it seem that the propensity toward censorship and sensitivity toward criticism follow the Irish even when they leave home—possibly a carry-over from their centuries-old struggle for independence from Great Britain.

---

[4] Robert Hogan, "O'Casey and the Archbishop," *New Republic,* 138:29 (May 19, 1958).

Marion Witt
"GREAT ART BEATEN DOWN": YEATS ON CENSORSHIP

When William Butler Yeats made his first visit to America in 1903, the political and religious tolerance on all sides amazed and delighted him in contrast to the hard intolerance of every group in his native Ireland. After many years of effort to foster in Ireland what he had admired in the United States, Yeats recognized sadly, as his life neared its end in the thirties, that in a world hastening toward war fewer and fewer people anywhere stood independently against the increasing efforts to curtail freedom of thought and opinion in the name of some orthodoxy. Some of Yeats's biographers and critics, emphasizing his romantic nationalism and the supposed authoritarianism of his later years, have neglected his fight against censorship in Ireland, his sustained struggle to keep the human mind everywhere free to criticize, speculate, and create. The latest historian of the Abbey Theatre, Peter Kavanagh, makes clear that such success as Yeats had in Ireland was personal, since within a few months after his death in 1939 many pressure groups wrecked completely the artistic standards of the famous institution he had defended for forty years. Today the Abbey languishes with plays chosen not for excellence but because they are written in Gaelic or because they are theologically or politically "correct"; and Ireland maintains a moral censorship of printed matter so strict as to make her absurd— the 1948 list of *Books Prohibited in Eire* contains over two thousand titles. Yet from the beginning to the end of his life, as poet, playwright, theatre manager, and public man, Yeats never surrendered to the forces of repression.

Yeats always believed that any kind of censorship is dangerous, and he repeatedly stated that unless the Abbey could be free of government or mob interference, he preferred to close its doors. He early protested censorship by the Anglican or Roman Catholic clergy, by supersensitive Irish nationalists, or by the English government in Ireland. He inveighed against a boycotting philistinism that thought Rossetti's women "guys," Rodin's women "ugly," and Ibsen "immoral"; against the scorn of the Anglo-Irish (as represented by Trinity College, Dublin) for Irish myth of the past or Irish life in the present; against the fixed conventions of the commercial theatre. Theatrical orthodoxy, Yeats said, is "much less pliant than the orthodoxy of the church, for there is nothing so passionate as a vested interest disguised as an intellectual conviction." In the theatre he found, too, that the English censor rarely interfered with anything that made money, "for money is always respectable." All these—Irish patriots, pulpits, philistines, the English governing classes, the subservient critics of the commercial theatre —used as tool a venal press which gladly whipped up an artificial frenzy. Yeats scorned "that defense of virtue by those who have but little, which is the pomp and gallantry of journalism and its right to govern the world." The press employed, too, a method still effective. To Yeats it was "the greatest and most ignoble power of journalism, the art of repeating a name again and again with some ridiculous or evil association."

The support Yeats gave to men he personally disliked or to works he did not admire is more significant than his championship of the plays of his friend Synge. Yeats's blindness to Shaw's artistry, for example, in no way affected his defense against the English government of the Abbey Theatre's right in 1909 to play *The Shewing-Up of Blanco Posnet*, which had been banned in England. Though the English government threatened to revoke the patent of the Abbey and Yeats and Lady Gregory actually faced the closing of their little theatre and the loss by fine of a small capital slowly accumulated, they stood firm and triumphed over the Castle. In part they won because they had already successfully resisted the Catholic church over Yeats's *Countess Cathleen* and the Irish nationalists over Synge's *Playboy of the Western World*. In his late years when Yeats rarely devoted his energy to reviewing, it is significant that his comment in 1933 on an unknown young Irishman's new book emphasizes not so much the excellence of the book as Ireland's need for

---

Marion Witt, " 'Great Art Beaten Down': Yeats on Censorship," *College English*, 13:248–58 (February, 1952), copyright 1952 by the National Council of Teachers of English. Reprinted (without footnotes) by permission of the publisher.

unpurged naturalism and Yeats's own desire to protect works for which he could not feel sympathy:

> Much modern Irish literature is violent, harsh, almost brutal, in its insistence upon the bare facts of life. Again and again I have defended plays or novels unlike anything I have myself attempted, or anything in the work of others that has given me great pleasure, because I have known that they were medicinal to a people struggling against second-hand thought and insincere emotion.

In 1927 when the Irish Dail was moving toward a law on censorship, Yeats wrote a friend:

> Have you read Liam O'Flaherty's *Informer* or his *Mr. Gilhooley?* I think they are great novels and too full of abounding natural life to be terrible despite their subjects. They are full of that tragic farce we have invented. I imagine that part of the desire for censorship here is the desire to keep him out.

This praise carries no hint of a venomous attack O'Flaherty had made on Yeats in the preceding year (1926) because of the way Yeats had defended O'Casey's *Plough and the Stars*. In a hysterical letter printed in the *Irish Statesman* O'Flaherty classed Yeats with "pompous fools" and said he had risen to fame on the shoulders of the heroic Irish nationalists of the preceding generation. O'Flaherty's raging anger and absurd charges in no way affected Yeats's literary judgment that the ebullient young novelist should be heard.

From the beginning Yeats's arguments against censorship grew out of his firm conviction that literature, supremely important, should never be a servant to morals or politics. In 1896 he wrote:

> Ireland . . . is so busy with opinions that she cannot understand that imaginative literature wholly, and all literature in some degree, exists to reveal a more powerful and passionate, a more divine world than ours; and not to make our ploughing and sowing, our spinning and weaving, more easy or more pleasant, or even to give us a good opinion of ourselves by glorifying our past or our future.

Deprived of the religious beliefs of his youth, Yeats made for himself a kind of religion of the truths revealed in the world's great books. Literature, he soon insisted, is "the great teaching power of the world, the ultimate creator of all values . . . not only in the sacred books whose power everybody acknowledges, but by every movement of imagination in song or story or drama that height of intensity and sincerity has made literature at all." Every masterpiece, then, is "a portion of the conscience of mankind."

If literature is the great teaching power, as Yeats assumed, charges of immorality hurled against it by press and pulpit will be found most frequent exactly when men of letters illuminate some obscure corner of the conscience. Every increase in conscience, therefore, as men of letters understand the term, will make literature, especially drama, its most immediately powerful form, "more daring, more logical, more free-spoken," and, to "the rough and ready conscience of the newspaper and pulpit," more immoral. In an appeal to nationalism, Yeats told the Irish that this moral puritanism, "a pretended hatred of vice and a real hatred of intellect," was not Irish at all but an "English cuckoo." To the clergy who wanted "all mankind painted with a halo or with horns," Yeats insisted that "there is no evil that men and women may not be driven into by their virtues all but as readily as by their vices." To all those who believe every work must support a moral law he said that "the subject of art is not law, which is a kind of death, but the praise of life, and it has no commandments that are not positive."

When a Connaught bishop charged his people that they "should never read stories about the degrading passion of love," Yeats wrote that the bishop must be ignorant of "a chief glory of his Church." Yet the "English cuckoo" of puritanism nested itself so well in Ireland that a quarter of a century later, when the Irish were ready to pass their Censorship of Publications Bill, Yeats used more elaborately the same arguments he had addressed to the bishop of Connaught. "The Censorship and St. Thomas Aquinas" begins with a sentence from the proposed bill: "The word 'indecent' shall be construed as including 'calculated to excite sexual passions.'" Such a definition, Yeats observed, "ridiculous to a man of letters, must be sacrilegious to a Thomist." Quoting Cardinal Mercier, Yeats pointed out that St. Thomas, unlike Plato (or Descartes) held "that the soul is wholly present in the whole body and all its parts." Then in an eloquent passage Yeats showed how in the abstract splendor of Byzantine basilicas, "stood saints with thought-tortured faces and bodies, . . . a Christ with a face of pitiless intellect, or a pinched, flat-breasted virgin holding a child like a wooden doll." An art of the body, "an especial glory of the Catholic Church," within half a century after St. Thomas' death, inspired Giotto, and within three centuries bodies natural and beautiful and "represented with all the patience of 'sexual passion'" came from Andrea del Sarto or Raphael or Titian. Yeats ended his argument by asking: "Are we prepared to exclude such art from Ireland and to sail in a ship of fools, fools that dressed bodies Michael Angelo left naked, Town Councillors of Montreal who hid Discobolus in the cellar?" Despite Yeats's plea, A. E.'s temperate arguments, and Shaw's vivid diatribe against a legal censorship, Ireland was prepared to sail in a ship with no berths for recalcitrant genius. In 1929 the Censorship of Publications Bill became law.

Yeats realized fully that literature, always personal, always "one man's vision of the world, one man's experience, . . . can only be popular when men are ready to welcome the visions of others. A community that is opinion-ridden," he added, "even when those opinions are in themselves noble, is likely to put its creative minds into some sort of a prison." When in 1905 Synge's *Well of the Saints* was played in Dublin in an atmosphere of quiet, deep hostility, Yeats reported to John Quinn, "We will have a hard fight before we get the right of every man to see the world in his own way admitted." Synge's intense personality raised well an issue previously unknown in Ireland: the creative man of letters unacceptable to the public because of the very freshness of his moral judgment, the originality and depth of his imagination. The objection to Synge was, Yeats said, "not mainly that he makes the country people unpleasant and immoral, but that he has got a standard of morals and intellect." The public "shrink from Synge's harsh, heroical, clean, windswept view of things." Later Yeats insisted that Synge was "but the more hated because he gave his country what it needed, an unmoved mind where there is a perpetual last day, a trumpeting, and coming up to judgement." Forging the uncreated conscience of a race is, as Joyce also learned, a task for which the smith receives belated thanks. Yeats experienced no deeper bitterness than the recognition that the excellent is hated simply because it is excellent: that Parnell and Hugh Lane were repudiated because of the very originality and nobility of what they would do for their people.

Years after Synge was dead, Yeats was insisting again on the need for audacity of thought in an essay so pointed that even a friendly and sympathetic editor, A. E., dared not publish it for fear it would endanger the very existence of the *Irish Statesman.* In the *Dial,* accordingly, Yeats held up to ridicule two particularly foolish examples of Irish clerical censorship. One of the censored works was an old masterpiece; the other, a modern imaginative recreation of a religious story. The Christian Brothers had put out a circular headed "A Blasphemous Publication," which told of a "horrible insult to God, . . . a Christmas Carol set to music and ridiculing in blasphemous language the Holy Family." The editor of a Catholic boys' paper burned copies in the Dublin streets with filming of the ceremony. The "devilish literature" burned was the *Cherry Tree Carol.* Yeats said he resented educators so ignorant "that they do not recognize the most famous Carol in the English language"; but his weightiest argument, aside from the fact that the *Cherry Tree Carol* is a masterpiece, "because something of great moment is there completely stated," is that the whole carol follows from a belief in the Incarnation. Obviously, Yeats said, the churchmen who condemned it did not believe in that event. Though Yeats himself did not, he desired belief; hence the old carol and all similar art delighted him.

The modern work banned and defended for audacity of thought, Lennox Robinson's story, "The Madonna of Slieve Dun," though earlier rejected by an English editor because it might give offense, had already been published in an American periodical with no word of reproach from its readers. When "The Madonna of Slieve Dun" appeared in Dublin in the first issue of *Tomorrow* (1924), the magazine was immediately banned, and in the resulting furor Mr. Robinson was discharged from his position on the National Library Board. The story tells of a religious girl who dreamed of the Second Coming, was ravished while unconscious, convinced herself and her family that the child was the Redeemer until all was revealed by the tramp who had raped her. Because Roberto Rossellini's film, *The Miracle,* banned as blasphemous in New York in 1950, is closely parallel in concept, Yeats's arguments in defense of Robinson are still pertinent. Robinson's enemies forgot, said Yeats, that "we cannot understand any historical event till we have set it amidst new circumstance"; for minds that have belief "grow always more abundant, more imaginative, more full of fantasy even, as its object approaches; and to deny that play of mind is to make belief impossible." Yeats thought that "the intellect of Ireland is irreligious, and its moral system, being founded upon habit, not intellectual conviction, has shown of late that it cannot resist the onset of modern life." Moreover, the Irish, "quick to hate and slow to love, . . . have never lacked a press to excite the most evil passions." The whole, Yeats pointed out, is a European problem (he might have said world-wide), shown in an acute form in Ireland. The only solution lies in "audacity of speculation and creation," in a new consideration of the foundations of existence. A couple of years later, apropos of the censorship bill, Yeats wrote in England that, because all great literature engages in just such audacity of speculation, the proposed outrageous censorship law would ban all great love poetry and such writers as Darwin, Marx, Flaubert, Balzac, and Proust. The Irish, he said, "do not understand that you cannot unscramble eggs, that every country passing out of automatism passes through demoralization, and that it has no choice but to go on into intelligence." *Playboy* and *Plough and the Stars* were attacked because, like the *Cherry Tree Carol,* "they contain what a belief, tamed down into a formula, shudders at, something wild and ancient."

Yeats's views on the rights of the individual conscience, expressed often in his remarks on censorship, nowhere are shown more clearly than in his protest as Irish senator against the divorce bill, aimed to impose on the Protestant minority the views on divorce of the Catholic majority. Yeats's speech, which criticized both Catholic and Anglican ecclesiastics, defended the liberty of minorities, the right of the individual conscience, rather than divorce as such. Never did Yeats speak more eloquently, and the whole led to what Joseph Hone called "the proud and justifiable peroration":

> We against whom you have done this thing are no petty people. We are one of the great stocks of Europe. We are the people of Burke; we are the people of Grattan; we are the people of Swift, the people of Parnell. We have created the most of the modern literature of this country. We have created the best of its political intelligence.

On the issues joined in the Free State, Yeats spoke even more frankly in the *Irish Statesman* than he had on the floor of the senate. He told his readers that there had been no such spectacle of Catholic majority ruling for the non-Catholic minority since medieval Spain. He reminded Irishmen that the church had been wrong to fight against the union of Italy and that the divorce bill was a blow against the union of Ireland, since Ulster Protestants must be convinced that in joining Eire they will not lose their right of individual judgment. Insisting that laws should be made "by statesmen and not by a celibate clergy, however patriotic or public-spirited," Yeats urged the minority to resist, since fanaticism had won this victory and might win more.

Against the forces of repression Yeats advised continual vigilance, but he suggested more positive measures. The first of these was education. Years before he became a senator, Yeats had noted that education in Irish secondary schools, especially the Catholic schools, substituted pedantry for taste, "pedantry, which opens to the mind a kind of sensual ease." He found "no young man out of these schools who has not been injured by the literature and the literary history learned there." Young Catholics, however, who had not been through these schools Yeats thought more imaginative than Protestant boys and girls of the same age. This led him to the conclusion that "Catholic secondary education destroys . . . much that the Catholic religion gives. Provincialism destroys the nobility of the Middle Ages." In a speech before the Irish Literary Society in 1925, based on his experience as inspector of schools for the senate, Yeats pleaded anew for the arts in Ireland, held back by ignorance and by defective education. Base the curriculum, he said, for children on the old folk life, and for the mature intellect upon Berkeley's philosophy and Burke's view of history, "and Ireland is reborn, potent, armed and wise." If this curriculum seems a shade simple to achieve so large a purpose, Yeats concluded that religion should be taught as "the most powerful part" of the history of the world and that the child must know the religious part of its whole inheritance, "not as a mere thought . . . but as part of its emotional life."

Yeats, like most other Irish men of letters, insisted, too, that children should be taught in what was for most of them their native tongue, English. The effort to restore by law a primitive language was aimed, Yeats believed, at isolating Ireland from the world. In a symposium he wrote on "Compulsory Gaelic," Peter (certainly Yeats himself) probes the psychology which makes a nation long subject to another wish, in turn, to enslave its own citizens. "We . . . prefer," says Peter, "to make men servile, rather than permit their opinions to differ from our own, and if there is a man notable for intellect and sincerity, we fit some base motive to his every act that he may not prevail against us." When Paul defends the right of the government to compel instruction in Gaelic and even urges that certain literatures like those of Spain or Italy "would go better into Gaelic than into English," Peter comes to the center of his argument:

> As soon as a play or book is translated, which goes deep into human life, it will be denounced for immorality or irreligion. Certain of our powerful men advocate Gaelic that they may keep out the European mind. They know that if they do not build a wall, this country will plunge, as Europe is plunging, into philosophic speculation.

Timothy, the third in the symposium, tries unsuccessfully to make peace between the contestants by urging the possibility of "a kind of politics where one need not be certain," for "imitation is automatic, but creation moves in a continual uncertainty"; and he concludes ironically: "There are moments—unpractical moments, perhaps—when I think the State should leave the mind free to create."

Not all Yeats's forays for literary freedom were solemn affairs, for he often displayed that love of mischief he had thought near the core of the Irish intellect. In the course of his earnest speech on divorce he paused to ask whether the stern moralists considered removing from Dublin streets the statues of Nelson, O'Connell, and Parnell, whose private lives would not meet standards of conduct that the new state meant to set up. Lord Glenavy, presiding over the senate, asked whether the debate might not leave the dead alone; but Yeats refused to do so either in legislative halls or later in an amusing poem. "The Three Monuments" quotes the popular statesmen who, in the shadow of the statues of Ireland's most renowned patriots, stand and urge the nation to cling to purity, shun ambition:

> For intellect would make us proud
> And pride bring in impurity:
> The three old rascals laugh aloud.

The whole project of *Tomorrow,* founded at Yeats's suggestion on a real belief in the immortality of the soul and charging bishops with heresy in a fashion Lionel Johnson had indulged in during Yeats's youth, was conceived, no doubt, as mischief. That the first issue contained this statement on immortality (certainly suggested by Yeats and probably his work), Lennox Robinson's madonna story, and Yeats's great sonnet, "Leda and the Swan," made banning inevitable. When the ban came, Yeats was in highest spirits and dreamed of a wild paper for the young, which would suffer suppression, he hoped, many times, "for the logical assertion, with all fitting deductions, of the immortality of the soul." When Frank O'Connor, F. R. Higgins, and Yeats protested the ban on Shaw's *The Adventures of the Black Girl in Her Search for God,* Yeats carried, to the amazement of the younger men, a roll of photographs of Michelangelo's frescoes in the Sistine Chapel to prove to the Irish official that nudity is endurable in the Vatican. This argument was hardly more serious than Shaw's suggestion that the Black Girl wear petticoats in an Irish version. Yeats had his fun baiting the official, and the ban on *Black Girl* remained in Ireland until 1947.

Yeats lived almost ten years after the passage of the Irish censorship bill, and all who, like T. S. Eliot, think the "principle" of censorship is tenable may well brood on his experience under government rule of the intellectuals. Yeats's first move, as Sean O'Casey has recently reported, was to propose and secure the appointment of a Protestant cleric to the censorship committee. Since any ban had to be unanimous, Yeats thought his candidate would vote against the Roman Catholic members and thus make censorship harmless. To his consternation the Protestant cleric, stricter than his colleagues, demanded banning of books the others were ready to pass. Yeats's positive contribution to the struggle in the thirties was founding the Irish Academy of Letters to add dignity to literature and to unite the intellectuals against the ridiculous censorship of books. Significantly, Yeats recorded in his diary of 1930 that Synge "must have felt compelled to his conflict with the pasteboard morality of political Dublin to make the world of his imagination more and more complete." Perhaps some such impulse motivated the older Yeats as ill and tired he continued his campaign in the face of defeat.

Though Yeats's own printed works escaped the official Irish ban, his poems were not welcomed by Irish editors or critics, and the Abbey Theatre was under constant attack. Sir Herbert Grierson has noted since Yeats's death that Yeats often said to him in their early meetings "that once the fight with England was over it would be followed by the fight for intellectual freedom against the domination of the priesthood." In New York, where Yeats was in 1932 gathering funds for the Irish Academy, Grierson reminded Yeats, "The clergy seem to have won a pretty complete victory," and Yeats "acknowledged somewhat sadly that it was so." In 1935 Yeats arrived in Dublin to find wild denunciations of the Abbey for blasphemy and appeals to the government to withdraw the subsidy and introduce a censorship of the stage. The offense was producing O'Casey's *The Silver Tassie.* Yeats, as a director of the theatre and still its guiding spirit, was especially denounced by the *Standard,* the chief clerical newspaper. In all this furor he said that the educated Catholics, clerics and laymen, knew that his fight was against ignorance but that they could not openly support the Abbey in the contest. In the next year, 1936, aroused by the Civil War in Spain, a gathering of bigots in a new Christian Front threatened mob violence against the Irish Academy of Letters and against Yeats in particular. He was much disturbed when the Abbey wanted to do his new play, *The Herne's Egg,* and a little later greatly relieved when the production was abandoned; for he found himself no longer fit for riots and a bad one seemed almost certain.

In 1934 Yeats wrote that the Abbey Theatre of world fame and the Irish Academy were held in low regard because the upper class cared for Ireland only as a place for sport, while the rest of the population was "drowned in religious and political fanaticism." When he had protested to members of the government over some attack on the theatre or the banning of a book, Yeats said he came away feeling that the minister felt as he did, "but was helpless; the mob reigned." Though Yeats still faintly hoped for

> Might of the Church and the State,
> Their mobs put under their feet,

he at once warned the poet,

> Wander in dreams no more;
> What if the Church and the State
> Are the mob that howls at the door!

At this point Yeats made the gloomiest prophecy he ever made for Ireland:

> If that reign [of the mob] is not broken our public life will move from violence to violence or from violence to apathy, our Parliament disgrace and debauch those that enter it; our men of letters live like outlaws in their own country.

As Yeats's *saeva indignatio* deepened in his last decade, he inevitably questioned the importance of the nationalism and racism he had long advocated; but he never openly admitted his doubts. Instead, he continued to make what he called "necessary" senatorial speeches, claiming the Irish literary movement essential to holding together the thirty million Irish scattered over the world and insisting that all his work had been to that end; yet in a letter reporting one such speech to Dorothy Wellesley, he added, "My dear, I am anarchic as a sparrow," and quoted Blake on the worthlessness of kings and parliaments. The mask is torn away for a moment, too, in a poem, "A Parnellite at Parnell's Funeral" (1934), where the Parnellite, convinced of the guilt of all the people, not of any man or men, thirsting for accusation of himself, insists:

> All that was sung,
> All that was said in Ireland is a lie
> Bred out of the contagion of the throng,
> Saving the rhyme rats hear before they die.

Purgatory (1938), the terrible last play, is a palinode of Yeats's earlier nationalism. He said himself that a spirit in the play "suffers because of its share, when alive, in the destruction of an honoured house. That destruction is taking place all over Ireland today." Before the ruined house "the remorse of the dead" for their part in this ruin and "the misery of the living" are linked in the final line of *Purgatory.* No sharper contrast could be conceived than between *Purgatory* and that early bit of patriotic sentimentality, *Cathleen ni Houlihan,* of the four beautiful green fields and the fighting Irish sons. If Ireland had come to such a state as *Purgatory* symbolizes, Yeats's talk of "our Irish fight" was meaningless. A. E., equally helpless in the new Ireland, told an American audience that 100 per cent Irishmen, Englishmen, or Americans are "the most perfectly intolerable people, at least from the artist's and poet's point of view." Yeats never publicly agreed. Only in a letter did he concede that the fight for right and justice had nothing to do with this or that country, that it was Shaw's fight, every man's fight, to stiffen the spines of the wise and the good against the stupid and the evil in Ireland, in England, everywhere.

On the Boiler, published in the year after Yeats's death and directed to Irish readers, attributed all oppressions in Ireland to the new representative government which gave Ireland over to the incompetent. After accounts of burning of books by mobs who invaded public libraries—or even, in Galway, the solemn disposal by a library committee of all of Shaw's works—Yeats scornfully thought it probable that many men in Irish public life should never have been taught to read or write. The half-education doled out by government incompetents he found a total evil. Yet once more he suggested a curriculum for Irish schools and once more he insisted that the requirement of Gaelic as a spoken language must come slowly; for "a sudden or forced change of language may be the ruin of the soul." Bitter, violent, outspoken, Yeats perched "on the boiler," the platform used by a fanatic Irishman of his youth; and here ended his fight with those he believed to be enemies of all his imagination valued.

Every important account of Irish life and literature since 1930 notes how the censorship outlaws Irish men of letters in their own country or sends them to Paris, London, or New York. Leslie Daiken in 1936 wrote that "as a result of veto, ban and boycott the whole social atmosphere tends not only to thwart, but atrophy, the creative impulse among poets, and reduce the rising generation to one of cultural frustrates." In 1949 Sean O'Faolain complained as a Catholic writer that "the Church relies on the weapon of rigid authority" and that the priest "takes the easy way out by applying to all intellectual ideas the test of their effect on the poor and the ignorant." L. A. G. Strong, also in 1949, said:

> Ireland today persecutes every writer who is not content to make his act of submission and accept a censorship which in this country [England] would be thought excessive for a girls' school. Her rulers, spiritual and temporal, seem resolved to keep her in a preadolescent stage. Few artists are able to endure this.

In the nineties Yeats had planned to found a system of libraries to educate the Irish for wider tolerance in the arts; but today, as Frank O'Connor has pointed out, no Protestant may be a librarian in Eire, nor may the patrons of libraries read most modern literature.

Yeats lost his battle in Ireland and added his name to the roster of great men who have struggled for the freedom of the human mind against powers that would enslave it. As his friend Sir William Rothenstein wrote, "Yeats, like Shaw, was a man of great courage who championed losing causes and men who were unfairly assailed." Rothenstein has noted, too, how Yeats risked the American popularity he depended on when he protested in the New York press against the moral refusal of hotels to admit Gorki and his mistress. Today in the United States the issues are greater than a hotel room for Gorki. Books and films and plays are banned and boycotted not because they are pornographic or dangerous to the national security but because they represent a group unflatteringly or displease a powerful organization or shock an adolescent sense of reality or even because, though the work is innocent, the author is suspected of having once been "subversive." Yeats's arguments against censorship in Ireland are unhappily more pertinent in the United States today than when, almost fifty years ago, he rejoiced in the easy tolerance he found in the new world.

William Butler Yeats
THE IRISH CENSORSHIP

The other night I woke with a sense of wellbeing, of recovered health and strength. It took me a moment to understand that it had come to me because our men and women of intellect, long separated by politics, have in the last month found a common enemy and drawn together. Two days before I had gone to see an old friend, from whom I had been separated for years, and was met with the words, "We are of the same mind at last." The Free State Government has in a month accomplished what would, I had thought, take years, and this it has done by drafting a Bill which it hates, which must be ex-

---

William Butler Yeats, "The Irish Censorship," *Spectator*, 141:391–92 (September 29, 1928), copyright 1928 by the Spectator Ltd. Reprinted by permission of the publisher.

pounded and defended by Ministers full of contempt for their own words.

Ecclesiastics, who shy at the modern world as horses in my youth shied at motor-cars, have founded a "Society of Angelic Welfare." Young men stop trains, armed with automatics and take from the guard's van bundles of English newspapers. Some of these ecclesiastics are of an incredible ignorance. A Christian Brother publicly burnt an English magazine because it contained the Cherry Tree Carol, the lovely celebration of Mary's sanctity and her Child's divinity, a glory of the mediaeval church as popular in Gaelic as in English, because, scandalized by its *naïveté,* he believed it the work of some irreligious modern poet; and this man is so confident in the support of an ignorance even greater than his own, that a year after his exposure in the Press, he permitted, or directed his society to base an appeal for public support, which filled the front page of a principal Dublin newspaper, upon the destruction of this "infamous" poem.

> Then out and spoke that little Babe
> Which was within Her womb:
> "Bow down, bow down thou cherry tree
> And give my Mother some."

The Bill is called "Censorship of Publications Bill, 1928," and empowers the Minister of Justice to appoint five persons, removable at his pleasure, who may, if that be his pleasure, remain for three years apiece, and to these persons he may on the complaint of certain "recognized associations" (The Catholic Truth Society and its like) submit for judgment book or periodical. These five persons must then say whether the book or periodical is "indecent," which word "shall be construed as including calculated to excite sexual passions or to suggest or incite to sexual immorality or in any other way to corrupt or deprave," or whether, if it be not "indecent" it inculcates "principles contrary to public morality," or "tends to be injurious or detrimental to or subversive of public morality." If they decide it is any of these things the Minister may forbid the post to carry it, individual or shop or library to sell or lend it. The police are empowered by another section to go before a magistrate who will be bound by the Bill's definition of the word "indecent" and obtain, without any reference to the committee or the Minister, a right to seize in a picture-dealer's shop, or at a public exhibition where the pictures are for sale, an Etty, or a Leighton—the police have already objected to "The Bath of Psyché"—and fine or imprison the exhibitor. Another section forbids the sale or distribution of any "appliance to be used for," or any book or periodical which advocates or contains an advertisement of any book or periodical which advocates "birth control." The *Spectator,* the *Nation,* the *New Statesman,* and *Nature,* are, I understand, liable to seizure.

This Bill, if it becomes law, will give one man, the Minister of Justice, control over the substance of our thought, for its definition of "indecency" and such vague phrases as "subversive of public morality," permit him to exclude *The Origin of Species,* Karl Marx's *Capital,* the novels of Flaubert, Balzac, Proust, all of which have been objected to somewhere on moral grounds, half the Greek and Roman Classics, Anatole France and everybody else on the Roman index, and all great love poetry. The Government does not intend these things to happen, the Commission on whose report the Bill was founded did not intend these things to happen, the holy gunmen and "The Society of Angelic Welfare" do not intend all these things to happen; but in legislation intention is nothing, and the letter of the law everything, and no Government has the right, whether to flatter fanatics or in mere vagueness of mind to forge an instrument of tyranny and say that it will never be used. Above all, they have no right to say it here in Ireland, where until the other day the majority of children left school at twelve years old, and where even now, according to its own inspectors, no primary schoolmaster opens a book after school hours.

It will, of course, appoint a "reasonable committee," and, unless the Minister of Justice decides to remove one or more of its members, four out of five must agree before anything happens. I know those reasonable committee-men who have never served any case but always make common cause against the solitary man of imagination or intellect. Had such a committee, with even those two Protestant clergymen upon it somebody suggests, censored the stage a while back, my theatre, now the State theatre, would never have survived its first years. It now performs amid popular applause four plays, of which two, when first performed, caused riots, three had to be protected by the police, while all four had to face the denunciations of Press and pulpit. Speaking from the stage, I told the last rioters—to-day's newspaper burners—that they were not the first to rock the cradle of a man of genius. By such conflict truth, whether in science or in letters, disengages itself from the past. The present Bill does not affect us, but if it passes into law the next will bring the stage under a mob censorship acting through "recognized associations."

The well-to-do classes practise "birth control" in Ireland as elsewhere, and the knowledge is spreading downwards, but the Catholic Church forbids it. If those men of science are right, who say that in a hundred years the population will overtake the food supply, it will doubtless direct the married to live side by side and yet refrain from one another, a test it has not imposed upon monk and nun, and if they do not obey—well, Swift's "Modest Proposal" remains, and that, at any rate, would make love self-supporting.

Although it was almost certain that Catholic Ireland, thinking "birth control" wrong in principle, would follow the lead of countries that, being in sore need of soldiers and cheap labour, think it undesirable and legislate against it, those who belong to the Church of Ireland or to neither Church should compel the fullest discussion. The Government is forbidden under the Treaty to favour one religion at the expense of another, which does not mean that they may not propose legislation asked for by one Church alone, but that they must show that the welfare of the State demands it. "You Mahommedans must not quote your Koran because the Christians do not believe in it, you Christians must not quote your Bible," said the chairman at the religious meeting in ancient Damascus—or was it Bagdad?—which scandalized the Spanish Traveller. Those who think it wrong to bring into the world children they cannot clothe and educate, and yet refuse to renounce that "on which the soul expands her wing," can say "no man knows whether the child is for love's sake, the fruit for the flower, or love for the child's sake, the flower for the fruit"; or quote the words of St. Thomas: *"Anima est in toto corpore."*

The enthusiasts who hold up trains are all the better pleased because the newspapers they burn are English, and their best public support has come from a newspaper that wants to exclude its rivals; but their motives may be, in the main, what they say they are, and great numbers of small shopkeepers and station-masters who vaguely disapprove of their methods approve those motives. A Government official said of these station-masters and shopkeepers the other day: "They are defending their sons and daughters and cannot understand why the good of the nine-tenths, that never open a book, should not prevail over the good of the tenth that does." Twenty years ago illegitimacy was almost unknown, infanticide unknown, and now both are common and increasing, and they think that if they could exclude English newspapers, with their police-court cases which excite the imagination, their occasional allusions to H. G. Wells which excite the intellect, their advertisements of books upon birth control which imply safety for illicit love, innocence would return. They do not understand that you cannot unscramble eggs, that every country passing out of automatism passes through demoralization, and that it has no choice but to go on into intelligence. I know from plays rejected by the Abbey Theatre that the idealist political movement has, after achieving its purpose, collapsed and left the popular mind to its own lawless vulgarity. Fortunately, the old movement created four or five permanent talents.

There are irresponsible moments when I hope that the Bill will pass in its present form, or be amended by the Republicans, as some foretell, into a still more drastic form, and force all men of intellect, who mean to spend their lives here, into a common understanding. One modern-minded Catholic writer has been hawking a letter round the Press threatening anti-clericalism; but if that come, and I do not expect it in my time, it will not come in the old form. No Irishman wants the fourteenth century, even though most damnably compromised and complicated by modern Rathmines, driven from his back door so long as the front door opens on the twentieth. Our imaginative movement has its energy from just that combination of new and old, of old stories, old poetry, old belief in God and the soul, and a modern technique. A certain implacable and able Irish revolutionary soldier put me to read Berkeley with the phrase: "There is all the philosophy a man needs"; and I have long held that intellectual Ireland was born when Berkeley wrote in that famous notebook of his after an analysis of contemporary mechanistic thought: "We Irish do not think so," or some such words. The power to create great character or possess it cannot long survive the certainty that the world is less solid than it looks and the soul much solider—"a spiritual substance" in some sense or other—and our dramatists, when they leave Ireland, or get away from the back door in some other fashion, prefer cause or general idea to characters that are an end to themselves and to each other. Synge's "Playboy" and O'Casey's "Plough and the Stars" were attacked because, like "The Cherry Tree Carol," they contain what a belief, tamed down into a formula, shudders at, something wild and ancient.

AE
THE CENSORSHIP IN IRELAND

The Irish Free State, through the publicity given to its Censorship Bill, and because of other activities by its moralists, has become, with Tennessee, a butt for the wits of the world. I am glad, both for Ireland and Tennessee, that it should be so. Light is the great germicide. When we lift a stone we see multitudes of little black creatures scurrying about, frightened by the light, trying to find some hole to hide in. Our little black creatures are scurrying about, angry and confused because of the light flung on their mentality. To what must we attribute the Bill? It is, I think, a consequence of arrested growth; or, in other words, moral infantilism. Hell is more open for Christians in Ireland than in any other country of which I have knowledge. It lies all about us in our infancy. Millions of children over the world are terrified by talk of death, hell, and the eternal damnation which follows sin. But most, as they grow up, by contact with literature or life, liberate themselves from the grosser form of these terrors, and come to a true moral wisdom. In Ireland people read but little. About 95 per cent. of boys under the old regime left the national schools at the age of twelve before any real education could begin. These semi-illiterates remain with the intellectual nature and the moral nature stunted in a permanent moral infantilism. Sex in Ireland has come to have an obscene significance, a fact on which a Freudian psychologist would have much to say. Sexual sins are almost the only ones seriously regarded by our moralists. Men may perjure themselves, rob, or commit murder, and these are but venial acts in comparison with any violation of the sex taboos.

Love itself is regarded with suspicion. Our delicacy in these matters is so refined that in a school reader the line of Goldsmith about the seat under the shade—

For talking age or whispering lovers made—

was altered, and "weary travellers" substituted for the immoral "whispering lovers." Only moral infantilism could prompt that change. A few years ago an advertisement which displayed a naked baby outraged our moral guardians so that the billposters in two counties had to go out with paintpot and brushes and put trousers on that infant. That also was moral infantilism. Again to illustrate this sensitiveness, public controversy arose over a song in the Feis competition because the word "kiss" occurred in it. Moral infantilism was rampant in that controversy. We have many, many thousands of such people, seemingly grown up, but stunted and terrified, creeping on all fours in their souls, which are in a state of infancy, feeling still all the terrors of hell with which they were made familiar so early. They form associations whose activities in other countries would bring them to jail. They invade public libraries and burn books which they have heard were evil. Of course, they have never read them themselves. Tolstoy, Shaw, Maeterlinck, Turgenieff, and Balzac are some of the authors whose books were banned or burned.

It was, I believe, members of one of these associations who drafted the Censorship Bill and forced it on Ministers. Why do Ministers accept it? They, I believe, loathe the Bill and its creators, and I imagine the Catholic hierarchy is very dubious about it indeed. These laymen outdo their own Bishops in virtue, and they, no more than Ministers, can stand up against associations of fanatical laymen, who wear a threatening halo around their heads and speak loudly in the name of virtue. Of course, our Puritans are uncultivated, and being in a state of stunted

---

AE, "The Censorship in Ireland," London *Nation & Athenaeum*, 44:435-36 (December 22, 1928), copyright 1928 by the Nation & Athenaeum. Reprinted by permission of the publisher.

moral growth they do not know their own religion. That is obvious from the definition of indecency in the Bill they drafted. It is only moral infantilism could define indecent literature as anything "calculated to excite sexual passion." These poor children did not know that they were reviving an ancient Manichean heresy by this definition, a heresy which the greatest schoolmen of their own faith had denounced. This definition would suppress in Ireland half the literature of the world which deals with the passionate love between men and women.

They do not trust either Church or State to suppress evil literature. In their Bill they throw the responsibility of rooting out what is evil on bodies which are called "recognized associations"—that is, on themselves. The original draft of their Bill had provisions enabling search to be made in private houses, so that no person could retain a copy of a book the censors had prohibited. There is no damnable outrage on the high soul of man these obscene fanatics would not commit so that none might outgrow their own ignorance, prejudices, limitations, and terrors. The associations are like witch doctors in African kraals who smell out evil. They are to discover the evil in books, and judgment is to be pronounced by a Board of Censors, whose members must know that if they do not prohibit the works denounced they themselves will be denounced as immoral pagans and their characters blackened as only the highly moral can blacken character. There is to be no defence permitted. Justice is not a virtue at all esteemed by our moralists. Let us suppose an Irish publisher to have spent some hundreds of pounds on the printing of a book. The witch doctors have smelled something evil in it. It is denounced to the Censors. The Censors prohibit it. The police must then seize and destroy every copy of the book. The publisher is ruined by order of a Board which conducts its business in secret. Neither publisher nor author has any right to appear before the Board or to defend the work. There is no right of appeal. The Courts of the Free State are set aside by the fanatics. Can we conceive of any other kind of property being so dealt with by a secret tribunal? Can we imagine in the modern world a State giving five men sitting in secret the power of taking house or field from a man, or burning his share certificates without trial or defence permitted?

It seems incredible, but our moralists have terrified Ministers so that they accept the Bill as their own. Moralists on the scent of evil will perpetrate any villainy in the name of God. Our associations seem quite ready to commit murder, for they are armed with revolvers when they descend on some unfortunate bookseller and burn his stock. The Bill gives them power to range over the whole field of thought. It is not merely what is pornographic which is aimed at. If the Bill was directed solely against pornographic literature, I would have nothing to say. But science, philosophy, political theory, are in danger, for any literature which can be regarded as "tending to be detrimental to public morality" can legally be denounced and suppressed. We know from the marauders' activities in libraries and bookshops that there is no famous author in the world who would not offend these little ones. The Hop-o'-my-Thumbs in life as in fairy tales have a hatred of the giants. Literature among the ignorant in Ireland has come to have much the same sinister significance that Bolshevism has among the readers of the more Conservative Press.

I do not deny that there is a kind of idealism behind this agitation for the suppression of evil literature. It is an idealism which is quite genuine, and it would be pleasant to think of these young warriors for heaven if they were not so childish, if they knew the first thing about the soul of man, that its virtue is to be free, to choose between the light and the dark, and that there is no virtue where there is no free choice. I think this fanaticism is a mood which will pass. It certainly is generating its own anti-toxin, for the educated in Ireland, Catholic and Protestant alike, are bitter in their hatred of the fanatics. It will not be long, I think, before this hatred becomes public, and once this happens there will be an intellectual conflict which will end, as all such conflicts do, in the victory of the free soul. The fanatics are making life so disagreeable and uncomfortable for the average man that revolt is inevitable. They denounce everything in the name of God—dances, short skirts, books, newspapers, theatres, moving pictures. I am an artist, and if they were angry because the country was becoming vulgarized, I would be in sympathy. But they do not denounce these things because they are vulgar or unbeautiful. They do not try to create a superior beauty, which is the only way to overcome bad literature. They create nothing, and their publications do not rise in literary merit beyond the penny tract. I will believe in no prophet of the Lord unless his words, even in anger, break in a foam of beauty on the ear.

Francis Hackett
A MUZZLE MADE IN IRELAND

There exists in this country a community of men and women of free minds. Some of them are Catholic by religion, some Protestant, but they have a conception of intellectual freedom in common, and with them are a number, of whom I happen to be one, who belong to no Church yet take religion seriously.

To this community I should like to address myself on the Censorship law, under which my own novel, "The Green Lion," has recently been banned.

A book is officially banned on the ground that in its general tendency it is obscene and indecent. As a piece of property it is instantly and irrevocably destroyed by this official ukase; one's livelihood, in so far as derived from Irish sales, is taken away, as well as access to the Irish public for whom the book was intended.

The material injury caused by this Censorship is evident. Less evident, and more important, is the moral injury, which is extremely serious. To protest against this injury is a public duty.

Whether a book is, in fact, indecent or the reverse, most readers cannot hope to judge since they cannot buy the book. But it is not really on this ground—whether or not a book is indecent—that the principle of Censorship can usefully be discussed. To me, I may say, it is simply incredible that any honest person could call "The Green Lion" obscene or indecent, but to assert the decency of my own work would put me in a false position. Apart from the fact that no man is a good judge in his own cause, the large question arises, What is decency? Decency varies with habit, since habit goes a long way toward making decency. What is indecent in Persia is decent in Cavan. It is still indecent in Persia, I think, for a woman to expose her face to the public gaze, yet the most prudish in Cavan do not lose their self-respect when gazed upon. In tough Chicago, I believe, the law still governs the bathing costume and calls for the concealment of nude female legs, while in Ireland one-piece bathing suits are to be seen on every beach. Once you study morals comparatively you become a little dizzy. Stonewall Jackson thought it immoral to fight a battle on a Sunday and though a professor he refused to read by any light except God's sunlight. There are certain rules of conduct, of course, which can be reduced to law, and administered as law, but there are others still in flux, subject to private judgment, and the objection to a Star Chamber is its making up the law on these open questions as it goes along. Hence the warning, Judge not and ye shall not be judged.

To argue about the decency of any specific book is the wrong approach to the Censorship. Nor is the situation helped by relying on the fact that the Censors are sincere. The men who condemned Socrates undoubtedly thought themselves sincere. Bernard Shaw, in what has been called the noblest play since Shakespeare, has insisted how sincere were the judges who condemned Saint Joan of Arc. To come closer home, I can believe that the men who condemned our Easter patriots in 1916 were also sincere. But when a government appoints men to make policy by consulting their own personal opinions without any process of restriction or revision, it is clear that mistakes and injustices are invited. On the issue of decency, certainly, the most tyrannical opinions have been and can be sincerely maintained. And it is a commonplace that such tyranny breeds a revolt against decency as such, by exasperating human nature.

What I wish to lay before the community of free minds in Ireland is not the conundrum of the metaphysics on which our five Censors act, but the intolerable outrage of having them empowered to ban any book at all.

The Censorship law is repugnant to every instinct of a free man, ignorant in its conception, ridiculous in its method, odious in its fruits, bringing the name of self-governing Irishmen into contempt wherever the freedom of literature is understood, and revealing the muddle and

---

Francis Hackett, "A Muzzle Made in Ireland," *Dublin Magazine*, N.S. 11:8–17 (October, 1936), copyright 1936 by the Dublin Magazine. Reprinted by permission of the author and of the publisher.

immaturity of our statecraft. The worst law we tolerate in Ireland is possibly the Military Tribunal law. Next to it is this law by which a Censorship Board was imposed by President Cosgrave and accepted without the customary repudiation or revision by the present De Valera government. That the men most honoured in the republic of letters should have been besmirched by it is enough to bring it under suspicion, but those of them who are not citizens of Ireland cannot appeal to Irish opinion. It is, therefore, doubly laid on Irishmen whose work has been smudged by these Censors to revolt against an act that should stir every reader as well as every writer who has the spark of freedom in him.

For this Censorship is not aimed solely at those whose very life it is to be expressive. It tries to cripple the minds of the reading public as well. Curtailing here, repressing there, lopping off at one end, deterring at the other end, it eventually, by an action on which there is no power of restriction whatever, begins to limit and direct the reading of a whole people. It intimidates the booksellers, of course. It frightens the book reviewers and the editors. The very names of the books it debars from the public are not communicated by most of the Press. The assassination of these books is stealthy and the news of it would be entirely hidden if the Censors carried to its logical end the exercise of their pernicious principle. That is the path on which the Cosgrave government set the Irish readers, and it is down this degraded path that the De Valera government has guided them.

Pooh pooh, says the friend of the Censorship. Most of the books condemned are cheap and nasty. Only a few of them are by serious authors, and they can well afford to lose their Irish sales.

One is familiar with this sort of Laodicean in Ireland. But to anyone who knows the price that has had to be paid for the bare conditions of intellectual freedom in Europe since 1500, this return to the Black List is not indifferent. It is a caricature of democracy and all that is meant by it. And it is from the standpoint of democracy and the civic liberty it has won that the Censorship is mainly obnoxious.

A Church can endorse or restrict any reading it likes, so long as it is a voluntary association. The Presbyterian Truth Society, the Methodist Truth Society, the Catholic Truth Society, may dictate as seems fit to their members. But the State is an instrument fashioned by and for a heterogeneous society. The modern State has worked out democratic association on the very basis of intellectual freedom, and it is this multiplicity-in-unity which is the supreme hope for the development of the individual.

It is also, as Ranke has so well defined, the hope of nationality, and no one has insisted more intelligently on this division between the political and the ecclesiastical.

"Nations cannot suffer themselves to be debarred from exercising the understanding bestowed on them by nature, or the knowledge acquired by study, or an investigation of its truth. In every age, therefore, we see diversities in the views of religion arise in different nations, and these again react in various ways on the character and condition of the State. It is evident, from the nature of this struggle, how mighty is the crisis which it involves for the destiny of the human race. Religious truth must have an outward and visible representation, in order that the State may be perpetually reminded of the origin and end of our earthly existence; of the rights of our neighbours, and the kindred of all the nations of the earth; it would otherwise be in danger of degenerating into tyranny, or of hardening into inveterate prejudice—into intolerant conceit of self, and hatred of all that is foreign. On the other hand, a free development of the national character and culture is necessary to the interest of religion. Without this, its doctrines can never be truly understood nor profoundly accepted: without incessant alternations of doubt and conviction, of assent and dissent, of seeking and finding, no error could be removed, no deeper understanding of truth attained. Thus, then, independence of thought and political freedom are indispensable to the Church herself; she needs them to remind her of the varying intellectual wants of men, of the changing nature of her own forms; she needs them to preserve her from the lifeless iteration of misunderstood doctrines and rites, which kill the soul.

"It has been said," the great German goes on, "the State is itself the Church, but the Church has thought herself authorised to usurp the place of the State. The truth is, that the spiritual or intellectual life of man—in its intensest depth and energy unquestionably one—yet manifests itself in these two institutions, which come into contact under the most varied forms; which are continually striving to pervade each other, yet never entirely coincide; to exclude each other, yet neither has ever been permanently victor or vanquished. . . ."

It is in the striving for "independence of thought and political freedom," even as against the Church, that democracy has made the modern State what it is, the emancipator of the individual.

It is quite true that countries which became poisoned by the War of 1914–18—a war carried beyond the point of sane endurance—have, in the past twenty years, injected into peace organization the mad intolerance of war, the corpses of eleven million Europeans festering in their sick memories. This does not alter the fact that, as between Church and State, the modern democracies have accepted the principles of free worship, a free press, free speech, free association. To deny these conditions is to imperil the State, since "intolerance is of the essence of every church, an immediate consequence of its faith that it possesses the only effective means for the salvation of the soul."

The standards of democracy, in this respect, are maintained by any Church that is temporarily at a disadvantage. When Russia is considered, or Mexico, or Spain, we know how promptly they are measured by the standards of Western liberalism. "When error prevails, it is right to invoke liberty of conscience: but when, on the contrary, the truth predominates, it is just to use coercion!" That, unfortunately, is the Augustinian opportunism we are too familiar with.

But the root of the Irish State is in "independence of thought and political freedom." And it is by this we must judge Censorship.

Without unimpeded access to books, books of every kind, there cannot be a free people or an intellectual aristocracy. There cannot be true public opinion. There cannot be a sound resort to the public mind. Once you begin censoring literature, you begin to de-cerebrate the public. Then the psychological defences are wiped out, and in the end any adventurer who covers the Parliament Buildings with enough machine guns, and seizes the microphone and the rotary press, can call himself to power. It is not armour-plate that has made England proof against dictatorship since Cromwell. It is a free political literature and the open process of intellectual discussion. The ambitions of dictatorship are bred like maggots in England as elsewhere, but they die with exposure to free opinion. That is the open, the many-sided process that a Censorship cripples. We have official Black Listers here, masquerading of course as a moral agency, helping the infant Irish to pick their steps through the mire of sex, but in reality foot-binding the Irish in other ways, so that our liberation, won after years of effort, is subordinated to a policy that authorizes intellectual boycott.

The Censorship is illiberal in its essence. It stands above the ordinary revisions of the law. It is arbitrary and irresponsible, denying the right of appeal or else granting appeal to a Minister of Justice who has never seen fit to lift the ban. To bind a reputable author hand and foot, to affix the words "obscene and indecent" to him, is of itself contrary to elemental justice, but the final venom of this law is to allow interested parties to pass on books that concern them.

It may be said that this is a Catholic country; and that the more Catholic the State is, the better it represents the majority of the people. If the object of the Church is to produce stagnation, the argument is sound. But no State is sound which does not accommodate its minorities. The more Catholic the Irish State makes itself, the more the Six Counties are alienated. The Irish State may, as Sean T. O'Kelly says, endorse wholeheartedly the Catholic system of education and co-operate with it fully; but the necessary corollary of this statement is the sinister assertion that "the lost territory will be, with God's help, restored, *perhaps without bloodshed.*" Perhaps without bloodshed! A religious war is not the sane prescription for an United Ireland.

Yet from this identification of Church and State there can only come the bullying of minorities.

President de Valera has refused to submit the question of annuities to a Commonwealth Tribunal which, he holds, might not be disinterested when Ireland is in the minority position. Yet President de Valera allows any book that is outspoken about the clergy to be submitted to a Board packed by the Catholic Church. How righteous he waxes when he lectures England on a just tribunal. How eloquent he was at Geneva when he took the Russians to task on religious tolerance, pointing to Ireland with unction. Yet in Ireland this censoring then existed and it had already been applied to the greatest living authors by men whose approach to literature necessarily leads with the most excruciating stupidity to sheer intolerance.

President de Valera is ever prompt to raise the cry of "justice." What justice is it to have a Board consisting of two priests, a Catholic ex-librarian and a Papal Chamberlain to decide whether or not a book on religion by Bernard Shaw is to be banned. I know, of course, that the nominal objection was to the woodcuts with which the book was illustrated, an objection so silly as to be unbelievable. I know also that there is a fifth wheel on the Censorship machine, a hostage Protestant. His could be the Diary of a Superfluous Man. It is quaint that so nationalist a government as ours should have installed a Thrift of Yorkshire to censor Irish reading.

But the Board has to be composed of men who misunderstand the liberal arts and lend themselves to obscurantism. This Board has, and must have, a Catholic bias. In Tennessee it would have the Calvinist bias. In Moscow it would have the Marxian bias. In Harlem it would have the Negro bias. The Cosgrave government made an attempt to recruit "liberal" censors, but this animal is not to be found in captivity. How could any free man of letters stoop to class H. G. Wells and Bernard Shaw with lewd authors? To class them with lewd authors is on the same level as classing political prisoners with criminals. President de Valera has been in prison under sentence of death. Was he a criminal to be thumb-printed with murderers? Yet he accepts a Board that thumb-prints authors of world reputation, and brands them as obscene and indecent in company with lewd writers who should be handled like all other criminals, by the police power.

The smug may say that in the matter of sex behaviour the level of the Irish is so much higher than the rest of the world, we must ban any literature that could contaminate us.

Complacency about our sex behaviour is not tenable. The Bishops' pastorals, to take one bit of evidence, do not permit it. No sociologist, in any event, could judge on this delicate matter until the government gave him the Crimes Report. Rape, incest, infanticide, homosexuality are to be found in Ireland, and the question of Irish sex superiority cannot be begged.

Let us admit that another campaign is tied up with the Censorship. Let us admit that to keep up discipline through regulating sex conduct is beyond doubt the aim of the Church, and that the Censorship was designed to serve this object: then we know that by obscene and indecent the Irish censors really mean any sex conduct not regulated according to Catholic practice. The Irish State, in other words, lends itself to a specific theology, and arms its theologians with the powers of the State.

This is the basic evil of the Censorship. "Religious liberty," as Ruggiero has said, "is violated by an ecclesiastical institution only when it attempts to enforce its intolerant prescriptions by invoking the sanctions of the civil power, either through the authority which it may itself possess under a theocratic form of government or through an external secular government." That is the harm the Catholic Church is doing to its free citizens through the Irish Free State. It amounts to demanding that, to be deemed Irish, they must be specifically Catholic.

The injustice does not turn on the value of Catholic ideology. It turns on the imposition of this ideology by the State, with one Protestant Censor as a decoy.

What makes Censorship malign is its interference with the process of lay opinion. My opinion on sex behaviour, to take an example, may not be valuable, but in a free country it ought to be judged on its merits and not on its orthodoxy. The public should be allowed to judge, if freedom of speech means anything.

The basic evil of the Censorship is the invoking of the civil power by a religion; and this, as its history in Ireland has now fully shown to every free man, is due to the perfect incapacity of a Censorship to keep from turning into a heresy hunt.

The world has every reason to rule out heresy hunting. Quite good men worked for the Inquisition in Spain, but the ugly fruits of their protected intolerance are not yet fully harvested. Quite good men were no doubt employed in Russia to black out the free opinions of Tolstoy, but there too the crop is not yet cut. The well-meaning obscurantists in Tennessee who attack Darwin, on the other hand, are disinfected from the surrounding community, just as the new bourgeoisie in France, who prosecuted Gustave

Flaubert in the effervescence of their fresh culture, came to be subdued by the free minds whose concepts had been maturing in France from Rabelais through Montaigne and Voltaire.

What handicaps Ireland at present is the cultural division between those who care for national liberty and those who care for intellectual liberty. It is a natural result of the historic struggle. But the time has come for those now moulding the State to admit that the problem of intellectual freedom exists.

The fallacy of the Censor everywhere is that free literature can be, or can have to be, orthodox. Ranke knew that the deeper understanding of truth is only attained by "incessant alternations." If literature is free, it must incessantly test orthodoxy. School-boards, universities, academies, churches, police courts—they can make their orthodoxies and fight for them, but when it comes to the public as a whole, to taxpayers as a whole, to modern citizens, any interference with their literary supply is a betrayal of the spontaneities that keep the national mind moving and alive. To dam up this source is to empoison the best minds. What good was it for England and Ireland to block ultimate candour until a "Ulysses" ripened and burst? Can any Censorship shut off that explosion? The prim Irish in America did their best to sit on it, but the Federal Court of Appeals stepped between these zealots and a geyser of Dublin candour, so that the Dublin which is now imprinted on educated Americans is not the Dublin of decorum but this festering Dublin of James Joyce.

If enlightened public opinion in America has insisted on the free circulation of "Ulysses," how futile it must seem to have Aldous Huxley fanned out of here, and Ernest Hemingway, and Shaw and Wells. It makes us ridiculous. Such narrowness and bigotry in those who talked of "Freedom," such crude efforts to curb free writing and free reading, have reinforced the prejudices that, in America, have so long debarred Catholic Irish-Americans from important national office, or else admit them only if they leave Irishness behind. President de Valera is careful to talk "democracy" when he talks to America by microphone, but he does not tell American publicists that in free Ireland one can only criticize the Catholic clergy on terms that are acceptable to a national Censorship packed by the Church. And when Catholics of the Six Counties come to Dublin to enlist him on the side of tolerance, the fact that Shaw and Wells are to be banned in a "free" Belfast is naturally not dilated on.

Under guise of hunting out obscenity and indecency, the Catholic Church is giving the lie to every nationalist who, like myself, insisted day in and day out that Home Rule would not mean Rome Rule. Home Rule, through the action of the Censorship, does mean Rome Rule. My "Green Lion," I venture to think, is a case in point. It has been reviewed on every Continent since it was published and nowhere has it been said to be obscene, so far as I have learned. The Catholic librarian of a great Catholic university in the United States could not find anything to take exception to. I have just heard that one school in the United States asks its pupils to read it during vacation. Yet in this country it has been banned, to the best of my belief, because it speaks candidly of the Jesuit system of education, and of the gross intolerance of the clergy in the Parnell era, with its spiritual consequences to one youth in particular. The reasons for calling it indecent come, in my opinion, from a parti-pris so outrageous as to be beyond argument.

Yet one must be above-board. Our Censorship law has this merit: it is a flower of our native genius.

Around our necks, on our wrists and ankles, there have been many traditional gyves, many "galling chains." These restraints were put on us from outside, and to be enraged by them was highly natural when we thought of our rights as free men. But the Censorship is from inside. We cannot blame the wicked English for it. The nose-ring that our literature now wears is not a sign of conquest. It is a native Celtic ornament.

To disengage this little fact from our tangle of heaving historic memories is not to minimize the memories: to unload responsibility for as many of our blemishes as possible is in order, since a history of injured citizenship like ours does relieve us of nearly all blame. But in the seductive shade of historic grievance we are tempted to browse on the past, to indulge in patience and procrastination. The Censorship is not of the past. It is in the open, and of the present. The responsibility is ours.

It is this voluntary character of the Censorship that should finally be dwelt on. No one forced us to pass it. No one threatened us with instant and terrible war if we did not pass it. If it is evil and bigoted, it is we, the Irish people, who willed it. Do we intend to perpetuate it? That is the question I suggest to our community of free minds.

Margaret Barrington
THE CENSORSHIP IN EIRE

It is difficult to approach the subject of our censorship of books in Eire in an absolutely unbiased spirit. Bigotry begets bigotry, even in a good cause. Whenever the subject comes up, tempers run high and manners go by the board. This lack of manners, understandable in the minority party, is even more apparent in the majority which supports censorship. You have only to read the Dail debates on the subject to be deeply shocked at the baseness of abuse and innuendo, coming from men and women unfailingly courteous in the ordinary walks of life.

I myself am biased; there's no getting away from it. Not only do I live by the profession of letters but I regard it as an impertinence that a group of five "addlepated old men," as Sean O'Faolain called the Board of Censors, should confine my reading matter to the level of what is fit for the adolescent girl. I regard these men as not only addlepated but capable of seeing indecency where there is none. The Chairman of the Board, Professor Magennis, once described the effect on him of seeing the drawings in the medical books for students displayed in a bookshop. I do not know if I am more shocked at the Professor's sensitivity or amazed that a man of his age should react in so robust, so adolescent, a manner. That is the truth of the matter. These men who are set to judge our reading, are still emotionally adolescent. It is not an uncommon complaint in any country. Only here we do not recognize it as a failing.

The idea of a censorship of publications came up as soon as we had a government of our own. The Cosgrave party resisted the pressure which was brought to bear on it, not only by the Church but even more strongly by the religious lay bodies, such as The Catholic Truth Society. Though it is quite true that many clergymen and bishops, of both the Catholic and Protestant Churches, were in favor of a censorship, the real impetus came from laymen. This is a national, not a religious censorship.

At first the threatened reading public, which is relatively small, took the matter lightly. A few intellectuals tried to band together to agitate against it, mostly young writers and painters. But nothing came of it but a few merry jests and rude verses of no great merit. They simply did not realize what was coming.

But it was not until Mr. De Valera's party (Fianna Fail) came to power that matters took a serious turn. Those who voted for Fianna Fail, under the impression that they were voting for a more revolutionary form of government, soon saw their mistake. By 1929, the Board of Censorship was established and working. And the Irish writers who had laughed found themselves among its first victims. There is now not a single Irish writer of repute, Catholic as well as non-Catholic, and scarcely a well-known foreign writer whose work has not been banned. One is forced to believe when one finds a decent book to read, that it is because the Board of Censors has not got round to it yet.

The Board consists of five members, chosen by the Government. Three are Catholics, two Protestants, only one is a priest. Senator Professor Magennis is chairman. They are supposed to read the books and advise the Minister of Justice who does the banning. If a majority of three decides that a book is to be banned and the other two object, setting out their objections in writing to the Minister, he cannot ban the book. But so far as the public is aware this has not happened. The only set-back the Censorship Board has suffered was when Mr. Lynn Doyle, like the proverbial worm, turned and resigned. But that set-back was only momentary. Sublime, self-confident, above criticism, the Board goes its way, banning an average of three books a week.

It may seem impossible that three men, who receive no salary for their work and must earn their livings otherwise, could possibly find time to read all those books, not only the ones banned, but the unbanned. It is generally accepted that they rely on the fervid enthusiasts

---

Margaret Barrington, "The Censorship in Eire," *Commonweal*, 46:429–32 (August 15, 1947), copyright 1947 by the **Commonweal** Publishing Co., Inc. Reprinted by permission of **the publisher**.

for the bulk of their information, i.e., the common informer. This purity fifth column scours the libraries and bookshops in search of material to turn in, neatly marked and docketed. Little escapes them. Every small town has its willing band of helpers. The lives of most librarians and booksellers cannot be easy. They are obliged, in self-defense, to do the Censors' work for them. Otherwise they would incur losses through confiscation of stock. There is virtually no black market in banned books, because the reading public is not large enough, nor rich enough, to make it worth the risk. In a country where—to quote Senator Fitzgerald—over twenty-five million dollars is spent annually teaching the people to read and write without giving them any real education, the majority of the people want only such reading matter as requires the least mental effort. Consequently, there is no real opposition to the censorship. The fight goes on between ten percent of bigots backed by eighty-nine percent of indifferent yes-men and a handful of vociferous intellectuals.

For by no means all the intellectuals fight on the side of liberty. There are many second-rate men who believe that the banning of the books of better-known writers leaves the market open to them without competition. But a few writers, such as Sean O'Faolain, Peadar O'Donnell, Teresa Deevy and some others, have consistently kept up the fight, partly through the columns of *The Irish Times,* the only daily paper open to them and the only daily paper which publishes the list of banned books, and *The Bell,* a monthly magazine run by O'Faolain and O'Donnell. And in the Senate, the fight has been carried on by Senator Sir John Keane.

This continued buzzing of the wasps, who though small in number, have pens and tongues and wits to aid them, has led to one change. A Board of Appeal has been set up to which writer or publisher can appeal in the case of a banned book. So far this has happened only once, in the case of Mr. Frank O'Connor's translation of "The Midnight Court." But since the judges of the Court of Appeal are hand-picked by the same powers which set up the Board of Censors, there is little sense and much expense in appealing to them. In the case of "The Midnight Court," where it was contended by the publisher that the poem was one of the finest in the Gaelic language; that it could be bought and read any day of the week in that language; that it had been previously translated by Arland Ussher and that translation uncensored; that the work was scholarly and exact; it transpired during an acrimonious correspondence in the columns of *The Irish Times* that the judges had not even read the work, relying on the reports of those they called "experts." The very fact that they must know Gaelic to hold their positions, and yet had not read this classic, was in itself a shocking admission. They even asserted, without reading it, or having read the original, that certain passages must be interpolations or bad translations.

On what grounds can a book be banned? Section 6 of the *Censorship of Publications Act, 1929,* lays it down that:

Whenever a complaint is duly made under this act to the Minister to the effect that a book or a particular edition of a book is indecent or obscene or advocates the unnatural prevention of conception or the procurement of abortion by miscarriage or the use of any method, treatment or appliance for the purpose of such procurement, the Minister may refer such complaint to the Board.

The word *indecent* is the catch. Very reluctantly, under pressure from Sir John Keane, the Government conceded this definition of "indecent":

The word "indecent" shall be construed as including anything *suggestive of,* or inciting to sexual immorality or unnatural vice or *likely in any other similar way to corrupt or deprave.*

The italics are mine. It is because these words can be used to cover almost anything that so many works, which seem utterly harmless to an educated reader, or for that matter, to an ignorant one, are banned. One outraged gentleman wrote to *The Cork Examiner,* in a tone of bitter levity, to say that he thought his son ought not to be taught to read and write, otherwise he might get hold of a dictionary and learn indecent words he had no right to know. The idea is not so preposterous. Certainly one wonders why Professor Magennis has not got round to having a bowdlerized edition of the dictionary published.

From time to time the controversy dies down, only to spring up again with renewed bitterness. The last big fight was staged during the war. On the 18th of November, 1942, Sir John Keane tabled a motion in the Senate that the Censorship Act had ceased to retain public confidence. With the good manners which have always characterized this gentleman of the old school, Sir John had previously informed the Minister of Justice of the names of the three books he intended to bring into question. They were: "The Tailor and Ansty," by Eric Cross; "The Land of Spices," by Kate O'Brien; and "The Laws of Life," by Halliday Sutherland; possibly so that the Minister might go to the trouble of reading them, a vain hope. There followed one of the most unpleasant debates I have ever read, enlivened here and there with unconscious humor.

After Sir John Keane had stated his case, the Minister, Mr. Boland, modestly replied, saying that he was not a literary man, and acted on the advice of the Board of Censors. He passed the debate on to Professor Magennis and his satellites, who moved into the attack, no holds barred, a fine old-fashioned free-for-all. Not only were Sir John's disinterested motives attacked, but all authors who were banned were stigmatized as smut-hounds, and panderers to man's lowest instincts.

Senator Goulding moved in with a description of the pure Irish fireside, so misrepresented in "The Tailor and Ansty." This somewhat idealized picture makes one wonder if Senator Goulding could ever have sat at one, or emptied a pint in a local snug. Senator Goulding went on to demand a doubled censorship. He asked the Senate to look at the state of England where juvenile crime was on the increase due to unfettered reading. Let us save our young people from a like fate. Evidently Mr. Goulding thought the criminal classes were confirmed readers, and that all the spivs, pimps and cat-burglars of Soho were anxiously waiting for the publication of Sylvia Townsend Warner's book on White's tortoise. Or that all readers were incipient if not actual criminals. "A single passage in a book may degrade and corrupt," he declared. "A single passage or two or three passages make a book liable to censorship." He accused Irish writers of so far forgetting themselves and the pure Irish hearths from which they sprang, as to give the rest of the world the impression that we were not only all drunkards, but immoral into the bargain. He ended by thanking God fervently that we were not as the English.

Then, after Senator Johnston, in a mild and cultured speech, urged in support of the motion, that many works of literary value, both ancient and modern, were by these standards indecent, Senator Kehoe raised his voice:

"This affects our national reputation, I am told. I do not know. Does it, I wonder? The fact of having fathered George Moore and others of his ilk—I do not know if that added one jot to our national reputation. Our reputation is built on other things than on literature which is indecent in its tendency. . . ." From this he passed on to an attack on those Irish writers who "purvey their wares for gold." He demanded a sterner censorship. "We hear about authors of repute. Authors of repute from what point of view? From the point of view of world standards, which, mark you, are not the standards of Ireland. . . ." He ended with a warning: "But I will quote the Bible again for Sir John Keane: 'You cannot touch pitch and not be defiled by it.'"

Senator Fitzgerald raised the tone of the debate in a speech which brought comfort to neither party. He disagreed with Sir John Keane. He saw no evidence of any dislike of the censorship among the people. They were too ignorant and badly educated to trouble their heads one way or another. As a people we were without any literary standards. We had no critics worthy of the name. He made a plea for books of literary merit; especially for the works of Graham Greene. He ended . . . "I hate to hear people talking as though anything not suitable for a girl of 14 or for a typist going on the bus to the office must necessarily be condemned and excluded."

There followed another speech from the Minister. Mr. Boland seemed to have forgotten his earlier modesty. He denied any literary merit whatever to books which had been banned. They were "Filth, pure filth," he asserted. He went so far as to say that in his opinion writers inserted filth to get banned and in this way get cheap advertisement in England and Northern Ireland.

It was now that Senator Mrs. Concannon advanced to the attack. Mrs. Concannon is herself a writer, chiefly of books of a religious nature. She began by saying that if Dante (to whose work Senator Fitzgerald had referred) could have thought of a worse punishment for his enemies than the torments of hell then he would have made them read "The Tailor and Ansty." (I myself can think of little worse than a wet day in an Irish seaside hotel with nothing to read except Mrs. Concannon's lives of the Irish female saints.) Mrs. Concannon then went on to paint a moving picture of Professor Magennis, a "man of outstanding ability" who might well have chosen to sit in his study and write philosophical masterpieces. Instead he offered up his great intellect and pure mind to the constant contamination of filthy and indecent literature in order to serve his country and save its inhabitants from pollution. And all this without monetary reward or compensation of any kind. She called for a stricter censorship.

Heralded by this outburst of praise, Senator Professor Magennis, the martyr to the cause of purity, stepped forward. He talked and talked. His speech was full of innuendoes, hints at underhand conspiracies, red herrings by the dozen and half-dozen. He attacked Sir John Keane who was there, and many who were not. All his enemies, or those he fancied were his enemies, were dragged in by reference or name. From *The Irish Times* and the Academy of Letters, to Teresa Deevy, Sean O'Faolain, Frank O'Connor and Deputy Dillon. Finally he turned on Sir John Keane and accused him of falling asleep.

"No, no," said Sir John. "It is a modified form of coma."

The result of the debate was a foregone conclusion. The motion was defeated as all knew it would be. The few gallant fighters realized once again that there was no hope of even a modification of the censorship so long as Mr. De Valera's government remained in power, or even afterwards. The only hope now lies in the fact that so many books will be banned that it will become impossible to keep track of them. As it is, it is the name of the author which remains in the bookseller's mind. I have bought books openly and innocently exposed for sale which were on the banned list.

But it is not only the official censorship the reader is up against. Pressure is often brought to bear on booksellers to suppress certain books. Librarians in public libraries are forced by their committees to remove certain books from the shelves and deny them, even to students. These include Hobbes's "Leviathan," Sigrid Undset's "Kristin Lavransdatter," Tolstoy's "Anna Karenina," and other such. I made a list of the unbanned books of the best known Irish writers.

It was pathetically small. Then, as an interested stranger, I made the rounds of the Dublin bookshops. Not one was in stock, and only one shop would place an order for me. Not that booksellers cooperate willingly in this form of tyranny. It gives them additional work. But if they do not, they lose large orders from the religious bodies, and most of the educational establishments in the country are run by the religious orders.

The reasons for this puritanical censorship are many and involved. It is caused partly by the ignorance of the bulk of the people and those who represent them, and by our low standard of education. We still think that swotting up textbooks for an examination is education. At present there is no hope of this standard being raised. In other countries of Western Europe, there has been for centuries an educated middle class, which has not existed here. Until the turn of the century we had in Southern Ireland only a peasantry and a landlord class. It takes time and security to build up culture and an appreciation of the arts. The new middle class is too uncertain, too anxious to hold a hard-won power to think of the finer things of life. And a censorship can be used to prevent the infiltration of ideas which might disturb their peace. But there is something else, which springs from the very heart of the people, from that dark undercurrent of superstition which lies heavily on our land. It is the fear of the written word.

If you listen to ordinary people talking in Ireland, you will find their conversation no more inhibited than anywhere else. It is often free and racy. It is wonderfully alive, for the Irish still use language as a living thing. They do not mind very much what they say, for the spoken word vanishes. The written word remains. And it is just this quality of permanence which makes them timorous. The written word is magic.

The effects of the censorship are being felt in more ways than one. The most serious is the effect on the younger generation, which has now just reached maturity. They have been cut off not only from their own writers but from the fine modern literature which has been written in other countries. There has lately been a series of broadcasts on the State of Irish Letters and it was noticeable that not only were all the speakers, but the writers they discussed, men and women of the older generation, who had made their reputations before the days of the censorship. The youngest of the speakers was Denis Johnston and he is over forty. The well is drying up. To quote Pascal: "We think we are shutting in the light; what we are really shutting in is the dark."

It is impossible to give a list of the books which have been banned. There are too many. But here is a list of a few of the authors. Irish authors: G. B. Shaw, George Moore, Frank O'Connor, Liam O'Flaherty, Sean O'Faolain, Austin Clarke, Francis Stuart, Norah Hoult, Sean O'Casey, Samuel Beckett, Kate O'Brien, Con O'Leary and others. English and American authors: Graham Greene, Henry Green, Christopher Isherwood, Ralph Bates, the Powys Brothers, Frederic Prokosch, Michael Sadleir, Storm Jameson, Sylvia Townsend Warner, Aldous Huxley, Eric Linklater, H. E. Bates, Gerald Bullett, V. S. Pritchett, James Laver, Thomas Wolfe, William Faulkner, Kay Boyle, John Dos Passos, Ernest Hemingway, Maurice Hindus, Martha Gellhorn, Joseph Hergesheimer and others. European writers: Ignazio Silone, Montherlant, Kastner, De Castro, Celine, Remarque, Zweig, Léon Blum, Jules Romains, Robert Neumann, Alfred Neumann, Anatole France, Sholem Asch, Boccaccio, Max Brod, Gina Kaus, Leonhard Frank, André Malraux, Ramón Sender, Unamuno, Ibáñez, Knut Hamsun, Mikhail Sholokhov and others.

Brian Inglis
SMUGGLED CULTURE

We Irish are a touchy people when it comes to reading about ourselves in newspapers and periodicals from abroad. We have not yet reached the stage when the sight of our dirty linen exposed to a neighbour's view causes us only a mild amusement, or even gratification at an ability to enjoy our own discomfiture. But there are two institutions which are exempt from the protective howl that goes up when their doings are noised broad. One is the present Abbey Theatre, whose protective lease, it is felt,

---

Brian Inglis, "Smuggled Culture," *Spectator*, 189:726 (November 28, 1952), copyright 1952 by the Spectator Ltd. Reprinted by permission of the publisher.

has run long enough. The other is the Censorship of Publications Board.

Every month the Censorship Board issues a list of books that have been banned for indecency or obscenity. For the month of October, 1952, it excelled itself. Eighty-five books were prohibited, including—it sounds better if they are read aloud—

Three Pair of Heels, by Neil Bell.
The Sun Dances at Easter, by Austin Clarke.
Doting, by Henry Green.
The Good Soldier Schweik, by Jaroslav Hasek.
The Walnut Trees of Altenburg, by André Malraux.
Honey, Not Now, by Steve Markham.
Hellbox, by John O'Hara.
Glamour of Desire, by Alan Roscoe.
Phoenix Rising, by Marguerite Steen.
Young Man on a Dolphin, by Anthony Thorne.
Hemlock and After, by Angus Wilson.
Bedtime Blonde, by John Wilstach.

—altogether a nice, all-round selection, with perhaps a little less emphasis than usual on the "No orchids" school, which is usually represented by more lurid titles. (*"Hotsy, You'll Be Chilled"* was a recent one.)

The culprit who immediately catches the eye is that hardened old sinner Schweik, who has been lurking here undetected in English translations for over twenty years. The Censorship Board appears to have no statute of limitations; longevity is no protection from disgrace. Years after it appeared as a "Penguin," Miss E. Arnot Robertson's *Four Frightened People* came under the ban, and Nigel Balchin's *Small Back Room* suffered almost as belatedly. In the case of the Balchin it has since transpired that the Board was sent an American pocket-edition with a suggestive picture on the cover; that was sufficient.

The way in which the Censorship Board works was disclosed, not for the first time, in 1949, when one of its members, resigning, sent a statement of his reasons to the Press. He had apparently been anxious to obey the clause in the Censorship Act which enjoins the Board to have regard "to the literary, artistic, scientific, or historic merit, or importance, and the general tenor of the book." But so many books came before the Board that he found this was impossible. Books were sometimes handed round for the first time at the meeting which banned them, and his colleagues appeared satisfied on occasion to ban a book on the strength of a passage marked by the reader who had sent it in.

As it happened, the resigning member's statement was a less effective exposure of the Board's methods than the Board's letter in reply. Not only did it defend the practice of judging books from marked passages, but it went further and boasted that on one occasion a book was banned before the Censors had had a chance to study it, on the strength of a denunciation which had appeared in an English Sunday newspaper. The Board's inability to supply a ruling under which it claimed to be acting—a ruling not found in the Censorship Act—was excused on the grounds of the imminence of the holiday season. The letter went on to explain that, if a Censor had no time to read a particular book, he would always have "the opinion of his colleagues to guide him, in addition to a quick examination during the meeting." Finally, a statement made by a Minister for Justice was quoted in defence of the Board's policy. "There are books which are blatantly indecent and known to be indecent," the Minister had said. "Should the members of the Board, for instance, be compelled to read every line of *Ulysses,* a book which has been universally condemned?"

The position is less bad than it sounds, because some years ago the censorship situation became so farcical that the Government had to intervene, to set up an Appeal Board. This consisted of a more enlightened group of citizens, who have since busied themselves unbanning books ranging from *Brave New World* and Shaw's *Black Girl* to *For Whom the Bell Tolls* and *The Cruel Sea*. But the Appeal Board works under difficulties. It has to receive formal notice of appeal, with several copies of the book from the publishers; and the Irish market is not so profitable that many publishers consider the money well spent—especially as the reader who can afford to buy books is often in a position to get a copy from England smuggled in.

Alternatively, an appeal can be made by five members of the Irish Parliament—a procedure which, it is to be hoped, will be adopted in the case of old Schweik. The unbanning of books, incidentally, is not well received by the Censorship Board. On one occasion recently it instructed its secretary to reaffirm its original conviction about a book which the Appeal Board had taken off the banned list—in a letter to the Press. It was as if a circuit court judge were to tell the judges of the Court of Appeal that they were all wrong to acquit a citizen whom he had convicted.

It has now become apparent that the Censorship Board, irritated by the establishment of the higher court, is interpreting its duties more rigidly than when it was alone in the field. Some of its decisions have been astonishing. It banned Dr. Halliday Sutherland's *The Laws of Life* in spite of the fact that it had received the *Permissu Superiorum* of the Catholic Archbishop of Westminster. Of two books by Irish authors banned recently, one became the Catholic book-of-the-month in America and the other the Catholic book-of-the-month in Holland. On the day that Graham Greene's *The Heart of the Matter* was published, the *Irish Times* carried an advertisement quoting from a review in which Evelyn Waugh had called it a book which only a Catholic could write, and only a Catholic could understand. On another page of the *Irish Times* was the announcement that *The Heart of the Matter* had been banned as indecent or obscene. More recently an English author wrote sorrowfully to the same newspaper to ask how it could come about that his book had been banned, when such was its propriety that it had been chosen by the B.B.C. for the series *A Book at Bedtime*. Nobody could enlighten him.

Significantly, strictures on the Board have even appeared in a leading article in the *Irish Press*. The *Press* is the organ of Mr. de Valera's party, and is not much given to criticism of that party's handiwork. Nevertheless, it felt obliged to tell the censors that they were making public asses of themselves by banning the British White Paper on population. Such an action, the *Press* thought, could only bring ridicule on the country. And there lies the only hope of a change in the present system. No real demand exists for the abolition of censorship in Ireland—and, if an English visitor is inclined to scoff at our apathy on the subject, he is quickly reminded that there is no official censorship of the theatre in Ireland, which is more than can be said for the theatre of a certain neighbour. But Irish Governments, and the Irish people, are sensitive to ridicule. They do not like the way in which the censors' absurdities are pounced upon for use by the Northern Irish politicians, as justification for the continuance of the Border. They do not like having their legs pulled at Strasbourg, or other international gatherings, about the fact that much of the best work of the outstanding Irish writers of the present day, O'Connor and O'Faolain and the rest, cannot be obtained in Ireland. A few more lists like this last October effort, and who knows but that the Government may once again be jogged into action, unable to tolerate such nonsense any longer?

Heywood Broun
IT SEEMS TO HEYWOOD BROUN

The Irish are always being insulted by somebody. They take more umbrage than is good for them. At least they sometimes fail to carry it with becoming dignity. The fine old fighting Gael of the legends has dwindled into a whimperer who cries out, "There ought to be a law," whenever he is hit. And now the proposal has been made in New York City that the toes of every Irishman shall be made a special government preserve with punitive penalties for each trespasser. Joseph McKee, president of the Board of Aldermen, wants a new ordinance empowering the Commissioner of Licenses to close any motion-picture theater if it shows a film which tends "to ridicule, disparage, or hold up to obloquy or contempt any race, creed, or nationality." Also the commissioner is to be empowered to proceed against such movies as are "calculated to arouse racial, national, or religious prejudice, or do in fact give offense to a considerable number of any race, creed, or nationality." The members of the oppressed nationality are instructed that they "shall report same to the Commissioner of Licenses who shall thereupon abrogate and cancel the license or licenses of the theater or theaters exhibiting such motion pictures."

It is true that the proposed ordinance does not specify offenses against Irish sensitivity, but Mr. McKee stated that his bill was based on a complaint from the American Irish Vigilance Committee and that the particular films which he had in mind were "The Callahans and the Murphys," "Irish Hearts," "The Shamrock and the Rose," and "The Garden of Allah."

Of the works listed, I have seen only "The Callahans and the Murphys." It seemed to me a silly and vulgar production and yet I cannot agree that the legal system of a great city should be radically altered because of this unhappy film. Concerning the other three upon the black list I can only guess. The inclusion of "The Garden of Allah" puzzles me. I had been under the impression that this was a story dealing chiefly with camels. Possibly it is insulting to the Arabs of New York who are prepared to come forward and protest in considerable numbers. It is fair for us to assume that none of the scorned scenarios offends against purity as there is already ample machinery in the State of New York to deal with such transgressions. The crime which they commit must consist of ridicule. Possibly the authors of these impertinent stories have been devilishly malignant in scoffing at the greatness of the Irish people.

And even so I think it a grave mistake to summon censors. Possibly Mr. McKee has not considered the potentialities of his little ordinance. After all, polyglot New York harbors nationals less rich than the Irish in humorous appreciation. I should like to state the sort of case which might arise under the proposed law. Recently, within a great cinema temple, I saw a motion picture which contained the caption: "What is the difference between a Scotchman and a canoe? A canoe tips."

This did not move me to enormous merriment, for I had heard the joke some several years ago. Still, I had not regarded it as insidious propaganda calculated to arouse national prejudice. Under the law my feelings in the matter would be wholly irrelevant. This would be a matter for Scotchmen to decide. Let us suppose, then, that thirty thousand Caledonians marched to the license office with bagpipes skirling to keep their anger hot. Even the city official would be without the power to reason why. Under the law the decision would lie wholly with the offended nationality, and the Commissioner of Licenses would be compelled to say, "Thirty thousand Scotchmen can't be wrong" and close the theater.

Because of one small sorry jest "The Dance

Heywood Broun, "It Seems to Heywood Broun," *Nation*, 125:444–45 (October 26, 1927), copyright 1927 by the Nation Associates, Inc. Reprinted by permission of the publisher.

of the Hours" could never more be heard in that great gilded auditorium and the passing multitude of merry-makers would be compelled to walk full half a block to find another theater in which to get a baritone version of "The End of a Perfect Day." Mr. Cecil de Mille might some day, God forbid, produce "Hamlet" upon the silver screen. What if the director were incautious enough to let the harassed Prince exclaim, "There's something rotten in the state of Denmark"? This should be enough to make Danes descend upon the City Hall in clusters crying out for cloture.

Atheists might with perfect logic protest against that great million-dollar Biblical masterpiece "The King of Kings" on the ground that this Gospel narrative tended to hold the creed of unbelief up to contempt. I'm afraid they would not get far, for it is always difficult to gather atheists together in considerable numbers for any purpose. Generally they are too busily engaged in good deeds to take up organization. The Chinese, also, might fail in procuring the suppression of "Broken Blossoms," though this tale from "Limehouse Nights" most certainly falls within the classification of themes disparaging a race. It might be remembered parenthetically that when the Negroes of New York asked for action against "The Birth of the Nation" they received but scant official attention.

Under a strict interpretation of the McKee ordinance things might come to such a pass that the scenario writer wishing to include a villain among his characters would have to make him a Moabite or Hittite or a member of some other civic minority not numerous enough to muster considerable numbers even under provocation.

As a matter of fact, no other nationals have come forward to join the Irish in their plea for censorship along racial lines. The Jews of New York have always been patient with the Perlmutters and Potashes. No Frenchman as far as I know has objected to the film tradition that every Gaul is a waiter whose articulation is limited to "Où là là." Not all the pictures dealing with the war have been wholly sympathetic with the Germans, but as yet Mr. Viereck has failed to raise a finger. The Portuguese and the Argentines and the Greeks, all these are mute.

I think it is fair to say that of the proud peoples who dwell within the borders of New York none approaches the Irish in the demand for special fictional and dramatic favors. Sidney Howard's play "They Knew What They Wanted" was refused by dozens of managers before it found shelter within the chill arms of the Theater Guild. The commercial producers knew well enough that here was an excellent play, but they feared to put it on because an Irish priest was represented as being a little less than superbly educated. The notion of a rascally Irish prelate is unthinkable upon the stage of New York. No producer in the city would have dared to touch "Rain" if the unfortunate missionary had been called Father Kelly.

The present protest against cheap and vulgar films of Irish life and character would win more sympathy from me if the Celts had not been so ready in the past to accept and even applaud so large an amount of trash if only it were sentimental. I have yet to hear of any vigilance committee raising a single shillelagh against the noxious banalities of "Abie's Irish Rose." The sons of Erin were enraptured when Chauncey Olcott and his many imitators pictured the Irishman as a fellow with a heart of gold and a brain of some much softer metal, but when a truly great comedy came out of the very peat smoke of Ireland they would have none of it and rioted at the opening.

I was at the first performance of Synge's "Playboy of the Western World" and heard the snarl go up—"It never happened in Ireland." After that the potatoes and stink bombs began to fly and Marie O'Neill was stunned when hit by a missile thrown by some man who had familiarized himself with Irish life through long residence in Elmhurst.

To be fair, which is not altogether my intention, not all the Irish in America were gathered in the Maxine Elliott Theater, but it sounded to me as if they were present in considerable numbers. Undoubtedly there were many Gaels who recognized the fine flash of Synge's play and when the piece was done again in later years there was no riot. Still, I think it is not unjust to say that the pseudo-Irishman holds greater appeal for the Irish-American public than the more authentic fellow. The Clan-na-Gael failed to decree dancing in the streets in honor of "John Bull's Other Island."

If there is to be any sort of nationalistic censorship I think it might be an excellent idea to provide for a rotation of the function. Thus, the Jews could be empowered to decide what is offensive to the Irish, the French might act as censors for the Germans, and the Irish call a halt at themes too libelous toward England. This is much the better way. Surely no nationalistic decision should be left to a people whose representatives in New York seem to believe that Donn Byrne is a greater Irish writer than George Bernard Shaw.

Chapter XI

Books under dictators red and black

THROUGHOUT history the evidence is piled high that whenever and wherever tyrants and authoritarian regimes have wanted to suppress opposition and to kill ideas, their first thought, almost invariably, has been to destroy books of contrary view, and oftentimes their authors. Conversely, they have cunningly turned to their own advantage, to tighten their grip on the people, certain other books: for example, Adolf Hitler's *Mein Kampf,* Karl Marx's *Das Kapital,* and the voluminous writings of Lenin and Stalin. No one realizes better than the despot the enormous explosive forces pent up in books.

In a 1951 Phi Beta Kappa address, Professor Harry Fuller made the following discerning comments: "Recent history has demonstrated that dictators fear books and that, as a consequence of that fear, they ban, censor and burn books. Without moralizing, those of us who are devoted to the liberal studies can make a telling argument by indicating the kind of books which dictators burn and the kinds which they spare. Hitler, Mussolini, and Stalin, to the best of my knowledge, never burned books on dairy science, bridge construction, surgical practice, soil physics, electrical engineering, tax laws, and human nutrition. The books which they have most feared and which they have delivered to the flames were books on philosophy, history, political science, literature, the fine arts, and the pure sciences."

With the coming of Adolf Hitler to power in 1934, a wave of horror went through the civilized world at the reports of book-burnings in Germany. To millions of people the action signified a return to the Dark Ages and to the methods of the Inquisition. In case there were still those who thought the democratic nations could do business with Hitler, the true nature of fascism was revealed for all to see.

Red dictatorship is no improvement over the black- or brown-shirt variety. In his *The Challenge of Soviet Education,* Professor George S. Counts, one of the most knowledgeable interpreters of the Soviet Union, wrote: "The point should be made that a truly free library is dangerous to any authoritarian or totalitarian system. If the people were permitted to read books containing materials subversive of the system, literacy itself could scarcely be tolerated. Consequently, the Bolsheviks have followed the policy of the 'permanent purge' in the realm of books as well as in the realm of personnel. As the Party line has changed, as 'truth' has been altered by political fiat, books have been removed from and placed on the shelves of both bookstores and libraries . . . The library, being a component part of the Soviet system for the education of the people, is a political weapon. It therefore cannot be allowed to develop according to its own laws. It must always be held tightly in the hands of the Party." [1]

The fate of books under Fascist and Communist dictatorships is graphically described in the following accounts from the pens of several seasoned reporters and literary figures.

G. E. R. Gedye's "What a Book Famine Means" was written just five years after the Nazi purge began. He presents a vivid description of what happened to bookstores in countries suffering Fascist conquest during the 1934–39 period. Gedye has had a long career as an international newspaper correspondent for the London *Times,* the *New York Times,* the *Manchester Guardian,* and other papers. Since 1954, he has been with Radio Free Europe.

G. E. R. Gedye
WHAT A BOOK FAMINE MEANS

Strolling through one of New York's great bookstores just off Fifth Avenue this afternoon my fancy led me to make a rapid estimate of how such a store would look by tomorrow afternoon were the same political tornado to strike it as I saw break over one of the great capitals of Europe barely six weeks ago. Twenty-four hours is longer than it took to effect the devastation of my favorite bookshop in Prague. There four working hours sufficed to sweep away every trace of freedom of choice and variety from the display and to give it a grey monotone. In this bookshop—I will not give you the name, for I would hate to see one bookseller more than necessary vanish into prison—I was known, although not by name until the afternoon of March 14th. As I was paying for a couple of books which I was particularly keen to read—they still stand unpacked on a table in my flat in Prague as I put them down that same evening before the Gestapo got on my track—the manager looked keenly at me and said "I seem to recognise you from a photograph I have just seen. Aren't you Mr. Gedye, author of 'Betrayal in Central Europe,' the newly published book which tells the fate of my country?" I am still a young enough author, however venerable a foreign correspondent, to feel a little thrill at such recognition in a bookstore, and admitted the fact with an appropriate blush. A large consignment of the English edition ("Fallen Bastions") of my book had just arrived, and the manager showed me the fine display he was just putting into the window. He asked me to inscribe a copy for him personally and I dated it "March 14th, 1939—Bastion besieged again." He asked if I could let him see a copy of the American edition as he thought the title "Betrayal in Central Europe" would be more familiar and therefore more saleable to American tourists. I sent him round a copy and he telephoned an hour later saying that he was ordering himself a supply. He will never get them.

Seven hours later that Bastion had fallen for a second time. Fourteen hours later it was in the occupation of the enemy as the German troops marched into Prague. Within two hours of opening on March 15th, every copy of my book had vanished from the displays of every bookstore

---

[1] George S. Counts, *The Challenge of Soviet Education* (New York: McGraw-Hill, 1957), p. 196.

G. E. R. Gedye, "What a Book Famine Means," *Publishers' Weekly,* 135:1754–55 (May 13, 1939), copyright 1939 by R. R. Bowker Co. Reprinted by permission of the publisher.

in the city. World's record best seller? No, for although there was an unprecedented rush for my book the moment that the thousands of "tourists" in field-grey reached Prague next morning, they did not pay for copies. Furthermore, it was not many days before other books dealing in any way critically with the policies of the Third Reich shared the distinction; they were just as unobtainable as my own. Running my eye this afternoon over the nearest counter in that New York bookstore, I estimated that were the opening of the World's Fair tomorrow to be signalized by the arrival of those same visitors in the same field-grey uniforms, eighty per cent of the display would be unobtainable (though not sold out!) next morning. A similar calculation of the contents of one window showed that from 25 per cent to 30 per cent of the books shown there would have disappeared.

I wonder whether the American bookseller and the American book-loving public can really picture to themselves what a dreary spectacle is presented by the average bookstore counter in the greater part of the continent of Europe today? I believe statistics showing the disastrous result for the German book trade are available, but even these give no picture of the mental desert through which the book-buyer in Germany, Italy and all other countries subjected to the influence of these Fascist States is compelled to wander. For the book trade, statistics are improved by the inclusion of masses of Party literature which it is sometimes compulsory, sometimes highly advisable to buy, even though the purchaser may be in the comparatively fortunate position of not having to read it. This barrenness of thought is seen not only in the field of political books but equally in that of fiction. Not only have books to be tested, not by the standards of literature or selling qualities but by that of conformity to the interests of the existing regime; it is not the author's pen but his grandmother which decides whether or not his works may be put on sale. Nor is it enough for his book, even though it be purely a work of fiction, to be politically innocuous. If it is to stand any chance of sales its heroine must be a flaxen-haired Brünnhilde, its hero one of Nietzsche's blue eyed Nordic giants in a brown shirt—or at the least a spiritually brown coat of mail, bear skin or tincture of woad. Its villains must all be bow-legged, flat-footed, hook-nosed mental degenerates conspiring the enslavement of the Nordic blondes. At the very least they must be Nordic "race traitors" in the pay of the very dangerous, yet always overthrown, conspirators from the East. Poetry, science and drama have equally to become the handmaidens and slaves of the cast-iron creed of the dictators. Is it any wonder that under these conditions the voluntary purchasing of books in countries where they obtain has slumped to unheard-of depths?

For any reader of books I can imagine no better antidote to incipient Nazism than compulsory residence for a period in a Fascist country. In Vienna I knew a young English colleague who after a short residence there felt Nazi conspiracies against the Schuschnigg regime to be rather good fun, the young conspirators good sports and who consequently began to feel a sneaking sympathy with their aims. As luck would have it he was transferred to Berlin. Twelve months later he was passing through Prague and had lunch with me. He was extremely bitter about the Third Reich and all traces of his former Nazi leanings had disappeared. I did not like to ask him outright what had disillusioned him, but walking up the Vaclavske Namesti after lunch, I discovered the reason for myself. It proved almost impossible to drag my friend past the many big bookstore windows there. Devouring their contents with hungry eyes like a man emerging from a twelve months mental fast he said:

"Gedye, you can have no idea what it means to be able to see books—real books again. It is not merely that Germany has no money for the importation of foreign books; I am just as happy reading German as English, but there is literally nothing which anyone with a grain of intelligence can read. Even the average thriller swindles you by selling excitement and delivering political propaganda. I have stuffed my bags here with good fiction. Political books, although they may be in English and French, I dare not take across the frontier, but even so it helps one's sanity just to look into these windows and realize that 'the other side' really does exist and can be vocal."

I can imagine no reading public—not even that of Great Britain—which would suffer more acutely from such a mental famine than the American public. As correspondent of the New York *Times* for Central and Southeastern Europe I have long realized the keen interest taken by newspaper readers over here in European affairs. In the New York *Times* offices this week I was shown the museum—"The History of the Recorded Word"— and pondered with interest and satisfaction over that magnificent paragraph of the American Constitution which forbids Congress ever to pass a law which should interfere with the liberties of free speech and publication. In the windows of the bookstores there seems to me to be a greater variety and a better display of books dealing with the European political situation than even in London, despite the fact that London should be still more closely concerned with questions which may now at any hour bring the threat of war to that capital. On this, my first visit to New York, it strikes me as a fine thing that the people of the United States should be equipping themselves so well to meet the menace already so close to Great Britain, which the width of the Atlantic certainly does not suffice to hold off from the United States. The avalanche of requests for speeches on the Central and Eastern European situation, for interviews, articles and photographs, which descended on me despite my entirely unadvertised arrival furnished further proof. It was naturally extremely gratifying to me to find the sales of my new book keeping pace very well with those in London—apart, of course, from the figure of 60,000 copies in a special cheap "Book Club" edition in Great Britain. It encourages me to contemplate the work a little later of adding some final chapters which will have to bring right up to date the tragic story of betrayal which my book tells.

America's troubadour, favorite poet, and Lincoln biographer, Carl Sandburg, expresses his wrath against the "Murderers of Books" in a piece taken from his *Home Front Memo* (1943).

Carl Sandburg
MURDERERS OF BOOKS

In a Library of Congress hall a peculiar little memorial program was given. And why not?

Carl Sandburg, *Home Front Memo* (New York: Harcourt, Brace, 1943), pp. 59–60, copyright 1941 by Carl Sandburg. Reprinted by permission of the publisher.

Why shouldn't a living library, representing a nation and a people building an arsenal of democracy, memorialize certain books?

Over Nazified Europe these books have been put to death. With grimaces, jeers, maledictions, these books have been burned, banned, published as dead, cremated, and the epitaphs well chosen.

Einstein, the German Jew, the mathematician with a hair-trigger imagination, his works are verboten, three strikes and out. The little song of the Lorelei by Heinrich Heine, the wit, the lyric writer whose bittersweet is better than straight sweet, you can't read him nor sing him except behind closed doors with an eye and ear ready for the Gestapo, who might have heard about your personal taste in literature and music.

Karel Capek, the Czech who had something on the ball in drama and whimsy, who invented Rossum's Universal Robots, who put an ant colony on the stage as a forecast of the "New Order" and the wave of the future, who died in part of sheer heartbreak, not wanting to live any more after Czechoslovakia died its political death preparatory to dying other deaths—Capek is verboten, nix, his books legally and by decree dead as a dead mackerel in the moonshine.

And the living Thomas Mann, who got out while the going was good, when they read him in the original German as once published in what was then his country—when in Berlin, Bremen, Breslau, Munich they read Mann—they do it in secret and hide the forbidden book where they hope no informer might find it.

Many more authors and books could be named. The theory of the authorities is that these books are washed up and destroyed for all time, or at least a thousand years, the time limit calculated by the Leader.

Maybe this is so. Maybe not. Maybe this is partly what the shooting is about. At least in this United States of America an organization has well under way the reprinting and restoration of every book of permanent value officially destroyed, purged, assassinated, in Europe. These books have crossed the Atlantic Ocean for a rebirth and a resurrection, available in the original languages for any one the wide earth over who wishes to read them.

Among those who now favor all-out aid to Britain are men and women who can't think of human freedom except as it touches the human mind. They look at what has happened to the human mind in Nazified Europe and see it as a vast atrocity.

To kill the books of Heine and Capek is a more dirty and bloody form of human murder than leading handcuffed authors out to have their heads hacked off by an official axman with an official napkin for wiping the gore off the edge of the ax blade.

Why the murder of a book is worse than the murder of a man you may find argued well in the works of John Milton who is dead and Archibald MacLeish who is alive.

There are Irish books that will go down if and when Britain goes down and Ireland with her. There are Swiss, Swedish, and Finnish books that will meet the deaths now being given to Norwegian books in the latest Nazi bans in Oslo—if and when Britain goes down.

The "New Order" in Europe requires death, as public policy and surgical procedure, for all outspoken believers in freedom—along with death for the books of such believers.

One Washington correspondent quotes a church dignitary as charging that the majority of the 800,000 prisoners in German concentration camps are Catholics. This is an estimate that cannot be verified. What needs no verification is the dank and clammy fact that in the Nazi realm every book that advocates freedom of conscience and worship has been called in, made verboten, and when seized burned to a nice black and gray crisp that stinks.

It is well to say 1941 is not 1914 or 1915. The conflicting aims are not the same. The atrocities are different. The possible consequences are different. The time for crossing the Atlantic Ocean has been reduced since 1927, when the top record was thirty-three hours, to the month of March in 1941, when a bomber flew from Newfoundland to Britain in nine hours, a later flight making it in seven and a half hours.

A potent critic of totalitarianism in any guise, the English novelist George Orwell will be longest remembered perhaps for his *Animal Farm* (1946), a devastating satire on Stalin's Russia, and *Nineteen Eighty-Four* (1949), a terrifying look into the future, when a collectivist government has taken over society. Orwell served as a volunteer in the Spanish Civil War, and in fighting against Franco came to detest every form of tyranny, whether of Communist or Fascist origin.

George Orwell
THE PREVENTION OF LITERATURE

Freedom of speech and of the press are usually attacked by arguments which are not worth bothering about. Anyone who has experience in lecturing and debating knows them backwards. Here I am not trying to deal with the familiar claim that freedom is an illusion, or with the claim that there is more freedom in totalitarian countries than in democratic ones, but with the much more tenable and dangerous proposition that freedom is undesirable and that intellectual honesty is a form of antisocial selfishness.

Though other aspects of the matter are usually in the foreground, the controversy over freedom of speech and of the press is at bottom a controversy over the desirability, or otherwise, of telling lies. What is really at issue is the right to report contemporary events truthfully, or as truthfully as is consistent with the ignorance, bias, and self-deception from which every observer necessarily suffers. In saying this I may seem to be saying that straightforward reportage is the only branch of literature that matters; but I will try to show later that at every literary level, and probably in every one of the arts, the same issue arises in more or less subtilized forms. Meanwhile, it is necessary to strip away the irrelevancies in which this controversy is usually wrapped up.

The enemies of intellectual liberty always try to present their case as a plea for discipline versus individualism. The issue truth-versus-untruth is as far as possible kept in the background. Although the point of emphasis may vary, the writer who refuses to sell his opinions is always branded as a mere egoist. He is accused, that is, either of wanting to shut himself up in an ivory tower, or of making an exhibitionist display of his own personality, or of resisting the inevitable current of history in an attempt to cling to unjustified privileges. The

---

George Orwell, "The Prevention of Literature," *Atlantic Monthly*, 179:115–19 (March, 1947), copyright 1947 by the Atlantic Monthly Co. Reprinted by permission of the publisher.

Catholic and the Communist are alike in assuming that an opponent cannot be both honest and intelligent. Each of them tacitly claims that "the truth" has already been revealed, and that the heretic, if he is not simply a fool, is secretly aware of "the truth" and merely resists it out of selfish motives.

In Communist literature the attack on intellectual liberty is usually masked by oratory about "petty-bourgeois individualism," "the illusions of nineteenth-century liberalism," etc., and backed up by words of abuse such as "romantic" and "sentimental," which, since they do not have any agreed meaning, are difficult to answer. In this way the controversy is maneuvered away from its real issue. One can accept, and most enlightened people would accept, the Communist thesis that pure freedom will only exist in a classless society, and that one is most nearly free when one is working to bring about such a society. But slipped in with this is the quite unfounded claim that the Communist Party is itself aiming at the establishment of the classless society, and that in the U.S.S.R. this aim is actually on the way to being realized. If the first claim is allowed to entail the second, there is almost no assault on common sense and common decency that cannot be justified. But meanwhile, the real point has been dodged. Freedom of the intellect means the freedom to report what one has seen, heard, and felt, and not to be obliged to fabricate imaginary facts and feelings. The familiar tirades against "escapism," "individualism," "romanticism," and so forth, are merely a forensic device, the aim of which is to make the perversion of history seem respectable.

Fifteen years ago, when one defended the freedom of the intellect, one had to defend it against Conservatives, against Catholics, and to some extent—for in England they were not of great importance—against Fascists. Today one has to defend it against Communists and "fellow travelers." One ought not to exaggerate the direct influence of the small English Communist Party, but there can be no question about the poisonous effect of the Russian *mythos* on English intellectual life. Because of it, known facts are suppressed and distorted to such an extent as to make it doubtful whether a true history of our times can ever be written.

Let me give just one instance out of the hundreds that could be cited. When Germany collapsed, it was found that very large numbers of Soviet Russians—mostly, no doubt, from nonpolitical motives—had changed sides and were fighting for the Germans. Also, a small but not negligible proportion of the Russian prisoners and displaced persons refused to go back to the U.S.S.R., and some of them, at least, were repatriated against their will. These facts, known to many journalists on the spot, went almost unmentioned in the British press, while at the same time Russophile publicists in England continued to justify the purges and deportations of 1936–1938 by claiming that the U.S.S.R. "had no quislings." The fog of lies and misinformation that surrounds such subjects as the Ukraine famine, the Spanish Civil War, Russian policy in Poland, and so forth, is not due entirely to conscious dishonesty, but any writer or journalist who is fully sympathetic to the U.S.S.R.—sympathetic, that is, in the way the Russians themselves would want him to be—does have to acquiesce in deliberate falsification on important issues.

2

I have before me what must be a very rare pamphlet, written by Maxim Litvinoff in 1918 and outlining the recent events in the Russian Revolution. It makes no mention of Stalin, but gives high praise to Trotsky, and also to Zinoviev, Kamenev, and others. What could be the attitude of even the most intellectually scrupulous Communist towards such a pamphlet? At best, he would take the obscurantist attitude that it is an undesirable document and better suppressed. And if for some reason it should be decided to issue a garbled version of the pamphlet, denigrating Trotsky and inserting references to Stalin, no Communist who remained faithful to his party could protest. Forgeries almost as gross as this have been committed in recent years. But the significant thing is not that they happen, but that even when they are known, they provoke no reaction from the left-wing intelligentsia as a whole. The argument that to tell the truth would be "inopportune" or would "play into the hands of" somebody or other is felt to be unanswerable, and few people are bothered by the prospect that the lies which they condone will get out of the newspapers and into the history books.

The organized lying practiced by totalitarian states is not, as is sometimes claimed, a temporary expedient of the same nature as military deception. It is something integral to totalitarianism, something that would still continue even if concentration camps and secret police forces had ceased to be necessary. Among intelligent Communists there is an underground legend to the effect that although the Russian government is obliged now to deal in lying propaganda, frame-up trials, and so forth, it is secretly recording the facts and will publish them at some future time. We can, I believe, be quite certain that this is not the case, because the mentality implied by such an action is that of a liberal historian who believes that the past cannot be altered and that a correct knowledge of history is valuable as a matter of course. From the totalitarian point of view history is something to be created rather than learned.

A totalitarian state is in effect a theocracy, and its ruling caste, in order to keep its position, has to be thought of as infallible. But since, in practice, no one is infallible, it is frequently necessary to rearrange past events in order to show that this or that mistake was not made, or that this or that imaginary triumph actually happened. Then, again, every major change in policy demands a corresponding change of doctrine and a revaluation of prominent historical figures. This kind of thing happens everywhere, but clearly it is likelier to lead to outright falsification in societies where only one opinion is permissible at any given moment. Totalitarianism demands, in fact, the continuous alteration of the past, and in the long run probably demands a disbelief in the very existence of objective truth. The friends of totalitarianism in England usually tend to argue that since absolute truth is not attainable, a big lie is no worse than a little lie. It is pointed out that all historical records are biased and inaccurate, or, on the other hand, that modern physics has proved that what seems to us the real world is an illusion, so that to believe in the evidence of one's senses is simply vulgar philistinism.

A totalitarian society which succeeded in perpetuating itself would probably set up a schizophrenic system of thought, in which the laws of common sense held good in everyday life and in certain exact sciences, but could be disregarded by the politician, the historian, and the sociologist. Already there are countless people who would think it scandalous to falsify a scientific textbook, but would see nothing wrong in falsifying a historical fact. It is at the point where literature and politics cross that totalitarianism exerts its greatest pressure on the intellectual. The exact sciences are not, at this date, menaced to anything like the same extent. This difference partly accounts for the fact that in all countries it is easier for the scientists than for the writers to line up behind their respective governments.

It may seem that all this time I have been talking about the effects of censorship, not on literature as a whole, but merely on one department of political journalism. Granted that Soviet Russia constitutes a sort of forbidden area in the British press, granted that issues like Poland, the Spanish Civil War, the Russo-German pact, and so forth, are debarred from serious discussion, and that if you possess information that conflicts with the prevailing orthodoxy you are expected either to distort it or to keep quiet about it— granted all this, why should literature in the wider sense be affected? Is every writer a politician, and is every book necessarily a work of straightforward reportage? Even under the tightest dictatorship, cannot the individual writer remain free inside his own mind and distill or disguise his unorthodox ideas in such a way that the authorities will be too stupid to recognize them? And if the writer himself is in agreement with the prevailing orthodoxy, why should it have a cramping effect on him? Is not literature, or any of the arts, likeliest to flourish in societies in which there are no major conflicts of opinion and no sharp distinctions between the artist and his audience? Does one have to assume that every writer is a rebel, or even that a writer as such is an exceptional person?

Whenever one attempts to defend intellectual liberty against the claims of totalitarianism, one meets with these arguments in one form or another. They are based on a complete misunderstanding of what literature is, and how—one should perhaps rather say *why*—it comes into being. They assume that a writer is either a mere entertainer or else a venal hack who can switch from one line of propaganda to another as easily as an organ grinder changes tunes. But after all, how is it that books ever come to be written? Above a quite low level, literature is an attempt to influence the views of one's contemporaries by recording experience. And so far as freedom of expression is concerned, there is not much difference between a mere journalist and the most "unpolitical" imaginative writer. The journalist is unfree, and is conscious of unfreedom, when he is forced to write lies or suppress what seems to him important news: the imaginative writer is unfree when he has to falsify his subjective feelings, which from his point of view are facts. He may distort and caricature reality in order to make his meaning clearer, but he cannot misrepresent the scenery of his own mind: he cannot say with any conviction that he likes what he dislikes, or believes what he disbelieves. If he is forced to do so, the only result is that his creative faculties dry up.

Nor can the imaginative writer solve the problem by keeping away from controversial topics. There is no such thing as genuinely non-political literature, and least of all in an age like our own, when fears, hatreds, and loyalties of a directly political kind are near to the surface of everyone's consciousness. Even a single taboo can have an all-round crippling effect upon the mind, because there is always the danger that any thought which is freely followed up may lead to the forbidden thought. It follows that the atmosphere of totalitarianism is deadly to any kind of prose writer, though a poet, at any rate a lyric poet, might possibly find it breathable. And in any totalitarian society that survives for more than a couple of generations, it is probable that prose literature, of the kind that has existed during the past four hundred years, must actually *come to an end.*

3

Literature has sometimes flourished under despotic regimes, but, as has often been pointed out, the depotisms of the past were not totalitarian. Their repressive apparatus was always inefficient, their ruling classes were usually either corrupt or apathetic or half-liberal in outlook, and the prevailing religious doctrines usually worked against perfectionism and the notion of human infallibility. Even so, it is broadly true that prose literature has reached its highest levels during periods of democracy and free speculation. What is new in totalitarianism is that its doctrines are not only unchallengeable but also unstable. They have to be accepted on pain of damnation, but on the other hand they are always liable to be altered at a moment's notice.

Consider, for example, the various attitudes, completely incompatible with one another, which an English Communist or "fellow traveler" has had to adopt towards the war between Britain and Germany. For years before September, 1939, he was expected to be in a continuous stew about "the horrors of Nazism" and to twist everything he wrote into a denunciation of Hitler; after September, 1939, for twenty months, he had to believe that Germany was more sinned against than sinning, and the word "Nazi," at least so far as print went, had to drop right out of his vocabulary. Immediately after hearing the eight o'clock news bulletin on the morning of June 22, 1941, he had to start believing once again that Nazism was the most hideous evil the world had ever seen.

Now, it is easy for a politician to make such changes; for a writer the case is somewhat different. If he is to switch his allegiance at exactly the right moment, he must either tell lies about his subjective feelings, or else suppress them altogether. In either case he has destroyed his dynamo. Not only will ideas refuse to come to him, but the very words he uses will seem to stiffen under his touch. Political writing in our time consists almost entirely of prefabricated phrases bolted together like the pieces of a child's Meccano set. It is the unavoidable result of self-censorship. To write in plain, vigorous language one has to think fearlessly, and if one thinks fearlessly one cannot be politically orthodox.

It might be otherwise in an "age of faith," when the prevailing orthodoxy has been long established and is not taken too seriously. In that case it would be possible, or might be possible, for large areas of one's mind to remain unaffected by what one officially believed. Even so, it is worth noticing that prose literature almost disappeared during the only age of faith that Europe has ever enjoyed. Throughout the whole of the Middle Ages there was almost no imaginative prose literature and very little in the way of historical writing; and the intellectual leaders of society expressed their most serious thoughts in a dead language which barely altered during a thousand years.

Totalitarianism, however, does not so much promise an age of faith as an age of schizophrenia. A society becomes totalitarian when its structure becomes flagrantly artificial: that is, when its ruling class has lost its function but succeeds in clinging to power by force or fraud. Such a society, no matter how long it persists, can never afford to become either tolerant or intellectually stable. It can never permit either the truthful recording of facts, or the emotional sincerity, that literary creation demands. But to be corrupted by totalitarianism one does not have to live in a totalitarian country. The mere prevalence of certain ideas can spread a poison that makes one subject after another impossible for literary purposes. Wherever there is an enforced orthodoxy—or even two orthodoxies, as often happens—good writing stops. This was well illustrated by the Spanish Civil War. To many English intellectuals the war was a deeply moving experience, but not an experience about which they could write sincerely. There were only two things that you were allowed to say, and both of them were palpable lies; as a result, the war produced acres of print but almost nothing worth reading.

4

It is not certain whether the effects of totalitarianism upon verse need be so deadly as its effects on prose. There is a whole series of converging reasons why it is somewhat easier for a poet than for a prose writer to feel at home in an authoritarian society. To begin with, bureaucrats and other "practical" men usually despise the poet too deeply to be much interested in what he is saying. Secondly, what the poet is saying— that is, what his poem "means" if translated into prose—is relatively unimportant even to himself. The thought contained in a poem is always simple, and is no more the primary purpose of the poem than the anecdote is the primary purpose of a picture. A poem is an arrangement of sounds and associations, as a painting is an arrangement of brush marks. For short snatches, indeed, as in the refrain of a song, poetry can even dispense with meaning altogether. It is therefore fairly easy for a poet to keep away from dangerous subjects and avoid uttering heresies; and even when he does utter them, they may escape notice.

But above all, good verse, unlike good prose, is not necessarily an individual product. Certain kinds of poems, such as ballads, or, on the other hand, very artificial verse forms, can be composed coöperatively by groups of people.

Whether the ancient English and Scottish ballads were originally produced by individuals, or by the people at large, is disputed; but at any rate they are non-individual in the sense that they constantly change in passing from mouth to mouth. Even in print no two versions of a ballad are ever quite the same. Many primitive peoples compose verse communally. Someone begins to improvise, probably accompanying himself on a musical instrument, somebody else chips in with a line or a rhyme when the first singer breaks down, and so the process continues until there exists a whole song or ballad which has no identifiable author.

In prose, this kind of intimate collaboration is quite impossible. Serious prose, in any case, has to be composed in solitude, whereas the excitement of being part of a group is actually an aid to certain kinds of versification. Verse—and perhaps good verse of its kind, though it would not be the highest kind—might survive under even the most inquisitorial regime. Even in a society where liberty and individuality had been extinguished, there would still be need either for patriotic songs and heroic ballads celebrating victories, or for elaborate exercises in flattery; and these are the kinds of poetry that can be written to order, or composed communally, without necessarily lacking artistic value. Prose is a different matter, since the prose writer cannot narrow the range of his thoughts without killing his inventiveness.

But the history of totalitarian societies, or of groups of people who have adopted the totalitarian outlook, suggests that loss of liberty is inimical to *all* forms of literature. German literature almost disappeared during the Hitler regime, and the case was not much better in Italy. Russian literature, so far as one can judge by translations, has deteriorated markedly since the early days of the Revolution, though some of the verse appears to be better than the prose. Few if any Russian novels that it is possible to take seriously have been translated for about fifteen years. In Western Europe and America large sections of the literary intelligentsia have either passed through the Communist Party or been warmly sympathetic to it, but this whole leftward movement has produced extraordinarily few books worth reading. Orthodox Catholicism, again, seems to have a crushing effect upon certain literary forms, especially the novel. During a period of three hundred years, how many people have been at once good novelists and good Catholics?

The fact is that certain themes cannot be celebrated in words, and tyranny is one of them. No one ever wrote a good book in praise of the Inquisition. Poetry *might* survive in a totalitarian age, and certain arts or half-arts, such as architecture, might even find tyranny beneficial, but the prose writer would have no choice between silence and death. Prose literature as we know it is the product of rationalism, of the Protestant centuries, of the autonomous individual. And the destruction of intellectual liberty cripples the journalist, the sociological writer, the historian, the novelist, the critic, and the poet, in that order. In the future it is possible that a new kind of literature, not involving individual feeling or truthful observation, may arise, but no such thing is at present imaginable. It seems much likelier that if the liberal culture that we have lived in since the Renaissance actually comes to an end, the literary art will perish with it.

5

Meanwhile totalitarianism has not fully triumphed anywhere. Our own society is still, broadly speaking, liberal. To exercise your right of free speech you have to fight against economic pressure and against strong sections of public opinion, but not, as yet, against a secret police force. You can say or print almost anything so long as you are willing to do it in a hole-and-corner way. But what is sinister is that the conscious enemies of liberty are those to whom liberty ought to mean most. The public do not care about the matter one way or the other. They are not in favor of persecuting the heretic, and they will not exert themselves to defend him. They are at once too sane and too stupid to acquire the totalitarian outlook. The direct, conscious attack on intellectual decency comes from the intellectuals themselves.

It is possible that the Russophile intelligentsia, if they had not succumbed to the Russian myth, would have succumbed to another of much the same kind. But at any rate the Russian myth is there, and the corruption it causes stinks. When one sees highly educated men looking on indifferently at oppression and persecution, one wonders which to despise more, their cynicism or their shortsightedness. Many scientists, for example, are uncritical admirers of the U.S.S.R. They appear to think that the destruction of liberty is of no importance so long as their own line of work is for the moment unaffected. The U.S.S.R. is a large, rapidly developing country which has acute need of scientific workers and, consequently, treats them generously. Provided that they steer clear of dangerous subjects such as psychology, scientists are privileged persons.

Writers, on the other hand, are viciously persecuted. It is true that literary prostitutes like Ilya Ehrenburg or Alexei Tolstoy are paid huge sums of money, but the only thing which is of any value to the writer as such—his freedom of expression—is taken away from him. Some, at least, of the English scientists who speak so enthusiastically of the opportunities enjoyed by scientists in Russia are capable of understanding this. But their reflection appears to be: "Writers are persecuted in Russia. So what? I am not a writer." They do not see that *any* attack on intellectual liberty, and on the concept of objective truth, threatens in the long run every department of thought.

For the moment, the totalitarian state tolerates the scientist because it needs him. Even in Nazi Germany, scientists, other than Jews, were relatively well treated, and the German scientific community, as a whole, offered no resistance to Hitler. At this stage of history, even the most autocratic ruler is forced to take account of physical reality, partly because of the lingering on of liberal habits of thought, partly because of the need to prepare for war. So long as physical reality cannot be altogether ignored, so long as two and two have to make four when you are, for example, drawing the blueprint of an aeroplane, the scientist has his function, and can even be allowed a measure of liberty. His awakening will come later, when the totalitarian state is firmly established. Meanwhile, if he wants to safeguard the integrity of science, it is his job to develop some kind of solidarity with his literary colleagues and not regard it as a matter of indifference when writers are silenced or driven to suicide, and newspapers systematically falsified.

But however it may be with the physical sciences, or with music, painting, and architecture, it is—as I have tried to show—certain that literature is doomed if liberty of thought perishes.

Not only is it doomed in any country which retains a totalitarian structure; but any writer who adopts the totalitarian outlook, who finds excuses for persecution and the falsification of reality, thereby destroys himself as a writer. There is no way out of this. No tirades against "individualism" and "the ivory tower," no pious platitudes to the effect that "true individuality is only attained through identification with the community," can get over the fact that a bought mind is a spoiled mind. Unless spontaneity enters at some point or another, literary creation is impossible, and language itself becomes ossified. At some time in the future, if the human mind becomes something totally different from what it now is, we may learn to separate literary creation from intellectual honesty. At present we know only that the imagination, like certain wild animals, will not breed in captivity. Any writer or journalist who denies that fact—and nearly all the current praise of the Soviet Union contains or implies such a denial—is, in effect, demanding his own destruction.

The articles by Michel Gordey, "What You Can Read in Russia," and John MacCormac, "Reading by Red Star Light," are complementary. Gordey, the son of White Russian parents, was active in the Free French Movement with the OWI, 1941–45, and has since been correspondent for *France-Soir*, largest daily in France. He speaks Russian fluently, and his observations are based on visits to the Soviet Union. MacCormac was a veteran European correspondent for the *New York Times* until his death in 1958.

Michel Gordey
WHAT YOU CAN READ IN RUSSIA

There is in the Soviet Union one field where statistics abound and figures are almost too plentiful. Here, the usual veil of military secrecy has been deliberately cast aside by the regime. This is the field of the state publishing activities, of the printing of books. Here are some figures, which speak for themselves:

Michel Gordey, *Visa to Moscow* (New York: Alfred A. Knopf, 1952), pp. 195–209, copyright 1952 by Alfred A. Knopf, Inc. Reprinted by permission of the publisher.

Total number of books brought out in the USSR from 1918 to 1949: 13,000,000,000 copies.
Books printed in the USSR in the single year 1949: 683,000,000 copies.
"Classics of Marxism" (Marx, Engels, Lenin, Stalin) printed between 1918 and 1949: 802,000,000 copies (works of Lenin: 190,600,000; works of Stalin: 540,000,000).
Children's books printed between 1945 and 1949: 200,000,000 copies.

If one takes into account the fact that in 1918 more than half the adult population of the Soviet Union could not read or write, and that in 1950 the proportion of illiterates was less than 10 per cent, the scope and result of this effort appear remarkable.

The figures I have quoted, for a total population that in the past thirty-two years has fluctuated between 150,000,000 and 200,000,000, might well set any publishing expert in the Western countries to dreaming. When one considers that a printing of a hundred thousand copies, even in countries like France, England, and the United States, constitutes an exceptional success, one may realize the prodigious labor accomplished by Soviet *kultura*.

What does *kultura* mean? Strictly translated, it means "culture," but in actual fact its connotation is immeasurably more comprehensive and complex. Is a salesman polite to his customers? He is showing *kultura*. Has the central Post Office in Moscow installed leather chairs for the use of citizens who want to sit down to write? That is a triumph of *kultura*. Is a woman ticket-taker churlish with the passengers? "Comrade, you are lacking *kultura!*" Are the washrooms in some restaurant or theatre particularly badly kept? A hand has scribbled on the walls: "Comrade manager, a little more *kultura,* please!" Intangible and omnipresent, this term denotes all amelioration, but also all modernization of human living and human relations. Under this head the politeness of the citizens, the installation of gas in Moscow, a leather armchair, or the mass production of baby carriages rests on *kultura* just as does the latest discovery of a great scientist, or an edition of several hundred thousand copies of the complete works of Chekhov.

But in the field of publishing, as opposed to that of manufacturing trains or tractors, the Soviet statistics do not spring from propaganda and have not been subject to any clever manipulation. The attentive observer cannot doubt their truth. Some of my own experiences make it possible for me to illustrate the dry language of figures in living terms.

When I took the subway or the trolley-bus in Moscow in the spring of 1950, I used to be struck, from the first, by the large number of passengers reading books. I found it particularly noteworthy that these people, who seemed lost in their reading to the point of forgetting the people around them, the noise, and the weather, were not on the whole intellectuals. They were, for the most part, laborers, peasants, ordinary people in general, plainly and cheaply dressed. It likewise impressed me that they were usually reading bulky volumes and not little booklets or easily digestible stories. When I scrutinized the titles of these books, I found a striking proportion of classic authors, both Russian and foreign. How many times, riding around Moscow, have I not noted that the old woman in a woolen scarf, or the young man with hands blackened by toil, sitting beside me, was reading Tolstoi, Pushkin, Gogol, Chekhov, Gorky, or Balzac, Shakespeare, Dickens, Victor Hugo! Innumerable others were bent over textbooks of high-school or college level, books on science or technological manuals. To a Western point of view, nearly all these books seemed out of keeping with their obviously "lower-class" readers.

I noticed the same thing in other cities, as well as in the waiting rooms of railroad stations and airports, in trains and planes, and even in very small towns that I went through by chance. I was, in fact, rather surprised by the small number of people reading newspapers or illustrated weeklies. To fill the long hours of waiting or of the leisure forced upon them by daily journeys, the Russian crowd very clearly preferred big books to the publications of the Soviet press.

When I spoke with workmen or small employees I was able to verify that these people read a great deal. I often checked up on their knowledge of books that I had read myself. In schools and workers' clubs I found libraries of from twenty to forty thousand volumes. The directors, far from being proud of these libraries, considered them comparatively meager. A large factory in Stalingrad, for instance, which must employ from ten to fifteen thousand workers (the actual figure was, of course, kept secret), had in its House of Culture fifty thousand volumes at the free disposal of its personnel. Library stocks were augmented by three to five thousand volumes a year. The workers had not only a magnificent choice of technical books and Soviet literature, but also a very fine collection of foreign classics in translation. These were greatly in demand (I consulted, just be to sure, the slips that registered the French classics borrowed to take home).

By spending hours at a time in bookshops I was able to form an idea of the extent to which the Soviet population is hungry for books. I did this in Moscow, Leningrad, Stalingrad, Rostov, and Tiflis. Everywhere the salesmen were besieged. People of all ages and conditions were demanding works in all categories. The demand was so great that new shipments of books were exhausted in a few hours. One morning, in a large bookshop in Leningrad, I myself saw a case containing three hundred copies of a new novel; in the afternoon there was not a single copy left. There are second-hand bookshops, run by the state (like all retail commerce), in the USSR; and here again I constantly found throngs of customers who were asking for books published in 1945 and 1946, already out of print and unobtainable in the stores for new books. Yet Soviet books are brought out in large printings: several hundred thousand copies for contemporary novels, from fifty to a hundred thousand for a single edition of a classic author, more than a hundred thousand for certain scientific works or manuals in current use. Even collections of poetry sometimes have printings of fifty thousand copies; and those of the most popular poets, like Konstantin Simonov, run to two and three hundred thousand! As for Stalin's works, some of them have gone beyond 18,000,000 copies in the Russian language.

Furthermore, books are published in the USSR in 119 different languages. In 1946 the total printing of books in Russian amounted to 364,000,000, but that of works brought out in the country's other languages numbered 100,000,000 copies. When one compares the 1913 printings—80,200,000 in the Russian language and 6,500,000 in the others—one can measure numerically the progress achieved by *sovietskaya kultura*.

II

These statistics and personal authentications would excite unreserved admiration if there were not, also, the reverse of the medal. It is this reverse side that makes the evaluation of the term *kultura* so delicate and controversial for the Western mind. It is the Soviet state that publishes all books. It is therefore the Bolshevist party and the Soviet regime that decide what is and what is not to be published. The government has decreed constant reprintings since 1945 of Stalin's book *On the Patriotic War,* to the number of more than 18,000,000 copies. The government has also, for fifteen years, failed to bring out any new editions of the works of Dostoevsky. Finally, it is again the "ideological administration" of the party that explicitly prescribes what the contemporary Soviet authors must and must not write. Thus the intellectual elements of this vast country find themselves subject to a rigid censorship, at once positive and negative. These directives, which anticipate, down to the least detail, all that *is* to be published and also all that *is not,* govern literature, science, art, and the most innocent books for children. They prescribe in advance the numerical dose of such works that is to be administered to the Soviet public. The control of written thought is thus total and unlimited.

In its quantitative aspect the production of state publications is incontestably admirable. The fact that about eighty books per capita have been printed in the USSR since 1918 requires no comment. But the qualitative aspect—that is, the nature of the books that have been published and also of those that have been forbidden (before or after publication)—poses problems that are infinitely grave. The theories of Leninism-Stalinism officially assert the necessity for ideological control in order to consolidate proletarian dictatorship. But one must closely consider the present and future result of this directing of collective thought. It has cut a rude chasm, which grows deeper each year, between the Soviet Union and the rest of the world. Seen from this angle, a certain proportion of the 683,000,000 books printed in the USSR in 1949 may present a danger, if not to the peace of the world, at any rate to the full development of the intellectual faculties of the Soviet peoples. Here, as in many places, one must ask oneself if the Soviet rulers are not really committing a crime in distrusting their people, in doubting their intellectual maturity, in treating tens of millions of intelligent, responsible human beings like children whose least thought must be at the same time controlled and shielded from "pernicious influences."

Consider, first, the negative aspect of this ideological censorship. Let us take an example. Dostoevsky is regarded by the Soviet regime as a pernicious writer, dangerous for youth, reactionary in his political thought, "useless" in his philosophical thought. In this specific case, however, censorship does not go so far as to ban openly the works of an author whose reputation in Russia is, after all, too well established. During the past fifteen or twenty years, nevertheless, Dostoevsky's novels have not been reprinted. Even more, his books evidently figure on the black list of the second-hand bookshops. It is thus impossible today to get any work whatever by Dostoevsky in a bookstore. Though his works have not been removed from certain public libraries, which usually possess a single copy of them, there is not one book by this ill-esteemed writer in the school libraries or libraries for workers that I visited myself. Now, to my great surprise, on several occasions I saw torn, dog-eared copies of Dostoevsky's novels in the hands of my neighbors in the theaters, restaurants, or busses. These readers—most of them young— had had to go to great pains to procure these rare books. Of course, in spite of ideological directives, Dostoevsky did not disappear overnight from the shelves of private libraries. But the practical difficulty of finding his books, and the fact that he is no longer mentioned in the literature courses in the secondary schools, give ground for predicting his gradual and inevitable disappearance from the intellectual field of vision of future Soviet generations.

Let us go further and consider books strictly prohibited in the USSR. To justify these prohibitions, the champions of the Soviet regime often assert that they apply to works that are immoral, pornographic, prejudicial to youth, or, in general, "devoid of all literary value." These partisans then lash out at the Western countries, which, in the name of liberty, would demoralize or stultify their populations by a flood of books that are trash. It is true that such books do not appear in the USSR. It is true that they are published in the West. For us they are the inevitable cost of freedom. But the Soviet book prohibitions are infinitely more serious. They are not inspired by moral considerations alone—far from it.

On this black list appear not only most of the contemporary works produced in the non-Communist world but a part of the literary, scientific, and political output of the Soviet peoples themselves. Total suppression, which the regime has not dared to invoke against Dostoevsky, is actively enforced against thousands of other books, especially works of the past fifty years. The black list varies from month to month, constantly adjusted to the latest orders of the ideological administration. What is the practical significance of this black list?

It is rigorously applied, as we have seen, in second-hand bookstores. Also, the condemned works find no more mention in the different grades of public education (secondary schools, universities, scientific institutes, and so on). Finally, they are withdrawn from public use in the libraries, large and small, which serve the mass of the population. It is for this reason that the Lenin Library in Moscow, which is proud to be counted among the five richest libraries in the world, sometimes prints on its catalogue cards: "This work *cannot* be consulted." (These prohibitions apply to the mass of ordinary mortals. People who have a special and officially approved reason for consulting the forbidden books may be allowed to do so, by exceptional privilege, in a special little room in the public library.)

These prohibitions do not apply solely to the books of the great heretics of the regime, such as Trotsky or Bukharin. They even cover particular editions of the works of Lenin. They extend to the work of all those authors (novelists, scholars, historians) who were purged before the war during the trials of "right and left deviationists." Hence not one of the novels of Babel or Pilnyak, two of the most gifted writers since the Revolution, is at the present time available in the USSR. Yet Babel's *Red Cavalry* and Pilnyak's *The Volga Flows to the Caspian Sea* were considered for years—up to around 1935—as classics of the Civil War period. Then Babel and Pilnyak were accused of Trotskyite sympathies and disappeared without leaving any trace. Their books soon followed them into oblivion.

In the same way, once Lysenko's theories had been officially ratified by Stalin, the biologists who opposed them suffered more than rebuke or demotion. All their works were automatically placed on the black list. Nowadays there is no trace of their writings in Moscow's bookstores and libraries.

The range and ramifications of this censorship can hardly be appreciated. Yessenin was in 1940 still considered one of the greatest poets of the Revolution and a loyal Bolshevist. Attacked expressly in the late Andrei Zhdanov's literary decrees, the works of this poet (who killed himself in 1927) disappeared instantly from all the stores. A small collection of Yessenin's verse has recently been printed; it contains insignificant and frankly bad poems that have been deemed "publishable" by the ideological authorities. The rest are doomed to complete oblivion, once the last copies owned by private individuals have fallen into bits.

The successive changes in official party doctrine concerning history have given rise to personal tragedies: eminent historians have been first deported to Siberia, then recalled to activity, then dismissed anew and consigned to disgrace. The learned works published by these victims met with a fate exactly identical with that of their authors. They vanished; then they reappeared on the counters of shops and in the public libraries. These alternations were very rapid: I heard of one case in which a book made its reappearance in the shops before its author could complete the train ride from Siberia to Moscow.

One of my Western friends who had lived for several years in Moscow began to collect Russian books and regularly made a tour of second-hand bookshops. He hunted for months for a certain historical work without finding it. When he questioned the salesmen, they were evasive. Plainly this book was on the black list—a matter kept strictly secret. One day when my friend was browsing in a second-hand shop, a man came in and offered to sell a book to the clerk. It was the elusive history my friend had hunted in vain. After a brief trip to the back room of the shop, the clerk bought the book for twenty rubles. My friend asked for it at once.

"Very well," said the salesman. "It will cost twenty-two rubles; our legal commission is 10 per cent."

My friend was reaching into his pocket when the salesman said, with a smile: "Just a minute. We have to perform an operation."

With a pair of scissors he cut out the first twenty pages, depriving the book of its preface. This excision was clearly compulsory. Then, methodically, with a little knife, he scraped from the cover the name of the author of the censored preface (he had been a victim of the 1936 purge of historians). My friend received his mutilated book in silence.

The episode may, and should, shock a Western mind. I do not know whether any Soviet citizens could be revolted by it, but certainly none can be surprised. Constant revisions of the ideological line, with their instantaneous repercussions on the sale or suppression of books in the USSR, sometimes produce grotesque results. These official interventions are publicly admitted. While I was in Moscow, several large papers reported (*Pravda* May 14, 1950) that a historian of Soviet Azerbaijan, G. Guseinov, whose book published in 1949 had won the supreme recognition of a Stalin Prize, had given evidence of "mistaken political and theoretical attitudes" in discussing certain movements of national liberation in the Caucasus in the nineteenth century.

He had praised an insurrection that, according to Marx and Engels, had really been backed by Turkey and England. These "bourgeois and nationalist uncertainties" of the scholar "must be energetically condemned," said *Pravda*. The Stalin Prize was consequently withdrawn, a few days later, from Comrade Professor Guseinov.

About this time *Pravda* published an article vigorously criticizing a volume of the *Great Soviet Encyclopedia*, which is checked by personages as important as Voroshilov and Vishinsky. Nevertheless, its volume on the United States (published in 1945) sinned through excess of sympathy for the principal enemy of the USSR. The official organ of the Russian Communist party therefore condemned it in a long article.

On the succeeding days I tried to get the two incriminated works, searching for them in the largest bookshops and second-hand stores in Moscow. Already, they had vanished from the showcases and display counters, never to reappear—unless there should be a sudden shift in the party's policy.

III

But the ideological administration does not confine itself to laying an interdict upon authors or published works of undesirable tendencies. A still more important function of this supercensorship consists in dictating the contents of works in preparation. It is unnecessary to enlarge on this subject; examples are too numerous in all fields of publishing. In the years immediately following the end of the war, all books of fiction and history were devoted to descriptions of the Soviet feats of arms in the struggle against Hitler's Germany. There was not a single novel and very few pieces of historical work that in 1945–47 dealt with other subjects. Then came the peacetime directive: all new novels were consecrated henceforth to the description of "the new Soviet man in the struggle for the reconstruction of the socialist fatherland." This directive was still in force in 1950. In this year and through 1949 the novels that received official rewards, and had the advantage of heavy initial promotion (through the dithyrambic praises of all the newspapers and the figures of their exceptionally large first printings), were almost all based on the same theme: the veteran's return to his peacetime place of work; the ensuing psychological and political conflicts; the advances achieved in all branches of industry and agriculture, thanks to the good ideology of these demobilized heroes.

I asked some Soviet intellectuals, who were entirely devoted to the regime, to suggest the best novels that had appeared in the USSR in 1949 and 1950. Their replies were almost unanimous, and I bought the three books most highly recommended: *The Knight of the Golden Star*, by Semyon Babayevsky, Stalin Prize; *Far from Moscow*, by the young author Ajaev, Stalin Prize; and *The Luminous Shore*, by Vera Panova, Stalin Prize.

All three had subjects strictly in conformity with the general line mentioned above. The writers handled these subjects with indisputable talent, and there was no doubt of the literary value of their works. But I cannot believe that the three authors by themselves would have selected almost identical themes. And if this phenomenon appears altogether normal to Soviet readers, I cannot, for my part, help seeing in it the proof of what I call the positive function of the Soviet censorship, which dictates when it does not ban.

Similarly, at intervals of a few months, several works intended to expose the horrors of American life and civilization made their appearance in the Soviet bookshops. One collection, *Here Is America,* contained extracts from books put out by twentieth-century Russian writers, Soviet and pre-Soviet, beginning with Maxim Gorky. This anthology drew a terrifying picture of American existence. Its jacket showed a policeman, with the face of a brute, brandishing a blackjack; the content was like the cover. Another book, *Reports on America,* was a different sort of anthology: here the editor had collected texts from American authors, describing the horrors of unemployment, the poverty, the exploitation of the workers, and the merciless brutality of American capitalists. The cover depicted an angry crowd of laborers dashing forward, flags in their hands —doubtless to show that the American working class would end, one day, by revolting.

What is significant here is not so much the content of the books as their simultaneous publication, and the chorus of applause in the Soviet press which greeted the appearance of these anti-American works. Here, again, the ideological administration had decreed the political line, the size of the printings, and the widespread distribution of this literature. Nothing is left to chance in Soviet publishing. Everything follows a plan strictly laid down in advance.

I observed, nevertheless, that readers did not always happily accept the decrees of the supreme ideological authority. In visiting bookshops, I often witnessed the intense interest in contemporary foreign authors that is felt by the Soviet public. Often I heard people of all ages and conditions ask the salesmen: "Haven't you something new in the way of foreign translations?" And when the salesmen would suggest a book like the anti-American anthology, or a novel by Theodore Dreiser or Louis Aragon or some German Communist writer, I would hear a dissatisfied voice say: "Oh no, not that. Haven't you Roger Martin du Gard or Hemingway? Or Priestley?"

The reply was, of course, always in the negative. But I was surprised to discover that in spite of all barriers the Soviet public still knew outstanding names in contemporary world literature. And I was dumbfounded one day to discover that a pale young man sitting beside me in a bus was reading Marcel Proust's *Remembrance of Things Past,* in an old edition, as torn and dog-eared as the copies of Dostoevsky that I mentioned.

In the field of contemporary foreign literature there has been a progressive and now almost complete contraction in the last five or ten years. Before the war, authors like Hemingway, Richard Wright, André Malraux, J. B. Priestley, Upton Sinclair, Thomas Mann, Sinclair Lewis, were very popular. At the present time most of these men's books have disappeared from the display counters and have joined the ranks of the black list. The only foreign authors now living who may still be published in the Soviet Union are writers faithful to the Stalinist doctrine, such as Aragon, Howard Fast, or Andersen Nexö. The censorship that has fallen upon others is explained either by the political evolution of these authors (Wright, Hemingway, and Malraux have in one way or another made plain their opposition to Communism) or by the new doctrine known as "the fight against cosmopolitanism."

The famous conference-decrees of Andrei Zhdanov, in 1946 and 1947, inaugurated a merciless war against "the dangerous influences of Western bourgeois culture" and also against what is called, in a phrase constantly recurring in postwar intellectual discussions, "subservience to the West." An entire volume would not be large enough to reproduce the texts hurled against the eagerness of certain Soviet intellectuals to "westernize" Soviet culture. This campaign gave rise to successive purges in the domains of literature, painting, music, history, pure and applied science, literary and art criticism. The campaign against the West was part of that wave of nationalism which broke over the various branches of Soviet life after the war. The disappearance of non-Communist foreign authors from the bookshops and libraries was one more manifestation of it. As I have just said, it does not seem to me that Soviet readers have accepted these new rigors of censorship with alacrity; but what can they do against the decisions made at the Kremlin by the chief directors of the Soviet Union?

Some very popular Soviet authors, outstandingly gifted, were hard hit by this campaign. The poets Pasternak and Anna Akhmatova and the humorist Mikhail Zochtchenko were its first victims. They were accused, respectively, of "Western formalism" and of "the *petit-bourgeois* spirit of disparagement." Their works were placed on the black list, and the Soviet literary world waited patiently for the three culprits to make their apology. But only one of them officially repented: Anna Akhmatova, a sensitive lyric poet (condemned specifically for her bourgeois sentimentality, which brought nothing constructive to the forward march of socialism). It took this old and ailing poet three years, after the promulgation of the Zhdanov decrees, to do it. Rumor had it that she was driven to desperation by extreme poverty, as her royalties were no longer paid her (an inexorable result of the black list). She then published, in the illustrated review *Ogonyok,* in April 1950, five poems: on Stalin, on the Communist man, on the Stalinist plan for reforestation, and so on. These poems were execrable and had no relation to Akhmatova's lifelong style. But the old woman was thus assured of avoiding starvation, and no one in Moscow blamed her for capitulating.

The other two great culprits have not, up to the present, made known their contrition. It must not be imagined that their life or their personal liberty has been threatened, as was rumored in anti-Soviet reviews. The reality is more subtle. The period of firing squads for unruly intellectuals seems to have served its turn in the USSR. The present penalty is not imprisonment or exile any longer, unless it is a matter of clearly defined political offense. These two recalcitrants offer interesting examples.

Zochtchenko has reportedly retired to a little farm in the vicinity of Leningrad which belongs to him. He occupies himself with—raising chickens. From time to time he even publishes an inoffensive little story in some minor paper or magazine. His books have disappeared from the shop counters, and he no longer receives the substantial royalties he used to collect for the satiric writings that lashed (no doubt too rudely) the Soviet bureaucracy. But he has enough of his savings left to end his days in peace.

The case of Boris Pasternak is more interesting. This man is probably at the present time the greatest living Russian poet and one of the greatest in the world. He was denounced and covered with abuse by Zhdanov and the party's official critics because of his abstruse style, which was called "formalist" and "incomprehensible to the people." In spite of his "formalism" (or perhaps because of it), Pasternak had enjoyed an extraordinary popularity among Soviet intellectual youth. I was told that in 1947, just before the Zhdanov decrees, at a poetry reading in one of the large Moscow auditoriums, Pasternak received a long ovation. When he began to recite his poems, he several times paused for a few seconds to search his memory for the next line; each time the entire hall chanted in chorus the words momentarily forgotten by this poet "incomprehensible to the people."

The first result of Pasternak's condemnation was the disappearance of all his books from the bookshops and public libraries. They became unobtainable. My own requests for them came up against the icy or dismayed air of the salesmen confronted by such lack of tact. But Pasternak has not suffered any financial privation from having been put on the index. Well before 1947 he had undertaken the poetic translation of the complete works of Shakespeare and of Goethe's *Faust.* He is continuing this work and receives a considerable monthly stipend from the government publishing office. I am informed that Pasternak at the present time makes about ten thousand rubles a month and thus remains in the privileged category of great Soviet intellectuals. He has a beautiful apartment in the Writers' House, and a villa outside Moscow. He even has an automobile at his disposal. In short, he lives in great material comfort. Does he continue to write his "formalist and abstruse" poems? That seems highly probable. What also seems certain is that his poetic works will remain shut up in his desk drawers, and that his admirers will never be able to buy them in the bookshops, either during his lifetime or later (Pasternak is in his sixties). Evidently the truth about *kultura* is not so simple as is claimed, alike by the advocates and the adversaries of the USSR.

There are, indeed, so many complexities and contradictions in the Soviet literary domain that a simple judgment of ideological administration is impossible. I have already pointed out the popularity and large printings of Russian and foreign classics in the USSR. Some of these authors—and especially Pushkin, Gogol, and

Saltykov-Shchedrin—devoted a mass of their writing to the struggle against tyranny, against the tsarist bureaucracy of the nineteenth century, against the police system of the old days. Their works ought to embarrass the present regime, which shares the faults denounced—and with what talent!—by the great Russian writers of the nineteenth century. Nothing impedes today's Soviet reader from making, in his own mind, the transition from the abuses of the last century to present Soviet reality.

But classical authors of this type are wholly exempt from "ideological" cutting. Indeed, works suppressed in former days by the tsarist censorship because of their attacks on authority have been published for the first time under the Stalin regime. Stalin proclaims in his writings and his speeches his profound respect for the great nineteenth-century writers who fought for liberty and democracy. This stand taken by Stalin is enough in itself to assure Soviet readers that the rigors of the black list are in no danger of depriving them of certain somewhat daring passages in the works of these classical authors. If a contemporary author had ventured to put into his writing one one-hundredth of the virulence to be found in certain chapters or poems of Pushkin and Saltykov, the censorship would have clamped down mercilessly upon him. But, as one sees, here again *kultura* is not simple or easy to grasp.

A still more substantial contradiction exists between the campaign against "Western cosmopolitanism" and the publication and distribution of great foreign classics in the USSR. From 1918 to 1947 the printings were considerable: Byron, 500,000; Goethe, 586,000; Heine, 1,100,000; Balzac, 2,000,000; Dickens, 2,200,000; Victor Hugo, 4,100,000; Guy de Maupassant, almost 4,000,000; Shakespeare, 1,600,000; Zola, 2,500,000. Postwar editions of all these authors (and of Voltaire, Diderot, and Mark Twain) have augmented these figures. It is not an empty formula when the Soviet ideological administration proclaims the respect of *kultura* for the intellectual heritage of all peoples. These huge editions of foreign classics are exercising their influence on Soviet youth, as I discovered in conversation with young intellectuals. There remains such a contradiction between the encouragement lavished by the regime upon this spread of Western influence in its forms of greatest genius, and the barrier raised against the same influence in the contemporary world, that one can find in it no logic whatsoever. We come always to the same conclusion: simplified judgments of *sovietskaya kultura* are impossible.

John MacCormac
READING BY RED STAR LIGHT

Scarcely two months ago *Pravda* of Prague, in an article calling for "More Vigilance on the Cultural Front," declared: "Let's look in the windows of the bookshops. Beside the works of Sholokhov stands 'The Grapes of Wrath,' by Steinbeck. Beside the Slovakian fiction writer Peter Jilemnick stands Somerset Maugham's 'The Moon and Sixpence'; beside Ilya Ehrenburg a book of Louis Bromfield's; beside Fadeyev's 'Young Guard,' Vercors' 'Silence of the Sea'; Cronin's romances next to the Soviet poet Mayakovski; beside the progressive works of Louis Aragon the reactionary François Mauriac and Agatha Christie's 'The Unknown Threatens.' "

Why did *Pravda* object to this juxtaposing of Soviet and non-Soviet writers? The reasons may sound strange to Western ears: "Steinbeck's 'Grapes of Wrath,' which describes the wandering of farmers beggared by the banks through 'God's own land of California' served the cause of capitalism by its 'social sympathies' since it demanded measures against the proletarianization, and the agricultural laws which were then enacted were designed to avert the danger that the oppressed would organize themselves collectively." More comprehensible, if no better grounded, was *Pravda's* complaint that the works of Somerset Maugham could still be bought in Prague although "he had fought as an agent in 1917 against the Bolshevist Revolution."

The same kind of lament can be heard in Hungary. Last September the *Nepszava* of Budapest complained that the library of the former Shell Oil Company "contains mainly Fascist, semi-Fascist, and destructive books, such as the works of Bromfield, Upton Sinclair, and the

---

John MacCormac, "Reading by Red Star Light," *Saturday Review*, 33:9–10+ (February 25, 1950), copyright 1950 by the Saturday Review Associates, Inc. Reprinted by permission of Mrs. John MacCormac and of the publisher.

works of the Chinese philosopher Lin Yutang. One of the comrades wished to keep the works of the Chinese philosopher, saying they were quite harmless. In answer he was shown the chapter entitled 'The Doctrine of Personality' and this made him realize that the 'wise' Chinese philosopher is a dangerous political enemy."

This proscription of books from the West is a recent but increasingly common development in the Soviet-controlled "people's democracies." The Communist regimes of Czechoslovakia, Hungary, Rumania, Bulgaria, and Poland are just as anxious as were the Nazis that ideas which fail to jibe with their own dogmas be prevented from circulating. The Nazis burned the books of which they did not approve. In the Soviet satellites today paper is too scarce a commodity to permit so fiery a form of disapproval. Instead, in an effort to quarantine themselves from Western ideas, they turn books by non-Soviet writers into pulp so that their newly nationalized presses may print books with approved messages.

This Communist form of book-burning is one of the negative measures of a system of thought control by which Stalin is recreating the 70,000,000 inhabitants of the people's democracies in his own image. The positive measures include the alteration of their old moral and cultural traditions—and even of their history—and the virtually compulsory reading of the works of Stalin and his local imitators. In this ambitious reconditioning project scientists, artists, and teachers are all required to play their part, but the most important role is reserved for writers.

To make the role easier to fill the writers are being offered "direction," direction that is also extended to the reader by librarians trained not only to follow the Party line but to retail it. The gradual elimination of translations of their Western rivals assures authors who can learn to write in the prescribed spirit of "Socialist realism" a monopoly. Even should the public not appreciate their products, the situation is not hopeless for them. As Pavel Reiman recently wrote in the Czechoslovakian weekly *Tvorba*: "A book which does not help us reeducate the people in the spirit of Socialism and Marxist-Leninist theory is a harmful book, more harmful than other damaged goods since it fills people's brains with the poison of reactionary bourgeois literature. The Communist Party has effective means to compel the purchase of political literature."

A poll conducted just before Christmas by the *Lidove Noviny* of Prague suggests that Mr. Reiman was right. Dividing the book field into three categories, *Lidove Noviny* declared that seven of the ten most popular books in Czechoslovakia in Category I, eight of the first ten in Category II, and four of the first ten in Category III (books from which the reader derived the greatest pleasure) were by Soviet Russian authors. Stalin, of course, led the list in popularity.

In every Soviet satellite the publishing industry has been nationalized, libraries have been taken over by the State, and writers have been required to organize themselves into new federations under official guidance. Art, music, and the stage have also been brought under Government control. In Poland, which has succumbed more slowly than its neighbors, the Warsaw Radio admitted on June 30 that all private printing works had been expropriated and on November 8 the Ministry of Culture and Art established a "General Theatre, Opera, and Orchestra Authority" to guide, coordinate, and supervise the activities of all theatres, opera houses, symphony orchestras, artistic ensembles, circuses, and fairs. The Czechoslovakian nationalization decree went further since it envisaged even the taking over of second-hand bookshops. In Czechoslovakia no author who does not belong to the Union of Czechoslovakian Writers may have his books published.

This also holds true in Rumania. The task which the Rumanian Union of Writers is expected to fulfil was indicated on August 2 of last year by the Communist newspaper *Scanteia,* which said that the union must help build up "new cadres of literary critics more in tune with Marxist-Leninist reality." On June 10 *Scanteia* chided Rumanian theatres which "prefer the old plays" although new ones based on the life of workers and peasants had been introduced, and said the General Directorate of the Theatres would expel those with "outmoded mentality." In Bulgaria not only the theatre directors but the actors had been criticized by the Committee of Arts and Science for their ideological failings. It was decided that modern Soviet and Bulgarian plays should be produced and acting modeled on the Stanislavsky-Denchenko realistic school. Some Western classics would also be permitted.

This sounded like a concession but is not necessarily so. A solution of the problem presented by Western classics in art and literature has been found in their "reinterpretation." For instance, the Hungarian newspaper *Szabad Szo,* commenting on October 17 on a Shakespeare series at the Budapest National Theatre, declared "the correct interpretation of Shakespeare began in the Soviet Union. In Shakespeare's tragedies feudalism is falling to pieces. 'Hamlet,' 'Macbeth,' 'King Lear,' and 'Richard III' all show the dismay caused by the disintegration of the ideology of the Middle Ages in human souls. . . . Shakespeare expresses in the language of passion the struggle which will be decided in the decades before us."

Not only the classics of the drama but of opera are reinterpreted in the light of Socialist "realism." Mozart's "Abduction from the Seraglio" might not seem to have any close connection with Marxism but one was found and expressed in a presentation of this work in Prague's German Theatre at the end of November. Among other changes the great C major coloratura aria was deleted perhaps because its lyric "Tortures of every kind may await me, I laugh at pain and suffering" might be thought to carry "Socialist realism" too far.

Although the reinterpretation of Western classics may still earn them a place in the satellite world it would seem bound to be a modest one at best. As the Hungarian Communist Party organ, *Szabad Nep,* remarked on December 8 in a criticism of a new textbook on literature issued by the Pedagogic Institute for high-school students: "The masterpieces of Greek and Roman literature are much less important than the Western European literature of modern times and the Russian literature of the nineteenth century. . . . The 'humanism' of the ancient times sees 'great human qualities in the enemy' and even 'fine examples of self-sacrificing patriotism.' We, of course, are not sorry for the fall of imperialist agents. Our humanism is Socialist humanism, which demands that 'the enemy must be destroyed if he does not surrender' [Gorky] in the interest of humanity."

The first books to fall victims of the new regime in the people's democracies were, of course, the school books. As *Szabad Nep* remarked on September 28, "The curriculum had to be purged from clerical and nationalist trends which distorted science. It had to be completed . . . with the decisive achievements of Soviet scientists." This has been done throughout the people's democracies, and to reach the child of pre-reading age texts have been prepared for kindergarten nurses. According to an article on November 16 in *Közneveles,* a publication devoted to educational matters, this was necessary because the kindergarten nurses "must clearly see their place in the camp of peace-living people. They must learn to hate the imperialists and have a right view concerning the culture and moral superiority of the Soviet Union. . . . The children must learn to love the Soviet Union."

Next to be pulped and rewritten were the history books. In Czechoslovakia this coincided with the *coup d'état* of February 1948 and was carried out by the "action committees," who were the driving force of that revolution. It is recorded that in Prague alone 184 tons of pulp were obtained in this manner. As Kopecky, the Minister of Information, remarked during the celebration of the thirtieth anniversary of the founding of the Czechoslovakian Republic, "Hitherto history has been written by the bourgeoisie and their historians. That's at an end. Now we shall write the history of our Republic from the standpoint of our class, the working class."

Scientific writing was the next to be *"gleichgeschaltet."* As Professor Jan Mukarovsky, rector of Charles University in Prague put it, "Almost all scientists hitherto have been educated to believe that science must be classless and non-political and that every linking-up of scientific and non-scientific opinions must be at the expense of research. Today it is clear, however, that the so-called non-partisan science is as great a fiction as non-partisan art." Professor Mukarovsky was rewarded for this speech with the "State Prize." Professor Istvan Rusznyak, new president of the Hungarian Academy, put it more strongly in his inaugural address on December 20 in Budapest. "It cannot be sufficiently stressed," he said, "that science is not independent of social conditions, class, or party. Science is the product of social work and will remain a means and a weapon of class warfare as long as rival classes exist. . . . A proletarian partisan outlook insures *de facto* objective knowledge and proletarian partisanship is a *sine qua non* of real science."

How proletarian partisanship can be employed to assess the value of scientific writing was well illustrated by Professor Traian Savulescu in a statement to the Rumanian Academy of Science criticizing "the cosmopolitan, antipatriotic, and anti-scientific position adopted by the *Revista de Oftalmologie"* on June 29 last. Professor Savulescu declared that "numerous Soviet ophthalmologists, guided by the scientific conception—the only correct conception—of dialectical materialism, under the direction of the Communist Party of Soviet Russia and with the strong support of the Soviet Government, have succeeded in raising the ophthalmological science of their country to a level which has made possible the solution of the main problems in this field." The *Revista de Oftalmologie,* which neglected the progress made by Soviet medical science, has since been disciplined.

In all satellite countries the state publishing houses are linked with the respective Soviet Friendship Society and with the libraries, including those established in the factories or agricultural cooperatives. The purpose of the librarians is to bring about what the Budapest newspaper *Szabad Szo* referred to as "collective reading." Commenting on the announcement that "a literary movement which requires all workers to read four books by Sayers Khan, Smirnov, Iljin, and Bela Illes, after which authors and critics are to discuss the works with the workers," is to be started in Budapest factories and is then to be extended to the whole of Hungary, the newspaper continues: "This means an enterprise which is without example. Not only reactionaries but honest people ask whether 'a collective reading movement' is possible, reading being a private affair. . . . Free choice of books, however, was not possible under the capitalist system. The worthless best sellers were propagated apparently for political reasons. . . . A new movement had to be organized to direct our working people to the true sources of culture."

On October 27 *Nepszava,* the Hungarian trade-union organ, announced that future plant librarians are being trained in the Academy of Free Education at Szentendre. "The curriculum is: 'Social Conditions Mirrored in Literature,' 'Thirty Years of Soviet Literature,' 'The Party Line in Literature,' and 'The Fight Against Inimical Ideologies.'"

This training soon bore fruit. Not long after it was begun *Szabad Nep* recorded with satisfaction that 570 out of a total of 1,200 books had been eliminated from the Ganz Shipyard Library in Budapest and that 12,000 had been removed from the MAVAG factory library on the ground that they were Fascist or destructive. "We cannot speak of progress, however," *Szabad Nep* complained, "as long as in the Ganz Wagon factory a book by Tibor Joo, 'Hungarian Nationalism,' published in 1943, is still available, while the new librarian in the MAVAG is a man who maintains the view that religious instruction is inseparable from morality! At the Ganz Electric factory a young worker dared to state that the task of a librarian was to 'serve the readers and if a reader wished to read Cronin, it was the librarian's task to put Cronin at the reader's disposal.' This young worker had no idea that the librarian . . . is a propagandist and an agitator of Bolshevik culture."

The Socialist organ announced that "library committees" were to be organized in Budapest, which among other duties would launch "a book campaign which is to serve to increase hatred against the imperialists and their base agents and increase the love of the Soviet Union. All these books will unmask nationalism as an arm of the imperialists. Their heroes are the heroes of Soviet production."

Hungary is not the only satellite where a sharp eye is being kept on the libraries. On June 9 last the Bucharest newspaper *Romania Libera* complained that the Craiova public library "contains remnants of the writings with which the exploiting bourgeoisie sought to darken the minds of the working people in our country. For example, we found Aristide Bazilescu's 'Political Economy' on the shelves of this library. The Craiova Provisional Committee should immediately remove this book and others of this type still to be found in this institution, where the workers come to find new and progressive culture."

The problem of providing "progressive culture" has also been tackled at the source. Like the Rumanian Federation of Writers' Unions or the Union of Czechoslovakian Writers, the Federation of Hungarian Authors has been instructed "not only to debate literary problems but implement directing principles in literature." Joseph Darvas, Minister of Construction, who wrote an article about this on October 17 in Budapest, continued: "Yes, it must direct. This does not imply a restriction of literary freedom but points the way in a jungle which obstructs our adequate literary development. Like the Federation of Soviet Authors, the Federation of Hungarian Authors must become an operative body, the chief director of literary life."

The Rumanian Federation of Writers' Unions has already become an operative body. According to an article in *Flacăra* on December 28 "the federation, in order to raise writers' political and ideological level, has organized courses in Marxism-Leninism and esthetics and, to raise their professional level, a series of discussions about the main problems of literary creation."

What does the "direction" of literature imply? Among other things, according to a recent article in *Nepszava,* Hungarian writers and poets "shall be sent to work in plants, tractor and machine stations or join the Army in order to acquaint themselves with the lives of workers and soldiers and to enable them to represent the heroes of work." The Rumanian Federation of Writers was able to record in December that as a result of such direction "works of prose and poetry could be created which show the reader living pictures of the activity of miners in the Jiu Valley or of the builders of the Danube–Black Sea canal."

Another task of the writers' federation will be to introduce the Communist institution of "criticism and self-criticism" in literary life. As Sos Endre pointed out in an article on November 3 in the *Magyar Nemzet* of Budapest, "Criticism and self-criticism should never be restricted to a narrow sphere but should take place in public." The first public example was provided by György Lukács, whose political and literary attitude had been sharply criticized last summer by his fellow writer Laszlo Rudas. Lukács in reply admitted he had been guilty of a grave mistake in neglecting the importance of Soviet literature and giving too much consideration to progressive Western literature. But he denied that he had "slandered Lenin" or been guilty of "cosmopolitanism." He recalled that he had "fought against decadent trends in Hungarian and Western art alike when Leftist politicians considered James Joyce and Dos Passos as novelists of great value."

It was a dangerous situation for Comrade Lukács since Joszef Revai, Minister of the People's Culture, had declared on September 27 that "those who oppose the Party line on questions of literature, art, and ideology . . . fight in fact for re-establishment of the former capitalist exploiting system. Art and literature cannot be neutral. They must be warlike, partial." During a debate at the Hungarian Authors' Federation on November 12 Comrade György Szudi had asserted that "any author maintaining a passive attitude toward things happening in the country is a counter-revolutionary." Finally, on December 21, Geza Losonczy, under-secretary for the People's Culture, had laid it down in a Parliamentary speech that "indifference and contempt of Soviet art and literature is an important manifestation of reaction. Relations to Soviet culture are a testing block just as, in political life, relations to the Soviet Union."

Comrade Lukács was in hot water and may still be there since, in an article in the authoritative *Szabad Nep* on December 25, Marton Horvath commented severely: "Comrade Lukács has admitted part of his mistakes. But if we consider that Comrade Lukács's mistakes have distorted the literary policy of the Party for years and have influenced a significant part of Hungarian authors unfavorably we must state that Comrade Lukács's self-criticism was not thorough enough."

The prospect for literature and the artist in the Soviet satellites is bleak enough in all conscience. Yet just the other day I came across a faintly heartening item. The Brothers Grimm, who enchanted my bourgeois childhood, are of course *verboten* in their original state. But for them, like Shakespeare, there is hope: they can be "reinterpreted." The Budapest newspaper *Kis Ujsag* told the story on December 20:

"On Stalin's seventieth birthday the puppet theatre will perform the story of Red Riding Hood as staged by the Soviet author Chorny. In the Soviet transcription the romantic darkness of the Grimm fairy tale is changed into a story with logical characters."

Chapter XII

The broad view: past, present, future

Over the years, America has always been exceedingly fortunate in possessing eloquent and convincing spokesmen for freedom, liberty, and justice. When misguided pressure groups and demagogic individuals have called for conformity, for unanimity of opinion, for eliminating all ideas with which they happen to disagree, these clearheaded, courageous molders of public opinion have aided immeasurably in bringing us back to our senses. They have pounded home the fact that by seeking to kill freedom of expression, freedom of information and inquiry, and allied rights, certain veterans organizations, religious bodies, congressional committees, headline-seeking politicians, and the like would destroy the basic concepts upon which America was founded.

Every era of our history has been afflicted with this problem in one form or another. Unquestionably, therefore, "eternal vigilance is the price of liberty" if we are "to avoid tyranny over the mind of man." Among the writers who have manned the ramparts most effectively during the last generation, a few stand out. Of these, we think immediately of Elmer Davis, Zechariah Chafee, Jr., and Gerald W. Johnson. The case for the defense is ably summed up by the statements which follow from their pens; those by Davis and Chafee were written shortly prior to their deaths.

A complementary point of view is set forth by another ardent advocate of free expression—Curtis Bok.

Elmer Davis' *But We Were Born Free* (1954), from which "Are We Worth Saving?" is taken, is a fighting book, described by one reviewer as "a hard-hitting and exhilarating book: crisply written, humorous, full of quietly murderous thrusts at the heresy-sniffers, the doublethinkers, the would-be thought-controllers, the cowardly conformists, and at absolutists of various stripes." In this work Davis draws on a remarkably full background of experience, including service on the staff of the *New York Times,* Director of the U.S. Office of War Information during World War II, and news analyst first of the Columbia Broadcasting System and later of the American Broadcasting Company. Though the author of *But We Were Born Free* is somewhat preoccupied with that strange phenomenon of the early fifties known as "McCarthyism," the truths enunciated in "Are We Worth Saving?" are timeless.

Elmer Davis
ARE WE WORTH SAVING? AND IF SO, WHY?

A century or so ago a Harvard graduate wrote a hymn whose opening line, plausible enough when written, turned out to be one of the most inaccurate forecasts ever set down:

The morning light is breaking, the darkness disappears.

The final couplet of that stanza, however, would—with the omission of a single word—be a fairly accurate picture of the world today:

Each breeze that sweeps the ocean brings tidings from afar
Of nations in commotion, prepared for Zion's war.

Commotion indeed; but it is not Zion's war for which they are preparing. Yet in his day the Reverend Samuel F. Smith seemed to have good reason for his confidence in the success of the missionary enterprises that were then spreading over the world, and not only in their direct success but in the derivative benefits that would flow from them. He had faith—not only faith in his religion; but back of that, like most men of his day, he had the general confidence of the Western world in that golden afternoon, the immensely successful nineteenth century; an assurance that it had not only a religion but a culture which was so good in itself that it was the Christian duty of all who possessed it to extend it to less favored races.

To its intended beneficiaries that assurance must often have seemed arrogance. Especially as expressed in the most famous missionary hymn of the time:

By many an ancient river, from many a palmy plain,
They call us to deliver their souls from error's chain.

The call was audible mostly to the inner ear, but there it rang loudly.

Shall we whose souls are lighted by wisdom from on high,
Shall we to men benighted the lamp of life deny?

Responding to that appeal, many men and women went forth into the foreign field, performed the most heroic, arduous and often hazardous labors, and sometimes laid down their lives. We owe them the utmost respect; yet I am sure we all wish that the appeal had been phrased more tactfully. The missionary techniques of Olaf Trygvasson no longer commend themselves; but at least, when he gave his subjects the choice between accepting the lamp of life and getting their throats cut, he didn't pretend that they had asked for it.

But Bishop Heber and the Reverend Samuel Smith profoundly believed what they wrote, as did most men of their time. The principal group that disagreed with them, the Hardshell Baptists, did so only in an even greater faith—that when God chose to save the heathen He could do it by Himself, without the help of contributors to foreign missions. Logically and theologically they seem to have had the better of the argument; but they were a feeble and dwindling group because the vast majority was inspired, for the most part unconsciously, by a faith which comprehended and transcended theology. The great Protestant missionary effort of the nineteenth century, like the great Catholic missionary effort of the sixteenth century, was the expression of a strong and vigorous culture—different phases only of the culture of what we call the Western world; though a Polynesian or even a Japanese might reasonably ask, West of what? In the sixteenth century the West was just

---
Elmer Davis, *But We Were Born Free* (Indianapolis: Bobbs-Merrill, 1954), pp. 204-29, copyright 1952, 1954 by Elmer Davis. Reprinted by permission of the publisher.

awakening, with a delighted surprise, to an awareness of its own strength, which had seemed gravely in question in the opening phases of the Turkish onslaught. By the nineteenth century the West had no doubt that it was the culmination of all human progress to date, with even more dazzling achievements lying beyond.

In the middle of the twentieth century the principal questions in dispute among Western intellectuals seem to be whether the West can be saved, and if it is worth saving. The two most popular of recent historical philosophers both think the Western world is going downhill, and one of them seems to feel that it won't be much loss. Spengler appreciated the loss more than Toynbee; if he felt that it was inevitable, that was perhaps because he was an artist rather than a philosopher. Yet, though it may be only a coincidence, it is certainly a disquieting one that he and Toynbee, starting from very different premises, come out to about the same conclusion as to the phase of development that our civilization has reached; and still more disquieting, as to what lies ahead—what Spengler called Caesarism, and Toynbee the universal state.

There are optimists, of course, who think that a really universal state—a world-wide state—could be created by some other means than military force; Spengler and Toynbee are not among them nor, to compare small things with great, am I. So long as Communists remain Communists any world coalition government would be subject to the same dangers, and likely to meet the same fate, as the coalition governments of Poland and Czechoslovakia; and there is still wisdom enough in the West not to run that risk. Others think that even if a universal state were created by military force the result would not be Caesarism—provided, of course, that our side won. A couple of years ago Bertrand Russell was one of these; lately he seems to have become discouraged, and offers us the variant but not very cheerful prospect of a dual Caesarism, with Premier Malenkov and President McCarthy dividing the world between them and collaborating to suppress dissent in both their realms. I do not suppose that Russell was entirely serious in suggesting this; he may only have been reading Orwell's *1984,* or he may have been reading the *Congressional Record.* Such a future seems improbable; but in the world we live in, no one can be sure that it is impossible.

Spengler is dead and can write no more; he has said his say; within his artistic scheme, the progressive deterioration of any culture seemed inevitable. Any man who keeps on writing and talking is likely to contradict himself; Toynbee has written so much that he has involved himself in about as many contradictions as Dr. John H. Watson, when he set down the history of Sherlock Holmes. A few years ago Toynbee seemed to have some hope that the creative minority of our civilization had not yet lost its creativity, not yet become a merely dominant minority, for the inadequacy of whose rule the internal proletariat would have to compensate by creating or adopting a universal religion; now he seems to think we have passed the point of no return. We passed it, apparently—or at least so he thought when he delivered the Reith Lectures last year; he may since have changed his mind again—we passed it toward the end of the seventeenth century, when men became disgusted with the endless religious wars which neither side ever decisively won, and turned to secular interests—turned from preoccupation with preparation for the next world to consideration of what could be done with this one; and, increasingly, to what could be done with it through technology.

And for this apostasy, thinks Toynbee, God has punished us—punished the West by the loss of the East; not only our territorial possessions and our commerce there but our moral influence in an East which increasingly turns toward our Communist enemy. The East rejected our religion, and our technology with it, when they were parts of an indivisible way of life; it accepted our technology when it was divorced from our religion (and incidentally had become far more efficient; that is to say, far more worth accepting) with consequences which became apparent at Pearl Harbor in 1941 and more recently in Korea. "The fortunes," he says, "of Western civilization in the mission field veered right around from conspicuous failure to conspicuous successes as soon as its attitude toward its own ancestral religion had veered around from a warm devotion to a cool skepticism." Which appears to mean, when the mission field had become the field of a new kind of missionary, offering no longer the lamp of life but oil for the lamps of China, and all that went with it.

History does not support this interpretation.

It has been subjected to a number of searching criticisms—notably by Professor Michael Karpovitch in the *New Leader* and by G. F. Hudson in *Commentary*. Karpovitch, after pointing out that Toynbee is wrong on all the things that Karpovitch knows most about, suavely admits that no doubt he is right in other fields. Hudson makes a more general attack on the entire doctrine, to which a layman can offer only a couple of corroborative footnotes. The great success of Protestant missions—not to mention a vigorous revival of Catholic missions and the beginnings of the penetration of the East by Western technology as well—came at a time when the cool skepticism of the eighteenth century had been buried under a new wave of evangelical fervor, when Protestantism was not only as vigorous but as dogmatic as the Catholicism of the Counter-Reformation. (I do not know whether Toynbee regards Modernist Protestantism as a religion at all; but he can hardly deny that title to Fundamentalist Protestantism.)

What at present appears to be the failure of Protestantism in China seems to be due less to divine wrath at apostasy than to an intensified form of the thing that caused the eventual failure of Catholicism in Japan, when it had lost little if any of its energy and fervor in Europe—the fear of a suspicious and despotic government that religion had been merely the cover for imperialistic political intrigues. In either case there was little evidence on which to base that fear; but despots need little evidence—especially despots newly come to power, who still feel insecure.

It might indeed be argued that the West, in its relation with the East, is being punished for its sins. But the sin is not apostasy; it is too great faith. We have all observed that the sin that is most surely and sharply punished is a mistake—however well intended, however it may have seemed at the time the thing to do. The punishment is often delayed, and falls on the descendants of those who made the mistake—often on innocent bystanders. "Those eighteen upon whom the tower of Siloam fell, and slew them—think ye that they were sinners above all men that dwelt in Jerusalem?" We are authoritatively assured that they were not. The sin was that of the architect or the contractor; the punishment fell on people who only happened to be around. Many Europeans and Americans have suffered in Asia, and may presently suffer in Africa, for mistakes for which they were in no way responsible—mistakes made from the highest motives, as a result of faith.

For alongside the theological religion of the West, which in the past two and a half centuries has had its ups as well as its downs, there was growing up in Western Europe and America a secular religion, held as fervently by devout Christians as by rationalists—the faith in freedom, in self-government, in democracy. (Indeed the only living ex-president of Columbia University has more than once implied that only believers in a theological religion can believe in this secular religion too. The evidence for this cannot be found in history.) The Westerners who interpenetrated the East in the nineteenth century, whether missionaries, engineers, businessmen or administrators, mostly carried this religion with them. They made many mistakes; but it was devotion to this secular religion that led them to make what, from the standpoint of practical consequences, was the worst mistake the West ever made in dealing with the East. They educated the natives.

Not merely in the operation of modern weapons, though they did that first, for the greater convenience of Western powers warring among themselves; these were men of faith, faith in the whole Western culture of which this secular religion was becoming steadily a more important part. Many of those whom they educated sprang from cultures far older than ours and in some respects more distinguished. But it was the Western culture that seemed to work, so it did not have to be forced on them; in this case they really did call us to deliver their minds, at least, from error's chain. We educated them in Western medicine and engineering, in Western government and law. And in the course of that education the pupils were exposed to the fact that there were such things as freedom and self-government and democracy—things which the educators obviously regarded as good for themselves; it was only a question of time till the pupils began to suspect that they might be good for everybody. Educate any man, of whatever race or color, in what he didn't know before and you are taking a chance; how he will turn out will depend somewhat on the education but more on his background and environment and on what was in him to start with; you may get a Nehru and you may get a Jomo Kenyatta. The only thing they have in common is a conviction that those who educated them, having fulfilled that function, ought to get out.

I have enough faith in that secular religion to believe that in the long run the consequences of this will be beneficial—as they seem to be already in the successor states of the Indian Empire. But that is no consolation to those on whom various towers of Siloam have fallen elsewhere.

This digression was necessitated by the fact that the most popular of contemporary historians has offered an explanation not only for our unsatisfactory relations with Asia and Africa but for the general dilemma of our times—an explanation which not only to me but to many of my betters seems no explanation at all. But what then is the matter with us? What have we left, if anything, that is worth saving?

This first and obvious answer, of course, is "If we aren't worth saving, who is?" Faulty as we are, we seem infinitely preferable—by our standards—to the moral nihilism and intellectual rigidity of the Soviet system which is competing with us for the allegiance of the East; competing indeed, though with little success outside of France and Italy, for the allegiance of our own citizens. Unfortunately, we do not always seem preferable to those among whom our missionaries, and those of the opposition, are working; and if through force or deception they have once accepted the opposition's gospel, they find that the choice is irrevocable. Rebels on the barricades would be blown to pieces by tanks and bombing planes; indeed the secret police would never let anybody get to the barricades in the first place.

G. F. Hudson—following Orwell—holds that modern totalitarian techniques would make impossible even Toynbee's last refuge for the disconsolate, wheresoe'er they languish—the creation by the internal proletariat of a universal church to compensate for the shortcomings of a universal state. "If Nero," says Hudson, "had had the resources of the MVD at his disposal, the early Christians would have been publicly confessing how in their vileness they had set fire to Rome on instructions of the King of Parthia." In the world we live in, freedom once lost is lost to stay lost. We had better remember that, in dealing with our internal even more than with our external problems.

Granted, however, that from anything that could be called an ethical viewpoint we are better worth saving than our adversaries, this is no proof that we are going to be saved unless we have the qualities that enable us to save ourselves. The western Roman Empire was far more worth saving than the barbarian tribal dominions that surrounded it and eventually overran it; but its own faults brought it down. This is worth mentioning since not only Spengler and Toynbee but lesser men have dealt with our predicament in terms of what befell civilizations of the past; and these analyses, however embellished with facts, or conjectures, from Chinese and Mayan and Sumerian history, all rest pretty much on the one case about which we have tolerably complete information—the decline and fall of the Roman Empire. Many historians have attempted to explain it; almost all of them, even Gibbon—even Rostovtzeff—seem to me to explain it largely in terms of their own experience, and observation of their own times.

I shall not add to that confusion, but shall only point out one or two details in which our situation is different. We know now that the happiness and prosperity of the age of the Antonines, which so impressed Gibbon, was only relative—considerable no doubt compared to what had gone before and what was to come afterward, but behind the splendid front there was a dry rot inside. Economically the Empire was deteriorating, and intellectually, too.

Economically the Western world is doing pretty well nowadays; and in the English-speaking and Scandinavian countries (Switzerland and the Low Countries as well) the problem that Rome never solved and that finally did more than anything else to bring Rome down has been solved with a fair degree of success—the problem of passing prosperity around, of seeing that everybody gets some of it. If France and Italy solved that problem too, the Communist parties in those countries would soon shrink to the hard core. Our civilization, said Rostovtzeff thirty years ago—lately echoed and emphasized by Professor Robinson of Brown—our civilization will not last unless it be a civilization not of one class but of the masses. This is a warning that might more pertinently be directed toward the Soviet Union than the United States, in so far as what exists in the Soviet Union can be called a civilization. As for Rostovtzeff's last despairing question, "Is not every civilization bound to decay as soon as it penetrates the masses?" We can only say that we shall in due course find out. We have started in that direction and we can't turn back.

The Romans, outside of the cities, never got started; and even there civilization was a narrowing pyramid, with a hollow top. The most notable thing about the age of the Antonines was its intellectual sterility, in a period of rest between calamities when the Western world might have made vast advances and fortified itself against the calamities that were to come—the classic case of what Toynbee calls the loss of creativity in the dominant minority. Are we losing it? Dr. J. G. de Beus of the Netherlands Embassy in Washington, who has lately analyzed these forecasts of the future, thinks the Western world is still vigorously creative—not only in science and technology but in politics, domestic and foreign, and in art and letters as well.

It is perhaps fortunate that this optimistic view was set down before the recent sculptural competition in London for a statue of the Unknown Political Prisoner, where the prize was given to a contraption in wire that looked like nothing, unless perhaps a television aerial. As for letters, most of the most admired literature of the Western nations—especially the English-speaking nations—for thirty-five years past has been to all appearance the effluvium of a sick society. English literature, between wars, gave us an almost unrelieved picture of a nation in process of dissolution from its own internal weakness—a nation that would collapse in ruins as soon as somebody pushed. But the time came when somebody pushed, and it did not collapse; indeed the people who did the pushing eventually did the collapsing too.

Many American novelists have written about the late war or about American society in the years just before it and since. Most of their works would be intelligible if written by Frenchmen after 1870, or Spaniards after 1898—mercilessly candid pictures of the inner decay that led to calamitous defeat. But since we happened to win the war, something seems to have been wrong with the picture—not perhaps with the individual picture which each man saw, but with the total picture which few of them ever noticed.

This phenomenon is a symptom of what has been called the alienation of "intellectuals" from the life around them, which is taken very seriously by many intellectuals. I cannot see that it makes much difference, with intellectuals like these. They wrote their books, which often sold widely; the society around them bought the books, read them and ignored them. Indeed their authors usually ignored them when the chips were down; men who had spent their lives proving that the United States was not worth fighting for went out and fought for it like everybody else.

This naturally does not mean that I share the scorn of Senator Ferguson and his type for eggheads, radical or otherwise. It depends on what you call an intellectual. Franklin and Jefferson were not alienated from the society around them, either in America or when they lived in France; yet they qualified as intellectuals in about the fastest company the world has known since Periclean Athens. It seems doubtful, however, if the more rigorous intellectuals of our time would acknowledge them as members of the club.

The first condition of the survival of any civilization is that it should win its wars. Rome did, till its armies wore themselves out fighting one another. I think that from the military point of view we could win the next war, if we should have to fight it, despite the weakness of our air defense in the northeastern approaches. But to win a war under modern conditions requires more than military strength—more even than preservation of a sound dollar. It requires political shrewdness, domestic and foreign, to a degree the Romans seldom had to practice. For five centuries after the battle of Magnesia they had virtually no need for a foreign policy, till the degenerate days when they found it necessary to make an alliance with one German tribe against another. The United States, as the *prima inter pares* of a coalition, has to deal with complexities convincingly set forth not long ago by the President, who has had more experience in dealing with coalitions than any other man since Metternich. It would not be easy to cope with them, even if he had the actual (though not the theoretical) power of a Roman Emperor; still less is it easy in a republic whose Constitution, as Woodrow Wilson once put it, permits the

President to be as big a man as he can. If he cannot be or does not want to be a big man, there will be plenty of others who will volunteer to fill the vacancy. Every American President must conduct his foreign policy against and in spite of men who, if they no longer think we should not have a foreign policy at all, at least think it should not be his policy. In the circumstances, we have in recent years done remarkably well.

What a civilization like ours, which is not a universal state but a coalition of independent powers, can do to insure its own continuance depends quite as much on how each state manages its own internal affairs. Here the Romans met the proximate cause of their disaster. When they had a good man at the head of the state all went well—unless he was a good man like Antoninus Pius—perhaps the most virtuous of all rulers of a great realm and certainly pre-eminent in manly beauty, but he appears to have been only a glorified Calvin Coolidge, who sat there and went through the motions while the problems piled up for his unhappy successor. But when the Romans got a bad man in, there was no way to get him out except by assassination or revolution. Over a period of ninety years almost every Emperor—and they were many—was got out by one or the other of those methods—good men as well as bad.

The nations which embody Western civilization are no longer subject to that danger, but their political systems have other defects. Mr. Walter Lippmann remarks that if the free world is in peril, it is not because our enemies are so strong but because the free nations are so badly governed; and they are badly governed because of the usurpation of power by the national legislatures. . . . Well—we must discriminate. In the nations of the British Commonwealth the supremacy of the legislature is the essence of their constitutions, and they have learned how to make it work. In the French Republic it is also the essence of the constitution; in the three quarters of a century of the Third and Fourth Republics they have not learned how to make it work. In our own republic it is in flat conflict with the Constitution, and no wonder it doesn't work. It is an old story; long before the recent publicized attacks on the State Department, and on the President's control of foreign policy, the principal problem of our government was Congressional usurpation, usually through committees, of executive functions. Congress not only tells administrators what they must do, which is its right, but how to do it, which is not its right and is wholly outside Congress's field of practical competence as well as of authority.

A Congress which ate raw meat during the last few years of a Democratic administration has shown that it is not going back to a milk diet just because the Republicans are in power. Nor would it do so even in wartime unless compelled, as it has been compelled by every strong President. Until the question whether it would be so compelled again may arise, we might reflect that all the periods of Congressional government in our history have been periods either of bad government or of do-nothing government. There have been times when we could afford a do-nothing government; we can afford it no longer. Still less a bad government.

But to return from this digression into the factors that will make it practically possible—or practically impossible—to save us; back to the original question, Why should we be saved? What have we got that our adversaries have not that makes us worth saving? Our faults, God knows, are numerous and glaring enough; recognition of those faults is the chief cause of the loss of confidence that has afflicted so many people of the Western world. But we do recognize them; we do not pretend that our failures were decreed by ineluctable historical necessity; nor do we rewrite history according to the precepts of Double-think, to prove that they never happened at all.

What we have to offer, to the contemporary world and to the future, is a method—and the freedom of the mind that makes that method possible. Not an infallible method, but the best yet discovered for reaching increasingly closer approximations to the truth. It will never offer its conclusions with such assurance as does dialectical materialism—which, by a singular coincidence, always seems to produce the conclusions that are convenient for the men in power. It can only say, We have kept the door open for exploration of all possibilities, consideration of all objections, application of all possible tests; and this is what seems to be true. Maybe something else will seem more probable later on, but this is the best we can do now. Or, as the method was summarized long ago—Prove all things; hold fast that which is good.

This method has been responsible for almost all human progress. Outside the Western world it does not exist, except in those parts of the East which have been influenced by Western thought; if it died here, it would die there too. Ex-President Conant of Harvard has remarked that the right to think and question and investigate is the basic difference between the free world and the world of totalitarianism. It might well be the basic difference that would save us, if it came to a shooting war; and whether it does that or not, this one thing—the scientific method, and above all the freedom of the mind that makes it possible—is what makes us worth saving. As G. F. Hudson has observed, "To repudiate faith in freedom is to abandon Western civilization."

The founders of this republic held that faith so firmly that its guarantee was embedded in the very first amendment to the Constitution, almost as soon as the Constitution was adopted. Yet lately that faith has been repudiated by many of our fellow citizens, if indeed they ever held it, and in that repudiation lies our greatest danger; it is this, rather than any external attack, that might bring us down. That repudiation takes various forms and appears on various levels. One phase of it was the recent attack on the Bureau of Standards and particularly the manner in which the Secretary of Commerce questioned its objectivity. As Eugene Rabinowitch commented in the *Bulletin of the Atomic Scientists,* the government has the right, if it should so choose, to subordinate the findings of science to the demands of business; but it has no right to attempt to coerce the scientists into adjusting their findings to those demands. That is Lysenkoism; it is something we had better leave to the enemy. Happily, the Secretary of Commerce now seems to have come around to that point of view.

But far more widespread and more dangerous is the general attack on the freedom of the mind. George Kennan said at Notre Dame that it springs from forces too diffuse to be described by their association with the name of any one man or any one political concept—forces which perhaps were summarized by John Duncan Miller of the London *Times,* in the early days of McCarthyism, as a revolt of the primitives against intelligence. Unfortunately, it cannot be denied that after centuries of education we will have plenty of primitives—some of them white-collar or even top-hat primitives; a sediment, a sludge, at the bottom of American society—and I am afraid a fairly deep layer at that; people who seem actuated only by hatred and fear and envy. All the products of ignorance, for their fear is not a rational fear of a very formidable and unfriendly foreign power. I have received thousands of letters from people like that in recent years and they do not seem interested in Russia at all: what they hate and fear is their own neighbors who try to think. In the name of anti-Communism they try to strike down the freedom of the mind, which above all things differentiates us from the Communists; in the name of Americanism they try to suppress the right to think what you like and say what you think, in the evident conviction—in so far as they have reasoned conviction at all—that the principles on which this Republic was founded and has been operated will not bear examination. People like that are not merely un-American; they are anti-American.

It is people who feel that way who provide the mass support for McCarthy—though of course he has an elite support as well, if it may be so termed, in the reactionary press and the Texas oil billionaires. He has already done serious injury to the United States Government—especially to the State Department, on which we must chiefly rely for avoidance of war; and he has done more than any other man to encourage the spread of suspicion and distrust and hatred among ourselves, which is the best formula for losing a war.

We have now reached the point where, if agents of the FBI appear in the home town of a prominent man and begin asking questions about him, his neighbors know that he is either on his way to jail or to high public office. I doubt if such confusion is healthy. Judge Learned Hand, in that speech I mentioned earlier, a speech so often quoted that perhaps everybody now knows it by heart, has said that he believes that that community is already in process of dissolution where each man begins to eye his neighbor as a possible enemy, where nonconformity with the accepted creed is a mark of disaffection, where denunciation takes the place of evidence and orthodoxy chokes freedom of dissent.

If we are not to become such a community, the friends of freedom will have to stand up and fight.

In saying all this I am talking not about Western civilization but about the United States. And without apology, for we are the principal component of Western civilization, at least in the material sense. If we go down it all goes down—and when we confront a totalitarian dictatorship, whatever goes down stays down; it doesn't get up again. And we shall go down, unless we recognize what we have to fight for and have the courage to fight for it. What makes Western civilization worth saving is the freedom of the mind, now under heavy attack from the primitives—including some university graduates—who have persisted among us. If we have not the courage to defend that faith, it won't matter much whether we are saved or not.

I do not think Stalin could have licked us; I do not think that whoever now may be running Russia can lick us. But McCarthy and the spirit of McCarthyism could lick us—no doubt without intention, but they could—by getting us to fighting among ourselves like the Romans, by persuading every man that he must keep on looking over his shoulder, to make sure that the man beside him doesn't stab him in the back. There is still enough vitality in Western civilization to save us, unless we insist on disemboweling ourselves.

I should perhaps have begun this sermon with a text, a text taken from the fourth chapter of the first book of Samuel, the eighth and ninth verses—the mutual exhortations of the Philistines before the battle of Ebenezer. "Woe unto us!" they said when they realized that the Israelites had brought the Ark of God with them to battle. "Woe unto us! Who shall deliver us out of the hands of these mighty gods?" But then, realizing that nobody else was going to deliver them, they said to one another, "Be strong, and quit yourselves like men; and fight." And they did fight, and delivered themselves. So may we; but only if we quit ourselves like men. This republic was not established by cowards; and cowards will not preserve it.

Another champion of civil liberties throughout a long lifetime was Zechariah Chafee, Jr., a member of the Harvard University Law School faculty from 1916 until his retirement in 1950. Chafee called himself "a conservative with an old-fashioned concern about the Bill of Rights." In 1948 he served as the U.S. delegate to the UN Conference on Freedom of Information at Geneva. His absorbed interest in civil liberties is revealed by the titles of some of his books: *Freedom of Speech, Free Speech in the United States, The Inquiring Mind, Documents on Fundamental Human Rights, How Human Rights Got Into the Constitution.* "Why I Like America" appears in his last book, *The Blessings of Liberty* (1956).

Zechariah Chafee, Jr.
WHY I LIKE AMERICA

> I will build a motor car for the great multitude. It will be large enough for the family but small enough for the individual to run and care for. It will be constructed of the best materials, by the best men to be hired, after the simplest designs that modern engineering can devise. But it will be so low in price that no man making a good salary will be unable to own one—and enjoy with his family the blessing of hours of pleasure in God's great open spaces.
> *Henry Ford, about 1907*

For many reasons I am happy to be an American though I had nothing whatever to do with being born in Providence, Rhode Island. This is no mood of complacent satisfaction. Each of my hopes is matched by fears. Whether the nation changes for better or worse will depend on the readers of this book and its writer and people like us. What kind of country do we want to serve in the years ahead?

First, I like America because of the land itself. Although American scenes have not brought me quite so much happiness as those of Europe, here I have much to remember and long to see again. I recall the Parapets of Mount Madison in late afternoon, Northeast days off the Maine coast, the Connecticut Valley anywhere above Holyoke, the Hudson River from the Cloisters, Aiken pines, Point Lobos in the swirling fog, the silence of the Grand Canyon, the unbroken poppy-fields which stretched in my boyhood from Pasadena to the foothills of the Sierra

---

Zechariah Chafee, Jr., *The Blessings of Liberty* (Philadelphia: J. B. Lippincott, 1956), pp. 39–63, copyright © 1956 by Zechariah Chafee, Jr.; copyright 1954 by Zechariah Chafee, Jr. Reprinted (without footnotes) by permission of the publisher.

Madre. Aside from such rewards of long journeys, beauty lies within reach of an afternoon or a weekend from most of our crowded cities. On a more utilitarian level, the fullness and variety of our natural resources bring the exhilaration felt in Archibald MacLeish's account of the Lewis and Clark expedition:

Many men will have living on these lands.
There is wealth in the earth for them all and the wood standing
And wild birds on the water where they sleep.
There is stone in the hills for the towns of a great people. . . .

We can never be thankful enough that Fate brought our ancestors to these shores.

Yet all this can easily go the way of the buffalo and the passenger pigeon. The poppyfields north of Pasadena have vanished and today I can barely see the Sierra Madre in the smog. We have suddenly been aroused to the evils of redwood stumps and topsoil forever lost. Only vision and hard work will keep the riches we were given for the asking.

Nor can we separate the land from what we have put on the land. Buildings and roads can be as satisfying as mountains. Witness the University of Virginia and U.S. 202. Or they can be as meaningless as the imperial frigidity of Constitution Avenue in Washington, as ugly as the factory on the Sheepscot River below Wiscasset. And it is for us to decide whether our main highways shall multiply Walter Prichard Eaton's description of the Mohawk Trail:

Most of its length it is a swiftly moving steel and rubber river between banks of "hot-dog" kennels, fried clam stands, filling stations, and other odoriferous and ugly reminders of this progressive age.

I refuse to believe that progress is incompatible with beauty. The great advance in housing for those of moderate means, the New York sky-line, the San Francisco bridges, the Trailridge Road in Colorado, the hillside drive above Bar Harbor, all show what can be done. Surprisingly little money is sometimes enough to save a delightful landscape or building, but it has to be saved now or never.

Second, our heritage from the men of the past. Our settlers were neither conquistadores nor convicts. They were men and women with a deep sense of the purposefulness of life. We were especially fortunate in having the founders of the United States free from faults which might later infect our ideals. The nation was not based on Bismarck's "blood and iron" like Germany, or like Italy on the craftiness of Cavour. Our first leader willingly laid down his military command and later his power as President. We disagree but we do not hate. The adherents of Hamilton admire Jefferson, the adherents of Jefferson recognize Hamilton's greatness. The South honors Lincoln, the North honors Lee. We have been spared the calamity of the French where the heroes of half the nation are monsters of depravity to the other half.

At one time our national heroes seemed likely to become plaster saints, but the lights and shades with which they have been painted lately make them more impressive than before. There is a risk that our pride in Americans of the past may make us ignore the benefits brought us by later-comers from abroad, always excepting of course the group which included our own ancestors. The immigrants outside that group are regarded as "foreigners" whose descendants had better cut themselves loose from their European heritage as fast as possible.

Third, the pooling of peoples for freedom and friendliness. Class distinctions no longer seem permanent as they did before the Depression. When I visited the South after an absence of thirty years, I felt a marked decline in racial antagonism. This seems partly caused by the higher economic level on which both races are living. When there is money to go around, people get along better with each other. And the equally shared sacrifices during the Second World War made us increasingly conscious of the injustice of withholding other equalities.

Yet disquieting factors persist. The situation of the Negroes continues to be our biggest single domestic problem. I anticipate that desegregation will spread southward from state to state until defiance of the Supreme Court is confined to a few isolated areas, where eventually the white people will get weary of banging their heads against a stone wall. We shall be lucky if those who rejoice in resisting the inevitable do so peacefully. Again, general condemnations of religious intolerance are likely to be futile unless the specific causes of intolerance are frankly and wisely faced. Yet any attempt to examine a definite issue is likely to produce a free-for-all fight participated in by many who show very little wisdom.

Fourth, Americans have a healthy attitude toward the family. Perhaps I like our prevailing ideals of marriage and parenthood just because I was brought up among them, but I should hate to have to adjust myself somehow to polygamy or the complete legal subjection of women. I am glad my wife is not to be burned alive on my funeral pyre if I should die first, and it is pleasant to be able to take a walk without seeing bodies of exposed female infants as in China or the Athens of Pericles. Coming closer to our own civilization, I prefer our norm of a married couple who "live happily ever after," despite its occasional absurdities, to the Parisian norm of the Eternal Triangle. I should not want marriages arranged by the parents as in France. The demands of the frontier for youthful independence and enterprise freed us centuries ago from the traditional subordination of children to parents which lasted in England until after 1850. It is good that Thanksgiving, our most characteristic festival, symbolizes the essential unity of the procession of the generations.

We have a sound norm, but we deal stupidly with departures from this norm. When the varied relationships between men and women are sought to be explored sincerely and thoughtfully in a radio program or a motion-picture produced in the United States all sorts of obstacles are raised. Yet at the same time, an actual scandal, with no lessons except the general messiness of immorality, is recounted at length on the front pages of newspapers. Broken homes are bound to occur, but they are handled by divorce laws which are a conglomerate of inconsistencies and hypocrisies. We deliberately prolong and intensify the unhappiness of unhappy marriages and fool ourselves into the belief that this will make happy marriages more frequent.

Fifth, opportunities for productive enterprise at all the essential stages. In the past the situation was excellent for inventors and men who wanted to start new businesses, but too many people were just cogs in the industrial machine. During my lifetime I have seen purely manual labor almost disappear with the advent of new devices. There is a much greater opportunity than formerly for all who work to feel themselves part of a creative process and contributing to a satisfying product. Also the constant warfare between employers and unions has to a considerable extent been transformed into something approaching an orderly adjustment of disputes.

These improvements, however, are overcast by the curse of bigness—big corporations, big unions, big government agencies, each of them inclined to make its own decisions for its own benefit. The old-fashioned, enterprising, hard-working citizen feels lost in this play of enormous economic forces, in the same way that his vote seems insignificant in the great electorate of today. He just does not count. Frankly, I do not see the way out. The Socialists tell us that these gigantic groups are the last step to an all-absorbing state. That would not relieve us from the curse of bigness. We should merely get something still bigger.

Sixth, we now have abundant leisure with abundant opportunities for its fruitful use. Leisure until very recently was the privilege of only the favored few, but in the United States today leisure belongs to everybody. The normal forty-hour week in factories, stores, and offices is less than a quarter of the whole week of 168 hours. In homes and on farms, labor-saving devices and machinery have similarly released many hours of free time. All this would have brought little enjoyment to our ancestors. Only a few recreations were open to them, especially in cities. Rich men could drive fast horses and educated men could read, but the working man whose schooling had been cut short was largely limited to the poolroom and the saloon. In 1870, drunkenness and street-fighting were so prevalent in Boston that there were more crimes in proportion to the population than now. What else was there to do in a man's spare time? He had no access to the wide range of enjoyment which has since been opened by inventiveness and organization and by the knowledge of literature and art made possible through the great increase of enrollment in high schools.

Yet even now, the existence of leisure carries no guarantee that it will be used fruitfully. The knowledge how to employ it must come in part from formal education. On this account the current demand for vocational training at the expense of the humanities seems to me particularly calamitous. We are determined to give more training for work at the very time when work is a smaller part of a man's life than ever before.

Seventh, freedom for the life of the mind and the spirit. The hope of Roger Williams for "full liberty in religious concernments" has been realized all over the United States, as a later chapter will tell. Equally precious are freedom of speech, press, and assembly, which are also assured by the First Amendment. These are peculiarly sensitive to insidious attacks, and freedom is in large measure indivisible. When liberty of speech was lost in Nazi Germany, liberty of the person soon became gravely impaired. So we ought to cling resolutely to the primary freedoms of the mind.

Nevertheless, liberties of speech, press, and assembly which were universally cherished by Americans in my boyhood have been eroded during the past forty years by law after law, and only scattered protests have been heard. Much of the rest of this book will show how the whittling away of these liberties has increased notably during the last decade. Just as truly now as in Jefferson's day: "Eternal vigilance is the price of liberty."

Eighth, our courageous response to crises. We rose to the emergency of Fort Sumter and Pearl Harbor. We were much more baffled by the Depression of 1929, but when we had been shown by Mr. Roosevelt what we might do to end it, we did with determination whatever we were asked to do.

There is more doubt of the wisdom of some of our responses and of our ability to work out solutions for ourselves. Thus we were completely at a loss from 1929 until 1933. Sometimes we have a predilection for over-simplified solutions and cling to them with prolonged obstinacy as in the case of Prohibition. To use good old New England words, we have more guts than gumption.

Ninth, I am proud of the honorable part which America has, on the whole, played in the world. Here again our nation has been peculiarly fortunate. Much of our expansion has been accomplished without attacking our neighbors, a fate denied to most nations. There were regrettable phases of our history, such as breaches of faith with the Indians, but these are so far in the past that they have left no running sores to bother us now. We have no Alsace-Lorraines. We have not acted the bully.

The difficulty now is, of course, that we can no longer pursue a policy of benevolent isolation, whether we want to or not. The only question is whether we shall belong to a struggling mob or a town meeting. The fact that our people and our Congress have never before been forced to think so much about other national governments makes it hard for us to participate patiently in a world organization. We shall have to learn as we go along.

Tenth, and last, the satisfying nature of the governmental framework. I like the separation of national and regional problems by the device of federalism; the division of governmental powers among three distinct groups of men; and the safeguards of liberty in the Bill of Rights.

The trouble is that we are like a boy who has outgrown his clothes, and nobody lets them out. The main features of our government seem to me as sound as ever; but, because of new conditions, details have gone wrong at several points. This leads to plenty of grumbling, but there is very little systematic effort to discover and adopt suitable remedies for the maladjustments. I am especially troubled by the lack of popular confidence in the agencies of government which are closest to the people, for example, Congress and city governments. A French writer says that a country is in danger when the voters hate and despise the very men for whom they vote. Sighs of relief go up whenever Congress adjourns, and editorials in thoughtful newspapers denouncing municipal inefficiency and corruption often sound uncomfortably like what Hitler used to say against democracy.

Beard wrote of Congress in his stimulating little book, *The Republic*:

> The framers of the Constitution expected . . . that Congress should be the dominant branch of the Federal Government. They put it first in order in the Constitution. . . . They gave it the power of the purse and the power of the sword—the two mighty engines of government.

If the President rather than Congress occupies the dominant place today, may not Congress itself be partly to blame? I do not mind that Congress should differ from the President. God forbid that any single man should be thought entitled to have everything his own way in these United States. The historic function of the legislature since the days of the Stuart kings is to make the popular will operate as a check on the power of the Executive. What disturbs me is that in these clashes the President seems to be closer than Congress to what the people want. The fault is not mainly, I believe, with the calibre of the men who get elected. I known from long experience the ability and devotion of many men in both Houses. But their ability is not canalized so as to work responsibly and effectively.

Nobody can read a dozen pages of the *Congressional Record* straight through without feeling either ridicule or shame. I have sometimes thought of rewriting a day of the debates in the Constitutional Convention of 1787 as if they took place in the United States Senate in 1955. Three times in the same morning, delegates at Philadelphia would stop all business as follows:

MR. X: Mr. President, I suggest the absence of a quorum.
THE PRESIDENT: The clerk will call the roll.
The clerk proceeded to call the roll [showing far more than a quorum, as was obvious to anybody with eyes].
MR. X: Mr. President, I ask unanimous consent that the order for the quorum call be rescinded.
THE PRESIDENT: Without objection, it is so ordered.

The discussion of the conflict between large and small states would be interrupted by the request for leave to print a rabble-rousing speech of Sam Adams to the Boston wharf rats on the anniversary of the Boston Tea Party. Then some member from New Hampshire would talk for an hour on the bravery of the New Hampshire soldiers at the Battle of Bennington, winding up with a glowing eulogy of Molly Stark.

The most striking example of our distrust of democracy is the City of Washington. Taxation without representation and government without the consent of the governed prevail within sight of the Capitol. This was not always so. Until 1871 Washingtonians chose their own mayor and council, who (it is said) rivaled the Tweed Ring in New York. After a few years of appointed and elected officials combined, Congress established the present system in 1878. For over three-quarters of a century Washington has been under a triumvirate about as absolute as Caesar, Pompey, and Crassus. Congress did not even try to make Washington safe for democracy. Nor does it appear that the inhabitants, then or subsequently, cared very much about their loss.

How many other American cities, I wonder, would willingly abandon self-government if in return they could get rid of padded payrolls, endlessly dug-up streets, and a $65 tax rate?

While discussing each of my first nine reasons for liking America, I have in the end expressed confidence that my hopes will prevail over my fears. I feel considerably more anxiety about the actual operation of our national, state, and local governments. Although I am by no means discouraged, this anxiety leads me to reflect at greater length on our ideals of government than on the other matters with which this chapter deals.

Woodrow Wilson described our political institutions and our hopes for their future by the single word "democracy." Although some influential Americans have recently insisted that our country is a republic and not a democracy, it can be both. No doubt, "democracy" is one of the words which the Soviet bloc has tried to take away from us and transform into something else. All the more reason why we should hold on to it and understand better what makes it precious to us. The best way to protect democracy against insidious onslaughts is to give this ideal solid substance to which our minds can firmly attach themselves. That will put us on guard when anybody is persuading us to give some of it away.

What is this democracy which most Americans have long wanted to preserve and strengthen? Everybody knows that it comes from two Greek words meaning "people" and "rule" or "govern," but this is just a start. Who are the people and how are they to govern?

Take a test case: Is Great Britain a democracy, although it is surely not a republic? Many American students of politics and history would answer "Yes," at least if they do not go back of the Reform Bills of the Nineteenth Century. Yet much depends on what definition of "democracy" is chosen. Turn to the highest authority in England, the Oxford Dictionary in many volumes. Here the principal definition of "democracy" begins: "Government by the people; that form of government in which the sovereign power resides in the people as a whole, and is exercised either directly by them (as in the small republics of antiquity) or by officers elected by them." So far, this may include England, but look at the next sentence: "In modern use often more vaguely denoting a social state in which all have equal rights, without hereditary or arbitrary differences of rank or privilege." Surely this does not apply to a nation with a royal family, hereditary nobles and baronets, and a House of Lords. The second definition in the same dictionary raises even more perplexities: "A state or community in which the government is vested in the people as a whole." Was there ever such a government, where even babies in arms were carried to the polls? More satisfactory is the Funeral Oration of Pericles: "We are called a democracy, for the administration is in the hands of the many and not of the few." And yet a century later we find Aristotle using "democracy" to describe mob rule in contradiction to "commonwealth." According to him, the United States is a commonwealth, as Massachusetts, Pennsylvania, Virginia, and Kentucky call themselves. A definition of "democracy" with a thrill to it is Mazzini's: "Progress of all through all, under the leading of the best and wisest." Excellent though rare. Contrast Lord Byron's diary, "What is democracy?—an aristocracy of blackguards."

All this brings about my chief conclusion. Democracy is not a single thing like oxygen. There are several kinds of democracies just as there are several kinds of beauty. Possibly there is a least common denominator which inheres in all the different kinds, but it is by no means easy to frame a definition which will include them all.

Nevertheless, as a convenient starting-point, political democracy will be loosely defined as any system of government in which a considerable portion of the population exercises a substantial control. Then to bring out the wide range of such systems and the limits at which a government ceases to be a democracy, I shall consider in detail three questions: Control by whom? Control over what? Control for what?

Who exercises control? We think of democracy as government by the people, but who are the people? If they be the whole population of the territorial unit, then it is plain that a good many of them do not do any governing. A very large number of citizens cannot vote, namely, persons under twenty-one. Of course, some of them do not know how to talk, but the bright boys of sixteen know more than most of us ever will again. Even if the voting age is reduced to eighteen, as is now proposed, the younger teenagers will still be disfranchised. They may fairly argue that they are affected by the expenditure of a big fraction of the public revenue on schools and are subjected to stricter regulations than the rest of us. At any rate, youths will become adults if they go on living, but women will never be anything else than women. Must we say that democracy did not exist in the United States until 1920 except in Wyoming and a few other western regions which opened voting booths to pioneering wives? Or that Switzerland is not a democracy today? And if we can surmount these obstacles by the dubious argument that voting men represent their families, we still have to decide whether democracy is possible when males are barred by drastic property qualifications like those at the time of the Constitution or by failure to pay poll taxes or pass literacy tests.

Now comes another point. No official who serves is the choice of the entire electorate. A substantial minority of those who voted wanted somebody else. And many citizens stayed away from the polls. For example, it would be very unusual for the winning candidate in a Presidential election to receive sixty per cent of the popular vote or for the votes cast to run much over sixty per cent of the electorate. It is convenient and, I believe, desirable to say that government by the President thus elected is government by the people, but the bare fact is that he was named by only about a third of the qualified voters and by a much smaller fraction of the whole population of the United States. No doubt, those who fail to register a choice have themselves to blame, but the smallness of the vote often deprives an election of some of the impressiveness we like to attach to it. This is especially true of votes on the ratification of amendments to a state constitution, which sometimes attract much less attention than contests over minor offices and yet are treated as the highest manifestation of the will of the people of the state.

Finally, we ought never to forget that some of the citizens who are concerned with the acts of a government cannot possibly vote with reference to such acts. Edmund Burke described constitutional government as "a partnership between those who are living, those who are dead and those who are to be born."

Thus the phrase "the people" can be used to describe at least five different groups of persons in a political community: (1) the whole body of inhabitants past, present, and future; (2) the entire population at the time of speaking; (3) the electorate; (4) those who actually vote at a given election; (5) the victors at that election. Theoretical defenders of democracy are tempted to obscure the important distinctions between these groups. The idea of all the men, women, and children in a nation or state or city glows in our imaginations and rightly so, especially when it embraces the dead who made possible so much of our happiness, and the unborn generations for whom we plan and sacrifice. But there is nothing sacred about the individuals who happened to be on the winning side at the last election. Yet by sliding the word "people" hither and thither, writers and orators contrive to surround the momentary majority with a bright halo.

Talk about "the will of the people" makes eloquent perorations, but persons subject to the actual strains of campaigning and being governed are bound to disbelieve it. The voter who sees his honest candidate for mayor defeated by a crook knows very well that he and his associates are not identical with the majority. Large taxpayers are constantly indignant about the burdens imposed on them by citizens who are taxed little or nothing.

In truth, the relation between the momentary majority and the whole population is a central problem of democracy. The two are not the same and yet they ought to be closely linked. The manner in which the connecting cord is woven determines the strength of self-government in that nation. The whole system really rests on the willingness of the losers to accept the decision against them and carry it out loyally. When this willingness breaks down, serious trouble is likely, as during National Prohibition. It is true that stable governments could hardly exist if men felt that their consciences entitled them to disobey whatever laws they disliked, and yet there is a limit to what the majority can safely try to do in coercing opponents. The outstanding example of this is the repeated failure of religious persecutions. One of the chief purposes of the Bill of Rights is to prevent the momentary majority from undertaking legal action which diverges widely from the deep-seated desires of the rest of the population.

The foregoing discussion of the question: Who controls? leads me to three further reflections. In the first place, since the electorate is always smaller than the whole body of persons affected by government, it follows that voters, like legislators, are representatives. They do not act merely for themselves, but for others—the living who cannot or do not vote, the dead, the unborn. The voter, like the legislator and the officeholder, is a trustee for the public. Like them, he has duties as well as rights, and is bound by grave responsibilities—not just out to get what he can like the sinecurists of old.

Secondly, democracy is consistent with varying extensions of the franchise. The whole body of citizens never governs, and those who do may be more or fewer without the government's ceasing to be democratic. There are limits, however. Democracy becomes doubtful when the right to hold office or to vote is based on rank or inheritance, although we still have to allow for the House of Lords and remember that slavery was extensive in two of the greatest of democracies—ancient Athens and the United States of America until 1865. Democracy also becomes questionable when the franchise is based on property beyond what almost every citizen can probably acquire by moderate diligence. Furthermore, although control is never actually exercised by everybody, the opportunity to share in control must be open at least to all or nearly all heads of families, even if women be disfranchised. So democracy is evidently a single name for several types of popular government.

It may also be regarded as a term of degree like "hot." A government is said to become more democratic as the right to vote and hold office is widened. Are we bound to conclude that because democracy is good, the more the better? That line of reasoning is not valid for some other things like mince pie or small babies. For example, it is arguable that a citizen must prove his fitness to vote by his ability to save two dollars a year for a poll tax to help support his community or by learning to read and write. However, fitness is only part of the story. The poor and the uneducated may need the ballot to protect themselves from exploitation. Another argument for a wide franchise at some sacrifice is that no community can afford to let a considerable part of its working strength nourish resentment at being permanently deprived of privileges.

In short, the exact point at which the franchise should stop is a question for sound judgment. Still, the American experience throws a heavy burden of proof on those who urge disqualifying citizens for any reasons except immaturity, mental disease, or conviction for a really serious crime.

My last point about the franchise is its immense educational value. John Stuart Mill emphasized this as the great argument for representative government. Except for jury service, voting is the only opportunity most men have for directly engaging in the business of governing. Furthermore, the prolonged discussion before elections on the part of most voters is a strong mental stimulus. On the other hand, deprivation of the ballot encourages intellectual sluggishness and the feeling that one is not really part of the community. Even if we could obtain more efficient government by diminishing the electorate, we might very well refuse to stop the teaching which the ballot gives.

Look, for example at the effects of women suffrage. Its supporters who prophesied that skirts at the polls would bring housecleaning into politics and peace for the world were as sadly wrong as the anti-suffragists who predicted the disintegration of the home if women left it on election-day. Nobody foresaw that the greatest visible gain from the Nineteenth Amendment would be the League of Women Voters, which does a job of public education men were not bright enough to plan and too busy with their own affairs to carry out.

Our second main question is: Over what do the people exercise control? Of course, they have have considerable influence through refusing to re-elect officials and through public opinion, but I am asking now about actual power. How far do they govern directly in a democracy? Here again there are plainly many different types of democracies. The share taken by the electorate in the management of the state may vary widely.

At one extreme lies ancient Athens where the citizens did most of the business of government themselves. The whole body of qualified voters could throng to the market-place for the purpose of enacting laws. They administered justice as large juries without any judges. They did delegate executive power, but only for brief periods running as short as a day. With this rapid rotation and the choice of many officers by lot, any citizen might look forward to being an official. So we can almost say that the executive functions were also in the hands of the electorate. At all events, the Athenian voters made important decisions of military policy which, in this country, would be made by the President with the advice of the Joint Chiefs of Staff. Thus Alcibiades brought about the disastrous expedition to Sicily by a popular referendum. Then, just as it was about to start under his command, the voters recalled Alcibiades and put in another general to take its great fleet to ruin.

In Rome there was somewhat more stability. The executive power was delegated to consuls and judicial power was exercised by judges, sometimes with small juries of knights. Still, such powers were kept in close check by annual elections and by the queer Roman custom of giving almost every job to two or more persons, from consuls down. Moreover, great masses of Roman citizens enacted statutes. This shifting system conquered the world, but probably because a permanent balance-wheel was supplied by the Senate, composed of past officials who sat for life.

When Roman citizenship was extended over the whole of Italy, the system broke down. Everybody realized that things were wrong, yet nobody did anything about it in the way of permanent, unselfish remedies. Tiberius Gracchus was a lone exception, and he was soon put to death for his unusual inventiveness. Cicero had the most capacity to devise a solution, but he was too timid and he never commented on the Gracchi except to denounce them. All he could suggest was to go back to the good old days. There is no way back out of political crises, only forward. So long as the population of all Italy was entitled to make or reject laws by traveling hundreds of miles to gather in a city square too small to hold more than a fraction of them, any decision was bound to depend on accident and manipulation. The only solution which would have preserved the Roman Republic was representative government. This had been used in the Achaean League. Yet the

Romans did not even consider it. The truth is that political inventiveness is a very rare quality. This fact entitles the Philadelphia Convention of 1787 to great praise.

Not until democracy was supplemented by representative government, was it able to succeed over large areas. The Dominican Order thought up this device when its scattered monasteries sent delegates to its councils. Afterwards, in the later Middle Ages, many European countries had assemblies of estates, but only the English Parliament kept power into modern times. In the rest of Europe powerful nobles were the chief rivals of the monarch, but the English nobles rendered a great service to democracy by killing each other off during the Wars of the Roses. This left a clear field in England for the King and Parliament, either to work together or to struggle for power. Thus, by the time the American colonies were settled, it was a matter of course for the inhabitants to send delegates to a law-making body roughly resembling the House of Commons.

With the invention of representation, citizens once more participated directly in government although their functions were obviously much more limited than in ancient Athens and Rome. Most of the decisions were not made by them, but by the men they elected. The voters had a wider scope in a considerable part of this country because they could go to town meetings, fix taxes, authorize public works, and generally supervise the governmental affairs which come closest to men's lives. However, the direct political powers of American citizens shrank during the Nineteenth Century as towns grew into cities. The urban population could do no more law-making, only electing.

The Twentieth Century brought a fresh expansion of the powers of the electorate. By the recall, citizens can take a man out of office as well as put him in. By the initiative and referendum they can enact laws. The desirability of these new devices is fiercely debated; but in Massachusetts at least, the voters have made some good decisions on important issues which the legislators lacked courage to touch. For example, the censorship of motion-pictures was defeated, and labor union officials were required to file annual financial reports. The high-water mark of the new tendency was the demand, some years ago, that war should be declared only after a national referendum. The Gallup Polls have made it practicable to refer almost any question to a popular vote. The radio and the progress of electronics might enable every voter each morning to press a black or a white button in order to decide about the enactment of every bill in the state legislature, whether income taxes should be lowered, how many billions are to be spent on the Air Force, and whether a prominent general ought to be retired.

Once more, we are confronted with the argument that if we favor democracy we ought to have as much of it as possible. Hence there should be popular election of federal judges and more and more referenda. Here too, however, it may be true that you can have too much of a good thing. We have to consider sound finance—the people may be inclined to eat up the seed corn. Governmental efficiency, fruitful negotiations with foreign nations, the welfare of groups like business corporations or labor unions which may be temporarily disliked by a great many voters, the freedom of individuals who happen to be in a small minority—these are all desirable purposes which have to be weighed alongside the advantages of increased democracy. Moreover, it is well known that election-days are subject to the law of diminishing returns. The more often people are asked to vote, the fewer votes you get, as time goes on. The size of the dinner must be limited by the capacity of the stomach, else indigestion follows. Experience suggests the wisdom of confining the voter's annual task to choosing between candidates for a few important offices and to answering a very few questions about the adoption or defeat of measures, and, further, that such questions will not be satisfactorily decided unless they call for a plain "Yes" or "No."

The lesson of all I have said, is that democracy is not enough. It must be supplemented by numerous political devices and practices to make it effective. Of this truth the framers of our government were well aware. Safeguards to prevent a government from being too strong are indeed desirable, but it is also important not to have it too weak. "The first business of a government is to govern." If the rules on paper do not permit this, one of two things is bound to happen. One possibility is that a many-headed and inefficient government will break down in a crisis or even be unable to cope with ordinary routine, like that of Poland in the Eighteenth Century. With the commoner alternative, the pressure of hard facts causes concentration of power in somebody without regard to the rules on paper.

To illustrate this last situation, I recall that Athens, despite its extreme democracy, came under the leadership of Pericles and then of Cleon the sausage maker, neither of whom held an official position. And I think of my native state of Rhode Island during the closing years of the Nineteenth Century. The state constitution set up two headless branches of the General Assembly and a governor who had no veto and no genuine power to appoint anybody. Although nominally chief of the state, he could really do nothing except preside over a joint session of these two branches. Thus the rules on paper left power as little concentrated as it possibly could be. Nevertheless, power was concentrated in fact in a single man, Charles R. Brayton, the blind boss, for whom the constitution made no provision whatever.

The phenomenon of the American boss like Brayton can, I believe, be somewhat explained as the devious effort of facts to cure a bad defect in the existing rules on paper. Of course, there were other causes like the prevalence of bribery and corruption among voters, legislators, and officeholders and the opportunities for looting public funds. Things are not perfect today, but nobody under the age of forty can possibly realize what the political atmosphere was in many states and cities during my boyhood. Still, the bosses were in part a response to genuine needs of the community which the rules on paper had failed to satisfy.

I like America in its governmental aspects much better than I did fifty years ago, leaving out of consideration for the moment deprivations of liberty which are discussed elsewhere in this book. We have got rid of the disgusting pretense that states and cities were governed by the men who were elected or appointed to legally created offices, whereas in fact (as most citizens knew) they were governed by a very different set of men unknown to the law. We owe this enormous improvement in government during the past half century to the tireless work of scores of men who combined vision with hard heads. Not content with slogans like, "Turn the rascals out," they changed the rules on paper so as to confer real power on executive officers whom the voters chose and on the associates chosen by these officers. And at the same time more and more men emerged, like Alfred E. Smith, Robert M. La Follette, and Tom Johnson (to name only a few), who were capable of exercising power with wisdom and bravery. All this shows the importance of supplementing democracy by making it possible that the genuine needs which used to be taken care of by bosses and party machines can be adequately met by the established governments of states and cities. Let me run over some of these needs.

First and foremost, a focus of power has to exist. Somebody must really be able to do something.

Second, modern regulation of business, labor, and other important elements in our complex industrial communities gives rise to a sort of collective bargaining between such private groups and government, or perhaps it may better be called negotiation. There needs to be some outstanding representative of government to whom a power company or a labor union or an association of parents or some other group can go to present its claims, some of which are likely to be legitimate even if others selfishly ignore the interests of the rest of the community. A weak executive and a headless legislature do not take care of this real need. It was met by a boss, at least in response to groups who could make some return for his services. It is met far more satisfactorily by a governor or mayor with power, or by the head of a properly organized department who possesses wide and definite authority over a specific section of governmental activities.

Third, the regulations of a modern government affect all sorts of people very intimately. Yet the organization of various bureaus and departments of a city or state—and this is even more true of the numerous alphabetical agencies in Washington—has become so complex and overlapping, that the ordinary citizen who wants to oppose or obtain governmental action is completely baffled. He is in a bewildering labyrinth. Consequently, he looks eagerly for some kind of information bureau, which will straighten out his perplexities and put him in touch with the right officials. The boss was such an information bureau, and so was welcomed by honest as well as dishonest citizens. Might it be worth while for any government to recognize this persistent need, and establish such a bureau itself?

Fourth, the need for a different kind of information bureau has been created by the length of the modern ballot. On election-day a voter is asked to express his judgment about filling a dozen or more offices. No citizen who works hard at his own job can possibly acquire for himself adequate information about two or more candidates for each of these numerous positions. Nowadays he is still more bewildered by several requests at the bottom of the ballot for his opinion about rather complicated laws on all sorts of subjects outside his own range of knowledge. He may vote by guesswork or not vote at all—either course is a breakdown of democracy. Or else he has to go to somebody to learn how to vote. The boss and his subordinates have always taken great pains to supply this information. Today the need is partly met by the more disinterested methods of the League of Women Voters. Yet I believe that, so long as a voter is confronted with an indigestible mass of choices, his genuine exercise of political judgment is impossible. Here is a strong argument for the short ballot which would in state and local elections resemble a federal election. Most voters might be glad to concentrate their attention on the few most important offices, leaving the rest to be filled by appointment just as the President selects his Cabinet and other national officials. It is harder to find a good way to cut down the number of measures submitted by initiative and referendum.

Finally, there is the need of the less fortunate members of the community for help—help in getting jobs, in being kept going while out of work, in finding legal defense, and so forth. In the old days, the orthodox view was that all this was none of the government's business except in cases of extreme poverty. So the help was obtained from the boss and his machine, largely at the expense of the taxpayers. They still foot the bill, but do so through the established government. There have been mistakes and waste, no doubt, but the great change in policy has given us a better country. A citizen participates in the government with a stronger sense of obligation when he knows that it will protect him from major disasters, like mass unemployment, against which he can do very little to guard.

The foregoing discussion of the extent to which citizens should be able to make decisions themselves about public affairs has necessarily been imperfect, but I want to stress factors which have to be considered as possible limitations on democracy. One is the need for concentration of power. The other cannot be stated so simply. Any person who governs in any way ought to be able to put his mind and heart into his particular job of governing. Voting is a kind of governing. Therefore, a ballot becomes wrong when it asks the voter to make choices into which he does not put his mind and heart—choices which are perfunctory, haphazard, or made for him by others.

The essentials of democracy are plainly compatible with a wide range of political structures—republics or constitutional monarchies as in most of Europe and the British Dominions, nations with a permanent executive officer like our President or executive officers chosen by the legislature like the British Cabinet, with or without a written constitution, with or without judicial power to invalidate statutes, and colonies like our own before the Revolution. There are many different ways in which peoples have learned to govern themselves, directly or indirectly. Each has come to fit pretty well the country in which it developed, but this does not prove it would operate successfully if transplanted to another soil.

Our last question about democracy is: Control for what? The purposes of government are manifold; a democracy faces pretty much the same tasks as any other system. Still, the ideal of government for the people requires it to work for the general welfare and not for that of a few. Thus a danger is presented by groups which are organized for political pressure. Since most elections are carried by a margin of less than ten per cent, the result would be changed by a shift of five per cent. Consequently, any group comprising five per cent of the voters stands a good chance of getting whatever its leaders want because of the assumption by politicians and legislators that everybody in this group will follow its leaders' orders and vote solidly against a candidate who has failed to comply with their demands. Yet the occasional man who will not give in to such pressure and steadily pursues the course he believes right often finds himself re-elected. My classmate Robert Taft put through the Taft-Hartley Act against the wishes of the leaders of powerful labor unions and then carried Ohio by half a million votes. Regardless of the merits of the Act, it was good to see the assumption of group solidarity shot to pieces. Politicians underestimate the admiration of American citizens for courage.

Unorganized small minorities, on the other hand, are especially vulnerable in a democracy because of the craving for conformity, which was noted here by De Tocqueville a century ago. Fortunately, realization of this danger led to the Bill of Rights. Perhaps freedom of religion, speech, and assembly are not inevitable accompaniments of democracy, but they have often gone with it since the Sixteenth Century. This has been true in Switzerland, Holland, and modern England, as well as in the United States, where, Justice Brandeis said, "Those who won our independence believed that the final end of the state was to make men free to develop their faculties."

Having tried to show very sketchily what democracy is, I shall go on to say why I like it.

In the first place, I cannot conceive of any alternative which would be tolerable. No doubt, Plato's theory that permanent control should be vested in "the wise" has always been tempting to many. Thus Van Bibber, the man about town in amusing stories by Richard Harding Davis, wanted the Mayor of New York to be elected by graduates of Harvard College. There are great differences of opinion about who are "the wise," and the misery through which recent dictators have dragged their countries shows that men who possess absolute power are likely to make more disastrous mistakes and commit far greater wrongs than the least estimable products of democracy. Such terrible experiences reenforce homely sayings that it is better to count heads than break them and to govern by ballots instead of bullets.

However, the argument that we must turn to democracy as a last resort, because, whatever its faults, everything else would be still worse, may be sound but arouses no enthusiasm. A man falls in love with a girl for what she is and not by deciding that all the other girls are even more disagreeable. This argument is not enough to make men die for democracy, or—what is perhaps harder—live for democracy.

Something of what we need was said by Robert Burns:

A man's a man for a' that.

The differences between men count for less than what they have in common. Those who favor setting up the few "wise" as rulers invariably expect those few to include themselves, or at least their friends. The multitude whom they want to leave out would look at the matter quite differently. When you strip off the non-essentials of inherited or accidental possessions, attempts to create different levels of power become either arbitrary or ridiculous. I am reminded of the time a Columbia professor took me for a swim in a pool where bathing suits are ignored. While we were all standing around as nature made us, a student engaged my friend in some sort of scholarly conversation, in which I joined. Afterwards my friend apologized for not introducing me, but I remarked that such formalities were superfluous between people who had no clothes on.

Thus far I have spoken mostly about political democracy, and said little about social and economic democracy, which have their own crop of problems. The three types are not coextensive, but they do help each other. Equal political power tends to diffuse the means of subsistence and control over the conditions of work. The absence of hereditary rank removes some of the barriers to association, friendship, and marriage. On the other hand, the undemocratic political thesis of the Nazis contemplated voteless millions living in serfdom and ghettos. The converse is also true, that social and economic democracy tend to produce political democracy. Many of us look forward to a classless society in the United States without many very rich or very poor, where everybody will have the oppportunity to get as much education as he needs and then obtain work into which he can put the best of himself, and with a widespread distribution of the material things which make for a happy and fruitful life. It is hard to think of such a society tolerating an undemocratic form of government. Men with an approximately equal chance of earning and achieving in their work would not long consent to be outlawed politically.

It is no accident that democracies have arisen in communities with a strong religious consciousness, in the broadest sense of religion to embrace all kinds of faith in the brotherhood of men and their equality before the Spirit of the Universe, however conceived. Forgetting differences, we turn to each other for help and strength in a cause which belongs to all of us and not just to a few.

The biggest danger from communism is the possibility that it will win masses of men away from democracy, here and in Western Europe and Asia. I regret the fashionable phrase "the cold war" because it has made us feel as if we were in a real war and confine our thinking to military might and catching spies, whereas the contest with communism is in large measure a contest of ideas. Ideas and the emotions which give ideas their drawing-power have to be met with stronger ideas possessing a stronger emotional force.

So far as I can judge the attraction which communism has had for some law-abiding men and women, it filled a void in their minds and hearts. A man becomes resentful over conditions he regards as unjust and degrading. He is disillusioned by the claptrap of both our major parties. So he turns to communism because it promises a new earth, if not a new heaven. The oppression which actually takes place in Russia or China today is for him irrelevant—the man is converted by a vision.

Yet Jefferson and Lincoln had a great vision. It also promised to remedy injustices and degrading inequalities. During the Nineteenth Century, it drew millions to our shores. If democracy has lost some of this former vitality, the fault (I believe) is in us, its adherents, and not in democracy. The best way for Americans to combat the ideas of communism here and in the rest of the world is to give increased drawing-power to our great traditions of democracy and freedom. We must show how much they mean to us.

This task requires stirring reaffirmations of our faith. The vision of Jefferson and Lincoln will not be revealed to men with disturbed minds through catchwords like "the American way" and "free enterprise." Only memorable sentences, close to their experience and their dreams, will make them see the vision of democracy and freedom. Nor is it enough for us to repeat the Declaration of Independence and the Gettysburg Address. Noble words lose something of their biting edge with time. In order to win over men of the Twentieth Century, we have to use the language of the Twentieth Century.

The trouble is that we ourselves are not fully aware how much can be said for our ideals. About twenty years ago a *Soviet Primer* was widely sold in this country. I wish we might get out a *Primer of Democracy*. A short book could contain stirring expositions of self-government and freedom, from the Funeral Oration of Pericles down to statements by men and women of today. In it might be David Lilienthal's reply to those who opposed his appointment as head of the Atomic Energy Commission:

> I conceive the Constitution of the United States to rest—as does religion—[upon] the fundamental proposition of the integrity of the individual; and that all government and private institutions must be designed to protect the integrity and the dignity of the individual. . . . The tenets of democracy . . . grow out of this central core of a belief that the individual comes first, that all men are the children of God and their personalities are therefore sacred. . . .

Such a book might reprint the statement of Secretary of State George Marshall to a conference at Moscow about what "democracy" means to us:

> We believe that human beings have . . . rights that may not be given or taken away. They include the right of every individual to develop his mind and his soul in the ways of his own choice, free of fear and coercion—provided only that he does not interfere with the rights of others. . . . To us, a society is not free if law-abiding citizens live in fear of being denied the right to work or deprived of life, liberty and the pursuit of happiness.

Without ignoring past shortcomings, we Americans ought to stress our progress and our hopes, so as to make the great vision of democracy shine before the eyes of multitudes at home and abroad who are now disheartened by these troublesome times.

"Of all contemporary writers about the American scene," a *Saturday Review* editorial writer commented, "none more nearly deserves the title of Democratic Liberal than Gerald W. Johnson." During H. L. Mencken's lifetime, Johnson was referred to as "the second ranking Sage of Baltimore." With Mencken's passing, Johnson automatically assumed the number one position. Before Johnson joined the Baltimore "Sunpapers," Mencken described him as "the best editorial writer in the South, a very excellent critic, and a highly civilized man." A biographer, historian, critic, and journalist, Johnson with his fertile pen has produced some two dozen books and scores of newspaper and magazine articles. "Freedom of Inquiry Is for Hopeful People" is taken from his *This American People* (1951).

Gerald W. Johnson
FREEDOM OF INQUIRY IS FOR HOPEFUL PEOPLE

When Jefferson listed "the pursuit of happiness" as one of the rights which government cannot justly take from any man, except as punishment for crime, he stepped into a dark and mysterious corner of the realm of ideas. Nobody denies the truth of what he said; but the reason for that is that nobody knows exactly what it means.

The word "happiness" cannot be defined precisely because it means different things to different people, or to the same people at different times or in different circumstances. The word "pursuit" is almost as vague. Together, they express an idea that a man cannot always comprehend as it applies to himself, and that he can rarely, if ever, comprehend as it applies to anyone else.

The only interpretation of this phrase that is not open to some fatal objection seems to be this: the right to the pursuit of happiness is the right to be let alone.

Instantly, this raises the question, how is government going to govern if it lets people alone? The function of government is not to let people alone, but to interfere with them. Government is instituted to protect certain inalienable rights, among them life, liberty, and the pursuit of happiness; therefore its business, its reason for being, is to interfere with those who would infringe these rights, and not merely to interfere, but to prevent their doing what they would like to do. These people may be wrong, but they are nevertheless people, and they do not like it when government stops them from doing as they please.

There is no logical answer to this. The only answer is an illogical one—consider what would happen if government were abolished altogether. In that case, the right to the pursuit of happiness would not be respected at all. The strongest would impose his will on all others, and there would be no liberty except the liberty of the strongest. This is anarchy; and it was the secret fear of some founders of the republic that democracy must inevitably degenerate into anarchy.

Furthermore, there are some men—never a majority, but a definite number, and important out of all proportion to their number—for whom the pursuit of happiness consists in finding out what is true. They are critics of everything; and among other things they are critics of government, which lays upon the American government the duty of protecting those who attack it. This is the basis of the maxim beloved of early liberals, "That government is best that governs least." It means that government should interfere with the individual only as far as is absolutely necessary to protect the general welfare.

Two factors work constantly against this ideal —one is human nature, the other is the passage of time. Any group of men given a chance to wield power—and a government is just that— will try to extend that power. This is the first factor. As more people are crowded together in the same area, more activity by government is required to maintain order. This is the second factor. Neither can be eliminated. Each is capable of becoming a threat to all liberty. Since some extension of governmental power is necessary as the population grows, it is easy for governors to convince themselves that any extension of their power is justifiable. This tendency must be held within bounds by steady counterpressure from people who know their rights and mean to maintain them.

But steady counterpressure is extremely irritating to government officials. It irritates shrewd fellows who are in politics solely for what they can get out of it to their own advantage, but it is even more exasperating to sincere men who are working honestly to promote the general welfare. Dogged opposition slows down, even when it does not stop, the operations of government, and when men are opposed on what they consider frivolous and unreasonable pretexts, they tend to lose their tempers. This is the trap into which liberal leaders are most likely to fall; men as great as Andrew Jackson, Woodrow Wilson, and

---

Gerald W. Johnson, *This American People* (New York: Harper & Bros., 1951), pp. 88–111, copyright 1951 by Gerald W. Johnson. Reprinted (without footnotes) by permission of the author and of the publisher.

both Roosevelts stepped into it more than once, and the supremacy of Jefferson and Lincoln is due in part to their success in keeping out of it.

The mental process that betrays men in this respect is easy to understand. When opposition is unreasonable and insincere it is thoroughly bad. Opposition frequently is unreasonable and insincere; hence opposition is frequently bad. Thus far, the reasoning is perfectly sound, but at this point the human mind, and especially the mind of a harassed political leader, is likely to slip a cog, and go on to argue that since opposition is frequently bad it may be presumed to be bad until it is proved to be otherwise.

That is not the American doctrine. True Americanism holds the right to the pursuit of happiness to be inalienable, and if a man chooses to pursue happiness by opposing the government, his opposition must be presumed to be good until it is definitely proved to be bad. When the government molests a citizen in any way, it must show cause. The burden of proof is on the government, not on the citizen. In pursuing happiness he is within his rights up to the moment when he pursues it into territory that belongs to some other citizen, or to society as a whole. Those who assert that he has crossed the line must put up the proof; for when they molest him they are in the wrong unless they can show clearly that he was out of bounds, and the molestation was therefore necessary.

This is not merely difficult, it is next to impossible for men in power to remember. This is one case in which the maxim "Power corrupts and absolute power corrupts absolutely" is sustained by the evidence; for in every case in which absolute power has been gained in this century, the holder of that power has come to believe that the mere spirit of opposition is as much a crime as an overt act. Lenin, Mussolini, Hitler, Tojo, Stalin—all have felt compelled to stamp out what the Russians call "deviationism" and the franker Japanese "dangerous thoughts." Some centuries ago, when the English kings were absolute, the same idea was embodied in the law making "imagining the king's death" a crime; and in 1951 Madame Shih Liang, the woman Minister of Justice of Communist China, proclaimed the necessity of punishing not only those who act against the state, but also those who are merely hoping for an opportunity to act.

America, so far, has escaped both absolute kings and absolute dictators, so we have escaped the worst abuses of this kind. Nevertheless, even in this republic we have had proof of the way people in power tend to try to suppress freedom of thought when they feel their power threatened.

The most conspicuous instance—although by no means the only one—was connected with the abolition of slavery. The slave States did not stop with making it a crime even to advocate the abolition of slavery; they also attempted to prevent anyone's thinking of such a thing by preventing the circulation of books, magazines and newspapers containing arguments against slavery. Their great advocate in Congress, John C. Calhoun, demanded that the free States do likewise. In speech after speech he proclaimed that enforcement of the Fugitive Slave Law and other laws designed to prevent interference with slavery would not be enough; the North, he said, must cease agitating the question, which was tantamount to saying that the North must stop thinking about it.

It was an error. Far from persuading the North, Calhoun's speeches merely convinced many moderate Northerners that the South was utterly beyond reason. Under some circumstances a man may agree not to act on his beliefs, and it is permissible to ask him not to act; but to ask him not to think is too much. Anyone who makes such a request is asking him to submit his mind to tyranny, to surrender one of his inalienable rights, and the request is an insult.

At any rate, this was the way the American people regarded the matter in the Civil War period. Up to the time of Calhoun's death, in 1850, the Abolitionists were far from popular in the North. Even in 1860 Abraham Lincoln, campaigning for the Presidency, was careful to keep clear of them. They were, as a matter of fact, as unreasonable as Calhoun. William Lloyd Garrison, borrowing eloquence from the Prophet Isaiah, called the Constitution "a covenant with death and an agreement with hell" and publicly burned it because it recognized slavery as legal. Nonsense of that kind made people shy away from the movement; but when Calhoun undertook to tell them that they *must* close their minds to Abolitionist argument, the shoe was on the other foot. Americans of the period were not disposed to accept dictation from either side, and the foolish effort of the South to establish an Iron

Curtain did its own cause more damage than all the Abolitionist arguments.

Calhoun's error was in assuming that the danger to the cause of the South was the Abolitionist propaganda. The truth was the reverse. Such extreme statements as that of Garrison were making friends for the South among sensible Northerners. If the Southern leaders had had courage enough to remain silent the Abolitionists would have done them more good than harm. But they did not have that courage and it is probable that they lacked it because at heart they knew that their cause was a bad one. The greatest of their own leaders, Washington and Jefferson, had admitted that slavery was an evil, and innumerable other Southerners, smaller than these giants, but still big men, down as far as John Randolph of Roanoke in his early years, has regretted the existence of the "peculiar institution." Therefore such men as Calhoun, Jefferson Davis, Yancey, and Rhett felt that they were standing on slippery ground; and when men are uncertain of their own footing they become more violent and aggressive than those who know they are standing on solid earth.

The only man who can heartily favor complete freedom of inquiry is the man who is so certain that his own cause is right that further inquiry can only strengthen it. Truth has nothing to fear from the fullest investigation. If an idea is true, then the more it is investigated the better; for the more it is investigated, the more people will see that it is unquestionably true, and the fullest investigation will simply result in convincing everybody.

But a man who is not quite certain that his own cause is just is full of fears, and well he may be; for an idea that is plausible on the surface but unsound at heart cannot stand investigation. Little by little sharply inquiring minds will uncover the rotten spots, and soon or late that idea will be exposed as false. It may take a long time. Men have constructed many theories so beautiful on the surface that generations of persistent inquiry were necessary to show up what was wrong with them. Human slavery was one such theory. It lasted, not for generations, but for centuries. As acute a thinker as Plato never questioned it. The writers of the New Testament accepted it. Fifteen centuries of our era had passed before it was challenged seriously. Nevertheless, the thing was rotten at the heart, and as the power of reason was refined and sharpened, and as men learned more and more about the world they live in, it was inevitable that the rottenness should be exposed; and it was just as inevitable that men committed to that theory should become more and more uneasy, therefore more and more arrogantly and violently opposed to further investigation.

This explains the attitude of the Communists in 1951. They are committed to the theories of Karl Marx, all of them. Many other people have been impressed by some of Marx's ideas, but only the Communists swallow the doctrine whole. Yet they lack the courage of their convictions. They are not willing to permit complete, persistent, unrestricted examination of that doctrine, so they have lowered the Iron Curtain between the areas they control and the rest of the world. They may not realize it themselves, but at heart they are uncertain of the truth of that doctrine and so dare not submit it to what Justice Holmes called "the competition of the market."

In Russian Communists this attitude is not hard to understand, for they have had nothing like the American experience to contradict it. Up to 1917 Russia had been a despotism of one kind or another throughout its history. Mongol conquerors ruled most of the country for four hundred years before the Czars took over; and Mongol and Czar, if they agreed on nothing else, were both convinced that the state could not endure if the people were encouraged to think for themselves.

So when Czarism broke down in 1917, it was easy for the Russians to transfer from the despotic theory that one man must dictate to the Marxian theory that one class must dictate, if public order is to be preserved. If, as Marx believed, it is impossible for people with different interests on different economic levels—rich men and poor men, scholars, merchants, artists, craftsmen, dull men and brilliant men, the religious and the irreligious—to work out a compromise under which each will respect the rights of the others, then it is clear that someone must dictate. The Czars favored a despot, Marx favored the proletariat; but on the main fact, that there must be a dictator, they were agreed, so the transition from the Czar to Marx was not difficult.

Americans, however, have behind them the

experience of a hundred and sixty-two years flatly contradicting the Marxist-Czarist idea. We tried the experiment of working out a compromise based on the theory that each class is capable of enough self-restraint to permit other classes not only to live, but to enjoy the rights of liberty and the pursuit of happiness; and for a hundred and sixty-two years it has worked, not perfectly, indeed, but well enough for the country to be built up into the wealthiest and most powerful nation on the globe.

After all, what more is to be expected of any form of government? None will ever be perfect as long as greed, envy, and ambition exist among men; so if one works well enough over a long enough period to permit the construction of a great nation, it is obviously a good form, even though it may not be ideal. Furthermore, this form has been constructed on the theory that the people can think for themselves and it is advisable to encourage them to do so. Clearly, then, it is a good theory, or at least a tenable one; the American experiment has demonstrated that freedom of thought does not necessarily destroy the state but that, on the contrary, a state may flourish prodigiously where freedom of thought is encouraged. Communists may argue that we would have flourished even more prodigiously under a wise and benevolent dictatorship, but it is their business to prove it and they have submitted no sort of proof as yet. If Russia a hundred and thirty years hence is still Communist, and rich, powerful, and happy, they will have something like proof; but they haven't it as yet....

So communism has made little impression on this country. Thirty-odd years of incessant propaganda have produced, according to the Federal Bureau of Investigation, about fifty-five thousand card-carrying Communists, which, in a population of a hundred and fifty millions is thirty-six thousandths of one per cent. This is at the rate of slightly over one thousandth of one per cent a year; at which rate it would take something over forty thousand years to make Communists of a majority. The danger may be called remote.

Unfortunately, though, belief in dictatorship in the form of thought control is not confined to Communists, nor to Fascists, nor to Czarists, nor to the Lamaists of Tibet. It is shared by some people who hate communism and who regard themselves as being as far from communism as the poles are apart. It is shared, or at least it is tolerated, by all those whose fear of the future is greater than their hope; and this is characteristic of many native-born Americans, some of them highly intelligent.

For it is true that any man who thinks may think up devilment, and where there are many thinkers some are sure to do so.

This is a disturbing fact to those who believe that the power of thought is the greatest power in the universe; but that it is disturbing is no reason for ignoring it. The founders of this republic realized it, and it appalled some of them. Since their day every student of public affairs whose ideas carry any weight has realized it, and some of them, Brooks Adams for instance, have been staggered by it. Freedom of thought is dangerous. There is no doubt about it, and any serious consideration of the American tradition must take the fact into account.

In recent years it has been brought home sharply to men who are not philosophers, and who may not even call themselves thinkers, by one event that has startled and scared the world. This was the invention of the atomic bomb.

This article was the product of freedom of inquiry, not in this country alone, but throughout the scientific world. The principle of atomic fission was not the discovery of any one man, but had been approached, little by little, by many men of many nations. Germans had contributed much to it, and Italians, French, British, Danes, Swedes, Russians. It mattered little, as far as the result was concerned, who made any particular step, for what one physicist discovered he promptly made known to all other physicists and to anyone else capable of reading and understanding scientific journals.

But as late as 1940 it was still in the realm of theory. Mathematical calculations so intricate that the layman is incapable of reading them, not to speak of making them, had proved that if certain radioactive material were brought into a certain relation with certain other material, atomic fission would follow and the release of energy would be very great. This was known wherever a physicist had kept abreast of his science. To bring those materials into that relation was not a simple matter; in fact, it would require enormously abstruse calculations, so many and so difficult that nobody had time or inclination to undertake the labor; but everyone knew that, theoretically, it could be done.

After the attack on Pearl Harbor it was done. Two thousand scientists labored for nearly five years to accomplish it, but it was done. Relatively few of these scientists fooled around with test tubes and retorts, or stood at a workbench with precision instruments in a laboratory. What they did was think. They knew that if they worked out the correct formula, competent mechanics could design and manufacture the parts and fit them together. The scientists' job was to calculate in advance what would happen in an experiment that had never been tried.

They made that calculation. In fact, they made it in four different ways, all of which turned out to be workable. It was a triumph of thought, not of manual dexterity. It was one of the most gigantic achievements in the history of thought. Even laymen can understand that much, and laymen readily grant it.

But the outcome of this prodigious labor, utterly impossible without the freedom of inquiry that physics had enjoyed for nearly three hundred years, was the most dreadful engine of destruction that the world had ever seen. For the first time nonscientific Americans realized that the same science of which they had been inordinately proud and which had, indeed, largely created the American way of life, was also capable of creating an American way of death swifter and more overwhelming than any lethal machine hitherto contrived. If that is the result of freedom of inquiry, some people began to ask, is the game worth the candle?

They had at least one distinguished precedent for arguing that it is not. Once before ingenious armorers had devised a weapon so deadly in its effects that sober men feared it might depopulate the nations and the Pope issued an encyclical condemning its use by any Christian warrior against any other Christian, no matter what the circumstances. The Pope was Innocent II, the year 1197, the weapon the crossbow. So the feeling that a weapon may be so lethal as to discredit the science that produces it is at least seven hundred years old and has been shared by persons of high character and great eminence.

In 1951 so many persons of that type were coming to Pope Innocent's point of view that scientists were beginning to forecast a retrograde movement in science comparable to that which Greek astronomy suffered after the time of Hipparchus. This pessimistic view assumes that men have come to fear more than they hope from the advance of science; and, in fact, if science is to be devoted to purposes of destruction that fear is justified. The atomic bomb is by no means the worst of it; science has developed a threat even more grisly in bacteriological warfare. Time was, and within the memory of living men, when the utmost loathing and contempt for an enemy beyond the pale of civilization, even beyond the limits of humanity, was expressed in the phrase, "they fight with stink-pots and contagious diseases." But there is a very real threat that in the next World War all nations, including the United States, will be reduced to fighting with such weapons, put into our hands by the advance of science. Thus we are compelled to face the fact that science, the same science that has so largely created our material welfare, can take the opposite direction and drag us down toward the level of the beasts.

It is folly to dismiss this airily as the figment of a fevered imagination. It is nothing of the sort. It is a very real peril that may be the end of us as a civilized race. But it is not new and the men who founded the United States of America were well acquainted with it. Jefferson, for example, at least once was utterly defeated by the fear of freedom of inquiry; it was when he attempted to bring Dr. Thomas Cooper, the British-born chemist and philosopher, to a professorship in the newly-founded University of Virginia. Fear of what Cooper's inquiring mind might do to orthodox opinions defeated the effort, although in this case the opposition was theological, not scientific. Chemistry had not yet exhibited its power to destroy the world, but philosophical speculation was as much feared then as scientific investigation is now. The Virginians had no idea that Cooper, the chemist, might blow up the earth, but they had a lively dread that Cooper, the philosopher, might blow up religion, so they banned him and he had to go instead to what is now the University of South Carolina, where he made a great record—and did not demolish religion.

Fear of freedom of inquiry was thus familiar to the men who wrote the Constitution. It was not fear of physical destruction through the advance of science so much as it was fear of moral destruction through the questioning of philosophers; but to assume that the fear was any less real is to take a light-minded view of humanity; on the contrary, fear of the destruction of religion and morality appalls men who can face death without a quiver. There is no doubt that many honest and able men believed then, as some believe now, that unrestricted inquiry into the literal truth of the Bible or the then accepted dogmas of theology would so undermine morality that men would no longer hesitate to commit perjury, theft, and violence of all sorts including murder. There would be no safety of life or property, no public order, in short, no civilization if men were permitted to express freely any arguments they might find against religion.

Nevertheless, the official American doctrine is the exact opposite. Fully aware of the risk, the men who wrote the Constitution accepted it, for they hoped more than they feared from the process of pushing knowledge to the furthest bound attainable. In the Sixth Article they wrote, "No religious test shall ever be required as a qualification to any office or public trust under the United States." The religious test was the only one seriously considered at the time; but there is hardly room to doubt that if anyone had suggested a scientific test, or a philosophic test, they would have banned it just as vigorously.

The argument that led them to commit themselves to this risk, and to commit us to it ("no religious test shall *ever* be required") is itself to be found in that very Bible that the apprehensive were anxious to protect from investigation. It is in the Gospel according to St. John 8:32: "Ye shall know the truth, and the truth shall make you free."

This is one of the most hotly debated texts in Scripture, because it is extremely far-reaching. In the short run, it is flatly not true. Every man has found by experience that in many cases knowing the truth, far from making him free, binds him; for if he is a decent sort of man, when he knows the truth he is bound to act accordingly, even though he may very much dislike doing so. The truth is frequently hateful, and where ignorance is bliss 'tis folly to be wise. Nevertheless, when a man has had much experience, it dawns upon him that in the long run the words of the text are quite accurate; for when he knows what is what, he can form an opinion on which he can act with confidence, whereas before he had to accept the opinion of someone else and therefore was not a free agent.

It is an astonishing fact that some people can take almost any amount of formal schooling without becoming educated; for a man is not educated until he learns how to think. The beginning of thinking is realization that one has no opinion until he has learned the facts. On any subject whatever, before he has mastered the facts the best any man can have is a prejudice. If he has many prejudices, the laws of chance guarantee that some of them will be right, but the fact that he is occasionally right is small credit to the prejudiced man.

Life is so vastly complicated that most of us, even the wisest, make most of our decisions on prejudice, not on opinion. Sometimes prejudice is not ill-founded. We have discovered, say, that Mr. A is, in most things, a man of good judgment; therefore when he remarks that B's restaurant is an excellent one, we go there to dine, although we may never have heard of the place until he mentioned it. Our going there is not based on an opinion, but on a prejudice in favor of Mr. A's judgment of food. It may be erroneous, but it is not unreasonable, for a man who has shown good judgment in other things—in speech, in manners, in dress, and in general deportment—may reasonably be supposed to have good judgment about food. Oftener than not the restaurant will, in fact, turn out to be good, so we are justified in acting on that kind of prejudice.

Life is too short for a man to undertake to acquire a sound opinion on everything. In a thousand details he must act on supposition, because if he did not he would be dead of old age before he could make up his mind how to act at all. The great peril of democracy is that a majority of us may carry this habit over into things of the utmost importance, and so become no longer a self-governing people, but a people manipulated by a few shrewd men who know how to play on our prejudices.

We cannot flatter ourselves that we have never fallen into this error. A very slight and superficial examination of the history of the United States will show that the people have made error after error by acting on prejudice instead of on facts perfectly well known to a majority. The wisest men in the Constitutional Convention of 1787 wished to include in the document a provision for the gradual elimination of slavery, but prejudice blocked it. Even in 1860 the wisest men in the South realized that slavery was a social, political, and most emphatically an economic evil, and Abraham Lincoln stood ready to assist them in eliminating it by any means that did not involve disruption of the Union; but prejudice blocked it. In 1865 the wisest men in the North realized that a policy of reconciliation and rehabilitation was indicated, but prejudice blocked that, too.

In each case, the opinion of the wise men was based on facts known to them and easily available to all others. But an effective majority—which is not always the same as a numerical majority—either did not know the facts, or refused to believe them, and the greatest single tragedy in American history was the result.

To say that this was a departure from the essential American idea is not quite exact. It was rather a case of ignoring the idea. The Founding Fathers did not hold with compelling the people to do anything, not even compelling them to subordinate prejudice to informed opinion. They held only that it is absolutely essential to prevent the prejudiced from stopping or silencing any man who is attempting to get at the facts so that he may form a sound opinion. They believed that if the facts are made available, eventually the people will accept and act upon them, even though waves of hysteria may delay that acceptance for some time.

This is the basis of what is generally termed academic freedom, that is, the right of a scholar to pursue truth, no matter where the pursuit may take him. Unfortunately, since the truth is unknown (or there would be no occasion to look for it) this necessarily involves granting learned fools the right to pursue crazy ideas, and this liberty has brought academic freedom into disrepute with hasty and impatient people.

There is really nothing to be done about this, because the most brilliant advances in human thought have borne, at first, the appearance of utterly crazy ideas. Pliny the Younger, far from being a fool, was one of the shrewdest fellows of his time, a brilliant writer, an excellent administrator, and always interested in new ideas; yet when Christianity was first brought to his attention he wrote to the Emperor Trajan that in it "I could discover nothing more than an absurd and excessive superstition." For the time, even this was mild, and it brought upon Pliny charges of what we would now call whitewashing a bad situation. He was denounced very much as modern university presidents are denounced almost every day for not choking off some professor whose search for truth is not revealing truth exactly as it is known to the denouncers.

It is perfectly true that not every man who claims academic freedom is entitled to it, but the soundness of his claim cannot be determined in advance. Holmes' observation that the best test of truth is its ability to get itself accepted in the competition of the market was conservative; he might have called it not the best, but the only practical test. The American way, or at least the way the Constitution writers chose, is to permit the idea to enter the market without let or hindrance. Its collision with opposing ideas will test it, and if it survives it may be accepted.

But the search for truth was never pursued with much success by a man walking alone. This was abundantly demonstrated during what we are accustomed to call the Dark Ages, when Europe had almost completely forgotten the classical learning of Greece and Rome. Some of the most brilliant intellects of all time appeared during that period, but they worked for the most part with little and uncertain knowledge of what had been done before and less of what was being done in their own time, so their labors were ineffectual. Abélard, Roger Bacon, Paracelsus, for sheer brain-power have rarely been surpassed; but all of them fell into blatant absurdities for lack of information that had been known at one time or another to one man or another, but that was cut off from them by the Iron Curtain of prejudice and superstition.

No man is great enough to avoid error altogether, and the greater the mind the greater its need of constant correction and stimulation by other first-rate minds. For the error of a great man is much more serious than that of a small one. Paracelsus, by his mistaken treatments, undoubtedly poisoned far greater numbers than could have been killed by any doctor with a tenth of his reputation. Albert Einstein, cut off from communication with all other mathematicians, might have evolved false theories that would have misled the world for generations, and Toynbee, had he possessed only fragments, or none, of the writings of Gibbon, Ibn-Khaldun, and Thucydides, could have constructed a theory of history more fantastic than Friar Bacon's Brass Head.

This is the risk that the people who fear the search for truth overlook, but it was seen plainly by the men who wrote the Constitution, and they regarded it as far greater than the risk of permitting error to be proclaimed in the market. Their attitude has been until recently the American attitude, the essence of American tradition regarding freedom of the mind.

Perhaps it is still the essential American tradition, but there is at present a vigorous effort being made to change it. Since Russia has dropped the Iron Curtain between her thinkers and the rest of the world, there have been those who maintain that we must, in self-defense, impose an Iron Curtain between ours and the rest of the world. The science of nuclear physics has already been cut off, because nuclear physics can devise the highest of all high explosives. The fact that its methods of releasing atomic energy might theoretically be turned to the uses of peaceful industry is ignored in the general fear that some enemy might use atomic bombs against us. That is to say, our fear has grown greater than our hope.

This is a departure from the American tradition. This is, indeed, the utter repudiation of the American tradition; and if the fathers of the republic were right, it is a self-defeating movement. For it was their opinion that to permit fear to override hope is to abandon the great experiment and to admit that the thesis that "governments derive their just powers from the consent of the governed" is a lie. For consent is never freely given by people who are afraid. It is extorted from them, and an extorted consent is not self-government.

Furthermore, a thinking man is not stopped from thinking by laws, nor by Iron Curtains. Outside forces can only prevent him from thinking accurately. American scientists, cut off from intellectual contact with their fellows in the rest of the world, would not sink into lethargy. They would continue to use their powers, but they would probably use them erratically. Unaware of the needs, the efforts, the failures, and the successes of their fellow scientists, they would be unable to view science as a whole. They could only peep at it from their national angle, and a distorted conception would be the result. But it does not follow that they would be idle. Nuclear physicists are anything but idle in the United States today; on the contrary, fear of what may be going on behind the Iron Curtain has spurred them into furious activity and will continue to spur them. The destructive power of atomic energy is being developed as completely and as rapidly as is humanly possible. Unfortunately, there is no equivalent drive behind development of its constructive power. A science afraid of itself can be wonderfully productive of weapons and armor, but not of improvements and restoratives. From a distorted and truncated science we may expect ever larger and deadlier bombs, but not many engines.

In 1776 and 1787 American hope of the future overrode fear of the future and to fit that condition the American system was devised. In 1951 if fear is permitted to override hope, the system will no longer fit the condition, for freedom of inquiry is of small value to hopeless men. But the question cannot be answered by examining the system; the answer is to be found in the attitude of the people. The confidence of the fathers made it work then, and only a similar confidence in the sons can make it work now.

Judge Curtis Bok, author of "The Duty of Freedom," is represented by another contribution in the present compilation—in the chapter, "The Courts Look at Books."

Curtis Bok
THE DUTY OF FREEDOM

Behind our freedom to read is the freedom of others to speak and to write. Legally, these freedoms are at a high point: any blatancy, however strident, is protected, and the temper of the times is such that at least in the field of the written word, obscenity, blasphemy, public criticism, and general outcry go relatively unscathed.

At the same time the freedom of silence is at a low ebb. If challenged or if seeking public employment, no person may safely refuse to state his loyalty, and it is the temper of the times to regard silence on this subject either as suspicious or as fatal to a man's desire to serve his community. This is nothing new in itself, since the

---

Curtis Bok, "The Duty of Freedom," *Saturday Review*, 36: 27–28 (July 11, 1953), copyright 1953 by the Saturday Review Associates, Inc. Reprinted by permission of the author and of the publisher.

refusal to speak required words has cost the lives of many people, from Jesus down through the saints and martyrs.

What gives the subject a fresh twist is that the suppression of silence, hitherto a weapon of tyrants, should make headway in a nation founded upon freedom of conscience. It is incredible that any part of American freedom should be considered weaker than the dangers that confront the country. Principles considered good enough to live by should be considered good enough to die for, if it comes to that. Since it hasn't come fully to that, we must be in a phase when weakness is being experimented with, as it was in Germany during the Thirties.

Our Anglo-Saxon system of law is not considered divinely inspired except as it reflects the best faith and conscience of those who live by it. It may therefore be regarded as an anvil on which we hammer out our social experiments, like prohibition, censorship, and ideological conformity. Behind the anvil is the force of public opinion, the real censor who controls our freedom to read, to be spoken to, and to be silent.

When I say that I believe in censorship, I trust you will read on. The following things are forms of censorship in which one may believe to greater or lesser extent: the general idea of law and order, the penal and civil codes, the tax law, Emily Post, custom and habit, conscience, religion, and the editorial process—not necessarily in that order. At the bottom of the list stand a few pale and timid moral laws, some of which become energized on rare occasions by the First Amendment to the Constitution. This Amendment compels us, if we think about it, to speak freely and fully, or answer for it. Nothing less than the whole truth will do, in the long run, provided it be in fact the truth; but the full light of the First Amendment becomes a bit embarrassing when turned upon some of the darker corners of our living. The trouble is not with free speech but with free truth, and this may be one reason why a book that has become a classic has little to fear from the law. Two things have happened to it: it has been accepted as truth, and perhaps on that account it has ceased to be interesting. We think we love truth more than we actually do.

Truth has a way of shifting under pressure. If you must know what truth is, Holmes said that it was what he couldn't help thinking, with the surmise that his "can't helps" were not necessarily cosmic. It is largely a matter of what agitates society at the moment, for while men are always on fire over their opinions, they are rarely so on more than one front at a time. For a long time the front was religious heresy, then it was political nonconformity, then it was sexual immorality, and recently it has swung to treason. Primary attention just now does not focus on heresy, political independence, or immorality so long as we are concerned with annihilation by the hydrogen bomb.

The real question is not the freedom to read, to speak, or to be silent. It is rather the courage to do these things. The legal freedoms exist, but now and then a price is put upon them. And it is the price that effectively destroys the freedom, people being what they are. This can be vicious, for the freedoms ostensibly remain. So long as a man howl with the wolves, he may say whatever monstrous thing occurs to him; if he howls against the wolves, it may cost him his job, his social position, and perhaps his liberty. Free speech is at a minimum in the areas of the fighting faiths.

The reading public has little to fear at present from the legal censor. Last December a Congressional Committee published its report on pornographic material. It found that an appalling amount of it exists, mostly in little books. The Committee's conclusions are interesting. They begin with the statement that the members had found it necessary during the hearings to make public announcements that the very idea of censorship was as repugnant to them as it was to the publishing industry. Three recommendations followed: one, legislation making illegal the distribution of obscene material in interstate commerce; two, legislation authorizing the Postmaster General to impound mail pending hearings and exempting the Post Office Department from certain delaying procedures; three, an appeal to the publishing industry to eliminate "borderline" literature on its own initiative.

This very modest effort does illuminate, I think unconsciously, the real answer. Communications that reach the widest audiences are as pure as the driven snow through voluntary censorship. The movie industry has censored itself almost to the point of chronic anemia; state censors have little to do but look. Magazines with circulations in the millions are morally unobjectionable because of a sound balance between decency in their publishers and the knowledge that the public will not stand for lesser values. As for the nasty little books that circulate from beneath the counter, the best law to deal with them would be one to compel their display on top of the counter: dirt for dirt's sake flourishes best in the dark.

Books appear to offend mostly because their circulation is in thousands rather than millions, and because what might otherwise be pure obscenity takes its place, as valid as it may be unpleasant, in any serious effort to show life as it is. Given such an effort, obscenity stubbornly defies all efforts to define it. Even the Congressional Committee could do no better, although it tried hard, than to assert that everybody knows what obscenity is, even if it is difficult to define.

This, of course, is arrant nonsense. The conception of obscenity has run the gamut from the Victorian editor who deleted the word "chaste" because it was suggestive, to the United States Courts that cleared Joyce's "Ulysses," which contains all the four-letter words in the lexicon of impurity.

You need not worry about your freedom to read. There will always be a law against obscenity, for it is considered a handy gun to be kept hanging on the wall in case the situation should get out of control. But it is not the temper of the times to enforce it: even in Massachusetts, where they try the book rather than the publisher, the question is becoming residual and censorship is at most a minor annoyance.

It is not legal censorship that I believe in but the kind that exists in every person and flowers best in the free air of competitive discussion. It forwards the development of taste, and in the public market no holds need be barred. Justice Brandeis said in the case of Whitney v. California: "No danger flowing from speech can be deemed clear and present unless the incidence of the evil apprehended is so imminent that it may befall before there is opportunity for full discussion." It is hard to see how obscene speech could result in danger before the community had a chance to answer back. The public has been answering back since the time when Plato said that Homer should be expurgated before Greek children should be allowed to read him.

We are a very moral nation, and our high divorce rate has little to do with it. The primary cause of divorce is marriage, not sexual irregularity, and divorce will not slacken until we learn better how to marry. I do not believe that our morality was born of any law against obscene speech and behavior. The United States took its law from England as it existed at the time of the Revolution, and the entire English law against obscenity rests upon one Court decision in 1727 and one statement by Blackstone that obscenity was indictable at common law. On these two commandments hang all the law and the prophets.

For almost a hundred years after the Revolution we got along without laws on the subject. Suppression has been a phase. Today the consensus of preference is for disclosure rather than stealth, and that in itself is a moral code. The present public attitude is that of the thoughtful gentleman who invented an eleven-foot pole so he could touch all the things he wouldn't touch with a ten-foot pole. Hence I believe in the censorship of the open market rather than of the police station. A ban keeps up both the demand and the profits; when the market is open the demand seals itself off and is limited to the sick in mind and spirit who will be with us until we become wise enough to heal them.

Above the bare legal right to speak or to read is the courage to use these rights well: to speak clearly, bravely, and accurately, and to read with understanding. On the other side is the right to maintain a lighted silence, and this right must still be fought for.

For the first time in our history we are positively required to speak when we may choose not to speak, or we are frightened into silence when we might otherwise choose to speak out. This is a new kind of censorship for us, although it is not new in the long record of man's repression of man. If free and loyal men must swear fealty by words more stringent on the conscience than those required by the Constitution itself, then why not fealty to a particular church or political party or code of conduct? Men have had to do these things in the past, with their necks as hostage if they refused. It was not for fealty by fear that America was discovered, colonized, and matured. This is not the voice of America at Valley Forge, the Alamo, or the Bulge. It is the voice of the enemy within imitating the methods of the enemy without.

The freedom to read does not mean the right to sit by the fire with a book. It means the right to listen to a free voice speaking from the page, the right of that voice to speak fully to our condition, and our right to reply in freedom or to remain quiet if we will.

The voice is what matters, its quality of speech and its quality of expressive silence. It must be the voice of Jefferson speaking of the illimitable freedom of the human mind, and with him Washington and Hamilton and Lincoln and Wilson and Roosevelt. Why should the conscience of America be of less worth than when our enemy was on our soil? Unless that conscience is as good now as it was then, there has been a wastage of history. It is time, in the vitality of our liberty, to turn to the first principles of the American revolution, not to the fear or imitation of the methods of any other.

Index

Abbey Theatre, 381, 382, 387, 390
Abbott, Lyman, 188
Abrams Case, 314
Adams, Brooks, 453
AE (George William Russell), 379, 381, 384, 387; "The Censorship in Ireland," 381, 391–93
Aeschylus, 279
Ajaev, *Far from Moscow,* 421
Akhmatova, Anna, 423
Alcott, Louisa May, 182
Alexandrian Library, 3
Algren, Nelson, 137
Alien and Sedition Acts, 228
Allen, Hervey, 379; *Anthony Adverse,* 305; *Toward Morning,* 305
Allwardt, Elizabeth, 305
Alpert, Leo M., 123; "Judicial Censorship of Obscene Literature," 52–67; "Naughty, Naughty!" 4–8

Alsop, Joseph and Stewart, 245
American Bar Association, "On the Freedom to Read," 302, 341–42
American Book Publishers Council, 134, 302, 306, 333, 337
American Civil Liberties Union, 134–38, 141, 142, 189
American Legion, 134, 145, 305, 308, 332, 352, 363
American Library Association, xii, 134, 302, 306, 333; Freedom To Read, 337–39; Intellectual Freedom Committee, 307, 351; Library Bill of Rights, 336, 371; Overseas Libraries Statement, 339–40; Statement on Labeling, 336–37
American Mercury, 202, 278
American Parents Committee on Education, 345

American Youth Commission, 66
Americans for Democratic Action, 370
Andersen, Hans Christian, 125, 146, 147, 148
Anderson, Archibald W., "'The Nation' Case," 353–59
Anderson, Margaret, 186
Anderson, Sherwood, 333; *Dark Laughter,* 166, 184
Anniston Star, 375
Apuleius, Lucius, 379; *The Golden Ass,* 83, 181, 184
Arabian Nights, 59, 83, 88, 164, 180
Aragon, Louis, 422, 424
Archdiocese Council of Catholic Women of Chicago, 29, 326
Aretino, Pietro, 164
Aristophanes, 87, 103, 171; *Lysistrata,* 37, 127, 218

462 Index

Arlen, Michael, 163; *The Green Hat,* 321; *Young Men in Love,* 184
Armstrong, O. K., "Treason in the Textbooks," 345
Arnold, Thurman, 89
Aronson, Jacob, 364
Arthur, T. S., *Ten Nights in a Bar Room,* 282
Asbury, Herbert, "Hatrack," 184, 202
Asch, Sholem, 402
Association of the Bar of the City of New York, 247
Auchincloss, Louis, 137
Authors League of America, "Freedom To Write," 252–53

Babayevsky, Semyon, *The Knight of the Golden Star,* 421
Babel, Isaak E., *Red Cavalry,* 420
Balchin, Nigel, *Small Back Room,* 402
Balzac, Honoré de, 164, 279, 391, 418, 424; *Droll Stories,* 118–19, 127
Band, William and Claire, *Two Years with the Chinese Communists,* 306
Banning, Margaret Culkin, 196, 201; "The Restricted Shelf," 320–23
Bard, Guy K., 286–301
Barrington, Margaret, 378; "The Censorship in Eire," 381, 398–402
Barth, Alan, *Government by Investigation,* 243
Bartlesville, Oklahoma, Public Library, 303, 304
Bates, H. E., 402
Bates, Ralph, 402
Baum, Vicki, 137
Bazilescu, Aristide, *Political Economy,* 427
Beard, Charles A., 346; *The Republic,* 440
Becker, Carl, 129
Beckett, Samuel, 402
Bell, Neil, *Three Pair of Heels,* 402
Bell, 399
Berkeley, William, 129
Berninghausen, David K., 351
Besant, Annie, 75, 102, 186
Bible, 123, 135, 149, 165, 186, 286, 333
Birth control, 192, 193, 390
Birth of a Nation (film), 145, 153, 155, 405
Black, Douglas M., 205
Black Lust, 64
Blackstone, William, 68, 100, 459

Blaich, Theodore P., and Baumgartner, J. C., *The Challenge of Democracy,* 375
Blanshard, Paul, 316, 353; *American Freedom and Catholic Power,* 180; "Sex and Obscenity," 181–93
Blasphemy, 98
Bloy, Leon, 151
Blum, Léon, 402
Boak, A. E. R., and others, *World History,* 368
Boccaccio, Giovanni, 87, 149; *Decameron,* 59, 83, 88, 127, 150, 180, 184, 320, 402
Bok, Curtis, 115, 119, 131, 148–49, 185, 187, 201, 206–7, 429; "Commonwealth v. Gordon et al.," 93–114; "The Duty of Freedom," 457–60
Bolte, Charles G., "Security through Book Burning," 242–47
Bonner, Paul Hyde, 137, 138
Borrow, George, *Lavengro,* 379
Boston Herald, 304, 305
Boston Post, 304
Boston Public Library, 304–5
Bourdet, Édouard, 279
Bow, Frank, 248
Bowdler, Thomas, *The Family Shakespeare,* 14–18, 65
Bowles, Paul, 137
Boyd, Julian P., "Subversive of What?" 224–30
Boyle, Kay, 402
Boynton, Edward C., 367
Bradlaugh, Charles, 75
Bradley, F. H., 320
Brandeis, Louis D., xi, 92, 108–9, 113, 116, 314, 315, 316, 448, 459
Brayton, Charles R., 446
Brennan, Mrs. Martin J., 367
Brentford, William, "Censorship of Books," 179
Bridges v. *California,* 110
Brieux, Eugène, 262; *Maternité,* 265; *The Three Daughters of Monsieur Dupont,* 265
Briffault, Robert, *Europa,* 320
Brod, Max, 402
Brogan, Denis, 231
Bromfield, Louis, 248, 424; *A Good Woman,* 320
Brontë, Charlotte, 75; *Jane Eyre,* 46, 99, 162–63, 173, 174
Broun, Heywood, 381; "Censoring the Censor," 273–75; "It Seems to Heywood Broun," 404–6
Brown, Courtney C., 364
Brown, John Mason, "Wishful Banning," 155–58
Brown, Ruth, 303, 304, 309
Browning, Elizabeth Barrett, *Aurora Leigh,* 99, 163

Browning, Robert, *Men and Women,* 182
Brustat, August W., 368–69
Budenz, Louis F., *Men without Faces,* 368–69
Bukharin, Nikolai I., 420
Bullett, Gerald, 402
Burke, Edmund, 442
Burns, John Horne, 137
Burstyn v. *Wilson,* 51–52
Butler, Samuel, 255
Butler v. *Michigan,* 51
Buxton, Frank W., 304
Byrne, Donn, 406
Byron, George Gordon, 65, 75, 89, 279, 424, 442; *Cain,* 4, 56; *Don Juan,* 4–5, 46

Cabell, James Branch, 279; *Jurgen,* 163, 184, 274, 275, 277, 280, 322
Caesar, Julius, 3
Cain, James M., 137
Cairns, Huntington, 151, 317
Caldwell, Erskine, 137, 286, 379; *God's Little Acre,* 7, 60–61, 95, 96, 187, 320; *Tobacco Road,* 7, 95
Calhoun, John C., 451, 452
Campbell, John, 50, 74–75, 102
Camus, Albert, 379
Canfield, Dorothy, *Her Son's Wife,* 320
Capek, Karel, 410, 411
Cardozo, Benjamin N., 60, 162; *The Paradoxes of Legal Science,* 105
Carlyle, Thomas, 255, 260
Carnovsky, Leon, "The Obligations and Responsibilities of the Librarian concerning Censorship," 312–20
Carson, Ellis H., 363
Cary, Joyce, 137, 138, 379
Casanova, Giovanni, *Memoirs,* 83, 184
Case, Herbert W., 146–48, 149
Cather, Willa, *Death Comes to the Archbishop,* 379
Catholic Church, 8–9, 316, 353–59
Catholic Truth Society, 378, 389, 398
Catton, Bruce, xii
Causton, Bernard, *Keeping It Dark,* 272–73
Celine, Louis Ferdinand, 402
Celler, Emmanuel, 207, 333
Cellini, Benvenuto, *Life,* 180
Censorship: Chinese, 2–3; Irish, 68, 378–406
Cerf, Bennett, 186
Chafee, Zechariah, Jr., 29, 38, 54, 130, 316, 317, 318, 319, 429; *Free Speech in the United States,* 315; "Why I Like America," 437–49
Chalmers, Ruth Nash, 361, 365

Channing, William Ellery, 235
Chaplinsky v. *New Hampshire,* 110
Chase, J. Franklin, 183, 184, 202
Chaucer, Geoffrey, 87, 102, 127, 147
Chekhov, Anton, 299, 418
Cherry Tree Carol, 384, 385, 389, 391
Chesterfield, Philip, Earl of, *Letters to His Son,* 182
Chesterton, G. K., 26
Chicago Sun-Times, 334
Chicago Tribune, 133
Chicago Vice Commission, 190
Christian Science Monitor, 305
Christian Scientists, 145, 316
Christie, Agatha, *The Unknown Threatens,* 424
Churchill, Winston, 155–56
Clark, Tom C., 52, 123, 124, 125
Clarke, Austin, 402; *The Sun Dances at Easter,* 402
Clift, David H., "Enduring Rights," 331–36
Cockburn, Alexander, 22, 50–51, 57, 61, 63–64, 73, 75, 102, 122, 148, 149, 185, 317
Comic books, 72, 125, 126
Commager, Henry Steele, "Free Enterprise in Ideas," 230–35
Commonweal, 378
Commonwealth v. *Gordon,* 93–114
Commonwealth v. *Landis,* 101
Comstock, Anthony, 39, 62, 93, 165, 182–83, 184, 192, 195, 273, 276–77, 279
Conant, James B., 436
Concannon, Helena, 400
Conference of American Small Business Organizations, 343
Confessional Unmasked, 50, 57, 103, 317
Congressional Record, 441
Connell, Vivian, *The Chinese Room,* 37
Connelly, Marc, *The Green Pastures,* 145, 157
Connors, Bradley, 308
Consumer's Research, 303
Consumers Union, *Report on Contraceptive Materials,* 192
Coolidge, Albert Sprague, 327–29
Coolidge, Elizabeth Sprague, 327
Cooper, Thomas, 454
Corbin (Ky.) Public Library, 284–86
Cork Examiner, 399
Coudert, Frederic R., Jr., 249
Coughlin, Charles E., 362
Counterattack, 361, 363
Counts, George S., *The Challenge of Soviet Education,* 408
Cousins, Norman, 231
Cozzens, James G., 286

Crist, Judith, 363
Cronin, A. J., 424, 427
Cross, Eric, *The Tailor and Ansty,* 400
Cunningham, Charles, 305
Curll, Edmund, 4, 53
Curran, Henry, 96, 187
Cutting, Bronson, 6, 164

Daiken, Leslie, 388
Daily Worker, 304, 365
Dakin, Edward, 316
Daniels, Jonathan, 323
Dante, *Divine Comedy,* 135
Darvas, Joseph, 427
Darwin, Charles, 255, 268, 396; *The Origin of Species,* 389
Daughters of the American Revolution, 352
Davie, Emily, "'Profile' and the Congressional Censors," 247–50; *Profile of America,* 247–50
Davis, Elmer, 429; "Are We Worth Saving?" 430–37
Davis, Jefferson, 452
Davis, Katharine, 168
Davis, Maxine, *Woman's Medical Problems,* 192
Davis, Richard Harding, 448
Dean, Vera Micheles, 368
De Beus, J. G., 434
De Castro, Fernando Bermúdez, 402
Deevy, Teresa, 399, 401
De Jonge v. *Oregon,* 109
Dennett, Mary Ware, *The Sex Side of Life,* 63, 76–80, 82–83, 189
Detroit Police License and Censor Bureau, 29, 30–31, 135, 146–48
De Valera, Eamon, 395–96, 397, 398, 401, 403
De Voto, Bernard, 188, 210, 286; "The Case of the Censorious Congressmen," 205–9; "The Easy Chair," 201–5
Dewey, John, 365; *Human Nature and Conduct,* 293
Dial, 384
Dickens, Charles, 69, 123, 272–73, 418, 424; *American Notes,* 154; *Martin Chuzzlewit,* 154; *Oliver Twist,* 145, 152, 153–54, 156, 362
Diderot, Denis, 424
Dilling, Elizabeth, *The Red Network,* 345
Disney, Walt, "Uncle Remus," 153
Dohrenwend, Otto, 361, 362, 363, 364, 366, 367, 368
Donahue, Frank J., 304
Dos Passos, John, 137, 138, 147, 149, 161, 379, 402, 428; *Manhattan Transfer,* 184; *1919,* 147; *Three Soldiers,* 166; *U.S.A.,* 99

Dostoevski, Feodor, 162, 290, 419; *Crime and Punishment,* 379
Douglas, William O., 116, 142; "Censorship and Prior Restraint," 41–45; "Hannegan, Postmaster General, v. Esquire, Inc.," 89–92
Downs, R. B., 340–41; "The Book Burners Cannot Win," 310–12
Doyle, Lynn, 398
Dreiser, Theodore, 275, 280, 286, 422; *An American Tragedy,* 6, 42, 58, 65, 106, 164, 165, 184, 278, 333; *The Genius,* 6, 59, 184, 277; *Jennie Gerhardt,* 6, 163; *Sister Carrie,* 6, 59, 276, 280
Dublin International Theatre Festival, 381
Dufief, Nicholas, 224–25, 227
Du Gard, Roger Martin, 422
Du Maurier, George, *Trilby,* 99, 163
Du Maurier, Guy, *An Englishman's Home,* 260

Eaton, Walter Prichard, 438
Eddy, Mary Baker, 316
Educational Reviewer, 343, 350
Edwardes, George, 261
Ehrenburg, Ilya, 416, 424
Einstein, Albert, 410; *Theory of Relativity,* 306
Eisenhower, Dwight, 29, 244, 250, 302, 303, 332, 336, 434; "Letter on Intellectual Freedom," 340–41
Eldon, John Scott, 4, 55–56, 63, 89
Eliot, George, 75; *Adam Bede,* 99, 163; *Mill on the Floss,* 174
Eliot, T. S., 386
Ellis, Havelock, 60, 67, 83, 181, 279, 320; "Obscenity and the Censor," 168–70; *Studies in the Psychology of Sex,* 147, 186
Encyclopaedia of the Social Sciences, 312
Encyclopaedia Britannica, 127
Endre, Sos, 428
Engels, Friedrich, 417
Ernst, Morris, 148, 156, 166, 186; *The Censor Marches On,* 99; *To the Pure,* 99, 167–70, 186
Erskine, John, *The Private Life of Helen of Troy,* 184
Ervine, St. John, *The Wayward Man,* 166
Esquire, 89–93
Euripides, 263
Evans, Augusta J., *Beulah,* 282; *Inez,* 282; *St. Elmo,* 282
Evans, Ifor, 70
Evans, Luther H., 351

Fadeyev, Aleksandr, *Young Guard,* 424

464 Index

Farmer, Arthur E., 287–90, 294, 300, 301
Farnham, Marynia, 205
Farrell, James T., 137, 146, 161, 379; "The Author as Plaintiff," 286–301; *Father and Son*, 289; *Judgment Day*, 94, 286, 287; *My Days of Anger*, 289; *No Star Is Lost*, 289; *Studs Lonigan*, 286, 287–94; *A World I Never Made*, 95, 96, 148, 187, 289, 297, 298, 299; *Young Lonigan*, 94, 286, 287; *The Young Manhood of Studs Lonigan*, 94, 286, 287–94
Fast, Howard, 360, 361, 362, 365, 367, 422; *The American*, 362; *Citizen Tom Paine*, 366, 367; *Haym Salomon*, 362
Faulkner, William, 137, 138, 149, 161, 163, 166, 379, 402; *Sanctuary*, 95, 187, 322; *Wild Palms*, 95
Feder, Edward L., *Comic Book Regulation*, 125
Federation of Women's Clubs, 352
Fellman, David, "The Censorship of Books," 51, 223–24
Feuchtwanger, Lion, 162; *Power*, 184
Fielding, Henry, 273; *Tom Jones*, 59, 120, 127, 165
Fine, Benjamin, "The Truth about Schoolbook Censorship," 349–52
Finney, Burnham, 363
Fischer, John, "The Harm Good People Do," 138–41
Fisher, Dorothy Canfield, *Fables for Parents*, 306
Fison, Lorimer, 182
Fitzgerald, Barry, 381, 399, 400
Fitzgerald, F. Scott, 379; *This Side of Paradise*, 203
Fitzgerald, Thomas J., 136, 138
Flaubert, Gustave, 289, 396–97; *November*, 61
Flues, A. Gilmore, 331
Flynn, John, 306
Forbes, Bertie C., 345, 346
Ford, Henry, 437
Ford, John Anson, "We Will Gamble on the American," 329–31
Foreign Agents Registration Act, 33–35
Foreign Policy Association, 368
Forster, E. M., 167
Fortune, 192
France, Anatole, 379, 389, 402
Frank, Jerome, "Roth v. Goldman," 115–19; "United States v. Roth," 119–32
Frank, Leonhard, 402
Frankel, Nathan, 357
Frankfurter, Felix, 51, 92–93, 111, 115, 116
"Frankie and Johnnie," 106

Franklin, Benjamin, 101, 120, 235, 434
Freedom To Read Statement, 306, 333, 337–39
Freud, Sigmund, 167, 188; *General Introduction to Psychoanalysis*, 181
Friedman, Lee M., 304
Fries, Amos A., 345
Fuller, Harry, 407
Fund for the Republic, xii

Galion (Ohio) *Inquirer*, 305
Galsworthy, John, 379; "About Censorship," 265–70
Garland, Hamlin, *Rose of Dutcher's Coolly*, 163
Garnett, Edward, *The Breaking Point*, 265
Garrison, William Lloyd, 451, 452
Gaskell, Elizabeth Cleghorn, 75
Gathings Committee, 147, 149, 185, 196–98, 201, 205–9, 458
Gautier, Théophile, *Mademoiselle de Maupin*, 60, 87, 106, 164, 277
Gedye, G. E. R., *Betrayal in Central Europe*, 408; "What a Book Famine Means," 408–10
Gellhorn, Martha, 402
Gellhorn, Walter, 358; *Individual Freedom and Governmental Restraints*, 51; "Restraints on Book Reading," 19–41; *Security, Loyalty, and Science*, 233
Georgia State Literature Commission, 29, 30
Gibbon, Edward, 433; *Decline and Fall of the Roman Empire*, 14
Gide, André, *If It Die*, 7, 61, 68
Gitlow v. New York, 109
Glueck, Sheldon and Eleanor, 25, 123; *Unravelling Juvenile Delinquency*, 72
Glyn, Elinor, *Three Weeks*, 23, 57–58, 214, 276
Goethe, 116, 129, 424; *Faust*, 423
Gogarty, St. John, 68
Gogol, Nikolai V., 418, 423
Goldman, Emma, 280
Goodman, Walter, "How To Deal with Obscene Books," 161
Gordey, Michel, "What You Can Read in Russia," 417–24
Gordon, Robert, 363, 364, 367
Gorer, Geoffrey, 191
Gorky, Maxim, 418, 422
Goslin, Ryllis Clair, and others, *American Democracy Today and Tomorrow*, 368
Goslin, Willard E., 133–34
Gosse, Edmund, 1–2
Gotshal, Sylvan, 363
Graham, Shirley, 362, 368

Granville-Barker (Barker), Harley, *Waste*, 265
Gray, James, *Shoulder the Sky*, 320
Great Britain, *Report of the Royal Commission on Population*, 68
Great Soviet Encyclopedia, 421
Green, Henry, 402; *Doting*, 402
Greene, Graham, 379, 400, 402; *The End of the Affair*, 68; *The Heart of the Matter*, 68, 403
Gregory, Horace, 170–71
Grierson, Herbert, 387
Griffin, John H., *The Devil Rides Outside*, 148; "Prude and the Lewd," 148–51
Grimm, Jacob, 125, 428
Griswold, Whitney, 41
Grosjean v. American Press Co., 45
Grothaus, Julia, 306–7
Guseinov, G., 421
Guthrie, A. B., Jr., *The Big Sky*, 284–86; "The Peter Rabbit Library," 285–86

Hackett, Francis, *The Green Lion*, 381, 393, 397; "A Muzzle Made in Ireland," 381, 393–98
Haight, Anne Lyon, *Banned Books*, 100
Haines, Helen, 322
Halecki, Oscar, 363, 365
Hall, Radclyffe, 137; *The Well of Loneliness*, 7, 60, 75, 186, 191
Halpenny, Marie Sien, 307
Hamilton, Alexander, 101, 438, 460
Hamsun, Knut, 402
Hance, Mildred G., 306, 307
Hancock, John M., 364
Hand, Augustus N., 63, 74, 104–5, 113, 115, 118, 189, 206; "United States v. Dennett," 76–80; "United States v. 'Ulysses,'" 86–89
Hand, Learned, 28, 63, 64, 149, 167, 185, 223, 436
Hannegan, Robert E., 89–93
Hannegan, Postmaster General, v. Esquire, Inc., 43, 89–93
Hanser, Richard, "Shakespeare, Sex ... and Dr. Bowdler," 15–18
Hardy, Thomas, 75, 162; *Jude the Obscure*, 99; *Tess of the d'Urbervilles*, 99, 379
Harlow, Ralph V., *Story of America*, 368
Harris, Frank, *My Life and Loves*, 215
Harris, M. H., 307
Harrison, Austin, "Literature and the Policeman," 46–49
Hart, Merwin K., 233, 345, 346
Hasek, Jaroslav, *The Good Soldier Schweik*, 402
Hawthorne, Nathaniel, *Scarlet*

Letter, 23, 99, 135, 182, 333
Hays, Arthur Garfield, 58
Hayworth, Rita, 200
Heggen, Thomas, 137; *Mister Roberts,* 139
Heine, Heinrich, 410, 411, 424
Heller, Louis B., 190
Helmholtz, Hermann L. F. von, 255
Hemingway, Ernest, 137, 138, 146, 147, 149, 161, 166, 284, 286, 326, 379, 397, 402, 422; *Across the River and into the Trees,* 148; *For Whom the Bell Tolls,* 99, 403; *The Sun Also Rises,* 166, 184; *To Have and Have Not,* 146, 320, 321
Henderson, Archibald, 253
Heptameron of Queen Margaret of Navarre, 59, 88, 102, 103
Herbert, Alan, 160
Hergesheimer, Joseph, 402
Herndon v. Lowry, 109
Hetherington, Henry, 5
Higgins, F. R., 386
Himes, Norman, 192; *Your Marriage,* 189-90
Hindus, Maurice, 402
Hitler, Adolf, *Mein Kampf,* 320, 330, 407
Hobbes, Thomas, 272; *Leviathan,* 401
Hogan, Robert, 381
Holmes, John Haynes, "Sensitivity as Censor," 152-55
Holmes, Oliver Wendell, 44, 92, 105, 108-9, 113, 116, 126, 243, 313, 314, 315, 452, 456, 458
Homer, 103; *Odyssey,* 135
Homosexuality, 191, 200
Hoover, J. Edgar, 24
Hornung, Ernest W., *Raffles,* 320
Horvath, Marton, 428
Hotten, John Camden, 6
Hoult, Norah, 402
Housman, Laurence, *Bethlehem,* 265
Howard, Sidney, *They Knew What They Wanted,* 405
Hudson, G. F., 432, 433, 436
Hughes, Charles Evans, 42, 110, 315-16
Hughes, Langston, 368
Hugo, Victor, 418, 424; *The Hunchback of Notre Dame,* 379
Hullfish, H. Gordon, 358
Humphreys, Harry E., 364
Hurst, Fannie, *Back Street,* 99
Huxley, Aldous, 137, 149, 161, 186, 379, 397, 402; *Antic Hay,* 184; *Brave New World,* 403; "Censorship," 272-73; *Eyeless in Gaza,* 321; *Point Counter Point,* 68; "Vulgarity in Literature," 210-13
Huxley, Thomas Henry, 255, 268

Ibáñez, Vicente Blasco, 402
Ibsen, Hendrik, 262, 382; *A Doll's House,* 262; *Ghosts,* 262, 263, 265
Illes, Bela, 427
Index Librorum Prohibitorum, 1-2, 97, 217, 222
Inglis, Brian, *The Freedom of the Press in Ireland, 1784-1841,* 381; "Smuggled Culture," 381, 402-04
Institute for American Democracy, 362
Irish Censorship Board, 68
Irish Press, 403
Irish Statesman, 381, 384, 385
Irish Times, 399, 401, 403
Irving, Henry, 153, 258
Isherwood, Christopher, 137, 402
Izvestia, 244, 304

Jackson, Andrew, 450
Jackson, Charles, *Fall of Valor,* 191
Jackson, Robert H., 32, 124
Jahoda, Marie, 25; *The Impact of Literature,* 124, 125
James, Henry, 123; *The Turn of the Screw,* 135
James, William, 233
Jameson, Storm, 402
Jansen, William, 353-59
Jefferson, Thomas, 101, 113-14, 117, 120, 121, 129, 224-30, 434, 438, 440, 449, 452, 454, 460
Jehovah's Witnesses, 315
Jersey City Board of Education, 370, 371
Jersey City Junior College, 370
Jilemnick, Peter, 424
Johnson, Gerald W., 429, 449-50; "Freedom of Inquiry Is for Hopeful People," 450-57
Johnson, Robert L., 308
Johnson, Samuel, *Dictionary,* 65
Johnston, Denis, 402
Jones, James, 137, 161; *From Here to Eternity,* 37, 139, 148, 183-84
Joo, Tibor, *Hungarian Nationalism,* 427
Joyce, James, 75, 428; *Ulysses,* 7, 51, 63-64, 74, 83-89, 98, 104, 118, 163, 167, 186, 318, 326, 381, 397, 403, 459
Jung, Carl Gustav, 167
Juvenile delinquency, 72, 123-26

Kafka, Franz, 294
Kamenev, Lev Borisovich, 412
Karpovitch, Michael, 432
Kauffmann, Sidney, *The Philanderer,* 51
Kaus, Gina, 402
Kavanagh, Peter, 382
Keane, John, 399, 400, 401

Keats, John, 46, 65
Kelly, Walt, 242
Kempton, Murray, 244
Kennan, George, 28, 436
Kennedy, John F., 141
Kennedy, Renwick C., "Alabama Book-Toasters," 375-77
Kent, Rockwell, 31
Kenworthey, Charles E., 287, 290, 291, 292
Kernan, William C., 362, 363, 365, 366, 367, 368
Khan, Sayers, 427
Kilgore, Harley M., 249
King of Kings (film), 405
Kinsey, Alfred, 31, 99; *Sexual Behavior in the Human Female,* 71, 190, 191; *Sexual Behavior in the Human Male,* 190
Kirkpatrick, William H., 82
Knopf, Alfred, 203
Koch, Henry C., 363
Koestler, Arthur, 137, 138, 161, 379; *Arrival and Departure,* 99
Kopecky, Vaclav, 426
Kovacs v. Cooper, 111
Krebiozen Research Foundation v. Beacon Press, 43
Kronenberger, Louis, 156

La Follette, Robert M., 446
Lardner, John, 134; "Let 'em Eat Newspapers," 146-47; "The Smut Detective," 147-48
Larmon, Sigurd S., 364
Larrabee, Eric, 23; "The Cultural Context of Sex Censorship," 193-201
Laski, Harold, 230
Laski, Marghanita, 159-60
Lasky, Victor, 247
Lasswell, Harold D., "Politics and Subversion," 235-42
Laver, James, 402
Lawrence, D. H., 67-68, 69, 137, 161, 163, 326; *Lady Chatterley's Lover,* 6, 58, 106, 170, 186, 272; "Pornography and Obscenity," 171-80; *The Rainbow,* 75, 170
Lawrence, T. E., *The Mint,* 70
Leabharlann, An, 379-80
Leach, John, 4, 56
Leach v. Carlile, 44, 93
League of Women Voters, 444, 447
Leclercq, Jacques, 140, 217
Lee, Robert E., 438
Legman, Gershon, *Love and Death,* 200
Lenin, Nikolai, 27, 243, 417, 420
Leo XIII, 222
Lerner, Max, "On Lynching a Book," 209-10
Lewis, C. S., 69

466 Index

Lewis, Sinclair, 275, 286, 379, 422; *Ann Vickers,* 321; *Elmer Gantry,* 166, 184
Lewis, Theodore N., 156
Life, 27, 188, 305, 379; "Birth of a Baby," 99
Lilienthal, David, 449
Lincoln, Abraham, 438, 449, 456, 460
Lindbergh, Charles A., 248
Lindey, Alexander, 186
Link, Henry C., *The Return to Religion,* 363
Linklater, Eric, 379, 402
Linnaeus, Carolus, 255
Lin Yutang, 425
Lippmann, Walter, 435
Little Black Sambo, 157
Little Review, 7, 186
Litvinoff, Maxim, 412
Liveright, Horace B., 65
Loewenberg, Bert James, 368
Long, Huey, 45
Loos, Anita, *Gentlemen Prefer Blondes,* 279
Lord, Milton E., 304, 305
Lord, Robert H., 304
Losonczy, Geza, 428
Louisville Times, 333
Lovell v. Griffin, 44–45, 109, 315
Lowell, James Russell, 335
Lukács, György, 428
Lyndhurst, John S. Copley, 75
Lyon, George W., "Book Burners in History," 2–3
Lysenko, Trofim D., 420

McAllister, G. Stanley, 367, 369
Macaulay, Thomas B., 25–26, 114
MacCarthy, Desmond, 74
McCarthy, Joseph R., 233, 302, 306, 307, 308, 436, 437; *McCarthyism and the Fight for America,* 304
McClelland, Allan, *Bloomsday,* 381
McConahay, Edward O., 368
MacCormac, John, "Reading by Red Star Light," 417, 424–28
MacDonald, Patrick F., 304, 305
McKee, Joseph, 404
Mackenzie, Compton, *Greek Memories,* 162
MacLeish, Archibald, 353–59, 411, 438; "A Tower Which Will Not Yield," 323–29
Madeleine, 59, 106
Madison, James, 117, 120, 121
Maeterlinck, Maurice, 391; *Monna Vanna,* 265
Magennis, William, 398, 399, 400, 401
Magruder, Frank, *American Government,* 350

Mailer, Norman, 137, 161; *Barbary Shore,* 148; *The Naked and the Dead,* 319
Malinowski, Bronislaw, 181, 273
Malraux, André, 379, 402, 422; *The Walnut Trees of Attenburg,* 402
Mann, Thomas, 410, 422; *Joseph in Egypt,* 306; *The Magic Mountain,* 306
Manton, Martin T., 104
Marcus, J. Anthony, 365
Markham, Steve, *Honey, Not Now,* 402
Marshall, George, 449
Martin v. Struthers, 109
Marx, Karl, 324, 374, 417, 452; *Communist Manifesto,* 304; *Das Kapital,* 326, 389, 407
Mason, F. Van Wyck, 137
Masters, John, 137
Maugham, Somerset, 160, 379; *The Moon and Sixpence,* 424; *Of Human Bondage,* 99; *The Painted Veil,* 68
Maupassant, Guy de, 424
Mauriac, François, 149, 424
Maverick, Maury, 307
Mayakovski, Vladimir V., 424
Mazzini, Giuseppe, 442
Meiklejohn, Alexander, 357
Melville, Herman, 245; *Moby Dick,* 147
Memoirs of a Woman of Pleasure, 57
Memoirs of Fanny Hill, 166
Mencken, H. L., 59, 184, 202, 203, 204, 273, 275, 449; "Comstockery," 276–77
Meyer, Arthur S., 364
Midgard, Edward, *The Perfect Embrace,* 189
Mill, John Stuart, 129, 130, 444; *On Liberty,* 232, 313, 314
Miller, Arthur, *The Death of a Salesman,* 145
Miller, John Duncan, 436
Milton, John, 70, 122, 130, 155, 235, 411; *Areopagitica,* 8–14, 42, 129, 314
Milwaukee Publishing Co. v. Burleson, 92
Minneapolis Star-Tribune, 191
Miracle (film), 51–52, 142, 144, 384
Mitchell, Katharine, 306
Monroe, Marilyn, 199
Monsarrat, Nicholas, *The Cruel Sea,* 403
Montaigne, Michel, 181; *Essay on Some Lines of Virgil,* 127
Montgomery Advertiser, 375, 377
Montherlant, Henry Millon de, 402

Moore, George, 46, 47, 73, 75, 379, 400, 402
Moore, Kingsmill, 68
Moravia, Alberto, 9, 137; *Woman of Rome,* 37
Morgan, Charles, 379; *The Fountain,* 68, 99; *The Voyage,* 99
Morgan, James B., 375
Morley, John, 65
Motley, John L., *Rise of the Dutch Republic,* 66, 72, 123
Mt. Lebanon (Pa.) Public Library, 306
Moving-picture censorship, 142–43, 144
Moxon, Edward, 5
Mozart, Wolfgang, *Abduction from the Seraglio,* 426
Mukarovsky, Jan, 426
Mumford, L. Quincy, 327–28
Mumford, Lewis, 355, 359
Murad, Anatol, and others, *Basic Economics,* 350
Murdock v. Pennsylvania, 45
Murphy, Frank, 110
Murray, John Courtney, 136–37, 140, 161; "Literature and Censorship," 215–22
Musser v. Utah, 111
Muste, A. J., 34

Nagle, Alexander C., 364
Nathan, George Jean, 90; "On Censorship," 278–79; "A Programme for Censorship," 279–80
Nation, 27, 144, 145, 153, 154, 155, 157, 180, 303, 316, 353–59
Nation (London), 389
Nation, Carrie, 183
National Association for the Advancement of Colored People, 134, 145
National Book Awards, 136, 137, 138
National Council for Youth, 191
National Institute of Arts and Letters, 287
National Organization for Decent Literature, 29, 134–41, 150, 161, 192, 246
National Police Gazette, 101
National Society of College Teachers of Education, 358–59
Nature, 389
Near v. Minnesota, 42, 43, 110
Nearing, Scott, 279
Negro Digest, 303
Negroes, 438
Nelson, Lester W., 361
Neumann, Alfred, 162, 402
Neumann, Robert, 402
New England Watch and Ward Society, 6, 57, 134, 164, 165, 183, 184, 188, 202

Index 467

New Republic, 27, 303
New Statesman, 389
New World Review, 304
New York City Board of Education, 352
New York City Bureau of Social Hygiene, 66, 71–72
New York Herald Tribune, 363
New York News, 191
New York Society for the Suppression of Vice, 6, 7, 58, 59, 134, 165, 182–83, 184, 273
New York State Economic Council, 345
New York Times, 189, 190, 408, 409–10
New York University, 368
New Yorker, "Comments on New York Textbook Censorship," 352
Newlin, A. Chauncey, 363, 366, 367
Newman, Cardinal John Henry, 151
Newsweek, 140
Nexö, Andersen, 422
Nichols, Anne, *Abie's Irish Rose,* 405
Nobel Prize, 136, 137, 138, 149
North Carolina, University, 333

O'Brien, Kate, 68, 402; *The Land of Spices,* 400
Obscenity (definition), 82, 93–94, 98, 106–7, 112–13, 117, 194–95
O'Casey, Sean, 379, 386, 402; *The Drums of Father Ned,* 381; *The Plough and the Stars,* 381, 383, 385, 391; *The Shadow of a Gunman,* 379; *The Silver Tassie,* 387; *Within the Gates,* 162
O'Connor, Frank, 379, 386, 388, 401, 402, 404; *The Midnight Court,* 399
O'Donnell, Peadar, 399
O'Donnell, Thomas E., 363
O'Faolain, Sean, 68, 379, 388, 398, 399, 401, 402, 404
O'Flaherty, Liam, 68, 379, 381, 402; *The Informer,* 383; *Mr. Gilhooley,* 383
O'Hara, John, 137, 138, 161; *Appointment in Samarra,* 323; *The Farmer's Hotel,* 148; *Hellbox,* 402
O'Kelly, Sean T., 395
Olcott, Chauncey, *Abie's Irish Rose,* 405
O'Leary, Con, 402
O'Meara, Joseph, 141
O'Neill, Eugene, *Ah, Wilderness!* 249; *Anna Christie,* 99; *Desire under the Elms,* 29; *Hairy Ape,* 99; *Strange Interlude,* 162, 321
Ortega y Gasset, José, 28

Orwell, George, 72, 138, 433; *Animal Farm,* 411; *1984,* 68, 411, 431; "The Prevention of Literature," 411–17
Otis, James C., 192
Oursler, Will, 137
Ovid, *Art of Love,* 59, 88, 120, 127

Page, Walter Hines, 99, 166
Paine, Thomas, 256, 366, 367
Panova, Vera, *The Luminous Shore,* 421
Paperback books, 22, 206, 207
Pareto, Vilfredo, *Le Mythe Vertuiste,* 272
Parker, Dorothy, 368
Parsons, Edward L., 357
Partridge, Eric, *Shakespeare's Bawdy,* 17–18
Pascal, Blaise, 151, 402
Pasternak, Boris, 423
Paulus, John D., 306
Payne, James Bertrand, 5–6
Peters, J., *Manual on Party Organization,* 304
Petry, Ann, 137; *The Street,* 158
Phelps, William Lyon, 90
Philbrick, Herbert, *I Led Three Lives,* 304
Pierce v. *United States,* 315
Pilnyak, *The Volga Flows to the Caspian Sea,* 420
Pilot, 305
Pittsburgh Press, 306
Pius XII, 71
Planned Parenthood Federation of America, 192
Plato, 129; *The Republic,* 374
Plutarch, 336
Popenoe, Paul, *Preparing for Marriage,* 189
Postal censorship, 89–93
Potter, Thomas, 54
Pound, Cuthbert W., 106
Powys, John Cowper, 402
Pravda, 244, 304
Priestley, J. B., 106, 422
Prior restraint, 41–45
Prokosch, Frederic, 402
Proudhon, Pierre Joseph, 256
Proust, Marcel, 167, 179; *Remembrance of Things Past,* 68, 422
Publishers' Weekly, 335
Pulitzer Prize, 136, 137, 138, 149
Pushkin, Aleksandr S., 418, 423, 424
Putnam, Herbert, 328

Qua, Stanley E., 317
Quakers, 332
Queen v. *Read,* 53
Quinn, John, 384

Rabelais, François, 59, 83, 88, 120, 127, 164, 184
Rabinowitch, Eugene, 436
Randolph, John, 452
Ranke, Leopold von, 397
"Red Riding Hood," 428
Redman, Ben Ray, "Is Censorship Possible?" 213–15
Reed, Stanley F., 111
Regina v. *Hicklin,* 50, 56–57, 61, 63–64, 73–74, 79, 88, 100, 102, 103, 104, 105, 114, 122, 148, 185, 186, 195, 197
Reiman, Pavel, 425
Remarque, Erich Maria, 162, 402; *All Quiet on the Western Front,* 99, 163, 183; *Arch of Triumph,* 99
Revai, Joszef, 428
Rex v. *Curl,* 100
Rex v. *Wilkes,* 100
Rice, Elmer, *Imperial City,* 321, 323; "New Fashions in Censorship," 141–46
Richardson, Samuel, *Pamela,* 174
Ricksecker, Robert, 305
Riesman, David, 27
Robbins, Harold, 137; *Never Love a Stranger,* 96
Robertson, E. Arnot, *Four Frightened People,* 402
Robeson, Paul, 365
Robin Hood, 332
Robinson, James Harvey, 28
Robinson, Lennox, "The Madonna of Slieve Dun," 384
Romains, Jules, 402
Rooney, Hugh J., 368
Rooney, John J., 248, 249
Roosevelt, Franklin D., xi, 116, 130, 371, 440, 460
Rorty, James, "The Attack on Our Libraries," 303–10
Rosen v. *United States,* 132
Rossetti, Dante Gabriel, 382
Rostovtzeff, Michael Ivanovich, 433
Roth, Samuel, 114–132
Rothenstein, William, 388
Rousseau, J. J., *Confessions,* 59, 83, 164
Ruark, Robert, *Something of Value,* 184
Rudas, Laszlo, 428
Rudd, Augustin G., 345, 346
Rugg, Harold, "A Study in Censorship," 344–49
Ruggiero, Guido de, 396
Ruskin, John, 49, 65, 255
Russell, Bertrand, 160, 191, 431
Russell, George William, *see* AE
Rusznyak, Istvan, 426
Rutherford, George, 367

468 Index

Rutledge, Wiley B., 45, 110, 111
Ryan, James Francis, 287, 290, 291, 292, 293, 294, 295, 296, 298, 299, 300, 301

Sadleir, Michael, 402
St. George, Katharine, 248
St. Hubert Guild v. *Quinn*, 59
St. John-Stevas, Norman, "Obscenity, Literature and the Law," 67–75
Salinger, J. D., 137, 161; *The Catcher in the Rye*, 147–48
Saltykov-Shchedrin, 424
San Antonio Minute Women, 306, 307
San Antonio News, 307
San Antonio Public Library, 306–7
Sand, George, 119
Sandburg, Carl, "Murderers of Books," 410–11
Sanger, Margaret, *Family Limitation*, 192
Sappho, 99
Sapulpa High School Library, 350
Sarah Lawrence College, 368
Sardou, Victorien, 261
Saroyan, William, "A Cold Day," 281–84
Sartre, Jean Paul, 379; *The Respectful Prostitute*, 157
Savulescu, Traian, 427
Scarsdale Inquirer, 361, 364, 365, 369
Schaumber, I. H., 363, 365
Schenck v. *United States*, 108–9, 113, 314
Schnitzler, Arthur, 279; *Casanova's Homecoming*, 7, 60; *Reigen*, 7, 60
Scholastic, 345
Schroeder, Theodore, 168, 188
Schulberg, Budd, 137, 161
Scott, S. Spencer, 363
Scott, Walter, *Ivanhoe*, 152, 154, 156
Sedition, 98
Sedley, Charles, 4, 39, 52–53
Seldes, Gilbert, 90
Sender, Ramón, 402
Seymour, Gideon, 191
Shakespeare, William, 14–18, 102, 135, 286, 418, 423, 424, 426; *Hamlet*, 87, 156, 262; *Henry IV*, 152; *Julius Caesar*, 257–58; *The Merchant of Venice*, 145, 152, 153, 155, 156, 362; *Othello*, 152, 379; *Romeo and Juliet*, 63, 87; *Venus and Adonis*, 65, 87, 127
Shaplen, Robert, "Scarsdale's Battle of the Books," 359–70
Shapley, Harlow, 361
Sharp, Margery, 137
Sharpless v. *Commonwealth*, 100

Shaw, Archibald B., 361, 366, 369
Shaw, George Bernard, 47, 379, 391, 396, 397, 402, 406; *The Adventures of the Black Girl in Her Search for God*, 386, 403; *Androcles and the Lion*, 279; *Arms and the Man*, 257; *Mrs. Warren's Profession*, 71, 99, 265; "The Rejected Statement," 254–65; *The Shewing-Up of Blanco Posnet*, 254, 382
Shaw, Irwin, 137, 161; *The Young Lions*, 319
Shelley, Percy Bysshe, 46, 75, 270; *The Cenci*, 265; *Queen Mab*, 5, 56, 63, 89; *Swellfoot the Tyrant*, 5
Sholokhov, Mikhail A., 402, 424
Silone, Ignazio, 402
Simenon, Georges, 146
Simonov, Konstantin, 418
Sinclair, Upton, 422, 424; *Oil!* 164, 165, 184
Sitwell, Osbert, "On the Burning of Books," 270–71
Smart, Anne, 307
Smith, Alfred E., 446
Smith, Lillian, *Strange Fruit*, 38, 106, 146, 148, 188, 209–10, 317, 319
Smith, Samuel F., 430
Smith, William Gardner, *The Last of the Conquerors*, 158
Smollett, Tobias, 279
Smoot-Hawley Tariff Act, 83
Smyth, George W., 25
Society for the Suppression of Vice (England), 5, 15
Socrates, 279
Sokolsky, George E., 345
Sons of the American Revolution, 349
Sophocles, 263; *Oedipus Rex*, 265
Southey, Robert, 89; *Wat Tyler*, 4–5, 55–56, 63
Soviet Russia Today, 303
Spaulding, William E., 32
Spectator, 389
Spencer, Herbert, 255
Spengler, Oswald, 431, 433
Spillane, Mickey, 200
Spinoza, Baruch, 131
Spitz, David, "Milton's Testament," 8–14
Sproul, Allan, 364
Stable, Wintringham N., 51, 73
Stalin, Joseph, 412, 417, 423, 424, 425; *On the Patriotic War*, 419
Stall, Sylvanus, 277; *What a Man of 45 Ought To Know*, 189; *What a Young Girl Ought To Know*, 189
Stead, W. T., 168

Steen, Marguerite, *Phoenix Rising*, 402
Steinbeck, John, 280, 286, 379; *The Grapes of Wrath*, 424; "Some Random and Randy Thoughts on Books," **284**
Stephen, *Digest of Criminal Law*, 74
Stone, Harlan Fiske, 116
Stopes, Marie, 177–78, 192; *Contraception*, 112; *Married Love*, 80–83, 112
Strauss, Richard, *Salome*, 99
Streibert, Theodore, 249
Strong, Anna Louise, 361, 362, 365
Strong, L. A. G., 388
Stuart, Francis, 402
Stull, De Forest, *Our World Today*, 368
Styron, William, 137
Summerfield v. *Sunshine Book Co.*, 44
Summerfield, Arthur, 193
Sumner, John S., 59–61, 165, 202, 208, 273, 274
Sumner, William G., 83
Sutherland, Halliday, *Laws of Life*, 68, 400, 403
Swearingen v. *United States*, 98
Swift, Jonathan, 279
Swinburne, Algernon Charles, 75; *Poems and Ballads*, 5–6, 65, 270
Synge, J. M., 382; *The Playboy of the Western World*, 378, 381, 382, 385, 391, 405; *Well of the Saints*, 384
Szudi, György, 428

Taber, John, 249
Taft, Robert, 447
Tennyson, Alfred, 75
Textbooks (censorship), 32–33, 343–77
Thacher, Russell, *The Captain*, 148
Thackeray, William Makepeace, 69
Thomas v. *Collins*, 45, 111
Thoreau, Henry David, 243; *Walden*, 249
Thorne, Anthony, *Young Man on a Dolphin*, 402
Thornhill v. *Alabama*, 109
Three Musketeers (film), 157
Time, 27
Times (London), 265
Tocqueville, Alexis de, 129, 231, 310, 448
Toksvig, Signe, *Eve's Doctor*, 381
Tolin, Ernest, 24
Tolstoy, Alexei, 416
Tolstoy, Leo, 115, 162, 290, 391, 396, 418; *Anna Karenina*, 174, 379, 401; *Kreutzer Sonata*, 101
Torres, Tereska, *Women's Barracks*, 191

Toynbee, Arnold, 431, 433
Treacy, C. S., 365–66, 368
Tree, Herbert Beerbohm, 261
Trotsky, Leon, 412, 420
Trygvasson, Olaf, 430
Turgenev, Ivan, 391
Twain, Mark, 242, 424; *The Adventures of Tom Sawyer*, 99, 333; *Huckleberry Finn*, 99
Tyndall, John, 255

Unamuno, Miguel de, 402
Uncle Tom's Cabin (play), 145, 152–53, 157
Undset, Sigrid, *Kristin Lavransdatter*, 401
UNESCO, 310
United Nations, xi, 310
United States v. *Bennett*, 88
United States v. *Dennett*, 63, 64, 76–80, 81, 88, 112–13
United States v. *Dennis*, 223
United States v. *Kennerley*, 51, 105, 123, 149, 185
United States v. *Levine*, 64
United States v. *Limehouse*, 316
United States v. *One Book Called "Ulysses,"* 52, 83–89
United States v. *Roth*, 119
U.S. Chamber of Commerce, *A Program for Community Anti-Communist Action*, 361
U.S. Customs Bureau, 35–36
U.S. Information Agency, 247–50, 303, 307, 311
U.S. Library of Congress, 310, 327–29
U.S. Post Office Department, 28, 36–37, 44
U.S. State Department, 307, 308, 311
Untermeyer, Louis, 361, 362, 367, 368
Uris, Leon, 137; *Battle Cry*, 148
Ussher, Arland, 399

Vanderbilt, Arthur T., 125
Van Doren, Mark, 335; "If Anybody Wants To Know," 370–74
Vanguard Press, 286–87
Van Vechten, Carl, *Nigger Heaven*, 184
Velde, Theodoor H. van de, *Ideal Marriage*, 189
Venereal diseases, 193
Vercors, Jean Bruller, *Silence of the Sea*, 424
Vidal, Gore, 137

Vishinsky, Andre, 421; *Law of the Soviet State*, 304
Vizetelly, Henry, 47
Voltaire, 279, 286, 424; *Candide*, 83, 164; *The Maid of Orleans*, 59; *Philosophical Dictionary*, 59
Voroshilov, Kliment, 421

Waggish Tales from the Czechs, 114–15, 118, 119
Wagner, Richard, *Tristan and Isolde*, 173, 174
Waite, Morrison Remick, 108
Walker, Frank C., 89, 189
Walker, James J., 123, 196
Walker v. *Popenoe*, 105
Wallace, Alfred Russel, 255, 268
Walter, Francis E., 201, 207
Warner, Sylvia Townsend, 400, 402
Warren, Mortimer A., *Almost Fourteen*, 188
Washburn, Claude, 322
Washington, Booker T., 157
Washington, George, 452, 460
Washington Post, 193
Waugh, Evelyn, 403
Weaver, Warren, 364
Webster, Margaret, 145
Weeks, Edward, 183; "Sex and Censorship," 162–67
Weinberg, Sidney J., 364
Welles, Orson, 17
Wellesley, Dorothy, 387
Wells, H. G., 48, 390, 396, 397; *Ann Veronica*, 163; *The World of William Clissold*, 166, 184
Wells, Herman B., 190
Wertham, Frederic, 24; *Seduction of the Innocent*, 72, 125, 126
Wesberry, James Pickett, 22, 23, 150
West, E. H., 345, 346
West, Nathanael, 137
Western Society for the Suppression of Vice, 165
Weybright, Victor, 150
White, E. B., "Censorship," 160–61
White, Jack, 306
White, Walter, *A Man Called White*, 158
White Plains Reporter-Dispatch, 365
Whitman, Walt, 279; *Leaves of Grass*, 99, 163, 182, 276, 319, 333; "Song of Myself," 170
Whitney v. *California*, xi, 108–9, 113, 459

Wiener, Norbert, *Cybernetics*, 306
Wiggins, J. R., xiii
Wilde, Oscar, 170
Wilkes, John, 4, 53–55
Williams, Roger, 440
Willingham, Calder, *End as a Man*, 95–96, 148
Wilson, Angus, *Hemlock and After*, 402
Wilson, Charles E., 364
Wilson, Edmund, *Memoirs of Hecate County*, 42–43, 110, 187, 317
Wilson, Lewis A., 352
Wilson, Woodrow, 434, 441, 450, 460; *Constitutional Government in the United States*, 224
Wilstach, John, *Bedtime Blonde*, 402
Winsor, Kathleen, 137; *Forever Amber*, 106, 188
Winters v. *New York*, 111, 112
Wise, John B., 165
Witt, Marion, "Great Art Beaten Down," 381, 382–88
Wolfe, Thomas, 379, 402
Wolfert, Ira, 137
Wood, John S., 208
Woolf, Virginia, 69, 73
Woolsey, John M., 51, 98, 104, 112–13, 167, 186, 206, 318; "*United States* v. 'Married Love,'" 81–83; "*United States* v. 'Ulysses,'" 83–89
Wormser, Isaac M., 105–6
Wright, Richard, 137, 422; *Black Boy*, 99, 158; *Native Son*, 305
Wylie, Philip, 199

Yeats, W. B., 378, 381, 382–88; *Cathleen ni Houhilan*, 387; *Countess Cathleen*, 382; *The Herne's Egg*, 387; "The Irish Censorship," 388–91; *Leda and the Swan*, 386; *On the Boiler*, 388; *Purgatory*, 387
Yerby, Frank, 137
Yessenin, Sergei, 420
Young, G. Gordon, *Keeping It Dark*, 272–73

Zhdanov, Andrei, 420, 422, 423
Zinoviev, Grigori E., 412
Zochtchenko, Mikhail, 423
Zola, Émile, 75, 137, 138, 149, 161, 279, 289, 424
Zook, Allen, 233
Zweig, Stefan, 162, 402

2714410

KH
4/6/15

DISCARDED
MILLSTEIN LIBRARY

Z657
.D76

Downs
The first freedom

DATE DUE			
AP 15 '77	DEC 17 '91	FEB 21 2000	
MR 18 '82	APR 11 '92	MAR 15 2000	
NO 4 '82	APR 21 '93	APR 05 2000	
NO 23 '82	MAY 16 '93	OCT 18 2000	
JE 22 '	NV 15 '93	MAY 03 2001	
AP 11 '85	MY 03 '94		
DE 15 '86	DEC 14 '94		
AP 06 '87	MAR 09 1995		
SE 22 '	APR 14 1997		
FE 28 '			
NOV 26 '90	DEC 08 1997		
MAR 20 '91			

UNIVERSITY OF PITTSBURGH
AT GREENSBURG